KARL MARX
FREDERICK ENGELS
COLLECTED WORKS
VOLUME
3

KARL MARX
FREDERICK ENGELS

**COLLECTED
WORKS**

LAWRENCE & WISHART
LONDON

KARL MARX
FREDERICK ENGELS

Volume
3

MARX AND ENGELS: 1843-44

1975
LAWRENCE & WISHART
LONDON

This volume has been prepared jointly by Lawrence & Wishart Ltd., London, International Publishers Co. Inc., New York, and Progress Publishers, Moscow, in collaboration with the Institute of Marxism-Leninism, Moscow.

Editorial commissions:
GREAT BRITAIN: Jack Cohen, Maurice Cornforth, Maurice Dobb, E. J. Hobsbawm, James Klugmann, Margaret Mynatt.
USA: James S. Allen, Philip S. Foner, the late Howard Selsam, Dirk J. Struik, William W. Weinstone.
USSR: for Progress Publishers — N. P. Karmanova, V. N. Pavlov, M. K. Shcheglova, T. Y. Solovyova; for the Institute of Marxism-Leninism — P. N. Fedoseyev, L. I. Golman, A. I. Malysh, A. G. Yegorov, V. Y. Zevin.

Copyright © Progress Publishers, Moscow, 1975

All rights reserved. Apart from any fair dealing for the purpose of private study, research, criticism or review, no part of this publication may be reproduced, stored in a retrieval system, or transmitted, in any form or by any means, electronic, electrical, chemical, mechanical, optical, photocopying, recording or otherwise, without the prior permission of the copyright owner.

ISBN 0 85315-293-4

First printing 1975

Printed in the Union of Soviet Socialist Republics in 1974

Contents

Preface XI

KARL MARX
WORKS
March 1843-August 1844

1. Contribution to the Critique of Hegel's Philosophy of Law 3
2. A Passage from the Kreuznach Notebooks of 1843 130
3. Draft Programme of the *Deutsch-Französische Jahrbücher* 131
4. Letter to the Editor of the *Démocratie pacifique* 132
5. Letters from the *Deutsch-Französische Jahrbücher* 133
6. On the Jewish Question 146
7. Contribution to the Critique of Hegel's Philosophy of Law. Introduction 175
8. Letter to the Editor of the *Allgemeine Zeitung* (Augsburg) 188
9. Critical Marginal Notes on the Article "The King of Prussia and Social Reform. By a Prussian" 189
10. Illustrations of the Latest Exercise in Cabinet Style of Frederick William IV 207
11. Comments on James Mill, *Élémens d'économie politique* 211
12. Economic and Philosophic Manuscripts of 1844 229
    Preface 231
    First Manuscript 235
    Wages of Labour 235
    Profit of Capital 246

1. Capital 246
2. The Profit of Capital 247
3. The Rule of Capital Over Labour and the Motives of the Capitalist 250
4. The Accumulation of Capitals and the Competition Among the Capitalists 250
Rent of Land 259
Estranged Labour 270
Second Manuscript 283
Antithesis of Capital and Labour. Landed Property and Capital 283
Third Manuscript 290
Private Property and Labour. Political Economy as a Product of the Movement of Private Property 290
Private Property and Communism 293
Human Requirements and Division of Labour Under the Rule of Private Property 306
The Power of Money 322
Critique of the Hegelian Dialectic and Philosophy as a Whole 326

LETTERS
October 1843-August 1844

1. To Ludwig Feuerbach, *October 3, 1843* 349
2. To Julius Fröbel, *November 21, 1843* 351
3. To Ludwig Feuerbach, *August 11, 1844* 354

FROM THE PREPARATORY MATERIALS

1. From the *Mémoires de R. Levasseur (De La Sarthe)*. Paris, 1829 ... 361
2. Summary of Frederick Engels' Article "Outlines of a Critique of Political Economy" 375

FREDERICK ENGELS
WORKS
May 1843-June 1844

1. Letters from London (I-IV) 379
2. Progress of Social Reform on the Continent 392
3. Progress of Communism in Germany. Persecution of the Communists in Switzerland 409

4. The *Times* on German Communism. To the Editor of the *New Moral World* 410
5. French Communism. To the Editor of the *New Moral World* 414
6. Continental Movements 415
7. The Press and the German Despots 417
8. Outlines of a Critique of Political Economy 418
9. The Condition of England. *Past and Present* by Thomas Carlyle, London, 1843 444
10. The Condition of England. I. The Eighteenth Century 469
11. The Condition of England. II. The English Constitution 489
12. Letter to the Editor of *The Northern Star* 514
13. The Situation in Prussia 515
14. News from Germany 517
15. Fate of a Traitor 519
16. Beer Riots in Bavaria 521
17. Parsonocracy in Prussia 523
18. News from St. Petersburg 524
19. The Civil War in the Valais 525
20. News from France 527
21. News from Prussia 530
22. Further Particulars of the Silesian Riots 532

SUPPLEMENT

Cola di Rienzi 537

APPENDICES

1. Marriage Contract Between Karl Marx and Jenny von Westphalen 571
2. Extract from the Register of Marriages of the Registry Office of Bad Kreuznach for the Year 1843 573
3. Jenny Marx to Karl Marx, *about June 21, 1844* 575
4. Jenny Marx to Karl Marx, *between August 4 and 10, 1844* 580
5. Jenny Marx to Karl Marx, *between August 11 and 18, 1844* 581

NOTES AND INDEXES

Notes 587
Name Index 625
Index of Quoted and Mentioned Literature 639
Index of Periodicals 647
Subject Index 651

ILLUSTRATIONS

A page from Marx's manuscript *Contribution to the Critique of Hegel's Philosophy of Law* 125
Cover of the *Deutsch-Französische Jahrbücher* 135
First page of the Preface to the *Economic and Philosophic Manuscripts of 1844* 240-41
A page from the *Economic and Philosophic Manuscripts of 1844* (beginning of the first manuscript) 256-57
A page from issue No. 70 of *Vorwärts!*, carrying Engels' article "The Condition of England. The Eighteenth Century" 478-79
Pages from the manuscript of *Cola di Rienzi* 544-45
Jenny von Westphalen in the early 1840s 576-77
Pages from the Register of Marriages showing the official entry of the marriage between Karl Marx and Jenny von Westphalen 576-77

TRANSLATORS

JACK COHEN: Marx: Works 8; Letters 1-3; From the Preparatory Materials 1
RICHARD DIXON: Appendices: 2
CLEMENS DUTT: Marx: Works 2, 3, 4, 5, 6, 9, 10, 11; From the Preparatory Materials 2;
  Engels: Article 1, Appendices 1, 3-5
ALEX MILLER: Supplement
MARTIN MILLIGAN AND BARBARA RUHEMANN: Marx: Works 1
MARTIN MILLIGAN AND DIRK J. STRUIK: Marx: Works 12
MARTIN MILLIGAN: Engels: Works 8
CHRISTOPHER UPWARD: Engels: Works 9, 10 and 11

Preface

The third volume of the works of Marx and Engels covers the period between March 1843 and August 1844, before their close collaboration began. The contents fall into two parts; the first consists of Marx's works, letters and preparatory material from March 1843 to August 1844; the second contains Engels' writings from May 1843 to June 1844. Included as appendices are biographical documents of Marx and letters which his wife Jenny wrote to him between June and August 1844.

This period marked an important stage in the formation of the world outlook of both Marx and Engels, each of whom accomplished in 1843 the transition from idealism to materialism and from the standpoint of revolutionary democracy to that of communism. The development of each proceeded in the main independently of the other, although they showed a growing interest in each other's writings and activity.

By late 1843 and early 1844 Marx and Engels were alike opponents not only of the existing political systems of feudal absolutism and bourgeois monarchy, but of any kind of social system resting on private property and exploitation of the working people. They both saw in the emancipation movement of the working class the only way to free humanity from social inequality and oppression. It was at this time that Marx and Engels made their first contacts with the working class. After moving to Paris in October 1843 Marx found himself in an atmosphere of intense socialist agitation and activity of workers' groups and secret societies. And during the same year, Engels, who had been living in England since November 1842, established close links with the Chartists and the Owenite Socialists and became a contributor to their periodicals.

The main efforts of Marx and Engels during this period were directed towards working out the scientific basis of a new, revolutionary-proletarian world outlook. Each had arrived at materialist and communist convictions, and set about studying a broad spectrum of philosophical, historical, economic and political problems. Marx was engaged upon a number of theoretical projects: he began writing a work on Hegel's philosophy of law, intended to write a history of the Convention, and was also planning works devoted to the criticism of politics and political economy; Engels, for his part, was studying social developments in England, the condition of the English working class. Each clearly realised the necessity to dissociate himself from current economic, philosophical and sociological doctrines; each considered the criticism of these essential if the theoretical principles of a new world outlook were to be arrived at. They both clearly understood the inconsistency of Hegel's idealism, the narrow-mindedness of the bourgeois economists, and the weaknesses of the Utopian Socialists, but at the same time they tried to make use of all that was rational in the views of their predecessors. They were deeply impressed by Feuerbach's materialism, but had already gone far beyond Feuerbach in their approach to theoretical and practical problems, particularly in interpreting the life of society.

The works included in this volume register the completion of Marx's and Engels' transition to materialism and communism and the initial stage in synthesising the emerging revolutionary-communist and dialectical-materialist views into a qualitatively new theory. The contribution each made to this complex process may be seen. Evident too are the common features in their views which led them later to unite their efforts in the theoretical and practical struggle.

The volume opens with Marx's extensive though incomplete manuscript *Contribution to the Critique of Hegel's Philosophy of Law* (written in the spring and summer of 1843). The object of this study was not only Hegel's philosophy. Marx studied a broad range of problems in the history and theory of the state and law, world history, the history of separate countries (England, France, Germany, the USA, Italy, Sweden), the English Revolution of the seventeenth century, and the French Revolution at the end of the eighteenth century. All this was reflected in his manuscript and in his notebooks of excerpts (the so-called Kreuznach Notebooks). Although he was strongly influenced by Feuerbach's materialism, Marx did not approach the criticism of Hegel through an analysis of religion, as Feuerbach had done, but through an investigation of social relations. For this reason what interested Marx most in Hegel was his philosophy of law, his teaching on the state and society. In the process of criticising Hegel's philosophy of law, Marx was led to the conclusion that the state is determined by civil society, that is, the sphere of private — first and foremost material — interests, and the social relations connected with them, and not civil society by the state, as Hegel had asserted.

Marx wished to define the concept of civil society in concrete terms, to bring out the essential features of its historical evolution, and in particular to analyse the stage at which bourgeois private property began to play the dominant role in the field of material relationships. Giving a materialist explanation of the mutual connection between the state in his time and bourgeois ownership, Marx wrote that the existing political constitution in the developed countries was "the *constitution of private property*" (see this volume, p. 98).

Later, in 1859, in the Preface to *A Contribution to the Critique of Political Economy,* Marx recalled the important part his work on the critique of Hegel's philosophy of law had played in the formation of his materialist views: "My inquiry led me to the conclusion that neither legal relations nor political forms could be comprehended either by themselves or on the basis of a so-called general development of the human mind, but that on the contrary they originate in the material conditions of life, the totality of which Hegel, following the example of English and French thinkers of the eighteenth century, embraces within the term 'civil society'; that the anatomy of this civil society, however, has to be sought in political economy."

From the criticism of the conservative aspects of Hegel's philosophy, such as the idealisation of monarchical and bureaucratic institutions, Marx went on to a critical reconsideration of the very basis of Hegel's idealism. He arrived at the conviction that idealism inevitably leads to religion and mysticism. But Marx did not reject the rational content of Hegel's philosophy or his dialectics, and stressed that Hegel had succeeded in presenting, though in an abstract, mystified form, many of the real processes of social life. Contrary to Feuerbach, Marx continued to attach great importance to Hegel's dialectical method and made the first step towards a materialist transformation of dialectics, towards freeing it from its mystical shell.

In his manuscript Marx put forward his own, essentially communist conception of democracy as a social system free from social oppression and worthy of man. We can, he stressed, acquire genuine freedom by throwing off the impositions of both the bureaucratically organised state and of a civil society resting on the egoistic principles of private property. But "for a *new* constitution a real revolution has always been required" (see this volume, p. 56).

Closely connected with the manuscript of 1843 is Marx's note on Hegel taken from the Kreuznach Notebooks, which is included in this volume. It bears witness to the internal connection between the manuscript and the notebooks, which were compiled because Marx felt the necessity to supplement his philosophical investigation with concrete historical material. In this note Marx criticises Hegel for separating the abstract idea of the state from its real historical form.

Marx's final transition to the standpoint of communism was associated with the preparation and publication of the journal *Deutsch-Französische Jahrbücher.*

Marx's draft programme of this journal and his correspondence with the co-founder, the radical philosopher and publicist Arnold Ruge, which are included in this volume, reflect the different approaches of the editors to the journal's tasks. Contrary to Ruge, who wanted to give it a more moderate, purely enlightening character, Marx held that the main theme of the journal, the purpose of which was to unite the German and French Socialists and democrats, should be relentless criticism of the existing world order. Accordingly, in the letters published in the *Deutsch-Französische Jahrbücher,* Marx had no use for speculative theories divorced from life and the practical struggle of the masses, and demanded the embodiment of theoretical criticism in practical revolutionary activity, "making ... *real* struggles the starting point of our criticism" (see this volume, p. 144). He expressed here one of the principal ideas of the emerging revolutionary-communist world outlook — the idea of the unity of theory and practice.

In his article "On the Jewish Question", Marx attacked Bruno Bauer's idealistic, narrowly theological presentation of the problem of Jewish emancipation. As opposed to his former fellow thinkers, the Young Hegelians, Marx saw criticism of religion, as well as of politics, not as the final aim but as a tool to be used in the revolutionary struggle, and he wanted to go further and deeper in the critical reconsideration of all existing relationships. Marx's polemic with Bauer provided him with the occasion for a broader materialist examination of the problem of mankind's emancipation not only from national, religious and political, but also from economic and social oppression. In this work Marx developed the concept of the limited nature of the bourgeois revolution, which he called "political emancipation". He put forward the idea of the necessity for a deeper-going revolution aiming at the real elimination of all social antagonisms. This kind of revolution he called "human emancipation".

In another of his works published in the *Deutsch-Französische Jahrbücher*—"Contribution to the Critique of Hegel's Philosophy of Law. Introduction", Marx continued his analysis of the problem of "human emancipation". Here he comes to the crucial conclusion of the historical role of the proletariat in the revolutionary transformation of the world. For the first time he declared that the proletariat is the social force capable of carrying out the complete emancipation of mankind. In this work Marx also came to another important conclusion: the profound revolutionising significance of advanced theory. "The weapon of criticism cannot, of course, replace criticism by weapons, material force must be overthrown by material force; but theory also becomes a material force as soon as it has gripped the masses" (see this volume, p. 182).

Lenin considered Marx's articles in the *Deutsch-Französische Jahrbücher* as the final link in his transition from revolutionary democracy to proletarian revolution: "Marx's articles in this journal showed that he was already a revolutionary, who advocated 'merciless criticism of everything existing', and in particular the 'criticism by weapons', and appealed to the *masses* and to the *proletariat*" (V. I. Lenin, *Collected Works*, Vol. 21, p. 47).

After the journal *Deutsch-Französische Jahrbücher* ceased publication, Marx wrote several articles for *Vorwärts!*, the German emigrants' paper in Paris. His articles in this newspaper, his direct participation in the editorial work from September 1844, and his enlistment of Frederick Engels, Heinrich Heine and Georg Herwegh as contributors, made this journal a militant political weapon in the struggle against both Prussian absolutism and German moderate liberalism. Under the influence of Marx and Engels the paper began to assume a communist character.

Marx's article "Critical Marginal Notes on the Article 'The King of Prussia and Social Reform. By a Prussian'", dealing with the uprising of the Silesian weavers in 1844, was published in *Vorwärts!* It was directed against Ruge, who considered the Silesian uprising a futile revolt of the desperate poor. Marx, on the other hand, regarded it as the first major class action of the German proletariat against the bourgeoisie, a testimony to the broad revolutionary possibilities of the working class. Developing the idea he had already expressed in the *Deutsch-Französische Jahrbücher* about the world-historical role of the proletariat, Marx pointed out that "it is only in the *proletariat* that" the German people "can find the dynamic element of its emancipation" (see this volume, p. 202).

Having arrived at a materialist position, Marx came to the conclusion that an extensive study of economic relations had to be undertaken. From this time until the end of his life the study of political economy occupied the central place in his scientific activity. Marx made numerous excerpts from the works of Adam Smith, Ricardo, Say, Skarbek, List, James Mill, Destutt de Tracy, McCulloch, Boisguillebert, Lauderdale, Schütz and other economists, in many cases accompanying these excerpts with his own comments and critical remarks. The most extensive of these are the "Comments on James Mill, *Élémens d'économie politique*", which formed part of Marx's summary of this work and are included in the present volume. From these comments it is clear that although Marx's own economic views were still in the initial stage of formation, he nevertheless succeeded in noting the main defect of bourgeois political economy—its anti-historical approach to capitalism. He pointed out that Mill, like other bourgeois economists, thought capitalist relations eternal and immutable, corresponding to "man's nature" (see this volume, p. 217).

Many of the thoughts expressed in the "Comments" have much in common with the unfinished, only partially extant work which has editorially been given the title *Economic and Philosophic Manuscripts of 1844*. This was Marx's first attempt at a critical examination, from the standpoint of the dialectical-materialist and communist conclusions he had reached, of the economic bases of bourgeois society and the views of the bourgeois economists. At the same time, these manuscripts were the first attempt of synthesising the new philosophical, economic and historical-political ideas of the integral world outlook of the proletariat.

The *Economic and Philosophic Manuscripts of 1844* embrace various fields of the social sciences. In all these fields Marx used and developed materialist dialectics as a penetrative instrument of knowledge. He achieved a new stage of comprehension of the structure and development of society. Marx emphasised here for the first time the decisive role of production in the social process and pointed out that private property and the division of labour are the material basis of society's division into classes. Analysing the economic structure of bourgeois society, he stressed that the class contradictions of capitalism would inevitably grow deeper as wealth became concentrated in the hands of capitalist owners. Extremely penetrating are Marx's thoughts on the influence of man's productive labour and his social relations on science and culture. He noted in particular the process not only of social enslavement, but also of spiritual impoverishment of the working man resulting from the domination of private property.

In his manuscripts Marx put forward materialist criteria for assessing the development of economic thought, a development which, he explained, is a reflection in the ideological sphere of the evolution of actual economic relations. The development of science, according to Marx, repeats the development of society itself. He considered the teaching of the leading bourgeois economists — Adam Smith, Ricardo and others — as the highest achievement of political economy. But although he had not yet undertaken an analysis of the labour theory of value, he at the same time noted the limitations of their views — their failure to understand the true internal connections and dynamics of the economic phenomena described, and their metaphysical approach to them. In their striving to perpetuate artificially the basis of capitalism and the relationships of inhuman exploitation, Marx discerned the anti-humanist tendencies of the bourgeois economists.

In the manuscripts of 1844, as in his other works of this period, Marx used the traditional terminology, partly of Feuerbach and partly of Hegel. Thus, in accordance with Feuerbach's usage Marx wrote that "communism, as fully developed naturalism, equals humanism, and as fully developed humanism equals naturalism". In fact, however, Marx gave these terms an essentially new content, and put forward views which were in many respects opposed to Feuerbach's abstract humanism and supra-class anti-historical anthropologism. His manuscripts are pervaded with the sense of history and understanding of the significance of revolutionary practice, and are distinguished by their class approach to the social phenomena under consideration. As regards Hegel, it can be seen from the manuscripts of 1844 that Marx had achieved a quite mature understanding of the relationship between the rational and conservative aspects of his teaching. Marx showed the groundlessness of Hegel's attempts to transform nature into another mode of existence of the mystical Absolute Idea. At the same time he also stressed the positive aspects of the Hegelian dialectic and in particular the significance of Hegel's conception—although it was expressed in an idealistic form—of the development and resolution of contradictions.

One of the central problems in the *Economic and Philosophic Manuscripts of 1844* is the problem of estrangement or alienation. Hegel had already made extensive use of this concept. With him, however, it is not real living people but the Absolute Idea that undergoes alienation. Feuerbach operates with a similar concept in his theory of the origin of religion, reducing it to the alienation of the universal (generic) qualities of abstract man, which are imputed to an illusory divinity.

Marx used the concept of alienation for purposes of a profound analysis of social relations. For him alienation was characteristic of those social relations under which the conditions of people's life and activity, that activity itself, and the relations between people, appear as a force which is alien and hostile to people. So in Marx's interpretation alienation is by no means a supra-historical phenomenon. Marx was the first to link alienation with the domination of private property and the social system it engenders. He saw that alienation could be overcome only by the liquidation of private property and of all the consequences of its domination.

Marx's views on alienation appeared in a concentrated form in his treatment of "estranged labour". The concept of "estranged labour" summed up the enslaved condition of the worker in capitalist society, his being tied down to a definite job, his physical and moral crippling as a result of labour which is forced on him, "the loss of his self" (see this volume, p. 274). The concept of "estranged labour" in the *Economic and Philosophic Manuscripts of 1844* constituted in particular the initial expression of the future Marxist theory of the appropriation of labour of others by capital, a preliminary approach to the important ideas later developed especially in *Capital*.

The wide application of the concept of alienation was distinctive of the initial stage in the shaping of Marx's economic teaching. In his subsequent works this concept was superseded to a considerable degree by other, more concrete determinations revealing more completely and more clearly the substance of the economic relations of capitalism, the exploitation of wage-labour. However, as a philosophically generalised expression of the exploiting, inhuman character of the social system based on private property, and of the destitution of the working masses in that society, it continues to be used in Marx's later works.

In the *Economic and Philosophic Manuscripts of 1844* Marx clearly formulated his conclusion that the system of private property can be overthrown only as a result of the revolutionary struggle of the broad masses. "In order to abolish the *idea* of private property, the *idea* of communism is quite sufficient. It takes *actual* communist action to abolish actual private property" (see this volume, p. 313).

As Marx saw it, the future social system represents the antipode of the existing society of exploitation. At that stage of social development man will have become capable of freeing himself from social antagonisms and all forms of alienation. Marx criticised the various primitive theories of egalitarian communism, with their tendencies towards asceticism, social levelling, and a return to the "*unnatural* simplicity of the *poor* and crude man who has few needs" (see this volume, p. 295). The future society must give scope for the all-round satisfaction of man's requirements, and the full flowering of the human personality.

The second section of the first part of this volume contains letters written by Marx which provide supplementary material showing the development of his views and his political activity during the period.

Of special interest are two letters from Marx to Ludwig Feuerbach. Marx wanted to draw the great materialist philosopher into active political and ideological struggle. In his letter of October 3, 1843, inviting Feuerbach to contribute to the *Deutsch-Französische Jahrbücher*, Marx mentioned how important it would be if his authority as a philosopher could be used to discredit Schelling's reactionary and idealist philosophy. The idea that philosophical materialism and idealism are irreconcilable likewise runs through another letter, written on August 11, 1844. In it Marx stressed that progressive philosophy should serve the most revolutionary social force, the proletariat. At that time Marx still regarded Feuerbach's materialism as the theoretical substantiation of the necessity for the revolutionary transformation of society. He considered that Feuerbach had provided "a philosophical basis for socialism" (see this volume, p. 354). However, it soon became obvious to Marx that such a foundation could be laid only by overcoming the weak sides of Feuerbach's philosophy, with its tendency towards abstraction from real social relations, and by working out a theory that would reveal the objective dialectical laws of social development.

The section "From the Preparatory Materials" contains a conspectus of the memoirs of the Jacobin Levasseur made by Marx after his move to Paris, most probably in connection with his unrealised intention to write a history of the Convention. This conspectus, entitled by Marx "The Struggle Between the Montagnards and the Girondists", demonstrates Marx's sustained interest in the French Revolution of the late eighteenth century as a major event of world history. It contains few of Marx's own remarks, but the selection of the material shows that he was particularly interested in the influence of the popular masses on the course of the Revolution. It was precisely the growing revolutionary activity of the masses after the fall of the monarchy on August 10, 1792, and their increasing discontent with the administration of the Girondists—who represented the moderate bourgeoisie, as the facts quoted by Marx eloquently prove — that led to the establishment of the revolutionary dictatorship of the Jacobins. His study of these events undoubtedly played a major part in the formation of his views of the determining role of the working masses in history and the class struggle as the most important factor in historical development.

This section also includes a short summary made by Marx of Engels' article "Outlines of a Critique of Political Economy". This article was one of the causes which led Marx to study political economy. Marx recognised in Engels a philosophical and political fellow thinker, and was deeply influenced by Engels' initiative in dealing with problems of economics from the standpoint of communism — a field in which his future associate was then a pioneer.

The second part of the volume contains the works of Engels written from May 1843 to June 1844. Living in England, the most highly developed capitalist country of the time, Engels studied with a profound interest its economic and political life and social relations. He devoted himself especially to the study of British political economy and the works of the English Utopian Socialists, in particular Robert Owen.

The key problem in Engels' series of articles "Letters from London", printed in the Swiss progressive journal *Schweizerischer Republikaner* in May and June 1843, concerns the social structure of English society. In analysing it, Engels laid bare the class character of the English political parties. He noted the important role of the Socialist and Chartist movements and stressed that Chartism "has its strength in the working men, the proletarians" (see this volume, p. 379). The "Letters from London" mark a new stage in the development of Engels' revolutionary-materialist world outlook since his arrival in England in the autumn of 1842. The thoughts he expressed in them show that he appreciated the part played by the class struggle in social development, and understood the role of the proletariat as the force capable of accomplishing a social revolution in England.

By his writings in the English and continental press Engels sought to bring about an international rapprochement in the field of ideas between the proletariat and the Socialists. He considered that the English Socialists were doing great service by making known to the workers the ideas of the eighteenth-century French Enlightenment. Engels himself thought it his duty to inform the English Chartists and Owenists about the socialist and communist movements in other countries. For this purpose he wrote a number of articles for the

Owenist paper *The New Moral World*, including the essay "Progress of Social Reform on the Continent". Engels linked the inception and development of socialist and communist teachings with the social protest of the working masses against oppression and exploitation, and showed that socialist views came into being as a reflection of that protest in the consciousness of progressive thinkers. Drawing attention to the common underlying social base and international character of the socialist and communist movement, he wrote: "... Communism is not the consequence of the particular position of the English, or any other nation, but ... a necessary conclusion, which cannot be avoided to be drawn from the premises given in the general facts of modern civilisation" (see this volume, p. 392). At the same time he noted the influence of each people's national peculiarities on the development of socialist thought.

Engels followed the history of socialist and communist ideas in France, Germany and Switzerland. He brought out the rational elements in the teaching of the various schools of utopian socialism and communism and at the same time he indicated the inconsistencies and immature features inherent in them. The article shows that he was clearly aware of the need to overcome the defects of previous socialist ideas, to deepen the theoretical understanding of communism and unite it with advanced philosophy.

The article "Outlines of a Critique of Political Economy" published in the *Deutsch-Französische Jahrbücher* was Engels' first work on economics. In it, Lenin wrote, he "examined the principal phenomena of the contemporary economic order from a socialist standpoint, regarding them as necessary consequences of the rule of private property" (V. I. Lenin, *Collected Works*, Vol. 2, p. 24). Engels' work is remarkable for its profound revolutionary purposefulness, its materialist proletarian class approach to economic phenomena and theories, and its clear understanding of the failure of the metaphysical method used by the bourgeois economists. His article was the first experiment in applying the materialist world outlook and materialist dialectics to the analysis of economic categories.

The work is devoted mainly to a critical examination of the economic basis of the capitalist system — private property. Engels proved that the main cause of the social antagonisms in the bourgeois world and the cause of the future social revolution was the development of the contradictions inherent in and engendered by private property. He investigated the dialectical interconnections between competition and monopoly resulting from the nature of private property, and the profound contradictions between labour and capital.

While criticising the bourgeois economists, Engels made no distinction at that time between the representatives of the classical school, Smith and Ricardo, and vulgar economists of the type of Say, McCulloch and others. At this stage he had not yet accepted Smith's and Ricardo's labour theory of value and was unable properly to assess its place in the development of economic teachings. At the same time he put forward the profound concept of the correspondence between the development of political economy and the level of economic relations achieved. He vehemently criticised the unscientific misanthropic population theory of Malthus and proved that poverty and destitution are in no way to be accounted for by allegedly limited possibilities of production and of applied science. On the contrary, Engels stressed that "the productive power at mankind's disposal is immeasurable" (see this volume, p. 436). Social calamities, he concluded, are engendered by the existing economic system, which must be subjected to a revolutionary communist reconstruction.

Engels' review—also published in the *Deutsch-Französische Jahrbücher*—of Carlyle's *Past and Present*, which he criticised from the standpoint of materialism and atheism, took issue with Carlyle's idealist interpretation of history, his hero-worship and romantic idealisation of the Middle Ages. In opposition to these views Engels emphasised that at the basis of the historical process lies the concrete activity of people, their hard struggle both to subjugate nature and to establish social relationships corresponding to man's dignity and genuine interest. Engels rejected Carlyle's view of the working class as a mere suffering mass. He expressed faith in the creative role of the proletariat, in its ability to carry out radical social changes.

In the articles continuing this review and published in the newspaper *Vorwärts!*—"The Condition of England. I. The Eighteenth Century" and "The Condition of England. II. The English Constitution"—Engels performed pioneering work in the materialist interpretation of the history of England, and this was a most important premise for the subsequent elaboration by Marx and Engels of the materialist understanding of the whole historical process. Engels traced the part played by the industrial revolution of the late eighteenth and early nineteenth century in England's development and analysed in detail its social and political consequences. Examining the English political system, he showed the limitations of bourgeois democracy. Opposing to it the idea of "social democracy", Engels arrived at the conclusion that the conquest of political power by the working class was the necessary condition for the transition to socialism.

This volume contains a large group of articles previously unknown as written by Engels from the Chartist paper *The Northern Star*, to which he began to contribute at the end of 1843. They had a common theme—the democratic and socialist movement in the countries of Central Europe, and exposure of the reactionary policy pursued by the governments of those states. Engels demonstrated the common condition of the working class in different countries and the identity of the social causes giving rise to the class actions of the workers.

Particularly notable are the articles "News from Prussia" and "Further Particulars of the Silesian Riots" because they are the first comments on the uprising of the Silesian weavers from the standpoint of revolutionary communism. Engels saw in the uprising the confirmation of the universal character of the contradictions of capitalism and pointed out that the emergence of the factory system would have the same effects in every country as it had in England. The account of the Silesian uprising in these articles coincided in many respects with Marx's assessment of it in his work "Critical Marginal Notes on the Article 'The King of Prussia and Social Reform. By a Prussian'".

The evolution of Engels' views led him to the same conclusions at which Marx was arriving. The ensuing steps in developing the scientific principles of the revolutionary world outlook were made by them jointly in their unique collaboration, which began after their meeting in Paris at the end of August 1844.

* * *

Some of the works included in this volume have never before been translated into English. Published for the first time in English are an extract from the Kreuznach Notebooks of 1843; "Draft Programme of the *Deutsch-Französische Jahrbücher*"; letters to the editors of the newspapers *Démocratie pacifique* and *Allgemeine Zeitung*; "Illustrations of the Latest Exercise in Cabinet Style of Frederick William IV"; Marx's letter of November 21, 1843, to Julius Fröbel, all the items in the section "From the Preparatory Materials" and also the letters of Jenny Marx published in the Appendices.

The works of Engels not previously published in English include the first three articles in the series "Letters from London" and one article in the series "The Condition of England". The eleven articles from the newspaper *The Northern Star* have been collected together for the first time.

Those works included in this volume which have been previously published in English are given either in new or in carefully revised translations. Peculiarities in the arrangement of the text of some works, in particular the manuscripts, are described in the notes.

Publishers and translators express their gratitude to Clarendon Press, Oxford, and Professor Sir Malcolm Knox for their kind permission to take as a basis for some of the quotations in the *Contribution to the Critique of Hegel's Philosophy of Law* the text of *Hegel's Philosophy of Right* translated and edited by Professor Knox. Certain changes have been introduced in the translation and some passages retranslated to render Marx's interpretation of the respective passages.

All the texts have been translated from the German except where otherwise indicated.

The volume was compiled and the preface and notes written by Velta Pospelova and edited by Lev Golman (Institute of Marxism-Leninism of the CC CPSU). Indexes of names and of books and periodicals mentioned or quoted were prepared by Kirill Anderson, and the subject index by Boris Gusev (Institute of Marxism-Leninism of the CC CPSU).

The translations were made by Jack Cohen, Clemens Dutt, Martin Milligan, Barbara Ruhemann, Dirk J. Struik and Christopher Upward, and edited by James S. Allen (International Publishers), Maurice Cornforth, Martin Milligan, Margaret Mynatt, Barbara Ruhemann, the late Alick West (Lawrence and Wishart) and Salo Ryazanskaya (Progress Publishers). The supplement was translated by Alex Miller in consultation with Diana Miller and Victor Schnittke.

The volume was prepared for the press by the editors Maria Shcheglova, Tatyana Grishina and Lyudgarda Zubrilova, and the assistant-editor Tatyana Butkova, for Progress Publishers, and Larisa Miskievich, scientific editor, for the Institute of Marxism-Leninism of the CC CPSU.

KARL MARX

WORKS

March 1843-August 1844

CONTRIBUTION TO THE CRITIQUE
OF HEGEL'S PHILOSOPHY
OF LAW[1]

Written in the spring and summer of 1843

First published in: Marx/Engels, *Gesamtausgabe*, Abt. 1, Bd. 1, Hb. 1, 1927

Printed according to the manuscript

261. "Over against the spheres of civil law and personal welfare, the family and civil society, the state is **on the one hand** an *external* necessity and their superior authority, and both their laws and interests are subordinate to and dependent upon the nature of this authority. **On the other hand**, however, the state is their *immanent* end, and its strength lies in the unity of its ultimate general purpose with the particular interest of individuals—in the fact that they have *duties* towards the state since they have rights as well (para. 155)."[2]

The previous paragraph [i. e., para. 260] tells us that *concrete freedom* consists in the identity (as an ought, a dual identity) of the system of particular interest (the family and civil society) with the system of general interest (the state). The relation between these spheres has now to be more precisely defined.

On the one hand, the state, over against the sphere of the family and civil society, is an "*external* necessity", an authority, in relation to which "laws" and "interests" are "subordinate and dependent". That the state is an "*external* necessity" over against the family and civil society was already implied to some extent in the category of "transition" and to some extent in the *conscious relation* of family and civil society to the state. The "subordination" to the state, too, corresponds completely to this relation of "*external* necessity". What Hegel means by "dependence", however, is shown by the following sentence in the Remark to this paragraph:

"It was Montesquieu above all who kept in view [...] both the thought of the **dependence** of civil law in particular on the specific character of the state, and also the philosophical notion of always treating the part in its relation to the whole", etc.

Hegel is thus speaking here of the fact that civil law, etc., is *intrinsically* dependent on, or determined in its essence by, the state.

At the same time, however, he subsumes this dependence under the relation of "*external* necessity" and contrasts it with the other relation in which the family and civil society have the state as their "*immanent* end".

"External necessity" can only be taken to mean that where a collision occurs, the "laws" and "interests" of family and society must give way to the "laws" and "interests" of the state; that they are subordinate to it; that their existence is dependent on its existence; or again that its will and its laws appear to their "will" and their "laws" as a necessity!

However, Hegel is not here speaking of empirical collisions: he is speaking of the relation of the "*spheres* of civil law and personal welfare, the family and civil society" to the state. What is at issue is the *essential relationship* of these spheres themselves. Not only their "interests", but also their "laws", their "fundamental characteristics" are "dependent" on the state, "subordinate" to it. It stands to their "laws and interests" as "superior *authority*". Their "interest" and "law" stand as its "subordinate". They live in "dependence" on it. Precisely because "subordination" and "dependence" are *external* relations which constrain and run counter to independent being, the relation of the "family" and of "civil society" to the state is that of "*external* necessity", of a necessity which goes against the inner nature of the thing. This fact itself, that the "civil law" depends on and is modified by "the specific character of the state", is therefore subsumed under the relation of "*external necessity*", precisely because "civil society and family" in their true (i. e., in their independent and complete) development are antecedent as particular "spheres" to the state. "*Subordination*" and "*dependence*" are the expressions for an "external", *imposed,* illusory identity, as the logical expression for which Hegel rightly uses "*external necessity*". In "subordination" and "dependence" Hegel has further developed one side of the dual identity, namely, the aspect of the estrangement within the unity;

> "on the other hand, however, the state is their *immanent* end, and its strength lies in the unity of its *ultimate* **general** *purpose* with the **particular** *interest* of individuals — in the fact that they have *duties* towards the state since they have rights as well."

Hegel here sets up an unresolved *antinomy. On the one hand* external necessity, *on the other hand* immanent end. The unity of the *ultimate general purpose* of the state with the *particular interest of individuals* is supposed to consist in the fact that their *duties* to the state and *their rights* in the state are identical. (Thus, for example, the duty to respect property is supposed to coincide with the right to property.)

In the Remark [to para. 261] this identity is explained thus:
"*Duty* is primarily behaviour *towards* something which is for me *substantial* and which is intrinsically universal; right, on the other hand, is actually *existence* of this substance, and is thus the aspect of its *particularity* and of my *particular* freedom. Consequently, at formal levels both duty and right appear allocated to different sides or different persons. In the state, as something ethical, as the interpenetration of the substantial and the particular, my obligation to what is substantial is at the same time the form of existence of my particular freedom: in the state, that is, duty and right are *united in one and the same relation.*"

262. "The actual idea, mind, divides itself into the two ideal spheres of its concept, family and civil society, that is, its **finite** phase, so as to emerge from their ideality as **explicitly infinite** actual mind. Accordingly, it assigns to these spheres the material of this, its finite actuality, individuals as a *multitude*, in such a way that with regard to the individual this assignment appears *mediated* by circumstances, caprice and the individual's own choice of vocation."

Translated into prose, the above yields this:

The way in which the state effects its self-mediation with the family and civil society is decided by "circumstances, caprice and the individual's own choice of vocation". Political reason has therefore nothing to do with the distribution of the material of the state to the family and civil society. The state arises from them in an unconscious and arbitrary fashion. The family and civil society appear as the dark natural ground from which the light of the state arises. The material of the state is taken as comprising the *concerns* of the state, namely, the family and civil society, insofar as they form parts of the state and participate in the state as such.

This exposition is remarkable in two respects.

1) Family and civil society are conceived as *spheres of the concept* of the state, namely, as the spheres of its *finite* phase, as *its finiteness*. It is the state which *divides* itself into them, which *presupposes* them, and it *does* this "so as to emerge from their ideality as *explicitly infinite* actual mind". "It divides, so as to." It "*accordingly assigns* to these spheres the material of its actuality *in such a way that* this assignment, etc., *appears* mediated". The so-called "actual idea" (mind as infinite and actual) is presented as if it acted on a specific principle and with specific intent. It divides into finite spheres; it does this "so as to return into itself, to be conscious of itself"; and this it does indeed so that what comes to pass is precisely what actually exists.

At this point the logical, pantheistic mysticism becomes very clear.

The *actual* relation is this: "with regard to the individual the assignment of the material of the state is mediated by circumstances, caprice and the individual's own choice of vocation". Speculative philosophy expresses this fact, this *actual relation* as *appearance,* as *phenomenon.* These circumstances, this caprice, this choice of vocation, this *actual mediation*—these are merely the *appearance of a mediation* which the actual idea effects with itself, and which goes on behind the scenes. Reality is expressed not as itself but as another reality. Ordinary empirical fact has not its own but an alien spirit for its law; whereas the form of existence of the actual idea is not an actuality evolved from itself, but ordinary empirical fact.

The idea is made the subject and the *actual* relation of family and civil society to the state is conceived as its *internal imaginary* activity. Family and civil society are the premises of the state; they are the genuinely active elements, but in speculative philosophy things are inverted. When the idea is made the subject, however, the real subjects, namely, civil society, family, "circumstances, caprice, etc.", become *unreal* objective elements of the idea with a changed significance.

The assignment of the material of the state "with regard to the individual ... mediated by circumstances, caprice and the individual's own choice of vocation" is not expressly stated to be what is true, necessary and absolutely warranted. These [circumstances, caprice, etc.] are *as such* not presented as rational. And yet, on the other hand, they are so presented simply by being presented as a *seeming* mediation, by being left as they are but at the same time acquiring the significance of being an attribute of the idea, a result, a product of the idea. The difference lies not in the content but in the method of approach or in the *manner of speaking.* There is a double history, an esoteric and an exoteric. The content lies in the exoteric part. The interest of the esoteric part is always that of finding again in the state the history of the logical concept. It is on the exoteric side, however, that development proper takes place.

Rationally interpreted, Hegel's propositions would only mean this:

The family and civil society are parts of the state. The material of the state is distributed amongst them "by circumstances, caprice and the individual's own choice of vocation". The citizens of the state are members of families and members of civil society.

"The actual idea, mind, *divides itself* into the two ideal spheres of its concept, family and civil society, that is, *its finite* phase"—hence, the division of the state into family and civil society is *ideal,* i. e., necessary as part of the essence of the state. Family and civil society are actual components of the state, actual spiritual existences of the will; they are modes of existence of the state. Family and civil society constitute *themselves* as the state.

They are the driving force. According to Hegel, they are on the contrary *produced* by the actual idea. It is not the course of their own life which unites them in the state; on the contrary, it is the idea which in the course of its life has separated them off from itself. Indeed, they are the finiteness of this idea. They owe their presence to another mind than their own. They are entities determined by a third party, not self-determined entities. Accordingly, they are also defined as "finiteness", as the "actual idea's" own *finiteness*. The purpose of their being is not this being itself; rather, the idea separates these presuppositions off from itself "so as to emerge from their ideality as explicitly infinite actual mind". That is to say, there can be no political state without the natural basis of the family and the artificial basis of civil society; they are for it a *conditio sine qua non*. But the condition is postulated as the conditioned, the determinant as the determined, the producing factor as the product of its product. The actual idea only degrades itself into the "finiteness" of the family and civil society so as by transcending them to enjoy and bring forth its infinity. "*Accordingly*" (in order to achieve its purpose), it "assigns to these spheres the material of this, its finite actuality" (this? which? these spheres are indeed its "finite actuality", its "material"), "individuals as a multitude" ("the individuals, the multitude" are here the material of the state; "the state consists of them": this composition of the state is here expressed as an act of the idea, as an "allocation" which it undertakes with its own material. The fact is that the state issues from the multitude in their existence as members of families and as members of civil society. Speculative philosophy expresses this fact as the idea's deed, not as the idea of the multitude, but as the deed of a subjective idea different from the fact itself), "in such a way that with regard to the individual this assignment" (previously the discussion was only about the assignment of individuals to the spheres of the family and civil society) "appears mediated by circumstances, caprice, etc." Empirical actuality is thus accepted as it is. It is also expressed as rational, but it is not rational on account of its own reason, but because the empirical fact in its empirical existence has a different significance from it itself. The fact which is taken as a point of departure is not conceived as such, but as a mystical result. The actual becomes a phenomenon, but the idea has no other content than this phenomenon. Nor has the idea any other purpose than the logical one of being "explicitly infinite actual mind". The entire mystery of the philosophy of law and of Hegel's philosophy as a whole is set out in this paragraph.

263. "In these spheres in which its elements, individuality and particularity, have their **immediate** and **reflected** reality, mind is present as their objective generality *shining into them*, as the power of the rational in necessity [(para. 184)], i. e., as the *institutions* considered above."

264. "Since **they themselves** possess spiritual natures and therefore unite in themselves the two poles, namely, *explicitly* knowing and willing *individuality*, and the *generality* which knows and wills what is substantial, the individuals who make up the multitude acquire their rights on these two counts only insofar as they are actual both as private and as substantial persons. In these spheres [the family and civil society] they attain partly the first of these rights directly, and partly the second, in that they have their essential self-consciousness in the institutions as the inherently *general* aspect of their particular interests, and partly in that these institutions furnish them in the corporation with an occupation and an activity directed to a general purpose."

265. "These institutions are the components of the *constitution* (i.e., of developed and actualised rationality) *in the sphere of particularity*. They are, therefore, the firm foundation of the state as well as of the individual's confidence in it and disposition towards it, and the pillars of public freedom, since in them particular freedom is realised and rational, so that in themselves there is *implicitly* present the union of freedom and necessity."

266. "**But** mind is objective and actual to itself not merely as this" (which?) "necessity [...], but also as the *ideality* and the heart of this necessity. In this way this substantial generality is *itself* its *own* object and purpose, and therefore this necessity is equally present to itself in the *shape* of freedom."

The transition of the family and civil society into the political state is, therefore, this: the mind of these spheres, which is *implicitly* the mind of the state, now also behaves to itself as such and is *actual* for itself as their inner core. The transition is thus derived, not from the *particular* nature of the family, etc., and from the particular nature of the state, but from the *general* relationship of *necessity* to *freedom*. It is exactly the same transition as is effected in logic from the sphere of essence to the sphere of the concept. The same transition is made in the philosophy of nature from inorganic nature to life. It is always the same categories which provide the soul, now for this, now for that sphere. It is only a matter of spotting for the separate concrete attributes the corresponding abstract attributes.

267. "*Necessity* in ideality is the *development* of the idea within itself. As *subjective* substantiality it is **political** *conviction*, as *objective* substantiality, in distinction therefrom, it is the *organism* of the state, the strictly *political* state and *its constitution*."

The *subject* here is "necessity in ideality"—the "idea within itself". The *predicate: political conviction* and the *political constitution*. In plain language *political conviction* is the subjective and the *political constitution* the *objective substance* of the state. The logical development from family and civil society to the state is thus sheer *pretence*. For it is not explained how family sentiment, civic sentiment, the institution of the family and social institutions as such are related to political conviction and to the political constitution, and how they are connected.

The transition in which mind exists "not merely as this necessity and as a *realm of appearance*" but is actual for itself and has a particular existence as "the ideality [...] of this necessity", as the soul of this realm, this transition is no transition at all, for the soul of the family exists for itself as love, etc. The pure ideality of an actual sphere, however, could exist only as *science*.

It is important that Hegel everywhere makes the idea the subject and turns the proper, the actual subject, such as "political conviction", into a predicate. It is always on the side of the predicate, however, that development takes place.

Paragraph 268 contains a fine disquisition on political *conviction, patriotism,* which has nothing in common with logical exposition, except that Hegel describes this conviction as "*only* the result of the institutions existing in the *state*, in which rationality is *actually* present"; whereas on the contrary, these institutions are just as much an *objectification* of political conviction. Cf. the Remark to this paragraph.

269. "This conviction gets its distinctive *content* from the various aspects of the **organism** of the state. This *organism* is the development of the idea into its distinct aspects and their objective actuality. These different aspects are **thus** the *various authorities* and their functions and activities, through which the **general** continually *engenders* itself, and that in a *necessary* fashion, since they are determined by the *nature of the concept*; and through these authorities the general also *preserves* itself, being likewise presupposed in its own production. This organism is the *political constitution.*"

The political constitution is the organism of the state, or the organism of the state is the political constitution. That the various aspects of an organism stand to one another in a necessary connection arising out of the nature of the organism is sheer tautology. That if the political constitution is defined as an organism, the various aspects of the constitution, the various authorities, behave as organic features and stand to one another in a rational relationship, is likewise a tautology. It is a great advance to treat the political state as an organism and therefore to look upon the variety of authorities no longer as something [in]organic,[a] but as a living and rational differentiation. But how does Hegel present this discovery?

1) "This *organism* is the development of the idea into its distinct aspects and their objective actuality." It does not say: this

---

[a] Marx has written *organische* (organic) here, but this seems to be a slip of the pen. It should probably read *anorganische* (inorganic) or *mechanische* (mechanical).— *Ed.*

organism of the state is the development of the state into distinct aspects and their objective actuality. The genuine thought is this: the development of the state or the political constitution into distinct aspects and their actuality is an *organic* development. The *actual distinct aspects* or *various facets of the political* constitution are the premise, the subject. The predicate is their characterisation as *organic*. Instead of this, the idea is made the subject, and the distinct aspects and their actuality are conceived as the idea's development and product; whereas, on the contrary, the idea has to be developed from the actual distinct aspects. The organic is just the *idea of the distinct aspects*, their ideal definition. Here, however, the *idea* is spoken of as a subject, which develops itself into *its* distinct aspects. Besides this inversion of subject and predicate, the impression is given that some other idea than organism is meant here. The point of departure is the abstract idea, whose development in the state is the *political constitution*. What is therefore being treated here is not the political idea, but the abstract idea in the political element. By saying "this organism" (of the state, the political constitution) "is the development of the idea into its distinct aspects, etc.", I have said nothing at all about the *specific idea* of the political constitution; the same statement can be made with the same truth about the *animal* as about the *political* organism. By what, then, is the *animal* organism *distinguished* from the *political*? This cannot be deduced from this general definition. But an explanation which does not provide the *differentia specifica* is *no* explanation. The sole interest is in rediscovering "the idea" pure and simple, the "logical idea", in every element, whether of the state or of nature, and the actual subjects, in this case the "political constitution", come to be nothing but their mere *names,* so that all that we have is the appearance of real understanding. They are and remain uncomprehended, because they are not grasped in their specific character.

"These different aspects are *thus* the *various authorities* and their functions and activities." By means of the little word "thus", the appearance is given of logical sequence, of deduction and explanation. We must rather ask "why?" That "the various aspects of the organism of the state" are "the various authorities" and "their functions and activities" is an empirical fact; that they are members of an "organism" is the philosophical "predicate".

Here we note a stylistic peculiarity in Hegel which often recurs, and which is a product of mysticism. The whole paragraph runs:

"This conviction gets its distinctive content from the **various aspects** of the **organism** of the state. *This organism* is the development of the idea into its distinct aspects and their objective actuality. *These different aspects* are **thus** the *various authorities* and their functions and activities, through which the general continually *engenders* itself, and that in a *necessary* fashion, since they are determined by the *nature of the concept*; and through these authorities the general also *preserves* itself, being likewise presupposed in its own production. This organism is the *political constitution*."

(1) "This conviction gets its distinctive content **from the various aspects** of the organism of the state." "These different aspects are ... the *various authorities* and their functions and activities."

(2) "This conviction gets its distinctive content from the various aspects of the **organism** of the state. **This** *organism* is the development of the idea into its distinct aspects and their objective actuality ... through which the general continually *engenders* itself, and that in a *necessary* fashion, since they are determined by the *nature of the concept*; and through these authorities the general also *preserves* itself, being likewise presupposed in its own production. **This organism** is the *political constitution*."

As can be seen, Hegel uses two subjects, the "various aspects of the organism" and the "organism", as the point of departure for further definitions. In the third sentence [of Hegel's original para. 269] the "different aspects" are described as the "various authorities". By the inserted word "*thus*" it is made to seem as if these "various authorities" had been derived from the preceding sentence about the organism as the development of the idea.

Then comes more about the "various authorities". The statement that the general continually "engenders" itself and thereby preserves itself says nothing new, for this is already implied in the description [of these authorities] as "aspects of the organism", as "organic" aspects. Or rather this characterisation of the "various authorities" is nothing but a paraphrase of the statement that the organism is "the development of the idea into its distinct aspects, etc."

The propositions that this organism is "the development of the idea into its distinct aspects and their objective actuality" or into distinct aspects through which "the general" (the general is here the same as the idea) "continually *engenders* itself, and that in a *necessary* fashion, since they are determined by the *nature of the concept*; and [...] also *preserves* itself, being likewise presupposed in its own production"—these propositions are identical. The latter is merely a more detailed elaboration of "the development of the idea into its distinct aspects". Hegel has thereby not advanced one step beyond the general concept of "the idea" or at most of the "organism" as such (for really it is this specific idea which is in question). What, then, entitles him to the final sentence: "This organism is the political constitution"? Why not "This organism is the solar system"? Because he has subsequently described "the various aspects of the state" as the "various authorities". The proposition that "the various aspects of the state are the various authorities" is an empirical truth and cannot be presented as a philosophical discovery, nor has it in any way emerged as a result of an earlier stage in the argument. By describing the organism, however, as the "development *of* the idea", by speaking of distinct aspects *of* the idea, and then inserting the concrete phrase "the various *authorities*", the impression is created that a *specific* content has been evolved. To the sentence "This conviction gets its distinctive content from the various aspects of the *organism of the state*" Hegel ought not to have conjoined "*this* organism" but rather "*the* organism is the development of the idea, etc." At any rate, what he says holds good of every organism, and there is no predicate present which would justify the subject "*this*". The actual result he wants to attain is the description of the *organism* as the *political constitution*. But no bridge has been built *whereby one could pass from the general idea of organism to the specific idea of the organism of the state or the political constitution*, and no such bridge can ever be built. The opening sentence speaks of "the various aspects of the organism of the state", which are later defined as "the various authorities". What is said, therefore, is merely this: "*the various authorities of the organism of the state*" or "*the state organism of the various authorities*" is the "*political constitution*" of the state. It is not from "organism", "*the* idea", its "distinct aspects", etc., that the bridge to the "*political* constitution" is built, but rather from the presupposed concept "various authorities", "organism of the *state*".

In truth, Hegel has done nothing but dissolve the "political constitution" into the general abstract idea of "organism"; but in appearance and in his own opinion he has evolved something determinate from the "general idea". He has turned the subject of the idea into a product, a predicate, of the idea. He does not develop his thinking from the object, but expounds the object in accordance with a thinking that is cut and dried — already formed and fixed in the abstract sphere of logic. It is not a question of evolving the specific idea of the political constitution, but of establishing a relationship of the political constitution to the abstract idea, of placing it as a phase in the life-history of the idea, a manifest piece of mystification.

Another statement is that the character of the "various authorities" is "determined by the *nature of the concept*", and therefore that the general "engenders" them "in a *necessary* fashion". The various authorities are therefore not determined by their "own nature", but by a nature alien to them. Similarly, the *necessity* is not derived from their own essence, still less critically established. Rather, their fate is predetermined by the "nature of the concept", sealed in "the sacred registers of the Santa Casa",[a] of logic. The soul of objects, in this case of the state, is cut and dried, predestined, prior to its body, which is really mere appearance. The "concept" is the Son in the "idea", in God the Father, the *agens*, the determining, differentiating principle. "Idea" and "concept" are here hypostatised abstractions.

270. "The fact that the purpose of the state is the general interest as such and the conservation therein of particular interests, the general interest being their substance, is, firstly, the *abstract actuality* or substantiality of the state. But it [this abstract actuality or substantiality of the state] is, secondly, its *necessity*, since it divides up into the conceptual *differentiations* of its activities which by virtue of that substantiality are equally actual, *concrete* attributes [of the state]—the **authorities**. Thirdly, however, this very substantiality, *having passed through the phase of education*, is mind knowing and willing itself. The state therefore *knows* what it wills, and knows it in its *generality*, as something *thought*. Hence it works and acts according to consciously adopted ends, known principles, and laws which are not merely *implicit* but are actually present to consciousness; and further, it acts with precise knowledge of existing conditions and circumstances, inasmuch as its actions have a bearing on these."

(The Remark to this paragraph on the relation of state and church [is to be considered] later.[3])

The application of these logical categories deserves quite special scrutiny.

"The fact that the **purpose** of the state is the **general interest** as such and the conservation therein of particular interests, the general interest being their substance, is, firstly, the *abstract actuality* or substantiality of the state."

The fact that the general interest as such and as the existence of particular interests is the *purpose of the state*—this fact constitutes the actuality of the state, its existence, abstractly defined. The state is not actual without this purpose. This is the essential object of its willing—but at the same time it is only a quite general definition of this object. This purpose as being is for the state the element of existence.

"But it" (the abstract actuality, substantiality [of the state]) "is, secondly, its *necessity*, since it divides up into the conceptual *differentiations* of its activities which by virtue of that substantiality are equally actual, *concrete* attributes—the authorities."

---

[a] Friedrich Schiller, *Don Carlos*, Act V, Scene 10. Santa Casa—literally "the holy house"—the Inquisition's prison in Madrid.—*Ed.*

It (the abstract actuality, the substantiality) is its (the state's) *necessity*, since its actuality divides up into *distinct activities*, whose differentiation is rationally determined and which are moreover concrete attributes. The abstract actuality of the state, its substantiality, is necessity, inasmuch as it is only in the existence of the different state authorities that the true purpose of the state and the true existence of the whole are realised.

That is clear. The first description of the state's actuality was *abstract*: the state cannot be regarded as simple actuality; it has to be seen as activity — and as differentiated activity.

"The *abstract actuality* or substantiality of the state [...] is its *necessity*, since it [the abstract actuality or substantiality] divides up into the conceptual differentiations of its activities which by virtue of that **substantiality** are equally actual, *concrete* attributes — the authorities."

The substantiality-relation is a relation of necessity: that is to say, substance appears divided into independent, but essentially determinate *actualities* or *activities*. These abstractions will be applicable to anything and everything actual. If I first regard the state under the heading of "abstract actuality", I shall subsequently have to regard it under the heading of "concrete actuality", of "necessity", of realised difference.

"Thirdly, however, this very substantiality, *having passed through the phase of education*, is mind knowing and willing itself. The state therefore *knows* what it wills, and knows it in its *generality*, as something *thought*. Hence it works and acts according to consciously adopted ends, known principles, and laws which are not merely *implicit* but are actually present to consciousness; and further, it acts with precise knowledge of existing conditions and circumstances, inasmuch as its actions have a bearing on these."

Now let us translate this whole paragraph into plain language.

1) *Mind knowing and willing itself* is the substance of the state (mind, *educated and self-aware*, is the subject and the foundation of the state, its independent existence).

2) *The general interest and, therein, the conservation of particular interests* constitutes the general purpose and content of this mind — the enduring substance of the state, the political aspect of self-knowing and self-willing mind.

3) Self-knowing, self-willing, self-aware, educated mind achieves the *actualisation* of this abstract content only in the form of differentiated *activities* — as the existence of the *various authorities*, as *articulated power*.

About Hegel's presentation of this the following should be noted:

a) It is *abstract actuality*, *necessity* (or difference of substance), *substantiality* — hence *abstractly logical categories* — that are made into

I. THE INTERNAL CONSTITUTION AS SUCH

272. "The constitution is rational insofar as the state internally differentiates and defines its activity *in accordance with the nature of the concept*; and that in such a way that *each* of these *authorities* is in itself the *totality*, by containing the other elements in an operative form in itself, and that these authorities, since they express the differentiation of the concept, remain wholly within its ideality and constitute a *single individual* whole."

The constitution is thus rational insofar as its elements can be dissolved into abstractly logical elements. The state has to differentiate and define its activity not in accordance with its specific nature, but in accordance with the nature of the concept, which is the mystified movement of abstract thought. The rationale of the constitution is thus abstract logic and not the concept of the state. In place of the concept of the constitution we get the constitution of the concept. Thought does not conform to the nature of the state; but the state to a ready-made system of thought.

273. "The political state thus" (why?) "divides up into the following substantial divisions:

"a) The power to determine and lay down the general, *legislative power*;

"b) The power to subsume *particular* spheres and individual cases under the general, *executive power*;

"c) The power of **subjectivity** as the will which makes the final decision, the *power of the monarch*, in which the different powers are bound together into an individual unity, and which is therefore the summit and the source of the whole, i.e., of the *constitutional monarchy*."

We shall return to this division [of powers] after examining the details of its exposition separately.

274. "**Mind is actual** only as that which it knows itself to be, and the state, being the mind of a people, is at the same time the law *permeating all its relationships* and the customs and consciousness of its individual members. Hence the constitution of any given people generally depends on the **character and development of its self-consciousness**. Its subjective freedom and with this the **actuality of the constitution** is rooted in its self-consciousness.... Every nation, therefore, has the constitution appropriate to it and suitable for it."

All that follows from Hegel's argumentation is that a state in which there is a contradiction between "character and development of self-consciousness" and "constitution" is no true state. That the constitution which was the product of a bygone consciousness can become a heavy fetter on an advanced consciousness, etc., etc., these are surely trivial truths. What would really follow would be simply the demand for a constitution which contains within itself the designation and the principle to advance along with consciousness, to advance as actual men advance, this is only possible when "man" has become the principle of the constitution. Hegel here is a *sophist*.

a) *The Monarch's Authority*

275. "The monarchical authority contains in itself the three elements of the whole [(para. 272)], the *general element* of the constitution and the laws, consultation as the relation of the *particular* to the general, and the element of final *decision*, as the *self-determination* to which everything else can be traced back and from which everything else derives its actuality. This absolute self-determination forms the **distinctive principle** of the monarchical authority as such, which has yet to be expounded."

The beginning of this paragraph says first of all no more than this: "The general element of the constitution and the laws" is the *monarchical authority. Consultation*, or the relation of the *particular* to the general, is the *monarchical authority*. The authority of the monarch does not stand outside the general system of the constitution and the laws, once it is taken to refer to the authority of the (constitutional) monarch.

What Hegel really wants to establish, however, is only that "the general element of the constitution and the laws" is the monarchical authority, the sovereignty of the state. It is wrong, then, to make the *monarchical authority* into the *subject*, and to make it seem, since the monarchical authority can also be taken as referring to the authority of the monarch, as if he, the monarch, were the master of *this* element, its subject. But let us turn now to what Hegel presents as "*the distinctive principle of the monarchical authority as such*"—namely, "the element of final *decision*, as the *self-determination* to which everything else can be traced back and from which everything else derives its actuality"—"absolute self-determination".

Here Hegel is simply saying that the *actual*, i.e., *individual, will* is the *monarchical authority*. Thus in paragraph 12 he says:

"In giving itself the form of *individuality* [...] the will is that which resolves, and only as the will that resolves is it an **actual** will."

Insofar as this element of "final decision" or "absolute self-determination" is separated from the "general element" of the contents and from the particularity of consultation, we have *actual will* as *arbitrariness*. Or:

"*Arbitrariness* is the monarchical authority", or "the monarchical authority is arbitrariness".

276. "The fundamental attribute of the political state is substantial unity as the *ideality* of its elements. In this unity

"α) The particular powers and functions of the state are as much dissolved as preserved, and they are preserved only insofar as they have no independent justification but are justified only to the extent determined by **the idea of the** *whole*, since they issue *from the power of the whole*, and are flexible limbs of it, as their single self."

Addition: "With this ideality of the elements it is much as with life in the physical organism."

Of course. Hegel is speaking purely of the idea of the "particular powers and functions" ... they are to be justified only to the extent determined in the idea of the whole; they are to issue only "from the power of the whole". That this *ought* to be so is implied in the idea of *organism*. What really called for explanation, however, was just how this is to be brought about. For what must prevail in the state is *conscious reason*; and *substantial* necessity, a necessity which, being purely internal, is also purely external, the accidental [intertwining]^a of "powers and functions", cannot be passed off as something rational.

277. "β) The particular functions and activities of the state, being its essential elements, are *peculiar to the state* and are associated with the *individuals* by whom they are applied and exercised not on the strength of their immediate personalities but only by virtue of their general and objective qualities. Hence the functions and affairs of the state are linked with a particular personality as such only formally and accidentally. State functions and powers cannot therefore be *private property*."

It goes without saying that if *particular* functions and activities are described as functions and activities of *the state*, as *state functions* and *state powers* they are not *private property* but *state property*. That is a tautology.

The functions and activities of the state are associated with individuals (the state is only effective through individuals), but with the individual not as a *physical* but as a *political* being, that is, with the *political quality* of the individual. It is therefore ridiculous of Hegel to say that *they* are "linked with a particular personality *as such only formally and accidentally*". On the contrary, they are linked with the individual by a *vinculum substantiale*,^b by an essential quality of the individual. They are the natural expression in action of his essential quality. This nonsense comes in because Hegel takes state functions and activities in abstract isolation, and the particular individual in antithesis to them. He forgets, though, that the particular individual is human and that the functions and activities of the state are human functions. He forgets that the essence of a "particular personality" is not its beard, its blood, its abstract physical character, but its *social quality*, and that state functions, etc., are nothing but modes of being and modes of

---

^a There is an unclear word at this point in Marx's manuscript. The word may be *Verschränkung* or *Verschlingung*— "intertwining" or "intermingling".— *Ed.*
^b Deep bond.— *Ed.*

action of the social qualities of men. Clearly, therefore, insofar as individuals are bearers of state functions and powers, they must be regarded in the light of their social and not of their private quality.

278. "That the particular functions and powers of the state are not self-sufficient or firmly based either on themselves or in the particular will of individuals, but have their ultimate root, rather, in the **unity of the state** as their **single self**, these two attributes together constitute *state sovereignty*."

"Despotism generally means the condition of lawlessness where the particular will as such, whether of a monarch or of a nation [...], counts as law, or rather, takes the place of law; whilst sovereignty by contrast forms the aspect of the ideality of the particular spheres and functions found precisely in a legal, constitutional state of affairs, such that no one of these spheres is independent, something self-sufficient in its purposes and ways of working and immersing itself only in itself, but on the contrary these purposes and ways of working are determined by and dependent on the *purpose of the whole* (which has been denominated in general terms by the rather vague expression '*good of the state*').

"This ideality manifests itself in two ways.

"In *peaceful* conditions, the particular spheres and functions pursue the path of minding their own business [...], and it is in part only by way of the unconscious *necessity* of the thing that their self-seeking is *turned* into a contribution to the support of one another and of the whole [...]. In part, however, it is by *direct influence* from above that they are not only continually brought back to the purpose of the whole and restricted accordingly [...], but are also constrained to perform direct services for the support of the whole. In *time of need*, however, whether internal or external, the organism in all its particularity fuses into the single concept of sovereignty, and to sovereignty is entrusted the salvation of the state at the sacrifice of this otherwise legitimate particularity. It is then that the **ideality** attains its **own proper** actuality."

This idealism is therefore not developed into a conscious rational system. In *peaceful* conditions it appears either merely as an external constraint imposed on the prevailing power, on private life by "direct influence from above", or as a blind, unconscious result of self-seeking. This ideality finds its "own proper actuality" only when the state is in a "condition of war or emergency" so that its essential nature is expressed here in this "condition of war and emergency" of the actual, existing state; whereas its "*peaceful*" conditions are just the war and misery of selfishness.

Sovereignty—the idealism of the state—exists, therefore, only as *inner* necessity, as *idea*. Hegel is satisfied even with this, for all that is at issue is the *idea*. Sovereignty thus exists, on the one hand, only as *unconscious, blind substance*. We shall presently encounter its other actuality.

279. "Sovereignty, in the first place simply the *general* thought of this ideality, *exists* only as *subjectivity* sure of itself and as the will's abstract and to that extent unfounded *self-*

1) "Sovereignty, in the first place simply the general thought of this ideality, *exists* only as *subjectivity* **sure of itself** [...]. In its truth subjectivity exists only as *subject*, **personality** only as

determination with which lies the final decision. This is the state's individuality as such, and only in this is the state itself *one*. In its truth, however, subjectivity exists only as *subject*, personality only as *person*, and in the constitution which has developed into real rationality each of the three elements of the concept has its *explicitly actual* and separate form. This absolutely decisive element of the whole is therefore not individuality in general, but one individual, the *monarch*."

person. In the constitution which has developed into real rationality each of the three elements of the concept has [its] explicitly actual and separate form."

2) Sovereignty "exists only [...] as the will's abstract and to that extent unfounded *self-determination* with which lies the final decision. This is the state's individuality as such, and only in this is the state itself *one* [...] (and in the constitution which has developed into real rationality each of the three elements of the concept has its *explicitly actual* and separate form). This absolutely decisive element of the whole is **therefore** not individuality in general, but *one* individual, the *monarch*".

The first proposition means only that the general thought of this ideality, the sorry character of whose existence we have seen above, would have to be the self-conscious work of subjects and exist as such for them and in them.

If Hegel had set out from real subjects as the bases of the state he would not have found it necessary to transform the state in a mystical fashion into a subject. "In its truth, however," says Hegel, "subjectivity exists only as *subject*, personality only as *person*." This too is a piece of mystification. Subjectivity is a characteristic of the subject, personality a characteristic of the person. Instead of conceiving them as predicates of their subjects, Hegel gives the predicates an independent existence and subsequently transforms them in a mystical fashion into their subjects.

The existence of predicates is the subject, so that the subject is the existence of subjectivity, etc.; Hegel transforms the predicates, the objects, into independent entities, but divorced from their actual independence, their subject. Subsequently the actual subject appears as a result, whereas one must start from the actual subject and look at its objectification. The mystical substance, therefore, becomes the actual subject, and the real subject appears as something else, as an element of the mystical substance. Precisely because Hegel starts from the predicates of the general description instead of from the real *ens* (ὑποκείμενον, subject), and since, nevertheless, there has to be a bearer of these qualities, the mystical idea becomes this bearer. The dualism consists in the fact that Hegel does not look upon the general as being the actual nature of the actual-finite, i.e., of what exists and is determinate, or upon the actual *ens* as the *true subject* of the infinite.

So in this case sovereignty, the essential feature of the state, is treated to begin with as an independent entity, is objectified. Then, of course, this objective entity has to become a subject again. This subject then appears, however, as a self-incarnation of sovereignty; whereas sovereignty is nothing but the objectified mind of the subjects of the state.

Leaving aside this fundamental defect of the exposition, let us consider this first proposition of the paragraph. As it stands there it means no more than this: Sovereignty, the ideality of the state, exists as person, as "subject" — obviously, as many persons, many subjects, since no single person absorbs in himself the sphere of personality, nor any single subject the sphere of subjectivity. What sort of state idealism would that be which, instead of being the actual self-consciousness of the citizens, the collective soul of the state, were to be *one* person, *one* subject? In this proposition Hegel has not set forth anything else. But let us now look at the second proposition which is interlinked with this one. Hegel is concerned to present the monarch as the true "God-man", as the *actual incarnation* of the Idea.

> "Sovereignty ... *exists* only ... as the will's abstract and to that extent unfounded *self-determination* with which lies the final decision. This is the state's **individuality** as such, and only in this is the state itself *one*. ... In the constitution which has developed into real rationality each of the three elements of the concept has its *explicitly actual* and separate form. This absolutely decisive element of the whole is **therefore** not individuality in general, but *one* individual, the *monarch*."

We have already drawn attention to this proposition earlier. The moment of resolving, of arbitrary, because definite, decision, is the *monarchical authority* of the *will* as such. The idea of the *monarchical authority*, as Hegel expounds it, is nothing but the *idea* of the *arbitrary*, of the *decision* of the will.

But whereas Hegel conceives of sovereignty as the idealism of the state, as the actual regulation of the parts by the idea of the whole, now he makes it "the will's *abstract* and to that extent *unfounded* self-determination with which lies the final decision. This is the state's *individuality* as such". Previously the discussion was about subjectivity, now it is about individuality. The state as sovereign must be *one, one individual,* [it must] possess individuality. The state is *one* "not only" in this individuality. The individuality is only the *natural* element in the oneness of the state, the *natural attribute* of the state. "This absolutely decisive element is *therefore* not individuality in general, but *one* individual, the *monarch*." Why? Because "each of the three elements of the concept in the constitution which has developed into real rationality has *its explicitly actual* and separate form". One element of the concept is "individuality", but this is not yet *one individual*. And what sort of constitution would that be in which generality, particularity and individuality each had "its *explicitly actual* and separate form"? Since it is not at all a question of an abstract entity but of the state, of society, we can even accept Hegel's classification. What would follow from it? As determining the general the citizen is legislator; as the maker of individual decisions, as *actually* exercising his will, he is king. What is the meaning of [saying that] *the individuality of the state's will* is "*one individual*", one particular individual distinct from all others? The element of *generality*, legislation, also has an "explicitly actual and separate form". One could therefore conclude that "the legislature are these particular individuals".

The Common Man:	Hegel:
2) The monarch has sovereign power, sovereignty.	2) The *sovereignty* of the state is **the** monarch.
3) Sovereignty does what it wills.	3) Sovereignty is "the will's abstract and to that extent unfounded *self-determination* with which lies the final decision".

Hegel converts all the attributes of the constitutional monarch in the Europe of today into the absolute self-determinations of *the will*. He does not say "the monarch's will is the final decision", but "the will's final decision is the monarch". The first proposition is empirical. The second perverts the empirical fact into a metaphysical axiom.

Hegel mixes up the two subjects—sovereignty "as subjectivity sure of itself" *and* sovereignty "as the will's *unfounded* self-determination, as the individual will", so as to construc the "idea" as "*one* individual".

It is obvious that subjectivity sure of itself must also *actually* will, and will as a unity, as an individual. But who has ever doubted that the state acts through individuals? Should Hegel want to argue that the state must have *one* individual as the representative of its individual unity, he would not get the *monarch* out of this. The *positive* result of this paragraph which we set down is merely this:

In the state the *monarch* is the element of *individual will*, of unfounded self-determination, of arbitrariness.

Hegel's Remark to this paragraph is so remarkable that we must examine it closely.

"The immanent development of a science, the *derivation of its entire content* from the elementary *concept* ... exhibits this peculiarity, that one and the same concept, in this case the **will**, which is abstract to begin with (because this is the beginning), is maintained, but its attributes are condensed—and this, indeed, purely through the concept itself—and in this way it gains a concrete content. Thus it is the basic element of personality, abstract at first in the sphere of immediate law, which has evolved through its various forms of subjectivity, and here, in the sphere of absolute law, in the state, in the completely concrete objectivity of the will, it is the *personality of the state,* the *state's certainty of itself.* This last, which in its single self transcends all particularities, cuts short the weighing of pros and cons between which it is possible to oscillate perpetually, *concluding* with its 'I will' and initiating all activity and actuality."

In the first place, it is not a "peculiarity of science" that the fundamental concept of a subject always recurs.

But then no *advance* has taken place. *Abstract personality* was the subject of abstract law. It has not changed; it is as *abstract personality* again the *personality of the state.* Hegel ought not to have been surprised that the *actual person*—and persons make the state—everywhere recurs as the essence of the state. He would have had cause for surprise at the contrary—and even more so at the recurrence of the person as a political person in the same meagre abstraction as the person of civil law.

Hegel here defines the monarch as "the personality of the state, the state's certainty of itself". The monarch is "personified sovereignty", "sovereignty incarnate", political consciousness in the flesh; in consequence, therefore, all other people are excluded from this sovereignty, from personality, and from political consciousness. At the same time, however, Hegel knows of no other content to give to this "*souveraineté personne*" than the "I will", the element of arbitrary choice within the will. "Political reason" and "political consciousness" are a "single" empirical person to the exclusion of all others; but this personified reason has no content other than the abstraction of the "I will". *L'état c'est moi.*

"***Further***, however, personality, and subjectivity in general, as something infinitely self-relating, only has *truth,* and its most direct, immediate truth, as person, as a subject existing for itself; and what exists for itself is likewise simply *one.*"

It goes without saying that since personality and subjectivity are only predicates of person and subject, they exist only as person and subject; and a person is *one.* But, Hegel should have continued, the *one* only has truth as the *many ones.* The predicate, the essence, never exhausts the spheres of its existence in *one unit* but *in many units.*

Instead, Hegel concludes:

"The personality of the state is actual only as a *person,* the *monarch.*"

Hence, because subjectivity is actual only as subject and the subject is actual only as one, the personality of the state is actual only as one person. A fine conclusion! Hegel might as well have concluded that because the individual human being is a unit, the human species is only a single human being.

"Personality expresses the concept as such; **at the same time** the person contains the concept's actuality, and only when so determined is the concept *idea*, truth."

Without the person, *personality* is certainly a mere abstraction; but the person is only the *actual idea* of personality as the embodiment of the species, *as the persons*.

"A so-called *juridical* person, a society, a community or a family, however inherently concrete it may be, contains personality only as an element, only abstractly; in a juridical person personality has not attained to the truth of its existence. The state, however, is precisely this totality in which the elements of the concept achieve the actuality corresponding to the truth peculiar to each of them."

There is considerable confusion in this passage. The *juridical* person, a society, etc., is called abstract: that is to say, precisely those species-forms are termed abstract in which the *actual person* manifests what is actually within him, objectifies himself and abandons the abstraction of the "person *quand même*". Instead of recognising this *realisation* of the person as the most concrete thing of all, the state is supposed to have the distinction that [in it] "the element of the concept", the "individuality", attains a mystical "presence". Rationality consists not in the reason of actual persons achieving actuality but in the elements of the abstract concept doing so.

"The concept of the monarch is therefore of all concepts the most difficult for ratiocination, i.e., for the method of reflection employed by the understanding. For this way of thinking does not get beyond the standpoint of isolated categories, and therefore knows only reasons [for this and that], finite points of view and *derivation* from premises. It therefore presents the dignity of the monarch as something *derivative* not merely in form but in content; whereas the concept of the monarch, on the contrary, is not derivative but *originates purely in itself*. Most closely related" (indeed!) "to this view is the idea of regarding the royal prerogative as based on divine authority, since its unconditional character is contained therein."

In a certain sense every necessary being "originates purely in itself"—in this respect the monarch's louse is as good as the monarch. Hence Hegel here was not saying anything special about the monarch. But if something is supposed to appertain to the monarch which makes him different in kind from all the other objects of science and of the philosophy of law, then that is real tomfoolery; and only correct insofar as the *"one person-idea"* is indeed something not derivable from the understanding but only from the imagination.

"*National sovereignty* may be spoken of in the sense that a nation is indeed an independent unit *in its external relations* and constitutes a state of its own", etc.

That is triviality. If the king is the "actual sovereignty of the state", it ought to be possible for "the king" to count as an "independent state" also in external relations, even without the people. But if he is sovereign inasmuch as he represents the unity of the nation, then he himself is only the representative, the symbol, of national sovereignty. National sovereignty does not exist by virtue of him, but he on the contrary exists by virtue of it.

"We may also speak of *sovereignty in home affairs* residing in the people, provided that we are only speaking generally about the *whole* and meaning only what was shown above (paras. 277, 278), namely, that sovereignty belongs to the state."

As if the actual state were not the people. The state is an abstraction. The people alone is what is concrete. And it is remarkable that Hegel, who without hesitation attributes a living quality such as sovereignty to the abstraction, attributes it only with hesitation and reservations to something concrete.

"The usual sense, however, in which men have recently begun to speak of the sovereignty of the people is in *opposition to the sovereignty existing in the monarch*. In this antithesis the sovereignty of the people is one of those confused notions which are rooted in the *wild* idea of the *people*."

The "confused notions" and the "*wild* idea" are here exclusively Hegel's. To be sure, if sovereignty *exists* in the monarch, then it is foolish to speak of an antithetical sovereignty in the people; for it is implied in the concept of sovereignty that sovereignty cannot have a double existence, still less one which is contradictory. However:

1) This is just the question: Is not that sovereignty which is claimed by the monarch an illusion? Sovereignty of the monarch or sovereignty of the people—that is the question.[a]

2) One can also speak of a sovereignty of the people *in opposition to the sovereignty existing in the monarch*. But then it is not a question of *one and the same sovereignty* which has arisen on two sides, but two *entirely contradictory concepts of sovereignty*, the one a sovereignty such as can come to exist in a *monarch*, the other such as can come to exist only in a *people*. It is the same with the question: "Is God sovereign, or is man?" One of the two is an untruth, even if an existing untruth.

"Taken *without* its monarch and the *articulation* of the whole which is necessarily and directly **associated with the monarch**, the people is that formless mass which is no longer a state. It no longer possesses *any* of the attributes which are to be found only in an *internally organised* whole—sovereignty, government, courts of law, the administration, estates of the realm, etc. With the appearance in a nation of such factors, which relate to organisation, to the life of the state, a people ceases to be that indeterminate abstraction, which, as a purely general notion, is called the nation."

---

[a] Marx here uses the English word "question".— *Ed.*

All this is a tautology. If a people has a monarch and the structure that necessarily and directly goes with a monarch, i. e., if it is structured as a monarchy, then indeed, taken out of this structure, it is a formless mass and a purely general notion.

"If by sovereignty of the people is understood a *republican* form of government and, more specifically, democracy [...] then [...] there can be no further discussion of such a notion in face of the developed idea."

That is indeed right, if one has only "such a notion" and not a "developed idea" of democracy.

Democracy is the truth of monarchy; monarchy is not the truth of democracy. Monarchy is necessarily democracy inconsistent with itself; the monarchical element is not an inconsistency in democracy. Monarchy cannot be understood in its own terms; democracy can. In democracy none of the elements attains a significance other than what is proper to it. Each is in actual fact only an element of the whole demos [people]. In monarchy one part determines the character of the whole. The entire constitution has to adapt itself to this fixed point. Democracy is the genus Constitution. Monarchy is one species, and a poor one at that. Democracy is content and form. Monarchy is *supposed* to be only a form, but it falsifies the content.

In monarchy the whole, the people, is subsumed under one of its particular modes of being, the political constitution. In democracy the *constitution itself* appears only as *one* determination, that is, the self-determination of the people. In monarchy we have the people of the constitution; in democracy the constitution of the people. Democracy is the solved *riddle* of all constitutions. Here, not merely *implicitly* and in essence but *existing* in reality, the constitution is constantly brought back to its actual basis, the *actual human being,* the *actual people,* and established as the people's *own* work. The constitution appears as what it is, a free product of man. It could be said that in a certain respect this applies also to constitutional monarchy; but the specific distinguishing feature of democracy is that here the *constitution* as such forms only *one* element in the life of the people—that it is not the *political constitution* by itself which forms the state.

Hegel starts from the state and makes man the subjectified state; democracy starts from man and makes the state objectified man. Just as it is not religion which creates man but man who creates religion, so it is not the constitution which creates the people but the people which creates the constitution. In a certain respect the relation of democracy to all other forms of state is like the relation of Christianity to all other religions. Christianity is the religion κατ' ἐξοχήν,[a] the *essence of religion*—deified man as a *particular* religion. Similarly, democracy is the *essence of all state constitutions*—socialised man as a *particular* state constitution. Democracy stands to the other constitutions as the genus stands to its species; except that here the genus itself appears as an existent, and therefore as one *particular* species over against the others whose existence does not correspond to their essence. To democracy all other forms of state stand as its Old Testament. Man does not exist for the law but the law for man—it is a *human manifestation*; whereas in the other forms of state man is a *legal manifestation*. That is the fundamental distinction of democracy.

All other *state forms* are definite, distinct, *particular forms of state*. In democracy the *formal* principle is at the same time the *material* principle. Only democracy, therefore, is the true unity of the general and the particular. In monarchy, for example, and in the republic as a merely particular form of state, political man has his particular mode of being alongside unpolitical man, man as a private individual. Property, contract, marriage, civil society, all appear here (as Hegel shows quite correctly with regard to these *abstract* state forms, but he *thinks* that he is expounding the idea of the state) as *particular* modes of existence alongside the *political* state, as the *content* to which the *political state* is related as *organising form*: properly speaking, the relation of the political state to this content is merely that of reason, inherently without content, which defines and delimits, which now affirms and now denies. In democracy the political state, which stands alongside this content and distinguishes itself from it, is itself merely a *particular* content and particular *form of existence* of the people. In monarchy, for example, this particular, the political constitution, has the significance of the *general* that dominates and determines everything particular. In democracy the state as particular is *merely* particular; as general, it is the truly general, i.e., not something determinate in distinction from the other content. The French have recently interpreted this as meaning that in true democracy the *political state is annihilated*.[5] This is correct insofar as the political state qua political state, as constitution, no longer passes for the whole.

In all states other than democratic ones the *state*, the *law*, the *constitution* is what rules, without really ruling—i. e., without materially permeating the content of the remaining, non-political

---

[a] *Par excellence*—i.e., "Christianity is the pre-eminent religion".—*Ed.*

spheres. In democracy the constitution, the law, the state itself, insofar as it is a political constitution, is only the self-determination of the people, and a particular content of the people.

Incidentally, it goes without saying that all forms of state have democracy *for* their truth and that they are therefore untrue insofar as they are not democracy.

In the states of antiquity the political state makes up the content of the state to the exclusion of the other spheres. The modern state is a compromise between the political and the unpolitical state.

In democracy the *abstract* state has ceased to be the dominant factor. The struggle between monarchy and republic is itself still a struggle within the abstract state. The *political* republic is democracy within the abstract state form. The abstract state form of democracy is therefore the republic; but here it ceases to be the *merely political* constitution.

Property, etc., in short, the entire content of the law and the state, is the same in North America as in Prussia, with few modifications. The *republic* there is thus a mere state *form*, as is the monarchy here. The content of the state lies outside these constitutions. Hegel is right, therefore, when he says: The political state is the constitution, i.e., the material state is not political. What obtains here is merely an external identity, a determination of changing forms. Of the various elements of national life, the one most difficult to evolve was the political state, the constitution. It developed as universal reason over against the other spheres, as ulterior to them. The historical task then consisted in its [the constitution's] reassertion, but the particular spheres do not realise that their private nature coincides with the other-worldly nature of the constitution or of the political state, and that the other-worldly existence of the political state is nothing but the affirmation of their own estrangement. Up till now the *political constitution* has been the *religious sphere*, the *religion* of national life, the heaven of its generality over against the *earthly existence* of its actuality. The political sphere has been the only state sphere in the state, the only sphere in which the content as well as the form has been species-content, the truly general; but in such a way that at the same time, because this sphere has confronted the others, its content has also become formal and particular. *Political life* in the modern sense is the *scholasticism* of national life. *Monarchy* is the perfect expression of this estrangement. The *republic* is the negation of this estrangement within its own sphere. It is obvious that the political constitution as such is brought into being only where the private spheres have won an independent existence. Where trade and landed property are not free and have not yet become independent, the political constitution too does not yet exist. The Middle Ages were the *democracy of unfreedom*.

The abstraction of the *state as such* belongs only to modern times, because the abstraction of private life belongs only to modern times. The abstraction of the *political state* is a modern product.

In the Middle Ages there were serfs, feudal estates, merchant and trade guilds, corporations of scholars, etc.: that is to say, in the Middle Ages property, trade, society, man are *political*; the material content of the state is given by its form; every private sphere has a political character or is a political sphere; that is, politics is a characteristic of the private spheres too. In the Middle Ages the political constitution is the constitution of private property, but only because the constitution of private property is a political constitution. In the Middle Ages the life of the nation and the life of the state are identical. Man is the actual principle of the state—but *unfree* man. It is thus the *democracy of unfreedom*—estrangement carried to completion. The abstract reflected antithesis belongs only to the modern world. The Middle Ages are the period of *actual* dualism; modern times, one of *abstract* dualism.

"We have already noted the stage at which the division of constitutions into democracy, aristocracy and monarchy has been made—the standpoint, that is, of that unity which is still **substantial, which still remains within itself and has not yet come to its process of infinite differentiation and inner deepening**: at that stage, the element of the *final self-determining resolution of the will* does not emerge explicitly into its *own proper actuality* as an *immanent* organic factor in the state."

In the spontaneously evolved monarchy, democracy and aristocracy there is as yet no political constitution as distinct from the actual, material state or the other content of the life of the nation. The political state does not yet appear as the *form* of the material state. Either, as in Greece, the *res publica*[a] is the real private affair of the citizens, their real content, and the private individual is a slave; the political state, *qua* political state, being the true and only content of the life and will of the citizens; or, as in an Asiatic despotism, the political state is nothing but the personal caprice of a single individual; or the political state, like the material state, is a slave. What distinguishes the modern state from these states characterised by the substantial unity between people and state is not, as Hegel would have it, that the various elements of the

---

[a] i.e., state, republic; etymologically, "public affairs".—*Ed.*

constitution have been developed into *particular* actuality, but that the constitution itself has been developed into a *particular* actuality alongside the actual life of the people — that the political state has become the *constitution* of the rest of the state.

<blockquote>280. "This, the ultimate self of the state's will, is in its abstraction a single self and therefore *immediate* individuality. Its very concept thus implies its attribute of being something *natural*: the essential nature of the monarch is therefore to be *this* individual, in abstraction from any other content, and this individual is destined for the dignity of the monarch directly and naturally, by *birth* in the course of nature."</blockquote>

We have already heard that subjectivity is a subject and the subject necessarily an empirical individual, *one*. Now we learn that in the concept of *immediate* individuality is implied the attribute of *being natural*, corporeal. Hegel has proved nothing but what is self-evident, namely, that subjectivity *exists* only as the *corporeal* individual; and, of course, to the corporeal individual belongs *birth in the course of nature*.

Hegel thinks he has proved that the "essential nature" of the subjectivity of the state, of sovereignty, of the monarch, is "to be *this* individual, in abstraction from any other content, and [that] this individual is destined for the dignity of the monarch directly and naturally, by *birth* in the course of nature". Sovereignty, royal dignity, would therefore be born. The *body* of the monarch would determine the dignity of the monarch. Thus at the very summit of the state, instead of reason, the merely *physical* would be decisive. Birth would determine the quality of the monarch, as it determines the quality of cattle.

Hegel has proved that the monarch has to be born, which no one doubts; but he has not proved that birth makes a monarch.

That man becomes a monarch by birth can no more be made a metaphysical truth than can the immaculate conception of the Virgin Mary. But just as this latter notion, this fact of consciousness, can be understood in the light of human illusion and circumstances, so can this other empirical fact.

In the Remark [to para. 280] which we are about to examine more closely, Hegel indulges himself in the pleasure of having demonstrated the irrational as absolutely rational.

<blockquote>"This transition of the concept of pure self-determination into the immediacy of being and so into the realm of nature is of a purely speculative character, and cognition of it therefore belongs to logical philosophy."</blockquote>

This is indeed purely speculative, but not the leap from *pure* self-determination, an abstraction, to the other extreme, the *pure* realm of nature (the accident of birth) — *car les extrêmes se touchent*. What is purely speculative is calling this a "transition of the concept" and presenting complete contradiction as identity, and supreme inconsistency as consistency.

We may regard it as a positive admission by Hegel that with the hereditary monarch the place of self-determining reason is taken by the abstract natural order, not as what it is, not as the natural order, but as the supreme determinant of the state; that this is the *positive* point at which monarchy can no longer preserve the appearance of being the organisation of rational will.

"Moreover, this transition is **on the whole the same**" (?) "as that familiar to us in the **nature of volition in general**, it is the process of translating a content from the sphere of subjectivity (in the form of a preconceived purpose) into that of existence [...]. But the **peculiar** form of the idea and of the transition here under consideration is the *immediate transformation* of the **pure self-determination of the will** (**of the simple concept itself**) into a *this*, a natural form of existence without mediation by a *particular* content (by a purpose in action)."

Hegel is saying that the transformation of state sovereignty (of a self-determination of the will) into the body of the born monarch (into existence) is *on the whole* that transition of content in general effected by the will in order to *realise*, to translate into existence, a purpose *entertained in thought*. But Hegel says: on the *whole*. The *peculiar* difference which he specifies is so peculiar as to destroy all analogy and to put *magic* in the place of the "nature of volition in general".

In the first place, the *transformation* of the preconceived purpose into existence is here *immediate, magical*. Secondly, the subject here is the *pure self-determination* of the will, the *simple concept itself*, it is the essence of the will as a mystical subject that makes decisions. It is not an actual, individual, conscious willing, it is the abstraction of volition which turns into a natural form of existence, the pure idea which embodies itself as *one* individual.

Thirdly, as the actualisation of willing into a natural form of existence takes place *immediately*, i.e., without any *means*, which otherwise the will requires for its objectification, so there is even lacking any *particular*, i.e., determinate, purpose: "Mediation by a *particular* content, by a purpose in action" does not take place, clearly, because no *acting* subject is present, and the abstraction, the pure idea of will, in order to act, has to act mystically. A purpose which is not a *particular* purpose is no purpose, just as action without purpose is purposeless, meaningless action. Thus the whole comparison with the teleological act of the will reveals itself in the end to be a piece of mystification itself, and an *empty* action of the idea.

The means is the absolute will and the word of the philosopher; the particular purpose is again the philosophising subject's aim of constructing the *hereditary monarch* out of the pure idea. The realisation of the purpose is simply an *assertion* by Hegel.

> "In the so-called *ontological proof* of the existence of God we have the same transformation of the absolute concept into being" (the same mystification). "This transformation has constituted the depth of the idea in modern times, although recently it has been presented" (rightly) "as *inconceivable*."
>
> "But since the notion of the monarch is regarded as falling entirely within the scope of ordinary" (sc. intelligent) "consciousness, the intellect here persists all the more in its separation [of the concept and existence] and sticks to the results thus derived by its clever ratiocination: it therefore denies that the moment of final decision in the state *as such* (i.e., in the rational concept) is bound up with what is directly natural in character."

People deny that the *final decision* is *born* and Hegel asserts that the monarch is by birth the final decision; but who has ever doubted that the final decision in the state is attached to actual *corporeal* individuals, and that it is therefore "bound up with what is directly natural in character"?

> 281. "Both elements in their undivided unity—the will's ultimate unfounded self, and, consequently, existence, likewise unfounded, as the aspect committed to *nature*—this idea of *that which is unmoved* by caprice constitutes the *majesty* of the monarch. In this unity lies the *actual unity* of the state, and it is only through this, its inward and *outward immediacy*, that the unity of the state is raised above the possibility of being drawn down into the sphere of *particularity* and its caprice, aims and opinions, and it likewise remains above the war of factions round the throne and the weakening and shattering of state power."

The two elements are: the *accident of the will*—caprice—and the *accident of nature*—birth. So: *His Majesty Accident*. Accident is thus the *actual unity* of the state.

How an "inward and outward immediacy" is supposed to be free from collision, etc., is an assertion of Hegel's which is quite incomprehensible, for it is just this immediacy which is exposed to it.

What Hegel asserts about elective monarchy applies with still greater force to the hereditary monarch:

> "In an elective monarchy, because of the nature of that relationship within it which has made *particular* will the ultimate deciding power, the constitution becomes an elective *capitulation*"—etc., etc.—"becomes a surrender of state authority at the discretion of the particular will, from which proceeds the transformation of particular **offices of state into private property**", etc.
>
> 282. "The *right to pardon* criminals flows from the sovereignty of the monarch, for to this alone it falls to actualise mind's power to undo what has been done and by forgiving and forgetting to wipe out a crime."

The right of pardon [*Begnadigungsrecht*] is the prerogative of mercy [*Gnade*]. Mercy is the highest expression of *haphazard arbitrariness*, and it is significant that Hegel makes it the attribute proper to the monarch. In the Addition to this paragraph Hegel declares that "*unfounded decision*" is its source.

283. "The *second* element in the monarch's authority is *particularity* or determinate content and its subsumption under the general. Insofar as this is given a particular existence, it takes the form of supreme consultative bodies and individual advisers. They bring before the **monarch** for his decision the content of current affairs of state or the legal provisions required to meet existing needs, together with their *objective* aspects, i.e., the grounds on which decisions are to be based, the relevant laws, circumstances, etc. Because *individuals* who discharge these duties are in direct contact with the person of the monarch, their choice and dismissal alike rest with his **unrestricted arbitrariness**."

284. "Since it is solely with regard to the *objective* element in decision-making (the knowledge of a topic and its context, and the relevant legal and other considerations) that *responsibility* can exist, in other words, since solely this aspect is capable of objective proof and therefore subject to consultation which is distinct from the personal will of the monarch as such, only these consultative bodies or individual advisers can incur **responsibility**. The peculiar majesty of the monarch, however, as the subjectivity making the final decision, is raised above all accountability for acts of government."

Hegel here describes quite empirically the *ministerial function* as it is usually defined in constitutional states. All that philosophy adds is to interpret this "empirical datum" as the existence, the predicate, of the "element of *particularity* in the monarch's authority".

(The Ministers represent the rational, objective aspect of the sovereign will. To them, therefore, also falls the *honour* of responsibility, whilst the monarch is fobbed off with the peculiar fancy of "majesty".) The speculative element is thus very meagre. The argument in its particulars, on the other hand, is based on quite empirical grounds, and actually on very abstract, very bad empirical grounds.

Thus, for example, the choice of Ministers is placed within "the unrestricted arbitrariness" of the monarch "because they are in direct contact with the person of the monarch"—i.e., because they are Ministers. In the same way, the "unrestricted choice" of the monarch's *valet* can be derived from the absolute idea.

Better, at least, is the reason given for the *accountability* of Ministers: "it is solely with regard to the *objective* element in decision-making (the knowledge of a topic and its context, and the relevant legal and other considerations) that *responsibility* can exist, *in other words,* solely this aspect is capable of *objective proof*". Of course, when one individual is the *hallowed, sanctified embodiment* of caprice, then "the subjectivity making the final decision", pure subjectivity, pure caprice, is not objective, and thus cannot be established objectively or therefore be accountable. Hegel's proof is conclusive if one accepts the constitutional presuppositions, but by *analysing* their basic notion, Hegel has not proved these presuppositions. The *whole uncritical character* of Hegel's philosophy of law *lies in this confusion.*

285. "The *third* element in the monarchical authority concerns that which is the general as such, which exists subjectively in the *conscience* of the *monarch* and objectively *in the whole* of the *constitution* and in the *laws*. The monarchical authority in this respect **presupposes** the other elements in the state, **just as it is presupposed by each of them**."

286. "The *objective guarantee* of the monarchical authority, of the right of hereditary succession to the throne and so forth, consists in the fact that just as this sphere has its own actuality, **differentiated** from that of the other rationally determined elements of the state, so these others in themselves have the rights and duties proper to their own definition. In the rational organism of the state, each member, by maintaining itself as such, thereby maintains the others in their distinctiveness."

Hegel does not see that with this third element, "the general as such", he explodes the first two or vice versa. "The monarchical authority in this respect presupposes the other elements in the state, just as it is presupposed by each of them." If this positing is understood not in a mystical sense but in a real sense, then the authority of the monarch is established not by birth but by the other elements, and is therefore not hereditary but fluid, i.e., it is a state function which is varyingly distributed among individual members of the state in accordance with the organisation of the other elements. In a rational organism the head cannot be of iron and the body of flesh. If the members are to maintain themselves, they must be of *equal birth*, of one flesh and blood. But the hereditary monarch is not of equal birth, he is made of different stuff. The prose of the rationalist will of the other members of the state is here confronted by the magic of nature. Besides, members of an organism can only mutually support one another insofar as the whole organism is fluid and each of them is absorbed in this fluidity, and when, therefore, no one of them, such as in this case the head of the state, is "unmoved" or "unalterable". By this proposition, therefore, Hegel abolishes "sovereignty by birth".

Secondly, irresponsibility. If the monarch violates "the whole of the constitution", the "laws", his irresponsibility is at an end, because his constitutional existence is at an end. But it is precisely these laws and this constitution which make him irresponsible. They therefore contradict themselves, and this *one* clause abolishes law and constitution. The constitution of constitutional monarchy is *irresponsibility*.

However, if Hegel is content with the thought "that just as this sphere has its own actuality, *differentiated* from that of the other rationally determined elements of the state, so these others *in themselves* have the rights and duties *proper* to their own definition", then he ought to call the medieval constitution an organisation; then all he has is merely a mass of particular spheres connected by an external necessity. And, indeed, a personal monarch fits only such a situation. In a state in which each particular attribute exists *on its own*, the *sovereignty of the state*, too, must be attached to a *particular* individual.

Résumé of Hegel's Exposition of the Monarch's Authority, or of the Idea of State Sovereignty

279. In the Remark, p. 367, it is said:

"*Sovereignty of the people* may be spoken of, in the sense that a people as a whole is an independent unit *in its external relations* and constitutes a state of its own, like the people of Great Britain. But the people of England, Scotland or Ireland, or the people of Venice, Genoa, Ceylon, etc., are no longer sovereign now that they have ceased to have **their own rulers** or supreme governments."

Here, therefore, the *sovereignty of the people* is *nationality*: the sovereignty of the monarch is *nationality*, or the monarchical principle is *nationality*, which by itself and exclusively forms the sovereignty of a people. A people whose *sovereignty* consists *solely* in nationality has a *monarch*. Difference of nationality among peoples cannot be better established or expressed than by having different *monarchs*. The same cleft which separates one absolute individual from another separates these nationalities.

The *Greeks* (and Romans) were *national* because and insofar as they were the *sovereign peoples*. The Germans are *sovereign* because and insofar as they are national. (*Vid. pag.* XXXIV.)[a]

"a so-called *juridical* person," further says the same Remark, "a society, a community or a family, however inherently concrete it may be, contains personality only as an element, only **abstractly;** in a juridical person personality has not attained to the **truth of its existence.** The state, however, is precisely this totality in which the elements of the concept achieve the actuality corresponding to the truth **peculiar to each of them.**"

The juridical person, society, the family, etc., contains personality only abstractly. In the monarch, on the other hand, the *state* is contained *within the person*.

It is only within the *juridical* person, society, the family, etc., that the *abstract person* has truly brought his *personality* into real existence. But Hegel conceives society, the family, etc., the *juridical person* in general, not as the realisation of the actual empirical person, but as an *actual* person, who, however, contains the ele-

---

[a] This refers to the relevant sheet of the manuscript (see this volume, p. 110).— *Ed.*

ment of personality as yet only abstractly. Hence, too, in Hegel, actual persons do not come to the state; instead, the state must first come to the actual person. Hence, instead of the state being brought forth as the supreme actuality of the person, as the supreme social actuality of man, *one single* empirical man, the empirical person, is brought forth as the supreme actuality of the state. This perversion of the subjective into the objective and of the objective into the subjective is a consequence of Hegel's wanting to write the biography of abstract substance, of the idea, man's activity, etc., thus having to appear as the activity and result of something else, and of his wanting to make the human essence operate on its own, as an imaginary individuality, instead of in its *actual human* existence. The inevitable outcome of this is that an *empirical existent* is *uncritically* accepted as the actual truth of the idea; for it is not a question of bringing empirical existence to its truth, but of bringing truth to an empirical existent, and so what lies to hand is expounded as a *real* element of the idea. (On this necessary transforming of empirical fact into speculation and of speculation into empirical fact, more later.[a])

In this way, too, the impression is produced of something *mystical* and *profound*. It is common knowledge that men are born, and that what is brought into being by physical birth becomes a social person, etc., and eventually a citizen of a state; that it is via his birth that a man comes to be all that he is. But it is very profound, it is startling, to hear that the idea of the state is born without intermediary; that, in the birth of the monarch, this idea has given birth to its own empirical existence. No content is gained in this way, only the *form* of the old content is changed. It has received a philosophical *form*, a philosophical testimonial.

Another consequence of this mystical speculation is that a *particular* empirical existent, one individual empirical existent in distinction from the others, is regarded as the *embodiment of the idea.* Again, it makes a deep mystical impression to see a *particular empirical* existent posited by the idea, and thus to meet at every stage an incarnation of God.

If, for example, in the exposition of the family, civil society, the state, etc., these social modes of man's existence are regarded as the actualisation, the objectification, of his essence, then the family, etc., appear as qualities inherent in a subject. The human being remains always the essence of all these entities, but these entities also appear as man's *actual* generality, and therefore also as *something*

---

[a] See this volume, pp. 60-65.— *Ed.*

men have in common. But if on the contrary family, civil society, the state, etc., are attributes of the idea, of substance as subject, they must be given an empirical actuality, and that body of people among whom the idea of civil society unfolds are members of a civil society, that other body of people [among whom the idea of the state unfolds] being state citizens. Since all we have here, really, is *allegory*, for the sole purpose of conferring on some empirical existent or other the *significance* of being the actualised idea, it is clear that these vessels have fulfilled their function as soon as they have become specific embodiments of elements in the life of the idea. The general, therefore, appears everywhere as something specific, particular; and individuality, correspondingly, nowhere attains to its true generality.

It therefore necessarily seems that the most profound, most speculative level has been reached when the most abstract attributes, the natural bases of the state such as birth (in the case of the monarch) or private property (in primogeniture), which have not yet developed at all into genuine social actualisation, appear as the highest ideas directly personified.

And it is self-evident. The correct method is stood on its head. The simplest thing becomes the most complicated, and the most complicated the simplest. What ought to be the starting point becomes a mystical outcome, and what ought to be the rational outcome becomes a mystical starting point.

However, if the monarch is the abstract *person* who contains the *state within his own person*, this only means that the essence of the state is the abstract *private person*. Only in its flower does the state reveal its secret. The monarch is the one private person in whom the relation of private persons generally to the state is actualised.

The hereditary character of the monarch follows from his concept. He is to be the person specifically distinguished from the whole species, from all other persons. What is it, then, that ultimately and firmly distinguishes one person from all others? The *body*. The highest function of the body is *sexual activity*. The highest constitutional act of the king is therefore his sexual activity, for through this he *makes* a king and perpetuates his body. The body of his son is the reproduction of his own body, the creation of a royal body.

b) *The Executive*

287. There is a difference between the **decisions** of the monarch and the **execution** and **application** of these decisions and, in general, the prosecution and maintenance of past decisions, of existing laws, arrangements and institutions for

common purposes, and the like. This task of *subsumption* [...] falls within the scope of the *executive,* as do the *judicial* **and** *police* authorities, which have more direct relation to the particular concerns of civil society, and which assert the general interest within these aims."

The usual explanation of the executive. The only thing that can be said to be *original* in Hegel is that he *links* the *executive,* the police and the *judiciary,* whereas usually the administration and the judiciary are treated as antithetical.

288. "*Particular* common interests, which fall within civil society **and lie outside the intrinsically and explicitly general character of the state proper** (para. 256), are administered by the **corporations** (para. 251) of the municipalities and of other trades and estates with their authorities, officials, administrators and the like. These concerns are on the one hand the *private property* and *interest* of these *particular* spheres, and from this point of view the authority of these officials rests on the confidence of their social equals and the members of their communities, and on the other hand, these circles must be subordinated to the higher interests of the state. This being so, the filling of these official posts in the corporations will in general be effected by a mixture of popular election by those interested with ratification and appointment by a higher authority."

A straightforward description of the empirical position in some countries.

289. "The *maintenance* of the *general state interest* and of *legality* in this sphere of particular rights, and the relating back of these to the general interest and legality, require to be seen to by **representatives** of the executive — **executive** *civil servants* and higher advisory bodies inasmuch as they are constituted on collegiate lines — which converge at the top in chiefs who are in direct touch with the monarch."

Hegel has not *fully set forth executive authority.* But even taking this into account, he has not proved that the executive power is more than *one function,* one *attribute,* of state citizens as such. He has deduced the executive as a *particular, separated* power only by looking at the "particular interests of civil society" as such, which "lie outside the intrinsically and explicitly general character of the state".

"Just as **civil society is the battlefield of the individual private interests of all against all, so here the struggle of private interests against particular common concerns and of both these together** against the superior viewpoints and edicts of the state has its seat. At the same time the corporation spirit, generated by the vested rights of the particular spheres, is itself inwardly transformed into the spirit of the state, on finding in the state the means for the support of particular aims. It is the **secret** of the patriotism of the citizens in this respect, that they know the state to be their substance, **because** it is the state which backs their particular spheres, both their rights and authority, and their welfare. The corporation spirit, since it *directly* comprises the *rooting* of the *particular in the general,* therefore constitutes the depth and strength which the state possesses in the citizens' *frame of mind.*"

The above is remarkable

1) On account of the definition of civil society as *bellum omnium contra omnes*;

2) Because *private egoism* is revealed as the "*secret of the patriotism of the citizens*" and as the "depth and strength which the state possesses in the citizens' frame of mind";

3) Because the "citizen", the man of the particular interest as opposed to the general, the member of civil society, is looked upon as a "fixed individual", whereas the state also confronts the "citizens" in "fixed individuals".

Hegel, one would have thought, should have defined "civil society" as well as the "family" as an attribute of every individual member of the state, and therefore the subsequent "political qualities" too as attributes of the individual member of the state as such. But [with Hegel] it is not the self-identical individual who unfolds new attributes out of his social essence. It is the essence of the will which allegedly brings forth its attributes out of itself. The extant, various and disparate, empirical forms of existence of the state are looked upon as direct incarnations of one or other of these attributes.

The general as such being given an independent existence, it is directly confounded with the empirical form of existence, and the limited straightway accepted uncritically as the expression of the idea.

Hegel falls into self-contradiction here only inasmuch as he does not regard the "family man", like the citizen, as a fixed breed denied those other qualities.

290. "*Division of labour* [...] also occurs in the **business of the government.** The organisation of administrative bodies has this formal but difficult task insofar as below, where civil life is *concrete,* it must be governed concretely, while the business of the executive is nevertheless divided into its *abstract* branches, administered by special departments as distinct centres whose activities merge below, as well as at the top, in the supreme government authority, in a concrete survey."

The *Addition* to this paragraph is to be considered later.[6]

291. Government business is by nature *objective* and determined, explicitly and in substance, by decisions already taken (para. 287), and has to be carried through and realised by *individuals.* Between it and these individuals there is no immediate **natural** link. The individuals are therefore not destined for office by virtue of their birth or natural personality. The objective factor in their appointment is knowledge and proof of ability. Such proof guarantees that the state gets what it requires, and since it is the sole condition of appointment, it also guarantees to every citizen the **opportunity** to devote himself to the general estate."

292. "Since the objective element in appointing to office in the administration is not genius (as in art, for example), selection is of necessity from an indefinite *plurality* of individuals whose relative merits cannot be positively ascertained, and is therefore subjective. The selection of a *particular* individual for a post, his appoint-

ment, and his authorisation to conduct public business, this linking of the individual to the office, whose relation one to the other must always be fortuitous, is the prerogative of the monarch as the deciding and sovereign power in the state."

293. "The particular affairs of state which **monarchy** devolves to departments of state constitute one part of the *objective* aspect of the sovereignty dwelling in the monarch. Their specific *differentiation* is also given by the nature of the subject-matter. And whilst the activity of the departments is the fulfilment of a duty, their business is also a right relieved of contingency."

The only thing to note is the *"objective* aspect of the sovereignty *dwelling in* the monarch".

294. "The individual who is appointed by sovereign act (para. 292) to an official position has to fulfil the duties — the substantial feature — of his post as the condition of his appointment, where *as a consequence* of this substantial relationship he finds means and the assured satisfaction of his particularity (para. 264), and is freed in his external circumstances and his official activity from other kinds of subjective dependence and influence."

"The service of the state [...] requires," the Remark says, "the renunciation of independent and arbitrary satisfaction of subjective aims; and at the same time offers the right to find satisfaction in, but only in, the discharge of one's duties. In this fact, so far as this aspect is concerned, there lies the link between the general and the particular interests which constitutes both the concept of the state and its inner stability (para. 260)." "The assurance of satisfaction of particular needs removes the external pressure which may induce a man to seek means for their satisfaction at the expense of his work and his duty as an official. In the general power of the state, those entrusted with its affairs find protection against that other subjective aspect, the private passions of the governed, whose private interests, etc., suffer as the general interest is made to prevail against them."

295. "The security of the state and of the governed against the abuse of power by government departments and their officials lies, on the one hand, directly in their hierarchical structure and accountability and, on the other hand, in the rights vested in local authorities and corporations. This prevents the intrusion of subjective arbitrariness into the power entrusted to a civil servant, and supplements from below the control from above which does not reach down to the conduct of individuals."

296. "But the fact that behaviour marked by dispassionateness, uprightness and kindness becomes *customary* [among civil servants] is partly connected with direct *moral* and *intellectual education,* which provides a spiritual counterpoise to whatever there is of the mechanical and suchlike in the learning of the so-called sciences related to their spheres of work, in the requisite professional training, in the actual work itself, etc.; in part the *size* of the state is also an important factor, weakening the pressure of family and other personal ties, and making less potent and less keen such passions as hatred, revenge, etc. In preoccupation with the large interests present in a great state these subjective features disappear of themselves, and habituation to general interests, points of view, and concerns is produced."

297. "The members of the government and the civil servants constitute the major part of the *middle estate,* in which is concentrated the developed intelligence of the mass of a people and its consciousness of what is lawful. That this section should not assume the isolated position of an aristocracy or use education and ability as a means to arbitrary domination, depends on the **institutions of sovereignty** working from above and on the **corporate institutions' rights** exercised from below."

"*Addition*: In the middle estate, to which civil servants belong, there is consciousness of the state and the most pronounced degree of education. This estate therefore constitutes the pillar of the state in terms of uprightness and intelligence." "The education of this middle estate is a principal interest of the state, but this can only occur in an organic structure such as we have been considering, namely, as a result of the rights vested in particular, relatively independent circles, and through a **world of officials** whose arbitrariness is checked by those who possess such rights. Action in accordance with general law, and habituation to such action, is a consequence of the antithesis constituted by these independent circles."

What Hegel says about the "executive" does not deserve to be called a philosophical exposition. Most of the paragraphs could stand word for word in the Prussian Common Law.[7] And yet, the administration proper is the most difficult point of all in the exposition.

As Hegel has already assigned the "police" and the "judiciary" to the sphere of *civil society*, the *executive* is nothing more than the administration, which he expounds as *bureaucracy*.

The bureaucracy presupposes, firstly, the *"self-government"* of civil society in *"corporations"*. The only stipulation added is that the selection of administrators, officials, etc., for these corporations is a *mixed* responsibility, initiated by the citizens and ratified by the executive proper ("ratification by a *higher* authority", as Hegel puts it).

Over this sphere, for the "maintenance of the general state interest and of legality", stand *"representatives"* of the executive", the "executive civil servants" and the "collegiate bodies", which converge in the "monarch".

"Division of labour" takes place in the "business of the government". Individuals must prove their suitability for government service — i.e., pass examinations. The choice of *specific* individuals for public office is the prerogative of the monarchical state authority. The division of state business is "given by the nature of the subject-matter". The responsibility of office is the duty of civil servants and their life's vocation. They must therefore receive *salaries* from the state. The guarantee against the abuse of bureaucratic power is partly the hierarchical structure and accountability of the bureaucracy, and on the other hand the rights which communities and corporations possess. The humanity of the bureaucracy depends partly on the "direct moral and intellectual education", partly on the "size of the state". Officials form the "major part of the middle estate". Against their becoming an "aristocracy and arbitrary domination" protection is provided, partly by "the institutions of sovereignty working from above", and partly by "the corporate institutions' rights exercised from below". The "middle estate" is the estate of "education". *Voilà tout.* Hegel gives us an empirical description of the bureaucracy, partly as it is in actual fact, and partly as it is on its own estimation. And with this the difficult chapter on the "executive" is done with.

Hegel proceeds from the *separation* of the "state" and "civil" society, from "particular interests" and the "intrinsically and explicitly general"; and indeed bureaucracy is based on *this separation.* Hegel proceeds from the presupposition of the "corporations", and indeed the bureaucracy does presuppose the *corporations,* or at least the "spirit of the corporations". Hegel expounds no *content* for the bureaucracy, but only some general features of its *"formal"* organisation; and indeed the bureaucracy is only the "formalism" of a content which lies outside itself.

The *corporations* are the materialism of the bureaucracy, and the bureaucracy is the *spiritualism* of the corporations. The corporation is the bureaucracy of civil society; the bureaucracy is the corporation of the state. In actual fact, therefore, bureaucracy as the "civil society of the state" confronts the "state of civil society", the corporations. Wherever the "bureaucracy" is a new principle, wherever the general state interest begins to become something "distinctive and separate" and thus a "real" interest, the bureaucracy fights against the corporations, as every consequence fights against the existence of its premises. On the other hand, once the state actually comes to life and civil society frees itself from the corporations by its own rational impulse, the bureaucracy tries to restore them. For with the fall of the "state of civil society" goes the fall of the "civil society of the state". The spiritualism disappears along with the materialism which opposes it. The consequence fights for the existence of its premises as soon as a new principle challenges not their *existence,* but the *principle* of their existence. The same spirit which creates the corporation in society creates the bureaucracy in the state. Hence, the attack on the spirit of the corporations is an attack on the spirit of the bureaucracy; and if earlier the bureaucracy combated the existence of the corporations in order to make room for its own existence, so now it tries forcibly to keep them in existence in order to preserve the spirit of the corporations, which is its own spirit.

The "bureaucracy" is the *"state formalism"* of civil society. It is the "state consciousness", the "state will", the "state power", as *one corporation*—and thus a *particular, closed* society within the state. (The "general interest" can maintain itself against the particular as "something particular" only so long as the particular maintains itself against the general as "something general". The bureaucracy must therefore protect the *imaginary* generality of the particular interest, the spirit of the corporations, in order to protect the *imaginary* particularity of the general interest — its own spirit. The state has to be a corporation so long as the corporation wants to be a state.) The bureaucracy wants the corporation, however, as an *imaginary* power. To be sure, the individual corporation, too, on behalf of its *particular* interest, has the same wish as regards the bureaucracy, but it *wants* the bureaucracy against other corporations, against other particular interests. The bureaucracy as the *perfect corporation* is therefore victorious over the *corporation* as the imperfect bureaucracy. The bureaucracy reduces the corporation to an appearance, or wants to do so, but it wants this appearance to exist, and to believe in its own existence. The corporation is the attempt of civil society to become the state; but the bureaucracy is the state which has actually turned itself into civil society.

The "state formalism" which bureaucracy is, is the "state as formalism"; and it is as a formalism of this kind that Hegel has described bureaucracy. Since this "state formalism" constitutes itself as an actual power and itself becomes its own *material* content, it goes without saying that the "bureaucracy" is a web of *practical* illusions, or the "illusion of the state". The bureaucratic spirit is a jesuitical, theological spirit through and through. The bureaucrats are the jesuits and theologians of the state. The bureaucracy is *la république prêtre*.

Since by its *very nature* the bureaucracy is the "state as formalism", it is this also as regards its *purpose*. The actual purpose of the state therefore appears to the bureaucracy as an objective *hostile* to the state. The spirit of the bureaucracy is the "formal state spirit". The bureaucracy therefore turns the "formal state spirit" or the *actual* spiritlessness of the state into a categorical imperative. The bureaucracy takes itself to be the ultimate purpose of the state. Because the bureaucracy turns its "formal" objectives into its content, it comes into conflict everywhere with "real" objectives. It is therefore obliged to pass off the form for the content and the content for the form. State objectives are transformed into objectives of the department, and department objectives into objectives of the state. The bureaucracy is a circle from which no one can escape. Its hierarchy is a *hierarchy of knowledge*. The top entrusts the understanding of detail to the lower levels, whilst the lower levels credit the top with understanding of the general, and so all are mutually deceived.

The bureaucracy is the imaginary state alongside the real state — the spiritualism of the state. Each thing has therefore a double meaning, a real and a bureaucratic meaning, just as knowledge (and also the will) is both real and bureaucratic. The really existing, however, is treated in the light of its bureaucratic nature, its other-worldly, spiritual essence. The bureaucracy has the state, the spiritual essence of society, in its possession, as its *private property*. The general spirit of the bureaucracy is the *secret*, the mystery, preserved within itself by the hierarchy and against the outside world by being a closed corporation. Avowed political spirit, as also political-mindedness, therefore appear to the bureaucracy as *treason* against its mystery. Hence, *authority* is the basis of its knowledge, and the deification of authority is its *conviction*. Within the bureaucracy itself, however, *spiritualism* becomes *crass materialism*, the materialism of passive obedience, of faith in authority, of the *mechanism* of fixed and formalistic behaviour, and of fixed principles, views and traditions. In the case of the individual bureaucrat, the state objective turns into his private objective, into a *chasing after higher posts*, the *making of a career*. In the first place, he looks on actual life as something *material*, for the *spirit of this life has its distinctly separate existence* in the bureaucracy. The bureaucracy must therefore proceed to make life as material as possible. Secondly, actual life is material for the bureaucrat himself, i.e., so far as it becomes an object of bureaucratic manipulation; for his spirit is prescribed for him, his aim lies beyond him, and his existence is the existence of the department. The state only continues to exist as various fixed bureaucratic minds, bound together in subordination and passive obedience. *Actual* knowledge seems devoid of content, just as actual life seems dead; for this imaginary knowledge and this imaginary life are taken for the real thing. The bureaucrat must therefore deal with the actual state jesuitically, whether this jesuitry is conscious or unconscious. However, once its antithesis is knowledge, this jesuitry is likewise bound to achieve self-consciousness and then become deliberate jesuitry.

Whilst the bureaucracy is on the one hand this crass materialism, it manifests its crass spiritualism in the fact that it wants to *do everything*, i.e., by making the *will* the *causa prima*. For it is purely an *active* form of existence and receives its content from without and can prove its existence, therefore, only by shaping and restricting this content. For the bureaucrat the world is a mere object to be manipulated by him.

When Hegel calls the executive the *objective* aspect of the sovereignty dwelling in the monarch, that is right in the same sense in which the Catholic Church was the *real presence* of the sovereignty, substance and spirit of the Holy Trinity. In the bureaucracy the identity of state interest and particular private aim is established in such a way that the *state interest* becomes a *particular* private aim over against other private aims.

The abolition of the bureaucracy is only possible by the general interest *actually*—and not, as with Hegel, merely in thought, in *abstraction*—becoming the particular interest, which in turn is only possible as a result of the *particular* actually becoming the *general* interest. Hegel starts from an unreal antithesis and therefore achieves only an imaginary identity which is in truth again a contradictory identity. The bureaucracy is just such an identity.

Now let us follow his exposition in detail.

The sole philosophical statement Hegel makes about the *executive* is that he *"subsumes"* the individual and the particular under the general, etc.

Hegel contents himself with this. On the one hand, the category of "subsumption" of the particular, etc. This has to be actualised. Then he takes any one of the empirical forms of existence of the Prussian or modern state (just as it is), anything which actualises this category among others, even though this category does not express its specific character. Applied mathematics is also subsumption, etc. Hegel does not ask "Is this the rational, the adequate mode of subsumption?" He only takes the *one* category, and contents himself with finding a corresponding existent for it. Hegel gives *a political body to his logic*: he does not give the *logic of the body politic* (para. 287).

On the relation to the government of the corporations and the local bodies, we learn first of all that their *administration* (the appointment of their magistracy) requires "in general a mixture of popular election by those interested with *ratification* and appointment by a *higher* authority". The *mixed selection* of officials of local bodies and corporations would thus be the *first relationship* between civil society and state or executive, their *first identity* (para. 288). According to Hegel himself, this identity is very superficial—a *mixtum compositum,* a *"mixture"*. Superficial as is this identity, so the antithesis is sharp. Since "these concerns" (of the corporation, the local body, etc.) "are on the one hand the *private property* and *interest* of these *particular* spheres, and from this point of view the authority of these officials rests on the confidence of their social equals and the members of their communities, and on the other hand, these circles must be subordinated to the *higher interests of the state*", the outcome is the indicated *"mixed selection".*

The administration of the corporation therefore has this antithesis:

Private property and the interest of the particular spheres against the higher interest of the state; antithesis between private property and state.

It does not need to be remarked that the resolution of this antithesis in the *mixed selection* is a mere *compromise,* a treaty, a *confession* of unresolved dualism, itself a *dualism,* a *"mixture".* The *particular* interests of the corporations and local authorities have a dualism within *their own sphere*—a dualism which likewise shapes the character of their *administration.*

The well-marked antithesis only comes to the fore, however, in the relationship of these *"particular common* interests", etc., which "lie outside the intrinsically and explicitly general character of the *state"* on the one hand, and this *"intrinsically and explicitly general character of the state"* on the other. To begin with, it is again present within this latter sphere.

"The maintenance of the general state interest and of legality in this sphere of particular rights, and the relating back of these to the general interest and legality, require to be **seen to** by **representatives** of the **executive—executive** *civil servants* and higher advisory bodies inasmuch as they are constituted **on collegiate lines**—which converge at the top in chiefs who are in direct touch with the monarch." (Para. 289.)

Incidentally, let us note the construction of the administrative *councils* which are unknown in France, for instance. *"Inasmuch"* as Hegel adduces these bodies as *"advisory",* it is certainly obvious that they are "constituted on collegiate lines".

Hegel brings in the "state proper", the "executive", to "see to" the "general state interest and legality, etc.", within civil society through "representatives", and according to him it is really these "representatives of government", the "executive civil servants", who constitute the *true "representation of the state"*—not "of", but "against" "civil society". The antithesis of state and civil society is thus fixed: the state does not reside in, but outside civil society. It touches it only through its *"representatives"* who are entrusted with *"seeing to the state"* within these spheres. Through these "representatives" the antithesis is not transcended, but has become a "legal", "fixed", antithesis. By means of deputies the "state"—an entity alien and ulterior to the *essence* of civil society—asserts itself over against civil society. The "police", the "judiciary" and the "administration" are not deputies of civil society itself, in and through whom it administers its *own* general interest, but representatives of the state for the administration of the state over against civil society. Hegel further explains this *antithesis* in the frank Remark [to para. 289] examined above.

"Government business is by nature *objective* and determined, explicitly [...], by decisions already taken." (Para. 291.)

Does Hegel conclude from this that for this very reason this government business all the less requires any "hierarchy of knowledge", and that it can be completely carried out by "civil society itself"? On the contrary.

He makes the profound observation that this business has to be carried out by "individuals", and that "between it and these individuals there is no immediate *natural* link". This is an allusion to the monarch's power, which is nothing but the *"natural power of arbitrary choice"*, and so can be *"born"*. The "monarchical authority" is nothing but the representative of the element of nature in the will, of the "dominion of *physical nature in the state"*.

The "executive civil servants" are therefore essentially distinguished from the "monarch" in the way they acquire their offices.

"The **objective factor** in their appointment" (sc. to government) "is knowledge" (subjective arbitrariness lacks this factor) "and proof of ability. Such proof guarantees that the state gets what it requires, and since it is the sole condition of appointment, it also guarantees to **every citizen the opportunity** to devote himself to the **general** estate."

This *opportunity* for every citizen to become a civil servant is thus the second affirmative relationship between civil society and state, the *second identity*. It is of a very superficial and dualistic nature. Every Catholic has the opportunity to become a priest (i.e., to separate himself from the laity as from the world). Does the clergy confront the Catholic as an other-worldly power any the less on that account? The fact that anyone has the opportunity to acquire the right of *another* sphere merely proves that in *his own* sphere this right has no reality.

In the genuine state it is not a question of the opportunity of every citizen to devote himself to the general estate as one particular estate, but the capacity of the general estate to be really general—that is, to be the estate of every citizen. But Hegel proceeds from the premise of the pseudo-general, illusory-general estate—the premise of generality as a particular estate.

The identity which he has constructed between civil society and state is the identity of *two hostile armies,* where every soldier has the "opportunity" to become, by "desertion", a member of the "hostile" army; and indeed Hegel herewith correctly describes the present empirical position.

It is the same with his construction of the "examinations". In a rational state, to sit an examination should be demanded of a shoemaker rather than an executive civil servant. For shoemaking is a skill without which one can be a good citizen of the state and social human being; whereas the necessary "political knowledge" is a requirement without which a person in the state lives outside the state, cut off from himself, from the air. The "examination" is nothing but a Masonic rite, the legal recognition of a knowledge of citizenship as a privilege.

The *examination*—this "link" between the "office of state" and the "individual", this objective bond between the knowledge of civil society and the knowledge of the state—is nothing but the *bureaucratic baptism of knowledge,* the official recognition of the *transubstantiation* of profane into sacred knowledge (in every examination, it goes without saying, the examiner knows all). One does not hear that the Greek or Roman statesmen passed examinations. But of course, what is a Roman statesman against a Prussian government official!

Besides the *examination,* the *objective* bond between the individual and public office, there is another bond—the *arbitrary decision of the monarch.*

"Since the objective element in appointing to office in the administration is not genius (as in art, for example), selection is of necessity from an indefinite *plurality* of individuals whose relative merits cannot be positively ascertained, and is therefore subjective. The selection of a *particular* individual for a post, his appointment, and his authorisation to conduct public business, this linking of the individual to the office, whose relation one to the other must always be fortuitous, is the prerogative of the monarch as the deciding and sovereign power in the state." [Para. 292.]

The monarch is everywhere the representative of contingency. In addition to the objective element of the bureaucratic confession of faith (the examination) there is also needed the subjective element of monarchical *grace and favour,* so that the faith may bear fruit.

"The particular affairs of state which *monarchy* devolves to departments of state" (the monarchy distributes, devolves the particular activities of the state to the departments as *business, distributes the state amongst the bureaucrats*; it hands them over as the Holy Roman Church hands out ordination. The monarchy is a system of emanation; the monarchy leases out the functions of the state) "constitute one part of the *objective* aspect of the sovereignty dwelling in the monarch." Here Hegel distinguishes for the first time the *objective* from the *subjective* aspect of the sovereignty dwelling in the monarch. Previously he cast them both together. The sovereignty dwelling in the monarch is taken here in a clearly mystical sense, just as theologians find the personal God in nature. It was also stated that the monarch is the subjective aspect of the sovereignty dwelling in the *state* (para. 293).

In para. 294 Hegel deduces the *salary* of the civil servants from the idea. Here in the *salary* of the civil servants, or in the fact that the service of the state also guarantees security of empirical existence, the *real identity* of civil society and the state is established. The civil servant's *pay* is the highest identity which Hegel constructs. The transformation of *state activities* into *official posts* presupposes the separation of the state from society. Hegel says:

"The service of the state [...] requires the renunciation of independent and arbitrary satisfaction of subjective aims", which is what any service requires, "and at the same time offers the right to find satisfaction in, but only in, the discharge of one's duties. In this fact, so far as this aspect is concerned, there lies the link between the general and the particular interests which constitutes both the concept of the state and its inner stability."

(1) This holds good of every servant, and (2) it is true that civil service *pay* constitutes the inner stability of the deep[-rooted] modern monarchies. Only the existence of civil servants is *guaranteed*, in contrast to that of the member of civil society.

Now it cannot escape Hegel that he has constructed the executive as an *antithesis* to civil society, and indeed as a dominant pole. How does he now establish a relation of identity?

According to para. 295, "the security of the state and of the governed against the *abuse* of power by government departments and their officials" lies, on the one hand, directly in their "hierarchical structure". (As if the hierarchy were not the *chief abuse,* and the few personal sins of the officials not at all to be compared with their *inevitable* hierarchical sins. The hierarchy punishes the official if he sins against the hierarchy or commits a sin unnecessary from the viewpoint of the hierarchy. But it takes him into its protection whenever the hierarchy sins in him; moreover, the hierarchy is not easily convinced of the sins of its members.) And security against abuse also lies "in the rights vested in local authorities and corporations. This prevents the intrusion of subjective arbitrariness into the power entrusted to a civil servant, and supplements from below the control from above which does not reach down to the conduct of individuals" (as if this control were not exercised from the standpoint of the bureaucratic hierarchy).

Thus the privileges of the corporations are the second guarantee against the arbitrariness of the bureaucracy.

If we ask Hegel, then, what protection civil society has against the bureaucracy, his answer is:

1) "*Hierarchy*" of the bureaucracy; *control*. It is the fact that the adversary himself is bound hand and foot, and that if he is a hammer to those below, he is an anvil to those above. Where, then, is the protection against the "hierarchy"? The lesser evil is indeed abolished by the greater insofar as it vanishes by comparison.

2) The *conflict,* the unresolved conflict, between bureaucracy and corporation. *Struggle,* the *possibility* of struggle, is the guarantee against defeat. Later (para. 297) Hegel adds as a further guarantee the "institutions of sovereignty working from above", by which is meant again the hierarchy.

However, Hegel adduces two more factors (para. 296):

In the civil servant himself—and this is supposed to humanise him and make "behaviour marked by dispassionateness, uprightness and kindness" "customary"—"direct moral and intellectual education" is supposed to provide the "spiritual counterpoise" to the *mechanical character* of his knowledge and of his "actual work". As if the "mechanical character" of his "bureaucratic" knowledge and of his "actual work" did not provide the "counterpoise" to his "moral and intellectual education"! And will not his actual mind and his actual work as substance triumph over the accident of his other endowments? For his "post" is his "substantial" relationship and his "livelihood". Fine, except that Hegel sets "direct moral and intellectual education" against the "mechanical character of bureaucratic knowledge and work"! The man within the official is supposed to secure the official against himself. But what unity! *Spiritual counterpoise.* What a dualistic category!

Hegel also cites the "size of the state", which in Russia provides no guarantee against the arbitrariness of the "executive civil servants", and which in any case is a circumstance which lies "*outside*" the "*essential nature*" of the bureaucracy.

Hegel has expounded the "executive" as "state officialdom".

Here, in the sphere of the "intrinsically and explicitly general character of the state proper", we find nothing but unresolved conflicts. The final syntheses are the civil servants' *examinations* and their *livelihood.*

As the final consecration of the bureaucracy Hegel adduces its impotence, its conflict with the corporation.

In para. 297 an identity is established, insofar as "the members of the government and the civil servants constitute the major part of the *middle estate*". Hegel praises this "middle estate" as the "pillar of the state in terms of uprightness and intelligence". (Addition to the quoted paragraph.)

> "The education of this middle estate is a principal interest of the state, but this can only occur in an organic structure such as we have been considering, namely, as a result of the rights vested in particular, relatively independent circles, and through a **world of officials** whose arbitrariness is checked by those who possess such rights."

Certainly, only in such an organic structure can the nation appear as *one* estate, the *middle estate*. But is that an organic structure which keeps itself going by means of the counterposing of privileges? The executive power is the most difficult to expound. It belongs to the entire nation to an even much higher degree than the legislative power.

Later, in the Remark to para. 308, Hegel expresses the real spirit of the bureaucracy when he characterises it as "business routine" and the "horizon of a restricted sphere".

c) *The Legislature*

> 298. "The *legislative authority* is concerned with the laws as such, insofar as they require to be further determined, and with **internal** affairs in their **entirely general** aspects" (a very general expression). "This authority is itself a **part of the constitution,** which is antecedent to it and which accordingly lies wholly beyond direct determination by the legislature, but which undergoes further development by the elaboration of laws and by the dynamic character of government affairs in general."

The first thing that is striking is Hegel's emphasis on the point that "this authority is itself a part of the constitution, which is antecedent to it and which lies wholly beyond direct determination by the legislature", since he has not made this remark about either the monarchical or the executive authority, though it is equally true of them. Then, however, Hegel is constructing the constitution as a whole, and, thus, cannot presuppose it. However, we recognise the profundity in Hegel precisely in the fact that he everywhere begins with and lays stress on the *opposition* between attributes (as they exist in our states).

The "legislative authority is itself a part of the *constitution*" which "lies wholly beyond direct determination by the legislature". But, again, the constitution has surely not made itself spontaneously. The laws, which "require to be further determined", must surely have had to be formulated. A legislative authority *prior* to the constitution and *outside* of the constitution must exist or have existed. A legislative authority must exist beyond the actual, *empirical, established* legislative authority. But, Hegel will reply, we are presupposing an *existing* state. Hegel, however, is a philosopher of law and is expounding the genus of the state. He must not measure the idea by what exists, but what exists by the idea.

The collision is simple. The *legislative power* is the power to organise the general. It is the power of the constitution. It reaches beyond the constitution.

But, on the other hand, the legislative power is a constitutional power. It is therefore subsumed under the constitution. The constitution is *law* for the legislative authority. It *gave* and continues to give laws to the legislature. The legislative authority is only the legislative authority within the constitution, and the constitution would stand *hors de loi,* were it to stand outside the legislative authority. *Voilà la collision!* In recent French history this proved to be a hard nut to crack.

How does Hegel resolve this antinomy?

First he says:

The *constitution* is *"antecedent"* to the legislature; it *"accordingly* lies wholly *beyond* direct determination *by the legislature"*.

"But"—but "by the elaboration of laws" "and by the dynamic character of government affairs in general" it "undergoes" its "further development".

That is to say, then: directly, the constitution lies beyond the reach of the legislature; but indirectly, the legislature changes the constitution. The legislature does in a roundabout way what it cannot and must not do straightforwardly. It takes the constitution apart piecemeal, because it cannot change it wholesale. It does through the nature of things and circumstances what, from the nature of the constitution, it ought not to do. It does *materially* and *in fact* what *formally, legally,* and constitutionally it does not do.

Hegel has not herewith abolished the antinomy: he has transformed it into another antinomy. He has posed the *working* of the legislature—its *constitutional* working—in antithesis to its constitutional *designation.* The opposition between the *constitution and the legislature* remains. Hegel has depicted the *actual* and the *legal* action of the legislature as constituting a contradiction, or again depicted the contradiction between what the legislature is supposed to be and what it actually is, between what it thinks it is doing and what it really does.

How can Hegel present this contradiction as the truth? "The dynamic character of government affairs in general" explains just as little, for it is just this dynamic character that calls for explanation.

In the Addition Hegel contributes nothing, it is true, to the solution of these difficulties. But he sets them out still more clearly.

> "The constitution must be actually and explicitly the firm and recognised ground on which the legislature stands, and for this reason it must not initially be completed. Thus the constitution *is*, but just as essentially it *becomes*, i.e., its formation advances. This advance is an **alteration** which is **inconspicuous** and does not have the **form of alteration**."

That is to say: according to the law (illusion) the constitution *is*, but according to reality (the truth) it *develops*. According to its definition the constitution is unalterable, but actually it is altered; only, this alteration is unconscious, it does not have the form of alteration. The *appearance* contradicts the *essence*. The appearance is the *conscious* law of the constitution, and the essence is its *unconscious* law, which contradicts the former. What the thing is in its own nature is not in the law. In law it is rather the contrary.

Is this, then, the truth: that in the state, according to Hegel the highest presence of *freedom,* the presence of self-conscious reason, it is not the law, the presence of freedom, which rules, but blind natural necessity? And if the law of the thing is recognised as contradicting the legal definition, why not recognise the law of the thing, of reason, as the law of the state as well; why consciously cling to the dualism? Hegel wants everywhere to present the state as the actualisation of free mind, but *re vera* he resolves all the difficult collisions by means of a natural necessity which stands in opposition to freedom. Thus the transition of the particular interest into the general is likewise not a conscious law of the state, but is mediated by accident, proceeds *against* consciousness, and Hegel wants everywhere in the state the realisation of free will! (Here Hegel's *substantial* standpoint makes itself evident.)

The examples of *gradual* alteration of the constitution which Hegel gives are infelicitously chosen, like the transformation of the property of the German princes and their families from private estates into state domains, or the transformation of the personal administration of justice by the German emperors into administration by representatives. The first transition only worked out in such a way that all state property was transformed into private property of the monarch.

Besides, these are particular changes. Certainly, entire state constitutions have changed in such a way that gradually new needs arose, the old broke down, etc.; but for a *new* constitution a real revolution has always been required.

"Hence further development of a condition of affairs," Hegel concludes, "is something **apparently** tranquil and unnoticed. In this way, after a long time, a constitution passes into a condition quite different from what existed previously."

The category of *gradual* transition is, in the first place, historically false; and in the second place, it explains nothing.

If the constitution is not merely to suffer change; if, therefore, this illusory appearance is not finally to be violently shattered; if man is to do consciously what otherwise he is forced to do without consciousness by the nature of the thing, it becomes necessary that the movement of the constitution, that *advance,* be made the *principle of the constitution* and that therefore the real bearer of the constitution, the people, be made the principle of the constitution. Advance itself is then the constitution.

Does the "constitution" itself, then, properly belong to the domain of the "legislative authority"? This question can only be raised (1) when the political state exists as the mere formalism of the real state, when the political state is a distinct domain, when the political state exists as "constitution"; (2) when the legislative authority has a different source from that of the executive authority, etc.

The legislature made the French Revolution; in general, wherever it has emerged in its particularity as the dominant element, it has made the great, organic, general revolutions. It has not fought the constitution, but a particular, antiquated constitution, precisely because the legislature was the representative of the people, of the will of the species. The executive, on the other hand, has produced the small revolutions, the retrograde revolutions, the reactions. It has made revolutions not for a new constitution against an old one, but against the constitution, precisely because the executive was the representative of the particular will, of subjective arbitrariness, of the magical part of the will.

Posed correctly, the question is simply this: Has the people the right to give itself a new constitution? The answer must be an unqualified "Yes", because once it has ceased to be an actual expression of the will of the people the constitution has become a practical illusion.

The collision between the constitution and the legislature is nothing but a *conflict of the constitution with itself,* a contradiction in the concept of the constitution.

The constitution is nothing but a compromise between the political and the unpolitical state. Hence, it is necessarily in itself a treaty between essentially heterogeneous powers. Here, then, it is impossible for the law to declare that one of these powers, one part of the constitution, is to have the right to modify the constitution itself, the whole.

If we are to speak of the constitution as something particular, however, it must be considered, rather, as one *part* of the whole.

If by the constitution is understood the general, the fundamental attributes of rational will, then it is obvious that every people (state) has these as its basis, and that they must form its political credo. This is really a matter of knowledge and not of will. The will of a people can no more escape the laws of reason than the will of an individual. In the case of an irrational people one cannot speak at all of a rational organisation of the state. Here, in the philosophy of law, moreover, the will of the species is our subject-matter.

The legislature does not make the law; it only discovers and formulates it.

The resolution of this conflict has been sought in the distinction between *assemblée constituante* and *assemblée constituée*.

> 299. "These concerns" (of the legislature) "are more precisely defined in relation to individuals under two heads: (α) what advantages and benefits they receive from the state; and (β) what they have to contribute to the state. Under the former come the laws belonging to the sphere of civil law generally, laws concerning the rights of local bodies and corporations, and quite general arrangements; and, indirectly (para. 298), the whole of the constitution. As for the contributions [from individuals]: only if these contributions are reduced to *money*, as the existing general *value* of things and services, can they be fixed justly, and at the same time in such a way that the *particular* tasks and services which the individual can perform are mediated by his own choice."

With regard to this definition of the concerns of the legislature Hegel himself observes in the Remark to this paragraph:

> "In general, indeed, the way in which the concerns of general legislation can be distinguished from matters calling for decision by administrative departments or government regulation generally, is that to the former belongs what is **wholly general** in content—the legal enactments, whereas to the latter belongs the **particular** and the manner of *execution*. This distinction, however, is not a hard and fast one, because a law, to be a law and not a mere general command (such as 'Thou shalt not kill' [...], must in itself be something *definite*; and the more definite it is, the more its terms are capable of being carried out as they stand. At the same time, however, to give to laws such a very detailed determinacy would give them empirical features which would inevitably become subject to alterations in the course of being actually implemented, and this would jeopardise their character as laws. The **organic unity** of the state authorities itself implies that *one* spirit establishes the general and also brings it to its determinate actuality and carries it out."

But it is precisely this *organic* unity which Hegel has failed to construct. The different authorities have different principles.

They are, moreover, solid reality. To take refuge from their real conflict in an *imaginary* "organic unity", instead of expounding them as elements of an organic unity, is therefore mere empty, mystical evasion.

The first unresolved collision was that between the *constitution as a whole* and the *legislature.* The second is that between the *legislature* and the *executive,* between the law and its execution.

The second statement in the paragraph is that the only contribution which the state requires from individuals is *money.*

The reasons Hegel gives for this are:

1) Money is the existing general *value* of things and services;

2) The contributions can only be fixed *justly* by means of this reduction;

3) Only in this way can the contribution be fixed so that the *particular* tasks and services which an individual can perform are mediated by his own choice.

Hegel observes in the Remark:

On 1: "It may, in the first place, seem astonishing that of the numerous skills, possessions, activities and talents and the infinitely manifold living *properties*[a] this implies, which are at the same time associated with a definite frame of mind, the state demands no direct service, but lays claim only to the *one* kind of property,[a]—that which appears in the form of *money.*

"The services relating to the defence of the state against enemies pertain only to the duty considered in the next section." (Not because of the next section but for other reasons, it is only later that we shall come to the personal obligation to military service.[8])

"In fact, however, money is not one *particular* kind of property alongside the others but their general form, insofar as they are produced in the externality of concrete being, in which they can be grasped as a *thing.*"

"With us," he goes on in the *Addition,* "the state *buys* what it needs."

On 2: "Only at this extreme of externality" (sc. where *wealth* is produced in the externality of concrete being, in which its various forms can be grasped as *things*) "is *quantitative* precision, and therewith justice and **equality of contributions,** possible." In the *Addition* he says: "By means of money, however, the **justice of equality** can be much better achieved." "Otherwise the talented would be more taxed than the untalented, if it depended on concrete ability."

On 3: "In his state *Plato* has individuals assigned to the particular estates by the guardians and has their *particular* services imposed on them [...]; in feudal monarchy vassals had equally indeterminate services to perform, but they had also to serve in their *particular character*—e. g., as judges, etc. The services demanded in the East, in Egypt, for the immense architectural works, etc., are likewise of *particular* quality, etc. In these conditions the principle of *subjective freedom* is lacking—i. e., the principle that the individual's substantial activity, which in any case becomes something particular in content in services like those mentioned, shall

---

[a] The German word *Vermögen,* here rendered as "property", has a wide range of meanings including ability, capacity, faculty, power, etc., as well as fortune, wealth, riches.—*Ed.*

be mediated by his *particular will*. This is a right which can only be realised through the demand for services in the form of a general value, and it is the reason which has brought about this transformation."

In the Addition he says: "With us, the state *buys* what it needs, and this may at first seem abstract, dead and heartless, and it can also look as if the state were in decline because it is satisfied with abstract services. But the principle of the modern state requires that everything which the individual does shall be mediated by his will."

"...But nowadays **respect** for subjective freedom is publicly recognised precisely in the fact that the state lays hold of a man only by that by which he is capable of being seized."

Do what you will, pay what you must.
The beginning of the Addition reads:

"The two sides of the constitution relate to the rights and services of individuals. As regards services, they are now almost all reduced to money. Military service is now almost the only personal service."

300. "Effective in the legislative authority as a **totality** are, first, the other two elements—the *monarchy*, whose prerogative it is to make the supreme decisions, and the *executive*, as the advisory authority possessing the concrete knowledge and over-all view of the whole in its manifold aspects together with the actual principles which have become **firmly established** in it, and also a knowledge of the requirements of state power in particular; and finally the *estates* element."

The monarchical authority and the executive authority are ... legislative authority. If, however, the legislative authority is the *totality*, monarchical and executive authority would, rather, have to be elements of the legislative authority. The supervening *estates* element is legislative authority *alone*, or the legislative authority in *distinction* from the monarchical and executive authority.

301. "The *estates* element has this characteristic, that in it matters of general concern come to exist not merely *in themselves* but also *for themselves*; in it, that is to say, the element of subjective *formal freedom*, public consciousness as the *empirical generality* of the opinions and thoughts of the *many*, comes into existence."

The estates element is a deputation of civil society to the state, which it confronts as the "many". The many are to deal for a moment with matters of general concern *consciously*, as being their own, as objects of *public consciousness* which according to Hegel is nothing but the "*empirical generality* of the opinions and thoughts of the *many*" (and in fact in modern monarchies, including constitutional monarchies, it is nothing else). It is significant that Hegel, who has such a great respect for the state spirit, for the ethical spirit, for state consciousness, positively despises it when it confronts him in an actual, empirical form.

This is the enigma of mysticism. The same fantastic abstraction, which rediscovers *state consciousness* in the inadequate form of the *bureaucracy*, a hierarchy of knowledge, and which uncritically accepts this inadequate existent as the real existent and as *fully valid*, this same mystical abstraction just as candidly avows that the real, *empirical* state spirit, *public consciousness*, is a mere pot-pourri of "thoughts and opinions of the many". As it imputes to the bureaucracy an alien essence, so it leaves for the true essence the inadequate form of appearance. Hegel idealises the bureaucracy, and empiricises public consciousness. He can treat actual public consciousness as very special precisely because he has treated the special consciousness as the public consciousness. He needs to concern himself all the less about the actual existence of the state spirit since he believes he has already realised it properly in its so-called existences. As long as the state spirit mystically haunted the forecourt, many bows were made in its direction. Now, when we have caught it in person, it is scarcely regarded.

"The estates element has this characteristic, that in it matters of general concern come to exist not merely *in themselves* but also *for themselves*." And indeed they come to exist explicitly as "public consciousness", as the *"empirical generality* of the opinions and thoughts of the *many"*.

The process by which "matters of general concern" — which are in this way turned into an independent entity — come to be a subject, is here presented as a phase in the life-process of the "matters of general concern". Instead of the subjects making themselves objective in the "matters of general concern", Hegel brings the "matters of general concern" to the point of being the "subject". The subjects do not need the "matters of general concern" as their true concerns, but the matters of general concern require the subjects for their *formal* existence. It is a matter for "matters of general concern" that they exist also as subject.

What has especially to be kept in view here is the difference between the *"being in itself"* and the *"being for itself"* of the matters of general concern.

The *"matters of general concern"* already exist *"in themselves"* as the business of the government, etc. They exist, without *actually* being matters of *general* concern. They are on no account matters of general concern, for they are not the concern of *"civil society"*. They have already found their *essential*, actual existence. That they now also actually become "public consciousness", "empirical generality", is something purely formal and, as it were, only a *symbolic* attaining to actuality. The "formal" existence or the "empirical" existence of matters of general concern is separated from their *substantial existence*. The truth of this is that "matters of general concern" in their *being as such* are not *actually general*, and the actual, *empirical* matters of general concern are merely *formal*.

Hegel separates *content* and *form, being in itself* and *being for itself*, and brings in the latter externally as a *formal* element. The content is complete and exists in many forms, which are not the forms of this content; whereas clearly the form which is supposed to be the actual form of the content, has not the actual content for its content.

The *matters of general concern* are complete, without being actual concerns of the people. The actual business of the people has come into being without action by the people. The estates element is the *illusory existence* of matters of state as a public concern. [It is] the illusion that the *matters of general concern* are matters of general concern, public matters; or the *illusion* that the people's affairs are matters of general concern. Things have gone so far, both in our states and in Hegel's philosophy of law, that the tautological sentence "Matters of general concern are matters of general concern" can only appear as an *illusion of practical consciousness*. The *estates element* is the *political illusion of civil society*. Precisely because he does not establish objective freedom as the realisation, the practical manifestation of subjective freedom, *subjective* freedom appears in Hegel as *formal* freedom. (It is certainly important though that what is free is also done freely; that freedom does not prevail as the unconscious natural instinct of society.) Because he has given the presumed or actual content of freedom a mystical bearer, the actual subject of freedom acquires a formal significance.

The separation of the *in itself* and the *for itself*, of substance and subject, is abstract mysticism.

In the Remark Hegel explains the "estates element" very much as something "formal" and "illusory".

Both the *knowledge* and the *will* of the "estates element" are treated partly as unimportant, partly as suspect: i.e., the estates element is not a *substantial addition*.

1) "The idea uppermost in men's minds when they speak about the necessity or usefulness of summoning the estates is usually something of this sort, that the people's representatives, or even the people, *must best understand* what is best for them, and that they undoubtedly have the best intention to bring about this best. On the first point, it is rather the case that if by 'the people' is meant one particular section of the members of the state, then it is that section which *does not know what it wants*. To know what one wants, and, even more, to know what will, existing in and for itself, i.e., reason, wants, is the fruit of deep understanding" (confined, of course, to [government] offices) "and insight—which, of course, is not the people's affair."

Further on, he says with reference to the estates themselves:

"The highest civil servants necessarily have deeper and more comprehensive insight into the nature of the structure and the needs of the state, as well as being more skilled in, and more accustomed to, these affairs; without the estates they are therefore *able* to do what is best, as they constantly must do their best when the estates are in session."

And it stands to reason that in the organisation described by Hegel this is perfectly true.

2) "As for the estates' especially *good intention* to bring about the general good, it has already been pointed out [...] that to presume a bad or less good intention in the executive is characteristic of the vulgar crowd and of a negative outlook generally. If one were to answer in like manner, the countercharge would follow that since the estates have their origin in individuality, the private standpoint, and particular interests, they are inclined to use their powers on behalf of these at the expense of the general interest, whereas the other state authorities consciously adopt the standpoint of the state from the start, and are devoted to the common purpose."

Thus the *knowledge* and *will* of the estates are partly superfluous, partly suspect. The people do not know what they want. The estates do not possess knowledge of state affairs in the same degree as the officials, who have a monopoly of this knowledge. The estates are superfluous for the implementation of "matters of general concern", the officials are *able* to accomplish them without the estates, and indeed *have to* do what is best in spite of the estates. Thus from the point of view of content, the estates are a pure luxury. Their presence is therefore in the most literal sense a mere *form*.

Furthermore, with regard to the attitude, the *will* of the estates: this is suspect, for they issue from the private standpoint and from private interests. The truth is that private interest is their matter of general concern, and that matters of general concern are not their private interest. But what a state of things when "matters of general concern" assume the *form* of matters of general concern in a will which does not know what it wants, or at least does not possess any particular knowledge of the general, and which has as its real content an opposing interest!

In modern states, as in Hegel's philosophy of law, the *conscious, the true actuality* of *matters of general concern is merely formal*; or, *only what is formal is an actual matter of general concern.*

Hegel is not to be blamed for depicting the nature of the modern state as it is, but for presenting that which is as the *nature of the state*. That the rational is actual is proved precisely in the *contradiction* of *irrational actuality*, which everywhere is the contrary of what it asserts, and asserts the contrary of what it is.

Instead of showing how "matters of general concern" exist for themselves "subjectively, and therefore actually as such", and that they have also the form of matters of general concern, Hegel only shows that *formlessness* is their subjectivity, and a form without content must be formless. The form which matters of general concern gain in any state which is not the state of matters of general concern can only be a deformity, a self-deceiving, self-contradictory form, an *illusory form* which will reveal itself as this illusion.

Hegel wants the luxury of the estates element only for the sake of logic. The *being for themselves* of matters of general concern as empirical generality must have a specific presence. Hegel does not look for an adequate actualisation of the "being for themselves of matters of general concern", he is content to find an empirical existent which can be dissolved into this logical category; this is then the estates element, and Hegel himself does not fail to note how pitiful and full of contradictions this existent is. Yet he still reproaches ordinary consciousness for not being content with this logical satisfaction, and for wanting to see logic transformed into true objectivity rather than actuality dissolved into logic by *arbitrary* abstraction.

I say *arbitrary* abstraction; for, since the executive authority wills, knows and actualises the *matters of general concern*, has its source in the nation and is an empirical multiplicity (that it is not a question of totality Hegel himself tells us), why should it not be possible to define the executive as the "being for themselves of matters of general concern"? Or why not the "estates" as their *being in themselves*, since it is only in the executive that these matters reach the light and gain determinacy and implementation and independence?

The true antithesis, however, is this: "Matters of general concern" have to be *represented* somewhere in the state as "actual" and therefore "empirical matters of general concern". They must appear somewhere in the crown and robes of the general, which thereby automatically becomes a role, an illusion.

The antithesis in question here is that of the "general" as "*form*" — in the "form of generality" — and of the "general as content".

In science, for example, an "individual" can accomplish matters of general concern, and it is always individuals who do accomplish them. But these matters become truly general only when they are the affair no longer of the individual but of society. This changes not merely the form but also the content. In this case, however, the issue is the state, where the nation itself is a matter of general concern; in this case it is a question of the will, which finds its true presence as species-will only in the self-conscious will of the nation. In this case, moreover, it is a question of the idea of the state.

The modern state, in which "matters of general concern" and preoccupation with them are a monopoly, and in which, on the contrary, monopolies are the real matters of general concern, has invented the strange device of appropriating "matters of general concern" as a *mere form*. (The truth is that only the *form* is a matter of general concern.) With this it has found the corresponding form for its content, which is only seemingly composed of real matters of general concern.

The constitutional state is the state in which the state interest as the actual interest of the nation exists *only* formally but, at the same time, as a *determinate form* alongside the actual state. Here the state interest has again acquired actuality *formally* as the interest of the nation, but it is only this *formal actuality* which it is to have. It has become a *formality*, the *haut goût* of national life, a *ceremonial*. The *estates* element is the *sanctioned, legal lie* of constitutional states, the lie that the *state* is the *nation's interest*, or that the *nation* is the *interest of the state*. This lie reveals itself in its *content*. It has established itself as the *legislative* power, precisely because the legislative power has the general for its content, and, being an affair of knowledge rather than of will, is the *metaphysical* state *power*; whereas in the form of the executive power, etc., this same lie would inevitably have to dissolve at once, or be transformed into a truth. The metaphysical state power was the most fitting seat for the metaphysical, general illusion of the state.

[301.] "A little reflection will show that the guarantee of the common good and public freedom afforded by the estates lies not in their special insight [...] but partly indeed in an **additional**" (!!) "insight contributed by the deputies, principally into the doings of officials at some removes from direct supervision by the higher authorities, and particularly into the more pressing and specialised needs and deficiencies which these deputies have concretely before them; but partly, too, it lies in the effect which the criticism to be expected from the many, and public criticism at that, brings with it in inducing officials in advance to apply the greatest understanding to their tasks and to the projects they have to prepare, and to deal with them only in accordance with the purest motives — a compulsion which is equally effective in the case of the members of the estates themselves."

"As for the guarantee generally which the estates in particular are supposed to furnish, **each of the other institutions of the state** shares with them in being a guarantee of the public good and of rational freedom; and amongst these are institutions such as the sovereignty of the monarch, hereditary succession to the throne, the constitution of the courts, etc., which provide this guarantee in far greater measure than do the estates. The **distinctive** feature of the estates is to be sought, therefore, in the fact that in them the subjective element of general freedom—the specific insight and the specific will characteristic of that sphere which in this presentation has been called civil society—comes *into existence relative to the state*. That this element is an aspect of the idea as developed into a totality, this inner necessity, not to be confused with *external necessities* and *expediencies*, follows, as always, from the philosophical standpoint."

Public, general freedom *is* allegedly guaranteed in the other state institutions; the estates are its alleged self-guarantee. [But the fact is] that the people attach more importance to the estates, through which they believe themselves to be able to safeguard their own security, than to those institutions which without any action on their part are supposed to be safeguards of their freedom—being affirmations of their freedom without being manifestations of their freedom. The co-ordinate position which Hegel assigns to the estates alongside the other institutions, contradicts the nature of the estates.

Hegel solves the enigma by seeing the "distinctive feature of the estates" in the fact that in them "the specific insight and the specific will characteristic of [...] civil society comes *into existence relative to the state*". It is the *reflection of civil society on to the state*. As the bureaucrats are *representatives of the state* to civil society, so the estates are *representatives of civil society* to the state. It is always a case, therefore, of *transactions* between two *opposing wills*.

In the *Addition* to this paragraph he says:

"The attitude of the executive to the estates should not be **essentially** hostile, and the belief in the inevitability of such a hostile relationship is a sad mistake",

is a "sad truth".

"The government is not a party facing another party."

On the contrary.

"The taxes voted by the estates, furthermore, are not to be regarded as a **present** given to the state; they are voted, rather, for the good of the voters themselves."

In the constitutional state, the voting of taxes is inevitably *thought of* as a *present*.

"The real significance of the estates lies in the fact that through them **the state enters the subjective consciousness of the people**, and that the people begins to participate in the state."

This last point is quite right. In the estates the people *begins* to participate in the state, and likewise the state enters its subjective consciousness as an other-world. But how can Hegel present this *beginning* as the full *reality*?

302. "Considered as a *mediating* organ, the estates stand between the government as a whole on the one hand, and the nation on the other, resolved into particular spheres and individuals. Their function requires of them a *sense* and a *way of thinking* appropriate to the *state* and *government*, as well as to the *interests* of *particular* groups and *individuals*. At the same time, their position has the

significance of being, together with the organised^a executive, a mediating factor, so that neither the monarchical authority should appear isolated as an *extreme* and thus as exclusively the power of the sovereign and arbitrariness, nor should the particular interests of communities, corporations and individuals become isolated; and—still more important—that individuals should not come to form a *multitude* or a *crowd*, characterised by correspondingly non-organic views and intentions and constituting a mere massed force against the organic state."

On the one side are placed, always as identical, state and government; on the other, the nation, resolved into particular spheres and individuals. The estates stand between the two as a *mediating* organ. The estates are the centre where "sense and a way of thinking appropriate to the state and government" are supposed to coincide and be united with "sense and a way of thinking appropriate to particular groups and individuals". The identity of these two opposed senses and ways of thinking, in whose identity the state should properly be rooted, is given a *symbolic* representation in the *estates*. The transaction between state and civil society appears as a *particular* sphere. The estates are the *synthesis between state and civil society*. But how the estates are to set about uniting in themselves two contradictory ways of thinking is not indicated. The *estates* are the *posited contradiction* of the state and civil society within the state. At the same time, they are the *demand* for the *resolution* of this contradiction.

"At the same time, their position has the significance of being, together with the **organised**^a executive, a mediating factor, etc."

The estates not only *mediate* nation and government. They prevent the "monarchical authority" from appearing as an isolated *"extreme"* and thus as "exclusively the power of the sovereign and arbitrariness"; they likewise prevent the "isolation" of the "particular" interests, etc., and the "appearance of individuals as a *multitude* or *crowd*". This mediating function is common to the estates and to the organised executive. In a state where the "position" of the "estates" prevents "individuals from coming to form a *multitude* or a *crowd*, characterised by correspondingly non-organic views and intentions and constituting a mere massed force against the organic state", the *"organic* state" exists outside the "multitude" and the "crowd"; or there the "multitude" and the "crowd" do belong to the organisation of the state, only their "non-organic views and intentions" are not to become "views and intentions against the state"—for with such a *definite orientation* these views and intentions would become "organic". Similarly, this "massed force" is to remain only "mass", so that understanding

---

^a Marx wrote "organic".—*Ed.*

remains located outside the masses and hence they cannot set themselves in motion, but can only be moved, and exploited as a massed force, by the monopolists of the "organic state". Where "the particular interests of communities, corporations and individuals" are not isolated from the state, but "individuals come to form a *multitude* or a *crowd*, characterised by correspondingly non-organic views and intentions and constituting a mere massed force against the state", it becomes clear, of course, that it is no "particular interest" which contradicts the state, but that the "actual, organic, general thought of the multitude or the crowd" is not the "thought of the organic state" and does not find its realisation in it. What is it, then, that makes the estates appear as a mediating factor in relation to this extreme? Only the fact that "the particular interests of communities, corporations and individuals become isolated", or the fact that their isolated interests *balance their account with the state through the estates*; and also the fact that the "non-organic views and intentions of the multitude or the crowd" have occupied their *will* (their activity) in creating the estates, and occupied their "views" in judging the work of the estates, and have enjoyed the illusion of their own objectification. The "estates" preserve the state from the non-organic crowd only as a result of the disorganisation of this crowd.

But at the same time the mediation by the *estates* is intended to prevent the "isolation" of "the particular interests of communities, corporations and individuals". They mediate in this respect (1) by treating with the "state interest", (2) by themselves being the "*political* isolation" of these particular interests, by being this *isolation as a political act*, since through them these "isolated interests" attain the rank of the "general".

Finally, the estates are supposed to mediate in relation to the *"isolation"* of the authority of the monarch as an *"extreme"* (which "thus *would appear* as exclusively the power of the sovereign and arbitrariness"). This is correct insofar as the *principle* of the *authority of the monarch* (arbitrariness) is limited by the estates or at least is fettered in its operation, and inasmuch as the estates themselves become participants in, and accomplices of, the monarch's authority.

In this way either the power of the monarch actually ceases to be the extreme of the power of the monarch (and, since it is not an organic principle, the power of the monarch exists only as an extreme, as a one-sidedness), and becomes an *appearance of power*, a symbol; or else it only loses the *appearance* of being arbitrary and exclusively the power of the sovereign. The estates mediate to counter the "isolation" of particular interests by presenting this isolation as a *political* act. They *mediate* to counter the isolation of the authority of the monarch as an extreme, partly by themselves becoming a part of monarchical authority, and partly by putting the executive into the position of an *extreme*.

In the "estates" all the contradictions of the organisations of the modern state coalesce. The estates are the "mediators" in all directions, because in all respects they are "hybrids".

It should be noted that Hegel does not so much expound the content of the activity of the estates, the legislative power, as the *position* of the estates, their political rank.

It should further be noted that whereas, according to Hegel, the *estates* stand to begin with "between the *government as a whole on the one hand*, and the *nation on the other*, resolved into particular spheres and individuals", their position as expounded above "has the significance of being, *together* with the organised executive, a mediating factor".

With regard to the first point, the *estates* are the nation over against the government, but *the nation in miniature*. This is their posture in opposition.

With regard to the second point, the estates are the government over against the nation, but the government amplified. This is their conservative posture. They are themselves a part of the executive over against the nation, but in such a way as to have at the same time the significance of being the nation over against the executive.

Hegel, above, characterised the "legislative authority as a totality" (para. 300): the *estates* actually are this *totality*—the state within the state—but it is precisely in them that it *becomes apparent* that the state is not the totality, but a dualism. The estates represent the state in a society that *is no* state. The state is a *mere concept*.

In the Remark [to para. 302] Hegel says:

> "It is one of the most important insights of logic that a certain element which occupies the position of an extreme when standing within an antithesis, is at the same time a *middle term*, and thus ceases to be an extreme and is an *organic* element."

(Thus the estates element is (1) the extreme of the nation over against the government; but also (2) the middle term between nation and government; or it is the *antithesis within the nation* itself. The antithesis of government and nation is mediated by the antithesis between *estates* and *nation*. The estates occupy the position of the nation with regard to the government, but the position of the government with regard to the nation. The real antithesis between nation and government is overcome when the nation attains existence as a *notion,* as a fantasy, an illusion, a *representation*—as the *represented* nation, or the estates, which straightway finds itself, as a *particular power,* cut off from the real nation. Here the nation is displayed in just the way it must be displayed in the organism under consideration, so as not to have a clear-cut character.)

"In connection with the matter here being considered it is all the more important to stress this aspect because of the frequently-held, but most dangerous prejudice which regards the estates primarily from the point of view of *opposition* to the government, as if this were their essential attitude. Looked upon organically, i. e., as part of the totality, the **estates element** manifests itself **only through the function of mediation.** Thus the **antithesis** itself is reduced to an **appearance**. If this antithesis, when it **manifests** itself, were not merely something superficial but **actually** became a **substantial antithesis**, then the state would be in the throes of destruction. That the conflict is not of this kind is shown, in accordance with the nature of the thing, by the fact that it is not concerned with the essential elements of the state organism but with more specialised and less important things; and the passion nevertheless aroused by these matters becomes faction concerned with merely subjective interests such as higher state appointments."

In the *Addition* he says:

"The constitution is essentially a system of mediation."

303. "The *general* estate, or more precisely the estate which devotes itself to *government service,* is directly defined as having the general as the purpose of its essential activity. In the *estates* element of the legislature the *civil estate* acquires *political significance* and effectiveness. Now this civil estate can appear in this sphere neither as a mere undifferentiated mass nor as a multitude resolved into its atoms, but as that *which it already is,* namely, differentiated into the estate based on the substantial relationship and the estate based on specific needs and the labour satisfying them [...]. Only thus is the really *particular in* the state truly linked in this respect with the general."

Here we have the solution of the enigma. "In the estates element of the legislature the *civil estate* acquires *political significance."* Naturally, the *civil estate* acquires this significance in a way corresponding to what it is, corresponding to its *structure within civil society* (Hegel has already characterised the general estate as that which devotes itself to the service of the government; the general estate is thus represented within the legislative authority by the executive).

The estates element is *the political significance of the civil estate*, of the unpolitical estate—a contradiction in terms. Or in the estate described by Hegel, the *civil estate* (and further the distinction of the civil estate as such) has a *political* significance. The *civil estate* belongs to the essence, to the politics of this state. He, therefore, gives it a *political significance,* i. e., a significance other than its real significance.

In the Remark he says:

"This runs counter to another current notion, namely, that when the civil estate is elevated to the **participation** in general affairs in the legislature it ought to appear there in the form of *individuals* either by their choosing representatives for this function, or even by each individual himself exercising a vote there. This atomistic, abstract view disappears already within the family as well as within civil society, where the individual only makes his appearance as a member of something general. The state, however, is essentially an organisation consisting of components, each of which is *itself* a group; and no element should appear as a non-organic mass in the state. The *many* as individuals, which is what we readily take to be meant by 'people', are indeed an *assemblage*, but only as a *multitude*—a formless mass whose movement and action, accordingly, could only be elemental, irrational, savage and frightful."

"The notion which resolves the communities already existing in these groupings again into a multitude of individuals at the point where they enter the political realm, i. e., where they take up the standpoint of the *highest concrete generality*, thereby keeps **civil and political life separate** and suspends the latter, so to speak, in the air, since its basis would only be the abstract individuality of caprice and opinion, and thus the accidental, and not an absolutely *solid* and *legitimate* foundation."

"Although the *estates of civil society* in general and the *estates in the political sense* are widely separated in the concepts advanced by so-called theories, **language**, nevertheless, still preserves their unity, which moreover **formerly prevailed in fact**."

"The *general* estate, or more precisely the estate which devotes itself to *government service*."

Hegel takes it as a presupposition that the *general* estate is in the "service of the government". He takes it for granted that general intelligence "is both proper to the estates and is constant".

"In the *estates* element, etc." The "political significance and effectiveness" of the *civil estate* is a *particular* significance and effectiveness of the civil estate. The *civil estate* is not transformed into the *political estate*; on the contrary, it is as *civil estate* that it assumes its political effectiveness and significance. It does not have political effectiveness and significance in an unqualified way. Its political effectiveness and significance is the *political effectiveness and significance of the civil estate as civil estate*. Hence, the civil estate can only enter the political sphere in a way which corresponds to the *differentiation of estates in civil society*. The *differentiation of estates* within civil society becomes a political distinction.

Language itself, says Hegel, expresses the identity of *the estates of civil society* with the *estates in the political sense*—a "unity" "which moreover *formerly prevailed in fact*", and which, one must conclude, now no longer prevails.

Hegel finds that "the really *particular in* the state is truly linked in this respect with the general". *In this manner the separation of "civil and political life"* is supposed to be transcended and their *"identity"* established.

Hegel relies on the following:

"There are already existing *communities* in these groupings" (family and civil society). How can one, just "at the point where they enter the political realm, i.e., where they take up the standpoint of the *highest concrete generality*", wish "to resolve" them "again into a multitude of individuals"?

It is important to follow this argument closely.

The identity Hegel is asserting was at its most complete, as he himself admits, in the *Middle Ages*. Here the *estates of civil society* as such and the *estates in the political sense* were identical. One can express the spirit of the Middle Ages in this way: The estates of civil society and the estates in the political sense were identical, because civil society was political society—because the organic principle of civil society was the principle of the state.

Hegel, however, takes as his starting point the *separation* of *"civil society"* and the *"political state"* as two fixed opposites, two really different spheres. This separation does indeed *really* exist in the *modern* state. The identity of the civil and political estates was the *expression* of the *identity* of civil and political society. This identity has disappeared. Hegel takes it to have disappeared. "The identity of the civil and political estates", if it expressed the truth, *could* therefore now only be an expression of the *separation* of civil and political society. Or rather, only the *separation* of the civil and political estates[a] expresses the *true* relationship of *modern* civil and political society.

Secondly: Hegel is dealing here with *political* estates in a quite different sense from that of the *political* estates of the Middle Ages whose identity *with the estates of civil society* is asserted.

Their whole existence was political. Their existence was the existence of the state. Their *legislative activity*, their *voting of taxes for the Empire*, was only a *particular* expression of their *general* political significance and effectiveness. Their estate was their state. The relation to the Empire was merely a treaty relationship of these various states with *nationality*; for the political state as something distinct from civil society was nothing else but the *representation of nationality*. Nationality was the *point d'honneur*, the κατ' ἐξοχὴν,[b] political significance of these various corporations, etc., and the taxes, etc., had reference only to nationality. That

---

[a] In the manuscript: "society".— *Ed.*
[b] Pre-eminently.— *Ed.*

was the relationship of the legislative estates to the Empire. The position of the estates was similar *within the individual principalities*. Here the *princedom*, the *sovereignty*, was a *particular* estate, which had certain privileges but which was correspondingly restricted by the privileges of the other estates. (Among the Greeks civil society was the *slave* of political society.) The general *legislative effectiveness* of the estates of civil society was not at all an attaining to a *political* significance and effectiveness on the part of the *civil estate*, but rather a simple expression of their *actual and general* political significance and effectiveness. Their activity as a legislative power was simply a complement to their sovereign and governing (executive) power; it was rather their attaining to matters of wholly general concern as a *civil affair*, their attaining to sovereignty as a *civil estate*. In the Middle Ages the estates of civil society were as estates of *civil society* at the same time legislative estates, because they were *not* civil estates, or because the *civil estates* were political estates. The medieval estates did not acquire a new character as a political-estates element. They did not become *political* estates because they participated in legislation; on the contrary, they participated in legislation because they were *political* estates. What have they in common, then, with Hegel's *civil estate*, which as a *legislative* element attains a political aria di bravura, an ecstatic condition, an outstanding, striking, exceptional political significance and effectiveness?

All the *contradictions* characteristic of Hegel's presentation are to be found together in the exposition of this question.

1) He has presupposed the *separation* of civil society and the political state (a modern condition), and expounded it as a *necessary element of the idea*, as absolute rational truth. He has presented the political state in its *modern* form—in the form of the *separation* of the various powers. He has given the bureaucracy to the actual, *active* state for its body, and set the bureaucracy as mind endowed with knowledge above the materialism of civil society. He has counterposed the intrinsically and actually general aspect of the state to the particular interest and the need of civil society. In short, he presents everywhere the *conflict* between civil society and the state.

2) Civil society as *civil estate* is counterposed by Hegel to the political state.

3) He characterises the *estates* element of the legislature as the mere *political formalism* of civil society. He describes it as a *relationship of reflection in which civil society is reflected on to the state*, and as one which does not affect the *essence* of the state. And a

relationship of reflection is the highest form of identity between essentially different things.

On the other hand:

1) Hegel does not want to allow civil society to appear in its self-constitution as a legislative element either as a mere, undifferentiated mass or as a multitude dissolved into its atoms. He wants *no* separation of *civil and political life*.

2) He forgets that what is in question is a relationship of reflection, and makes the civil estates as such political estates, but again only in terms of legislative power, so that their activity is itself proof of the separation.

He makes the *estates element* the expression of the *separation*; but at the same time it is supposed to be the representative of an identity which is not there. Hegel is aware of the separation of civil society and the political state, but he wants the unity of the state to be expressed within the state, and this to be accomplished, in fact, by the estates of civil society, in their character as such estates, also forming the *estates* element of legislative society. (Cf. XIV.*)[a]

304. "The political-estates element contains at the same time in its own determination the distinctions of estates already present in the earlier spheres. Its initially abstract position, that of the *extreme of empirical generality* over against the *royal* or *monarchical* principle in general, a position which implies only the *possibility of harmony* and therefore likewise the *possibility of hostile* confrontation, this abstract position becomes a rational relation (a syllogism, cf. Remark to para. 302) only if its *mediation* is actually effected. Just as from the monarchical authority the executive already has this attribute (para. 300), so likewise one aspect of the estates must be adapted to the function of existing essentially as the middle element."

305. "One estate of civil society contains the principle which is of itself capable of being established in this political role—namely, the estate whose ethical life is natural, and whose basis is family life and, so far as its livelihood is concerned, landed property. Its specific feature, accordingly, is a will based on itself; it shares this and the natural attribute, which the monarchical element contains, with the latter."

306. "This estate is more particularly fitted for political position and significance in that its wealth is equally independent of the wealth of the state and of the uncertainty of business, the quest for profit, and any sort of fluctuation in possessions, independent both of the favour of the executive, and of the favour of the crowd. It is even safeguarded *against its own caprice* by the fact that the members of this estate who are called to fill this role lack the right of other citizens either to dispose freely of their entire property, or to know that it will pass to their children in accordance with the equality of their love for them. Their wealth thus becomes an *inalienable heritage*, burdened with primogeniture."

Addition: "This estate is more independent in its volition. Speaking generally, the landowning estate is divided into an educated section of landowners and the

---

[a] The asterisk apparently refers not to p. XIV of the manuscript but to p. XXIV since the same sign is repeated there by Marx (see this volume, p. 75).—*Ed.*

peasantry. But over against both these sorts of people stands the business estate, which is dependent on and orientated towards need, and the general estate, which is essentially dependent on the state. The security and stability of the [landowning] estate can be further enhanced by the institution of primogeniture, though this institution is desirable only from a political point of view, since it involves a sacrifice for the political purpose of enabling the first-born son to live independently. The justification for primogeniture is that the state must be able to count on a certain way of thinking not as a mere possibility, but as something necessary. Now this way of thinking is not, of course, tied to wealth, but the relatively necessary connection is that a man of independent means is not restricted by external circumstances and can thus come forward and act for the state without hindrance. Where political institutions are lacking, however, the establishment and encouragement of primogeniture is nothing but a fetter laid upon the freedom of civil right; this fetter must either acquire political meaning or move towards disintegration."

307. "Thus the rights of this section of the propertied estate are on the one hand no doubt founded on the **natural principle of the family**, but this principle is at the same time distorted by hard sacrifice for a *political purpose*; consequently this estate is essentially assigned to activity for this purpose, and is therefore also summoned and *entitled* to this activity by *birth*, without the fortuitousness of elections. Thus it occupies a stable, essential position between the subjective caprice or contingency of the two poles, and just as it [...] carries in itself a likeness of the element of the monarchical authority, so it shares with the other pole needs and rights which are in other respects similar and becomes the pillar both of the throne and of society."

Hegel has achieved the feat of deriving the born peers, the hereditary landed property, etc., etc.—this "pillar both of the throne and of society"—from the absolute idea.

*ᵃ It shows Hegel's profundity that he feels the separation of civil from political society as a *contradiction*. He is wrong, however, to be content with the appearance of this resolution and to pretend it is the substance, whereas the *"so-called theories"* he despises demand the *"separation"* of the civil from the political estates—and rightly so, for they voice a *consequence* of modern society, since there the *political-estates* element is precisely nothing but the factual expression of the actual relationship of state and civil society, namely, their *separation*.

Hegel does not call the matter here in question by its well-known name. It is the disputed question of a *representative* versus *estates* constitution. The representative constitution is a great advance, since it is the *frank, undistorted, consistent* expression of the *modern condition of the state*. It is an *unconcealed contradiction*.

Before we deal with the substance of the matter let us glance once more at Hegel's presentation.

"In the *estates* element of the legislature the *civil estate* acquires *political* significance." [Para. 303.]

ᵃ See footnote on p. 74.—*Ed.*

Earlier (Remark to para. 301) he said:

"The **distinctive** feature of the **estates** is to be sought, therefore, in the fact that in them ... the specific insight and the specific will characteristic of that sphere which in this presentation has been called **civil society**—*comes into existence relative to the state.*"

Summarising this definition, we get: "*Civil society* is the *civil estate*", or the *civil estate* is the direct, essential, concrete estate of civil society. It [civil society] acquires "political significance and effectiveness" only in the estates element of the legislature. This is something new, which is added to it, a *particular* function, for its very nature as *civil estate* expresses its *contrast* to political significance and effectiveness, the forfeiture of its political character, expresses the fact that civil society in and for itself is *without* political significance or effectiveness. The *civil estate* is the estate of civil society, or civil society is the *civil estate*. Hence Hegel also consistently excludes the "general estate" from the "estates element of the legislature".

"The *general* estate, or more precisely the estate which devotes itself to *government service*, is directly defined as having the general as the purpose of its essential activity." [Para. 303.]

Civil society or the civil estate is not so defined. Its essential activity is not defined as having the general as its purpose; or, its essential activity is not a characteristic of the general—does *not* have a *general* character. The civil estate is the estate of civil society *against* the state. The estate of civil society is *not* a political estate.

In describing civil society as civil estate, Hegel has declared the distinctions of estate in civil society to be *non*-political distinctions, and civil and political life to be heterogeneous, even *opposites*. How does he go on?

"Now this civil estate can appear in this sphere neither as a mere undifferentiated mass nor as a multitude resolved into its atoms, but as that *which it already is*, namely, differentiated into the *estate* based on the substantial relationship and the *estate* based on specific needs and the labour satisfying them (para. 201 ff.). Only thus is the really *particular in* the state truly linked in this respect with the general." [Para. 303.]

Civil society (the *civil estate*) can indeed not appear as a "mere undifferentiated mass" in its activity as legislative estate because the "mere undifferentiated mass" exists only as a "notion", only in the imagination, but not in *actuality*. Here there are only accidental masses of various sizes (cities, market towns, etc.). These masses or this mass not only *appears* but *is* everywhere "a multitude resolved into its atoms" in reality, and as thus atomised it *must* appear and proceed in its activity as *political* estate. The *civil estate*, civil society, cannot here appear "as that *which it already is*". For what is it already? *Civil estate*, i.e., antithesis to and separation from the state. To acquire "political significance and effectiveness" it must rather abandon itself as that which it already is, as *civil estate*. Only thus does it acquire its "*political* significance and effectiveness". This political act is a complete transubstantiation. In it, civil society must completely give itself up as civil society, as civil estate, and assert an aspect of its essence which not only has nothing in common with the real civil existence of its essence but stands in opposition to it.

The *general law* here appears in the individual. Civil society and state are separated. Hence the citizen of the state is also separated from the citizen as the member of civil society. He must therefore effect a *fundamental division* with himself. As an *actual citizen* he finds himself in a twofold organisation: the *bureaucratic* organisation, which is an external, formal feature of the distant state, the executive, which does not touch him or his independent reality, and the *social* organisation, the organisation of civil society. But in the latter he stands as a *private person* outside the state; this social organisation does not touch the political state as such. The former is a state organisation for which he always provides the *material*. The second is a *civil organisation* the material of which is not the state. In the former the state stands as formal antithesis to him, in the second he stands as material antithesis to the state. Hence, in order to behave as an *actual citizen of the state*, and to attain political significance and effectiveness, he must step out of his civil reality, disregard it, and withdraw from this whole organisation into his individuality; for the sole existence which he finds for his citizenship of the state is his sheer, blank *individuality*, since the existence of the state as executive is complete without him, and his existence in civil society is complete without the state. He can be a *citizen of the state* only in contradiction to these *sole available communities*, only as an *individual*. His existence as a citizen of the state is an existence outside his *communal* existences and is therefore purely *individual*. For the "legislative power" as "power" is only the *organisation*, the *common body*, which it *is to* receive. Civil society, the civil estate, does *not* exist as *state organisation prior to* the "legislative authority", and in order to come into existence as such the *real organisation* of the civil estate, its real civil life, must be posited as *non-existent*, for the estates element of the legislature has precisely the quality of positing the *civil estate, civil society*, as *non-existent*. The separation of civil society and political state necessarily appears as a separation of the *political* citizen, the citizen of the state, from civil society, from his own, actual, empirical reality, for as an idealist of the state he is *quite another being*, a *different*, distinct, opposed being. Civil society here effects within itself the relationship of state and civil society which already exists on the other side as *bureaucracy*. In the estates element the general really becomes *for itself* what it is *in itself*, namely, the *opposite* of the *particular*. The citizen must discard his estate, civil society, the *civil estate*, so as to acquire political significance and effectiveness, for it is this *estate* which stands between the *individual* and the *political state*.

If Hegel poses civil society as a whole, as the *civil estate*, in opposition to the political state, it stands to reason that the differences *within* the civil estate, the various civil estates, can in reference to the state have only a private significance, not a political significance. For the various civil estates are merely the realisation, the existence, of the *principle*, of the civil estate as the principle of civil society. But when the principle has to be given up, it stands to reason that the divisions *within* this principle exist all the *less* for the political state.

"Only thus," Hegel concludes the paragraph [303], "is the really *particular in* the state truly linked in this respect with the general."

But Hegel here confuses the state as the whole of the existence of a people with the political state. This particular is not the "*particular in*" but rather "*outside* the state", namely, the political state. Not only is it not "the really particular in the state", it is rather the "*unreality* of the state". Hegel seeks to demonstrate that the estates of civil society are the political estates, and to prove that, he assumes that the estates of civil society are the "particularisation of the political state", i.e., that civil society is political society. The expression "the particular *in* the state" can have here only the meaning "particularisation of the state". Bad conscience prompts Hegel to choose the vague expression. He himself has not only demonstrated the opposite, he again confirms this himself in the same paragraph when he describes civil society as the "civil estate". The statement that the particular "*is linked*" with the general is also very cautious. One can link the most heterogeneous things. It is here, however, not a question of a gradual *transition* but of a *transubstantiation* and it is useless to refuse to see the chasm to be jumped over, which the jump itself demonstrates.

Hegel says in the Remark [to para. 303]:

"This runs counter to another current notion", etc. We have just shown how consistent, how necessary, this current notion is, that it is a "necessary notion at the present stage of development of the nation", and that Hegel's notion, although also quite current in certain circles, is nevertheless an untruth. Returning to the current notion, Hegel says:

"This atomistic, abstract view disappears already within the family", etc., etc. "The state, however, is", etc. This view is indeed abstract, but it is the "abstraction" of the political state as Hegel himself expounds it. It is also atomistic, but it is the atomism of society itself. A "view" cannot be concrete when its *subject-matter* is abstract. The atomism into which civil society plunges in its *political act* follows necessarily from the fact that the community, the communal being in which the individual exists, is civil society separated from the state, or that the *political state* is an *abstraction* from it.

This atomistic view, although [it] disappears already in the family, and perhaps (??) in civil society as well, returns in the political state precisely because it is an abstraction from the family and from civil society. The reverse is also true. By expressing the *strangeness* of this phenomenon Hegel has not eliminated the *estrangement*.

"The notion," we read further, "which resolves the **communities** already **existing** in these groupings again into a multitude of individuals at the point where they enter the political realm, i.e., where they take up the standpoint of the *highest concrete generality*, thereby **keeps** civil and political life separate and suspends the latter, so to speak, in the air, since its basis would only be the abstract individuality of caprice and opinion, and thus the accidental, and not an absolutely *solid* and *legitimate* foundation." [Remark to para. 303.]

That notion does not *keep* civil and political life separate; it is merely the *notion of a really existing separation*.

That notion does not suspend political life in the air; it is rather that political life is *life in the airy regions*—the ethereal regions of civil society.

Now let us consider the *estates* system and the *representative* system.

It is an historical advance which has transformed the *political estates* into *social* estates, so that, just as the Christians are equal in heaven, but unequal on earth, so the individual members of the nation are *equal* in the heaven of their political world, but unequal in the earthly existence of *society*. The real transformation of the *political estates* into *civil* estates took place in the *absolute monarchy*. The bureaucracy maintained the notion of unity against the various states within the state. Nevertheless, the *social difference* of the estates, even alongside the bureaucracy of the absolute executive power, remained a political difference, *political within* and alongside the bureaucracy of the absolute executive power.

Only the French Revolution completed the transformation of the *political* into *social* estates, or changed the *differences of estate* of civil society into mere *social* differences, into differences of civil life which are without significance in political life. With that the separation of political life from civil society was completed.

The estates of civil society likewise were transformed in the process: civil society was changed by its separation from political society. *Estate* in the medieval sense continued only within the bureaucracy itself, where civil and political position are directly identical. As against this stands civil society as *civil estate*. Difference of estate here is no longer a difference of *needs* and of *work* as independent bodies. The only general, *superficial and formal* difference still remaining here is that of *town* and *country*. Within society itself, however, the difference was developed in mobile and not fixed circles, of which *free choice* is the principle. *Money* and *education* are the main criteria. However, this has to be demonstrated not here but in the critique of Hegel's presentation of civil society. Enough. The estate of civil society has for its principle neither need, that is, a natural element, nor politics. It consists of separate masses which form fleetingly and whose very formation is fortuitous and does *not* amount to an organisation.

Only one thing is characteristic, namely, that *lack of property* and the *estate of direct* labour, of concrete labour, form not so much an estate of civil society as the ground upon which its circles rest and move. The estate proper, in which political and civil position coincide, is confined to the *members of the executive authority*. The present-day estate of society already shows its difference from the earlier estate of civil society in that it does not hold the individual as it formerly did as something communal, as a community, but that it is partly accident, partly the work and so on of the individual which does, or does not, keep him in his estate, an *estate* which is itself only an *external* quality of the individual, being neither inherent in his labour nor standing to him in fixed relationships as an objective community organised according to rigid laws. It stands, rather, in no sort of *real* relation to his material actions, to his *real standing*[a]. The physician does not form a special estate within civil society. One merchant belongs to a different estate from another, to a different *social position*. For just as civil society is separated from political society, so civil society has within itself become divided into *estate* and *social* position, however many relations may occur between them. The principle of the civil

---

[a] The German word *Stand*—in this passage mostly rendered as "estate"—can also mean position, situation, rank, profession, standing, etc.—*Ed.*

estate or of civil society is *enjoyment* and the *capacity to enjoy*. In his political significance the member of civil society frees himself from his estate, his true civil position; it is only here that he acquires importance as a *human being*, or that his quality as member of the state, as social being, appears as his *human* quality. For all his other qualities in civil society *appear inessential* to the human being, the individual, as *external* qualities which indeed are necessary for his existence in the whole, i.e., as a link with the whole, but a link that he can just as well throw away again. (Present-day civil society is the realised principle of *individualism*; the individual existence is the final goal; activity, work, content, etc., are *mere* means.)

The *estates constitution*, where it is not a tradition of the Middle Ages, is the attempt to some extent in the political sphere itself to thrust the human being back into the narrowness of his individual sphere, to turn his particularity into his material consciousness, and because in the political sphere the differences of estate exist, to turn them again into social differences.

The *real human being* is the *private individual* of the present-day state constitution.

In general, the *estate* has the significance that *difference* and *separation* constitute the *very existence* of the individual. His way of life, activity, etc., instead of turning him into a member, a function of society, make of him an *exception* to society, are his privilege. That this *difference* is not merely *individual* but is established as a *community*, estate or corporation, not only does not cancel its exclusive nature but is rather an expression of it. Instead of the individual function being a function of society, it turns, on the contrary, the individual function into a society for itself.

Not only is the *estate* based on the *separation* of society as the prevailing law; it separates the human being from his general essence, it turns him into an animal that is directly identical with its function. The Middle Ages are the *animal history* of human society, its zoology.

The modern era, *civilisation*, makes the opposite mistake. It separates the *objective* essence of the human being from him as merely something *external*, material. It does not accept the content of the human being as his true reality.

This will be further considered in the section on "civil society".[9] We pass on to

304. "The political-estates element contains at the same time in its **own** significance[a] the distinctions of estates already present in the earlier spheres."

[a] In Hegel: *Bestimmung*, i.e., "determination", not *Bedeutung*, "significance". But on pp. 74 and 96, where Marx quotes the same passage, it is given as in Hegel.—*Ed.*

We have already shown that "the distinctions of estate already present in the earlier spheres" have either no significance for the political sphere at all, or only the significance of private, hence non-political, distinctions. According to Hegel, however, this distinction here does not have its "already existing significance" (the significance it has in civil society), but it is rather the "political-estates element", which, by absorbing it, affirms its essence; and, immersed in the political sphere, it acquires as its "own" significance a significance which belongs to *this element* and *not to it* [this distinction].

When the structure of civil society was still political and the political state was civil society, this *separation,* this *doubling* of the significance of the estates, was not present. They did not *signify one thing* in civil society and *something else* in the political world. They acquired no *significance* in the political world but *signified themselves*. The dualism of civil society and the political state, which the *estates* constitution seeks to resolve by a *harking-back,* appears in that constitution itself in such a way that the *difference of estate* (the differentiation within civil society) acquires a different significance in the *political* and the civil sphere. Here we are seemingly confronted by something identical, *the same subject,* but with *essentially different* attributes; hence it is really a *twofold* subject; and this *illusory identity* is artificially preserved by that reflection which at one time ascribes a character to the civil estate distinctions as such which is yet to accrue to them from the political sphere, and conversely, at another time ascribes to the distinctions of estate in the political sphere a character which does not arise from the political sphere but from the subject of the civil sphere. (This identity is illusory if only for the reason that although the human being, the *real subject*, does remain himself, whatever forms his essence takes, and does not lose his identity, here however the human being is not the subject but is identified with a predicate, the estate; and at the same time it is maintained that both in this *particular determination* and in some *other* determination, the human being, as this particular, exclusively limited entity, is something *other* than this limited entity.) In order to represent the one limited subject, the particular estate (the distinctions of estate) as the essential subject of both predicates, or in order to prove the identity of both predicates, they are both mystified and presented in an illusory, vague, twofold form.

The same subject is here taken in different *significances*, the significance however is not that determined by the subject itself, but an *allegorical,* substituted definition is given. The same significance could be assigned to a different concrete subject, and the same subject could be given a different significance. The significance acquired by the civil distinctions of estate in the political sphere does not arise from those distinctions but from the political sphere, and they could also here have a different significance, as was indeed historically the case. The reverse is also true. It is this *uncritical, mystical* way of *interpreting* an *old world-view* in terms of a new one which turns it into nothing better than an unfortunate hybrid, where form belies significance and significance belies the form, and where form does not acquire its significance and real form, nor does significance become form and real significance. This *uncritical approach*, this *mysticism*, is both the enigma of modern constitutions (κατ' ἐξοχήν,[a] the estates constitution) and the mystery of the Hegelian philosophy, particularly the *philosophy of law* and the *philosophy of religion*.

One can best rid oneself of this illusion by taking the significance as what it is, namely, as the *essential quality*, by making it as such the subject, and then considering whether the subject *allegedly* belonging to it is its *real predicate*, whether it represents its essence and true realisation.

"Its initially abstract position" (that of the political-estates element), "that of the extreme of *empirical generality* over against the *royal* or *monarchical principle* in general, a position which implies only the *possibility* of *harmony* and therefore likewise the *possibility of hostile* confrontation, this abstract position becomes a rational relation (a *syllogism*, cf. Remark to para. 302) only if its *mediation* is actually effected."

We have already seen that the estates together with the executive authority form the middle term between the monarchical principle and the people, between the will of the state as *one* empirical will and as *many* empirical wills, between *empirical singularity* and *empirical generality*. Since Hegel defined the will of civil society as *empirical generality*, he had to define the will of the monarch as *empirical singularity*, but he does not express the *antithesis* in all its sharpness.

Hegel continues:

"Just as from the monarchical authority the executive already has this attribute (para. 300), so likewise one aspect of the estates must be adapted to the function of existing essentially as the middle element."

The true opposites, however, are the monarch and civil society. And we have already seen that the estates element has with regard to the people the same significance which the executive has with

---

[a] Pre-eminently.—*Ed.*

regard to the monarch. As the latter is an *emanation* into a widespread circulation system, so the former is *condensation* into a miniature edition; for the constitutional monarchy can get on with the *people* only *en miniature*. The estates element is entirely the *same abstraction of the political state* in relation to civil society as is the executive in relation to the monarch. It seems, then, that the mediation has been completely effected. Both poles have lessened their harshness, the fires of their particular natures have met, and the *legislature,* whose elements consist of both the executive and the estates, seems not to need to initiate the *mediation,* but rather itself to be *mediation incarnate*. Hegel has also already described this *estates element together with the executive* as the *middle term* between people and monarch (and similarly, the estates element as the middle term between civil society and executive, etc.). Hence the rational relationship, the *conclusion,* appears to be complete. The *legislature,* the middle term, is a *mixtum compositum* of the two extremes, the monarchical principle and civil society, empirical singularity and empirical generality, subject and predicate. In general, Hegel takes the *conclusion* as the middle term, as a composite mixture. One may say that in his exposition of the rational deduction the whole transcendence and mystical dualism of his system is made apparent. The middle term is the wooden iron, the concealed opposition between generality and singularity.

First, let us notice with regard to this whole exposition that the "mediation" which Hegel here wants to effect is not a demand he derives from the *essence of the legislative power,* from its own character; it is rather derived from *consideration* for an existence which lies outside its essential character. It is a *construction from consideration*. The legislature in particular is only derived from consideration for a third thing. It is therefore pre-eminently the *construction of its formal being* which lays claim to all the attention. The legislature is constructed very *diplomatically*. This follows from the *false,* illusory, κατ' ἐξοχήν,[a] *political* position which the legislature occupies in the modern state (whose interpreter is Hegel). It follows as a matter of course that this state is no *true* state, since in it the *political attributes,* one of which is the legislature, have to be considered not in and for themselves, not theoretically, but practically, not as independent powers, but as powers afflicted with an antithesis, not according to the nature of things, but according to the rules of convention.

---

[a] Pre-eminently.—*Ed.*

Thus the estates element "together with the executive" should really be the middle term between the will of the empirical singularity, the monarch, and the will of the empirical generality, civil society; but in *truth,* in reality, "*its* position" is "initially an abstract position, that of the *extreme of empirical generality* over against the *royal* or *monarchical principle* in general, a position which implies only the *possibility of harmony* and therefore likewise the *possibility of hostile confrontation*"—an "abstract position", as Hegel correctly remarks.

First, it now appears that here neither the "*extreme of empirical generality*", nor the "royal or monarchical principle", the extreme of empirical singularity, confront each other. For the estates are *delegated* by civil society, as the executive is *delegated* by the monarch. As in the delegated executive authority the monarchical principle ceases to be the extreme of empirical singularity, and in it, really, gives up the "*unfounded*" will and condescends to the "*finiteness*" of knowledge and accountability and thinking, so in the estates element civil society no longer appears as empirical generality, but rather as a very definite whole which has the same "sense and a way of thinking appropriate to the state and government, as well as to the interests of particular groups and individuals" (para. 302). In its miniature edition, the estate edition, civil society has ceased to be "empirical generality". It is rather reduced to a committee, to a very limited number, and if in the executive the monarch has given himself empirical generality, then civil society has given itself in the estates empirical singularity or particularity. Both have become particularities.

The only opposition which is still possible here seems to be that between the two representatives of the two wills of the state, between the two emanations, between the *executive element* and the *estates* element of the legislature; and it therefore seems to be an *opposition within the legislature itself.* The "*joint*" mediation seems also well suited to get them into each other's hair. In the executive element of the legislature the empirical, inaccessible singularity of the monarch becomes *earthly* in a number of restricted, tangible, accountable personalities, and in the estates element civil society has become *heavenly* in a number of political men. Both sides have lost their impalpable quality, the monarchical authority [has lost] the inaccessible, purely *empirical unit*; civil society, the inaccessible, vague *empirical all*; the one [has lost] its inflexibility, the other its fluidity. Thus only in the estates element on the one hand and in the executive element of the legislature on the other, which together were supposed to mediate between civil society and the monarch, the *opposition* seems to have become an opposition set for battle and also an *irreconcilable contradiction.*

This *"mediation"*, therefore, has indeed a very great need, as Hegel rightly shows, for "*its mediation* to be *actually* effected". It is itself rather the existence of contradiction than of mediation.

Hegel seems to have no good reason for asserting that this mediation is effected by the *estates element.* He says:

> "Just as from the monarchical authority the executive already has this attribute (para. 300), so likewise one aspect of the estates must be adapted to the function of existing essentially as the middle element." [Para. 304.]

But we have already seen that Hegel here arbitrarily and inconsistently places monarch and estates in polar opposition. As the executive has this attribute from the monarch, so the estates element has this attribute from civil society. The estates not only stand jointly with the executive between the monarch and civil society; they also stand between the executive in general and the people (para. 302). They do more with regard to civil society than the executive does with regard to monarchical authority, since the latter itself stands in opposition to the people. It has therefore filled the measure of mediation. Why pack still more on the backs of these asses? Why must the estates element everywhere serve as the asses' bridge, even between itself and its opponent? Why is it everywhere so self-sacrificing? Is it expected to hack off *one* of its hands so as to be unable to hold off *with both* of them its opponent, the executive element of the legislature?

In addition, Hegel first made the estates arise from the corporations, the distinctions of estate, etc, so that they should not be "mere empirical generality", and now, in reverse, he turns them into "mere empirical generality" in order to make distinctions of estate arise from them! As the monarch mediates himself with civil society through the executive power as its Christ, so society mediates itself with the monarch through the estates as its priests.

It now appears rather to have to be the role of the extremes, the monarchical authority (empirical singularity) and civil society (empirical generality), to come as mediators between "their mediators" the more so as it is "one of the most important insights of logic that a certain element which occupies the position of an extreme when standing within an antithesis, is at the same time a *middle term,* and thus ceases to be an extreme and is an *organic* element". (Remark to para. 302.) Civil society seems not to be able to take on this role since in the "legislature" it has no seat as *itself,* as an extreme. The monarchical principle, the other extreme, which is situated *as such* in the midst of the legislature, therefore seems to have to be the mediator between the estates and the executive element. It also seems to have the necessary qualifications. For on the one hand the whole of the state, including therefore also civil society, is represented in it, and it has specifically the "empirical singularity" of will in common with the estates, since the empirical generality is only actual as empirical singularity. Furthermore, it does not confront civil society merely as a *formula,* as state *consciousness,* like the executive. It *is* itself the state; it has the *material,* the *natural* element in common with civil society. On the other hand, the monarch is the head and representative of the executive power. (Hegel, who stands everything on its head, turns the executive power into the representative, into the emanation, of the monarch. Since in speaking of the idea the existence of which is supposed to be the monarch, he has in mind not the real idea of the executive authority, not the executive authority as idea, but the subject of the absolute idea which exists *bodily* in the monarch, the executive authority becomes a *mystical extension of the soul which exists in* his body, *the body of the monarch.*)

In the legislature, the monarch had therefore to constitute the middle term between the executive and the estates element; but the executive is the middle term between him and the estates element, and the estates element is the middle term between him and civil society. How is he to mediate between what he needs for his middle term in order not to be a one-sided extreme? Here all the absurdity of these extremes which in turn play the role now of the extreme, now of the middle term, becomes obvious. They are Janus-faced, show themselves now from the front, now from the back and have different characters front and back. That which originally was defined as the middle term between two extremes now appears itself as an extreme, and one of the two extremes which through it was mediated with the other, now appears again as the middle term (because it is regarded in *its distinction* from the other extreme) between its extreme and its middle term. It is a mutual complimentation. As if a man were to step between two fighting men and then again one of the fighting men were to step between the mediator and the fighting man. It is the story of the man and his wife who fought, and the doctor who wanted to step between them as mediator, when in turn the wife had to mediate between the doctor and her husband, and the husband between his wife and the doctor. It is like the lion in *A Midsummer Night's Dream,* who shouts: "I am lion and I am not lion, I am Snug the joiner." So here every extreme is now the lion of opposition, now Snug the mediator. When one of the extremes calls "I am the middle term now!" the other two must not touch it, but only hit in the direction of the other which is now the extreme. One can see, it is a society which at heart is spoiling for a fight, but is too afraid of bruises to engage in a real fight, and the two who want to fight arrange things so that the third, who steps in between, is to get the hiding; but now one of the other two acts again as the third, and so from being so cautious they don't come to any decision. This system of mediation also comes about so that the same man who wants to beat up his opponent must protect him on all sides from the thrashing of other opponents, and so in this double occupation never comes to carry out his business. It is strange that Hegel, who reduces the absurdity of mediation to its abstract, logical, and therefore unadulterated, unique expression, describes it at the same time as the *speculative mystery* of logic, as the rational relationship, as the syllogism of reason. Real extremes cannot be mediated precisely because they are real extremes. Nor do they require mediation, for they are opposed in essence. They have nothing in common, they do not need each other, they do not supplement each other. The one does not have in its own bosom the longing for, the need for, the anticipation of the other. (But when Hegel treats generality and singularity, the abstract elements of the syllogism, as actual opposites, this precisely is the basic dualism of his logic. The further development of this point belongs to the criticism of Hegelian logic.)

To this the saying *"Les extrêmes se touchent"* seems to be opposed. North pole and south pole attract each other, female and male sexes also attract each other, and man is born only through the unifying of their polar differences.

On the other hand: every extreme *is* its other extreme. Abstract *spiritualism* is *abstract materialism*; *abstract materialism* is the *abstract spiritualism* of matter.

Concerning the first: north pole and south pole are both *pole*; their *essence* is identical; similarly, *female and male* sex are both one *species,* one *essence,* human essence. North and south are opposed aspects of *one* essence—the differentiation of one *essence* at the *height of its development.* They are *differentiated* essence. They are what they are *only* as a *distinct* attribute, and as *this* distinct attribute of the essence. *True actual* extremes would be pole and non-pole, human and *non*-human species. The difference in one case [i.e., between north and south poles, women and men] is a *difference of existence;* in the other [between pole and non-pole, human and non-human] a difference of *essences*—between *two* essences. Concerning the second: the chief feature here is that a *concept* (a form of existence, etc.) is taken *abstractly*, is considered to have significance not as something independent but as an *abstraction* of something else and only as this *abstraction*; thus spirit, for example, is regarded as merely the *abstraction* of matter. Then it is self-evident that precisely because this form is to constitute its content, this concept is rather the *abstract contrary*, the object, from which it is abstracted, in its abstraction, which constitutes the real essence, in this case abstract materialism. If the *difference* within the existence of *one* essence had not been confused on the one hand with the *hypostatised abstraction* (not, of course, an abstraction from something else, but really from itself), and on the other with the *actual* opposition of mutually exclusive essences, a threefold error would have been prevented: (1) that, since only the extreme is said to be true, every abstraction and one-sidedness thinks itself true, whereby a principle appears only as an abstraction of something else, instead of as a totality in itself; (2) that the *sharply-marked character* of *actual* opposites, their development into extremes, which is nothing else but their self-cognition and also their eagerness to bring the fight to a decision, is thought of as something possibly to be prevented or something harmful; (3) that their mediation is attempted. For however much both extremes come on to the scene in their existence as actual and as extremes, it lies only in the *essence* of one of them to be an extreme, while for the other this has not the *significance* of *true actuality*. The one overreaches the other. They do not occupy the same position: Christianity, for example, or religion in general, and philosophy are extremes. But in truth religion does not form a *true* opposite to philosophy. For philosophy comprehends *religion* in its *illusory* actuality. For philosophy, religion is therefore dissolved into itself, insofar as it wants to be something actual. There is no actual dualism of *essence*. More of this later.[a]

It may be asked, how does Hegel arrive at all at the need for a new *mediation* by the estates element? Or does Hegel share with [others][b] "the frequently-held, but most dangerous prejudice which regards the estates primarily from the point of view of *opposition* to the government, as if this were their essential attitude"? (Remark to para. 302.)

The position is simply this: On the one hand we have seen that

---

[a] See this volume, p. 92 et seq.—*Ed.*
[b] A word is missing: presumably *anderen.—Ed.*

only in the "legislature" civil society as "estates" element and the monarchical power as "executive element" have been actuated to real, direct, practical opposition.

On the other hand: The legislature is a totality. We find there the delegation of the monarchical principle, the "executive power"; (2) the delegation of civil society, the "estates" element; but in addition it also contains (3) the one *extreme as such*, the monarchical principle, while the other extreme, civil society, is not there as such. It is only thereby that the "estates" element becomes the extreme confronting the "monarchical" principle which really civil society should be. As we have seen, civil society becomes organised as *political* existence only as the "estates" element. The "estates" element is its *political* existence, its *transubstantiation* into the political state. Only the "legislature" is therefore, as we have seen, the *political state* proper in its totality. Here there are, therefore, (1) the monarchical principle; (2) the executive; (3) civil society. The "estates" element is "the *civil society of the political state*", of the "legislature". The opposite pole to the monarch, which should be formed by civil society, is therefore formed by the *"estates"* element. (Since civil society is the unreality of political existence, the political existence of civil society is its own dissolution, its separation from itself.) For the same reason it [the estates element] also forms an opposite to the executive.

Hegel therefore also describes the "estates" element again as the "extreme of empirical generality", which really is civil society itself. (Hegel therefore made the political-estates element arise from the corporations and the distinct estates to no good purpose. This would only be meaningful if the distinct estates as such were legislative estates, hence if the distinctions of civil society, the civil character, were in reality the political character. Then we would have not a *legislative power* of the whole state, but the *legislative power* of the different estates and corporations and classes over the state as a whole. The estates of civil society would not acquire a political determination, but on the contrary they would determine the political state. They would make their *particularity* the determining power of the whole. They would be the power of the particular over the general. We would have not one legislative power but several legislative powers which would negotiate with each other and with the executive. But Hegel has in mind the modern significance of the estates element as being the actualisation of state citizenship, of the citizen. He wants the "intrinsically and explicitly general", the political state, not to be determined by civil society, but, on the contrary, to determine the latter. Hence while taking the form of the medieval-estates element, he gives it the opposite significance of being determined by the nature of the political state. The estates as representatives of the corporations, etc., would not be "empirical generality", but "empirical particularity", the "particularity of empirical fact"!) The "legislature" therefore requires *mediation* within itself, i.e., a glossing-over of the opposition, and this mediation must come from the "estates element" since within the legislature the estates element loses the significance of being the representation of civil society and becomes the *primary* element, becomes itself the civil society of the legislature. The "legislature" is the totality of the political state, and for this very reason its *contradiction forced to the surface*. It is therefore also its *posited*[a] resolution. Very different principles collide within it. This certainly *appears* as the *opposition* between the elements of the monarchical principle and the principle of the estates element, etc. *Actually*, however, it is the antinomy of the *political state* and *civil society*, the self-*contradiction of the abstract political state*. The legislature is the *posited*[a] revolt. (Hegel's chief error is to conceive the *contradiction of appearances* as *unity in essence, in the idea*, while in fact it has something more profound for its essence, namely, an *essential contradiction*, just as here this contradiction of the legislative authority within itself, for example, is merely the contradiction of the political state, and therefore also of civil society with itself.

Vulgar criticism falls into an opposite, *dogmatic* error. Thus it criticises the constitution, for example. It draws attention to the antagonism of the powers, etc. It finds contradictions everywhere. This is still dogmatic criticism which *fights* with its subject-matter in the same way in which formerly the dogma of the Holy Trinity, say, was demolished by the contradiction of one and three. True criticism, by contrast, shows the inner genesis of the Holy Trinity in the human brain. It describes the act of its birth. So the truly philosophical criticism of the present state constitution not only shows up contradictions as existing; it *explains* them, it comprehends their genesis, their necessity. It considers them in their *specific* significance. But *comprehending* does not consist, as Hegel imagines, in recognising the features of the logical concept everywhere, but in grasping the specific logic of the specific subject.)

Hegel expresses this in such a way that the attitude of the political-estates element to the monarchical element "implies only

---

[a] In the manuscript: *gesetzt*, which means either posited or sedate, staid.—*Ed.*

the *possibility of harmony* and therefore likewise the *possibility of hostile* confrontation".

The possibility of confrontation is implied wherever *different* wills meet together. Hegel himself says that the "possibility of harmony" is the "possibility of confrontation". Hence he must now form an element which is the *"impossibility of confrontation"* and the *"actuality* of harmony". For him such an element would be the freedom of deciding and of thinking *vis-à-vis* the monarchical will and the executive. It would therefore no longer be part of the "estates-political" element. It would rather be an element of the monarchical will and the executive and would stand in the same opposition to the *actual* estates element as the executive itself.

This requirement is already much toned down in the conclusion of the paragraph:

"Just as from the monarchical authority the executive already has this attribute (para. 300), so likewise one aspect of the estates must be adapted to the function of existing **essentially** as the **middle element**."

The element which is delegated by the estates must have the *reverse* attribute to that which the executive has from the monarchs, since monarchical and estates elements are opposed extremes. As the monarch is democratised in the executive, so this "estates" element must be *monarchised* in its delegation. Hence what Hegel wants is a *monarchical element from the estates*. As the executive has an estates element with regard to the monarch, so there has to be a monarchical element with regard to the estates.

The "actuality of harmony" and the "impossibility of confrontation" is transformed into the following demand: "one aspect of the estates must be adapted to the *function* of *existing essentially* as the *middle element"*. Adapted to the *function*! According to para. 302 the estates have this function anyway. Here it should no longer be *"function"* but *"character"*.

And what kind of function is that anyway, "to exist essentially as the middle element"? Of being in "essence" "Buridan's ass".

The matter is simply this:

The estates are supposed to be "mediation" between monarch and executive on the one hand and the nation on the other, but they are not that, they are rather the organised *political* opposite of civil society. The "legislature" requires *mediation* within itself, namely, as has been shown, a mediation on the part of the estates. The presupposed *moral* harmony of the two wills, of which one is the will of the state as the monarchical will and the other the will of the state as the will of civil society, is not sufficient. Indeed, only the legislature is the organised, *total* political state, but precisely because the legislature is the highest development of the state, it is there that the unconcealed contradiction of the *political state* with itself becomes evident. Hence the *appearance* of an *actual identity* between the monarchical will and the will of the estates must be established. *The estates element must be posed as the monarchical will, or the monarchical will as the estates element.* The estates element must set itself up as the reality of a will which is not the will of the estates element. The *unity* which is not present in *essence* (otherwise it would have to prove itself by its *efficacy* and not by the *mode of being* of the estates element), must be present at least as an *existent*; or else an *existence* of the legislature (of the estates element) has the *attribute* of being this *unity* of the *non-united*. This component of the estates element, the House of Peers or Upper House, etc., is the highest *synthesis* of the political state within the organisation here considered. What Hegel wants, the "actuality of harmony", and the "impossibility of hostile confrontation", has indeed not been achieved thereby; we are rather left with the "possibility of harmony". But that is the *postulated illusion* of the *unity of the political state with itself* (of the unity of the will of the monarch with the will of the estates, and further the principle of the political state and civil society), of this *unity* as a *material* principle; that is to say, it is the illusion that not only two opposed principles are united but that their unity is [their] *nature*, the basis of [their] existence. This component of the estates element is the *romanticism* of the political state, the *dreams* of its substantiality or of its harmony with itself. It is an *allegorical* entity.

It now depends on the actual *status quo* of the relations between the estates element and the monarchical element whether this *illusion* is an effective illusion or *conscious self-deception*. So long as estates and monarchical power are in *actual* harmony, get on with each other, the *illusion* of their *essential* unity is an *actual*, hence *effective*, illusion. In the opposite case, where it ought to demonstrate its truth in practice, it becomes *deliberate untruth* and ridiculous

305. "One **estate of civil** society contains the principle which is of itself capable of being established in this **political** role—namely, the estate whose ethical life is natural, and whose basis is family life and, so far as its livelihood is concerned, landed property. Its specific feature, accordingly, is a will based on itself; it shares this and the natural attribute, which the monarchical element contains, with the latter."

We have already shown Hegel's inconsistency (1) in comprehending the political-estates element in its *modern* abstraction from civil society, etc., after having made it originate in the corporations; (2) in now again defining it in accordance with the *differentiation of estates in civil society,* after he has defined the political estates as such as the "extreme of empirical generality".

It would be *consistent* now to regard the *political estates* of themselves as a new element and from them now to construe the mediation stipulated in para. 304.

But now we see Hegel again dragging in the differentiation of civil estates and at the same time creating the appearance that the *reality* and the *particular essence* of the differentiation of civil estates do not determine the *highest political sphere,* the legislative power, but on the contrary, that they are reduced to a mere *material* which the political sphere moulds and shapes according to *its own* needs which arise from itself.

"One estate of civil society contains the **principle** which is of itself capable of **being established** in this **political role**—namely, the estate whose **ethical life is natural**." (The peasantry.)

Now in what does this *capability in principle,* or this *capability of the principle* of the peasantry consist?

It has as its "**basis family life** and, so far as its livelihood is concerned, **landed property.** Its **specific feature,** accordingly, is a will based **on itself;** it shares this and the **natural attribute,** which the **monarchical** element contains, with the latter."

The "will based on itself" refers to its livelihood, the "landed property"; the "natural attribute" shared with the monarchical element refers to "family life", regarded as the basis.

The livelihood based on "landed property" and a "will based on itself" are two different things. One should rather speak of a "will *based* on land". But one should rather speak not of a will based *on itself,* but of a will based *on the whole,* on a "political way of thinking".

The place of the "way of thinking", of the "possession of political spirit" is taken by the "possession of *land".*

Where, further, *"family life"* as a basis is concerned, the "social" ethical life of civil society would seem to stand above this "natural ethical life". Moreover, "family life" is the *"natural ethical life"* of *the other estates,* or of the middle-class estate of civil society as much as of the peasantry. But the fact that with the peasantry "family life" is not only the principle of the family but the basis of its social existence altogether, would seem rather to make it unfit for the highest political task, inasmuch as it will apply patriarchal laws to a non-patriarchal sphere and indicate child or father, master and man, where it is a question of the *political* state, of *citizenship.*

As for the *natural attribute* of the *monarchical* element, Hegel has deduced not a patriarchal, but a *modern constitutional* king. His natural attribute is to be the *bodily representative* of the state and to be born as *king,* or that kingship is his *family inheritance*; but what has that in common with family life as the basis of the peasantry? What has natural ethical life in common with natural destination by birth as such? The king shares this with the horse in that just as the horse is born as a horse, the king is born as a king.

If the differentiation of estates as such, which Hegel accepted, had been regarded by him as a political distinction, the peasantry as such would already have been an independent section of the estates element, and if as such it is an element of mediation with the monarchical element, what need is there for the construction of a *new* mediation? And why separate it from the estates element proper, since the latter gets into the "abstract" relation to the monarchical element only because of this separation from it? But after Hegel has just expounded the political-estates element as a particular element, as a *transubstantiation of the civil estate into state citizenship* and has found that for just this reason it needs mediation, how can he now dissolve this organism again into the distinctions of the civil estate, that is, into the civil estate, and from that derive the mediation of the political state with itself?

What an anomaly altogether, that the highest *synthesis* of the political state should be nothing but the synthesis of landed property and family life!

In one word:

As soon as the civil estates as such become political estates that mediation is not required, and as soon as that mediation is required the civil estate is not political, and so is not that mediation either. The peasant is then a part of the political-estates element not as peasant but as citizen, while in the reverse case ([when he is] a citizen as a *peasant,* or when he is a peasant as a citizen) his citizenship is his *being a peasant,* he is not a citizen as a peasant but a peasant as a citizen!

This is here therefore an inconsistency of Hegel *within his own* way of looking at things, and such an inconsistency is *accommodation.* In the modern sense, in the sense expounded by Hegel, the political-estates element is the *separation of civil society from its civil estate and its distinctions, assumed as accomplished.* How can Hegel turn the civil estate into a *solution* of the antinomies of the *legislature* within itself? Hegel wants the medieval-estates system, but in the modern sense of the legislature, and he wants the modern legislature, but in the body of the medieval-estates system! This is the worst kind of syncretism.

At the beginning of para. 304 he says:

"The political-estates element contains at the same time in its own determination the distinctions of estates already present in the earlier spheres."

But in its *own* definition the political-estates element contains these distinctions only by cancelling them, annulling them within itself, *abstracting from them.*

If the peasant estate, or, as we shall see later on, the peasant estate *raised to a higher power,* the landed aristocracy, is as such turned, in the manner described above, into the mediation of the total *political* state, of the legislative power in itself, then that is indeed the mediation of the political-estates element with the monarchical power in the sense that it is the *dissolution* of the political-estates element as an actual political element. Not the peasant estate, but the *estate,* the *civil estate,* the *analysis* (reduction) of the political-estates element to the civil estate is here the *restored unity of the political state with itself.* (Not the *peasantry* as such is here the *mediation* but its separation from the political-estates *element* in its quality as *civil estate:* the fact is that its civil estate gives it a particular position in the political-estates element, and therefore the other section of the political-estates element likewise acquires the position of a *particular* civil estate, and thus *ceases* to represent the state citizenship of civil society.) Here the *political* state is now no longer present as *two opposed wills,* but on the one hand there is the political state (executive and monarch) and on the other civil society as distinct from the political state. (The different estates.) With that the political state is, of course, annulled as a *totality.*

The next sense of the *duplication* of the political-estates element in itself as a mediation with the monarchical authority is, generally speaking, that the inner *division* of this element, its own opposition within itself, is its *restored* unity with the monarchical authority. The basic dualism between the *monarchical* and the estates elements of the legislative power is *neutralised* by the dualism of the estates element in itself. With Hegel, however, this neutralisation is effected by the political-estates element separating itself from its *political* element.

As regards *landed property* as *livelihood,* which is supposed to correspond to the *sovereignty* of the will, the *sovereignty of the monarch,* and *family life* as the basis of the peasantry, which is supposed to correspond to the *natural attribute* of monarchical authority, we shall return to this later.[a] Here in para. 305 the *"principle"* of the peasantry is expounded "which is of itself capable of being established in this political role".

---

[a] See this volume, pp. 98-104.—*Ed.*

In para. 306 this "establishing" of "political position and significance" is effected. It comes down to this: "wealth" "becomes an *inalienable heritage*, burdened with *primogeniture*". It is thus "primogeniture" which is supposed to establish the peasantry politically.

"The justification for primogeniture," says the Addition, "is that the state must be able to count on a certain way of thinking not as a **mere possibility**, but as something **necessary**. Now this way of thinking is not, of course, tied to wealth, but the **relatively necessary** connection is that a man of independent means is not restricted by external circumstances and **can** thus come forward and act for the state without hindrance."

First proposition. The state is not content with "a *certain way of thinking as a mere possibility*", it must count on it as something "*necessary*".

Second proposition. "The way of thinking is not tied to wealth", i. e., the mentality of wealth is a "*mere possibility*".

Third proposition. But there is a "*relatively necessary connection*", namely, "that a man of independent means, etc., *can* act for the state", i.e., *wealth* provides the "*possibility*" of a political way of thinking, but it is just the "possibility" which does not suffice according to the first proposition.

Moreover, Hegel has not shown that *landed property* is the only sort of "independent means".

The *establishment of its capacity*[a] *for independence* is what fits the peasantry "for political position and significance". Or, "the independence of wealth" *is* its "political position and significance".

This independence is further expounded as follows:

Its "*wealth*"[a] is "*independent* of the *wealth of the state*". The wealth of the state here evidently means the *government exchequer*. In this respect "the *general* estate" stands "*by contrast*" "as essentially dependent on the *state*". So we read in the Preface [to Hegel's *Philosophy of Law*], p. 13:

Moreover, **philosophy** with us is not, as it was with the Greeks for instance, practised as a private art", "but has an existence in the open, in contact with the public, and especially, or even *solely*, in the service of the state".

Hence, philosophy is also "*essentially*" dependent on the exchequer.

The *wealth* [of this estate] is *independent* "of the uncertainty of business, the quest for profit, and any sort of fluctuation in

---

[a] Here and in the following paragraph the German word *Vermögen* is used, which can mean ability, capacity, or wealth, fortune, etc.—*Ed.*

possessions". In this respect the "business estate" stands over against it as the estate "dependent on and orientated towards need".

This wealth is thus "independent both of the *favour* of the *executive*, and of the *favour* of the *crowd*".

Finally, it is even secured *against its own caprice* by the fact that the members of this estate called to fulfil this role "lack the right of other citizens either to dispose freely of their entire property, or to know that it will pass to their children in accordance with the equality of their love for them" [para. 306].

Here the antitheses have assumed an entirely new and very material form such as we could scarcely have expected in the heaven of the political state.

As expounded by Hegel, the antithesis is, expressed in all its sharpness, the antithesis of *private property* and *wealth*.

Landed property is *private property* κατ' ἐξοχήν,[a] it is private property *proper*. Its precisely *private* nature is evident (1) as "*independence* of the *wealth of the state*", of the "*favour of the executive*", of the property which exists as "general property of the political state", a *particular wealth* alongside others according to the construction of the political state; (2) as "*independence* of the *needs*" of society or of "social wealth", of the "favour of the crowd". (It is likewise significant that the share in the wealth of the state is conceived of as a "*favour* of the *executive*" and the share in social wealth as a "*favour* of the *crowd*".) The wealth of the "general estate" and of the "business estate" is not *private property proper* because it is there *directly*, here *indirectly*, conditioned by the connection with the general wealth or with property as social property—is a *participation* in it, and therefore indeed in both cases mediated by "favour", i.e., by the "accident of the will". Over against this stands *landed property* as *sovereign private property*, which has not yet the form of wealth, i. e., of property established by the *social will*.

The political constitution at its highest point is therefore the *constitution of private property*. The supreme *political conviction* is the *conviction of private property*. *Primogeniture* is merely the *external* appearance of the *inner* nature of *landed property*. The fact that it is *inalienable* cuts off its *social* nerves and ensures *its isolation from civil society*. The fact that it does not pass to their children in accordance with the "equality of their love for them" frees it, makes it independent even of the smaller society, the natural

---

[a] *Par excellence.*—*Ed.*

society of the *family,* and its will and its laws, thus preventing the *harsh* nature of *private property* from passing into *family property.*

In para. 305 Hegel declared the estate of landed property capable of being established in the "political role" because it has "family life" as its "basis". But he himself has declared "love" to be the basis, the principle, the *spirit* of family life. Hence in the estate which is based on family life, the *basis of family life,* love as the actual, and therefore effective and determining principle, is lacking. It is *spiritless* family life, the *illusion* of family life. In its highest development the *principle of private property contradicts* the *principle of the family.* In contrast with the *estate whose ethical life is natural,* the estate of family life, it is only in civil society that *family life* becomes the life of the family, the *life of love.* The former is rather the *barbarism* of private property *against* family life.

Such, then, is the alleged *sovereign magnificence of private property,* of *landed property,* on which so much sentimentality has been spent and so many multicoloured crocodile tears have been shed in recent times.

It does not help Hegel to say that *primogeniture* is only a *demand of politics* and must be understood in its *political* position and significance. It does not help him to say: "The security and stability of the [landowning] estate can be further enhanced by the institution of primogeniture, though this institution is desirable *only from a political point of view,* since it involves a sacrifice for the *political purpose* of *enabling* the first-born son *to live independently*" [Addition to para. 306]. It is a certain decency, a *decorum of thought* which induces Hegel to put it this way. He wants to justify and construe primogeniture not in and for itself, but only in reference to something else; not as something determined by itself, but as determined by something else, not as end but as *means* to an end. In truth, primogeniture is a consequence of *perfect* landed property, it is fossilised private property, private property (*quand même*) at the peak of its independence and intensity of its development, and that which Hegel represents as the purpose, the determining factor and prime cause of primogeniture, is rather its effect, its consequence, the power of *abstract private property* over the *political state;* whereas Hegel represents primogeniture as the *power of the political state over private property.* He makes the cause the effect and the effect the cause, the determining the determined and the determined the determining.

But what is the *content* of the political establishment, of the political purpose—what is the purpose of this purpose? What is its substance? *Primogeniture,* the *superlative of private property,* sovereign *private property*. What power does the political state exercise over private property in primogeniture? This, that it *isolates* private property from family and society, that it turns it into *something abstractly independent*. What then is the power of the political state over private property? The *power of private property itself*, its essence brought into existence. What remains for the political state in contrast with this essence? The *illusion* that the state determines, when it is being determined. It does, indeed, break the *will of the family and society*, but only so as to give existence to the *will of private property without family and society* and to acknowledge this existence as the supreme existence of the political state, as the supreme existence of *ethical* life.

Let us examine how the various elements conduct themselves here, in the *legislature,* the total state, the state come to actualisation and consequence, to consciousness, the *actual* political state with the *ideal*, the *logical* character and form of these elements, as they *ought to be*.

(Primogeniture is not, as Hegel says, "a fetter laid upon the freedom of civil right", it is rather the "freedom of civil right which has freed itself of all social and ethical ties".) ("The supreme political construction is here the construction of abstract private property.")

Before we make this comparison we must take a closer look at one statement in the paragraph, namely, that which says that through primogeniture the wealth of the peasantry, landed property, private property, is secured even *"against caprice on their own part* by the fact that the members of this estate who are called to fill this role lack the right of other citizens to dispose freely of their entire property".

We have already emphasised that by the "inalienability" of landed property the social nerves of private property are cut. Private property (landed property) is secured against the *caprice* of the owner *himself* by the fact that the sphere of his caprice has turned from being a generally human caprice into the *specific caprice of private property*; that private property has become the *subject* in volition; that will is merely now the *predicate* of private property. Private property is no longer a *distinct* object of free choice; instead, free choice is the *distinct* predicate of private property. But let us compare what Hegel himself says about the sphere of civil law:

65. "I can *alienate* my property, for it is mine only insofar as I put my will into it [...], provided always that the thing in question is a thing *external by nature*."

66. "Therefore those possessions, or rather those material attributes, which

constitute my innermost person and the general nature of my self-consciousness—such as my personality generally, my general freedom of will, my morality and my religion—are *inalienable*, just as the right to them is *imprescriptible*."

With primogeniture, therefore, landed property, perfect private property, becomes an *inalienable* possession, hence a *material attribute*, which constitutes the "innermost person, the general nature of the self-consciousness" of the estate of owners of entailed estates, its "personality generally, its general freedom of will, its morality and its religion". Hence it is also consistent with this that where private property, landed property, is *inalienable*, the "general freedom of will" (which includes the freedom to dispose of something external, such as landed property) and the *morality* (which includes *love* as the real spirit manifesting itself likewise as the true law of the family) are, by contrast, alienable. The *"inalienability" of private property* is one with the *"alienability" of the general freedom of will and morality*. Here property no longer exists "insofar as I put my will into it", but my will exists "insofar as it lies in property". My will here does not possess, it is possessed. That is just what is *romantically* titillating about the power of primogeniture, that private property, hence private caprice in its most abstract form, the *wholly narrow-minded*, unethical, crude will, appears here as the highest synthesis of the political state, as the supreme alienation of caprice, as the hardest, most self-sacrificing struggle with *human weakness*; for the *humanisation* of private property here appears as *human* weakness. Primogeniture is *private property* become a *religion* to itself, lost in itself, *elated* by its own independence and power. As the estate entailed in primogeniture is exempt from direct alienation, so it is also exempt from *contract*. Hegel represents the transition from property to contract as follows:

71. "Existence as determinate being is essentially being for something else; [...] one aspect of property is that it is an existent as an external thing, that is, it exists for other external things, and in the context of this necessity and contingency. But it is also an existent as an embodiment of *will*, and from this point of view the other for which it exists can only be *the will* of another person. This relation of will to will is the specific and true soil in which freedom *exists*. This mediation, to have **property** no longer only by means of **a thing and my subjective** will, but also by means of another will and, therewith, to hold it in a **common** will, constitutes the sphere of *contract*."

(For entailment by primogeniture it is laid down in public law that property is owned not in *a common* will but only "by means of a *thing* and my *subjective will*".) While Hegel here in *civil law* understands the *alienability* and dependence of private property on a *common* will as its *true idealism*, in *constitutional law*, on the contrary, the imaginary splendour of independent property is praised in contrast with the "uncertainty of business, the quest for profit, any sort of fluctuation in possessions, the dependence on the wealth of the state". What kind of state is this that cannot even tolerate the idealism of civil law? What kind of philosophy of law is that where the independence of private property has a different significance in civil law and in constitutional law?

Over against the *crass stupidity* of independent private property the uncertainty of business is elegiac, the quest for profit bombastic (dramatic), the fluctuations in possessions a serious fatality (tragic), dependence on the wealth of the state ethical. In brief, in all these qualities the beat of the *human heart*, that is, the dependence of man on man, sounds right through property. No matter how this dependence may be constituted in and for itself, it is *human* over against the slave, who thinks himself free because the sphere which restricts him is not society but the *soil*. The freedom of this will is its *lack* of any other content but that of *private property*.

To define monstrosities like primogeniture as a determination of private property by the political state is quite unavoidable when one interprets an old world-view in terms of a new one, when one gives to a thing, as to private property here, a double meaning, one in the court of abstract law, an opposite one in the heaven of the political state.

We now come to the comparison suggested above.

In para. 257 we read:

"The state is the actuality of the ethical idea—the ethical spirit as the *manifest*, substantial will, clear to itself.... In *custom* the state has its immediate existence, and in the *self-consciousness* of the individual ... its mediated existence; just as the self-consciousness of the individual, by virtue of the individual's conviction, finds *substantial freedom* in the state as its essence, purpose, and the product of its activity."

In para. 268 we read:

"Political *conviction, patriotism* in general, as certainty founded on *truth* [...] and willing which has become *habitual*, is only the result of the institutions existing in the state, in which rationality is *actually* present, just as action which is in conformity with these institutions is the practical expression of this conviction. This conviction is in general *trust* (which may turn into a more or less enlightened insight), the consciousness that my substantial and particular interest is preserved and contained in the interest and purpose of another (here the state) in relation to me as an individual; whereupon this other is directly for me no other, and in this consciousness I am free."

The *actuality* of the ethical idea here appears as the *religion of private property*. (Because in primogeniture private property regards itself in a religious manner, it has come about that in our modern times religion in general has become a quality inherent in landed property and that all writings on primogeniture are full of religious unction. Religion is the highest form of thought of this brutality.) The "*manifest,* substantial will, clear to itself", turns into a dark will, broken by the soil, intoxicated with the impenetrability of the element to which it is attached. The "certainty founded on truth", which is the "political conviction", is the certainty which stands on "its own ground" (in the literal sense). The political "willing", which "has become habitual", is no longer "only the result", etc., but an institution which stands outside the state. The political conviction is no longer "*trust*" but the "confidence, the consciousness that my substantial and particular interest" is "*independent* of the interest and purpose of another (here the state) in relation to me as an individual". That is the consciousness of my *freedom from the state.*

The "maintenance of the *general state interest*", etc., was (para. 289) the task of the "executive". In it there was concentrated the "developed intelligence of the mass of a people and its consciousness of what is lawful" (para. 297). It "actually renders the estates superfluous", for "without the estates" they[a] "are *able* to do what is best, as they constantly must do their best when the estates are in session" (Remark to para. 301). The "general estate, or more precisely the estate which devotes itself to government service, is directly defined as having the general as the purpose of its essential activity" [para. 303].

And how does the general estate, the executive, appear now? "As essentially dependent on the state", as the "wealth, *depending on the favour of the executive*". The same transformation has taken place with civil society, which earlier achieved its ethical character in the corporation. It is a wealth dependent on "the uncertainty of business", etc., on "the favour of the crowd".

What then is the allegedly specific quality of the owners of entailed estates? And in what can the *ethical* quality of *inalienable* wealth consist at all? In *incorruptibility. Incorruptibility* appears as the *supreme* political virtue, an abstract virtue. Moreover, in the state constructed by Hegel incorruptibility is something so singular that it must be constructed as a *special* political power; thus one becomes conscious of it precisely because incorruptibility is not the spirit of the political state, not the rule but the *exception;* and it is constructed as such an exception. One corrupts the owners of entailed estates through their independent property in order to

---

[a] The top bureaucrats (see this volume p. 63).—*Ed.*

preserve them from corruptibility. Whereas, according to the idea, *dependence* on the state and the feeling of this dependence is supposed to be the supreme political freedom, since it is the feeling of a private person as an abstract, dependent person, and this person rather feels and should feel *independent* only as a citizen of the state, here [on the other hand] the *independent private person* is constructed. "His wealth is [equally] independent of the wealth of the state and of the uncertainty of business", etc. He is confronted by the "business estate, which is dependent on and orientated towards need, and the general estate, which is essentially dependent on the state". Here we find, therefore, *independence* of the state and of civil society, and this realised abstraction of both, which in fact is the crudest *dependence on the soil*, constitutes in the legislature the mediation and the unity of both. *Independent private property*, i.e., abstract private property, and the corresponding *private person* are the supreme construction of the political state. Political "independence" is construed as "independent private property" and the "person of this independent private property". In the following we shall see how things are *re vera* with the "independence" and "incorruptibility" and the political conviction arising from that.

That *estates entailed in primogeniture* are *hereditary estates* goes without saying. More of this later.[a] That they go to the *first-born son* is purely historical, as Hegel observes in the Addition [to para. 306].

<small>307. "Thus the rights of this section of the propertied estate are on the one hand no doubt founded on the natural principle of the family, but this principle is at the same time distorted by **hard sacrifice** for a *political purpose*; **consequently** this estate is essentially assigned to activity for this purpose, and is therefore also summoned and *entitled* to this activity by *birth*, without the fortuitousness of elections."</small>

How far the rights of this propertied estate are based on the *natural principle* of the family is not demonstrated by Hegel, unless he means thereby that landed property exists as *hereditary property*. Thus no right of this estate in the political sense is demonstrated herein, but only the right by birth of the owners of entailed estates to their land. "But this", the natural principle of the family, is "at the same time distorted by hard sacrifice for a political purpose". We have indeed seen how "the natural principle of the family is distorted" here, but also that this is "no hard sacrifice for a political purpose", but merely the *realised abstraction of private property*. Rather, through this *distortion of the natural principle of the*

<small>[a] See this volume, p. 106 et seq.—*Ed.*</small>

family the political purpose is equally distorted, "*consequently* (?) this estate is essentially assigned to activity for this purpose"—by private property being made independent?—"and is therefore also summoned and entitled to this activity by birth, without the fortuitousness of elections".

Here therefore *participation in the legislature* is an *innate* human right. Here we have *born legislators*, the *born mediation of the political state with itself*. There has been much sneering at *innate human rights*, especially by the owners of entailed estates. Is it not even stranger that the right to the supreme dignity of the legislative authority is entrusted to a particular race of men? Nothing is more ridiculous than the fact that the appointment by "birth" of legislators, representatives of the citizens, should be opposed by Hegel to their appointment by "the fortuitousness of elections". As if *election*, the conscious product of civil confidence, did not stand in a very different, necessary, connection with the political purpose than the physical accident of birth. Hegel descends everywhere from his political spiritualism into the crassest *materialism*. At the summits of the political state it is everywhere birth which makes certain individuals the incarnations of the supreme offices of state. The supreme state activities coincide with the individual by birth, much as the position of the animal, its character, its way of life, etc., are directly innate in it. In its supreme functions the state acquires the reality of an *animal*. Nature avenges itself on Hegel for the contempt he has shown it. If matter is no longer to be anything for itself against the human will, so the human will here no longer retains anything for itself but matter.

The *false* identity, the *fragmentary*, *patchy* identity of nature and spirit, body and soul, appears as *incarnation*. Since birth gives to the human being only his *individual* existence, positing him in the first place only as a *natural* individual, whereas political attributes such as *legislative* power, etc., are *social products*, progeny of society, and not offspring of the natural individual, it is precisely the direct identity, the unmediated coincidence of the *birth of the individual* with the individual as *individualisation of a particular social position, function*, etc., which is the astonishing thing, the *miracle*. In this system nature directly *produces* kings, directly creates *peers*, etc., just as it makes eyes and noses. It is astonishing to see as a direct product of the physical species what is only a product of the self-conscious species. I am a human being by birth without the consent of society; a particular offspring becomes peer or king only by general consent. Only consent makes the birth of this human being the birth of a king: hence it is consent and not birth which makes a king. When birth, as distinct from the other determinants, directly gives a position to a human being, *his body* makes of him *this particular* social functionary. *His body* is his *social* right. In this system the *physical dignity of the human being* or the *dignity of the human body* (which can be further expanded to read: the dignity of the physical, natural element of the state) appears in such a way that certain dignities, and indeed the highest social dignities, are the *dignities of certain bodies predestined by birth*. It is therefore natural that the nobility should be proud of their blood, their descent, in short the *life-history of their bodies*; it is, of course, this *zoological* way of looking at things which has its corresponding science in *heraldry*. The secret of the nobility is *zoology*.

Concerning the entailment of estates in primogeniture two elements need stressing:

1) That which is enduring is the *ancestral estate*, the *landed property*. It is the lasting element in the relationship, the *substance*. The master of the entailed estate, the owner, is really a mere *accident*. The different generations represent *anthropomorphised* landed property. *Landed property*, as it were, continually *inherits* the first-born of the House as the attribute fettered to it. Every first-born in the series of landed proprietors is the *inheritance*, the *property* of the *inalienable estate*, the *predestined substance of its will* and its *activity*. The subject is the thing and the predicate the human being. The will becomes the property of the property.

2) The *political quality* of the owner of the entailed estate is the *political quality* of his ancestral estate, a *political quality* inherent in this estate. Hence the political quality also appears here as the *property* of *landed property*, as a quality which directly belongs to the *purely physical* earth (nature).

Concerning the first, it follows that the owner of an entailed estate is the *serf* of *landed property*, and nothing but the *practical* consequence of the *theoretical* relationship in which he himself stands to landed property becomes evident in the *serfs* who are subordinated to him. The depth of Germanic subjectivity appears everywhere as the crudeness of a spiritless objectivity.

Here one must explain the relation (1) between *private property* and *inheritance*, (2) between *private property*, inheritance, and through that the privilege of certain families to take part in political sovereignty, (3) the *real historical relationship* or the *Germanic* relationship.

We have seen that the right of primogeniture is the abstraction of *"independent private property"*. A second consequence follows from this. *Independence, self-reliance* in the political state, the construction of which we have been following up to now, means *private property* which at its summit appears as *inalienable landed property*. Political independence therefore does not flow *ex proprio sinu* of the political state; it is not a gift of the political state to its members; it is not the spirit animating it; but rather the members of the political state receive their independence from a factor which is not the essential factor of the political state, but from an essential factor of abstract civil law, from abstract *private property*. Political independence is not the substance of the political state, it is incidental to private property. The political state and the *legislative authority* in it, as we have seen, is the unveiled mystery of the *true value and essence* of the elements of the state. The significance which *private property* has in the political state is its *essential*, its *true*, significance; the significance which *differences of estate* have in the political state is the *essential significance* of differences of estate. Similarly the *essence* of monarchical [power] and the executive manifests itself in the *"legislative authority"*. It is here, in the sphere of the political state, that the individual elements of the state are related to themselves as the *essence of the species*, as the "species-being"; because the political state is the sphere of their general aspect, their *religious sphere*. The *political state* is the *mirror of truth* for the various elements of the *concrete* state.

Thus, when "independent private property" has in the political state, in the legislature, the *significance* of *political independence*, then it *is* the *political independence* of the state. "Independent private property" or *"real* private property" is then not only the "pillar of the constitution" but the *"constitution itself"*. And surely the pillar of the constitution is the constitution of constitutions, the primary, real constitution?

When constructing the hereditary monarch, Hegel, himself surprised as it were at "the immanent development of a science, the *derivation of its entire content* from the elementary *concept"* (Remark to para. 279), made this observation:

> "Thus it is the basic element of **personality, abstract** at first in the sphere of immediate law, which has evolved through its various forms of subjectivity, and here, in the sphere of absolute law, in the state, in the completely concrete objectivity of the will, it is the *personality of the state*, the state's *certainty of itself*."

That is to say, in the political state it becomes *apparent* that the *"abstract personality"* is the *supreme political* personality, the political basis of the whole state. Similarly, in primogeniture the right of this abstract personality, its *objectivity*, "abstract private property", comes into being as the supreme objectivity of the state, as its *supreme law*.

That the state is a hereditary monarch, an abstract personality, means nothing but that the personality of the state is abstract, or that it is the state of the abstract personality; just as the Romans expounded the royal prerogative purely within the norms of civil law, or civil law as the supreme norm of constitutional law.

The *Romans* are the rationalists, the Germans the *mystics* of sovereign private property.

Hegel describes civil law as the *right of abstract personality* or as *abstract right*. And, in truth, it must be expounded as the *abstraction* of right and thus as the *illusory right of abstract personality*, just as the morality expounded by Hegel is the *illusory being of abstract subjectivity*. Hegel expounds civil law and morality as such abstractions; from this he does not deduce that the state and the ethical life based on them can be nothing but the *society* (the social life) of these illusions, but on the contrary, he concludes that they are subordinate elements of this ethical life. But what is civil law other than the law, and what is morality other than the morality of these subjects of the state? Or rather, the person of civil law and the subject of morality are the *person* and the *subject* of the state. Hegel has been often attacked for his exposition of morality. He has done no more than expound the morality of the modern state and of modern civil law. People have wanted to separate morality more from the state, to emancipate it more. What have they proved thereby? That the separation of the present-day state from morality is moral, that morality is apolitical and the state is immoral. Rather, it is a great merit of Hegel to have assigned to modern morality its proper position, although in one respect this is an unconscious merit (namely, in that Hegel passes off the state which is based on such a morality for the actual idea of ethical life).

In the constitution where *primogeniture* is a guarantee, *private property* is the guarantee of the political constitution. In primogeniture this appears in such a way that a *particular* kind of private property serves as this guarantee. *Primogeniture* is merely a particular manifestation of the general relationship of *private property and political state*. Primogeniture is the *political* meaning of private property, private property in its political significance, i.e., in its general significance. The constitution is here therefore the *constitution of private property*.

Where we find primogeniture in *classical* form, in the Germanic nations, we find also the constitution of *private property*. *Private property* is the general category, the general political bond. Even the general functions appear as the private property now of a corporation, now of an estate.

The different subdivisions of trade and industry are the private property of different corporations. Court dignities, jurisdiction, etc., are the private property of particular estates. The various provinces are the private property of individual princes, etc. Service to the country, etc., is the private property of the ruler. The spirit is the private property of the clergy. My dutiful activity is the private property of another, as my rights are again a particular private property. Sovereignty, here *nationality*, is the private property of the emperor.

It has often been said that in the Middle Ages every form of right, of freedom, of social existence, appears as *privilege*, as an *exception* to the rule. In this context the empirical fact that all these privileges appeared in the form of *private property* could not be overlooked. What is the general cause of this coincidence? *Private property* is the *specific mode of existence of privilege,* of rights as *exceptions.*

Where, as in France, the monarchs attacked the *independence* of private property, they infringed the property of the *corporations* before that of *individuals.* But by attacking the private property of the corporations, they attacked private property as corporation, as a *social* bond.

In *feudal rule* it is directly apparent that the monarchical power is the power of private property, and in the *monarchical power* the mystery of the *general power,* the *power of all state circles,* is set down.

(What is *powerful* in the state finds its expression in the monarch as the representative of political power. The *constitutional* monarch therefore expresses the idea of the constitutional state in its sharpest abstraction. He is on the one hand the *idea* of the state, the sanctified majesty of the state, and precisely as *this* person. At the same time he is *mere* imagination, as person and as monarch he has neither real power nor real activity. Here the separation of political and real, of formal and material, of general and individual person, of human being and social person, is expressed in its supreme contradiction.)

In private property *Roman* intellect and *German* feeling are combined. At this point it will be instructive to make a comparison between these two extreme developments of private property. This will help us to solve the political problem discussed above. *Ad. pag.* XII.^a

It is really the Romans who first developed the *law of private property*, abstract right, civil law, the right of the abstract person. *Roman civil law* is *civil law* in its *classical form*. But nowhere do we find among the Romans that the law of private property is mystified, as is the case with the Germans. It nowhere becomes the *law of the state* either.

The right of private property is the *jus utendi et abutendi*,^b the right to *do what one likes* with the object. The main interest of the Romans is to set forth *relations* and to determine which of them prove to be *abstract* relations of private property. The true basis of private property, *possession*, is a *fact*, an *inexplicable fact, not a right*. Only through the juridical attributes which society gives to factual possession does it acquire the quality of legal possession, of *private property*.

Concerning the connection between political constitution and private property amongst the Romans the following would appear to have obtained:

1) The *human being* (as slave), as amongst the peoples of antiquity generally, is object of private property.

That is nothing specific.

2) The conquered lands are treated as private property; the *jus utendi et abutendi* is applied to them.

3) In their own history there appears the struggle between the poor and the rich (patricians and plebeians), etc.

For the rest, private property as a whole, as in general with the classical nations of antiquity, asserts itself as *public property*; either, as in good times, as expenditure by the republic, or as *luxurious and general benefits* (baths, etc.) for the masses.

The manner in which slavery is explained is through *military law*, the law of occupation: they are slaves precisely because their political existence has been destroyed.

We mainly emphasise two circumstances which differ from those obtaining among the Germans.

1) The *imperial* power was not the power of private property but the *sovereignty* of the *empirical will* as such, which was far from regarding *private property* as a bond between itself and its subjects, but on the contrary, dealt with private property as with all other social goods. The imperial power was therefore also *heritable only*

---

^a See this volume, p. 38.—*Ed.*
^b Right of use and of disposal.—*Ed.*

as a matter of fact. The highest development of the law of private property, of civil law, belongs to the imperial period, it is true; but it is a consequence of political disintegration rather than political disintegration having been a consequence of private property. Moreover, when civil law becomes fully developed in Rome, constitutional law is abolished or in its process of dissolution; whereas in Germany the opposite obtained.

2) State dignities are never hereditary in Rome, i.e., private property is not the dominant political category.

3) In contrast with German primogeniture, etc., in Rome *arbitrary testamentary disposition* seems to be the outcome of private property. This last contrast contains the *whole* difference between the Roman and German developments of private property.

(In primogeniture the fact that private property constitutes the relation to political functions appears in such a way that political existence is something inherent in, an adjunct of, *direct* private property, *landed property*. At the highest summits therefore the state appears as private property, whereas here private property should appear as state property. Hegel makes citizenship, political existence and political conviction attributes of private property, instead of making private property an attribute of citizenship.)

308. "The second section of the estates element comprises the *mobile* part of *civil society* which can enter it only through *delegates*, superficially because of the large number of its members, but essentially because of the nature of their vocation and pursuits. Since these representatives are delegated by civil society it is plain that the latter acts *as that which it is*—hence not as atomistically dispersed into individuals and assembled only for a moment, for a single and transient act, without continuing cohesion, but rather as articulated in its already instituted associations, communities and corporations which thus acquire political cohesion. The existence of the estates and their assembly finds a constitutional and fitting guarantee in their **entitlement** to such representation under the summons of the monarch, as in the entitlement of the first estate (para. 307) to appear in the assembly."

We find here a *new* antithesis within civil society and the estates—a *mobile*, and hence also an *immobile* part (that of landed property). This antithesis has also been presented as the antithesis of *space* and *time*, etc., of conservative and progressive. On this point see the previous paragraph. Moreover, with the corporations, etc., Hegel has turned the *mobile* part of society also into a *static* one.

The second antithesis is that the first section of the *estates element* which has just been expounded, the *owners of entailed estates*, are legislators in their own right; that the power to legislate is an attribute of their empirical persons; that they are not *delegates* but *themselves*; whereas with the second estate *election* and *delegation* takes place.

Hegel gives two reasons why this *mobile* part of civil society can enter the political state, the legislature, only through *representatives*. The first, their *large numbers*, he himself describes as *superficial* and so saves us a reply on this point.

The *essential* reason, however, he says, is the "nature of their vocation and pursuits". "Political activity" and "pursuits" are something alien to "the nature of their vocation and pursuits".

Hegel now returns to his old song, to these estates as "*delegates of civil society*". This must, he claims, "act *as that which it is*". It must rather act as what it is *not*, for it is *unpolitical* society, and it is here called upon to perform a *political* act as an' act *essential to it*, arising out of itself. In so doing, it is "atomistically dispersed into individuals" "and assembled only for a moment, for a single and transient act, without continuing cohesion". Firstly, its *political* act is a *single and transient* one and in its realisation can therefore appear only as such. It is a *sensational* act, an *ecstasy* of political society, and must also *appear* as such. Secondly: Far from objecting, Hegel has even construed it as necessary that, *materially*, civil society separates itself from its civil reality (appearing only as a *second society delegated by itself*), and that it puts forward what it is *not* as itself; how can he now wish *formally* to reject this?

Hegel thinks that since society delegates by its corporations, etc., "its already instituted associations", etc., "thus acquire *political* cohesion". But they acquire either a significance which is *not* their significance, or else their connection as such *is* political and does not just "*acquire*" a political complexion as set forth above, it being rather the case that "politics" acquires its cohesion from it [from the cohesion of civil society]. By designating only this part of the estates element as "delegated", Hegel has unwittingly described the essence of the two chambers (where they actually stand to each other in the relation which he describes). House of Representatives and House of Peers (or whatever else they are called) are here not different manifestations of the same principle but belong to *two* essentially *different principles* and social conditions. The House of Representatives is here the *political constitution* of civil society in the modern sense, the House of Peers in the estates sense. House of Peers and House of Representatives confront one another here as the *estate* and as the *political* representation of civil society. The one is the *existing* estate principle of civil society, the other is the realisation of its *abstract political* being. Hence it goes without saying that the latter cannot *exist* again as the representation of estates, corporations, etc., for it simply does not represent the estate aspect but the political aspect of civil society. Thus it is self-evident that in the Upper House only the *estate* part of civil society has seats, only "sovereign landed property", the hereditary landed aristocracy, for it is not *one* estate among others; rather the estate principle of civil society as an actual, social, that is, political, principle continues to exist *only* in it. It is *the* estate. Civil society thus has the representative of its medieval aspect in the *estate* House, that of its *political* (modern) aspect in the House of Representatives. Progress compared with the Middle Ages here consists only in the fact that the *estate politics* has been reduced to a special political existence alongside *civic* politics. The *empirical* political phenomenon which Hegel has in mind (*England*) has therefore a very different meaning from that which he imputes to it.

In this respect also the French constitution is an advance.[10] It has, it is true, reduced the House of Peers to a mere nullity, but *within the principle* of the constitutional monarchy, as Hegel alleged, this House by its nature can only be a *nullity*, the *fiction* of harmony between monarch and civil society, or the *legislature* or the *political state with itself* as a separate, and hence again *contradictory*, existence.

The French have allowed the *life membership* of the Peers to stand so as to express their independence of the choice both of government and people. But they have abolished the *medieval* expression of this—*hereditariness*. Their advance consists in the fact that they no longer make the *House of Peers* originate in *actual civil* society either, but have created it in *abstraction* from the latter. They cause their election to proceed from the *existing* political state, the *monarch*, without tying him to any other civil quality. In this *constitution* the *peerage* is actually an *estate in civil society* which is purely political, created from the point of view of the abstraction of the *political state*; but it appears more as *political embellishment* than as an actual *estate* endowed with particular rights. The House of Peers under the Restoration was a reminiscence of the past. The House of Peers of the July revolution is a *real* creation of the constitutional monarchy.

Since in modern times the idea of the state could not appear except in the *abstraction* of the "*merely* political state" or the *abstraction of civil society from itself*, from its actual condition, it is a merit of the French to have defined, produced this *abstract actuality*, and in so doing to have produced the *political* principle itself. The abstraction for which they are blamed is therefore not an abstraction but the true consequence and product of the *rediscovered political conviction*, rediscovered it is true in an antithesis, but in a necessary antithesis. Hence it is here the merit of the French to have instituted the House of Peers as a *peculiar* product of the political state, or, in general, to have made the political principle in its *peculiarity* the determinative and effective factor.

Hegel remarks further that with the representation he has construed, "the *existence* of the estates and their assembly finds a constitutional and fitting guarantee" in the "entitlement of the corporations, etc., to such representation". The *guarantee of the existence* of the assembly of the estates, its true, *primitive* existence, thus becomes the *privilege* of the corporations, etc. At this point Hegel has completely sunk back to the medieval standpoint and has entirely abandoned his "abstraction of the political state as the sphere of the state as state, the intrinsically and actually general".

In the modern sense the *existence* of the *assembly of the estates* is the *political existence* of civil society, the *guarantee* of its political being. To cast doubt on its existence is therefore to *doubt the existence of the state*. Just as previously "political conviction", the essence of the legislature, finds its guarantee according to Hegel in "independent private property", so its *existence* finds a guarantee in the "privileges of the corporations".

But one of the estates elements is rather the *political privilege* of civil society, or its *privilege* to be *political*. This element therefore cannot anywhere be the privilege of a particular, civil mode of the existence of civil society; still less can it find its guarantee in it, since on the contrary it is *supposed* to be the general guarantee.

Thus Hegel everywhere sinks to that level where the "political state" is not described as the highest actuality of social being, existing in and for itself, but where a precarious reality is granted to it, one which is *dependent on something else*; and where the political state is not depicted as the true being of the other sphere, but rather as something which finds in the other sphere *its true being*. Everywhere it requires the guarantee of spheres which lie outside it. It is not realised power. It is *supported* impotence, it is not power over these supports but the power of the support. The support is the paramount power.

What kind of august aspect is this whose existence requires a guarantee from outside itself, while it is itself supposed to be the *general* existence of this guarantee, and thus its actual guarantee? In general, in expounding the legislature Hegel everywhere falls back from the philosophical standpoint to that other standpoint where the matter is not dealt with *in its own terms*.

If the existence of the estates requires a guarantee, then they are *not an actual* but only a *fictitious mode of existence of the state*. In constitutional states the guarantee for the existence of the estates is the *law*. Their existence is therefore a *legal* existence dependent on the general nature of the state and not on the power or impotence of individual corporations or associations; they exist, rather, as the actuality of the *association of the state*. (It is precisely here that the corporations, etc., the particular circles of civil society, are to acquire their general existence, and Hegel now again *anticipates* this general existence as privilege, as the existence of these particular circles.)

Political right as the right of corporations, etc., wholly contradicts political right as *political* right, i.e., as the law of the state—the law of the citizens; for it is supposed to be not the law of a given mode of existence as a particular mode of existence, not the law representing this particular mode of existence.

Before we pass on to the category of *election* as the political act whereby civil society sets itself apart as a political body, let us add a few further points from the Remark to this paragraph.

"The idea that all should individually participate in deliberating and deciding on the general affairs of the state on the ground that they are all members of the state and that its affairs are the affairs of *all*, in which they are *entitled* to be involved with their knowledge and volition, this idea seeks to introduce the *democratic* element *without any rational form* into the state organism which is a state organism solely by virtue of such a form. This idea comes so readily to mind because it does not go beyond the *abstract* definition of being a member of the state, and superficial thinking clings to abstractions." [Para. 308.]

Firstly, Hegel calls "being a member of the state" an "*abstract* definition", although according to the *idea*, the *view* of his own expounding, it itself is the highest, *most concrete* social definition of the legal person, the member of the state. Not to go beyond the "definition of being a member of the state", and to regard the individual from this angle, would therefore not seem to be merely "superficial thinking which clings to abstractions". But that the "definition of being a member of the state" is an "*abstract*" definition is not the fault of that thinking but of Hegel's exposition and of the actual modern conditions which presuppose the separation of real life from the life of the state and make belonging to a state an "abstract definition" of the real member of the state.

According to Hegel the direct participation of *all* in deliberating and deciding on the general affairs of the state includes "the *democratic* element *without any rational form* into the state organism which is a state organism *solely* by virtue of such a form", i. e., the democratic element can be embodied only as a *formal* element in a state organism which is merely the formalism of the state. The democratic element must rather be the actual element which gives to itself its *rational form* in the state organism *as a whole*. But if on the other hand it enters the organism or formalism of the state as a *"particular"* element, then what is meant by the "rational form" of its being is a drill, an accommodation, a form in which the democratic element does not display the specific features of its nature; or what is meant is that it only enters as a *formal* principle.

We have already indicated once that Hegel only expounds a *state formalism*. The actual *material* principle is for him the *idea*, the abstract mental *form* of the state as a subject, the absolute idea which contains no passive, no *material* element. By contrast to the abstraction of this idea the characteristics of the actual, empirical state formalism appear as *content* and hence the *real* content appears as formless, inorganic matter (in this case the actual person, the actual society, etc.).

Hegel put the essence of the estates element in the concept that in this element the "empirical generality" becomes the subject of the intrinsically and actually general. What then should this mean but that the affairs of the state "are the affairs of *all*, in which they are *entitled* to be involved with their knowledge and volition", and is it not just the estates which should be this, their realised right? And is it then surprising that the all now also want the "reality" of this, their right?

> "That *all* should individually participate in deliberating and deciding on the general affairs of the state."

In a really rational state one might reply: "*All should* not *individually* participate in deliberating and deciding on the general affairs of the state", for the "individuals" participate in deliberating and deciding on the *general affairs* as "all", i.e., within the society and as members of society. Not all individually, but the individuals as all.

Hegel poses this dilemma for himself: Either civil society (the many, the crowd) participates in deliberating and deciding on the general affairs of the state through delegates, or *all* do this [as] *individuals*. This is no contrast of *essence*, as Hegel later seeks to represent it, but of *existence*, and indeed of existence at the most superficial level, of *numbers*; and hence the reason which Hegel himself has called *"superficial"*—the *large number of members*—remains the best reason that can be advanced against the direct participation of all. *The question* whether civil society should participate in the legislative power *either* by entering it through *delegates* or by "all individually" sharing directly, is itself a question within the *abstraction of the political state* or within the *abstract-political state*; it is an *abstract*-political question.

In both cases, as Hegel has himself shown, it is the political meaning of "empirical generality".

In its essential form the contrast is: the *individuals all do it*, or the *individuals* do it as *a few*, as *not-all*. In both cases the universality remains only as an *external* multiplicity or totality of the individuals. The universality is no essential, spiritual, actual quality of the individual. It is not something through which he would lose the attribute of abstract individuality; rather the universality is only the full *count* of *individuality*. *One* individuality, *many* individualities, *all* individualities. One, many or all—none of these descriptions alters the *essence* of the subject, individuality.

"All" are to participate "individually" in "deliberating and deciding on the general affairs of the state"; that means then: *All* shall not thus participate as all but as "individuals".

The question appears to stand in contradiction to itself in two ways.

The general affairs of the state are state affairs, the state as *actual affair*. Deliberating and deciding means *giving effect* to the state as an actual affair. Hence it appears to be self-evident that all members of the state have a *relation* to the state as their *actual affair*. Already the concept *members of the state* implies that they are *members* of the state, a *part* of it, that it takes them as *part of it*. But if they are a *part* of the state, then, of course, their social *being* is already *their real participation* in it. They *are* not only part of the state, but the state is *their* portion. To be a conscious part of something means consciously to acquire a part of it, to take a conscious interest in it. Without this consciousness the member of the state would be an *animal*.

When one says: "the general affairs of the state", the impression is given that the "general affairs" and the "state" are two *different* things. But the *state* is the "general affair", and thus in fact the "general affairs".

To participate in the general affairs of the state and to participate in the state is therefore one and the same thing. It is then a *tautology* that a member of the state, a part of the state, participates in the state and that this participation can only appear as *deliberating* or *deciding* or in some similar form, and hence that every member of the state participates in *deliberating* and *deciding* on the general affairs of the state (if these functions are understood as functions of the *real* participation in the state). Therefore, if one is speaking of *real* members of the state, one cannot speak of this participation as something which *ought* to be. Otherwise one would instead be speaking of subjects who *ought* to be and *want* to be, but *are* not really *members of the state*.

On the other hand: if one is speaking of *definite* affairs, of a particular act of the state, it is again self-evident that *all* do not perform that act *individually*. Otherwise the individual would be the *true* society and would make society superfluous. The individual would have to do everything at once; whereas society both lets him act for others and others for him.

The question whether *all* should *individually* "participate in deliberating and deciding on the general affairs of the state" is a question which arises from the separation of the political state and civil society.

As we have seen: The state exists *only* as the *political state*. The totality of the political state is the *legislature*. To take part in the legislature is therefore to take part in the political state, is to demonstrate and put into effect one's *being* as a *member of the political state*, as a *member of the state*. Hence that *all* wish *individually* to share in the legislature is nothing but the wish of *all* to be actual (active) *members of the state*, or to give themselves a *political being*, or to demonstrate and give effect to their being as a *political* being. We have further seen that the estates element is *civil society* as legislative power, its *political being*. Hence, that civil society should penetrate the *legislative* power *in the mass*, if possible *in its entirety*, that actual civil society wishes to substitute itself for the *fictitious* civil society of the legislative power, this is merely the striving of civil society to give itself *political* being or to make *political being* its actual being. The striving of *civil society* to turn itself into *political* society, or to turn *political* society into *actual* society, appears as the striving for as *general* as possible a participation in the *legislative power*.

Numbers here are not without significance. If the increase of the *estates element* is already a physical and intellectual increase of one of the *hostile* forces—and we have seen that the different elements of the legislative power oppose each other as hostile forces—on the other hand, the question as to whether all shall individually be members of the legislative power or whether they shall enter it through deputies puts in question the *representative* principle within the representative principle, within the basic conception of the political state which finds its existence in the constitutional monarchy.

(1) It is a notion belonging to the abstraction of the political state that the *legislature* is the *totality* of the political state. Because this *single* act is the only *political* act of civil society, *all* should, and wish to, share in it at once. (2) *All* as *individuals*. In the *estates element* the legislative activity is not regarded as a *social* function, as a function of *sociality*, but rather as the act through which the individuals first enter into actual and *conscious social* function, i. e., into a political function. The *legislative power* here is no outcome, no function of society, but only its *formation*. The forming of the legislative power requires that *all* members of civil society regard themselves as *individuals*; they actually face [each other] as *individuals*. The attribute "being members of the state" is an "abstract definition", an attribute which is not realised in their actual life.

Either: Separation of political state and civil society takes place, in which case *all* cannot *individually* share in the legislative power. The political state is a phenomenon *separated* from civil society. On the one hand, civil society would abandon itself if all were legislators; on the other, the political state, which confronts civil society, can bear it only in a form appropriate to the *scale* of the political state. Or it is precisely the participation of civil society in the political state through *delegates* that is the *expression* of their separation and of their merely dualistic unity.

Or, conversely: Civil society is *actual* political society. In this case, it is nonsense to raise a demand which has arisen only from the notion of the political state as a phenomenon separated from civil society, which has arisen only from the *theological* notion of the political state. In this situation the significance of the *legislative* power as a *representative* power completely disappears. The legislative power is representation here in the sense in which *every* function is representative—in the sense in which, e.g., the shoemaker, insofar as he satisfies a social need, is my representative, in which every particular social activity as a species-activity merely represents the species, i. e., an attribute of my own nature, and in which every person is the representative of every other. He is here representative not because of something else which he represents, but because of what he *is* and *does*.

"Legislative" power is striven for not because of its *content* but because of its *formal* political significance. Properly speaking *executive power*, e. g., rather than legislative power, the *metaphysical* state function, must be the goal of popular desire. The *legislative* function is the will not in its practical but in its theoretical energy. Here the *will* is not to have sway *instead* of the *law*: rather, the actual law has to be *discovered* and *formulated*.

This twofold nature of the legislature as the actual *legislative* function and as the *representative, abstract-political* function gives rise to a peculiarity which comes to the fore especially in France, the land of political culture.

(In the *executive power* we always have *two* things, the actual conduct of affairs and the political considerations behind it, as a second actual consciousness which in its total structure is the bureaucracy.)

The proper content of the legislative power (insofar as the existing particular *interests* do not come into any considerable conflict with the object of the investigation) is treated very much as separate, as a secondary matter. A question only arouses particular attention when it becomes *political*, i. e., either when it can be linked with a ministerial problem, and hence one involving the authority of the legislature over the executive, or as soon as it is in general a question of rights connected with the political formalism. Why is this so? Because the legislative power is at the same time the representation of the political being of civil society; because in general the political essence of a question consists in its relation to the various powers of the political state; because the legislative power represents political consciousness and because this can prove to be *political* only in conflict with the executive. This essential demand that every social need, law, etc., must be understood as *political*, that is, as *determined by the state as a whole* in its *social* sense, takes on a new turn in the state characterised by political abstraction, by being given—besides its actual content—a *formal* twist against another power (content). That is no abstraction of the French but rather a necessary consequence, since the actual state exists only as the *political state formalism* considered above. The *opposition* within the representative authority is the κατ' ἐξοχήν [a] *political* mode of being of the representative authority. Within this representative constitution, however, the question under consideration takes on a form different from that in which Hegel considered it. The question here is not whether civil society shall exercise the legislative power through representatives or by all individually; the question is rather one of the *extension* and greatest possible *generalisation* of *election*, both of the right to *vote* and the right to *be elected*. This is the real point of dispute concerning political *reform*, in France as in England.

One is not looking at *election* philosophically, i. e., in its specific character, if one takes it at once in relation to the *monarchical* or

---

[a] Pre-eminently.—*Ed.*

executive power. The *election* is the *actual relation* of *actual civil society* to the *civil society* of the *legislature*, to the *representative element*. Or, the *election* is the *immediate, direct* relation of civil society to the political state—a relation that is not *merely representative but actually exists*. It is therefore self-evident that *elections* are the chief political interest of actual civil society. Civil society has *really* raised itself to abstraction from itself, to *political* being as its true, general, essential mode of being only in *elections unlimited* both in respect of the franchise and the right to be elected. But the completion of this abstraction is at the same time the transcendence of the abstraction. In actually positing its *political existence* as its *true* existence, civil society has simultaneously posited its civil existence, in distinction from its political existence, as *inessential*; and the fall of one side of the division carries with it the fall of the other side, its opposite. *Electoral reform* within the *abstract political state* is therefore the demand for its *dissolution*, but also for the *dissolution of civil society*.

Later we shall encounter the question of electoral reform in a different form, namely, from the point of view of *interests*.[11] Likewise, we shall later discuss the other conflicts which arise from the twofold character of the *legislative power* (being at one time the *delegate*, mandatory of civil society, at another time on the contrary its *political* mode of being and *a distinctive mode of being* within the political state formalism[a]).

For the present we return to the Remark to our paragraph. [Para. 308.]

> "Rational consideration, the consciousness of the idea, is *concrete* and to that extent coincides with genuine *practical* sense, which itself is nothing but rational sense, the sense of the idea." "The **concrete** state is the *whole, articulated into its particular circles*; the member of the state is a *member* of one of these *estates*; and he can be taken into account in the state only in this objective character."

Everything which needs saying about this has already been said above.

> "His" (the member of the state's) "general character as such contains the twofold aspect of being a *private person* and also, as a *thinking being*, a person who is conscious of and wills the *general*. This consciousness and willing, however, is not empty but *complete* and truly *alive* only when it is filled with particularity, namely, the particularity of particular estate and character; or, the individual is a *species*, but has his *immanent* general *actuality* in the *next* species."

Everything that Hegel says is correct, with the reservations (1) that he treats *particular estate* and *character* as identical; (2) that this

---

[a] See this volume, pp. 122-23.—*Ed.*

character, the subspecies, the next species, should be posited *actually*, not only *in itself* but *for itself*, as *subspecies of the general species*, as *its* particularisation. But Hegel is content that in the state, which he demonstrates to be the self-conscious mode of being of ethical spirit, this ethical spirit should only *as such*, in the sense of the general idea, be the *determining factor*. He does not allow society to become the actually determining factor, because that requires an *actual* subject, and he has only an abstract one—an *imaginary* one.

> 309. "Since delegates are elected for the purpose of deliberating and deciding on matters of *general* concern, this means both that, on the strength of trust, individuals are chosen who understand these matters better than the electorate, and also that these persons do not champion the particular interests of a community or corporation against the general interest, but primarily assert the latter. Hence they are not in the position of commissioned or instruction-bearing mandatories—the less so since their assembly is meant to be a living body in which all members deliberate in common and reciprocally instruct and convince each other."

The delegates are (1) not to be "commissioned or instruction-bearing mandatories" because they must "not champion the particular interests of a community or corporation against the general interest, but primarily assert the latter". Hegel has first construed the delegates as delegates of corporations, etc., so as thereupon to bring in again the other political aspect that they are not bound to champion the *particular interests* of the corporations, etc. He thereby cancels his own characterisation, for in their *essential* character as representatives he completely separates them from their *corporation existence*. He thereby also separates the corporation from itself as its actual content, for it is not supposed to elect from *its own standpoint* but from the *standpoint of the state*; i. e., it is supposed to elect in its *non-being* as corporation. In the *concrete* definition he thus recognises what he reversed in the *formal* definition—civil society's own abstraction from itself in its political act; and its *political mode of being* is nothing but *this abstraction*. The reason Hegel gives is that they are elected precisely for the purpose of dealing with "matters of general concern"; but corporations do not exist as matters of general concern.

(2) "Election of delegates" is supposed to "mean" "that, on the strength of trust, individuals are chosen who understand these matters better than the electorate"; from which once again it is supposed to follow that the deputies do not stand in the position of "mandatories".

Only by a sophism can Hegel demonstrate that they understand these matters "better" and do not "simply" understand them. This could be concluded only if the electorate had the choice either to deliberate and decide on matters of general concern *themselves or* to elect certain individuals to fulfil this function; i. e., only if *election, representation*, were not essentially part of the nature of the *legislative power* of civil society, which constitutes precisely its *distinctive* character in the state construed by Hegel, as we have just shown.

This is a very characteristic example of how Hegel half deliberately turns away from the intrinsic character of the thing he is dealing with, and imputes to that thing in its restricted form a significance the very reverse of this restrictedness.

Hegel gives the real reason last. The deputies of civil society form an "assembly" and only this assembly is the *actual political mode of being* of civil society and the exercise of its *will*. The separation of the political state from civil society appears as the separation of the deputies from their mandators. Society delegates only elements from itself to its political mode of being.

The contradiction appears in two ways:

1) *Formally*. The delegates of civil society form a society which is not linked with those who commission them by the form of the "instruction", the mandate. Formally they are commissioned, but once they are *actually* commissioned they are *no* longer *mandatories*. They are supposed to *be delegates*, and they are *not*.

2) *Materially*. With reference to interests. We shall come to this later.[12] Here the reverse takes place. They are commissioned as representatives of *general* concerns, but they actually represent *particular* concerns.

It is significant that *Hegel* here describes trust as the substance of *delegation*, as the fundamental relation between electors and delegates. *Trust* is a personal relation. In the Addition [to para. 309] he goes on to say:

> "Representation is founded on trust, and trusting someone else is different from my voting as a particular person. Majority voting is also contrary to the principle that I as a particular person should be present when any decisions are made which are to be binding on me. I have trust in a person if I consider his discernment to be such as to enable him to treat my concern as his concern, to the best of his knowledge and conscience."
>
> 310. "The **guarantee** of the qualities and of the attitude [in delegates] corresponding to this purpose—since the right of independent wealth has already been asserted in the first section of the estates—is to be seen in the second section, the section drawn from the mobile and changeable element in civil society, particularly in the attitude, the skill and the knowledge of the institutions and interests of the state and of civil society gained in the *actual* conduct of affairs in *administrative* or *political office* and tested in *action*, and also in the *administrative* and *political sense* formed and tested in such experience."

First the Upper House, the *House of independent private property*, was constructed for the monarch and the executive as a *guarantee* against the attitude of the Lower House as the *political mode of existence* of the empirical generality, and now Hegel again demands a *new guarantee*, which is to guarantee the *attitude*, etc., of the Lower House itself.

First trust, the guarantee of the electors, was the guarantee of the delegates. Now, this trust itself requires a further guarantee of its soundness.

Hegel seems to be rather inclined to turn the Lower House into a chamber of civil service *pensioners*. He demands not only "political sense", but also "administrative", bureaucratic, sense.

What he demands here really is that the *legislature* should be the *actual governing* power. He expresses this by demanding bureaucracy *twice*, once as representing the monarch and again as the representative of the people.

Even if in constitutional states civil servants are allowed to be deputies, this occurs only because in general there is abstraction from *social rank*, from *civil* quality, and the abstraction of *citizenship* prevails.

Hegel forgets here that he made the representation originate in the *corporations* and that these are directly opposed by the executive. He goes so far in this forgetfulness—this forgetfulness in its turn is forgotten in the very next paragraph—that he carries it to the point of creating an *essential* distinction between delegates of the corporations and delegates of the estates.

In the Remark to this paragraph we read:

"Subjective opinion of oneself easily finds superfluous, or perhaps even offensive, the demand for such guarantees if it is made with regard to what is called the people. The state, however, is characterised by objectivity, not by a subjective opinion and its **self-confidence**; it can recognise in individuals only their objectively recognisable and tested qualities, and it must be all the more careful on this point in connection with this [the second] section of the estates since this section is rooted in interests and occupations directed towards the particular, i.e., in the sphere where chance, changeability, and caprice enjoy their right of free play."

Here the thoughtless inconsistency and the *"administrative"* sense of Hegel become truly *repulsive*. At the end of the Addition to the preceding paragraph [para. 309] he says:

"**The electors** require a guarantee that the delegate will further and secure this" (i. e., the task described above).

This guarantee *for the electors* has secretly been developed into a *guarantee against* the electors, against their *"self-confidence"*. In the estates element the "empirical generality" was to attain to "the element of subjective formal freedom". In it, "public consciousness as the *empirical generality* of the opinions and thoughts of the *many*" was to come into existence (para. 301).

A page from Marx's manuscript of the Contribution to the Critique of Hegel's Philosophy of Law

Now these "opinions and thoughts" are *first* to pass a *government* test to prove that they are *"its"* [the government's] opinions and thoughts. For Hegel here stupidly speaks of the state as a *finished* thing, although he is only now about to complete the construction of the state with the estates element. He speaks of the state as a concrete subject which "does not take into account subjective opinion and its self-confidence", and for which individuals must demonstrate their "recognisable" and "tested" qualities. All that is missing is for Hegel to demand that the *estates* should pass an *examination* set by their worshipful government. Hegel here descends almost to servility. We see him infected through and through with the miserable arrogance of the *Prussian* civil service which in its bureaucratic stupidity grandly looks down on the "self-confidence" of the "people's own subjective opinion". For Hegel the "state" is everywhere here identical with the "government".

In an actual state "mere trust", "subjective opinion", can indeed not suffice. But in the state constructed by Hegel, the *political* attitude of civil society is mere *opinion*, precisely because the political being of civil society is an *abstraction* from its actual being; precisely because the state as a whole is not the *objectification of the political attitude*. If Hegel wished to be consistent, he would on the contrary have to make every effort to construe the estates element in accordance with its *essential character* (para. 301) as the *being for themselves* of matters of general concern in the thoughts, etc., of the *many*, that is, to construe it quite independently of the other presuppositions of the political state.

Just as Hegel earlier described the view which presumes bad will in the government, etc., as the view of the vulgar crowd, so it is equally and still more characteristic of the vulgar crowd to presume bad will in the people. Hegel, then, must not find it either "superfluous" or "offensive" in the theoreticians, whom he despises, if they demand guarantees "with regard to *what is called*" the state, the *soi-disant* state, the government, if they demand guarantees that the attitude of the bureaucracy is the attitude of the state.

311. "Delegation, since it issues from civil society, means **furthermore** that the delegates are conversant with the special needs, difficulties and particular interests of civil society and share them. Since in accordance with the nature of civil society delegation is initiated by its various corporations (para. 308), and since the simplicity of this mode of appointment is not impeded by abstractions and atomistic notions, it is thus directly satisfactory from this point of view and elections are either something altogether superfluous or reduced to a minor play of opinion and caprice."

Firstly, Hegel links delegation in its character as "legislative power" (paras. 309, 310) to delegation as "issuing from civil society", i.e., to its representative nature, by a simple "furthermore". The huge contradictions which are implied in this "furthermore" are expressed equally thoughtlessly by him.

According to paragraph 309 the delegates are not to "champion the particular interests of a community or corporation against the general interest, but *primarily* assert the latter".

According to paragraph 311 they come from the corporations, represent these *particular* interests and needs and do not allow themselves to be impeded by "abstractions"—as if the "general interest" were not just such an abstraction, and an abstraction precisely from the interests of *their* corporations, etc.

In paragraph 310 it is stipulated that the delegates shall have acquired and tested an "administrative and political sense" through "the actual conduct of affairs, etc.". In paragraph 311 they are required to have a corporation and civil sense.

In the Addition to paragraph 309 we read that "representation is founded on *trust*". According to paragraph 311 "elections"—this realisation of trust, this giving effect to it and making it apparent—are "either something altogether superfluous or reduced to a minor play of opinion and caprice".

That on which representation is founded, its essence, is thus for representation "either something altogether superfluous", etc. In one breath Hegel thus utters the flat contradictions: Representation is founded on trust, on the reliance of one person on another, and it is not founded on that trust. This is merely an empty game.

Not the particular interest but the person and his citizenship, the general interest, is the object of representation. On the other hand, the particular interest is the substance of representation, the spirit of this interest is the spirit of the representative.

In the Remark to the paragraph which we are now considering, these contradictions are developed even more glaringly. At one time representation is the representation of the person; at another time, of a particular interest, a particular matter.

"It is obviously of advantage that amongst the delegates there should be individuals who can speak for each particular main branch of society—e. g., for trade, manufacture, etc.—who know that branch thoroughly, and themselves belong to it. With the notion of free, unrestricted elections this important consideration is left to chance only. Each of these branches, however, has the same right to be represented as the others. If the delegates are regarded as *representatives*, this has an organically rational meaning only when they are *representatives* not of *individuals*, of a conglomerate, but are *representatives* of one of the essential *spheres* of society, of its major interests. In this case representation no longer means that *one takes the place of another;* the point is rather that the interest itself is *actually present* in the representative, just as the representative is there for the sake of his own objective element.

"It may further be remarked that election by the many individuals necessarily brings with it *indifference* towards voting, especially in large states, since one vote has an insignificant effect where there are so many, and those who are entitled to vote, however much this right is brought to their notice as something valuable, simply do not turn up to vote. The result of this institution is thus the very opposite of that which it was meant to produce and election falls under the control of a few, of a party, and thus of some particular, chance interest, which is precisely what was to have been neutralised." [Para. 311.]

The two paragraphs 312 and 313 have been dealt with in what has gone before, and do not deserve any special discussion. We therefore simply quote them at this point:

312. "Each of the two sections contained in the estates element (paras. 305, 308) makes a particular contribution to the work of deliberation; and since, moreover, one of them has the specific function of mediation in this sphere, and of mediating in fact between existing entities, it follows that this itself, likewise, has a distinct and separate existence. The assembly of the estates will thus be divided into *two houses.*"

Good Lord!

313. "This division of the assembly, by providing more than one *decision-making body*, gives greater assurance of mature decisions, and eliminates both the fortuity of a passing mood and the accidental character which can belong to decision by a numerical majority. But above all, with this the estates element is less liable to confront the government in direct opposition; or in the event of the mediating element finding itself on the side of the second estate, the opinion of this estate will carry all the greater weight, since it will then seem more unbiassed, and its opposition will appear to be neutralised."[a]

---

[a] The manuscript ends at this point. The next sheet, which has no number, contains only the following words:

Contents

Concerning Hegel's Transition and Interpretation.—*Ed.*

[A Passage from
THE KREUZNACH NOTEBOOKS OF 1843][13]

Note. Under Louis XVIII, the constitution [by] grace of the king (Charter imposed by the king); under Louis Philippe, the king [by] grace of the constitution (imposed kingship).[14] In general we can note that the conversion of the subject into the predicate, and of the predicate into the subject, the exchange of that which determines for that which is determined, is always the most immediate revolution. Not only on the revolutionary side. The king makes the law (old monarchy), the law makes the king (new monarchy). Likewise in regard to the constitution. The reactionaries as well. Primogeniture is the law of the state. The state demands the law of primogeniture. Owing to the fact, therefore, that Hegel makes the elements of the state idea the subject, and the old forms of existence of the state the predicate, whereas in historical reality the reverse is the case, the state idea being instead the predicate of those forms of existence, he expresses only the general character of the period, its *political teleology*. It is the same thing as with his philosophical-religious pantheism. By means of it all forms of unreason become forms of reason. But essentially here in religion reason is made the determining factor, while in the state the idea of the state is made the determining factor. This metaphysics is the metaphysical expression of reaction, of the old world as the truth of the new world outlook.

Written in July-August 1843
First published in:
Marx/Engels, *Gesamtausgabe*,
Abt. 1, Bd. 1, Hb. 1, 1927

Printed according to the manuscript

Published in English for the first time

[DRAFT PROGRAMME OF THE *DEUTSCH-FRANZÖSISCHE JAHRBÜCHER*]¹⁵

The articles of our annals will be written by Germans or Frenchmen, and will deal with

1) Men and systems which have acquired a useful or dangerous influence, and political questions of the day, whether they concern constitutions, political economy, or public institutions and morals.

2) We shall provide a review of newspapers and journals which in some way will be a castigation and correction of the servility and baseness shown by some, and which will help to call attention to the worthy efforts on behalf of humanity and freedom shown by others.

3) We shall include a review of the literature and publications of the old regime of Germany which is decaying and destroying itself, and finally a review of the books of the two nations which mark the commencement and continuance of the new era that we are entering.

Written in August-September 1843
Published for the first time

Printed according to the manuscript
Translated from the French

LETTER TO THE EDITOR
OF THE *DÉMOCRATIE PACIFIQUE*[16]

No. 28 of the *Bien public* contains the following lines:
"The *Kölnische Zeitung* publishes a letter from Leipzig in which it is stated that a journal in French and German is due to appear shortly in Paris under the editorship of Dr. Ruge, to which M. de Lamartine and M. de Lamennais are said to have promised their collaboration.[17]

"It is not true that M. de Lamartine has undertaken to write in any journal and, in particular, in the one in question, with M. de Lamennais.

"M. de Lamartine, who is wholly absorbed in his parliamentary work, is reserving for the *Histoire des Girondins* the little leisure that politics leaves him."

It is true that M. de Lamartine has not undertaken to write for the journal in question with M. de Lamennais, but we affirm that he has let us hope for his collaboration in the journal that we are proposing to found.

In addressing ourselves separately to these two famous personages, we have been prompted by the belief that for a work such as that of an intellectual alliance between France and Germany one should seek the support of all eminent representatives of progress in France.

Furthermore, we declare that the letter from Leipzig published by the *Kölnische Zeitung*, which gave rise to the article in the *Bien public*, did not emanate from us or from any of our friends.

Arnold Ruge,
former editor of the *Deutsche Jahrbücher*

Charles Marx,
former editor of the *Rheinische Zeitung*

Paris, December 10, 1843

First published in the *Démocratie pacifique*, December 11, 1843

Printed according to the newspaper
Translated from the French
Published in English for the first time

LETTERS FROM THE *DEUTSCH-FRANZÖSISCHE JAHRBÜCHER*[18]

M. to R.[a]

On the canal-boat going to D.,
March 1843

I am now travelling in Holland. As far as I can judge from the Dutch and French newspapers, Germany is sunk deep in the mire and will sink still deeper. I assure you, even if one has no feeling of national pride at all, nevertheless one has a feeling of national shame, even in Holland. The most insignificant Dutchman is still a citizen compared with the greatest German. And the verdict of the foreigners on the Prussian Government! A horrifying unanimity prevails; no one is any longer deceived about the Prussian system and its simple nature. After all, therefore, the new school has been of some use. The mantle of liberalism has been discarded and the most disgusting despotism in all its nakedness is disclosed to the eyes of the whole world.

That, too, is a revelation, although one of the opposite kind. It is a truth which, at least, teaches us to recognise the emptiness of our patriotism and the abnormity of our state system, and makes us hide our faces in shame. You look at me with a smile and ask: What is gained by that? No revolution is made out of shame. I reply: Shame is already revolution of a kind; shame is actually the victory of the French Revolution over the German patriotism that defeated it in 1813. Shame is a kind of anger which is turned inward. And if a whole nation really experienced a sense of shame, it would be like a lion, crouching ready to spring. I admit that in Germany even shame is not yet felt; on the contrary, these miserable people are still patriots. But what system is capable of knocking the patriotism out of them if not this ridiculous system

---

[a] Marx to Ruge.—*Ed.*

of the new cavalier[a]? The comedy of despotism that is being played out with us is just as dangerous for him, as the tragedy once was for the Stuarts and Bourbons. And even if for a long time this comedy were not to be looked upon as the thing it actually is, it would still amount to a revolution. The state is too serious a thing to be turned into a kind of harlequinade. A ship full of fools[19] could perhaps be allowed to drift for quite a time at the mercy of the wind, but it would be driven to meet its fate precisely because the fools would not believe this. This fate is the impending revolution.

M. to R.[b]

Cologne, May 1843

Your letter, my dear friend, is a fine elegy, a funeral song[20] that takes one's breath away; but there is absolutely nothing political about it. No people wholly despairs, and even if for a long time it goes on hoping merely out of stupidity, yet one day, after many years, it will suddenly become wise and fulfil all its pious wishes.

Nevertheless, you have infected me, your theme is still not exhausted, I want to add the finale, and when everything is at an end, give me your hand, so that we may begin again from the beginning. Let the dead bury their dead and mourn them. On the other hand, it is enviable to be the first to enter the new life alive; that is to be our lot.

It is true that the old world belongs to the philistine. But one should not treat the latter as a bugbear from which to recoil in fear. On the contrary, we ought to keep an eye on him. It is worth while to study this lord of the world.

He is lord of the world, of course, only because he fills it with his society as maggots do a corpse. Therefore the society of these lords needs no more than a number of slaves, and the owners of these slaves do not need to be free. Although, as being owners of land and people, they are called lords, in the sense of being pre-eminent, for all that they are no less philistines than their servants.

As for human beings, that would imply thinking beings, free men, republicans. The philistines do not want to be either of these. What then remains for them to be and to desire?

What they want is to live and reproduce themselves (and no one, says Goethe, achieves anything more), and that the animal

---

[a] Frederick William IV.—*Ed.*
[b] Marx to Ruge.—*Ed.*

DEUTSCH-FRANZÖSISCHE

JAHRBÜCHER

herausgegeben

von

Arnold Ruge und Karl Marx.

1ste und 2te Lieferung.

PARIS,

IM BUREAU DER JAHRBÜCHER. } RUE VANNEAU, 22.
AU BUREAU DES ANNALES.

1844

Cover of the *Deutsch Französische Jahrbücher*

also wants; at most a German politician would add: Man, however, *knows* that he wants this, and the German is so prudent as not to want anything more.

The self-confidence of the human being, freedom, has first of all to be aroused again in the hearts of these people. Only this feeling, which vanished from the world with the Greeks, and under Christianity disappeared into the blue mist of the heavens, can again transform society into a community of human beings united for their highest aims, into a democratic state.

On the other hand, people who do not feel that they are human beings become the property of their masters like a breed of slaves or horses. The aim of this whole society are the hereditary masters. This world belongs to them. They accept it as it is and as it feels itself to be. They accept themselves as they are, and place their feet firmly on the necks of these political animals who know of no other function than to be "obedient, devoted and attentive" to their masters.

The philistine world is a *political world of animals*, and if we have to recognise its existence, nothing remains for us but simply to agree to this *status quo*. Centuries of barbarism engendered and shaped it, and now it confronts us as a consistent system, the principle of which is the *dehumanised world*. Hence the most complete philistine world, our Germany, was bound, of course, to remain far behind the French revolution, which once more restored man; and a German Aristotle who wanted to derive his politics from our conditions would write at the top of it: "Man is a social animal that is however completely unpolitical",[a] but he could not explain the state more correctly than has already been done by Herr Zöpfl, the author of *Constitutionellen Staatsrechts in Deutschland*.[b] According to him, the state is a "union of families" which, we continue, belongs by heredity and property to a most eminent family called the dynasty. The more prolific the families, the happier, it is said, are the people, the greater is the state, and the more powerful the dynasty, for which reason, too, in Prussia, an ordinary despotic state, a prize of 50 imperial talers is awarded for a seventh son.

The Germans are such circumspect realists that all their desires and their loftiest thoughts do not go beyond a bare existence. And this reality—nothing more—is taken into account by those who

---

[a] In contradistinction to the Greek Aristotle who in his *Politics* called man a political animal (*Zöön politicon*).—*Ed.*

[b] This is a reference to Zöpfl, *Grundsätze des Allgemeinen und Constitutionell-Monarchistischen Staatsrechts*....—*Ed.*

rule over them. These latter people, too, are realists, they are very far removed from any kind of thoughts and from any human greatness; they are ordinary officers and country squires, but they are not mistaken, they are right; just as they are, they are quite capable of making use of this animal kingdom and ruling over it, for here, as everywhere, ruling and using are a *single* conception. And when homage is paid to them and they survey the swarming mass of these brainless beings, what is more likely to occur to them than the thought that Napoleon had at the Berezina? It is said of Napoleon that he pointed to the crowd of drowning people below him and exclaimed to his companion: "*Voyez ces crapauds!*"[a] This is probably a fabrication, but it is nonetheless true. Despotism's sole idea is contempt for man, the dehumanised man, and this idea has the advantage over many others of being at the same time a fact. The despot always sees degraded people. They drown before his eyes and for his sake in the mire of ordinary life, from which, like toads, they constantly make their appearance anew. If such a view comes to be held even by people who were capable of great aims, such as Napoleon before his dynastic madness, how can a quite ordinary king in such surroundings be an idealist?

The monarchical principle in general is the despised, the despicable, *the dehumanised man*; and Montesquieu was quite wrong to allege that it is honour.[b] He gets out of the difficulty by distinguishing between monarchy, despotism and tyranny. But those are names for *one and the same* concept, and at most they denote differences in customs though the principle remains the same. Where the monarchical principle has a majority behind it, human beings constitute the minority; where the monarchical principle arouses no doubts, there human beings do not exist at all. Why should someone like the King of Prussia,[c] to whom it has never been demonstrated that his role is problematical, not be guided exclusively by his whims? And when he acts in that way, what is the result? Contradictory intentions? Well, then nothing will come of it. Impotent trends? They are still the sole political reality. Ridiculous and embarrassing situations? There is only *one* situation which is ridiculous and only *one* which is embarrassing, and that is abdication from the throne. So long as whim retains its place, it is in the right. It can be as unstable, senseless and contemptible as it chooses, it is still good enough for ruling a

---

[a] "Just look at these toads!"—*Ed.*
[b] Ch. L. Montesquieu, *De l'esprit des lois.*—*Ed.*
[c] Frederick William IV.—*Ed.*

people that has never known any other law but the arbitrary power of its kings. I do not say that a brainless system and loss of respect within the state and outside it will be without consequences, I do not undertake to insure the ship of fools, but I assert: the King of Prussia will remain the man of his time so long as the topsy-turvy world is the real world.

As you know, I have given much thought to this man. Already at the time when he still had only the *Berliner politische Wochenblatt* as his organ, I recognised his value and his role. Already when the oath of allegiance was taken in Königsberg, he justified my supposition that the question would now become a purely personal one.[21] He declared that his heart and his turn of mind would be the future fundamental law of the realm of Prussia, of *his* state, and in point of fact, in Prussia the king is the system. He is the sole political person. In one way or another, his personality determines the system. What he does or is allowed to do, what he thinks or what is attributed to him, is what in Prussia the state thinks or does. Therefore the present king has really performed a service by stating this so unambiguously.

But the mistake which people made for a time was to attach importance to the desires and thoughts that would be expressed by the king. This could not alter the matter in the slightest: the philistine is the material of the monarchy, and the monarch always remains only the king of the philistines; he cannot turn either himself or his subjects into free, real human beings while both sides remain what they are.

The King of Prussia has tried to alter the system by means of a theory which in this form his father[a] really did not have. The fate of this attempt is well known. It was a complete failure. This was to be expected. Once one has arrived at the political world of animals, reaction can go no farther, and there can be no other advance than the abandonment of the basis of this world and the transition to the human world of democracy.

The old king had no extravagant desires, he was a philistine and made no claim to intellect. He knew that the state of servants and his possession of it required only a prosaic, tranquil existence. The young king was more alert and brighter and had a much higher opinion of the omnipotence of the monarch, who is only limited by his heart and mind. The old ossified state of servants and slaves disgusted him. He wanted to enliven it and imbue it wholly and entirely with his own desires, sentiments and thoughts; and in *his*

---

[a] Frederick William III.—*Ed.*

state he could demand this, if only it could be brought about. Hence his liberal speeches and the outpourings of his heart. Not dead laws, but the full, vigorous heart of the king should rule all his subjects. He wanted to set all hearts and minds into motion for the benefit of his own heart's desires and long-cherished plans. A movement did result; but the other hearts did not beat like that of the king, and those over whom he ruled could not open their mouths without speaking about the abolition of the old domination. The idealists, who have the audacity to want to turn men into human beings, spoke out, and while the king wove fantasies in the old German manner, they considered they had the right to philosophise in the new German manner. Of course, this was shocking in Prussia. For a moment the old order of things seemed to have been turned upside-down; indeed things began to be transformed into human beings, there even appeared renowned persons, although the mention of names is not permitted in the Diets. But the servants of the old despotism soon put an end to this un-German activity. It was not difficult to bring about a marked conflict between the desires of the king, who is enthusing about a great past full of priests, knights and feudal serfs, and the intentions of the idealists, who want only the consequences of the French Revolution and therefore, in the final count, always a republic and an organisation of free human beings instead of the system of dead objects. When this conflict had become sufficiently sharp and unpleasant and the hot-tempered king was sufficiently aroused, his servants, who previously had so easily guided the course of affairs, approached him and asserted that he was not acting wisely in inducing his subjects to make useless speeches, and that his servants would not be able to rule this race of vociferous people. In addition, the sovereign of all the posterior-Russians was alarmed by the movement in the minds of the anterior-Russians[a] and demanded the restoration of the old tranquil state of affairs. And so the result was a new edition of the old proscription of all the desires and thoughts of people in regard to human rights and duties, that is to say, a return to the old ossified state of servants, in which the slave serves in silence, and the owner of the land and people rules, as silently as possible, simply through a class of well-bred, submissively obedient servants. It is not possible for either of them to say what he wants: the slave cannot say that he wants to become a human being, nor can the ruler say that he has

---

[a] **Marx** ironically calls the Prussians (in Latin *Borussen*) *Vorderrussen* (anterior-Russians), and Nicholas I the sovereign of all the *Hinterrussen* (posterior-Russians).—*Ed.*

no use for human beings in his country. To be silent, therefore, is the only way out. *Muta pecora, prona et ventri oboedientia.*[a]

That is the unsuccessful attempt to abolish the philistine state on its own basis; the result has been to make it evident to the whole world that for despotism brutality is a necessity and humanity an impossibility. A brutal relationship can only be maintained by means of brutality. And now I have finished with our common task, that of taking a close look at the philistine and his state. You will not say that I have had too high an opinion of the present time; and if, nevertheless, I do not despair of it, that is only because it is precisely the desperate situation which fills me with hope. I am not speaking of the incapacity of the masters and of the indifference of the servants and subjects who let everything happen just as God pleases—although both together would already suffice to bring about a catastrophe. I simply draw your attention to the fact that the enemies of philistinism, in short, all people who think and who suffer, have reached an understanding, for which previously the means were altogether lacking, and that even the passive system of reproduction of the subjects of the old type daily enlists recruits to serve the new type of humanity. The system of industry and trade, of ownership and exploitation of people, however, leads even far more rapidly than the increase in population to a rupture within present-day society, a rupture which the old system is not able to heal, because it does not heal and create at all, but only exists and consumes. But the existence of suffering human beings, who think, and thinking human beings, who are oppressed, must inevitably become unpalatable and indigestible to the animal world of philistinism which passively and thoughtlessly consumes.

For our part, we must expose the old world to the full light of day and shape the new one in a positive way. The longer the time that events allow to thinking humanity for taking stock of its position, and to suffering mankind for mobilising its forces, the more perfect on entering the world will be the product that the present time bears in its womb.

M. to R.[b]

Kreuznach, September 1843

I am glad that you have made up your mind and, ceasing to look back at the past, are turning your thoughts ahead to a new

---

[a] The herd is dumb, prostrate and obedient to its stomach.—*Ed.*
[b] Marx to Ruge.—*Ed.*

enterprise.[22] And so—to Paris, to the old university of philosophy—*absit omen!*[a]—and the new capital of the new world! What is necessary comes to pass. I have no doubt, therefore, that it will be possible to overcome all obstacles, the gravity of which I do not fail to recognise.

But whether the enterprise comes into being or not, in any case I shall be in Paris by the end of this month,[23] since the atmosphere here makes one a serf, and in Germany I see no scope at all for free activity.

In Germany, everything is forcibly suppressed; a real anarchy of the mind, the reign of stupidity itself, prevails there, and Zurich obeys orders from Berlin. It therefore becomes increasingly obvious that a new rallying point must be sought for truly thinking and independent minds. I am convinced that our plan would answer a real need, and after all it must be possible for real needs to be fulfilled in reality. Hence I have no doubt about the enterprise, if it is undertaken seriously.

The internal difficulties seem to be almost greater than the external obstacles. For although no doubt exists on the question of "Whence", all the greater confusion prevails on the question of "Whither". Not only has a state of general anarchy set in among the reformers, but everyone will have to admit to himself that he has no exact idea what the future ought to be. On the other hand, it is precisely the advantage of the new trend that we do not dogmatically anticipate the world, but only want to find the new world through criticism of the old one. Hitherto philosophers have had the solution of all riddles lying in their writing-desks, and the stupid, exoteric world had only to open its mouth for the roast pigeons of absolute knowledge to fly into it. Now philosophy has become mundane, and the most striking proof of this is that philosophical consciousness itself has been drawn into the torment of the struggle, not only externally but also internally. But, if constructing the future and settling everything for all times are not our affair, it is all the more clear what we have to accomplish at present: I am referring to *ruthless criticism of all that exists,* ruthless both in the sense of not being afraid of the results it arrives at and in the sense of being just as little afraid of conflict with the powers that be.

Therefore I am not in favour of raising any dogmatic banner. On the contrary, we must try to help the dogmatists to clarify their propositions for themselves. Thus, *communism,* in particular, is a

---

[a] May it not be an ill omen!—*Ed.*

dogmatic abstraction; in which connection, however, I am not thinking of some imaginary and possible communism, but actually existing communism as taught by Cabet, Dézamy, Weitling, etc. This communism is itself only a special expression of the humanistic principle, an expression which is still infected by its antithesis—the private system. Hence the abolition of private property and communism are by no means identical, and it is not accidental but inevitable that communism has seen other socialist doctrines—such as those of Fourier, Proudhon, etc.—arising to confront it because it is itself only a special, one-sided realisation of the socialist principle.

And the whole socialist principle in its turn is only one aspect that concerns the *reality* of the true human being. But we have to pay just as much attention to the other aspect, to the theoretical existence of man, and therefore to make religion, science, etc., the object of our criticism. In addition, we want to influence our contemporaries, particularly our German contemporaries. The question arises: how are we to set about it? There are two kinds of facts which are undeniable. In the first place religion, and next to it, politics, are the subjects which form the main interest of Germany today. We must take these, in whatever form they exist, as our point of departure, and not confront them with some ready-made system such as, for example, the *Voyage en Icarie*.[a]

Reason has always existed, but not always in a reasonable form. The critic can therefore start out from any form of theoretical and practical consciousness and from the forms *peculiar* to existing reality develop the true reality as its obligation and its final goal. As far as real life is concerned, it is precisely the *political state*—in all its *modern* forms—which, even where it is not yet consciously imbued with socialist demands, contains the demands of reason. And the political state does not stop there. Everywhere it assumes that reason has been realised. But precisely because of that it everywhere becomes involved in the contradiction between its ideal function and its real prerequisites.

From this conflict of the political state with itself, therefore, it is possible everywhere to develop the social truth. Just as *religion* is a register of the theoretical struggles of mankind, so the *political state* is a register of the practical struggles of mankind. Thus, the political state expresses, within the limits of its form *sub specie rei publicae*,[b] all social struggles, needs and truths. Therefore, to take

---

[a] Étienne Cabet, *Voyage en Icarie. Roman philosophique et social.—Ed.*
[b] As a particular kind of state.—*Ed.*

as the object of criticism a most specialised political question—such as the difference between a system based on social estate and one based on representation—is in no way below the *hauteur des principes*.ᵃ For this question only expresses in a *political* way the difference between rule by man and rule by private property. Therefore the critic not only can, but must deal with these political questions (which according to the extreme Socialists are altogether unworthy of attention). In analysing the superiority of the representative system over the social-estate system, the critic *in a practical way wins the interest* of a large party. By raising the representative system from its political form to the universal form and by bringing out the true significance underlying this system, the critic at the same time compels this party to go beyond its own confines, for its victory is at the same time its defeat.

Hence, nothing prevents us from making criticism of politics, participation in politics, and therefore *real* struggles, the starting point of our criticism, and from identifying our criticism with them. In that case we do not confront the world in a doctrinaire way with a new principle: Here is the truth, kneel down before it! We develop new principles for the world out of the world's own principles. We do not say to the world: Cease your struggles, they are foolish; we will give you the true slogan of struggle. We merely show the world what it is really fighting for, and consciousness is something that it *has to* acquire, even if it does not want to.

The reform of consciousness consists *only* in making the world aware of its own consciousness, in awakening it out of its dream about itself, in *explaining* to it the meaning of its own actions. Our whole object can only be—as is also the case in Feuerbach's criticism of religion—to give religious and philosophical questions the form corresponding to man who has become conscious of himself.

Hence, our motto must be: reform of consciousness not through dogmas, but by analysing the mystical consciousness that is unintelligible to itself, whether it manifests itself in a religious or a political form. It will then become evident that the world has long dreamed of possessing something of which it has only to be conscious in order to possess it in reality. It will become evident that it is not a question of drawing a great mental dividing line between past and future, but of *realising* the thoughts of the past. Lastly, it will become evident that mankind is not beginning a *new* work, but is consiously carrying into effect its old work.

ᵃ Level of principles.—*Ed.*

In short, therefore, we can formulate the trend of our journal as being: self-clarification (critical philosophy) to be gained by the present time of its struggles and desires. This is a work for the world and for us. It can be only the work of united forces. It is a matter of a *confession,* and nothing more. In order to secure remission of its sins, mankind has only to declare them for what they actually are.

Written in March, May and
September 1843

Printed according to the journal

First published in the
Deutsch-Französische Jahrbücher, 1844

ON THE JEWISH QUESTION [24]

1. BRUNO BAUER, *DIE JUDENFRAGE*, BRAUNSCHWEIG, 1843
2. BRUNO BAUER, "DIE FÄHIGKEIT DER HEUTIGEN JUDEN UND CHRISTEN, FREI ZU WERDEN". *EINUNDZWANZIG BOGEN AUS DER SCHWEIZ*, PUBLISHED BY GEORG HERWEGH. ZÜRICH AND WINTERTHUR, 1843, pp. 56-71

I

Bruno Bauer, *Die Judenfrage*, Braunschweig, 1843

The German Jews desire emancipation. What kind of emancipation do they desire? *Civic, political* emancipation.

Bruno Bauer replies to them: No one in Germany is politically emancipated. We ourselves are not free. How are we to free you? You Jews are *egoists* if you demand a special emancipation for yourselves as Jews. As Germans, you ought to work for the political emancipation of Germany, and as human beings, for the emancipation of mankind, and you should feel the particular kind of your oppression and your shame not as an exception to the rule, but on the contrary as a confirmation of the rule.

Or do the Jews demand the same status as *Christian subjects of the state?* In that case they recognise that the *Christian state* is justified and they recognise too the regime of general oppression. Why should they disapprove of their special yoke if they approve of the general yoke? Why should the German be interested in the liberation of the Jew, if the Jew is not interested in the liberation of the German?

The *Christian* state knows only *privileges*. In this state the Jew has the privilege of being a Jew. As a Jew, he has rights which the Christians do not have. Why should he want rights which he does not have, but which the Christians enjoy?

In wanting to be emancipated from the Christian state, the Jew is demanding that the Christian state should give up its *religious* prejudice. Does he, the Jew, give up *his* religious prejudice? Has he then the right to demand that someone else should renounce his religion?

By its very nature, the Christian state is incapable of emancipating the Jew; but, adds Bauer, by his very nature the Jew cannot be emancipated. So long as the state is Christian and the Jew is Jewish, the one is as incapable of granting emancipation as the other is of receiving it.

The Christian state can behave towards the Jew only in the way characteristic of the Christian state, that is, by granting privileges, by permitting the separation of the Jew from the other subjects, but making him feel the pressure of all the other separate spheres of society, and feel it all the more intensely because he is in *religious* opposition to the dominant religion. But the Jew, too, can behave towards the state only in a Jewish way, that is, by treating it as something alien to him, by counterposing his imaginary nationality to the real nationality, by counterposing his illusory law to the real law, by deeming himself justified in separating himself from mankind, by abstaining on principle from taking part in the historical movement, by putting his trust in a future which has nothing in common with the future of mankind in general, and by seeing himself as a member of the Jewish people, and the Jewish people as the chosen people.

On what grounds then do you Jews want emancipation? On account of your religion? It is the mortal enemy of the state religion. As citizens? In Germany there are no citizens. As human beings? But you are no more human beings than those to whom you appeal.

Bauer has posed the question of Jewish emancipation in a new form, after giving a critical analysis of the previous formulations and solutions of the question. What, he asks, is the *nature* of the Jew who is to be emancipated and of the Christian state that is to emancipate him? He replies by a critique of the Jewish religion, he analyses the *religious* opposition between Judaism and Christianity, he elucidates the essence of the Christian state—and he does all this audaciously, trenchantly, wittily, and with profundity, in a style of writing that is as precise as it is pithy and vigorous.

How then does Bauer solve the Jewish question? What is the result? The formulation of a question is its solution. The critique of the Jewish question is the answer to the Jewish question. The summary, therefore, is as follows:

We must emancipate ourselves before we can emancipate others.

The most rigid form of the opposition between the Jew and the Christian is the *religious* opposition. How is an opposition resolved? By making it impossible. How is *religious* opposition made impossible? By *abolishing religion*. As soon as Jew and Christian recognise that their respective religions are no more than *different stages in the development of the human mind,* different snake skins cast off by *history,* and that *man* is the snake who sloughed them, the relation of Jew and Christian is no longer religious but is only a critical, *scientific* and human relation. *Science* then constitutes their unity. But contradictions in science are resolved by science itself.

The *German* Jew in particular is confronted by the general absence of political emancipation and the strongly marked Christian character of the state. In Bauer's conception, however, the Jewish question has a universal significance, independent of specifically German conditions. It is the question of the relation of religion to the state, of the *contradiction between religious constraint and political emancipation.* Emancipation from religion is laid down as a condition, both to the Jew who wants to be emancipated politically, and to the state which is to effect emancipation and is itself to be emancipated.

"Very well," it is said, and the Jew himself says it, "the Jew is to become emancipated not as a Jew, not because he is a Jew, not because he possesses such an excellent, universally human principle of morality; on the contrary, the *Jew* will retreat behind the *citizen* and be a *citizen,* although he is a Jew and is to remain a Jew. That is to say, he is and remains a *Jew,* although he is a *citizen* and lives in universally human conditions: his Jewish and restricted nature triumphs always in the end over his human and political obligations. The *prejudice* remains in spite of being outstripped by *general* principles. But if it remains, then, on the contrary, it outstrips everything else." "Only sophistically, only apparently, would the Jew be able to remain a Jew in the life of the state. Hence, if he wanted to remain a Jew, the mere appearance would become the essential and would triumph; that is to say, his *life in the state* would be only a semblance or only a temporary exception to the essential and the rule." ("Die Fähigkeit der heutigen Juden und Christen, frei zu werden". *Einundzwanzig Bogen,* p. 57.)

Let us hear, on the other hand, how Bauer presents the task of the state.

"France," he says, "has recently shown us" (Proceedings of the Chamber of Deputies, December 26, 1840) "in connection with the Jewish question—just as it has continually done in all other *political* questions—the spectacle of a life which is free, but which revokes its freedom by law, hence declaring it to be an appearance, and on the other hand contradicting its free laws by its action." (*Die Judenfrage,* p. 64.)

"In France, universal freedom is not yet the law, the *Jewish question too* has *not* yet been solved, because legal freedom—the fact that all citizens are equal—is restricted in actual life, which is still dominated and divided by religious privileges, and this lack of freedom in actual life reacts on law and compels the latter to sanction the division of the citizens, who as such are free, into oppressed and oppressors." (P. 65.)

When, therefore, would the Jewish question be solved for France?

"The Jew, for example, would have ceased to be a Jew if he did not allow himself to be prevented by his laws from fulfilling his duty to the state and his fellow citizens, that is, for example, if on the Sabbath he attended the Chamber of Deputies and took part in the official proceedings. Every *religious privilege*, and therefore also the monopoly of a privileged church, would have been abolished altogether, and if some or many persons, or *even the overwhelming majority, still believed themselves bound to fulfil religious duties*, this fulfilment ought to be left to *them* as a *purely private matter.*" (P. 65.) "There is no longer any religion when there is no longer any privileged religion. Take from religion its exclusive power and it will no longer exist." (P. 66.) "Just as M. Martin du Nord saw the proposal to omit mention of Sunday in the law as a motion to declare that Christianity has ceased to exist, with equal reason (and this reason is very well founded) the declaration that the law of the Sabbath is no longer binding on the Jew would be a proclamation abolishing Judaism." (P. 71.)

Bauer therefore demands, on the one hand, that the Jew should renounce Judaism, and that mankind in general should renounce religion, in order to achieve *civic* emancipation. On the other hand, he quite consistently regards the *political* abolition of religion as the abolition of religion as such. The state which presupposes religion is not yet a true, real state.

"Of course, the religious notion affords security to the state. But to what state? *To what kind of state?*" (P. 97.)

At this point the *one-sided* formulation of the Jewish question becomes evident.

It was by no means sufficient to investigate: Who is to emancipate? Who is to be emancipated? Criticism had to investigate a third point. It had to inquire: *What kind of emancipation* is in question? What conditions follow from the very nature of the emancipation that is demanded? Only the criticism of *political emancipation* itself would have been the conclusive criticism of the Jewish question and its real merging in the "*general question of the time*".

Because Bauer does not raise the question to this level, he becomes entangled in contradictions. He puts forward conditions which are not based on the nature of *political* emancipation itself. He raises questions which are not part of his problem, and he solves problems which leave his question unanswered. When Bauer says of the opponents of Jewish emancipation: "Their error was only that they assumed the Christian state to be the only true one and did not subject it to the same criticism that they applied to Judaism" (op. cit., p. 3), we find that his error lies in the fact that he subjects to criticism *only* the "Christian state", not the "state as such", that he does not investigate *the relation of political emancipation to human emancipation* and therefore puts forward conditions which can be explained only by uncritical confusion of political emancipation with general human emancipation. If Bauer asks the Jews: Have you from your standpoint the right to want *political emancipation?* we ask the converse question: Does the standpoint of *political* emancipation give the right to demand from the Jew the abolition of Judaism and from man the abolition of religion?

The Jewish question acquires a different form depending on the state in which the Jew lives. In Germany, where there is no political state, no state as such, the Jewish question is a purely *theological* one. The Jew finds himself in *religious* opposition to the state, which recognises Christianity as its basis. This state is a theologian *ex professo*. Criticism here is criticism of theology, a double-edged criticism, criticism of Christian theology and of Jewish theology. Hence, we continue to operate in the sphere of theology, however much we may operate *critically* within it.

In France, a *constitutional* state, the Jewish question is a question of constitutionalism, the question of the *incompleteness of political emancipation*. Since the *semblance* of a state religion is retained here, although in a meaningless and self-contradictory formula, that of a *religion of the majority*, the relation of the Jew to the state retains the *semblance* of a religious, theological opposition.

Only in the North American states—at least in some of them—does the Jewish question lose its *theological* significance and become a really *secular* question. Only where the political state exists in its completely developed form can the relation of the Jew, and of the religious man in general, to the political state, and therefore the relation of religion to the state, show itself in its specific character, in its purity. The criticism of this relation ceases to be theological criticism as soon as the state ceases to adopt a *theological* attitude towards religion, as soon as it behaves towards religion as a state, i.e., *politically*. Criticism then becomes *criticism of the political state*. At this point, where the question ceases to be *theological*, Bauer's criticism ceases to be critical.

"*Il n'existe aux Etats-Unis ni religion de l'Etat, ni religion déclarée celle de la majorité ni prééminence d'un culte sur un autre. L'Etat est étranger à tous les cultes.*"[a] (*Marie ou l'esclavage aux Etats-Unis, etc.*, par G. de Beaumont, [t. II,] Paris, 1835, p. 214.) Indeed, there are some North American states where "*la constitution n'impose pas les croyances religieuses et la pratique d'un culte comme condition des privilèges politiques*".[b]

---

[a] "*In the United States there is neither a state religion nor a religion declared to be that of the majority, nor the predominance of one cult over another. The state stands aloof from all cults.*"—*Ed.*

[b] "*The constitution does not impose any religious belief or religious practice as a condition of political rights.*"—*Ed.*

(op. cit., p. 225.) Nevertheless, *"on ne croit pas aux Etats-Unis qu'un homme sans religion puisse être un honnête homme"*.[a] (op. cit., p. 224.)

Nevertheless, North America is pre-eminently the country of religiosity, as Beaumont, Tocqueville and the Englishman Hamilton unanimously assure us.[b] The North American states, however, serve us only as an example. The question is: What is the relation of *complete* political emancipation to religion? If we find that even in the country of complete political emancipation, religion not only *exists*, but displays a *fresh and vigorous vitality*, that is proof that the existence of religion is not in contradiction to the perfection of the state. Since, however, the existence of religion is the existence of a defect, the source of this defect can only be sought in the *nature* of the state itself. We no longer regard religion as the *cause*, but only as the *manifestation* of secular narrowness. Therefore we explain the religious limitations of the free citizens by their secular limitations. We do not assert that they must overcome their religious narrowness in order to get rid of their secular restrictions, we assert that they will overcome their religious narrowness once they get rid of their secular restrictions. We do not turn secular questions into theological questions. We turn theological questions into secular ones. History has long enough been merged in superstition, we now merge superstition in history. The question of the *relation of political emancipation to religion* becomes for us the question of the *relation of political emancipation to human emancipation*. We criticise the religious weakness of the political state by criticising the political state in its *secular* form, *apart* from its weaknesses as regards religion. The contradiction between the state and a *particular religion,* for instance *Judaism,* is given by us a human form as the contradiction between the state and *particular secular* elements; the contradiction between the state and *religion in general* as the contradiction between the state and its *presuppositions* in general.

The *political* emancipation of the Jew, the Christian, and in general of *religious* man is the *emancipation of the state* from Judaism, from Christianity, from *religion* in general. In its own form, in the manner characteristic of its nature, the state as a *state* emancipates itself from religion by emancipating itself from the

---

[a] "In the United States people do not believe that a man without religion could be an honest man."—*Ed.*

[b] A. de Tocqueville, *De la Démocratie en Amérique*; Thomas Hamilton, *Men and Manners in North America*, Edinburgh, 1833, 2 vols. Marx quotes from the German translation *Die Menschen und die Sitten in den Vereinigten Staaten von Nordamerika.*—*Ed.*

state religion, that is to say, by the state as a state not professing any religion, but, on the contrary, asserting itself as a state. The *political* emancipation from religion is not a religious emancipation that has been carried through to completion and is free from contradiction, because political emancipation is not a form of *human* emancipation which has been carried through to completion and is free from contradiction.

The limits of political emancipation are evident at once from the fact that the *state* can free itself from a restriction without man being *really* free from this restriction, that the state can be a *free state*[a] without man being a *free man.* Bauer himself tacitly admits this when he lays down the following condition for political emancipation:

"Every religious privilege, and therefore also the monopoly of a privileged church, would have been abolished altogether, and if some or many persons, or even the *overwhelming majority,* still believed themselves bound to fulfil religious duties, this fulfilment ought to be left to them as a *purely private matter.*" [Bruno Bauer, Die Judenfrage, p. 65.]

It is possible, therefore, for the *state* to have emancipated itself from religion even if the *overwhelming majority* is still religious. And the overwhelming majority does not cease to be religious through being religious *in private.*

But the attitude of the state, and of the *republic*[a] in particular, to religion is after all only the attitude to religion of the *men* who compose the state. It follows from this that man frees himself through the *medium of the state,* that he frees himself *politically* from a limitation when, in contradiction with himself, he raises himself above this limitation in an *abstract, limited,* and partial way. It follows further that, by freeing himself *politically,* man frees himself in a *roundabout way,* through an *intermediary,* although an *essential intermediary.* It follows, finally, that man, even if he proclaims himself an atheist through the medium of the state, that is, if he proclaims the state to be atheist, still remains in the grip of religion, precisely because he acknowledges himself only by a roundabout route, only through an intermediary. Religion is precisely the recognition of man in a roundabout way, through an *intermediary.* The state is the intermediary between man and man's freedom. Just as Christ is the intermediary to whom man transfers the burden of all his divinity, all his *religious constraint,* so the state is the intermediary to whom man transfers all his non-divinity and all his *human unconstraint.*

---

[a] A pun on the word *Freistaat,* i. e., republic, for if it is taken literally, it means "free state".

The *political* elevation of man above religion shares all the defects and all the advantages of political elevation in general. The state as a state annuls, for instance, *private property*, man declares by *political* means that private property is *abolished* as soon as the *property qualification* for the right to elect or be elected is abolished, as has occurred in many states of North America. *Hamilton* quite correctly interprets this fact from a political point of view as meaning: "*the masses have won a victory over the property owners and financial wealth*".[a] Is not private property abolished in idea if the non-property owner has become the legislator for the property owner? The *property qualification* for the suffrage is the last *political* form of giving recognition to private property.

Nevertheless the political annulment of private property not only fails to abolish private property but even presupposes it. The state abolishes, in its own way, distinctions of *birth, social rank, education, occupation*, when it declares that birth, social rank, education occupation, are *non-political* distinctions, when it proclaims, without regard to these distinctions, that every member of the nation is an *equal* participant in national sovereignty, when it treats all elements of the real life of the nation from the standpoint of the state. Nevertheless, the state allows private property, education, occupation, to *act* in *their* way, i. e., as private property, as education, as occupation, and to exert the influence of their *special* nature. Far from abolishing these *real* distinctions, the state only exists on the presupposition of their existence; it feels itself to be a *political state* and asserts its *universality* only in opposition to these elements of its being. *Hegel* therefore defines the relation of the *political state* to religion quite correctly when he says:

"In order [...] that the state should come into existence as the *self-knowing*, **moral reality** of the mind, its **distinction** from the form of authority and faith is essential. But this distinction emerges only insofar as the ecclesiastical aspect arrives at a **separation** within itself. It is **only** in this way that the state, **above** the *particular* churches, has achieved and brought into existence *universality* of thought, which is the principle of its form" (Hegel's *Rechtsphilosophie*, 1st edition, p. 346).[b]

Of course! Only in this way, *above* the *particular* elements, does the state constitute itself as universality.

The perfect political state is, by its nature, man's *species-life*, as *opposed* to his material life. All the preconditions of this egoistic life continue to exist in *civil society outside* the sphere of the state, but

---

[a] Thomas Hamilton, *Die Menschen und die Sitten in den Vereinigten Staaten von Nordamerica*, Bd. 1, S. 146.—*Ed.*

[b] Hegel, *Grundlinien der Philosophie des Rechts*. In this quotation words emphasised by Marx are set in bold italics, words emphasised by both Marx and Hegel in italics.—*Ed.*

as qualities of civil society. Where the political state has attained its true development, man—not only in thought, in consciousness, but in *reality*, in *life*—leads a twofold life, a heavenly and an earthly life: life in the *political community*, in which he considers himself a *communal being*, and life in *civil society*, in which he acts as a *private individual*, regards other men as a means, degrades himself into a means, and becomes the plaything of alien powers. The relation of the political state to civil society is just as spiritual as the relation of heaven to earth. The political state stands in the same opposition to civil society, and it prevails over the latter in the same way as religion prevails over the narrowness of the secular world, i.e., by likewise having always to acknowledge it, to restore it, and allow itself to be dominated by it. In his *most immediate* reality, in civil society, man is a secular being. Here, where he regards himself as a real individual, and is so regarded by others, he is a *fictitious* phenomenon. In the state, on the other hand, where man is regarded as a species-being, he is the imaginary member of an illusory sovereignty, is deprived of his real individual life and endowed with an unreal universality.

Man, as the adherent of a *particular* religion, finds himself in conflict with his citizenship and with other men as members of the community. This conflict reduces itself to the *secular* division between the *political* state and *civil society*. For man as a *bourgeois*,[a] "life in the state" is "only a semblance or a temporary exception to the essential and the rule".[b] Of course, the *bourgeois*, like the Jew, remains only sophistically in the sphere of political life, just as the *citoyen* only sophistically remains a Jew or a *bourgeois*. But this sophistry is not personal. It is the *sophistry of the political state* itself. The difference between the religious man and the citizen is the difference between the merchant and the citizen, between the day-labourer and the citizen, between the landowner and the citizen, between the *living individual* and the *citizen*. The contradiction in which the religious man finds himself with the political man is the same contradiction in which the *bourgeois* finds himself with the *citoyen*, and the member of civil society with his *political lion's skin*.

This secular conflict, to which the Jewish question ultimately reduces itself, the relation between the political state and its preconditions, whether these are material elements, such as private property, etc., or spiritual elements, such as culture or religion,

---

[a] Here meaning a member of civil society.—*Ed.*

[b] Bruno Bauer, "Die Fähigkeit der heutigen Juden und Christen, frei zu werden", p. 57 (see also this volume, p. 148).—*Ed.*

the conflict between the *general* interest and *private interest,* the schism between the *political state* and *civil society*—these secular antitheses Bauer allows to persist, whereas he conducts a polemic against their *religious* expression.

"It is precisely the basis of *civil society*, the need that ensures the continuance of this society and *guarantees its necessity*, which exposes its existence to continual dangers, maintains in it an element of uncertainty, and produces that continually changing mixture of poverty and riches, of distress and prosperity, and brings about change in general." (P. 8.)

Compare the whole section: "Civil Society" (pp. 8-9), which has been drawn up along the basic lines of Hegel's philosophy of law. Civil society, in its opposition to the political state, is recognised as necessary, because the political state is recognised as necessary.

Political emancipation is, of course, a big step forward. True, it is not the final form of human emancipation in general, but it is the final form of human emancipation *within* the hitherto existing world order. It goes without saying that we are speaking here of real, practical emancipation.

Man emancipates himself *politically* from religion by banishing it from the sphere of public law to that of private law. Religion is no longer the spirit of the *state*, in which man behaves—although in a limited way, in a particular form, and in a particular sphere—as a species-being, in community with other men. Religion has become the spirit of *civil society,* of the sphere of egoism, of *bellum omnium contra omnes*. It is no longer the essence of *community,* but the essence of *difference*. It has become the expression of man's *separation* from his *community,* from himself and from other men—as it was *originally*. It is only the abstract avowal of specific perversity, *private whimsy,* and arbitrariness. The endless fragmentation of religion in North America, for example, gives it even *externally* the form of a purely individual affair. It has been thrust among the multitude of private interests and ejected from the community as such. But one should be under no illusion about the limits of political emancipation. The division of the human being into a *public man* and a *private man,* the *displacement* of religion from the state into civil society, this is not a stage of political emancipation but its *completion*; this emancipation therefore neither abolishes the *real* religiousness of man, nor strives to do so.

The *decomposition* of man into Jew and citizen, Protestant and citizen, religious man and citizen, is neither a deception directed *against* citizenhood, nor is it a circumvention of political emancipation, it is *political emancipation itself,* the *political* method of emancipating oneself from religion. Of course, in periods when the political state as such is born violently out of civil society, when political liberation is the form in which men strive to achieve their liberation, the state can and must go as far as the *abolition of religion,* the *destruction* of religion. But it can do so only in the same way that it proceeds to the abolition of private property, to the maximum, to confiscation, to progressive taxation, just as it goes as far as the abolition of life, the *guillotine.* At times of special self-confidence, political life seeks to suppress its prerequisite, civil society and the elements composing this society, and to constitute itself as the real species-life of man devoid of contradictions. But it can achieve this only by coming into *violent* contradiction with its own conditions of life, only by declaring the revolution to be *permanent,* and therefore the political drama necessarily ends with the re-establishment of religion, private property, and all elements of civil society, just as war ends with peace.

Indeed, the perfect Christian state is not the so-called *Christian* state, which acknowledges Christianity as its basis, as the state religion, and therefore adopts an exclusive attitude towards other religions. On the contrary, the perfect Christian state is the *atheistic* state, the *democratic* state, the state which relegates religion to a place among the other elements of civil society. The state which is still theological, which still officially professes Christianity as its creed, which still does not dare to proclaim itself *as a state,* has, in its *reality* as a state, not yet succeeded in expressing the *human* basis—of which Christianity is the high-flown expression—in a *secular, human* form. The so-called Christian state is simply nothing more than a *non-state,* since it is not Christianity as a religion, but only the *human background* of the Christian religion, which can find its expression in actual human creations.

The so-called Christian state is the Christian negation of the state, but by no means the political realisation of Christianity. The state which still professes Christianity in the form of religion, does not yet profess it in the form appropriate to the state, for it still has a religious attitude towards religion, that is to say, it is not the *true implementation* of the human basis of religion, because it still relies on the *unreal, imaginary* form of this human core. The so-called Christian state is the *imperfect* state, and the Christian religion is regarded by it as the *supplementation* and *sanctification* of its imperfection. For the Christian state, therefore, religion necessarily becomes a *means;* hence it is a *hypocritical* state. It makes a great difference whether the *complete* state, because of the defect inherent in the general *nature* of the state, counts religion among its *presuppositions,* or whether the *incomplete* state, because of the defect inherent in its *particular existence* as a defective state, declares that religion is its *basis*. In the latter case, religion becomes *imperfect politics*. In the former case, the imperfection even of consummate *politics* becomes evident in religion. The so-called Christian state needs the Christian religion in order to complete itself *as a state*. The democratic state, the real state, does not need religion for its political completion. On the contrary, it can disregard religion because in it the human basis of religion is realised in a secular manner. The so-called Christian state, on the other hand, has a political attitude to religion and a religious attitude to politics. By degrading the forms of the state to mere semblance, it equally degrades religion to mere semblance.

In order to make this contradiction clearer, let us consider Bauer's projection of the Christian state, a projection based on his observation of the Christian-German state.

"Recently," says Bauer, "in order to prove the *impossibility* or *non-existence* of a Christian state, reference has frequently been made to those sayings in the Gospel with which the [present-day] state *not only does not* comply, but *cannot possibly comply, if it does not want to dissolve itself completely* [as a state]." "But the matter cannot be disposed of so easily. What do these Gospel sayings demand? Supernatural renunciation of self, submission to the authority of revelation, a turning-away from the state, the abolition of secular conditions. Well, the Christian state demands and accomplishes all that. It has assimilated the *spirit of the Gospel*, and if it does not reproduce this spirit in the same terms as the Gospel, that occurs only because it expresses this spirit in political forms, i.e., in forms which, it is true, are taken from the political system in this world, but which in the religious rebirth that they have to undergo become degraded to a mere semblance. This is a turning-away from the state while making use of political forms for its realisation." (P. 55.)

Bauer then explains that the people of a Christian state is only a non-people, no longer having a will of its own, but whose true existence lies in the leader to whom it is subjected, although this leader by his origin and nature is alien to it, i.e., given by God and imposed on the people without any co-operation on its part. Bauer declares that the laws of such a people are not its own creation, but are actual revelations, that its supreme chief needs privileged intermediaries with the people in the strict sense, with the masses, and that the masses themselves are divided into a multitude of particular groupings which are formed and determined by chance, which are differentiated by their interests, their particular passions and prejudices, and obtain permission, as a privilege, to isolate themselves from one another, etc. (P. 56.)

However, Bauer himself says:

"Politics, if it is to be nothing but religion, ought not to be politics, just as the cleaning of saucepans, if it is to be accepted as a religious matter, ought not to be regarded as a matter of domestic economy." (P. 108.)

In the Christian-German state, however, religion is an "economic matter" just as "economic matters" belong to the sphere of religion. The domination of religion in the Christian-German state is the religion of domination.

The separation of the "spirit of the Gospel" from the "letter of the Gospel" is an *irreligious* act. A state which makes the Gospel speak in the language of politics, that is, in another language than that of the Holy Ghost, commits sacrilege, if not in human eyes, then in the eyes of its own religion. The state which acknowledges Christianity as its supreme criterion and the *Bible* as its *Charter*, must be confronted with the *words* of Holy Scripture, for every word of Scripture is holy. This state, as well as the *human rubbish* on which it is based, is caught in a painful contradiction that is insoluble from the standpoint of religious consciousness when it is referred to those sayings of the Gospel with which it "not only does not comply, but *cannot possibly comply, if it does not want to dissolve itself completely as a state*". And why does it not want to dissolve itself completely? The state itself cannot give an answer either to itself or to others. In its *own consciousness* the official Christian state is an *imperative,* the realisation of which is unattainable, the state can assert the *reality* of its existence only by lying to itself, and therefore always remains in its own eyes an object of doubt, an unreliable, problematic object. Criticism is therefore fully justified in forcing the state that relies on the Bible into a mental derangement in which it no longer knows whether it is an *illusion* or a *reality,* and in which the infamy of its *secular* aims, for which religion serves as a cloak, comes into insoluble conflict with the sincerity of its *religious* consciousness, for which religion appears as the aim of the world. This state can only save itself from its inner torment if it becomes the *police agent* of the Catholic Church. In relation to the church, which declares the secular power to be its servant, the state is powerless, the *secular* power which claims to be the rule of the religious spirit is powerless.

It is indeed *estrangement* which matters in the so-called Christian state, but not *man*. The only man who counts, the *king*, is a being specifically different from other men, and is moreover a religious being, directly linked with heaven, with God. The relationships which prevail here are still relationships dependent on *faith*. The religious spirit, therefore, is still not really secularised.

But, furthermore, the religious spirit cannot be *really* secularised, for what is it in itself but the *non-secular* form of a stage in the development of the human mind? The religious spirit can only be secularised insofar as the stage of development of the human mind of which it is the religious expression makes its appearance and becomes constituted in its *secular* form. This takes place in the *democratic* state. Not Christianity, but the *human basis* of Christianity is the basis of this state. Religion remains the ideal, non-secular consciousness of its members, because religion is the ideal form of the *stage of human development* achieved in this state.

The members of the political state are religious owing to the dualism between individual life and species-life, between the life of civil society and political life. They are religious because men treat the political life of the state, an area beyond their real individuality, as if it were their true life. They are religious insofar as religion here is the spirit of civil society, expressing the separation and remoteness of man from man. Political democracy is Christian since in it man, not merely one man but every man, ranks as *sovereign*, as the highest being, but it is man in his uncivilised, unsocial form, man in his fortuitous existence, man just as he is, man as he has been corrupted by the whole organisation of our society, who has lost himself, been alienated, and handed over to the rule of inhuman conditions and elements — in short, man who is not yet a *real* species-being. That which is a creation of fantasy, a dream, a postulate of Christianity, i.e., the sovereignty of man — but man as an alien being different from the real man — becomes in democracy tangible reality, present existence, and secular principle.

In the perfect democracy, the religious and theological consciousness itself is in its own eyes the more religious and the more theological because it is apparently without political significance, without worldly aims, the concern of a disposition that shuns the world, the expression of intellectual narrow-mindedness, the product of arbitrariness and fantasy, and because it is a life that is really of the other world. Christianity attains here the *practical* expression of its universal-religious significance in that the most diverse world outlooks are grouped alongside one another in the form of Christianity and still more because it does not require other people to profess Christianity, but only religion in general, any kind of religion (cf. Beaumont's work quoted above). The religious consciousness revels in the wealth of religious contradictions and religious diversity.

We have thus shown that political emancipation from religion leaves religion in existence, although not a privileged religion. The contradiction in which the adherent of a particular religion finds himself involved in relation to his citizenship is only *one aspect* of the universal *secular contradiction between the political state and civil society*. The consummation of the Christian state is the state which acknowledges itself as a state and disregards the religion of its members. The emancipation of the state from religion is not the emancipation of the real man from religion.

Therefore we do not say to the Jews as Bauer does: You cannot be emancipated politically without emancipating yourselves radically from Judaism. On the contrary, we tell them: Because you can be emancipated politically without renouncing Judaism completely and incontrovertibly, *political emancipation* itself is not *human* emancipation. If you Jews want to be emancipated politically without emancipating yourselves humanly, the half-hearted approach and contradiction is not in you alone, it is inherent in the *nature* and *category* of political emancipation. If you find yourself within the confines of this category, you share in a general confinement. Just as the state *evangelises* when, although it is a state, it adopts a Christian attitude towards the Jews, so the Jew *acts politically* when, although a Jew, he demands civic rights.

But if a man, although a Jew, can be emancipated politically and receive civic rights, can he lay claim to the so-called *rights of man* and receive them? Bauer *denies* it.

"The question is whether the Jew as such, that is, the Jew who himself admits that he is compelled by his true nature to live permanently in separation from other men, is capable of receiving the *universal rights of man* and of conceding them to others."

"For the Christian world, the idea of the rights of man was only discovered in the last century. It is not innate in men; on the contrary, it is gained only in a struggle against the historical traditions in which hitherto man was brought up. Thus the rights of man are not a gift of nature, not a legacy from past history, but the reward of the struggle against the accident of birth and against the privileges which up to now have been handed down by history from generation to generation. These rights are the result of culture, and only one who has earned and deserved them can possess them."

"Can the Jew really take possession of them? As long as he is a Jew, the restricted nature which makes him a Jew is bound to triumph over the human nature which should link him as a man with other men, and will separate him from non-Jews. He declares by this separation that the particular nature which makes him a Jew is his true, highest nature, before which human nature has to give way."

"Similarly, the Christian as a Christian cannot grant the rights of man." (P. 19, 20.)

According to Bauer, man has to sacrifice the *"privilege of faith"* to be able to receive the universal rights of man. Let us examine for a moment the so-called rights of man, to be precise, the rights of man in their authentic form, in the form which they have among those who *discovered* them, the North Americans and the French. These rights of man are in part *political* rights, rights which can only be exercised in a community with others. Their content is *participation* in the *community*, and specifically in the *political* community, in the *life of the state*. They come within the category of *political freedom*, the category of *civic rights*, which, as we have seen, in no way presuppose the incontrovertible and positive abolition of religion, nor therefore of Judaism. There remains to be examined the other part of the rights of man, the *droits de l'homme*,^a insofar as these differ from the *droits du citoyen*.^b

Included among them is freedom of conscience, the right to practise any religion one chooses. The *privilege of faith* is expressly recognised either as a *right of man* or as the consequence of a right of man, that of liberty.

Déclaration des droits de l'homme et du citoyen, 1791, article 10: "Nul ne doit être inquiété pour ses opinions même réligieuses."^c "La liberté à tout homme d'exercer le *culte religieux* auquel il est attaché"^d is guaranteed as a right of man in Section I of the Constitution of 1791.

Déclaration des droits de l'homme, etc., 1793, includes among the rights of man, Article 7: "Le libre exercice des cultes."^e Indeed, in regard to man's right to express his thoughts and opinions, to hold meetings, and to exercise his religion, it is even stated: "La nécessité d'énoncer ces *droits* suppose ou la présence ou le souvenir récent du despotisme."^f Compare the Constitution of 1795, Section XIV, Article 354.[25]

Constitution de Pensylvanie, article 9, § 3: "Tous les hommes ont reçu de la nature le *droit* imprescriptible d'adorer le Tout-Puissant selon les inspirations de leur conscience, et nul ne peut légalement être contraint de suivre, instituer ou soutenir contre son gré aucun culte ou ministère religieux. Nulle autorité humaine ne peut, dans aucun cas, intervenir dans les questions de conscience et contrôler les pouvoirs de l'âme."^g

Constitution de New-Hampshire, article 5 et 6: "Au nombre des droits naturels, quelques-uns sont inaliénables de leur nature, parce que rien n'en peut être l'équivalent. De ce nombre sont les *droits* de conscience."^h (Beaumont, op. cit., [t. II,] pp. 213, 214.)

---

^a Rights of man.—*Ed.*

^b Rights of the citizen.—*Ed.*

^c *Declaration of the Rights of Man and of the Citizen*, 1791, Article 10: "No one is to be subjected to annoyance because of his opinions, even religious opinions."—*Ed.*

^d "The freedom of every man to practise the *religion* of which he is an adherent."—*Ed.*

^e *The Declaration of the Rights of Man*, etc., 1793, "The free exercise of religion."—*Ed.*

^f "The necessity of proclaiming these rights presupposes either the existence or the recent memory of despotism."—*Ed.*

^g *Constitution of Pennsylvania*, Article 9, § 3: "All men have received from nature the imprescriptible *right* to worship the Almighty according to the dictates of their conscience, and no one can be legally compelled to follow, establish or support against his will any religion or religious ministry. No human authority can, in any circumstances, intervene in a matter of conscience or control the forces of the soul."—*Ed.*

^h *Constitution of New Hampshire*, Articles 5 and 6: "Among these natural rights some are by nature inalienable since nothing can replace them. The *rights* of conscience are among them."—*Ed.*

Incompatibility between religion and the rights of man is to such a degree absent from the concept of the rights of man that, on the contrary, a man's *right to be religious* in any way he chooses, to practise his own particular religion, is expressly included among the rights of man. The *privilege of faith* is a *universal right of man.*

The *droits de l'homme,* the rights of man, are as *such* distinct from the *droits du citoyen,* the rights of the citizen. Who is *homme* as distinct from *citoyen?* None other than the *member of civil society.* Why is the member of civil society called "man", simply man; why are his rights called the *rights of man?* How is this fact to be explained? From the relationship between the political state and civil society, from the nature of political emancipation.

Above all, we note the fact that the so-called *rights of man,* the *droits de l'homme* as distinct from the *droits du citoyen,* are nothing but the rights of a *member of civil society,* i. e., the rights of egoistic man, of man separated from other men and from the community. Let us hear what the most radical Constitution, the Constitution of 1793, has to say:

> *Déclaration des droits de l'homme et du citoyen.*
> *Article 2.* "Ces droits, etc. (les droits naturels et imprescriptibles) sont: l'*égalité,* la *liberté,* la *sûreté,* la *propriété.*" [a]

What constitutes *liberty?*

> *Article 6.* "La liberté est le pouvoir qui appartient à l'homme de faire tout ce qui ne nuit pas aux droits d'autrui", or, according to the Declaration of the Rights of Man of 1791: "La liberté consiste à pouvoir faire tout ce qui ne nuit pas à autrui." [b]

Liberty, therefore, is the right to do everything that harms no one else. The limits within which anyone can act *without harming* someone else are defined by law, just as the boundary between two fields is determined by a boundary post. It is a question of the liberty of man as an isolated monad, withdrawn into himself. Why is the Jew, according to Bauer, incapable of acquiring the rights of man?

> "As long as he is a Jew, the restricted nature which makes him a Jew is bound to triumph over the human nature which should link him as a man with other men, and will separate him from non-Jews."

But the right of man to liberty is based not on the association of man with man, but on the separation of man from man. It is the

---

[a] *Declaration of the Rights of Man and of the Citizen. Article 2.* "These rights, etc., (the natural and imprescriptible rights) are: *equality, liberty, security, property.*"—*Ed.*

[b] *Article 6.* "Liberty is the power which man has to do everything that does not harm the rights of others", or... "Liberty consists in being able to do everything which does not harm others."—*Ed.*

right of this separation, the right of the *restricted* individual, withdrawn into himself.

The practical application of man's right to liberty is man's right to *private property*.

What constitutes man's right to private property?

Article 16 (Constitution de 1793): "Le droit de *propriété* est celui qui appartient à tout citoyen de jouir et de disposer *à son gré* de ses biens, de ses revenus, du fruit de son travail et de son industrie."[a]

The right of man to private property is, therefore, the right to enjoy one's property and to dispose of it at one's discretion (*à son gré*), without regard to other men, independently of society, the right of self-interest. This individual liberty and its application form the basis of civil society. It makes every man see in other men not the *realisation* of his own freedom, but the *barrier* to it. But, above all, it proclaims the right of man

"de jouir et de disposer *à son gré* de ses biens, de ses revenus, du fruit de son travail et de son industrie".[b]

There remain the other rights of man: *égalité* and *sûreté*.

Égalité, used here in its non-political sense, is nothing but the equality of the *liberté* described above, namely: each man is to the same extent regarded as such a self-sufficient monad. The Constitution of 1795 defines the concept of this equality, in accordance with its significance, as follows:

Article 3 (Constitution de 1795): "L'égalité consiste en ce que la loi est la même pour tous, soit qu'elle protège, soit qu'elle punisse."[c 26]

And *sûreté*?

Article 8 (Constitution de 1793): "La sûreté consiste dans la protection accordée par la société à chacun de ses membres pour la conservation de sa personne, de ses droits et de ses propriétés."[d]

Security is the highest social concept of civil society, the concept of *police,* expressing the fact that the whole of society exists only in order to guarantee to each of its members the preservation of his person, his rights, and his property. It is in this sense that Hegel calls civil society "the state of need and reason".[e]

---

[a] *Article 16* (Constitution of 1793): "The right of *property* is that which every citizen has of enjoying and of disposing *at his discretion* of his goods and income, of the fruits of his labour and industry."—*Ed.*

[b] "of enjoying and of disposing *at his discretion* of his goods and income, of the fruits of his labour and industry".—*Ed.*

[c] *Article 3* (Constitution of 1795): "Equality consists in the law being the same for all, whether it protects or punishes."—*Ed.*

[d] *Article 8* (Constitution of 1793): "Security consists in the protection afforded by society to each of its members for the preservation of his person, his rights, and his property."—*Ed.*

[e] Hegel, *Grundlinien der Philosophie des Rechts. Werke.* Bd. VIII, S. 242.—*Ed.*

The concept of security does not raise civil society above its egoism. On the contrary, security is the *insurance* of its egoism.

None of the so-called rights of man, therefore, go beyond egoistic man, beyond man as a member of civil society, that is, an individual withdrawn into himself, into the confines of his private interests and private caprice, and separated from the community. In the rights of man, he is far from being conceived as a species-being; on the contrary, species-life itself, society, appears as a framework external to the individuals, as a restriction of their original independence. The sole bond holding them together is natural necessity, need and private interest, the preservation of their property and their egoistic selves.

It is puzzling enough that a people which is just beginning to liberate itself, to tear down all the barriers between its various sections, and to establish a political community, that such a people solemnly proclaims (Declaration of 1791) the rights of egoistic man separated from his fellow men and from the community, and that indeed it repeats this proclamation at a moment when only the most heroic devotion can save the nation, and is therefore imperatively called for, at a moment when the sacrifice of all the interests of civil society must be the order of the day, and egoism must be punished as a crime. (Declaration of the Rights of Man, etc., of 1793.) This fact becomes still more puzzling when we see that the political emancipators go so far as to reduce citizenship, and the *political community*, to a mere *means* for maintaining these so-called rights of man, that therefore the *citoyen* is declared to be the servant of egoistic *homme*, that the sphere in which man acts as a communal being is degraded to a level below the sphere in which he acts as a partial being, and that, finally, it is not man as *citoyen*, but man as *bourgeois* who is considered to be the *essential* and *true* man.

"Le *but* de toute *association politique* est la *conservation* des droits naturels et imprescriptibles de l'homme." (Déclaration des droits, etc., de 1791, article 2.) "Le *gouvernement* est institué pour garantir à l'homme la jouissance de ses droits naturels et imprescriptibles." (Déclaration, etc., de 1793, article 1.)[a][27]

Hence even in moments when its enthusiasm still has the freshness of youth and is intensified to an extreme degree by the force of circumstances, political life declares itself to be a mere *means*, whose purpose is the life of civil society. It is true that its

---

[a] "The *aim* of all *political association* is the *preservation* of the natural and imprescriptible rights of man." (Declaration of the Rights, etc., of 1791, Article 2.) "*Government* is instituted in order to guarantee man the enjoyment of his natural and imprescriptible rights." (Declaration, etc., of 1793, Article 1.)—*Ed.*

revolutionary practice is in flagrant contradiction with its theory. Whereas, for example, security is declared one of the rights of man, violation of the privacy of correspondence is openly declared to be the order of the day. Whereas the "liberté *indéfinie* de la presse"[a] (Constitution of 1793, Article 122) is guaranteed as a consequence of the right of man to individual liberty, freedom of the press is totally destroyed, because "la liberté de la presse ne doit pas être permise lorsqu'elle compromet la liberté publique".[b] (Robespierre jeune, *Histoire parlementaire de la Révolution française par Buchez et Roux*, T. 28, p. 159.) That is to say, therefore: The right of man to liberty ceases to be a right as soon as it comes into conflict with *political* life, whereas in theory political life is only the guarantee of human rights, the rights of the individual, and therefore must be abandoned as soon as it comes into contradiction with its *aim*, with these rights of man. But practice is merely the exception, theory is the rule. But even if one were to regard revolutionary practice as the correct presentation of the relationship, there would still remain the puzzle of why the relationship is turned upside-down in the minds of the political emancipators and the aim appears as the means, while the means appears as the aim. This optical illusion of their consciousness would still remain a puzzle, although now a psychological, a theoretical puzzle.

The puzzle is easily solved.

Political emancipation is at the same time the *dissolution* of the old society on which the state alienated from the people, the sovereign power, is based. Political revolution is a revolution of civil society. What was the character of the old society? It can be described in one word—*feudalism*. The character of the old civil society was *directly political*, that is to say, the elements of civil life, for example, property, or the family, or the mode of labour, were raised to the level of elements of political life in the form of seigniory, estates, and corporations. In this form they determined the relation of the individual to the *state as a whole*, i.e., his *political* relation, that is, his relation of separation and exclusion from the other components of society. For that organisation of national life did not raise property or labour to the level of social elements; on the contrary, it completed their *separation* from the state as a whole and constituted them as *discrete* societies within society. Thus, the vital functions and conditions of life of civil society remained nevertheless political, although political in the feudal sense, that is

---

[a] "*Unlimited* freedom of the press".—*Ed.*

[b] "Freedom of the press should not be permitted when it endangers public liberty."—*Ed.*

to say, they secluded the individual from the state as a whole and they converted the *particular* relation of his corporation to the state as a whole into his general relation to the life of the nation, just as they converted his particular civil activity and situation into his general activity and situation. As a result of this organisation, the unity of the state, and also the consciousness, will and activity of this unity, the general power of the state, are likewise bound to appear as the *particular* affair of a ruler isolated from the people, and of his servants.

The political revolution which overthrew this sovereign power and raised state affairs to become affairs of the people, which constituted the political state as a matter of *general* concern, that is, as a real state, necessarily smashed all estates, corporations, guilds, and privileges, since they were all manifestations of the separation of the people from the community. The political revolution thereby *abolished* the *political character of civil society*. It broke up civil society into its simple component parts; on the one hand, the *individuals*; on the other hand, the *material* and *spiritual elements* constituting the content of the life and social position of these individuals. It set free the political spirit, which had been, as it were, split up, partitioned and dispersed in the various blind alleys of feudal society. It gathered the dispersed parts of the political spirit, freed it from its intermixture with civil life, and established it as the sphere of the community, the *general* concern of the nation, ideally independent of those *particular* elements of civil life. A person's *distinct* activity and distinct situation in life were reduced to a merely individual significance. They no longer constituted the general relation of the individual to the state as a whole. Public affairs as such, on the other hand, became the general affair of each individual, and the political function became the individual's general function.

But the completion of the idealism of the state was at the same time the completion of the materialism of civil society. Throwing off the political yoke meant at the same time throwing off the bonds which restrained the egoistic spirit of civil society. Political emancipation was at the same time the emancipation of civil society from politics, from having even the *semblance* of a universal content.

Feudal society was resolved into its basic element—*man*, but man as he really formed its basis—*egoistic* man.

This *man*, the member of civil society, is thus the basis, the precondition, of the *political* state. He is recognised as such by this state in the rights of man.

The liberty of egoistic man and the recognition of this liberty, however, is rather the recognition of the *unrestrained* movement of the spiritual and material elements which form the content of his life.

Hence man was not freed from religion, he received religious freedom. He was not freed from property, he received freedom to own property. He was not freed from the egoism of business, he received freedom to engage in business.

The *establishment of the political state* and the dissolution of civil society into independent *individuals*—whose relations with one another depend on *law,* just as the relations of men in the system of estates and guilds depended on *privilege*—is accomplished by *one and the same act.* Man as a member of civil society, *unpolitical* man, inevitably appears, however, as the *natural* man. The *droits de l'homme* appear as *droits naturels,* because *conscious activity* is concentrated on the *political act. Egoistic* man is the *passive* result of the dissolved society, a result that is simply *found in existence,* an object of *immediate certainty,* therefore a *natural* object. The *political revolution* resolves civil life into its component parts, without *revolutionising* these components themselves or subjecting them to criticism. It regards civil society, the world of needs, labour, private interests, civil law, as the *basis of its existence,* as a *precondition* not requiring further substantiation and therefore as its *natural basis.* Finally, man as a member of civil society is held to be man *in the proper sense, homme* as distinct from the *citoyen,* because he is man in his sensuous, individual, *immediate* existence, whereas *political* man is only abstract, artificial man, man as an *allegorical, juridical* person. The real man is recognised only in the shape of the *egoistic* individual, the *true* man is recognised only in the shape of the *abstract citoyen.*

Therefore Rousseau correctly describes the abstract idea of political man as follows:

"Celui qui ose entreprendre d'instituer un peuple doit se sentir en état de *changer* pour ainsi dire la *nature humaine, de transformer* chaque individu, qui par lui-même est un tout parfait et solitaire, en *partie* d'un plus grand tout dont cet individu reçoive en quelque sorte sa vie et son être, de substituer une *existence partielle* et *morale* à l'existence physique et indépendante. Il faut qu'il ôte à *l'homme ses forces propres* pour lui en donner qui lui soient étrangères et dont il ne puisse faire usage sans le secours d'autrui."[a] (*Contrat Social,* livre II, Londres, 1782, p. 67.)

---

[a] "Whoever dares undertake to establish a people's institutions must feel himself capable of *changing,* as it were, *human nature,* of *transforming* each individual, who by himself is a complete and solitary whole, into a *part* of a larger whole, from which, in a sense, the individual receives his life and his being, of substituting a

All emancipation is a *reduction* of the human world and relationships to *man himself*.

Political emancipation is the reduction of man, on the one hand, to a member of civil society, to an *egoistic, independent* individual, and, on the other hand, to a *citizen,* a juridical person.

Only when the real, individual man re-absorbs in himself the abstract citizen, and as an individual human being has become a *species-being* in his everyday life, in his particular work, and in his particular situation, only when man has recognised and organised his "*forces propres*"[a] as *social* forces, and consequently no longer separates social power from himself in the shape of *political* power, only then will human emancipation have been accomplished.

II

"Die Fähigkeit der heutigen Juden und Christen, frei zu werden".
Von Bruno Bauer (*Einundzwanzig Bogen,* pp. 56-71).

It is in this form that Bauer deals with the relation between the *Jewish and the Christian religions,* and also with their relation to criticism. Their relation to criticism is their relation "to the capacity to become free".

The result arrived at is:

"The Christian has to surmount only one stage, namely, that of his religion, in order to give up religion altogether", and therefore to become free. "The Jew, on the other hand, has to break not only with his Jewish nature, but also with the development towards perfecting his religion, a development which has remained alien to him." (P. 71.)

Thus Bauer here transforms the question of Jewish emancipation into a purely religious question. The theological problem as to whether the Jew or the Christian has the better prospect of salvation is repeated here in the enlightened form: which of them is *more capable of emancipation.* No longer is the question asked: Is it Judaism or Christianity that makes a man free? On the contrary, the question is now: Which makes man freer, the negation of Judaism or the negation of Christianity?

"If the Jews want to become free, they should profess belief not in Christianity, but in the dissolution of Christianity, in the dissolution of religion in general, that is to say, in enlightenment, criticism and its consequence, free humanity." (P. 70.)

---

limited and *mental existence* for the physical and independent existence. He has to take from *man his own powers,* and give him in exchange alien powers which he cannot employ without the help of other men."—*Ed.*

[a] Own powers.—*Ed.*

For the Jew, it is still a matter of a *profession of faith,* but no longer a profession of belief in Christianity, but of belief in Christianity in dissolution.

Bauer demands of the Jews that they should break with the essence of the Christian religion, a demand which, as he says himself, does not arise out of the development of Judaism.

Since Bauer, at the end of his work on the Jewish question, had conceived Judaism only as crude religious criticism of Christianity, and therefore saw in it "merely" a religious significance, it could be foreseen that the emancipation of the Jews, too, would be transformed into a philosophical-theological act.

Bauer considers that the *ideal,* abstract nature of the Jew, his *religion,* is his *entire* nature. Hence he rightly concludes:

"The Jew contributes nothing to mankind if he himself disregards his narrow law", if he invalidates his entire Judaism. (P. 65.)

Accordingly the relation between Jews and Christians becomes the following: the sole interest of the Christian in the emancipation of the Jew is a general human interest, a *theoretical* interest. Judaism is a fact that offends the religious eye of the Christian. As soon as his eye ceases to be religious, this fact ceases to be offensive. The emancipation of the Jew is in itself not a task for the Christian.

The Jew, on the other hand, in order to emancipate himself, has to carry out not only his own work, but also that of the Christian, i.e., the *Kritik der Synoptiker* and *Das Leben Jesu,*[a] etc.

"It is up to them to deal with it: they themselves will decide their fate; but history is not to be trifled with." (P. 71.)

We are trying to break with the theological formulation of the question. For us, the question of the Jew's capacity for emancipation becomes the question: What particular *social* element has to be overcome in order to abolish Judaism? For the present-day Jew's capacity for emancipation is the relation of Judaism to the emancipation of the modern world. This relation necessarily results from the special position of Judaism in the contemporary enslaved world.

Let us consider the actual, worldly Jew, not the *Sabbath Jew,* as Bauer does, but the *everyday Jew.*

Let us not look for the secret of the Jew in his religion, but let us look for the secret of his religion in the real Jew.

What is the secular basis of Judaism? *Practical* need, *self-interest.*

---

[a] A reference to Bruno Bauer, *Kritik der evangelischen Geschichte der Synoptiker,* and David Friedrich Strauss, *Das Leben Jesu.—Ed.*

What is the worldly religion of the Jew? *Huckstering.* What is his worldly God? *Money.*

Very well then! Emancipation from *huckstering* and *money,* consequently from practical, real Judaism, would be the self-emancipation of our time.

An organisation of society which would abolish the preconditions for huckstering, and therefore the possibility of huckstering, would make the Jew impossible. His religious consciousness would be dissipated like a thin haze in the real, vital air of society. On the other hand, if the Jew recognises that this *practical* nature of his is futile and works to abolish it, he extricates himself from his previous development and works for *human emancipation* as such and turns against the *supreme practical* expression of human self-estrangement.

We recognise in Judaism, therefore, a general *anti-social* element of the *present time,* an element which through historical development—to which in this harmful respect the Jews have zealously contributed—has been brought to its present high level, at which it must necessarily begin to disintegrate.

In the final analysis, the *emancipation of the Jews* is the emancipation of mankind from *Judaism.*[a]

The Jew has already emancipated himself in a Jewish way.

"The Jew, who in Vienna, for example, is only tolerated, determines the fate of the whole Empire by his financial power. The Jew, who may have no rights in the smallest German state, decides the fate of Europe. While corporations and guilds refuse to admit Jews, or have not yet adopted a favourable attitude towards them, the audacity of industry mocks at the obstinacy of the medieval institutions." (Bruno Bauer, *Die Judenfrage,* p. 114.)

This is no isolated fact. The Jew has emancipated himself in a Jewish manner, not only because he has acquired financial power, but also because, through him and also apart from him, *money* has become a world power and the practical Jewish spirit has become the practical spirit of the Christian nations. The Jews have emancipated themselves insofar as the Christians have become Jews.

Captain Hamilton, for example, reports:

"The devout and politically free inhabitant of New England is a kind of *Laocoön* who makes not the least effort to escape from the serpents which are crushing him. *Mammon* is his idol which he adores not only with his lips but with the whole force of his body and mind. In his view the world is no more than a Stock Exchange, and he is convinced that he has no other destiny here below than to become richer

---

[a] Here and elsewhere in this article Marx evidently uses the words *Jude* and *Judentum* also in the figurative sense, i.e., denoting usury, huckstering, trading, etc.—*Ed.*

than his neighbour. Trade has seized upon all his thoughts, and he has no other recreation than to exchange objects. When he travels he carries, so to speak, his goods and his counter on his back and talks only of interest and profit. If he loses sight of his own business for an instant it is only in order to pry into the business of his competitors." [a]

Indeed, in North America the practical domination of Judaism over the Christian world has achieved as its unambiguous and normal expression that the *preaching of the Gospel* itself and the Christian ministry have become articles of trade, and the bankrupt trader deals in the Gospel just as the Gospel preacher who has become rich goes in for business deals.

> "*Tel que vous le voyez à la tête d'une congrégation respectable a commencé par être marchand; son commerce étant tombé, il s'est fait ministre; cet autre a débuté par le sacerdoce, mais dès qu'il a eu quelque somme d'argent à la disposition, il a laissé la chaire pour le négoce. Aux yeux d'un grand nombre, le ministère religieux est une véritable carrière industrielle.*" [b] (Beaumont, op. cit., pp. 185, 186.)

According to Bauer, it is

> "a fictitious state of affairs when in theory the Jew is deprived of political rights, whereas in practice he has immense power and exerts his political influence *en gros*, although it is curtailed *en détail*." (*Die Judenfrage*, p. 114.)

The contradiction that exists between the practical political power of the Jew and his political rights is the contradiction between politics and the power of money in general. Although theoretically the former is superior to the latter, in actual fact politics has become the serf of financial power.

Judaism has held its own *alongside* Christianity, not only as religious criticism of Christianity, not only as the embodiment of doubt in the religious derivation of Christianity, but equally because the practical-Jewish spirit, Judaism, has maintained itself and even attained its highest development in Christian society. The Jew, who exists as a distinct member of civil society, is only a particular manifestation of the Judaism of civil society.

Judaism continues to exist not in spite of history, but owing to history.

The Jew is perpetually created by civil society from its own entrails.

What, in itself, was the basis of the Jewish religion? Practical need, egoism.

---

[a] Hamilton, op. cit., Bd. I, S. 109-10.—*Ed.*

[b] "*The man who you see at the head of a respectable congregation began as a trader; his business having failed, he became a minister. The other began as a priest but as soon as he had some money at his disposal he left the pulpit to become a trader. In the eyes of very many people, the religious ministry is a veritable business career.*"—*Ed.*

The monotheism of the Jew, therefore, is in reality the polytheism of the many needs, a polytheism which makes even the lavatory an object of divine law. **Practical need, egoism**, is the principle of *civil society*, and as such appears in a pure form as soon as civil society has fully given birth to the political state. The god of *practical need and self-interest* is *money*.

Money is the jealous god of Israel, in face of which no other god may exist. Money degrades all the gods of man—and turns them into commodities. Money is the universal self-established *value* of all things. It has therefore robbed the whole world—both the world of men and nature—of its specific value. Money is the estranged essence of man's work and man's existence, and this alien essence dominates him, and he worships it.

The god of the Jews has become secularised and has become the god of the world. The bill of exchange is the real god of the Jew. His god is only an illusory bill of exchange.

The view of nature attained under the dominion of private property and money is a real contempt for and practical debasement of nature; in the Jewish religion nature exists, it is true, but it exists only in imagination.

It is in this sense that Thomas Münzer declares it intolerable

"that all creatures have been turned into property, the fishes in the water, the birds in the air, the plants on the earth; the creatures, too, must become free".[28]

Contempt for theory, art, history, and for man as an end in himself, which is contained in an abstract form in the Jewish religion, is the *real, conscious* standpoint, the virtue of the man of money. The species-relation itself, the relation between man and woman, etc., becomes an object of trade! The woman is bought and sold.

The *chimerical* nationality of the Jew is the nationality of the merchant, of the man of money in general.

The groundless[a] law of the Jew is only a religious caricature of groundless[a] morality and right in general, of the purely *formal* rites with which the world of self-interest surrounds itself.

Here, too, man's supreme relation is the *legal* one, his relation to laws that are valid for him not because they are laws of his own will and nature, but because they are the *dominant* laws and because departure from them is *avenged*.

Jewish Jesuitism, the same practical Jesuitism which Bauer

---

[a] In German a pun on the term *grund- und bodenlos*, which can mean "without land" or "without reason".—*Ed.*

discovers in the Talmud, is the relation of the world of self-interest to the laws governing that world, the chief art of which consists in the cunning circumvention of these laws.

Indeed, the movement of this world within its framework of laws is bound to be a continual suspension of law.

Judaism could not develop further as a *religion,* could not develop further theoretically, because the world outlook of practical need is essentially limited and is completed in a few strokes.

By its very nature, the religion of practical need could find its consummation not in theory, but only in *practice,* precisely because its truth is practice.

Judaism could not create a new world; it could only draw the new creations and conditions of the world into the sphere of its activity, because practical need, the rationale of which is self-interest, is passive and does not expand at will, but *finds* itself enlarged as a result of the continuous development of social conditions.

Judaism reaches its highest point with the perfection of civil society, but it is only in the *Christian* world that civil society attains perfection. Only under the dominance of Christianity, which makes *all* national, natural, moral, and theoretical conditions *extrinsic* to man, could civil society separate itself completely from the life of the state, sever all the species-ties of man, put egoism and selfish need in the place of these species-ties, and dissolve the human world into a world of atomistic individuals who are inimically opposed to one another.

Christianity sprang from Judaism. It has merged again in Judaism.

From the outset, the Christian was the theorising Jew, the Jew is therefore the practical Christian, and the practical Christian has become a Jew again.

Christianity had only in semblance overcome real Judaism. It was too *noble-minded,* too spiritualistic to eliminate the crudity of practical need in any other way than by elevation to the skies.

Christianity is the sublime thought of Judaism, Judaism is the common practical application of Christianity, but this application could only become general after Christianity as a developed religion had completed *theoretically* the estrangement of man from himself and from nature.

Only then could Judaism achieve universal dominance and make alienated man and alienated nature into *alienable,* vendible objects subjected to the slavery of egoistic need and to trading.

Selling is the practical aspect of alienation.[a] Just as man, as long as he is in the grip of religion, is able to objectify his essential nature only by turning it into something *alien*, something fantastic, so under the domination of egoistic need he can be active practically, and produce objects in practice, only by putting his products, and his activity, under the domination of an alien being, and bestowing the significance of an alien entity—money—on them.

In its perfected practice, Christian egoism of heavenly bliss is necessarily transformed into the corporal egoism of the Jew, heavenly need is turned into worldly need, subjectivism into self-interest. We explain the tenacity of the Jew not by his religion, but, on the contrary, by the human basis of his religion—practical need, egoism.

Since in civil society the real nature of the Jew has been universally realised and secularised, civil society could not convince the Jew of the *unreality* of his *religious* nature, which is indeed only the ideal aspect of practical need. Consequently, not only in the Pentateuch and the Talmud, but in present-day society we find the nature of the modern Jew, and not as an abstract nature but as one that is in the highest degree empirical, not merely as a narrowness of the Jew, but as the Jewish narrowness of society.

Once society has succeeded in abolishing the *empirical* essence of Judaism—huckstering and its preconditions—the Jew will have become *impossible*, because his consciousness no longer has an object, because the subjective basis of Judaism, practical need, has been humanised, and because the conflict between man's individual-sensuous existence and his species-existence has been abolished.

The *social* emancipation of the Jew is the *emancipation of society from Judaism*.

Written in the autumn of 1843　　　　Printed according to the journal
First published in the *Deutsch-Französische Jahrbücher*, 1844
Signed: *Karl Marx*

---

[a] In the German original *Veräusserung*, here rendered as "selling", and *Entäusserung*, as "alienation".—*Ed.*

CONTRIBUTION TO THE CRITIQUE OF HEGEL'S PHILOSOPHY OF LAW

Introduction [29]

For Germany the *criticism of religion* is in the main complete, and criticism of religion is the premise of all criticism.

The *profane* existence of error is discredited after its *heavenly oratio pro aris et focis*[a] has been disproved. Man, who looked for a superhuman being in the fantastic reality of heaven and found nothing there but the *reflection* of himself, will no longer be disposed to find but the *semblance* of himself, only an inhuman being, where he seeks and must seek his true reality.

The basis of irreligious criticism is: *Man makes religion,* religion does not make man. Religion is the self-consciousness and self-esteem of man who has either not yet found himself or has already lost himself again. But *man* is no abstract being encamped outside the world. Man is *the world of man,* the state, society. This state, this society, produce religion, an *inverted world-consciousness,* because they are an *inverted world.* Religion is the general theory of that world, its encyclopaedic compendium, its logic in a popular form, its spiritualistic *point d'honneur,* its enthusiasm, its moral sanction, its solemn complement, its universal source of consolation and justification. It is the *fantastic realisation* of the human essence because the *human essence* has no true reality. The struggle against religion is therefore indirectly a fight against *the world* of which religion is the spiritual *aroma.*

Religious distress is at the same time the *expression* of real distress and also the *protest* against real distress. Religion is the sigh of the oppressed creature, the heart of a heartless world, just as it is the spirit of spiritless conditions. It is the *opium* of the people.

---

[a] Speech for the altars and hearths.—*Ed.*

To abolish religion as the *illusory* happiness of the people is to demand their *real* happiness. The demand to give up illusions about the existing state of affairs is the *demand to give up a state of affairs which needs illusions*. The criticism of religion is therefore *in embryo the criticism of the vale of tears*, the *halo* of which is religion.

Criticism has torn up the imaginary flowers from the chain not so that man shall wear the unadorned, bleak chain but so that he will shake off the chain and pluck the living flower.[a] The criticism of religion disillusions man to make him think and act and shape his reality like a man who has been disillusioned and has come to reason, so that he will revolve round himself and therefore round his true sun. Religion is only the illusory sun which revolves round man as long as he does not revolve round himself.

The *task of history*, therefore, once the *world beyond the truth* has disappeared, is to establish the *truth of this world*. The immediate *task of philosophy*, which is at the service of history, once the *holy form* of human self-estrangement has been unmasked, is to unmask self-estrangement in its *unholy forms*. Thus the criticism of heaven turns into the criticism of the earth, the *criticism of religion* into the *criticism of law* and the *criticism of theology* into the *criticism of politics*.

The following exposition[30]—a contribution to that task—deals immediately not with the original, but with a copy, the German *philosophy* of state and of law, for no other reason than that it deals with *Germany*.

If one wanted to proceed from the *status quo* itself in Germany, even in the only appropriate way, i.e., negatively, the result would still be an *anachronism*. Even the negation of our political present is a reality already covered with dust in the historical lumber-room of modern nations. If I negate powdered pigtails, I am still left with unpowdered pigtails. If I negate the German state of affairs in 1843, then, according to the French computation of time, I am hardly in the year 1789, and still less in the focus of the present.

Yes, German history flatters itself with a movement which no people in the firmament of history went through before it or will go through after it. For we shared the restorations of the modern nations although we had not shared their revolutions. We underwent a restoration, first because other nations dared to carry out a revolution and second because other nations suffered a counter-revolution, the first time because our rulers were afraid, and the

---

[a] Cf. Karl Marx, "The Philosophical Manifesto of the Historical School of Law" (see this edition, Vol. 1, p. 205).—*Ed.*

second because our rulers were not afraid. We—and our shepherds first and foremost—never found ourselves in the company of freedom except once—on the *day of its burial.*

A school which legitimates the baseness of today by the baseness of yesterday, a school that declares rebellious every cry of the serf against the knout once that knout is a time-honoured, ancestral, historical one, a school to which history only shows its *posterior* as the God of Israel did to his servant Moses[a]—the *historical school of law*[31]—would hence have invented German history had it not been an invention of German history. For every pound of flesh cut from the heart of the people the historical school of law—Shylock, but Shylock the bondsman—swears on its bond, its historical bond, its Christian-Germanic bond.

Good-natured enthusiasts, Germanomaniacs by extraction and free-thinkers by reflection, on the contrary, seek our history of freedom beyond our history in the primeval Teutonic forests. But what difference is there between the history of our freedom and the history of the boar's freedom if it can be found only in the forests? Besides, it is common knowledge that the forest echoes back what you shout into it. So let us leave the ancient Teutonic forests in peace!

War on the German conditions! By all means! They are *below the level of history, beneath any criticism,* but they are still an object of criticism like the criminal who is below the level of humanity but still an object for the *executioner.* In the struggle against those conditions criticism is no passion of the head, it is the head of passion. It is not a lancet, it is a weapon. Its object is its *enemy,* which it wants not to refute but to *exterminate.* For the spirit of those conditions is refuted. In themselves they are not objects *worthy of thought,* but *phenomena* which are as despicable as they are despised. Criticism does not need to make things clear to itself as regards this subject-matter, for it has already dealt with it. Criticism appears no longer as an *end in itself,* but only as a *means.* Its essential sentiment is *indignation,* its essential activity is *denunciation.*

It is a case of describing the dull reciprocal pressure of all social spheres on one another, a general inactive ill humour, a limitedness which recognises itself as much as it misjudges itself, within the frame of a government system which, living on the preservation of all wretchedness, is itself nothing but *wretchedness in office.*

What a sight! This infinitely proceeding division of society into

---

[a] The Holy Bible, Exodus 33:23.—*Ed.*

the most manifold races opposed to one another by petty antipathies, uneasy consciences and brutal mediocrity, and which, precisely because of their reciprocal ambiguous and distrustful attitude, are all, without exception although with various formalities, treated by their *rulers* as *licensed existences*. And they must recognise and acknowledge as a *concession of heaven* the very fact that they are *mastered, ruled, possessed*! On the other side are the rulers themselves, whose greatness is in inverse proportion to their number!

Criticism dealing with this content is criticism in *hand-to-hand combat*, and in such a fight the point is not whether the opponent is a noble, equal, *interesting* opponent, the point is to *strike* him. The point is not to allow the Germans a minute for self-deception and resignation. The actual pressure must be made more pressing by adding to it consciousness of pressure, the shame must be made more shameful by publicising it. Every sphere of German society must be shown as the *partie honteuse*[a] of German society; these petrified relations must be forced to dance by singing their own tune to them! The people must be taught to be *terrified* at itself in order to give it *courage*. This will be fulfilling an imperative need of the German nation, and needs of the nations are in themselves the ultimate reason for their satisfaction.

This struggle against the limited content of the German *status quo* cannot be without interest even for the *modern* nations, for the German *status quo* is the *open completion of the ancien régime*, and the *ancien régime* is the *concealed deficiency of the modern state*. The struggle against the German political present is the struggle against the past of the modern nations, and they are still troubled by reminders of that past. It is instructive for them to see the *ancien régime*, which has been through its *tragedy* with them, playing its *comedy* as a German ghost. *Tragic* indeed was the history of the *ancien régime* so long as it was the pre-existing power of the world, and freedom, on the other hand, was a personal notion, i.e., as long as this regime believed and had to believe in its own justification. As long as the *ancien régime*, as an existing world order, struggled against a world that was only coming into being, there was on its side a historical error, not a personal one. That is why its downfall was tragic.

On the other hand, the present German regime, an anachronism, a flagrant contradiction of generally recognised axioms, the nothingness of the *ancien régime* exhibited to the world, only

---

[a] Shameful part.— *Ed.*

imagines that it believes in itself and demands that the world should imagine the same thing. If it believed in its own *essence*, would it try to hide that essence under the *semblance* of an alien essence and seek refuge in hypocrisy and sophism? The modern *ancien régime* is only the *comedian* of a world order whose *true heroes* are dead. History is thorough and goes through many phases when carrying an old form to the grave. The last phase of a world-historical form is its *comedy*. The gods of Greece, already tragically wounded to death in Aeschylus' *Prometheus Bound*, had to re-die a comic death in Lucian's *Dialogues*. Why this course of history? So that humanity should part with its past *cheerfully*. This *cheerful* historical destiny is what we vindicate for the political authorities of Germany.

However, once *modern* politico-social reality itself is subjected to criticism, once criticism rises to truly human problems, it finds itself outside the German *status quo* or else it would reach out for its object *below* its object. An example. The relation of industry, of the world of wealth generally, to the political world is one of the major problems of modern times. In what form is this problem beginning to engage the attention of the Germans? In the form of *protective duties*, of the *prohibitive system*, of *national economy*. Germanomania has passed out of man into matter, and thus one morning our cotton barons and iron champions saw themselves turned into patriots. People are therefore beginning in Germany to acknowledge the sovereignty of monopoly within the country by lending it *sovereignty abroad*. People are thus about to begin in Germany with what people in France and England are about to end. The old corrupt condition against which these countries are rebelling in theory and which they only bear as one bears chains is greeted in Germany as the dawn of a beautiful future which still hardly dares to pass from *cunning*[a] theory to the most ruthless practice. Whereas the problem in France and England is: *Political economy* or the *rule of society over wealth*, in Germany it is: *National economy* or the *mastery of private property over nationality*. In France and England, then, it is a case of abolishing monopoly that has proceeded to its last consequences; in Germany it is a case of proceeding to the last consequences of monopoly. There it is a case of solution, here as yet a case of collision. This is an adequate example of the *German* form of modern problems, an example of how our history, like a clumsy recruit, still has to do extra drill in matters that are old and hackneyed in history.

[a] In the German *listig*, probably an allusion to Friedrich List, who was an advocate of protectionism.—*Ed.*

If therefore the *whole* German development did not exceed the German *political* development, a German could at the most participate in the problems of the present to the same extent as a *Russian* can. But, if the separate individual is not bound by the limitations of the nation, still less is the nation as a whole liberated by the liberation of one individual. The fact that Greece had a Scythian[a] among its philosophers did not help the Scythians to make a single step towards Greek culture.

Luckily we Germans are not Scythians.

As the ancient peoples went through their pre-history in imagination, in *mythology*, so we Germans have gone through our post-history in thought, in *philosophy*. We are *philosophical* contemporaries of the present without being its *historical* contemporaries. German philosophy is the *ideal prolongation* of German history. If therefore, instead of the *œuvres incomplètes* of our real history, we criticise the *œuvres posthumes* of our ideal history, *philosophy*, our criticism is among the questions of which the present says: *That is the question.*[b] What in advanced nations is a *practical* break with modern political conditions, is in Germany, where even those conditions do not yet exist, at first a *critical* break with the philosophical reflection of those conditions.

German philosophy of law and state is the only *German history* which is *al pari* with the *official* modern reality. The German nation must therefore take into account not only its present conditions but also its dream-history, and subject to criticism not only these existing conditions but at the same time their abstract continuation. Its future cannot be *limited* either to the immediate negation of its real conditions of state and law or to the immediate implementation of its ideal state and legal conditions, for it has the immediate negation of its real conditions in its ideal conditions, and it has almost *outlived* the immediate implementation of its ideal conditions in the contemplation of neighbouring nations. Hence it is with good reason that the *practical* political party in Germany[32] demands the *negation of philosophy*. It is wrong, not in its demand, but in stopping at the demand, which it neither seriously implements nor can implement. It believes that it implements that negation by turning its back on philosophy and with averted face muttering a few trite and angry phrases about it. Owing to the limitation of its outlook it does not include philosophy in the circle of *German* reality or it even fancies it is *beneath* German practice and the theories that serve it. You demand that *real living germs*

---

[a] Anacharsis.—*Ed.*
[b] This sentence is in English in the original.—*Ed.*

be made the starting point but you forget that the real living germ of the German nation has grown so far only inside its *cranium*. In a word—*you cannot supersede philosophy without making it a reality.*

The same mistake, but with the factors *reversed*, was made by the *theoretical* political party originating from philosophy.[33]

In the present struggle it saw *only the critical struggle of philosophy against the German world*; it did not give a thought to the fact that the *hitherto prevailing philosophy* itself belongs to this world and is its *complement*, although an ideal one. Critical towards its adversary, it was uncritical towards itself when, proceeding from the *premises* of philosophy, it either stopped at the results given by philosophy or passed off demands and results from somewhere else as immediate demands and results of philosophy, although these, provided they are justified, can be obtained only by the *negation of hitherto existing philosophy*, of philosophy as such. We reserve ourselves the right to a more detailed description of this party. Its basic deficiency may be reduced to the following: *It thought it could make philosophy a reality without superseding it.*

The criticism of the *German philosophy of state and law,* which attained its most consistent, richest and final formulation through *Hegel,* is both a critical analysis of the modern state and of the reality connected with it, and the resolute negation of the whole *German political and legal consciousness* as *practised* hitherto, the most distinguished, most universal expression of which, raised to the level of a *science*, is the *speculative philosophy of law* itself. If the speculative philosophy of law, that abstract extravagant *thinking* on the modern state, the reality of which remains a thing of the beyond, if only beyond the Rhine, was possible only in Germany, inversely the *German* thought-image of the modern state which disregards *real man* was possible only because and insofar as the modern state itself disregards *real man* or satisfies the *whole* of man only in imagination. In politics the Germans *thought* what other nations *did*. Germany was their *theoretical consciousness*. The abstraction and conceit of its thought always kept in step with the one-sidedness and stumpiness of its reality. If therefore the *status quo of German statehood* expresses the *perfection of the ancien régime*, the perfection of the thorn in the flesh of the modern state, the *status quo of German political theory* expresses the *imperfection of the modern state,* the defectiveness of its flesh itself.

Even as the resolute opponent of the previous form of *German* political consciousness the criticism of speculative philosophy of law turns, not towards itself, but towards *problems* which can only be solved by one means—*practice*.

It is asked: can Germany attain a practice *à la hauteur des principes*, i. e., a *revolution* which will raise it not only to the *official level* of the modern nations but to the *height of humanity* which will be the near future of those nations?

The weapon of criticism cannot, of course, replace criticism by weapons, material force must be overthrown by material force; but theory also becomes a material force as soon as it has gripped the masses. Theory is capable of gripping the masses as soon as it demonstrates *ad hominem*, and it demonstrates *ad hominem* as soon as it becomes radical. To be radical is to grasp the root of the matter. But for man the root is man himself. The evident proof of the radicalism of German theory, and hence of its practical energy, is that it proceeds from a resolute *positive* abolition of religion. The criticism of religion ends with the teaching that *man is the highest being for man*, hence with the *categorical imperative to overthrow all relations* in which man is a debased, enslaved, forsaken, despicable being, relations which cannot be better described than by the exclamation of a Frenchman when it was planned to introduce a tax on dogs: Poor dogs! They want to treat you like human beings!

Even historically, theoretical emancipation has specific practical significance for Germany. For Germany's *revolutionary* past is theoretical, it is the *Reformation*. As the revolution then began in the brain of the *monk*, so now it begins in the brain of the *philosopher*.

Luther, we grant, overcame the bondage of *piety* by replacing it by the bondage of *conviction*. He shattered faith in authority because he restored the authority of faith. He turned priests into laymen because he turned laymen into priests. He freed man from outer religiosity because he made religiosity the inner man. He freed the body from chains because he enchained the heart.

But if Protestantism was not the true solution it was at least the true setting of the problem. It was no longer a case of the layman's struggle against the *priest outside himself* but of his struggle against his *own priest inside himself*, his *priestly nature*. And if the Protestant transformation of the German laymen into priests emancipated the lay popes, the *princes*, with the whole of their priestly clique, the privileged and philistines, the philosophical transformation of priestly Germans into men will emancipate the *people*. But *secularisation* will not stop at the *pillaging of churches* practised mainly by hypocritical Prussia any more than emancipation stops at princes. The Peasant War, the most radical fact of German history, came to grief because of theology. Today, when theology itself has come to grief, the most unfree fact of German history, our *status quo*, will be shattered against philosophy. On the eve of the Reformation official Germany was the most unconditional slave of Rome. On the eve of its revolution it is the unconditional slave of less than Rome, of Prussia and Austria, of country squires and philistines.

A major difficulty, however, seems to stand in the way of a *radical* German revolution.

For revolutions require a *passive* element, a *material* basis. Theory can be realised in a people only insofar as it is the realisation of the needs of that people. But will the enormous discrepancy between the demands of German thought and the answers of German reality be matched by a corresponding discrepancy between civil society and the state and between civil society and itself? Will the theoretical needs be immediate practical needs? It is not enough for thought to strive for realisation, reality must itself strive towards thought.

But Germany did not go through the intermediary stages of political emancipation at the same time as the modern nations. It has not even reached in practice the stages which it has overtaken in theory. How can it do a *somersault*, not only over its own limitations, but at the same time over the limitations of the modern nations, over limitations which in reality it must feel and strive for as bringing emancipation from its real limitations? Only a revolution of radical needs can be a radical revolution and it seems that for this the preconditions and ground are lacking.

If however Germany has accompanied the development of the modern nations only with the abstract activity of thought without playing an effective role in the real struggle of that development, it has, on the other hand, shared the *sufferings* of that development, without sharing in its enjoyment or its partial satisfaction. To abstract activity on the one hand corresponds abstract suffering on the other. That is why Germany will one day find itself on the level of European decadence before ever having been on the level of European emancipation. It will be comparable to a *fetish worshipper* pining away with the diseases of Christianity.

If we now consider the *German governments* we find that because of the existing state of affairs, because of Germany's condition, because of the standpoint of German education and finally under the impulse of their own fortunate instinct, they are driven to combine the *civilised shortcomings of the modern political world*, the advantages of which we do not enjoy, with the *barbaric deficiencies of the ancien régime*, which we enjoy in full; hence Germany must share more and more, if not in the reasonableness, at least in the unreasonableness of those state formations which are beyond the bounds of its *status quo*. Is there in the world, for example, a country which shares so naively in all the illusions of the constitutional state without sharing in its realities as so-called constitutional Germany? And was it not perforce a German government's idea to combine the tortures of censorship with the tortures of the French September laws which presuppose freedom of the press?[34] As you could find the *gods* of all nations in the Roman Pantheon, so you will find in the Germans' Holy Roman Empire all the *sins* of all political forms.[35] That this eclecticism will reach a height never dreamt of before is guaranteed in particular by the *political-aesthetic gourmandising* of a German king[a] who intends to play all the roles of monarchy, whether feudal or bureaucratic, absolute or constitutional, autocratic or democratic, if not in the person of the people, at least in his *own* person, and if not for the people, at least for *himself*. *Germany, as the deficiency of the political present constituted as a particular world*, will not be able to throw down the specific German limitations without throwing down the general limitation of the political present.

It is not the *radical* revolution, not the *general human* emancipation which is a utopian dream for Germany, but rather the partial, the *merely* political revolution, the revolution which leaves the pillars of the house standing. On what is a partial, a merely political revolution based? On the fact that *part of civil society* emancipates itself and attains *general* domination; on the fact that a definite class, proceeding from its *particular situation*, undertakes the general emancipation of society. This class emancipates the whole of society but only provided the whole of society is in the same situation as this class, e.g., possesses money and education or can acquire them at will.

No class of civil society can play this role without arousing a moment of enthusiasm in itself and in the masses, a moment in which it fraternises and merges with society in general, becomes confused with it and is perceived and acknowledged as its *general representative*; a moment in which its demands and rights are truly the rights and demands of society itself; a moment in which it is truly the social head and the social heart. Only in the name of the general rights of society can a particular class lay claim to general domination. For the storming of this emancipatory position, and hence for the political exploitation of all spheres of society in the

---

[a] Frederick William IV.— *Ed.*

interests of its own sphere, revolutionary energy and intellectual self-confidence alone are not sufficient. For the *revolution of a nation* and the *emancipation of a particular class* of civil society to coincide, for *one* estate to be acknowledged as the estate of the whole society, all the defects of society must conversely be concentrated in another class, a particular estate must be the general stumbling-block, the incorporation of the general limitation, a particular social sphere must be looked upon as the *notorious crime* of the whole of society, so that liberation from that sphere appears as general self-liberation. For *one* estate to be *par excellence* the estate of liberation, another estate must conversely be the obvious estate of oppression. The negative general significance of the French nobility and the French clergy determined the positive general significance of the immediately adjacent and opposed class of the *bourgeoisie*.

But no particular class in Germany has the consistency, the severity, the courage or the ruthlessness that could mark it out as the negative representative of society. No more has any estate the breadth of soul that identifies itself, even for a moment, with the soul of the nation, the genius that inspires material might to political violence, or that revolutionary audacity which flings at the adversary the defiant words: *I am nothing and I should be everything.* The main stem of German morals and honesty, of the classes as well as of individuals, is rather that *modest egoism* which asserts its limitedness and allows it to be asserted against itself. The relation of the various sections of German society is therefore not dramatic but epic. Each of them begins to be aware of itself and to settle down beside the others with all its particular claims not as soon as it is oppressed, but as soon as the circumstances of the time, without the section's own participation, create a social substratum on which it can in turn exert pressure. Even the *moral self-confidence of the German middle class* rests only on the consciousness that it is the general representative of the philistine mediocrity of all the other classes. It is therefore not only the German kings who accede to the throne *mal à propos*; every section of civil society goes through a defeat before it has celebrated victory, develops its own limitations before it has overcome the limitations facing it and asserts its narrow-hearted essence before it has been able to assert its magnanimous essence. Thus the very opportunity of a great role has on every occasion passed away before it is to hand, thus every class, once it begins the struggle against the class above it, is involved in the struggle against the class below it. Hence the princes are struggling against the monarchy, the bureaucrats against the nobility, and the bourgeois against them all, while the proletariat is already beginning to struggle against the bourgeoisie. No sooner does the middle class dare to think of emancipation from its own standpoint than the development of the social conditions and the progress of political theory pronounce that standpoint antiquated or at least problematic.

In France it is enough for somebody to be something for him to want to be everything; in Germany one has to be nothing if one is not to forego everything. In France partial emancipation is the basis of universal emancipation; in Germany universal emancipation is the *conditio sine qua non* of any partial emancipation. In France it is the reality of gradual liberation, in Germany the impossibility of gradual liberation, that must give birth to complete freedom. In France every class is *politically idealistic* and becomes aware of itself at first not as a particular class but as the representative of social requirements generally. The role of *emancipator* therefore passes in dramatic motion to the various classes of the French nation one after the other until it finally comes to the class which implements social freedom no longer on the basis of certain conditions lying outside man and yet created by human society, but rather organises all conditions of human existence on the presupposition of social freedom. In Germany, on the contrary, where practical life is as spiritless as spiritual life is unpractical, no class in civil society has any need or capacity for general emancipation until it is forced by its *immediate* condition, by *material* necessity, by its *very chains*.

Where, then, is the *positive* possibility of a German emancipation?

Answer: In the formation of a class with *radical chains*, a class of civil society which is not a class of civil society, an estate which is the dissolution of all estates, a sphere which has a universal character by its universal suffering and claims no *particular right* because no *particular wrong* but *wrong generally* is perpetrated against it; which can no longer invoke a *historical* but only a *human* title; which does not stand in any one-sided antithesis to the consequences but in an all-round antithesis to the premises of the German state; a sphere, finally, which cannot emancipate itself without emancipating itself from all other spheres of society and thereby emancipating all other spheres of society, which, in a word, is the *complete loss* of man and hence can win itself only through the *complete rewinning of man*. This dissolution of society as a particular estate is the *proletariat*.

The proletariat is coming into being in Germany only as a result of the rising *industrial* development. For it is not the *naturally arising* poor but the *artificially impoverished*, not the human masses mechanically oppressed by the gravity of society but the masses resulting from the *drastic dissolution* of society, mainly of the middle estate, that form the proletariat, although it is obvious that gradually the naturally arising poor and the Christian-Germanic serfs also join its ranks.

By proclaiming the *dissolution of the hitherto existing world order* the proletariat merely states the *secret of its own existence,* for it *is in fact* the dissolution of that world order. By demanding the *negation of private property*, the proletariat merely raises to the rank of a *principle of society* what society has made the principle of the *proletariat,* what, without its own co-operation, is already incorporated in *it* as the negative result of society. In regard to the world which is coming into being the proletarian then finds himself possessing the same right as the *German king* in regard to the world which has come into being when he calls the people *his* people as he calls the horse *his* horse. By declaring the people his private property the king simply states that the property owner is king.

As philosophy finds its *material* weapons in the proletariat, so the proletariat finds its *spiritual* weapons in philosophy. And once the lightning of thought has squarely struck this ingenuous soil of the people the emancipation of the *Germans* into *human beings* will take place.

Let us sum up the result:

The only *practically* possible liberation of Germany is liberation that proceeds from the standpoint of *the* theory which proclaims man to be the highest being for man. In Germany emancipation from the *Middle Ages* is possible only as emancipation from the *partial* victories over the Middle Ages as well. In Germany *no* kind of bondage can be broken without breaking *every* kind of bondage. The *thorough* Germany cannot make a revolution without making a *thoroughgoing* revolution. The *emancipation of the German* is the *emancipation of the human being.* The *head* of this emancipation is *philosophy,* its *heart* is the *proletariat.* Philosophy cannot be made a reality without the abolition of the proletariat, the proletariat cannot be abolished without philosophy being made a reality.

When all inner requisites are fulfilled the *day of German resurrection* will be proclaimed by the *ringing call of the Gallic cock.*

Written at the end of 1843-January 1844   Printed according to the journal
First published in the *Deutsch-Französische Jahrbücher,* 1844
Signed: *Karl Marx*

LETTER TO THE EDITOR OF THE
ALLGEMEINE ZEITUNG (AUGSBURG)

The diverse rumours which have been spread by German newspapers concerning the discontinuation of the *Deutsch-Französische Jahrbücher* impel me to state that the Swiss publishers of the *Jahrbücher* suddenly withdrew from this enterprise for economic reasons and thus made impossible the continuation of this journal for the time being.[36]

Paris, April 14, 1844

Karl Marx

First published in the *Allgemeine Zeitung*, Augsburg, No. 3, April 20, 1844

Printed according to the newspaper

Published in English for the first time

CRITICAL MARGINAL NOTES ON THE ARTICLE
"THE KING OF PRUSSIA AND SOCIAL REFORM.
BY A PRUSSIAN" *[37]

(*Vorwärts!* No. 60)

[*Vorwärts!* No. 63, August 7, 1844]

No. 60 of *Vorwärts* contains an article headed "Der König von Preussen und die Sozialreform", signed *"A Prussian"*.

First of all this alleged Prussian sets out the content of the royal Prussian Cabinet order on the *uprising of the Silesian workers* and the opinion of the French newspaper *La Réforme* on the Prussian Cabinet order.[38] The *Réforme*, he writes, considers that the King's *"alarm* and *religious feeling"* are the source of the Cabinet order. It even sees in this document a *presentiment* of the great reforms which are in prospect for bourgeois society. The "Prussian" lectures the *Réforme* as follows:

"The King and German society has not yet arrived at the 'presentiment of their reform',** even the Silesian and Bohemian uprisings have not aroused this feeling. It is impossible to make such an *unpolitical* country as Germany regard the *partial* distress of the factory districts as a matter of general concern, let alone as an affliction of the whole civilised world. The Germans regard this event as if it were of the same nature as any *local* distress due to flood or famine. Hence the King regards it as due to *deficiencies in the administration or in charitable activity.* For this reason, and because a few soldiers sufficed to cope with the feeble weavers, the destruction of factories and machinery, too, did not inspire any *'alarm'* either in the King or the authorities. Indeed, the Cabinet order was not prompted even by *religious feeling*: it is a very sober expression of the Christian art of statesmanship

---

* Special reasons prompt me to state that the present article is the first which I have contributed to *Vorwärts*. K. M.

** Note the stylistic and grammatical lack of sense. "The King of Prussia and society *has* not yet arrived at the presentiment of *their* (to whom does this *"their"* relate?) reform".— *Note by Marx.*

and of a doctrine which considers that no difficulties can withstand its sole medicine—'the well-disposed Christian hearts'. Poverty and crime are two great evils; who can cure them? The state and the authorities? No, but the union of all Christian hearts can."

The alleged Prussian denies the King's "*alarm*" on the grounds, among others, that a few soldiers sufficed to cope with the feeble weavers.

Therefore, in a country where ceremonial dinners with liberal toasts and liberally foaming champagne—recall the Düsseldorf festival—inspired a royal Cabinet order[39]; where *not a single* soldier was needed to shatter the desires of the *entire* liberal bourgeoisie for freedom of the press and a constitution; in a country where passive obedience is the order of the day—can it be that in such a country the necessity to employ armed force against feeble weavers is *not an event*, and not an *alarming* event? Moreover, at the first encounter the feeble weavers were victorious. They were suppressed only by subsequent troop reinforcements. Is the uprising of a body of workers less dangerous because it did not require a whole army to suppress it? Let the wise Prussian compare the uprising of the Silesian weavers with the revolts of the English workers, and the Silesian weavers will be seen by him to be *strong* weavers.

Starting out from the *general* relation of *politics* to *social ills*, we shall show why the uprising of the weavers could not cause the King any special "*alarm*". For the time being we shall say only the following: the uprising was not aimed directly against the King of Prussia, but against the bourgeoisie. As an aristocrat and absolute monarch, the King of Prussia cannot love the bourgeoisie; still less can he be alarmed if the submissiveness and impotence of the bourgeoisie is increased because of a tense and difficult relationship between it and the proletariat. Further: the orthodox Catholic is more hostile to the orthodox Protestant than to the atheist, just as the Legitimist is more hostile to the liberal than to the Communist. This is not because the atheist and the Communist are more akin to the Catholic or Legitimist, but because they are more foreign to him than are the Protestant and the liberal, being *outside* his circle. In the sphere of politics, the King of Prussia, as a politician, has his direct opposite in liberalism. For the King, the proletariat is as little an antithesis as the King is for the proletariat. The proletariat would have to have already attained considerable power for it to stifle the other antipathies and political antitheses and to divert to itself all political enmity. Finally: in view of the well-known character of the King, avid for anything *interesting* and *significant*, it must have been a joyful surprise for him to discover this *"interesting"* and *"much discussed" pauperism* in his own territory and consequently a new opportunity for making people talk about him. How pleasant for him must have been the news that henceforth he possesses his *"own"*, royal Prussian *pauperism!*

Our *"Prussian"* is still more unlucky when he seeks to *deny* that *"religious feeling"* is the source of the royal Cabinet order.

Why is religious feeling not the source of this order? Because it is a "very *sober* expression of the Christian art of statesmanship", a *"sober"* expression of the doctrine which "considers that no difficulties can withstand its sole medicine — the well-disposed Christian hearts".

Is not *religious feeling* the source of the *Christian* art of statesmanship? Is a doctrine that has its panacea in the well-disposed *Christian hearts* not based on religious feeling? Does a *sober* expression of religious feeling cease to be an expression of religious feeling? Moreover, I maintain that it is a very *intoxicated* religious feeling with an extremely high opinion of itself which denies that the *"state and the authorities"* can *"cure great evils"* and seeks their cure in the *"union of Christian hearts"*. It is a very *intoxicated* religious feeling which — as the "Prussian" himself admits — sees the whole evil in the lack of Christian feeling and therefore refers the authorities to *"admonition"* as the only means of strengthening this feeling. According to the "Prussian", the *Christian frame of mind* is the aim of the Cabinet order. When it is intoxicated, when it is not sober, religious feeling, as a matter of course, considers itself the only good. Wherever it sees evils it ascribes them to *absence* of religious feeling, for if the latter is the only good, then it alone can produce what is good. Hence the Cabinet order, being dictated by religious feeling, consistently prescribes religious feeling. A politician with a *sober* religious feeling would not in his "perplexity" seek "aid" in the "pious preacher's admonition about a Christian frame of mind".

How then does the alleged Prussian prove in the *Réforme* that the Cabinet order is not a product of religious feeling? He does so precisely by everywhere depicting the Cabinet order as a product of religious feeling. Can one expect from such an *illogical* brain an insight into social movements? Listen to him *chatting* about the attitude of *German society* to the workers' movement and to social reform in general.

Let us *distinguish* — which the "Prussian" neglects to do — the different categories contained in the expression *"German society"*: the Government, the bourgeoisie, the press and, finally, the workers themselves. These are the *different* masses with which we are concerned here. The "Prussian" lumps all these masses together and, from his lofty stand, passes sentence on them *en bloc*. *German society*, in his opinion, "has not yet arrived even at the *presentiment* of their reform".

Why does German society lack this instinct?

"It is impossible to make such an *unpolitical* country as Germany," replies the Prussian, "regard the *partial* distress of the factory districts as a *matter of general concern*, let alone as an affliction of the whole civilised world. The Germans regard this event as if it were of the same nature as any *local* distress due to flood or famine. Hence the King regards it as due to *deficiencies in the administration* and *in charitable activity.*"

Thus the "Prussian" explains this *misinterpretation* of the distressed state of the workers as due to the *special character* of an *unpolitical* country.

It will be admitted that England is a *political* country. It will be admitted also that England is the *country of pauperism*, even the word itself is of English origin. Observing the state of things in England, therefore, is the surest means of learning the *attitude* of a *political* country to *pauperism*. In England, the distress of the workers is not *partial* but *universal*; it is not restricted to the factory districts, but extends to the rural districts. The movements here are not just beginning to arise, for almost a century they have periodically recurred.

What then is the view about *pauperism* held by the *English* bourgeoisie and the government and press connected with it?

Insofar as the English bourgeoisie acknowledges that *politics are to blame* for pauperism, the *Whig* regards the *Tory*, and the *Tory* regards the *Whig*, as the cause of pauperism. According to the Whig, the main source of pauperism is the monopoly of big landownership and the prohibitive legislation against the import of corn.[40] According to the Tory, the whole evil lies in liberalism, in competition, and in the excessive development of the factory system. Neither of the parties sees the cause in politics in general, but each sees it only in the politics of the opposing party; neither party even dreams of a reform of society.

The most definite expression of the English view of pauperism—we are speaking always of the view of the English bourgeoisie and government—is *English political economy*, i.e., the scientific reflection of English economic conditions.

One of the best and most famous English economists, McCulloch—a pupil of the cynical Ricardo—who is familiar with present-day conditions and ought to have a comprehensive view of the movement of bourgeois society, still dares in a public lecture, and with applause from the audience, to apply to political economy what *Bacon* says about philosophy:

> "The man who, with true and untiring wisdom, suspends his judgment, who goes forward step by step, surmounting one after the other the obstacles which, like mountains, hinder the course of study, will eventually reach the summit of science, where peace and pure air may be enjoyed, where nature presents itself to the eye in all its beauty, and from where it is possible to descend by a comfortably sloping path to the last details of practice."[41]

Good *pure air* — the pestilential atmosphere of English cellar dwellings! Great *beauty of nature* — the fantastic rags worn by the English poor, and the flabby, shrunken flesh of the women, undermined by labour and poverty; children crawling about in the dirt; deformity resulting from excessive labour in the monotonous mechanical operations of the factories! The most delightful *last details of practice*: prostitution, murder and the gallows!

Even that part of the English bourgeoisie which is impressed by the danger of pauperism conceives this danger, as also the means to remedy it, not merely in a *partial* way, but also, frankly speaking, in a *childish* and *stupid* way.

Thus Dr. *Kay*, for example, in his pamphlet *Recent Measures for the Promotion of Education in England* reduces everything to *neglected education*. Guess why! Owing to lack of education, the worker does not understand the *"natural laws of trade"*, laws which *necessarily* reduce him to pauperism. That is why he rebels. This could

> "*affect the prosperity* of English manufactures and English commerce, shake the mutual confidence of mercantile men, and *diminish* the *stability* of political and social institutions."[42]

So great is the mental vacuity of the English bourgeoisie and its press on the subject of pauperism, this national epidemic of England.

Let us suppose then that the reproaches our "Prussian" levels against *German* society are well founded. Does the reason lie in the *unpolitical* condition of Germany? But if the bourgeoisie of *unpolitical* Germany is unable to see that a *partial* distress is a matter of general significance, the bourgeoisie of *political* England, on the other hand, manages to misunderstand the general significance of a universal state of distress — a distress the general significance of which has been made evident partly by its periodical recurrence in time, partly by its extension in space, and partly by the failure of all attempts to remedy it.

Further, the "Prussian" makes the *unpolitical* condition of Germany responsible for the fact that the *King* of Prussia finds the cause of pauperism in *deficiencies in the administration and in charitable activity* and therefore seeks the means to counter pauperism in *administrative* and *charitable measures*.

Is this kind of view peculiar to the King of Prussia? Let us take a quick look at England, the only country where large-scale *political* action against pauperism can be said to have taken place.

The present English legislation on the poor dates from the Poor Law enacted in the 43rd year of the reign of Elizabeth.* What are the means adopted in this legislation? They consist in the obligation of the parishes to support their poor labourers, in the poor rate, and in legal charity. This legislation — charity carried out by administrative means — has lasted for two centuries. What attitude do we find adopted by Parliament, after long and painful experience, in its Amendment Bill of 1834?

First of all, it explains the frightful increase of pauperism by *"deficiencies in the administration"*.

Consequently, the administration of the poor rate, which was in the hands of officials of each of the parishes, is reformed. *Unions* are formed of about 20 parishes which are united in a single administration. A committee of officials, a Board of Guardians,[a] consisting of officials elected by the taxpayers, meets on an appointed day in the administrative centre of the Union and decides on the admissibility of relief. These Boards of Guardians are directed and supervised by government representatives sitting in a Central Commission at Somerset House, the *Ministry of Pauperism*, as a Frenchman[b] aptly calls it. The capital supervised by this administration is almost equal to the amount which the military administration in France costs. It employs 500 local administrative bodies, and each of these in its turn has at least 12 officials working for it.

The English Parliament did not restrict itself to a *formal* reform of the administration.

It found the main source of the *acute* state of English pauperism in the *Poor Law* itself. Charity, the means prescribed by law against the social malady, is alleged to promote the social malady. As far as pauperism *in general* is concerned, it is said to be an *eternal law of nature*, according to the theory of *Malthus*:

"Since population is constantly tending to overtake the means of subsistence, charity is folly, a public encouragement of poverty. The state can therefore do

* For our purpose it is not necessary to go back to the Statute of Labourers under *Edward* III.— *Note by Marx*.

[a] The words "Board of Guardians" are in English in the manuscript.— *Ed*.
[b] Eugène Buret.— *Ed*.

nothing but leave the poor to their fate and, at the most, make death easy for them."

With this philanthropic theory the English Parliament combines the view that pauperism is *poverty which the workers have brought upon themselves by their own fault,* and therefore it is not a misfortune which must be prevented, but rather a crime which has to be suppressed and punished.

Thus there arose the system of workhouses,[a] i. e., houses for the poor, the internal organisation of which tends to *deter* the poor wretches from seeking refuge in them from death by starvation. In the workhouses, charity is cunningly combined with *revenge* of the bourgeoisie on the poor who appeal to its charity.

At first, therefore, England tried to abolish pauperism by *charity* and *administrative measures.* Then it came to see in the progressive advance of pauperism not the inevitable consequence of modern *industry* but, on the contrary, the consequence of the *English poor rate.* It regarded the universal distress merely as a *specific feature* of English legislation. What was previously ascribed to a *lack of charity* now began to be attributed to an *excess of charity.* Finally, poverty came to be regarded as the fault of the poor themselves, and consequently they were punished for it.

The general significance which pauperism has acquired in *political* England is restricted to the fact that in the course of its development, in spite of all the administrative measures, pauperism has become a *national institution* and has therefore inevitably become the object of a ramified and widely extended administration, but an administration which *no longer* has the task of abolishing pauperism but of *disciplining* it, of perpetuating it. This administration has given up trying to stop pauperism at its source by *positive* methods; it is satisfied to dig a grave for it with policeman-like gentleness whenever it wells up to the surface of the official world. Far from going beyond administrative and charitable measures, the English state has taken a big step backwards from them. Its administration now extends only to *that* pauperism which is so desperate as to allow itself to be caught and locked up.

So far, therefore, the "Prussian" has not shown that there is anything *original* in the course adopted by the King of Prussia. But *why,* exclaims our great man with *rare naivety,*

"why does the King of Prussia *not at once issue a decree for the education of all uncared-for children?"*

---

[a] This word is here and further on given in English in the original.—*Ed.*

Why does he first turn to the authorities and await their plans and proposals?

Our super-clever "Prussian" will be reassured when he learns that the King of Prussia is as little original in this matter as in all his other actions, and that the course he has taken is even the only possible one a head of state *can* take.

Napoleon wanted to abolish mendicancy at a stroke. He charged his official bodies with the preparation of plans for *eradicating mendicancy* throughout France. The drawing-up of a project dragged on. Napoleon lost patience. He wrote to Crétet, his Minister of Internal Affairs, ordering him to abolish mendicancy within one month. Napoleon said:

> "One ought not to traverse this earth without leaving behind traces which would earn us the grateful memory of posterity. Do not ask me for another three or four months for collecting information. You have young judges, wise prefects, well-trained engineers from the department for roads and bridges; set them all in motion, do not go to sleep in performing ordinary office work."[a]

Within a few months everything was done. On July 5, 1808, the law abolishing mendicancy was promulgated. How? By means of the *dépôts*,[b] which so quickly became converted into punitive institutions that very soon the poor entered them only by order of the *police-court*. Nevertheless M. Noailles du Gard, a member of the Legislative Corps, exclaimed at the time:

> "Eternal gratitude to the hero who gave a refuge to those in need, and means of subsistence to the poor. Children will no longer be left to their fate; poor families will no longer be deprived of a source of sustenance, and the workers of encouragement and occupation. *Nos pas ne seront plus arrêtés par l'image dégoûtante des infirmités et de la honteuse misère.*"[c]

The final cynical passage is the only truth in this eulogy.

If Napoleon addresses himself to the intelligence of his judges, prefects and engineers, why should not the King of Prussia appeal to his official bodies?

Why did Napoleon not *at once* issue a decree for the abolition of mendicancy? This is on the same level as the "Prussian's" question: "Why does the King of Prussia not at once issue a decree for the education of all uncared-for children?" Does the "Prussian" know what the King would have to decree? Nothing less than the *abolition of the proletariat*. In order to educate children

---

[a] This passage is taken from E. Buret, *De la misère des classes laborieuses en Angleterre et en France...*, t. 1, p. 227.— *Ed.*

[b] *Dépôt de mendicité*—i.e., workhouse.— *Ed.*

[c] "No longer will the sight of disgusting afflictions and disgraceful poverty dog our footsteps." This passage is taken from E. Buret's book, t. 1, pp. 229-30.— *Ed.*

they have to be *fed* and freed from *wage-labour*. The feeding and education of uncared-for children, i. e., the feeding and education of the *entire rising generation* of the proletariat, would be the *abolition* of the proletariat and pauperism.

The *Convention* at one moment had the courage to *decree* the abolition of pauperism—though not *"at once"*, as the "Prussian" demands of his King, but only after it had instructed the Committee of Public Safety to draw up the necessary plans and proposals and after this Committee had made use of the extensive researches of the Constituent Assembly on the conditions of the French poor, and had proposed through Barère the institution of a *Livre de la bienfaisance nationale*, etc. What was the result of the Convention's decree? That one more decree came into the world and *one* year later starving women besieged the Convention.⁴³

Yet the Convention represented the *maximum of political energy, political power* and *political understanding*.

No government in the world has issued *regulations* regarding pauperism *at once*, without reaching agreement with the authorities. The English Parliament even sent representatives to all the countries of Europe to learn about the various administrative remedies for pauperism. But insofar as the states have occupied themselves with pauperism, they have either confined themselves to *administrative* and *charitable measures*, or they have retreated to less than administrative action and charity.

Can the state act in any other way?

The *state*—contrary to what the Prussian demands of his King—will *never* see in *"the state* and the *system of society"* the source of *social maladies*. Where political parties exist, each party sees the root of *every* evil in the fact that instead of itself an opposing party stands at the *helm of the state*. Even radical and revolutionary politicians seek the root of the evil not in the *essential nature* of the state, but in a definite *state form*, which they wish to replace by a *different* state form.

From the *political* point of view, the *state* and the *system of society* are not *two* different things. The state is the system of society. Insofar as the state admits the existence of *social* defects, it sees their cause either in the *laws of nature*, which no human power can command, or in *private life*, which does not depend on the state, or in the *inexpedient activity of the administration*, which does not depend on it. Thus England sees the cause of poverty in the *law of nature* by which the population must always be in excess of the means of subsistence. On the other hand, England explains *pauperism* as due to the *bad will of the poor*, just as the King of Prussia explains it by the *un-Christian feelings of the rich*, and just as the Convention explained it by the *suspect counter-revolutionary mentality of the property-owners*. Therefore England punishes the poor, the King of Prussia admonishes the rich, and the Convention cuts off the heads of the property owners.

Finally, *every* state seeks the cause in *accidental* or *deliberate shortcomings of the administration*, and therefore it seeks the remedy for its ills *in measures* of the administration. Why? Precisely because *administration* is the *organising* activity of the state.

The *contradiction* between the purpose and goodwill of the administration, on the one hand, and its means and possibilities, on the other hand, cannot be abolished by the state without the latter abolishing itself, for it is *based* on this contradiction. The state is based on the contradiction between *public* and *private life*, on the contradiction between *general interests* and *private interests*. Hence the *administration* has to confine itself to a *formal* and *negative* activity, for where civil life and its labour begin, there the power of the administration ends. Indeed, confronted by the consequences which arise from the unsocial nature of this civil life, this private ownership, this trade, this industry, this mutual plundering of the various circles of citizens, confronted by all these consequences, *impotence* is the *law of nature* of the administration. For this fragmentation, this baseness, this *slavery of civil society* is the natural foundation on which the *modern* state rests, just as the *civil society of slavery* was the natural foundation on which the *ancient* state rested. The existence of the state and the existence of slavery are inseparable. The ancient state and ancient slavery—these straightforward *classic* opposites—were not more intimately *riveted* to each other than are the modern state and the modern commercial world, these hypocritical *Christian* opposites. If the modern state wanted to abolish the *impotence* of its administration, it would have to abolish the *private life* of today. But if it wanted to abolish private life, it would have to abolish itself, for it exists *only* in the contradiction to private life. But no *living being* believes that the shortcomings of his existence have their basis in the *principle* of his life, in the essence of his life; everyone believes that their basis lies in circumstances *external* to his life. *Suicide* is against nature. Therefore the state cannot believe in the *inherent* impotence of its administration, i. e., in its own impotence. It can perceive *only* formal, accidental deficiencies in its administration and try to remedy them. And if these modifications prove fruitless, the conclusion is drawn that social ills are a natural imperfection independent of man, a *law of God* or—that the will of private individuals is too spoilt to be able to respond to the good intentions of the administration. And how preposterous these private individuals are! They grumble at the government whenever it restricts their freedom, and at the same time they demand that the government prevent the inevitable results of this freedom!

The mightier the state, and the *more political* therefore a country is, the less is it inclined to grasp the *general* principle of *social* maladies and to seek their basis in the *principle of the state,* hence in the *present structure of society,* the active, conscious and official expression of which is the state. The *political* mind is a *political* mind precisely because it thinks *within* the framework of politics. The keener and more lively it is, the *more incapable* is it of understanding social ills. The *classic* period of political intellect is the *French Revolution.* Far from seeing the source of social shortcomings in the principle of the state, the heroes of the French Revolution instead saw in social defects the source of political evils. Thus, *Robespierre* saw in great poverty and great wealth only an obstacle to *pure democracy.* Therefore he wished to establish a universal Spartan frugality. The principle of politics is the *will.* The more one-sided and, therefore, the more perfected the *political* mind is, the more does it believe in the *omnipotence* of the will, the more is it blind to the *natural* and spiritual *limits* of the will, and the more incapable is it therefore of discovering the source of social ills. There is no need of further argument against the "Prussian's" silly hope that "*political understanding*" is destined "to discover *the roots of social distress* in Germany".

It was foolish to expect from the King of Prussia not only a power such as the Convention and Napoleon together did not possess; it was foolish to expect from him a manner of viewing things that transcends the bounds of *all* politics and which the wise "Prussian" himself is no closer to possessing than is his King. This whole declaration was all the more foolish in that the "Prussian" admits to us:

"Good words and a good frame of mind are *cheap*; insight and successful deeds are *dear*; in the present case they are *more than dear,* they *are still not at all to be had.*"

If they are still not at all to be had, then one should appreciate the attempts of anyone to do whatever is possible for him in his situation. For the rest, I leave it to the tact of the reader to decide whether in this connection the commercial gipsy jargon, i.e., "cheap", "dear", "more than dear", "still not at all to be had", is to be included in the category of "*good*" words" and a "*good* frame of mind".

Let us suppose then that the "Prussian's" remarks about the German Government and the German bourgeoisie — after all the latter is included in "German society" — are entirely well founded. Is this section of society more at a loss in Germany than in England and France? Can one be more at a loss than, for example, in England, where *perplexity* has been made into a system? When today workers' revolts break out throughout England, the bourgeoisie and government there know no better what to do than in the last third of the eighteenth century. Their sole expedient is material force, and since this material force diminishes in the same proportion as the spread of pauperism and the understanding of the proletariat increase, England's perplexity inevitably grows in geometrical progression.

Finally, it is *untrue, actually untrue,* that the German bourgeoisie totally fails to understand the general significance of the Silesian uprising. In several towns the masters are trying to act jointly with the apprentices. All the *liberal* German newspapers, the organs of the liberal bourgeoisie, teem with articles about the organisation of labour, the reform of society, criticism of monopolies and competition, etc. All this is the result of the movements among the workers. The newspapers of Trier, Aachen, Cologne, Wesel, Mannheim, Breslau, and even of Berlin, often publish quite reasonable articles on social questions from which the "Prussian" could after all learn something. Moreover, letters from Germany constantly express surprise at the slight resistance shown by the bourgeoisie against *social* tendencies and ideas.

The "Prussian" — if he were more familiar with the history of the social movement — would have put his question the other way round. Why does even the German bourgeoisie interpret a partial state of distress in such a comparatively universal manner? Whence the *hostility* and *cynicism* of the *politically-minded* bourgeoisie towards the proletariat, and whence the *lack of resistance* and the *sympathy* towards it of the *non-politically-minded* bourgeoisie?

[*Vorwärts!* No. 64, August 10, 1844]

Let us pass now to the oracular pronouncements of the "Prussian" on the *German workers.*

"The German poor," he says wittily, "*are no wiser than the poor Germans,* i. e., nowhere do they see beyond their own hearth and home, their own factory, their own district; the whole question has *so far still* been ignored by the all-penetrating political soul."

In order to be able to compare the condition of the German workers with the condition of the French and English workers, the "Prussian" would have had to compare the *first form,* the *start,* of the English and French workers' movement with the *German* movement that is *just beginning.* He failed to do so. Consequently, his arguments lead to trivialities, such as that *industry* in Germany is not yet so developed as in England, or that a movement at its start looks different from the movement in its subsequent progress. He wanted to speak about the *specific character* of the German workers' movement, but he has not a word to say on this subject of his.

On the other hand, suppose the "Prussian" were to adopt the correct standpoint. He will find that *not one* of the French and English workers' uprisings had such a *theoretical* and *conscious* character as the uprising of the Silesian weavers.

First of all, recall the *song of the weavers,*[44] that bold *call* to struggle, in which there is not even a mention of hearth and home, factory or district, but in which the proletariat at once, in a striking, sharp, unrestrained and powerful manner, proclaims its opposition to the society of private property. The Silesian uprising *begins* precisely with what the French and English workers' uprisings *end,* with consciousness of the nature of the proletariat. The action itself bears the stamp of this *superior* character. Not only machines, these rivals of the workers, are destroyed, but also *ledgers,* the titles to property. And while all other movements were aimed primarily only against the *owner of the industrial enterprise,* the visible enemy, this movement is at the same time directed against the banker, the hidden enemy. Finally, not a single English workers' uprising was carried out with such courage, thought and endurance.

As for the educational level or capacity for education of the German workers in general, I call to mind *Weitling's* brilliant writings, which as regards theory are often superior even to those of *Proudhon,* however much they are inferior to the latter in their execution. Where among the bourgeoisie—including its philosophers and learned writers—is to be found a book about the emancipation of the bourgeoisie—*political* emancipation—similar to Weitling's work: *Garantien der Harmonie und Freiheit?* It is enough to compare the petty, faint-hearted mediocrity of German political literature with this *vehement* and brilliant literary debut of the German workers, it is enough to compare these gigantic *infant shoes* of the proletariat with the dwarfish, worn-out political shoes of the German bourgeoisie, and one is bound to prophesy that the *German Cinderella* will one day have the *figure of an athlete*. It has to be admitted that the German proletariat is the *theoretician* of the European proletariat, just as the English proletariat is its *economist*, and the French proletariat its *politician*. It has to be admitted that Germany is just as much *classically* destined for a *social* revolution as it is incapable of a *political* one. For, just as the impotence of the German bourgeoisie is the *political* impotence of Germany, so also the capability of the German proletariat—even apart from German theory—represents the *social* capability of Germany. The disparity between the philosophical and the political development of Germany is not an *anomaly*. It is an inevitable disparity. A philosophical people can find its corresponding practice only in socialism, hence it is only in the *proletariat* that it can find the dynamic element of its emancipation.

At the present moment, however, I have neither the time nor the desire to explain to the "Prussian" the relationship of "German society" to social revolution, and, arising from this relationship, on the one hand, the feeble reaction of the German bourgeoisie against socialism and, on the other hand, the excellent capabilities of the German proletariat for socialism. He will find the first rudiments for an understanding of this phenomenon in my "Einleitung zur Kritik der Hegelschen Rechtsphilosophie" (*Deutsch-Französische Jahrbücher*).[a]

The wisdom of the *German poor,* therefore, is in *inverse* ratio to the wisdom of *poor Germans.* But people for whom every subject has to serve as a vehicle for stylistic exercises performed in public hit upon a distorted content owing to this *formal* kind of activity, while the distorted content, for its part, puts its stamp of baseness on the form. Thus, the "Prussian's" attempt—when an opportunity such as the Silesian workers' disturbances presents itself—to develop his arguments in the form of an antithesis leads him to the greatest antithesis to the truth. Confronted with the first outbreak of the Silesian workers' uprising, the sole task of one who thinks and loves the truth consisted not in playing the role of *schoolmaster* in relation to this event, but instead in studying its *specific* character. This, of course, requires some scientific insight and some love of mankind, whereas for the other operation a glib phraseology, impregnated with empty love of oneself, is quite enough.

---

[a] "Contribution to the Critique of Hegel's Philosophy of Law. Introduction" (see this volume, pp. 175-87).—*Ed.*

Why does the "Prussian" judge the German workers so contemptuously? Because he finds that the "whole question"—namely, the question of the distressed state of the workers—has *"so far still"* been ignored by the "all-penetrating *political* soul". He expounds his platonic love for the *political soul* in more detail as follows:

> "All uprisings which break out in this disastrous *isolation of people from the community*, and of their *thoughts from social principles*, will be smothered in blood and incomprehension; but when distress produces understanding, and the *political* understanding of the Germans discovers the roots of social distress, then in Germany too these events will be appreciated as symptoms of a great revolution."

First of all, let the "Prussian" allow us to make a comment of a *stylistic* nature. His antithesis is defective. In the first half it says: "when *distress* produces *understanding*", but in the second it says: "when *political understanding* discovers the roots *of social distress*". The *simple* understanding of the first half of the antithesis becomes *political* understanding in the second half, just as the *simple* distress of the first half of the antithesis becomes *social* distress in the second half. Why does our stylistic artist endow the two halves of his antithesis so unequally? I do not think that he realised why he did it. I will explain to him his correct *instinct* here. If the "Prussian" had written "when *social* distress produces *political* understanding, and *political understanding* discovers the roots of *social* distress", no unbiassed reader could have failed to see the *nonsense* of this antithesis. Everyone would at once have asked himself: why does the anonymous author not couple social understanding with social distress, and political understanding with political distress, as the simplest logic requires? And now to the matter itself!

That *social distress* produces *political* understanding is so incorrect that, on the contrary, what is correct is the opposite: *social well-being* produces *political* understanding. *Political* understanding is a spiritualist, and is given to him who already has, to him who is already comfortably situated. Let our "Prussian" listen to a French economist, M. *Michel Chevalier*, on this subject:

> "When the bourgeoisie rose up in 1789, it lacked—in order to be free—only participation in governing the country. Emancipation consisted for it in wresting the control of public affairs, the principal civil, military and religious functions, from the hands of the privileged who had the monopoly of these functions. *Rich* and *enlightened*, capable of being self-sufficient and of managing its own affairs, it wanted to escape from the system of arbitrary rule."[a]

We have already shown the "Prussian" how incapable *political*

---

[a] M. Chevalier, *Des intérêts matériels en France*, p. 3 (Marx gives a free translation).— *Ed.*

understanding is of discovering the source of social distress. Just *one* word more on this view of his. The more developed and universal the *political* understanding of a people, the more does the *proletariat*—at any rate at the beginning of the movement—squander its forces in senseless, useless revolts, which are drowned in blood. Because it thinks in the framework of politics, the proletariat sees the cause of all evils in the *will,* and all means of remedy in *violence* and in the *overthrow* of a *particular* form of state. The proof: the first uprisings of the *French* proletariat.[45] The Lyons workers believed that they were pursuing only political aims, that they were only soldiers of the republic, whereas actually they were soldiers of socialism. Thus their political understanding concealed from them the roots of social distress, thus it falsified their insight into their real aim, thus their *political understanding deceived* their *social instinct.*

But if the "Prussian" expects understanding to be produced by distress, why does he lump together *"smothering in blood"* and *"smothering in incomprehension"*? If distress is in general a means of producing understanding, then *bloody* distress is even a *very acute* means to this end. The "Prussian" therefore should have said: smothering in blood will smother incomprehension and procure a proper current of air for the understanding.

The "Prussian" prophesies the smothering of uprisings which break out in *"disastrous isolation of people from the community,* and in the *separation of their thoughts from social principles".*

We have shown that the Silesian uprising occurred by no means in circumstances of the separation of thoughts from social principles. It only remains for us to deal with the *"disastrous isolation of people from the community".* By community here is meant the *political community,* the *state.* This is the old story about *unpolitical* Germany.

But do not *all* uprisings, without exception, break out in a *disastrous isolation of man from the community?* Does not *every* uprising necessarily presuppose isolation? Would the 1789 revolution have taken place without the disastrous isolation of French citizens from the community? It was intended precisely to abolish this isolation.

But the *community* from which the worker is *isolated* is a community the real character and scope of which is quite different from that of the *political* community. The community from which the worker is isolated by *his own labour* is *life* itself, physical and mental life, human morality, human activity, human enjoyment, *human* nature. *Human nature* is the *true community* of men. The disastrous isolation from this essential nature is incomparably more universal, more intolerable, more dreadful, and more contradictory, than isolation from the political community. Hence, too, the *abolition* of this isolation—and even a partial reaction to it, an *uprising* against it—is just as much more infinite as *man* is more infinite than the *citizen,* and *human life* more infinite than *political life.* Therefore, however *partial* the uprising of the *industrial workers* may be, it contains within itself a *universal* soul; however universal a *political* uprising may be, it conceals even in its *most grandiose* form a *narrow-minded* spirit.

The "Prussian" worthily concludes his article with the following sentence:

"*A social revolution without a political soul* (i.e., without an organising idea from the point of view of the whole) *is impossible.*"

We have already seen that a *social* revolution is found to have the point of view of the *whole* because—even if it were to occur in only *one* factory district—it represents man's protest against a dehumanised life, because it starts out from the *point of view of a separate real individual,* because the *community,* against the separation of which from himself the individual reacts, is man's *true* community, *human* nature. The *political soul* of revolution, on the other hand, consists in the *tendency* of classes having no political influence to abolish their *isolation* from *statehood* and *rule.* Its point of view is that of the state, of an *abstract* whole, which exists *only* through separation from real life, and which is *inconceivable* without the *organised* contradiction between the universal idea of man and the individual existence of man. Hence, too, a revolution with a *political soul,* in accordance with the *limited* and *dichotomous* nature of this soul, organises a ruling stratum in society at the expense of society itself.

We want to divulge to the "Prussian" what a "*social revolution* with a *political* soul" actually is; we shall thereby at the same time confide the secret to him that he himself is unable, even in *words,* to rise above the narrow-minded political point of view.

A "*social*" revolution with a *political* soul is either a nonsensical concoction, if by "social" revolution the "Prussian" means a "*social*" as *opposed* to a political revolution, and nevertheless endows the social revolution with a political soul instead of a social one; or else a "*social revolution with a political soul*" is only a *paraphrase* for what was usually called a "*political revolution*", or "*simply a revolution*". Every revolution dissolves the *old society* and to that extent it is *social.* Every revolution overthrows the *old power* and to that extent it is *political.*

Let the "Prussian" choose between the *paraphrase* and the *nonsense!* But whereas a *social revolution* with a *political soul* is a paraphrase or nonsense, a *political revolution* with a *social* soul has a rational meaning. *Revolution* in general — the *overthrow* of the existing power and *dissolution* of the old relationships — is a *political act.* But *socialism* cannot be realised without *revolution.* It needs this *political* act insofar as it needs *destruction* and *dissolution.* But where its *organising activity* begins, where its *proper object,* its *soul,* comes to the fore — there socialism throws off the *political* cloak.

How much detailed argument has been necessary to tear to pieces the *tissue* of errors concealed on a single newspaper column. Not all readers can have the education and time to get to the bottom of such *literary charlatanism.* Is it therefore not the anonymous "Prussian's" duty to the reading public to refrain for the time being from all writing on political and social matters, such as the declamations about conditions in Germany, and instead sincerely try to come to an understanding of his own condition?

Paris, July 31, 1844.

First published in *Vorwärts!* Printed according to the news-
Nos. 63 and 64, August 7 and 10, 1844 paper
(Paris)

Signed: *Karl Marx*

ILLUSTRATIONS OF THE LATEST EXERCISE IN CABINET STYLE OF FREDERICK WILLIAM IV

"I cannot leave the soil of the Fatherland, although only for a short time, without expressing publicly the deeply-felt gratitude in My and the Queen's[a] name by which Our heart has been moved. It has been produced by the innumerable verbal and written proofs of the love for Us which the attempt of July 26 has evoked—of the love which jubilantly acclaimed Us at the moment of the crime itself, when the hand of the Almighty cast the deadly bullet away from My breast to the ground. While looking upwards to the divine Saviour, I go with new courage about My daily work, to complete what has been begun, to carry out what has been prepared, to combat evil with new certainty of victory, and to be to My people what My high vocation imposes on Me, and My people's love merits.
"Erdmannsdorf, August 5, 1844

(signed) *Frederick William*"[46]

Immediate emotion is a bad writer. The letter which a lover writes in great excitement to his beloved is no model of style, but it is just this *confusion* of expression that is the *clearest*, most obvious and most moving expression of the power of love over the writer of the letter. The power of love over the letter-writer is the power of his beloved over him. That passionate unclarity and erratic confusion of style therefore flatters the heart of the beloved, since the reflected, general, and therefore untrustworthy nature of the language has assumed a directly individual, sensuously powerful, and hence absolutely trustworthy, character. The trusting faith in the truth of the love that the lover expresses for her, however, is the supreme joy of the loved one, her faith in herself.

From these premises it follows: We perform an inestimable service for the *Prussian* people when we put the inner *truth* of the

---

[a] Queen Elizabeth.— *Ed.*

royal gratitude beyond all doubt. We put this truth beyond all doubt, however, by proving the force of the thankful feeling over the royal writer, and we prove the force of this feeling over the royal writer by demonstrating the *stylistic confusion* of the cabinet edict in *expressing thanks*. Hence the aim of our patriotic analysis will not be misinterpreted.

> "I cannot leave the soil of the Fatherland, although only for a short time, without expressing publicly the deeply-felt gratitude in My and the Queen's name by which Our heart has been moved."

By the construction of the sentence, it might be thought at first glance that the royal bosoms were moved by their own *name*. If amazement at this peculiar movement makes one think again, one sees that the relative conjunction "*by which* our heart has been moved" refers not to the *name*, but to the more remotely situated *gratitude*. The singular "*Our heart*" for the heart of the king and the heart of the queen can be justified as poetic licence, as a cordial expression of the cordial unity of the cordial royal couple. The laconic brevity: "in My and the Queen's name", instead of "in My name and in the name of the Queen", can easily lead to a false interpretation. "My and the Queen's name" could be understood to mean the *simple* name of the king, since the name of the husband is the name of the husband and the wife. Now, it is true that it is a privilege of great men and of children to make their *name* the subject of the sentence instead of saying "I". Thus Caesar could say "Caesar conquered" instead of "I conquered". Thus children do not say "I want to go to the school in Vienna", but "Friedrich, Karl, or Wilhelm, etc., wants to go to the school in Vienna". But it would be a dangerous innovation to make one's "I" the subject of the sentence and at the same time to give an assurance that this "I" speaks in his "own" name. Such an assurance could seem to contain a confession that one did not usually speak from one's own inspiration. "I cannot leave the soil of the Fatherland, although only for a short time" is neither a very skilful nor a more easily intelligible rephrasing of "I cannot leave the soil of the Fatherland, even for a short time, without, etc." The difficulty is due to the combination of three ideas: (1) that the king is leaving his homeland, (2) that he is leaving it only for a short time, (3) that he feels a need to thank the people. The too compressed utterance of these ideas makes it appear that the king expresses his *gratitude* only because he is leaving his homeland. But if the gratitude was seriously meant, if it came from the heart, then its utterance could not possibly be linked with such a chance occurrence. Under all circumstances, the full heart speaks for itself.

> "It" (the gratitude) "has been produced by the innumerable verbal and written proofs of the love for Us *which* the attempt of July 26 has evoked — *of the* love which jubilantly acclaimed Us at the moment of the crime itself, when the hand of the Almighty cast the deadly bullet away from My breast to the ground."

It is not clear whether the attempt evoked the love or the proofs of the love, the more so because the genitive "of the love" after the parenthesis appears again as the governing and emphasised phrase in the sentence. The stylistic boldness of the repetition of the genitive is very noticeable. The difficulty increases when we examine the content of the sentence. Was it correct that the love which spoke and wrote was described directly as the subject which shouted in the street? Did not chronological truth require that one should begin with the love that was voiced at once in the presence of the occurrence and only then go on to the subsequent expressions of love in writing and speech?

Should one not have avoided the suspicion that the king desires simultaneously to flatter both the aristocracy and the people? *The aristocracy* because their written and verbal expressions of love, although coming later in time than the popular expressions of love, nevertheless by their effect were earlier able to arouse gratitude in the royal heart; the *people* because its jubilant love is declared to be essentially the same as the written and verbal love, that is, the hereditary nobility of love is abolished? Lastly, it does not seem altogether appropriate to cause the *"bullet"* to be warded off directly by the hand of God, since in this way even a slight degree of consistent thought will arrive at the false conclusion that God at the same time both guided the hand of the criminal and diverted the bullet away from the king; for how can one presume a one-sided action on the part of God?

> "While looking upwards to the divine Saviour, I go with new courage about My daily work, to complete what has been begun, to carry out what has been prepared, to combat evil with [...] certainty of victory, and to be to My people what My high vocation imposes on Me, and My people's love merits."

One cannot very well say: "I go" "to be something". At the most one can go "to become something". The motion involved in becoming appears at least as the result of the motion of going, although we would not recommend even the latter turn of phrase as correct. That His Majesty *"goes* while *looking upwards to God"* "to complete what has been begun, to carry out what has been prepared", does not seem to offer a good prospect for either the completion or the carrying out. In order to complete what has been begun and to carry out what has been prepared one must keep one's eyes firmly fixed on what has been begun and prepared and not look away from these objects to gaze into the blue sky. One who truly "goes while looking upwards to God", will he not be "*completely absorbed* by the sight of God"? Will he not *lose all interest* in *worldly* plans and ideas? The isolated final phrase, left on its own after a comma: "and My people's love merits", seems to point to an unexpressed, hidden subsequent clause, something like: "merits the knout of my brother-in-law Nicholas and the policy of our neighbour Metternich"; or also: "merits the petty constitution devised by the knightly Bunsen".[47]

Written about August 15, 1844

First published in *Vorwärts!*
No. 66, August 17, 1844

Printed according to the newspaper
Published in English for the first time

[COMMENTS ON JAMES MILL, *ÉLÉMENS D'ÉCONOMIE POLITIQUE*
Translated by J. T. Parisot, Paris, 1823][48]

|| XXVI[a] In the compensation of money and value of metal, as in his description of the cost of production as the only factor in determining value,[49] Mill commits the mistake—like the school of Ricardo in general—of stating the *abstract law* without the change or continual supersession of this law through which alone it comes into being. If it is a *constant* law that, for example, the cost of production in the last instance—or rather when demand and supply are in equilibrium which occurs sporadically, fortuitously—determines the price (value), it is just as much a *constant law* that they are not in equilibrium, and that therefore value and cost of production stand in no necessary relationship. Indeed, there is always only a momentary equilibrium of demand and supply owing to the previous fluctuation of demand and supply, owing to the disproportion between cost of production and exchange-value, just as this fluctuation and this disproportion likewise again follow the momentary state of equilibrium. This *real* movement, of which that law is only an abstract, fortuitous and one-sided factor, is made by recent political economy into something accidental and inessential. Why? Because in the acute and precise formulas to which they reduce political economy, the basic formula, if they wished to express that movement abstractly, would have to be: In political economy, law is determined by its opposite, absence of law. The true law of political economy is *chance*, from whose movement we, the scientific men, isolate certain factors arbitrarily in the form of laws.

---

[a] The Roman figures refer to Marx's Paris Notebook number four.—*Ed.*

Mill very well expresses the essence of the matter in the form of a concept by characterising *money* as the *medium* of exchange. The essence of money is not, in the first place, that property is alienated in it, but that the *mediating activity* or movement, the *human,* social act by which man's products mutually complement one another, is *estranged* from man and becomes the attribute of money, a *material thing* outside man. Since man alienates this mediating activity itself, he is active here only as a man who has lost himself and is dehumanised; the *relation* itself between things, man's operation with them, becomes the operation of an entity outside man and above man. Owing to this *alien mediator*—instead of man himself being the mediator for man—man regards his will, his activity and his relation to other men as a power independent of him and them. His slavery, therefore, reaches its peak. It is clear that this *mediator* now becomes a *real God,* for the mediator is the *real power* over what it mediates to me. Its cult becomes an end in itself. Objects separated from this mediator have lost their value. Hence the objects only have value insofar as they *represent* the mediator, whereas originally it seemed that the mediator had value only insofar as *it* represented *them.* This reversal of the original relationship is inevitable. This *mediator* is therefore the lost, estranged *essence* of private property, private property which has become *alienated,* external to itself, just as it is the *alienated* species-activity of man, the *externalised mediation* between man's production and man's production. All the qualities which arise in the course of this activity are, therefore, transferred to this mediator. Hence man becomes the poorer as man, i.e., separated from this mediator, the *richer* this mediator becomes.

Christ *represents* originally: 1) men before God; 2) God for men; 3) men to man.

Similarly, *money* represents originally, in accordance with the idea of money: 1) private property for private property; 2) society for private property; 3) private property for society.

But Christ is *alienated* God and alienated *man.* God has value only insofar as he represents Christ, and man has value only insofar as he represents Christ. It is the same with money.

Why must private property develop into the *money system?* Because man as a social being must proceed to *exchange* ||XXV|[a] and because exchange—private property being presupposed—must evolve value. The mediating process between men

---

[a] Two consecutive pages are numbered XXV.—*Ed.*

engaged in exchange is not a social or human process, not *human relationship*; it is the *abstract relationship* of private property to private property, and the expression of this *abstract* relationship is *value*, whose actual existence as value constitutes *money*. Since men engaged in exchange do not relate to each other as men, *things* lose the significance of human, personal property. The social relationship of private property to private property is already a relationship in which private property is estranged from itself. The form of existence for itself of this relationship, money, is therefore the alienation of private property, the abstraction from its *specific*, personal nature.

Hence the opposition of modern political economy to the monetary system, the *système monétaire*,[50] cannot achieve any decisive victory in spite of all its cleverness. For if the crude economic superstition of the people and governments clings to the *sensuous, tangible, conspicuous* money-bag, and therefore believes both in the absolute value of the precious metals and possession of them as the sole reality of wealth — and if then the enlightened, worldly-wise economist comes forward and proves to them that money is a commodity like any other, the value of which, like that of any other commodity, depends therefore on the relation of the cost of production to demand, competition, and supply, to the quantity or competition of the other commodities — this economist is given the correct reply that nevertheless the *real* value of things is their *exchange-value* and this in the last instance exists in money, as the latter does in the precious metals, and that consequently money represents the *true* value of things and for that reason money is the most desirable thing. Indeed, in the last instance the economist's theory itself amounts to this wisdom, the only difference being that he possesses the capacity of abstraction, the capacity to recognise the existence of money under all forms of commodities and therefore not to believe in the exclusive value of its official metallic mode of existence. The metallic existence of money is only the official palpable expression of the soul of money, which is present in all branches of production and in all activities of bourgeois society.

The opposition of modern economists to the monetary system is merely that they have conceived the *essence of money* in its abstract universality and are therefore enlightened about the *sensuous* superstition which believes in the exclusive existence of this essence in precious metal. They substitute refined superstition for crude superstition. Since, however, in essence both have the same root, the enlightened form of the superstition cannot succeed in supplanting completely the crude sensuous form, because the former does not attack the essence of the latter but only the particular form of this essence.

The *personal* mode of existence of money as money — and not only as the inner, implicit, hidden social relationship or *class relationship* between commodities — this mode of existence corresponds the more to the essence of money, the more abstract it is, the less it has a *natural* relationship to the other commodities, the more it appears as the product and yet as the non-product of man, the less *primitive* its sphere of existence, the more it is created by man or, in economic terms, the greater the *inverse* relationship of its *value as money* to the exchange-value or money value of the material in which it exists. Hence *paper money* and the whole number of *paper representatives of money* (such as bills of exchange, mandates, promissory notes, etc.) are the *more perfect* mode of existence of *money as money* and a necessary factor in the progressive development of the money system. In the *credit system,* of which *banking* is the perfect expression, it appears as if the power of the alien, material force were broken, the relationship of self-estrangement abolished and man had once more human relations to man. The *Saint-Simonists,* deceived by this *appearance,* regarded the development of money, bills of exchange, paper money, paper representatives of money, *credit, banking,* as a gradual abolition of the separation of man from things, of capital from labour, of private property from money and of money from man, and of the separation of man from man. An organised *banking system* is therefore their ideal. But this abolition of ||XXVI| estrangement, this *return* of man to himself and therefore to other men is only an *appearance*; the self-estrangement, the dehumanisation, is all the more *infamous* and *extreme* because its element is no longer commodity, metal, paper, but man's *moral* existence, man's *social* existence, the *inmost depths* of his heart, and because under the appearance of man's *trust* in man it is the height of *distrust* and complete estrangement. What constitutes the essence of *credit?* We leave entirely out of account here the *content* of credit, which is again money. We leave out of account, therefore, the *content* of this trust in accordance with which a man *recognises* another man by advancing him a certain quantity of value and — at best, namely, when he does not demand payment for the credit, i.e., he is not a usurer — showing his trust in his fellow man not being a swindler, but a "good" man. By a "good" man, the one who bestows his trust understands, like Shylock, a man who is "able to pay".

Credit is conceivable in two relationships and under two different conditions. The two relationships are: first, a rich man gives credit to a poor man whom he considers industrious and decent. This kind of credit belongs to the romantic, sentimental part of political economy, to its aberrations, excesses, *exceptions,* not to the *rule.* But even assuming this exception and granting this romantic possibility, the life of the poor man and his talents and activity serve the rich man as a *guarantee* of the repayment of the money lent. That means, therefore, that all the social virtues of the poor man, the content of his vital activity, his existence itself, represent for the rich man the reimbursement of his capital with the customary interest. Hence the death of the poor man is the worst eventuality for the creditor. It is the death of his capital together with the interest. One ought to consider how vile it is to *estimate* the value of a man in *money,* as happens in the credit relationship. As a matter of course, the creditor possesses, besides *moral* guarantees, also the guarantee of *legal* compulsion and still other more or less *real* guarantees for his man. If the man to whom credit is given is himself a man of means, *credit* becomes merely a *medium* facilitating exchange, that is to say, *money* itself is raised to a completely *ideal* form. *Credit* is the *economic* judgment on the *morality* of a man. In credit, the *man* himself, instead of metal or paper, has become the *mediator* of exchange, not however as a man, but as the *mode of existence of capital* and interest. The medium of exchange, therefore, has certainly returned out of its material form and been put back in man, but only because the man himself has been put outside himself and has himself assumed a material form. Within the credit relationship, it is not the case that money is transcended in man, but that man himself is turned into *money,* or money is *incorporated* in him. *Human individuality,* human *morality* itself, has become both an object of commerce and the *material* in which money exists. Instead of money, or paper, it is my own personal existence, my flesh and blood, my social virtue and importance, which constitutes the material, corporeal form of the *spirit of money.* Credit no longer resolves the value of money into money but into human flesh and the human heart. Such is the extent to which all progress and all inconsistencies within a false system are extreme retrogression and the extreme consequence of vileness.

Within the credit system, its nature, estranged from man, under the appearance of an extreme economic appreciation of man, operates in a double way:

1) The antithesis between capitalist and worker, between big and

small capitalists, becomes still greater since credit is given only to him who already has, and is a new opportunity of accumulation for the rich man, or since the poor man finds that the arbitrary discretion of the rich man and the latter's judgment over him confirm or deny his *entire* existence and that his existence is wholly dependent on this contingency.

2) Mutual dissimulation, hypocrisy and sanctimoniousness are carried to extreme lengths, so that on the man without credit is pronounced not only the simple judgment that he is poor, but in addition a pejorative moral judgment that he possesses no trust, no recognition, and therefore is a social pariah, a bad man, and in addition to his privation, the poor man undergoes this humiliation and the humiliating necessity of having to *ask* the rich man for credit.

||XXVII| 3) Since, owing to this completely *nominal* existence of money, *counterfeiting* cannot be undertaken by man in any other material than his own person, he has to make himself into counterfeit coin, obtain credit by stealth, by lying, etc., and this credit relationship — both on the part of the man who trusts and of the man who needs trust — becomes an object of commerce, an object of mutual deception and misuse. Here it is also glaringly evident that *distrust* is the basis of economic trust; distrustful calculation whether credit ought to be given or not; spying into the secrets of the private life, etc., of the one seeking credit; the disclosure of temporary straits in order to overthrow a rival by a sudden shattering of his credit, etc. The whole system of bankruptcy, spurious enterprises, etc.... As regards *government loans*, the state occupies exactly the same place as the man does in the earlier example.... In the game with government securities it is seen how the state has become the plaything of businessmen, etc.

4) The *credit system* finally has its completion in the *banking system*. The creation of bankers, the political domination of the bank, the concentration of wealth in these hands, this economic *Areopagus* of the nation, is the worthy completion of the money system.

Owing to the fact that in the credit system the *moral recognition of a man*, as also *trust in the state*, etc., take the form of *credit*, the secret contained in the lie of moral recognition, the *immoral* vileness of this morality, as also the sanctimoniousness and egoism of that trust in the state, become evident and show themselves for what they really are.

Exchange, both of human activity within production itself and of *human products* against one another, is equivalent to *species-activity* and species-spirit, the real, conscious and true mode of existence of which is *social* activity and *social* enjoyment. Since *human* nature is the *true community* of men, by manifesting their *nature* men *create*, produce, the *human community*, the social entity, which is no abstract universal power opposed to the single individual, but is the essential nature of each individual, his own activity, his own life, his own spirit, his own wealth. Hence this *true community* does not come into being through reflection, it appears owing to the *need* and *egoism* of individuals, i.e., it is produced directly by their life activity itself. It does not depend on man whether this community exists or not; but as long as man does not recognise himself as man, and therefore has not organised the world in a human way, this *community* appears in the form of *estrangement*, because its *subject*, man, is a being estranged from himself. Men, not as an abstraction, but as real, living, particular individuals, *are* this entity. Hence, *as* they are, so is this entity itself. To say that *man* is estranged from himself, therefore, is the same thing as saying that the *society* of this estranged man is a caricature of his *real community*, of his true species-life, that his activity therefore appears to him as a torment, his own creation as an alien power, his wealth as poverty, the *essential bond* linking him with other men as an unessential bond, and separation from his fellow men, on the other hand, as his true mode of existence, his life as a sacrifice of his life, the realisation of his nature as making his life unreal, his production as the production of his nullity, his power over an object as the power of the object over him, and he himself, the lord of his creation, as the servant of this creation.

The *community of men*, or the manifestation of the nature of *men*, their mutual complementing the result of which is species-life, truly human life — this community is conceived by political economy in the form of *exchange* and *trade*. Society, says Destutt de Tracy, is a *series of mutual exchanges*.[a] It is precisely this process of mutual integration. *Society*, says Adam Smith, is a *commercial society*. Each of its members is a *merchant*.[b]

It is seen that political economy *defines* the *estranged* form of social intercourse as the *essential* and *original* form corresponding to man's nature.

|XXVIII| Political economy—like the real process—starts out from the *relation of man to man* as that of *property owner to property owner*. If man is presupposed as *property owner*, i.e., therefore as

---

[a] See Destutt de Tracy, *Élémens d'idéologie*, IVe et V^e parties. Traité de la volonté et de ses effets, p.68.— *Ed.*

[b] See Adam Smith, *Wealth of Nations*, Book I, Ch. IV.—*Ed.*

an exclusive owner, who proves his personality and both distinguishes himself from, and enters into relations with, other men through this exclusive ownership—private property is his personal, *distinctive*, and therefore essential mode of existence—then the *loss* or *surrender* of private property is an *alienation of man*, as it is of *private property* itself. Here we shall only be concerned with the latter definition. If I give up my private property to someone else, it ceases to be *mine*; it becomes something independent of me, lying *outside* my sphere, a thing *external* to me. Hence I *alienate* my private property. With regard to me, therefore, I turn it into *alienated* private property. But I only turn it into an *alienated* thing in general, I abolish only my *personal* relation to it, I give it back to the *elementary* powers of nature if I alienate it only with regard to myself. It becomes alienated *private property* only if, while ceasing to be *my* private property, it on that account does not cease to be *private property* as such, that is to say, if it enters into the same relation to *another* man, *apart* from me, as that which it had to myself; in short, if it becomes the *private property* of *another* man. The case of *violence* excepted—what causes me to alienate *my* private property to another man? Political economy replies correctly: *necessity, need*. The other man is also a property owner, but he is the owner of *another* thing, which I lack and cannot and will not do without, which seems to me a *necessity* for the completion of my existence and the realisation of my nature.

The bond which connects the two property owners with each other is the *specific kind of object* that constitutes the substance of their private property. The desire for these two objects, i.e., the need for them, shows each of the property owners, and makes him conscious of it, that he has yet another *essential* relation to objects besides that of private ownership, that he is not the particular being that he considers himself to be, but a *total* being whose needs stand in the relationship of *inner* ownership to all products, including those of another's labour. For the need of a thing is the most evident, irrefutable proof that the thing belongs to *my* essence, that its being is for me, that its *property* is the property, the peculiarity, of my essence. Thus both property owners are impelled to give up their private property, but to do so in such a way that at the same time they confirm private ownership, or to give up the private property within the relationship of private ownership. Each therefore alienates a part of his private property to the other.

The *social* connection or *social* relationship between the two property owners is therefore that of *reciprocity* in *alienation*, positing the relationship of alienation on both sides, or *alienation* as the relationship of both property owners, whereas in simple private property, *alienation* occurs only in relation to oneself, one-sidedly.

Exchange or *barter* is therefore the social act, the species-act, the community, the social intercourse and integration of men within *private ownership*, and therefore the external, *alienated* species-act. It is just for this reason that it appears as *barter*. For this reason, likewise, it is the opposite of the *social* relationship.

Through the reciprocal alienation or estrangement of private property, *private property* itself falls into the category of *alienated* private property.[51] For, in the first place, it has ceased to be the product of the labour of its owner, his exclusive, distinctive personality. For he has alienated it, it has moved away from the owner whose product it was and has acquired a personal significance for someone whose product it is *not*. It has lost its personal significance for the owner. Secondly, it has been brought into relation with another private property, and placed on a par with the latter. Its place has been taken by a private property of a *different* kind, just as it itself takes the place of a private property of a *different* kind. On both sides, therefore, private property appears as the representative of a different kind of private property, as the *equivalent* of a *different* natural product, and both sides are related to each other in such a way that each represents the mode of existence of the *other,* and both relate to each other as *substitutes* for themselves and the other. Hence the mode of existence of private property as such has become that of a *substitute*, of an *equivalent*. Instead of its immediate unity with itself, it exists now only as a relation to *something else*. Its mode of existence as an *equivalent* is no longer its specific mode of existence. It has thus become a *value*, and immediately an *exchange-value*. Its mode of existence as *value* is an *alienated* designation ||XXIX| *of itself*, different from its immediate existence, external to its specific nature, a merely *relative* mode of existence of this.

How this *value* is more precisely determined must be described elsewhere, as also how it becomes *price*.

The relationship of exchange being presupposed, *labour* becomes *directly labour to earn a living*. This relationship of alienated labour reaches its highest point only when 1) on one side *labour to earn a living* and the product of the worker have no *direct* relation to his need or his *function as worker*, but both aspects are determined by social combinations alien to the worker; 2) he who *buys* the product is not himself a producer, but gives in exchange what someone else has produced. In the crude form of *alienated* private property, *barter*, each of the property owners has produced what his immediate need, his talents and the available raw material have impelled him to make. Each, therefore, exchanges with the other only the surplus of his production. It is true that labour was his immediate *source of subsistence*, but it was at the same time also the manifestation of his *individual existence*. Through exchange his *labour* has become partly a *source of income*. Its purpose differs now from its mode of existence. The product is produced as *value*, as *exchange-value*, as an *equivalent*, and no longer because of its direct, personal relation to the producer. The more diverse production becomes, and therefore the more diverse the needs become, on the one hand, and the more one-sided the activities of the producer become, on the other hand, the more does his labour fall into the category of *labour to earn a living*, until finally it has only this significance and it becomes quite *accidental* and *inessential* whether the relation of the producer to his product is that of immediate enjoyment and personal need, and also whether his *activity*, the act of labour itself, is for him the enjoyment of his personality and the realisation of his natural abilities and spiritual aims.

Labour to earn a living involves: 1) estrangement and fortuitous connection between labour and the subject who labours; 2) estrangement and fortuitous connection between labour and the object of labour; 3) that the worker's role is determined by social needs which, however, are alien to him and a compulsion to which he submits out of egoistic need and necessity, and which have for him only the significance of a means of satisfying his dire need, just as for them he exists only as a slave of their needs; 4) that to the worker the maintenance of his individual existence appears to be the *purpose* of his activity and what he actually does is regarded by him only as a means; that he carries on his life's activity in order to earn means of *subsistence*.

Hence the greater and the more developed the social power appears to be within the private property relationship, the more *egoistic*, asocial and estranged from his own nature does man become.

Just as the mutual exchange of the products of *human activity* appears as *barter*, as trade, so the mutual completion and exchange of the activity itself appears as *division of labour*, which turns man as far as possible into an abstract being, a machine tool, etc., and transforms him into a spiritual and physical monster.

It is precisely the *unity* of human labour that is regarded merely as *division* of labour, because social nature only comes into existence as its opposite, in the form of estrangement. *Division of labour* increases with civilisation.

Within the presupposition of division of labour, the product, the material of private property, acquires for the individual more and more the significance of an *equivalent*, and as he no longer exchanges only his *surplus*, and the object of his production can be simply a *matter of indifference* to him, so too he no longer exchanges his product for something directly *needed* by him. The equivalent comes into existence as an equivalent in *money*, which is now the immediate result of labour to gain a living and the *medium* of exchange (see above[a]).

The complete domination of the estranged thing *over* man has become evident in *money*, which is completely indifferent both to the nature of the material, i.e., to the specific nature of the private property, and to the personality of the property owner. What was the domination of person over person is now the general domination of the *thing* over the *person*, of the product over the producer. Just as the concept of the *equivalent*, the value, already implied the *alienation* of private property, so *money* is the sensuous, even objective existence of this *alienation*.

||XXX| Needless to say that political economy is only able to grasp this whole development as a fact, as the outcome of fortuitous necessity.

The separation of work from itself—separation of the worker from the capitalist—separation of labour and capital, the original form of which is made up of *landed property* and *movable*[b] *property*.... The original determining feature of private property is monopoly; hence when it creates a political constitution, it is that of monopoly. The perfect monopoly is competition.

To the economist, *production, consumption* and, as the mediator of both, *exchange* or *distribution*, are separate [activities].[52] The separation of production and consumption, of action and spirit, in different individuals and in the same individual, is the *separation of labour* from its *object* and from itself as something spiritual. *Distribution* is the power of private property manifesting itself.

The separation of labour, capital and landed property from one another, like that of labour from labour, of capital from capital, and landed property from landed property, and finally the separation of labour from wages, of capital from profit, and profit from interest, and, last of all, of landed property from land rent,

---

[a] See this volume, pp. 212-14.—*Ed.*
[b] "Movable" is not underlined in the manuscript.—*Ed.*

demonstrate self-estrangement both in the form of self-estrangement and in that of mutual estrangement.

"We have next to examine the effects which take place by the attempts of government to control the increase or diminution of money [....] When it endeavours to keep the quantity of money less than it would be, if things were left in freedom, it raises the value of the metal in the coin, and renders it the interest of every body, [who can,] to convert his bullion into money." People "have recourse to private coining. This the government must [...] prevent by punishment. On the other hand, were it the object of government to keep the quantity of money *greater* than it would be, if left in freedom, it would reduce the value of the metal in money, below its value in bullion, and make it the interest of every body to melt the coins. This, also, the government would have only one expedient for preventing, namely, punishment. But the prospect of punishment will prevail over the prospect of profit [,only if the profit is small]."[a] Pp. 101, 102 (pp. 137, 138).

Section IX. "If there were two individuals one of whom owed to the other £100, and the other owed to him £100", instead of paying each other this sum "all they had to do was to exchange their mutual obligations. The case" is the same between two nations.... Hence *bills of exchange*. "The use of them was recommended by a still stronger necessity [...], because the coarse policy of those times prohibited the *exportation* of the precious metals, and punished with the greatest severity any infringement...." Pp. 104-05, 106 (p. 142 et seq.).

Section X. Saving of *unproductive* consumption by paper money. P. 108 et seq. (p. 146 et seq.).

Section XI. "The inconveniencies" of paper money are ... "First,— The *failure* of the parties, by whom the notes are issued, to fulfil their engagements. Second,— Forgery. Third,— The alteration of the value of the currency". P. 110 (p. 149).

Section XII. "... the precious metals, are [...] that commodity [which is the most generally bought and sold...]. Those commodities alone can be exported, which are cheaper in the country from which they go, than in the country to which they are sent; and that those commodities alone can be imported, which are dearer in the country to which they come, than in the country from which they are sent". Accordingly it depends on the value of the precious metals in a country whether they are imported or exported. Pp. 128, 129 [p. 175 et seq.].

Section XIII. "When we speak of the value of the precious metal, we mean the quantity of other things for which it will exchange." This relation is different in different countries and even in different parts of the country. "We say that *living is more cheap*; in other words, commodities may be purchased with a smaller quantity of money." P. 131 [p. 177].

Section XVI. The relation between nations is like that between merchants.... "The merchants [...] will always buy in the cheapest market, and sell in the dearest." P. 159 (p. 215).

IV. *Consumption.*

"*Production, Distribution, Exchange* [...] are *means*. No man produces for the sake of producing [....] distribution and exchange are only the intermediate operations [for bringing the things which have been produced into the hands of those who are] to *consume* them." P. 177 (p. 237).

---

[a] The extracts quoted by Marx from Parisot's French translation of 1823 are reproduced here from the original English text of James Mill's book. The page references are to the English edition of 1821, Marx's page references to the French translation being given in brackets. In this and the following extracts Marx has summarised or paraphrased some passages.— *Ed.*

Section I. "Of Consumption, there are two species." 1) *Productive*. It includes everything "expended for the sake of something to be produced" and comprises "the necessaries of the labourer...." The second class then [...] "machinery; including tools [...], the buildings necessary for the productive operations, and even the cattle. The third is, the material of which the commodity to be produced must be formed, or from which it must be derived". Pp. 178, 179 (pp. 238, 239). "[Of these three classes of things,] it is only the second, the consumption of which is not completed in the course of the productive operations." P. 179 (loc. cit.).

2) *Unproductive* consumption. "The wages" given to a "footman" and "all consumption, which does not take place to the end that something, which may be an equivalent for it, may be produced by means of it, is unproductive consumption". Pp. 179, 180 (p. 240). "Productive consumption is itself a *means*; it is a means to production. Unproductive consumption [...] is not a means." It "is the end. This, or the *enjoyment* which is involved in it, is the good which constituted the *motive* to all the operations by which it was preceded". P. 180 (p. 241). "By productive consumption, nothing is lost [....] Whatever is unproductively consumed, is lost." P. 180 (loc. cit.). "That which is *productively* consumed is always *capital*. This is a property of productive consumption which deserves to be particularly remarked [....] Whatever is consumed productively" *is* capital and "*becomes* capital." P. 181 (p. [241,]242). "The whole of what the productive powers of the country have brought into existence in the course of a year, is called the gross annual produce. Of this the greater part is required to replace the capital which has been consumed [....] What remains of the gross produce, after replacing the capital which has been consumed, is called the net produce; and is always distributed either as profits of stock, or as rent." Pp. 181, 182 (pp. 242, 243). "This net produce is the fund from which all addition to the national capital is commonly made." (loc. cit.) "... the two species of *consumption*" are matched by "the two species of labour, *productive* and *unproductive*...." P. 182 (p. 244).

Section II. "... the whole of what is annually produced, is annually consumed; or [...] what is produced in one year, is consumed in the next." Either productively or unproductively. P. 184 (p. 246).

Section III. "Consumption is co-extensive with production." "A man produces, only because he wishes to *have*. If the commodity which he produces is the commodity which he wishes to have, he stops when he has produced as much as he wishes to have[....] When a man produces a greater quantity [...] than he desires for himself, it can only be on one account; namely, that he desires some other commodity, which he can obtain in exchange for the surplus of what he himself has produced.... If a man desires one thing, and produces another, it can only be because the thing which he desires can be obtained by means of the thing which he produces, and better obtained than if he had endeavoured to produce it himself. After labour has been divided [...] each producer confines himself to some one commodity or part of a commodity, a small portion only of what he produces is used for his own consumption. The remainder he destines for the purpose of supplying him with all the other commodities which he desires; and when each man confines himself to one commodity, and exchanges what he produces for what is produced by other people, it is found that each obtains more of the several things which he desires, than he would have obtained had he endeavoured to produce them all for himself." ||XXXI| "In the case of the man who produces for himself, there is no *exchange*. He neither offers to buy any thing, nor to sell any thing. He has the property; he has produced it; and does not mean to part with it. If we apply, by a sort of metaphor, the terms demand and supply to this case, it is implied [...] that the demand and supply are exactly proportioned to one another.

As far then as regards the demand and supply of the market, we may leave that portion of the annual produce, which each of the owners consumes in the shape in which he produces or receives it, altogether out of the question." Pp. 186, 187 (p. 251).

"In speaking here of demand and supply, it is evident that we speak of aggregates. When we say of any particular nation, at any particular time, that its supply is equal to its demand, we do not mean in any one commodity, or any two commodities. We mean, that the amount of its demand in all commodities taken together, is equal to the amount of its supply in all commodities taken together. It may very well happen, notwithstanding this equality in the general sum of demands and supplies, that some one commodity or commodities may have been produced in a quantity either above or below the demand for those particular commodities." P. 188 (pp. 251, 252). "Two things are necessary to constitute a *demand*. These are—A Wish for the commodity, and An Equivalent to give for it. A demand means, the *will* to purchase, and the *means* of purchasing. If either is wanting, the purchase does not take place. An equivalent is the necessary foundation of all demand. It is in vain that a man wishes for commodities, if he has nothing to give for them. The equivalent which a man brings is the *instrument* of demand. The extent of his demand is measured by the extent of his equivalent. The demand and the equivalent are convertible terms, and the *one* may be substituted *for the other*. [...] We have already seen, that every man, who produces, has a wish for other commodities, than those which he has produced, to the *extent* of all that he has produced beyond what he wishes to keep for his own consumption. And it is evident, that whatever a man has produced and does not wish to keep for his own consumption, is a stock which he may give in exchange for other commodities. His *will*, therefore, *to purchase*, and his *means of purchasing*—in other words, his demand, is exactly equal to the amount of what he has produced and does not mean to consume." Pp. 188-89 (pp. 252, 253).

With his customary cynical acumen and clarity, Mill here analyses exchange on the basis of private property.

Man *produces* only in order to *have*—this is the basic presupposition of private property. The aim of production is *having*. And not only does production have this kind of *useful* aim; it has also a *selfish* aim; man produces only in order to *possess* for himself; the object he produces is the objectification of his *immediate,* selfish *need*. For man himself—in a savage, barbaric condition—therefore, the amount of his production is determined by the *extent* of his immediate need, the content of which is *directly* the object produced.

Under these conditions, therefore, man produces *no more* than he immediately requires. The *limit of his need* forms the *limit of his production*. Thus demand and supply exactly coincide. The extent of his production is *measured* by his need. In this case no exchange takes place, or exchange is reduced to the exchange of his labour for the product of his labour, and this exchange is the latent form, the germ, of real exchange.

As soon as exchange takes place, a surplus is produced beyond the immediate limit of possession. But this surplus production does not mean rising above selfish need. On the contrary, it is only an *indirect* way of satisfying a need which finds its objectification not in *this* production but in the production of someone else. Production has become a *means of gaining a living,* labour to gain a living. Whereas under the first state of affairs, therefore, need is the measure of production, under the second state of affairs production, or rather *ownership of the product,* is the measure of how far needs can be satisfied.

I have produced for myself and not for you, just as you have produced for yourself and not for me. In itself, the result of my production has as little connection with you as the result of your production has directly with me. That is to say, our production is not man's production for man as a man, i.e., it is not *social* production. Neither of us, therefore, as a man stands in a relation of enjoyment to the other's product. As men, we do not exist as far as our respective products are concerned. Hence our exchange, too, cannot be the mediating process by which it is confirmed that my product ‖XXXII‖ is [for] you, because it is an *objectification* of your own nature, your need. For it is not *man's nature* that forms the link between the products we make for one another. Exchange can only set in *motion,* only confirm, the *character* of the relation which each of us has in regard to his own product, and therefore to the product of the other. Each of us sees in his product only the objectification of his *own* selfish need, and therefore in the product of the other the objectification of a *different* selfish need, independent of him and alien to him.

As a man you have, of course, a human relation to my product: you have *need* of my product. Hence it exists for you as an object of your desire and your will. But your need, your desire, your will, are powerless as regards my product. That means, therefore, that your *human* nature, which accordingly is bound to stand in intimate relation to my human production, is not your *power* over this production, your possession of it, for it is not the *specific character,* not the *power,* of man's nature that is recognised in my production. They [your need, your desire, etc.] constitute rather the *tie* which makes you dependent on me, because they put you in a position of dependence on my product. Far from being the *means* which would give you *power* over my production, they are instead the *means* for giving me power over you.

When I produce *more* of an object than I myself can directly use, my *surplus* production is cunningly *calculated* for your need. It is only in *appearance* that I produce a surplus of this object. In reality I produce a *different* object, the object of your production, which I intend to exchange against this surplus, an exchange which in my mind I have already completed. The *social* relation in which I stand to you, my labour for your need, is therefore also a mere *semblance*, and our complementing each other is likewise a mere *semblance*, the basis of which is mutual plundering. The intention of *plundering*, of *deception*, is necessarily present in the background, for since our exchange is a selfish one, on your side as on mine, and since the selfishness of each seeks to get the better of that of the other, we necessarily seek to deceive each other. It is true though, that the power which I attribute to my object over yours requires your *recognition* in order to become a real power. Our mutual recognition of the respective powers of our objects, however, is a struggle, and in a struggle the victor is the one who has more energy, force, insight, or adroitness. If I have sufficient physical force, I plunder you directly. If physical force cannot be used, we try to impose on each other by bluff, and the more adroit overreaches the other. For the *totality* of the relationship, it is a matter of chance who overreaches whom. The *ideal, intended* overreaching takes place on both sides, i.e., each in his own judgment has overreached the other.

On both sides, therefore, exchange is necessarily mediated by the *object* which each side produces and possesses. The ideal relationship to the respective objects of our production is, of course, our mutual need. But the *real, true* relationship, which *actually* occurs and takes effect, is only the mutually *exclusive possession* of our respective products. What gives your need of my article its *value, worth* and *effect* for me is solely your *object*, the *equivalent* of my object. Our respective products, therefore, are the *means*, the *mediator*, the *instrument*, the *acknowledged power* of our mutual needs. Your *demand* and the *equivalent of your possession*, therefore, are for me terms that are *equal in significance* and validity, and your demand only acquires a *meaning*, owing to having an effect, when it has meaning and effect in relation to me. As a mere human being without this instrument your demand is an unsatisfied aspiration on your part and an idea that does not exist for me. As a human being, therefore, you stand in no relationship to my object, because *I myself* have no human relationship to it. But the *means* is the *true power* over an object and therefore we mutually regard our products as the *power* of each of us over the other and over himself. That is to say, our own product has risen up against us; it seemed to be our property, but in fact we are its property. We ourselves are excluded from *true* property because our *property* excludes other men.

The only intelligible language in which we converse with one another consists of our objects in their relation to each other. We would not understand a human language and it would remain without effect. By one side it would be recognised and felt as being a request, an entreaty, ||XXXIII|| and therefore a *humiliation*, and consequently uttered with a feeling of shame, of degradation. By the other side it would be regarded as *impudence* or *lunacy* and rejected as such. We are to such an extent estranged from man's essential nature that the direct language of this essential nature seems to us a *violation of human dignity*, whereas the estranged language of material values seems to be the well-justified assertion of human dignity that is self-confident and conscious of itself.

Although in your eyes your product is an *instrument*, a *means*, for taking possession of my product and thus for satisfying your need; yet in my eyes it is the *purpose* of our exchange. For me, you are rather the means and instrument for producing this object that is my aim, just as conversely you stand in the same relationship to my object. But 1) each of us actually *behaves* in the way he is regarded by the other. You have actually made yourself the means, the instrument, the producer of *your* own object in order to gain possession of mine; 2) your own object is for you only the *sensuously perceptible covering*, the *hidden shape*, of my object; for its production *signifies* and seeks to *express* the acquisition of my object. In fact, therefore, you have become for yourself a *means*, an *instrument* of your object, of which your desire is the *servant*, and you have performed menial services in order that the object shall never again do a favour to your desire. If then our mutual thraldom to the object at the beginning of the process is now seen to be in reality the relationship between *master* and *slave*, that is merely the *crude* and *frank* expression of our *essential* relationship.

Our *mutual* value is for us the *value* of our mutual objects. Hence for us man himself is mutually of *no value*.

Let us suppose that we had carried out production as human beings. Each of us would have *in two ways affirmed* himself and the other person. 1) In my *production* I would have objectified my *individuality*, its *specific character*, and therefore enjoyed not only an individual *manifestation of my life* during the activity, but also when looking at the object I would have the individual pleasure of knowing my personality to be *objective*, *visible to the senses* and hence a power *beyond all doubt*. 2) In your enjoyment or use of my product I would have the *direct* enjoyment both of being conscious of having satisfied a *human* need by my work, that is, of having objectified *man's* essential nature, and of having thus created an object corresponding to the need of another *man's* essential nature. 3) I would have been for you the *mediator* between you and the species, and therefore would become recognised and felt by you yourself as a completion of your own essential nature and as a necessary part of yourself, and consequently would know myself to be confirmed both in your thought and your love. 4) In the individual expression of my life I would have directly created your expression of your life, and therefore in my individual activity I would have directly *confirmed* and *realised* my true nature, my *human* nature, my *communal nature*.

Our products would be so many mirrors in which we saw reflected our essential nature.

This relationship would moreover be reciprocal; what occurs on my side has also to occur on yours.

Let us review the various factors as seen in our supposition:

My work would be a *free manifestation of life*, hence an *enjoyment of life*. Presupposing private property, my work is an *alienation of life*, for I work *in order to live*, in order to obtain for myself the *means of life*. My work *is not* my life.

Secondly, the *specific nature* of my individuality, therefore, would be affirmed in my labour, since the latter would be an affirmation of my *individual* life. Labour therefore would be *true, active property*. Presupposing private property, my individuality is alienated to such a degree that this *activity* is instead *hateful* to me, a *torment*, and rather the *semblance* of an activity. Hence, too, it is only a *forced* activity and one imposed on me only through an *external* fortuitous need, *not* through an *inner, essential* one.

My labour can appear in my object only as what it is. It cannot appear as something which by its nature it is *not*. Hence it appears only as the expression of my *loss of self* and of my *powerlessness* that is objective, sensuously perceptible, obvious and therefore put beyond all doubt. |XXXIII||[53]

Written in the first half of 1844
First published in: Marx/Engels, *Gesamtausgabe*, Abt. 1, Bd. 3, 1932

Printed according to the manuscript

[ECONOMIC AND PHILOSOPHIC MANUSCRIPTS OF 1844[54]]

Written between April and August 1844
First published in full in: Marx/Engels, *Gesamtausgabe*, Abt. 1, Bd. 3, 1932

Printed according to the manuscript

Preface

|XXXIX| I have already announced in the *Deutsch-Französische Jahrbücher* the critique of jurisprudence and political science in the form of a critique of the *Hegelian* philosophy of law.[a] While preparing it for publication, the intermingling of criticism directed only against speculation with criticism of the various subjects themselves proved utterly unsuitable, hampering the development of the argument and rendering comprehension difficult. Moreover, the wealth and diversity of the subjects to be treated could have been compressed into *one* work only in a purely aphoristic style; whilst an aphoristic presentation of this kind, for its part, would have given the *impression* of arbitrary systematism. I shall therefore publish the critique of law, ethics, politics, etc., in a series of distinct, independent pamphlets, and afterwards try in a special work to present them again as a connected whole showing the interrelationship of the separate parts, and lastly attempt a critique of the speculative elaboration of that material. For this reason it will be found that the interconnection between political economy and the state, law, ethics, civil life, etc., is touched upon in the present work only to the extent to which political economy itself expressly touches upon these subjects.

It is hardly necessary to assure the reader conversant with political economy that my results have been attained by means of a wholly empirical analysis based on a conscientious critical study of political economy.

⟨Whereas the uninformed reviewer[b] who tries to hide his complete ignorance and intellectual poverty by hurling the "uto-

---

[a] See this volume, pp. 175-87.—*Ed.*
[b] Bruno Bauer.—*Ed.*

pian phrase" at the positive critic's head, or again such phrases as "quite pure, quite resolute, quite critical criticism", the "not merely legal but social—utterly social—society", the "compact, massy mass", the "outspoken spokesmen of the massy mass",[55] this reviewer has yet to furnish the first proof that besides his theological family affairs he has anything to contribute to a discussion of *worldly* matters.⟩

It goes without saying that besides the French and English socialists I have also used German socialist works. The only *original* German works of substance in this science, however—other than Weitling's writings—are the essays by *Hess* published in *Einundzwanzig Bogen*[56] and *Umrisse zu einer Kritik der Nationalökonomie* by *Engels*[a] in the *Deutsch-Französische Jahrbücher*, where also the basic elements of this work [*Economic and Philosophic Manuscripts of 1844*] have been indicated by me in a very general way.

⟨Besides being indebted to these authors who have given critical attention to political economy, positive criticism as a whole—and therefore also German positive criticism of political economy—owes its true foundation to the discoveries of *Feuerbach*, against whose *Philosophie der Zukunft* and *Thesen zur Reform der Philosophie* in the *Anekdota*,[b] despite the tacit use that is made of them, the petty envy of some and the veritable wrath of others seem to have instigated a regular conspiracy of *silence*.⟩

It is only with *Feuerbach* that *positive*, humanistic and naturalistic criticism begins. The less noise they make, the more certain, profound, extensive, and enduring is the effect of *Feuerbach*'s writings, the only writings since Hegel's *Phänomenologie* and *Logik* to contain a real theoretical revolution.

In contrast to the *critical theologian*[c] of our day, I have deemed the concluding chapter of this work—a critical discussion of *Hegelian dialectic* and philosophy as a whole—to be absolutely necessary, ||XL| a task not yet performed. This *lack of thoroughness* is not accidental, since even the *critical* theologian remains a *theologian*. Hence, either he has to start from certain presuppositions of philosophy accepted as authoritative; or, if in the process of criticism and as a result of other people's discoveries doubts about these philosophical presuppositions have arisen in him, he abandons them in a cowardly and unwarrantable fashion, *abstracts* from them, thus showing his servile dependence on these presup-

---

[a] See this volume, pp. 418-43.—*Ed.*
[b] *Anekdota zur neuesten deutschen Philosophie und Publicistik.*—*Ed.*
[c] Marx has in mind Bruno Bauer.—*Ed.*

positions and his resentment at this servility merely in a negative, unconscious and sophistical manner.

⟨He does this either by constantly repeating assurances concerning the *purity* of his own criticism, or by trying to make it seem as though all that was left for criticism to deal with now was some other limited form of criticism outside itself—say eighteenth-century criticism—and also the limitations of the *masses,* in order to divert the observer's attention as well as his own from the *necessary* task of settling accounts between *criticism* and its point of origin—Hegelian *dialectic* and German philosophy as a whole—that is, from this necessary raising of modern criticism above its own limitation and crudity. Eventually, however, whenever discoveries (such as *Feuerbach*'s) are made regarding the nature of his own philosophic presuppositions, the critical theologian partly makes it appear as if *he* were the one who had accomplished this, producing that appearance by taking the results of these discoveries and, without being able to develop them, hurling them in the form of *catch-phrases* at writers still caught in the confines of philosophy. He partly even manages to acquire a sense of his own superiority to such discoveries by asserting in a mysterious way and in a veiled, malicious and sceptical fashion elements of the Hegelian *dialectic* which he still finds lacking in the criticism of that dialectic (which have not yet been critically served up to him for his use) against such criticism—not having tried to bring such elements into their proper relation or having been capable of doing so, asserting, say, the category of mediating proof against the category of positive, self-originating truth, [...]^a in a way *peculiar* to Hegelian dialectic. For to the theological critic it seems quite natural that everything has to be *done* by philosophy, so that he can *chatter away* about purity, resoluteness, and quite critical criticism; and he fancies himself the true *conqueror of philosophy* whenever he happens to *feel* some element [57] in Hegel to be lacking in Feuerbach—for however much he practises the spiritual idolatry of *"self-consciousness"* and *"mind"* the theological critic does not get beyond feeling to consciousness.⟩

On close inspection *theological criticism*—genuinely progressive though it was at the inception of the movement—is seen in the final analysis to be nothing but the culmination and consequence of the old *philosophical,* and especially the *Hegelian, transcendentalism,* twisted into a *theological caricature.* This interesting example of historical justice, which now assigns to theology, ever philosophy's

---

^a Three words in the manuscript cannot be deciphered.— *Ed.*

spot of infection, the further role of portraying in itself the negative dissolution of philosophy, i.e., the process of its decay—this historical nemesis I shall demonstrate on another occasion.[58]

⟨How far, on the other hand, *Feuerbach*'s discoveries about the nature of philosophy still, for their *proof* at least, called for a critical discussion of philosophical dialectic will be seen from my exposition itself.⟩ |XL||

[*First Manuscript*]

WAGES OF LABOUR

|I,1| *Wages* are determined through the antagonistic struggle between capitalist and worker. Victory goes necessarily to the capitalist. The capitalist can live longer without the worker than can the worker without the capitalist. Combination among the capitalists is customary and effective; workers' combination is prohibited and painful in its consequences for them. Besides, the landowner and the capitalist can make use of industrial advantages to augment their revenues; the worker has neither rent nor interest on capital to supplement his industrial income. Hence the intensity of the competition among the workers. Thus only for the workers is the separation of capital, landed property, and labour an inevitable, essential and detrimental separation. Capital and landed property need not remain fixed in this abstraction, as must the labour of the workers.

The separation of capital, rent, and labour is thus fatal for the worker.

The lowest and the only necessary wage rate is that providing for the subsistence of the worker for the duration of his work and as much more as is necessary for him to support a family and for the race of labourers not to die out. The ordinary wage, according to Smith, is the lowest compatible with common humanity,[59] that is, with cattle-like existence.

The demand for men necessarily governs the production of men, as of every other commodity. Should supply greatly exceed demand, a section of the workers sinks into beggary or starvation. The worker's existence is thus brought under the same condition as the existence of every other commodity. The worker has become a commodity, and it is a bit of luck for him if he can find a buyer. And the demand on which the life of the worker depends, depends on the whim of the rich and the capitalists. Should supply ex[ceed]^a demand, then one of the consti[tuent] parts of the price—profit, rent or wages—is paid below its *rate*, [a part of these] factors is therefore withdrawn from this application, and thus the market price gravitates [towards the] natural price as the centre-point. But (1) where there is considerable division of labour it is most difficult for the worker to direct his labour into other channels; (2) because of his subordinate relation to the capitalist, he is the first to suffer.

Thus in the gravitation of market price to natural price it is the worker who loses most of all and necessarily. And it is just the capacity of the capitalist to direct his capital into another channel which either renders the worker,^b who is restricted to some particular branch of labour, destitute, or forces him to submit to every demand of this capitalist.

||II,1|| The accidental and sudden fluctuations in market price hit rent less than they do that part of the price which is resolved into profit and wages; but they hit profit less than they do wages. In most cases, for every wage that rises, one remains *stationary* and one *falls*.

The worker need not necessarily gain when the capitalist does, but he necessarily loses when the latter loses. Thus, the worker does not gain if the capitalist keeps the market price above the natural price by virtue of some manufacturing or trading secret, or by virtue of monopoly or the favourable situation of his land.

Furthermore, *the prices of labour are much more constant than the prices of provisions.* Often they stand in inverse proportion. In a dear year wages fall on account of the decrease in demand, but rise on account of the increase in the prices of provisions—and thus balance. In any case, a number of workers are left without bread. In cheap years wages rise on account of the rise in demand, but decrease on account of the fall in the prices of provisions—and thus balance.

Another respect in which the worker is at a disadvantage:

The labour prices of the various kinds of workers show much wider differences than the profits in the various branches in which capital is applied. In labour all the natural, spiritual, and social variety of individual activity is manifested and is variously rewarded, whilst dead capital always keeps the same pace and is indifferent to *real* individual activity.

---

^a The letters and words enclosed in square brackets in this sentence are indecipherable as they are covered by an inkspot.—*Ed.*

^b Here and occasionally later Marx uses the French word *ouvrier*.—*Ed.*

In general we should observe that in those cases where worker and capitalist equally suffer, the worker suffers in his very existence, the capitalist in the profit on his dead mammon.

The worker has to struggle not only for his physical means of subsistence; he has to struggle to get work, i. e., the possibility, the means, to perform his activity.

Let us take the three chief conditions in which society can find itself and consider the situation of the worker in them:

(1) If the wealth of society declines the worker suffers most of all, and for the following reason: although the working class cannot gain so much as can the class of property owners in a prosperous state of society, *no one suffers so cruelly from its decline as the working class.*[a]

||III,1|| (2) Let us now take a society in which wealth is increasing. This condition is the only one favourable to the worker. Here competition between the capitalists sets in. The demand for workers exceeds their supply. But:

In the first place, the raising of wages gives rise to *overwork* among the workers. The more they wish to earn, the more must they sacrifice their time and carry out slave-labour, completely losing all their freedom, in the service of greed. Thereby they shorten their lives. This shortening of their life-span is a favourable circumstance for the working class as a whole, for as a result of it an ever-fresh supply of labour becomes necessary. This class has always to sacrifice a part of itself in order not to be wholly destroyed.

Furthermore: When does a society find itself in a condition of advancing wealth? When the capitals and the revenues of a country are growing. But this is only possible:

(α) As the result of the accumulation of much labour, capital being accumulated labour; as the result, therefore, of the fact that more and more of his products are being taken away from the worker, that to an increasing extent his own labour confronts him as another man's property and that the means of his existence and his activity are increasingly concentrated in the hands of the capitalist.

(β) The accumulation of capital increases the division of labour, and the division of labour increases the number of workers. Conversely, the number of workers increases the division of labour, just as the division of labour increases the accumulation of capital. With this division of labour on the one hand and the accumulation of capital on the other, the worker becomes ever more exclusively dependent on labour, and on a particular, very one-sided, machine-like labour at that. Just as he is thus depressed spiritually and

---

[a] Cf. Adam Smith, *Wealth of Nations*, Vol. I, p. 230 (Garnier, t. II, p. 162).—*Ed.*

physically to the condition of a machine and from being a man becomes an abstract activity and a belly, so he also becomes ever more dependent on every fluctuation in market price, on the application of capital, and on the whim of the rich. Equally, the increase in the |IV,1| class of people wholly dependent on work intensifies competition among the workers, thus lowering their price. In the factory system this situation of the worker reaches its climax.

(γ) In an increasingly prosperous society only the richest of the rich can continue to live on money interest. Everyone else has to carry on a business with his capital, or venture it in trade. As a result, the competition between the capitalists becomes more intense. The concentration of capital increases, the big capitalists ruin the small, and a section of the erstwhile capitalists sinks into the working class, which as a result of this supply again suffers to some extent a depression of wages and passes into a still greater dependence on the few big capitalists. The number of capitalists having been diminished, their competition with respect to the workers scarcely exists any longer; and the number of workers having been increased, their competition among themselves has become all the more intense, unnatural, and violent. Consequently, a section of the working class falls into beggary or starvation just as necessarily as a section of the middle capitalists falls into the working class.

Hence even in the condition of society most favourable to the worker, the inevitable result for the worker is overwork and premature death, decline to a mere machine, a bond servant of capital, which piles up dangerously over and against him, more competition, and starvation or beggary for a section of the workers.

|IV,1| The raising of wages excites in the worker the capitalist's mania to get rich, which he, however, can only satisfy by the sacrifice of his mind and body. The raising of wages presupposes and entails the accumulation of capital, and thus sets the product of labour against the worker as something ever more alien to him. Similarly, the division of labour renders him ever more one-sided and dependent, bringing with it the competition not only of men but also of machines. Since the worker has sunk to the level of a machine, he can be confronted by the machine as a competitor. Finally, as the amassing of capital increases the amount of industry and therefore the number of workers, it causes the same amount of industry to manufacture a *larger amount of products*, which leads to over-production and thus either ends by throwing a large

section of workers out of work or by reducing their wages to the most miserable minimum.

Such are the consequences of a state of society most favourable to the worker—namely, of a state of *growing, advancing* wealth.

Eventually, however, this state of growth must sooner or later reach its peak. What is the worker's position now?

> 3) "In a country which had acquired that full complement of riches [...] both the wages of labour and the profits of stock would probably be very low [...] the competition for employment would necessarily be so great as to reduce the wages of labour to what was barely sufficient to keep up the number of labourers, and, the country being already fully peopled, that number could never be augmented."[a]

The surplus would have to die.

Thus in a declining state of society—increasing misery of the worker; in an advancing state—misery with complications; and in a fully developed state of society—static misery.

||VI,1|| Since, however, according to Smith, a society is not happy, of which the greater part suffers[b]—yet even the wealthiest state of society leads to this suffering of the majority—and since the economic system[60] (and in general a society based on private interest) leads to this wealthiest condition, it follows that the goal of the economic system is the *unhappiness* of society.

Concerning the relationship between worker and capitalist we should add that the capitalist is more than compensated for rising wages by the reduction in the amount of labour time, and that rising wages and rising interest on capital operate on the price of commodities like simple and compound interest respectively.

Let us put ourselves now wholly at the standpoint of the political economist, and follow him in comparing the theoretical and practical claims of the workers.

He tells us that originally and in theory the *whole product* of labour belongs to the worker. But at the same time he tells us that in actual fact what the worker gets is the smallest and utterly indispensable part of the product—as much, only, as is necessary for his existence, not as a human being, but as a worker, and for the propagation, not of humanity, but of the slave class of workers.

The political economist tells us that everything is bought with labour and that capital is nothing but accumulated labour; but at the same time he tells us that the worker, far from being able to buy everything, must sell himself and his humanity.

---

[a] Adam Smith, *Wealth of Nations*, Vol. I, p. 84 (Garnier, t. I, p. 193).—*Ed.*
[b] Cf. Adam Smith, *Wealth of Nations*, Vol. I, p. 70 (Garnier, t. I, pp. 159-60).—*Ed.*

Whilst the rent of the idle landowner usually amounts to a third of the product of the soil, and the profit of the busy capitalist to as much as twice the interest on money, the "something more" which the worker himself earns at the best of times amounts to so little that of four children of his, two must starve and die.

|VII,1-3| Whilst according to the political economists it is solely through labour that man enhances the value of the products of nature, whilst labour is man's active possession, according to this same political economy the landowner and the capitalist, who *qua* landowner and capitalist are merely privileged and idle gods, are everywhere superior to the worker and lay down the law to him.

Whilst according to the political economists labour is the sole unchanging price of things, there is nothing more fortuitous than the price of labour, nothing exposed to greater fluctuations.

Whilst the division of labour raises the productive power of labour and increases the wealth and refinement of society, it impoverishes the worker and reduces him to a machine. Whilst labour brings about the accumulation of capital and with this the increasing prosperity of society, it renders the worker ever more dependent on the capitalist, leads him into competition of a new intensity, and drives him into the headlong rush of over-production, with its subsequent corresponding slump.

Whilst the interest of the worker, according to the political economists, never stands opposed to the interest of society, society always and necessarily stands opposed to the interest of the worker.

According to the political economists, the interest of the worker is never opposed to that of society: (1) because the rising wages are more than compensated by the reduction in the amount of labour time, together with the other consequences set forth above; and (2) because in relation to society the whole gross product is the net product, and only in relation to the private individual has the net product any significance.

But that labour itself, not merely in present conditions but insofar as its purpose in general is the mere increase of wealth—that labour itself, I say, is harmful and pernicious—follows from the political economist's line of argument, without his being aware of it.

In theory, rent of land and profit on capital are *deductions* suffered by wages. In actual fact, however, wages are a deduction

First page of the Preface to the *Economic and Philosophic Manuscripts of 1844*

which land and capital allow to go to the worker, a concession from the product of labour to the workers, to labour.

When society is in a state of decline, the worker suffers most severely. The specific severity of his burden he owes to his position as a worker, but the burden as such to the position of society.

But when society is in a state of progress, the ruin and impoverishment of the worker is the product of his labour and of the wealth produced by him. The misery results, therefore, from the *essence* of present-day labour itself.

Society in a state of maximum wealth—an ideal, but one which is approximately attained, and which at least is the aim of political economy as of civil society—means for the workers *static misery*.

It goes without saying that the *proletarian*, i. e., the man who, being without capital and rent, lives purely by labour, and by a one-sided, abstract labour, is considered by political economy only as a *worker*. Political economy can therefore advance the proposition that the proletarian, the same as any horse, must get as much as will enable him to work. It does not consider him when he is not working, as a human being; but leaves such consideration to criminal law, to doctors, to religion, to the statistical tables, to politics and to the poor-house overseer.

Let us now rise above the level of political economy and try to answer two questions on the basis of the above exposition, which has been presented almost in the words of the political economists:

(1) What in the evolution of mankind is the meaning of this reduction of the greater part of mankind to abstract labour?

(2) What are the mistakes committed by the piecemeal reformers, who either want to *raise* wages and in this way to improve the situation of the working class, or regard *equality* of wages (as Proudhon does) as the goal of social revolution?

In political economy *labour* occurs only in the form of *activity as a source of livelihood.*[a]

||VIII, 1|| "It can be asserted that those occupations which presuppose specific talents or longer training have become on the whole more lucrative; whilst the proportionate reward for mechanically monotonous activity in which one person can be trained as easily and quickly as another has fallen with growing competition, and was inevitably bound to fall. And it is just *this* sort of work which in the present state of the organisation of labour is still by far the commonest. If therefore a worker in the first category now earns seven times as much as he did, say, fifty years ago, whilst the earnings of another in the second category have remained unchanged, then of course both are earning *on the average* four times as much. But if the first category comprises only a thousand workers in a particular

---

[a] In the manuscript a blank space is left here.— *Ed.*

country, and the second a million, then 999,000 are no better off than fifty years ago—and they are *worse off* if at the same time the prices of the necessaries of life have risen. With such superficial *calculations of averages* people try to deceive themselves about the most numerous class of the population. Moreover, the size of the *wage* is only one factor in the estimation of the *worker's income*, because it is essential for the measurement of the latter to take into account the certainty of its *duration*—which is obviously out of the question in the anarchy of so-called free competition, with its ever-recurring fluctuations and periods of stagnation. Finally, the *hours of work* customary formerly and now have to be considered. And for the English cotton-workers these have been increased, as a result of the entrepreneurs' mania for profit, ||IX,1| to between twelve and sixteen hours a day during the past twenty-five years or so—that is to say, precisely during the period of the introduction of labour-saving machines; and this increase in one country and in one branch of industry inevitably asserted itself elsewhere to a greater or lesser degree, for the right of the unlimited exploitation of the poor by the rich is still universally recognised." (Wilhelm Schulz, *Die Bewegung der Production*, p. 65.)

"But even if it were as true as it is false that the average income of *every* class of society has increased, the income-differences and *relative* income-distances may nevertheless have become greater and the contrasts between wealth and poverty accordingly stand out more sharply. For just *because* total production rises—and in the same measure as it rises—needs, desires and claims also multiply and thus *relative* poverty can increase whilst *absolute* poverty diminishes. The Samoyed living on fish oil and rancid fish is not poor because in his secluded society all have the same needs. But in a *state that is forging ahead*, which in the course of a decade, say, increased by a third its total production in proportion to the population, the worker who is getting as much at the end of ten years as at the beginning has not remained as well off, but has become poorer by a third." (op. cit., pp. 65-66.)

But political economy knows the worker only as a working animal—as a beast reduced to the strictest bodily needs.

"To develop in greater spiritual freedom, a people must break their bondage to their bodily needs—they must cease to be the slaves of the body. They must, above all, have *time* at their disposal for spiritual creative activity and spiritual enjoyment. The developments in the labour organism gain this time. Indeed, with new motive forces and improved machinery, a single worker in the cotton mills now often performs the work formerly requiring a hundred, or even 250 to 350 workers. Similar results can be observed in all branches of production, because external natural forces are being compelled to participate ||X,1| to an ever-greater degree in human labour. If the satisfaction of a given amount of material needs formerly required a certain expenditure of time and human effort which has later been reduced by half, then without any loss of material comfort the scope for spiritual activity and enjoyment has been simultaneously extended by as much.... But again the way in which the booty, that we win from old Cronus himself in his most private domain, is shared out is still decided by the dice-throw of blind, unjust Chance. In France it has been calculated that at the present stage in the development of production an average working period of five hours a day by every person capable of work could suffice for the satisfaction of all the material interests of society.... Notwithstanding the time saved by the perfecting of machinery, the duration of the slave-labour performed by a large population in the factories has only increased." (Schulz, op. cit., pp. 67, 68.)

"The transition from compound manual labour rests on a break-down of the latter into its simple operations. At first, however, only *some* of the uniformly-recurring operations will devolve on machines, while some will devolve on men. From the nature of things, and from confirmatory experience, it is clear that unendingly monotonous activity of this kind is as harmful to the mind as to the body; thus this *combination* of machinery with mere division of labour among a greater number of hands must inevitably show all the disadvantages of the latter. These disadvantages appear, among other things, in the greater mortality of factory ||XI,1| workers.... Consideration has not been given... to this big distinction as to how far men work *through* machines or how far *as* machines." (op. cit., p. 69.)

"In the future life of the peoples, however, the inanimate forces of nature working in machines will be our slaves and serfs." (op. cit., p. 74.)

"The English spinning mills employ 196,818 women and only 158,818 men. For every 100 male workers in the cotton mills of Lancashire there are 103 female workers, and in Scotland as many as 209. In the English flax mills of Leeds, for every 100 male workers there were found to be 147 female workers. In Druden[a] and on the east coast of Scotland as many as 280. In the English silk mills... many female workers; male workers predominate in the woollen mills where the work requires greater physical strength. In 1833, no fewer than 38,927 women were employed alongside 18,593 men in the North American cotton mills. As a result of the changes in the labour organism, a wider sphere of gainful employment has thus fallen to the share of the female sex.... Women now occupying an economically more independent position... the two sexes are drawn closer together in their social conditions." (op. cit., pp. 71-72.)

"Working in the English steam- and water-driven spinning mills in 1835 were: 20,558 children between the ages of eight and twelve; 35,867 between the ages of twelve and thirteen; and, lastly, 108,208 children between the ages of thirteen and eighteen.... Admittedly, further advances in mechanisation, by more and more removing all monotonous work from human hands, are operating in the direction of a gradual ||XII,1| elimination of this evil. But standing in the way of these more rapid advances is the very circumstance that the capitalists can, in the easiest and cheapest fashion, appropriate the energies of the lower classes down to the children, to be used *instead* of mechanical devices." (op. cit., pp. 70-71.)

"Lord Brougham's call to the workers—'Become capitalists'. ... This is the evil that millions are able to earn a bare subsistence for themselves only by strenuous labour which shatters the body and cripples them morally and intellectually; that they are even obliged to consider the misfortune of finding *such* work a piece of good fortune." (op. cit., p. 60.)

"In order to live, then, the non-owners are obliged to place themselves, directly or indirectly, *at the service* of the owners—to put themselves, that is to say, into a position of dependence upon them."[b] (Pecqueur, *Théorie nouvelle d'économie soc., etc.*, p. 409.)

Servants—pay; workers—wages; employees—salary or emoluments.[c] (loc. cit., pp. 409, 410.)

"To hire out one's labour", "to lend one's labour at interest", "to work in another's place".[d]

---

[a] This is probably a misspelling of Dundee.—*Ed.*

[b] "Pour vivre donc, les non-propriétaires sont obligés de se mettre directement ou indirectement *au service* des propriétaires, c.-à.-d. sous leur dépendance."—*Ed.*

[c] *Domestiques—gages; ouvriers—salaires; employés—traitement ou émoluments.*—*Ed.*

[d] "louer son travail", "prêter son travail à l'intérêt", "travailler à la place d'autrui".—*Ed.*

"To hire out the materials of labour", "to lend the materials of labour at interest", "to make others work in one's place".[a] (op. cit., p. 411.)

||XIII,1| "Such an economic order condemns men to occupations so mean, to a degradation so devastating and bitter, that by comparison savagery seems like a kingly condition...."[b] (op. cit., pp. 417, 418.) "Prostitution of the non-owning class in all its forms."[c] (op. cit., p. 421 f.) Ragmen.

Charles Loudon, in the book *Solution du problème de la population, etc.,* Paris, 1842,[61] declares the number of prostitutes in England to be between sixty and seventy thousand. The number of women of doubtful virtue is said to be equally large (p. 228).

"The average life of these unfortunate creatures on the streets, after they have embarked on their career of vice, is about six or seven years. To maintain the number of sixty to seventy thousand prostitutes, there must be in the three kingdoms at least eight to nine thousand women who commit themselves to this abject profession each year, or about twenty-four new victims each day—an average of *one* per hour; and it follows that if the same proportion holds good over the whole surface of the globe, there must constantly be in existence one and a half million unfortunate women of this kind."[d] (op. cit., p. 229.)

"The numbers of the poverty-stricken grow with their poverty, and at the extreme limit of destitution human beings are crowded together in the greatest numbers contending with each other for the right to suffer.... In 1821 the population of Ireland was 6,801,827. In 1831 it had risen to 7,764,010—an increase of 14 per cent in ten years. In Leinster, the wealthiest province, the population increased by only 8 per cent; whilst in Connaught, the most poverty-stricken province, the increase reached 21 per cent. (*Extract from the Enquiries Published in England on Ireland,* Vienna, 1840.)"[e] (Buret, *De la misère, etc.,* t. I, pp. 36, 37.)

Political economy considers labour in the abstract as a thing; labour is a commodity. If the price is high, then the commodity is

---

[a] "Louer la matière du travail", "prêter la matière du travail à l'intérêt", "faire travailler autrui à sa place".—*Ed.*

[b] "Cette constitution économique condamne les hommes à des métiers tellement abjects, à une dégradation tellement désolante et amère, que la sauvagerie apparaît, en comparaison, comme une royale condition."—*Ed.*

[c] "La prostitution de la chair non-propriétaire sous toutes les formes."—*Ed.*

[d] "La moyenne vie de ces infortunées créatures sur le pavé, après qu'elles sont entrées dans la carrière du vice, est d'environ six ou sept ans. De manière que pour maintenir le nombre de 60 à 70 000 prostituées, il doit y avoir, dans les 3 royaumes, au moins 8 à 9000 femmes qui se vouent à cet infâme métier chaque année, ou environ vingt-quatre nouvelles victimes par jour, ce qui est la moyenne *d'une* par heure; et conséquemment, si la même proportion a lieu sur toute la surface du globe, il doit y avoir constamment un million et demi de ces malheureuses."—*Ed.*

[e] "La population des misérables croît avec leur misère, et c'est à la limite extrême du dénûment que les êtres humains se pressent en plus grand nombre pour se disputer le droit de souffrir.... En 1821, la population de l'Irlande était de 6 801 827. En 1831, elle s'était élevée à 7 764 010; c'est 14 p. % d'augmentation en dix ans. Dans le Leinster, province où il y a le plus d'aisance, la population n'a augmenté que de 8 p. %, tandis que, dans le Connaught, province la plus misérable, l'augmentation s'est élevée à 21 p. %. (*Extraits des Enquêtes publiées en Angleterre sur l'Irlande,* Vienne, 1840.)"—*Ed.*

in great demand; if the price is low, then the commodity is in great supply: the price of labour as a commodity must fall lower and lower. (Buret, op. cit., p. 43.) This is made inevitable partly by the competition between capitalist and worker, partly by the competition amongst the workers.

"The working population, the seller of labour, is necessarily reduced to accepting the most meagre part of the product.... Is the theory of labour as a commodity anything other than a theory of disguised bondage?"[a] (op. cit., p. 43.) "Why then has nothing but an exchange-value been seen in labour?"[b] (op. cit., p. 44.)

The large workshops prefer to buy the labour of women and children, because this costs less than that of men. (op. cit.)

"The worker is not at all in the position of a *free seller vis-à-vis* the one who employs him.... The capitalist is always free to employ labour, and the worker is always forced to sell it. The value of labour is completely destroyed if it is not sold every instant. Labour can neither be accumulated nor even be saved, unlike true [commodities].

||XIV, 1|| "Labour is life, and if life is not each day exchanged for food, it suffers and soon perishes. To claim that human life is a commodity, one must, therefore, admit slavery."[c] (op. cit., pp. 49, 50.)

If then labour is a commodity it is a commodity with the most unfortunate attributes. But even by the principles of political economy it is no commodity, for it is not the *"free result of a free transaction"*. [op. cit., p. 50.] The present economic regime

"simultaneously lowers the price and the remuneration of labour; it perfects the worker and degrades the man".[d] (op. cit., pp. 52-53.) "Industry has become a war, and commerce a gamble."[e] (op. cit., p. 62.)

"The cotton-working machines"[f] (in England) alone represent 84,000,000 manual workers. [op. cit., p. 193, note].

Up to the present, industry has been in a state of war, a war of conquest:

---

[a] "...La population ouvrière, marchande de travail, est forcément réduite à la plus faible part du produit... la théorie du travail marchandise est-elle autre chose qu'une théorie de servitude déguisée?"—*Ed.*

[b] "Pourquoi donc n'avoir vu dans le travail qu'une valeur d'échange?"—*Ed.*

[c] "Le travailleur n'est point vis-à-vis de celui qui l'emploie dans la position d'un *libre vendeur* ... le capitaliste est toujours libre d'employer le travail, et l'ouvrier est toujours forcé de le vendre. La valeur du travail est complètement détruite, s'il n'est pas vendu à chaque instant. Le travail n'est susceptible ni d'accumulation, ni même d'épargne, à la différence des véritables [marchandises].
Le travail c'est la vie, et si la vie ne s'échange pas chaque jour contre des aliments, elle souffre et périt bientôt. Pour que la vie de l'homme soit une marchandise, il faut donc admettre l'esclavage."—*Ed.*

[d] "Abaisse à la fois et le prix et la rémunération du travail; il perfectionne l'ouvrier et dégrade l'homme".—*Ed.*

[e] "L'industrie est devenue une guerre et le commerce un jeu."—*Ed.*

[f] "Les machines à travailler le coton".—*Ed.*

"It has squandered the lives of the men who made up its army with the same indifference as the great conquerors. Its aim was the possession of wealth, not the happiness of men."[a] (Buret, op. cit., p. 20.) "These interests" (that is, economic interests), "freely left to themselves ... must necessarily come into conflict; they have no other arbiter but war, and the decisions of war assign defeat and death to some, in order to give victory to the others.... It is in the conflict of opposed forces that science seeks order and equilibrium: *perpetual war*, according to it, is the sole means of obtaining peace; that war is called competition."[b] (op. cit., p. 23.)

"The industrial war, to be conducted with success, demands large armies which it can amass on one spot and profusely decimate. And it is neither from devotion nor from duty that the soldiers of this army bear the exertions imposed on them, but only to escape the hard necessity of hunger. They feel neither attachment nor gratitude towards their bosses, nor are these bound to their subordinates by any feeling of benevolence. They do not know them as men, but only as instruments of production which have to yield as much as possible with as little cost as possible. These populations of workers, ever more crowded together, have not even the assurance of always being employed. Industry, which has called them together, only lets them live while it needs them, and as soon as it can get rid of them it abandons them without the slightest scruple; and the workers are compelled to offer their persons and their powers for whatever price they can get. The longer, more painful and more disgusting the work they are given, the less they are paid. There are those who, with sixteen hours' work a day and unremitting exertion, scarcely buy the right not to die." (op. cit., pp. 68-69.)

||XV,1|| "We are convinced ... as are the commissioners charged with the inquiry into the condition of the hand-loom weavers, that the large industrial towns would in a short time lose their population of workers if they were not all the time receiving from the neighbouring rural areas constant recruitments of healthy men, a constant flow of fresh blood."[c] (op. cit., p. 362.) |XVI|

PROFIT OF CAPITAL

1. CAPITAL

||I, 2|What is the basis of *capital*, that is, of private property in the products of other men's labour?

---

[a] "Elle a prodigué la vie des hommes qui composaient son armée avec autant d'indifférence que les grands conquérants. Son but était la possession de la richesse, et non le bonheur des hommes."—*Ed.*

[b] "Ces intérêts" (sc. économiques), "librement abandonnés à eux-mêmes... doivent nécessairement entrer en conflit; ils n'ont d'autre arbitre que la guerre, et les décisions de la guerre donnent aux uns la défaite et la mort, pour donner aux autres la victoire... C'est dans le conflit des forces opposées que la science cherche l'ordre et l'équilibre: la *guerre perpétuelle* est selon elle le seul moyen d'obtenir la paix; cette guerre s'appelle la concurrence."—*Ed.*

[c] "Nous avons la conviction... partagée par les commissaires chargés de l'enquête sur la condition des tisserands à la main, que les grandes villes industrielles perdraient, en peu de temps, leur population de travailleurs, si elles ne recevaient, à chaque instant des campagnes voisines, des recrues continuelles d'hommes sains, de sang nouveau."—*Ed.*

"Even if capital itself does not merely amount to theft or fraud, it still requires the co-operation of legislation to sanctify inheritance." (Say, [*Traité d'économie politique*,] t. I, p. 136, note.)[62]

How does one become a proprietor of productive stock? How does one become owner of the products created by means of this stock?

By virtue of *positive law*. (Say, t. II, p. 4.)

What does one acquire with capital, with the inheritance of a large fortune, for instance?

"The person who [either acquires, or] succeeds to a great fortune, does not necessarily [acquire or] succeed to any political power [....] The power which that possession immediately and directly conveys to him, is the *power of purchasing*; a certain command over all the labour, or over all the produce of labour, which is then in the market." (*Wealth of Nations*, by Adam Smith, Vol. I, pp. 26-27 [Garnier, t. I, p. 61].)[63]

Capital is thus the *governing power* over labour and its products. The capitalist possesses this power, not on account of his personal or human qualities, but inasmuch as he is an *owner* of capital. His power is the *purchasing* power of his capital, which nothing can withstand.

Later we shall see first how the capitalist, by means of capital, exercises his governing power over labour, then, however, we shall see the governing power of capital over the capitalist himself.

What is capital?

"A certain quantity of *labour stocked* and stored up to be employed." (Adam Smith, op. cit., Vol. I, p. 295 [Garnier, t. II, p. 312].)

Capital is *stored-up labour*.

(2) *Fonds*, or stock,[a] is any accumulation of products of the soil or of manufacture. Stock is called *capital* only when it yields to its owner a revenue or profit. (Adam Smith, op. cit., p. 243 [Garnier, t. II, p. 191].

2. THE PROFIT OF CAPITAL

The *profit* or *gain of capital* is altogether different from the *wages of labour*. This difference is manifested in two ways: in the first place, the profits of capital are regulated altogether by the value of the capital employed, although the labour of inspection and direction associated with different capitals may be the same. Moreover in large works the whole of this labour is committed to some principal clerk, whose salary bears no regular proportion to the |II,2| capital of which he oversees the management. And although the labour of the proprietor is here reduced almost to nothing, he still demands profits in proportion to his capital. (Adam Smith, op. cit., Vol. I, p. 43 [Garnier, t. I, pp. 97-99].)[64]

---

[a] Marx uses the English word "stock".—*Ed.*

Why does the capitalist demand this proportion between profit and capital?

He would have no *interest* in employing the workers, unless he expected from the sale of their work something more than is necessary to replace the stock advanced by him as wages and he would have no *interest* to employ a great stock rather than a small one, unless his profits were to bear some proportion to the extent of his stock. (Adam Smith, op. cit., Vol. I, p. 42 [Garnier, t. I, pp. 96-97].)

The capitalist thus makes a profit, first, on the wages, and secondly on the raw materials advanced by him.

What proportion, then, does profit bear to capital?

If it is already difficult to determine the usual average level of wages at a particular place and at a particular time, it is even more difficult to determine the profit on capitals. A change in the price of the commodities in which the capitalist deals, the good or bad fortune of his rivals and customers, a thousand other accidents to which commodities are exposed both in transit and in the warehouses—all produce a daily, almost hourly variation in profit. (Adam Smith, op. cit., Vol. I, pp. 78-79 [Garnier, t. I, pp. 179-180].)

But though it is impossible to determine with precision what are the profits on capitals, some notion may be formed of them from the *interest of money*. Wherever a great deal can be made by the use of money, a great deal will be given for the use of it; wherever little can be made by it, little will be given. (Adam Smith, op. cit., Vol. I, p. 79 [Garnier, t. I p. 181].)

The proportion which the usual market rate of interest ought to bear to the rate of clear profit, necessarily varies as profit rises or falls. Double interest is in Great Britain reckoned what the merchants call a *good, moderate, reasonable profit*, terms which mean no more than a *common and usual profit*. (Adam Smith, op. cit., Vol. I, p. 87 [Garnier. t. I, p. 198].)

What is the *lowest* rate of profit? And what the *highest*?

The *lowest rate* of ordinary profit on capital must always be *something more* than what is sufficient to compensate the occasional losses to which every employment of stock is exposed. It is this surplus only which is neat or clear profit. The same holds for the lowest rate of interest. (Adam Smith, op. cit., Vol. I, p. 86 [Garnier, t. I, p. 196].)

|| III,2| The *highest rate* to which ordinary profits can rise is that which in the price of the greater part of commodities *eats up the whole of the rent of the land*, and reduces the wages of labour contained in the commodity supplied to the *lowest rate*, the bare subsistence of the labourer during his work. The worker must always be fed in some way or other while he is required to work; rent can disappear entirely. For example: the servants of the East India Company in Bengal. (Adam Smith, op. cit., Vol. I, pp. 86-87 [Garnier, t. I, pp. 197-98].)

Besides all the advantages of limited competition which the capitalist may *exploit* in this case, he can keep the market price above the natural price by quite decorous means.

For one thing, by keeping *secrets in trade* if the market is at a great distance from those who supply it, that is, by concealing a price change, its rise above the natural level. This concealment has the effect that other capitalists do not follow him in investing their capital in this branch of industry or trade.

Then again by keeping *secrets in manufacture*, which enable the capitalist to reduce the costs of production and supply his commodity at the same or even at lower prices than his competitors while obtaining a higher profit. (Deceiving by keeping secrets is not immoral? Dealings on the Stock Exchange.) *Furthermore*, where production is restricted to a particular locality (as in the case of a rare wine), and where the *effective demand* can never be satisfied. *Finally*, through *monopolies* exercised by individuals or companies. Monopoly price is the highest possible. (Adam Smith, op. cit., Vol. I, pp. 53-54 [Garnier, t. I, pp. 120-24].)

Other fortuitous causes which can raise the profit on capital:

The acquisition of new territories, or of new branches of trade, often increases the profit on capital even in a wealthy country, because they withdraw some capital from the old branches of trade, reduce competition, and cause the market to be supplied with fewer commodities, the prices of which then rise: those who deal in these commodities can then afford to borrow at a higher rate of interest. (Adam Smith, op. cit., Vol. I, p. 83 [Garnier, t. I, p. 190].)

The more a commodity comes to be manufactured—the more it becomes an object of manufacture—the greater becomes that part of the price which resolves itself into wages and profit in proportion to that which resolves itself into rent. In the progress of the manufacture of a commodity, not only the number of profits increases, but every subsequent profit is greater than the foregoing; because the capital from which ||IV,2| it is derived must always be greater. The capital which employs the weavers, for example, must always be greater than that which employs the spinners; because it not only replaces that capital with its profits, but pays, besides, the wages of weavers; and the profits must always bear some proportion to the capital. (op. cit., Vol. I, p. 45 [Garnier, t. I, pp. 102-03].)

Thus the advance made by human labour in converting the product of nature into the manufactured product of nature increases, not the wages of labour, but in part the number of profitable capital investments, and in part the size of every subsequent capital in comparison with the foregoing.

More about the advantages which the capitalist derives from the division of labour, later.

He profits doubly—first, by the division of labour; and secondly, in general, by the advance which human labour makes on the natural product. The greater the human share in a commodity, the greater the profit of dead capital.

In one and the same society the average rates of profit on capital are much more nearly on the same level than the wages of the different sorts of labour. (op. cit., Vol. I, p. 100 [Garnier, t. I, p. 228].) In the different employments of capital, the ordinary rate of profit varies with the certainty or uncertainty of the returns.

The ordinary profit of stock, though it rises with the risk, does not always seem to rise in proportion to it. (op. cit., Vol. I, pp. 99-100 [Garnier, t. I, pp. 226-27].)

It goes without saying that profits also rise if the means of circulation become less expensive or easier available (e.g., paper money).

3. THE RULE OF CAPITAL OVER LABOUR AND THE MOTIVES OF THE CAPITALIST

The consideration of his own private profit is the sole motive which determines the owner of any capital to employ it either in agriculture, in manufactures, or in some particular branch of the wholesale or retail trade. The different quantities of *productive labour* which it may put into motion, ||V,2| and the different values which it may add to the annual produce of the land and labour of his country, according as it is employed in one or other of those different ways, never enter into his thoughts. (Adam Smith, op. cit., Vol. I, p. 335 [Garnier, t. II, pp. 400-01].)

The most useful employment of capital for the capitalist is that which, risks being equal, yields him the greatest profit. This employment is not always the most useful for society; the most useful employment is that which utilises the productive powers of nature. (Say, t. II, pp. 130-31.)

The plans and speculations of the employers of capitals regulate and direct all the most important operations of labour, and *profit* is the end proposed by all those plans and projects. But the rate of profit does not, like rent and wages, rise with the prosperity and fall with the decline of the society. On the contrary, it is naturally low in rich and high in poor countries, and it is always highest in the countries which are going fastest to ruin. The interest of this class, therefore, has not the same connection with the general interest of the society as that of the other two.... The particular interest of the dealers in any particular branch of trade or manufactures is always in some respects different from, and frequently even in sharp opposition to, that of the public. To widen the market and to narrow the sellers' competition is always the interest of the dealer.... This is a class of people whose interest is never exactly the same as that of society, a class of people who have generally an interest to deceive and to oppress the public. (Adam Smith, op. cit., Vol. I, pp. 231-32 [Garnier, t. II, pp. 163-65].)

4. THE ACCUMULATION OF CAPITALS AND THE COMPETITION AMONG THE CAPITALISTS

The *increase of stock*, which raises wages, tends to lower the capitalists' profit, because of the *competition* amongst the capitalists. (Adam Smith, op. cit., Vol. I, p. 78 [Garnier, t. I, p. 179].)

If, for example, the capital which is necessary for the grocery trade of a particular town "is divided between two different grocers, their competition will tend to make both of them sell cheaper than if it were in the hands of one only; and if it were divided among twenty, ||VI,2| their competition would be just so much the greater, and the chance of their combining together, in order to raise the price, just so much the less". (Adam Smith, op. cit., Vol. I, p. 322 [Garnier, t. II, pp. 372-73].)

Since we already know that monopoly prices are as high as possible, since the interest of the capitalists, even from the point of view commonly held by political economists, stands in hostile opposition to society, and since a rise of profit operates like compound interest on the price of the commodity (Adam Smith, op. cit., Vol. I, pp. 87-88 [Garnier, t. I, pp. 199-201]), it follows that the sole defence against the capitalists is *competition,* which according to the evidence of political economy acts beneficently by both raising wages and lowering the prices of commodities to the advantage of the consuming public.

But competition is only possible if capital multiplies, and is held in many hands. The formation of many capital investments is only possible as a result of multilateral accumulation, since capital comes into being only by accumulation; and multilateral accumulation necessarily turns into unilateral accumulation. Competition among capitalists increases the accumulation of capital. Accumulation, where private property prevails, is the *concentration* of capital in the hands of a few, it is in general an inevitable consequence if capital is left to follow its natural course, and it is precisely through competition that the way is cleared for this natural disposition of capital.

We have been told that the profit on capital is in proportion to the size of the capital. A large capital therefore accumulates more quickly than a small capital in proportion to its size, even if we disregard for the time being deliberate competition. |VII|

||VIII, 2|[65] Accordingly, the accumulation of large capital proceeds much more rapidly than that of smaller capital, quite irrespective of competition. But let us follow this process further.

With the increase of capital the profit on capital diminishes, because of competition. The first to suffer, therefore, is the small capitalist.

The increase of capitals and a large number of capital investments presuppose, further,[a] a condition of advancing wealth in the country.

"In a country which had acquired its full complement of riches [...] the ordinary rate of clear profit would be very small, so the usual [market] rate of interest which could be afforded out of it would be so low as to render it impossible for any but the very wealthiest people to live upon the interest of their money. All people of [...] middling fortunes would be obliged to superintend themselves the employment of their own stocks. It would be necessary that almost every man should be a man of business, or engage in some sort of trade." (Adam Smith, op. cit., Vol. I, p. 86 [Garnier, t. I, pp. 196-97].)[b]

This is the situation most dear to the heart of political economy.

"The proportion between capital and revenue, therefore, seems everywhere to regulate the proportion between industry and idleness; wherever capital predominates, industry prevails; wherever revenue, idleness." (Adam Smith, op. cit., Vol. I, p. 301 [Garnier, t. II, p. 325].)

What about the employment of capital, then, in this condition of increased competition?

---

[a] "Further" is not clearly decipherable in the manuscript.—*Ed.*

[b] After this paragraph Marx crossed out the sentence: "The less capitals are loaned at interest and the more they are thrown into manufacturing business or commerce, the stronger grows the competition between the capitalists."—*Ed.*

"As stock increases, the quantity of stock to be lent at interest grows gradually greater and greater. As the quantity of stock to be lent at interest increases, the interest ... diminishes...." (i) because the market price of things commonly diminishes as their quantity increases. ... and (ii) because *with the increase of capitals in any country,* "it becomes *gradually more and more difficult* to find within the country a profitable method of employing any new capital. There arises in consequence a competition between different capitals, the owner of one endeavouring to get possession of that employment which is occupied by another. But upon most occasions he can hope to jostle that other out of this employment by no other means but by dealing upon more reasonable terms. He must not only sell what he deals in somewhat cheaper, but in order to get it to sell, he must sometimes, too, buy it dearer. The demand for productive labour, by the increase of the funds which are destined for maintaining it, grows every day greater and greater. Labourers easily find employment, |IX, 2|but the owners of capitals find it difficult to get labourers to employ. Their competition raises the wages of labour and sinks the profits of stock." (Adam Smith, op. cit., Vol. I, p. 316 [Garnier, t. II, pp. 358-59].)

Thus the small capitalist has the choice: (1) either to consume his capital, since he can no longer live on the interest—and thus cease to be a capitalist; or (2) to set up a business himself, sell his commodity cheaper, buy dearer than the wealthier capitalist, and pay higher wages—thus ruining himself, the market price being already very low as a result of the intense competition presupposed. If, however, the big capitalist wants to squeeze out the smaller capitalist, he has all the advantages over him which the capitalist has as a capitalist over the worker. The larger size of his capital compensates him for the smaller profits, and he can even bear temporary losses until the smaller capitalist is ruined and he finds himself freed from this competition. In this way, he accumulates the small capitalist's profits.

Furthermore: the big capitalist always buys cheaper than the small one, because he buys bigger quantities. He can therefore well afford to sell cheaper.

But if a fall in the rate of interest turns the middle capitalists from rentiers into businessmen, the increase in business capital and the resulting smaller profit produce conversely a fall in the rate of interest.

"When the profits which can be made by the use of a capital are [...] diminished [...] the price which can be paid for the use of it [...] must necessarily be diminished with them." (Adam Smith, loc. cit., Vol. I, p. 316 [Garnier, t. II, p. 359].)

"As riches, improvement, and population have increased, interest has declined", and consequently the profits of capitalists, "after these [profits] are diminished, stock may not only continue to increase, but to increase much faster than before. [...] A great stock though with small profits, generally increases faster than a small stock with great profits. Money, says the proverb, makes money." (op. cit., Vol. I, p. 83 [Garnier, t. I, p. 189].)

When, therefore, this large capital is opposed by small capitals with small profits, as it is under the presupposed condition of intense competition, it crushes them completely.

The necessary result of this competition is a general deterioration of commodities, adulteration, fake production and universal poisoning, evident in large towns.

|X,2| An important circumstance in the competition of large and small capital is, furthermore, the relation between *fixed capital* and *circulating capital*.[a]

Circulating capital is a capital which is "employed in raising" provisions, "manufacturing, or purchasing goods, and selling them again. [...] The capital employed in this manner yields no revenue or profit to its employer, while it either remains in his possession, or continues in the same shape. [...] His capital is continually going from him in one shape, and returning to him in another, and it is only by means of such circulation, or successive exchanges" and transformations "that it can yield him any profit". *Fixed capital* consists of capital invested "in the improvement of land, in the purchase of useful machines and instruments of trade, or in such-like things". (Adam Smith, op. cit., Vol. I, pp. 243-44 [Garnier, t. II, pp. 197-98].)

"Every saving in the expense of supporting the fixed capital is an improvement of the net revenue of the society. The whole capital of the undertaker of every work is necessarily divided between his fixed and his circulating capital. While his whole capital remains the same, the smaller the one part, the greater must necessarily be the other. It is the circulating capital which furnishes the materials and wages of labour, and puts industry into motion. Every saving, therefore, in the expense of maintaining the fixed capital, which does not diminish the productive powers of labour, must increase the fund which puts industry into motion." (Adam Smith, op. cit., Vol. I, p. 257 [Garnier, t. II, p. 226].)

It is clear from the outset that the relation of fixed capital and circulating capital is much more favourable to the big capitalist than to the smaller capitalist. The extra fixed capital required by a very big banker as against a very small one is insignificant. Their fixed capital amounts to nothing more than the office. The equipment of the bigger landowner does not increase in proportion to the size of his estate. Similarly, the credit which a big capitalist enjoys compared with a smaller one means for him all the greater saving in fixed capital—that is, in the amount of ready money he must always have at hand. Finally, it is obvious that where industrial labour has reached a high level, and where therefore almost all manual labour has become factory labour, the entire capital of a small capitalist does not suffice to provide him even with the necessary fixed capital. *On sait que les travaux de la grande culture n'occupent habituellement qu'un petit nombre de bras.*[b]

It is generally true that the accumulation of large capital is also

---

[a] Marx uses the French terms *capital fixe* and *capital circulant*.—*Ed.*

[b] As is well known, large-scale cultivation usually provides employment only for a small number of hands.—*Ed.*

accompanied by a proportional concentration and simplification of fixed capital, as compared to the smaller capitalists. The big capitalist introduces for himself some kind ||XI, 2| of organisation of the instruments of labour.

"Similarly, in the sphere of industry every manufactory and mill is already a comprehensive combination of a large material fortune with numerous and varied intellectual capacities and technical skills serving the *common* purpose of production.... Where legislation preserves landed property in large units, the surplus of a growing population flocks into trades, and it is therefore as in Great Britain in the field of industry, principally, that proletarians aggregate in great numbers. Where, however, the law permits the continuous division of the land, the number of small, debt-encumbered proprietors increases, as in France; and the continuing process of fragmentation throws them into the class of the needy and the discontented. When eventually this fragmentation and indebtedness reaches a higher degree still, big landed property once more swallows up small property, just as large-scale industry destroys small industry. And as larger estates are formed again, large numbers of propertyless workers not required for the cultivation of the soil are again driven into industry." (Schulz, *Bewegung der Production*, pp. 58, 59.)

"Commodities of the same kind change in character as a result of changes in the method of production, and especially as a result of the use of machinery. Only by the exclusion of human power has it become possible to spin from a pound of cotton worth 3 shillings and 8 pence 350 hanks of a total length of 167 English miles (i.e., 36 German miles), and of a commercial value of 25 guineas." (op. cit., p. 62.)

"On the average the prices of cotton-goods have decreased in England during the past 45 years by eleven-twelfths, and according to Marshall's calculations the same amount of manufactured goods for which 16 shillings was still paid in 1814 is now supplied at 1 shilling and 10 pence. The greater cheapness of industrial products expands both consumption at home and the market abroad, and because of this the number of workers in cotton has not only not fallen in Great Britain after the introduction of machines but has risen from forty thousand to one and a half million. ||XII, 2| As to the earnings of industrial entrepreneurs and workers; the growing competition between the factory owners has resulted in their profits necessarily falling relative to the amount of products supplied by them. In the years 1820-33 the Manchester manufacturer's gross profit on a piece of calico fell from four shillings $1^1/_3$ pence to one shilling 9 pence. But to make up for this loss, the volume of manufacture has been correspondingly increased. The consequence of this is that separate branches of industry experience over-production to some extent, that frequent bankruptcies occur causing property to fluctuate and vacillate unstably *within* the class of capitalists and masters of labour, thus throwing into the proletariat some of those who have been ruined economically; and that, frequently and suddenly, close-downs or cuts in employment become necessary, the painful effects of which are always bitterly felt by the class of wage-labourers." (op. cit., p. 63.)

"To hire out one's labour is to begin one's enslavement. To hire out the materials of labour is to establish one's freedom.... Labour is man; the materials, on the other hand, contain nothing human."[a] (Pecqueur, *Théorie sociale, etc.*, pp. 411-12.)

---

[a] "Louer son travail, c'est commencer son esclavage; louer la matière du travail, c'est constituer sa liberté.... Le travail est l'homme, la matière au contraire n'est rien de l'homme."—*Ed*.

"The material element, which is quite incapable of creating wealth without the other element, *labour*, acquires the magical virtue of being fertile for them [who own this material element] as if by their own action they had placed there this indispensable element."ᵃ (op. cit.)

"Supposing that the daily labour of a worker brings him on the average 400 francs a year and that this sum suffices for every adult to live some sort of crude life, then any proprietor receiving 2,000 francs in interest or rent, from a farm, a house, etc., compels indirectly five men to work for him; an income of 100,000 francs represents the labour of 250 men, and that of 1,000,000 francs the labour of 2,500 individualsᵇ (hence, 300 million [Louis Philippe] therefore the labour of 750,000 workers)." (op. cit., pp. 412-13.)

"The human law has given owners the right to use and to abuse—that is to say, the right to do what they will with the materials of labour.... They are in no way obliged by law to provide work for the propertyless when required and at all times, or to pay them always an adequate wage, etc."ᶜ (loc. cit., p. 413.) "Complete freedom concerning the nature, the quantity, the quality and the expediency of production; concerning the use and the disposal of wealth; and full command over the materials of all labour. Everyone is free to exchange what belongs to him as he thinks fit, without considering anything other than his own interest as an individual."ᵈ (op. cit., p. 413.)

"Competition is merely the expression of the freedom to exchange, which itself is the immediate and logical consequence of the individual's right to use and abuse all the instruments of production. The right to use and abuse, freedom of exchange, and arbitrary competition—these three economic moments, which form one unit, entail the following consequences; each produces what he wishes, as he wishes, when he wishes, where he wishes, produces well or produces badly, produces too much or not enough, too soon or too late, at too high a price or too low a price; none knows whether he will sell, to whom he will sell, how he will sell, when he will sell, where he will sell. And it is the same with regard to purchases. ||XIII, 2| The producer is ignorant of needs and resources, of demand and supply. He sells when he wishes, when he can, where he wishes, to whom he wishes, at the price he wishes. And he buys in the same way. In all this he is ever the plaything of chance, the slave of the law of the strongest, of the least harassed, of the richest.... Whilst at one place there is scarcity, at another there is glut and waste. Whilst one producer sells a lot or at a very high price, and at an enormous

---

ᵃ "L'élément matière, qui ne peut rien pour la création de la richesse sans l'autre élément *travail*, reçoit la vertu magique d'être fécond pour eux comme s'ils y avaient mis de leur propre fait cet indispensable élément."—*Ed*.

ᵇ "En supposant que le travail quotidien d'un ouvrier lui rapporte en moyenne 400 fr. par an, et que cette somme suffise à chaque adulte pour vivre d'une vie grossière, tout propriétaire de 2000 fr. de rente, de fermage, de loyer, etc., force donc indirectement 5 hommes à travailler pour lui: 100 000 fr. de rente représentent le travail de 250 hommes, et 1000000 le travail de 2500 individus."—*Ed*.

ᶜ "Les propriétaires ont reçu de la loi des hommes le droit d'user et d'abuser, c.-à-d. de faire ce qu'ils veulent de la matière de tout travail ... ils sont nullement obligés par la loi de fournir à propos et toujours du travail aux non-propriétaires, ni de leur payer un salaire toujours suffisant etc."—*Ed*.

ᵈ "Liberté entière quant à la nature, à la quantité, à la qualité, à l'opportunité de la production, à l'usage, à la consommation des richesses, à la disposition de la matière de tout travail. Chacun est libre d'échanger sa chose comme il l'entend, sans autre considération que son propre intérêt d'individu."—*Ed*.

profit, the other sells nothing or sells at a loss.... The supply does not know the demand, and the demand does not know the supply. You produce, trusting to a taste, a fashion, which prevails amongst the consuming public. But by the time you are ready to deliver the commodity, the whim has already passed and has settled on some other kind of product.... The inevitable consequences: bankruptcies occurring constantly and universally; miscalculations, sudden ruin and unexpected fortunes, commercial crises, stoppages, periodic gluts or shortages; instability and depreciation of wages and profits, the loss or enormous waste of wealth, time and effort in the arena of fierce competition."[a] (op. cit., pp. 414-16.)

Ricardo in his book[b] (rent of land[c]): Nations are merely production-shops; man is a machine for consuming and producing; human life is a kind of capital; economic laws blindly rule the world. For Ricardo men are nothing, the product everything. In the 26th chapter of the French translation it says:

"To an individual with a capital of £20,000 whose profits were £2,000 per annum, it would be a matter quite indifferent whether his capital would employ a hundred or a thousand men.... Is not the real interest of the nation similar? Provided its net real income, its rent and profits be the same, it is of no importance whether the nation consists of ten or twelve millions of inhabitants."[d] [t. II,

---

[a] "La concurrence n'exprime pas autre chose que l'échange facultatif, qui lui-même est la conséquence prochaine et logique du droit individuel d'user et d'abuser des instruments de toute production. Ces trois moments économiques, lesquels n'en font qu'un: le droit d'user et d'abuser, la liberté d'échanges et la concurence arbitraire, entraînent les conséquences suivantes: chacun produit ce qu'il veut, comme il veut, quand il veut, où il veut; produit bien ou produit mal, trop ou pas assez, trop tôt ou trop tard, trop cher ou à trop bas prix; chacun ignore s'il vendra, à qui il vendra, comment il vendra, quand il vendra, où il vendra: et il en est de même quant aux achats. Le producteur ignore les besoins et les ressources, les demandes et les offres. Il vend quand il veut, quand il peut, où il veut, à qui il veut, au prix qu'il veut. Et il achète de même. En tout cela, il est toujours le jouet du hasard, l'esclave de la loi du plus fort, du moins pressé, du plus riche... Tandis que sur un point il y a disette d'une richesse, sur l'autre il y a trop-plein et gaspillage. Tandis qu'un producteur vend beaucoup ou très cher, et à bénéfice énorme, l'autre ne vend rien ou vend à perte... L'offre ignore la demande, et la demande ignore l'offre. Vous produisez sur la foi d'un goût, d'une mode qui se manifeste dans le public des consommateurs; mais déjà, lorsque vous êtes prêts à livrer la marchandise, la fantaisie a passé et s'est fixée sur un autre genre de produit ... conséquences infaillibles la permanence et l'universalisation des banqueroutes, les mécomptes, les ruines subites et les fortunes improvisées; les crises commerciales, les chômages, les encombrements ou les disettes périodiques; l'instabilité et l'avilissement des salaires et des profits, la déperdition ou le gaspillage énorme de richesses, de temps et d'efforts dans l'arène d'une concurrence acharnée."—*Ed.*

[b] *On the Principles of Political Economy, and Taxation.*—*Ed.*

[c] These words are in English in the manuscript.—*Ed.*

[d] "Il serait tout-à-fait indifférent pour une personne qui sur un capital de 20 000 fr. ferait 2000 fr. par an de profit, que son capital employât cent hommes ou mille... L'intérêt réel d'une nation n'est-il pas le même? pourvu que son revenu net et réel, et que ses fermages et ses profits soient les mêmes, qu'importe qu'elle se compose de dix ou de douze millions d'individus?"—*Ed.*

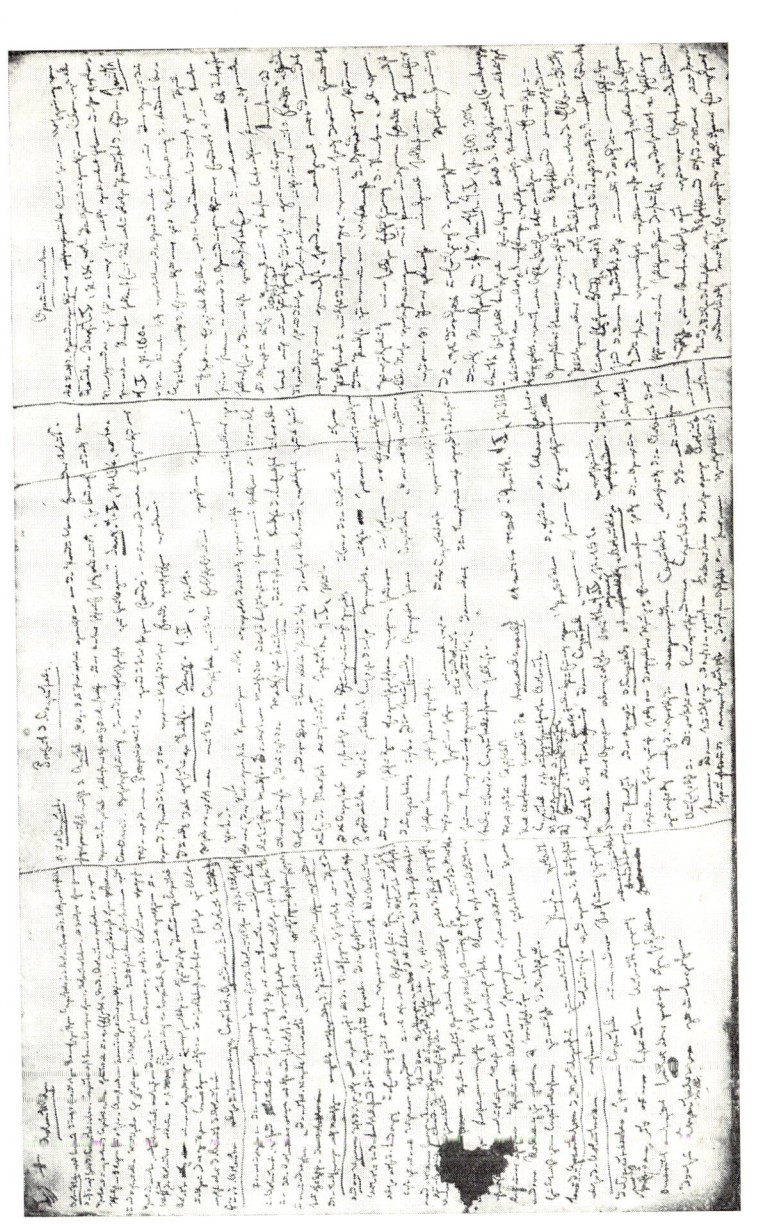

A page from the *Economic and Philosophic Manuscripts of 1844* (beginning of the first manuscript)

pp. 194, 195.] "In fact, says M. Sismondi ([*Nouveaux principes d'économie politique,*] t. II, p. 331), nothing remains to be desired but that the King, living quite alone on the island, should by continuously turning a crank cause automatons to do all the work of England." [a][66]

"The master who buys the worker's labour at such a low price that it scarcely suffices for the worker's most pressing needs is responsible neither for the inadequacy of the wage nor for the excessive duration of the labour: he himself has to submit to the law which he imposes.... Poverty is not so much caused by men as by the power of things." [b] (Buret, op. cit., p. 82.)

"The inhabitants of many different parts of Great Britain have not capital sufficient to improve and cultivate all their lands. The wool of the southern[c] counties of Scotland is, a great part of it, after a long land carriage through very bad roads, manufactured in Yorkshire, for want of capital to manufacture it at home. There are many little manufacturing towns in Great Britain, of which the inhabitants have not capital sufficient to transport the produce of their own industry to those distant markets where there is demand and consumption for it. If there are any merchants among them, ||XIV,2| they are properly only the agents of wealthier merchants who reside in some of the greater commercial cities." (Adam Smith, *Wealth of Nations*, Vol. I, pp. 326-27 [Garnier, t. II, p. 382].)

"The annual produce of the land and labour of any nation can be increased in its value by no other means but by increasing either the *number of its productive labourers*, or the *productive powers of those labourers* who had before been employed.... In either case an additional capital is almost always required." [d] (Adam Smith, op. cit., Vol. I, pp. 306-07 [Garnier, t. II, p. 338].)

"As the *accumulation* of stock must, in the nature of things, be previous to the division of labour, so labour can be more and more subdivided in proportion only as stock is previously more and more accumulated. The quantity of materials which the same number of people can work up, increases in a great proportion as labour comes to be more and more subdivided; and as the operations of each workman are gradually reduced to a greater degree of simplicity, a variety of new machines come to be invented for facilitating and abridging those operations. As the division of labour advances, therefore, in order to give constant employment to an equal number of workmen, an equal stock of provisions, and a greater stock of materials and tools than what would have been necessary in a ruder state of things, must be accumulated beforehand. But the number of workmen in every branch of business generally increases with the division of labour in that branch, or rather it is the increase of their number which enables them to class and subdivide themselves in this manner." (Adam Smith, op. cit., Vol. I, pp. 241-42 [Garnier, t. II, pp. 193-94].)

"As the accumulation of stock is previously necessary for carrying on this great

---

[a] "En vérité, dit M. de Sismondi, il ne reste plus qu'à désirer que le roi, demeuré tout seul dans l'île, en tournant constamment une manivelle, fasse accomplir, par des automates, tout l'ouvrage de l'Angleterre."—*Ed.*

[b] "Le maître, qui achète le travail de l'ouvrier à un prix si bas, qu'il suffit à peine aux besoins les plus pressants, n'est responsable ni de l'insuffisance des salaires, ni de la trop longue durée du travail: il subit lui-même la loi qu'il impose ... ce n'est pas tant des hommes que vient la misère, que de la puissance des choses."—*Ed.*

[c] In the manuscript: "eastern".—*Ed.*

[d] "Pour augmenter la valeur du produit annuel de la terre et du travail, il n'y a pas d'autres moyens que d'augmenter, quant au *nombre, les ouvriers productifs*, ou d'augmenter, quant à la puissance, la *faculté productive des ouvriers* précédemment employés... Dans l'un et dans l'autre cas il faut presque toujours un surcroît de capital."—*Ed.*

improvement in the productive powers of labour, so that accumulation naturally leads to this improvement. The person who employs his stock in maintaining labour, necessarily wishes to employ it in such a manner as to produce as great a quantity of work as possible. He endeavours, therefore, both to make among his workmen the most proper distribution of employment, and to furnish them with the best machines [...]. His abilities in both these respects ||XV, 2| are generally in proportion to the extent of his stock, or to the number of people whom it can employ. The quantity of industry, therefore, not only increases in every country with the *increase of the stock* which employs it, but, in consequence of that increase, the same quantity of industry produces a much greater quantity of work." (Adam Smith, op. cit., Vol. I, p. 242 [Garnier, t. II, pp. 194-95].)

Hence *over-production*.

"More comprehensive combinations of productive forces ... in industry and trade by uniting more numerous and more diverse human and natural powers in larger-scale enterprises. Already here and there, closer association of the chief branches of production. Thus, big manufacturers will try to acquire also large estates in order to become independent of others for at least a part of the raw materials required for their industry; or they will go into trade in conjunction with their industrial enterprises, not only to sell their own manufactures, but also to purchase other kinds of products and to sell these to their workers. In England, where a single factory owner sometimes employs ten to twelve thousand workers ... it is already not uncommon to find such combinations of various branches of production controlled by *one* brain, such smaller states or provinces within the state. Thus, the mine owners in the *Birmingham* area have recently taken over the *whole* process of iron production, which was previously distributed among various entrepreneurs and owners. (See "Der bergmännische Distrikt bei Birmingham", *Deutsche Vierteljahrs-Schrift* No. 3, 1838.) Finally in the large joint-stock enterprises which have become so numerous, we see far-reaching combinations of the financial resources of *many* participants with the scientific and technical knowledge and skills of others to whom the carrying-out of the work is handed over. The capitalists are thereby enabled to apply their savings in more diverse ways and perhaps even to employ them simultaneously in agriculture, industry and commerce. As a consequence their interest becomes more comprehensive, ||XVI,2| and the contradictions between agricultural, industrial, and commercial interests are reduced and disappear. But this increased possibility of applying capital profitably in the most diverse ways cannot but intensify the antagonism between the propertied and the non-propertied classes." (Schulz, op. cit., pp. 40-41.)

The enormous profit which the landlords of houses make out of poverty. House rent stands in inverse proportion to industrial poverty.

So does the interest obtained from the vices of the ruined proletarians. (Prostitution, drunkenness, pawnbroking.)

The accumulation of capital increases and the competition between capitalists decreases, when capital and landed property are united in the same hand, also when capital is enabled by its size to combine different branches of production.

Indifference towards men. Smith's twenty lottery-tickets.[67]

Say's net and gross revenue. |XVI||

RENT OF LAND

||I, 3| *Landlords' right* has its origin in robbery. (Say, t. I, p. 136, note.) The landlords, like all other men, love to reap where they never sowed, and demand a rent even for the natural produce of the earth. (Adam Smith, op. cit., Vol. I, p. 44 [Garnier, t. I, p. 99].)

"The rent of land, it may be thought, is frequently no more than a reasonable profit or interest for the stock laid out by the landlord upon its improvement. This, no doubt, may be partly the case upon some occasions.... The landlord demands" (1) "a rent even for unimproved land, and the supposed interest or profit upon the expense of improvement is generally an addition to this original rent." (2) "Those improvements, besides, are not always made by the stock of the landlord, but sometimes by that of the tenant. When the lease comes to be renewed, however, the landlord commonly demands the same augmentation of rent as if they had been all made by his own." (3) "He sometimes demands rent for what is altogether incapable of human improvement." (Adam Smith, op. cit., Vol. I, p. 131 [Garnier, t. I, pp. 300-01].)

Smith cites as an instance of the last case kelp,[a]

"a species of seaweed, which, when burnt, yields an alkaline salt, useful for making glass, soap, etc. It grows in several parts of Great Britain, particularly in Scotland, upon such rocks only as lie within the high-water mark, which are twice every day covered with the sea, and of which the produce, therefore, was never augmented by human industry. The landlord, however, whose estate is bounded by a kelp shore of this kind, demands a rent for it as much as for his corn fields. The sea in the neighbourhood of the Islands of Shetland[b] is more than commonly abundant in fish, which make a great part of the subsistence of their inhabitants. ||II, 3| But in order to profit by the produce of the water they must have a habitation upon the neighbouring land. The rent of the landlord is in proportion, not to what the farmer can make by the land, but to what he can make both by the land and by the water." (Adam Smith, op. cit., Vol. I, p. 131 [Garnier, t. I, pp. 301-02].)

"This rent may be considered as the produce of those *powers of nature*, the use of which the landlord lends to the farmer. It is greater or smaller according to the supposed extent of those powers, or in other words, according to the supposed natural or improved fertility of the land. It is the work of nature which remains after deducting or compensating everything which can be regarded as the work of man." (Adam Smith, op. cit., Vol. I, pp. 324-25 [Garnier, t. II, pp. 377-78].)

"The *rent of land,* therefore, considered as the price paid for the use of the land, is naturally a *monopoly price*. It is not at all proportioned to what the landlord may have laid out upon the improvement of the land, or to what he can afford to take; but to what the farmer can afford to give." (Adam Smith, op. cit., p. 131 [Garnier, t. I, p. 302].)

Of the three original classes, that of the landlords is the one "whose revenue costs them neither labour nor care, but comes to them, as it were, of its own accord, and independent of any plan or project[c] of their own". (Adam Smith, op. cit., Vol. I, p. 230 [Garnier, t. II, p. 161].)

---

[a] Adam Smith uses the general term "kelp". Marx writes "*Salzkraut (Seekrapp, Salicorne)*" which indicates species of saltwort (*Salsola*) or glasswort (*Salicornia*).—*Ed.*

[b] In the manuscript: "Scotland".—*Ed.*

[c] In the manuscript *Einsicht* (understanding) instead of *Absicht* (purpose, intention, project).—*Ed.*

We have already learnt that the size of the rent depends on the degree of *fertility* of the land.

Another factor in its determination is *situation*.

"The rent of land not only varies with its *fertility*, whatever be its produce, but with its *situation*, whatever be its fertility." (Adam Smith, op. cit., Vol. I, p. 133 [Garnier, t. I, p. 306].)

"The produce of land, mines, and fisheries, when their natural fertility is equal, is in proportion to the extent and proper ||III,3| application of the capitals employed about them. When the capitals are equal and equally well applied, it is in proportion to their natural fertility." (op. cit., Vol. I, p. 249 [Garnier, t. II, p. 210].)

These propositions of Smith are important, because, given equal costs of production and capital of equal size, they reduce the rent of land to the greater or lesser fertility of the soil. Thereby showing clearly the perversion of concepts in political economy, which turns the fertility of the land into an attribute of the landlord.

Now, however, let us consider the rent of land as it is formed in real life.

The rent of land is established as a result of the *struggle between tenant and landlord*. We find that the hostile antagonism of interests, the struggle, the war is recognised throughout political economy as the basis of social organisation.

Let us see now what the relations are between landlord and tenant.

"In adjusting the terms of the lease, the landlord endeavours to leave him no greater share of the produce than what is sufficient to keep up the stock from which he furnishes the seed, pays the labour, and purchases and maintains the cattle and other instruments of husbandry, together with the ordinary profits of farming stock in the neighbourhood. This is evidently the smallest share with which the tenant can content himself without being a loser, and the landlord seldom means to leave him any more. Whatever part of the produce, or, what is the same thing, whatever part of its price is over and above this share, he naturally endeavours to reserve to himself as the rent of his land, which is evidently the highest the tenant can afford to pay in the actual circumstances of the land.||IV,3| [...] This portion, however, may still be considered as the natural rent of land, or the rent for which it is naturally meant that land should for the most part be let." (Adam Smith, op. cit., Vol. I, pp. 130-31 [Garnier, t. I, pp. 299-300].)

"The landlords," says Say, "operate a certain kind of monopoly against the tenants. The demand for their commodity, site and soil, can go on expanding indefinitely; but there is only a given, limited amount of their commodity.... The bargain struck between landlord and tenant is always advantageous to the former in the greatest possible degree.... Besides the advantage he derives from the nature of the case, he derives a further advantage from his position, his larger fortune and greater credit and standing. But the first by itself suffices to enable him and him *alone* to profit from the favourable circumstances of the land. The opening of a canal, or a road; the increase of population and of the prosperity of a district, always raises the rent.... Indeed, the tenant himself may improve the ground at his own expense; but he only derives the profit from this capital for the duration of his lease, with the expiry of which it remains with the proprietor of the land; henceforth it is the latter who reaps the interest thereon, without having made the outlay, for there is now a proportionate increase in the rent." (Say, t. II, pp. 142-43.)

"Rent, considered as the price paid for the use of land, is naturally the highest which the tenant can afford to pay in the actual circumstances of the land." (Adam Smith, op. cit., Vol. I, p. 130 [Garnier, t. I, p. 299].)

"The rent of an estate above ground commonly amounts to what is supposed to be a third of the gross produce; and it is generally a rent certain and independent of the occasional variations ||V,3| in the crop." (Adam Smith, op. cit., Vol. I, p. 153 [Garnier, t. I, p. 351].) This rent "is seldom less than a fourth ... of the whole produce". (op. cit., Vol. I, p. 325 [Garnier, t. II, p. 378].)

Rent cannot be paid on all commodities. For instance, in many districts[a] no rent is paid for stones.

"Such parts only of the produce of land can commonly be brought to market of which the ordinary price is sufficient to replace the stock which must be employed in bringing them thither, together with its ordinary profits. If the ordinary price is more than this, the surplus part of it will naturally go to the rent of the land. If it is not more, though the commodity may be brought to market, it can afford no rent to the landlord. Whether the price is or is not more depends upon the demand." (Adam Smith, op. cit., Vol. I, p. 132 [Garnier, t. I, pp. 302-03].)

"Rent, it is to be observed, therefore, enters into the composition of the *price of commodities* in a *different way* from wages and profit. *High or low wages and profit* are the *causes* of high or low price; high or low rent is the *effect* of it." (Adam Smith, loc. cit., Vol. I, p. 132 [Garnier, t. I, pp. 303-04].)

Food belongs to the *products* which always yield a *rent*.

As men, like all other animals, naturally multiply in proportion to the means of their subsistence, food is always, more or less, in demand. It can always purchase or command a greater or smaller ||VI,3| quantity of labour, and somebody can always be found who is willing to do something in order to obtain it. The quantity of labour, indeed, which it can purchase is not always *equal* to what it could maintain, if managed in the most economical manner, on account of the high wages which are sometimes given to labour. But it can always purchase such a quantity of labour as it can maintain, according to the rate at which the sort of labour is commonly maintained in the neighbourhood.

"But land, in almost any situation, produces a greater quantity of food than what is sufficient to maintain all the labour necessary for bringing it[b] to market [....] The surplus, too, is always more than sufficient to replace the stock which employed that labour, together with its profits. Something, therefore, always remains for a rent to the landlord." (Adam Smith, op. cit., Vol. I, pp. 132-33 [Garnier, t. I, pp. 305-06].)

"Food is in this manner not only the original source of rent, but every other part of the produce of land which afterwards affords rent derives that part of its value from the improvement of the powers of labour in producing food by means of the improvement and cultivation of land." (Adam Smith, op. cit., Vol. I, p. 150 [Garnier, t. I, p. 345].)

"Human food seems to be the only produce of land which always and

---

[a] In the manuscript *Gegenständen* (objects) instead of *Gegen* (districts).—*Ed.*

[b] "It" refers to *food*, the manuscript however has *Arbeit* (labour).—*Ed.*

necessarily affords some rent to the landlord." (op. cit., Vol. I, p. 147 [Garnier, t. I, p. 337].)

"Countries are populous not in proportion to the number of people whom their produce can clothe and lodge, but in proportion to that of those whom it can feed." (Adam Smith, op. cit., Vol. I, p. 149 [Garnier, t. I, p. 342].)

"After food, clothing and lodging are the two great wants of mankind." They usually yield a rent, but not inevitably. (op. cit., Vol. I, p. 147 [Garnier, t. I, pp. 337-38].) | VI ||

||VIII,3|[68] Let us now see how the landlord exploits everything from which society benefits.

(1) The rent of land increases with population. (Adam Smith, op. cit., Vol. I, p. 146 [Garnier, t. I, p. 335].)

(2) We have already learnt from Say how the rent of land increases with railways, etc., with the improvement, safety, and multiplication of the means of communication.

(3) "Every improvement in the circumstances of the society tends either *directly* or *indirectly* to raise the real rent of land, to increase the real wealth of the landlord, his power of purchasing the labour, or the produce of the labour of other people.

"The extension of improvement and cultivation tends to raise it directly. The landlord's share of the produce necessarily increases with the increase of the produce.

"That rise in the real price of those parts of the rude produce of land [...] the rise in the price of cattle, for example, tends too to raise the rent of land directly, and in a still greater proportion. The real value of the landlord's share, his real command of the labour of other people, not only rises with the real value of the produce, but the proportion of his share to the whole produce rises with it. That produce, after the rise in its real price, requires no more labour to collect it than before. A smaller proportion of it will, therefore, be sufficient to replace, with the ordinary profit, the stock which employs that labour. A greater proportion of it must, consequently, belong to the landlord." (Adam Smith, op. cit., Vol. I, pp. 228-29 [Garnier, t. II, pp. 157-59].)

||IX,3| The greater demand for raw produce, and therefore the rise in value, may in part result from the increase of population and from the increase of their needs. But every new invention, every new application in manufacture of a previously unused or little-used raw material, augments rent. Thus, for example, there was a tremendous rise in the rent of coal mines with the advent of the railways, steamships, etc.

Besides this advantage which the landlord derives from manufacture, discoveries, and labour, there is yet another, as we shall presently see.

(4) "All those improvements in the productive powers of labour, which tend directly to reduce the real price of manufactures, tend indirectly to raise the real rent of land. The landlord exchanges that part of his rude produce, which is over and above his own consumption, or what comes to the same thing, the price of that part of it, for manufactured produce. Whatever reduces the real price of the latter,

raises that of the former. An equal quantity of the former becomes thereby equivalent to a greater quantity of the latter; and the landlord is enabled to purchase a greater quantity of the conveniencies, ornaments, or luxuries, which he has occasion for." (Adam Smith, op. cit., Vol. I, p. 229 [Garnier, t. II, p. 159].)

But it is silly to conclude, as Smith does, that since the landlord exploits every benefit which comes to society ||X,3| the interest of the landlord is always identical with that of society. (op. cit., Vol. I, p. 230 [Garnier, t. II, p. 161].) In the economic system, under the rule of private property, the interest which an individual has in society is in precisely inverse proportion to the interest society has in him—just as the interest of the usurer in the spendthrift is by no means identical with the interest of the spendthrift.

We shall mention only in passing the landlord's obsession with monopoly directed against the landed property of foreign countries, from which the Corn Laws,[69] for instance, originate. Likewise, we shall here pass over medieval serfdom, the slavery in the colonies, and the miserable condition of the country folk, the day-labourers, in Great Britain. Let us confine ourselves to the propositions of political economy itself.

(1) The landlord being interested in the welfare of society means, according to the principles of political economy, that he is interested in the growth of its population and manufacture, in the expansion of its needs—in short, in the increase of wealth; and this increase of wealth is, as we have already seen, identical with the increase of poverty and slavery. The relation between increasing house rent and increasing poverty is an example of the landlord's interest in society, for the ground rent, the interest obtained from the land on which the house stands, goes up with the rent of the house.

(2) According to the political economists themselves, the landlord's interest is inimically opposed to the interest of the tenant farmer—and thus already to a significant section of society.

||XI,3| (3) As the landlord can demand all the more rent from the tenant farmer the less wages the farmer pays, and as the farmer forces down wages all the lower the more rent the landlord demands, it follows that the interest of the landlord is just as hostile to that of the farm workers as is that of the manufacturers to their workers. He likewise forces down wages to the minimum.

(4) Since a real reduction in the price of manufactured products raises the rent of land, the landowner has a direct interest in lowering the wages of industrial workers, in competition amongst the capitalists, in over-production, in all the misery associated with industrial production.

(5) While, thus, the landlord's interest, far from being identical with the interest of society, stands inimically opposed to the interest of tenant farmers, farm labourers, factory workers and capitalists, on the other hand, the interest of one landlord is not even identical with that of another, on account of the competition which we will now consider.

In general the relationship of large and small landed property is like that of big and small capital. But in addition, there are special circumstances which lead inevitably to the accumulation of large landed property and to the absorption of small property by it.

||XII,3| (1) Nowhere does the relative number of workers and implements decrease more with increases in the size of the stock than in landed property. Likewise, the possibility of all-round exploitation, of economising production costs, and of effective division of labour, increases nowhere more with the size of the stock than in landed property. However small a field may be, it requires for its working a certain irreducible minimum of implements (plough, saw, etc.), whilst the size of a piece of landed property can be reduced far below this minimum.

(2) Big landed property accumulates to itself the interest on the capital which the tenant farmer has employed to improve the land. Small landed property has to employ its own capital, and therefore does not get this profit at all.

(3) While every social improvement benefits the big estate, it harms small property, because it increases its need for ready cash.

(4) Two important laws concerning this competition remain to be considered:

(α) The rent of the cultivated[a] land, of which the produce is human food, regulates the rent of the greater part of other cultivated land. (Adam Smith, op. cit., Vol. I, p. 144 [Garnier, t. I, p. 331].)

Ultimately, only the big estate can produce such food as cattle, etc. Therefore it regulates the rent of other land and can force it down to a minimum.

The small landed proprietor working on his own land stands then to the big landowner in the same relation as an artisan possessing his *own* tool to the factory owner. Small property in land has become a mere instrument of labour. ||XVI,1|[70] Rent entirely disappears for the small proprietor; there remains to him at the most the interest on his capital, and his wages. For rent can be driven down by competition till it is nothing more than the interest on capital not invested by the proprietor.

(β) In addition, we have already learnt that with equal fertility

---

[a] The manuscript has "produced" instead of "cultivated".— *Ed.*

and equally efficient exploitation of lands, mines and fisheries, the produce is proportionate to the size of the capital. Hence the victory of the big landowner. Similarly, where equal capitals are employed the product is proportionate to the fertility. Hence, where capitals are equal, victory goes to the proprietor of the more fertile soil.

(γ) "A mine of any kind may be said to be either fertile or barren, according as the quantity of mineral which can be brought from it by a certain quantity of labour is greater or less than what can be brought by an equal quantity from the greater part of other mines of the same kind." (Adam Smith, op. cit., Vol. I, p. 151 [Garnier, t. I, pp. 345-46].)

"The most fertile coal-mine, too, regulates the price of coals[a] at all the other mines in its neighbourhood. Both the proprietor and the undertaker of the work find, the one that he can get a greater rent, the other that he can get a greater profit, by somewhat underselling all their neighbours. Their neighbours are soon obliged to sell at the same price, though they cannot so well afford it, and though it always diminishes, and sometimes takes away altogether both their rent and their profit. Some works are abandoned altogether; others can afford no rent, and can be wrought only by the proprietor." (Adam Smith, op. cit., Vol. I, pp. 152-53 [Garnier, t. I, p. 350].)

"After the discovery of the mines of Peru, the silver mines of Europe were, the greater part of them, abandoned.... This was the case, too, with the mines of Cuba and St. Domingo, and even with the ancient mines of Peru, after the discovery of those of Potosi." (op. cit., Vol. I, p. 154 [Garnier, t. I, p. 353].)

What Smith here says of mines applies more or less to landed property generally:

(δ) "The ordinary market price of land, it is to be observed, depends everywhere upon the ordinary market rate of interest.... If the rent of land should fall short of the interest of money by a greater difference, nobody would buy land, which would soon reduce its ordinary price. On the contrary, if the advantages should much more than compensate the difference, everybody would buy land, which again would soon raise its ordinary price." (op. cit., Vol. I, p. 320 [Garnier, t. II, pp. 367-68].)

From this relation of rent of land to interest on money it follows that rent must fall more and more, so that eventually only the wealthiest people can live on rent. Hence the evergreater competition between landowners who do not lease their land to tenants. Ruin of some of these; further accumulation of large landed property.

‖XVII,2‖ This competition has the further consequence that a large part of landed property falls into the hands of the capitalists and that capitalists thus become simultaneously landowners, just as the smaller landowners are on the whole already nothing more than capitalists. Similarly, a section of large landowners become at the same time industrialists.

---

[a] The manuscript has "mine" instead of "coals".— *Ed.*

The final consequence is thus the abolition of the distinction between capitalist and landowner, so that there remain altogether only two classes of the population—the working class and the class of capitalists. This huckstering with landed property, the transformation of landed property into a commodity, constitutes the final overthrow of the old and the final establishment of the money aristocracy.

(1) We will not join in the sentimental tears wept over this by romanticism. Romanticism always confuses the shamefulness of *huckstering the land* with the perfectly rational consequence, inevitable and desirable within the realm of private property, of the *huckstering of private property* in land. In the first place, feudal landed property is already by its very nature huckstered land—the earth which is estranged from man and hence confronts him in the shape of a few great lords.

The domination of the land as an alien power over men is already inherent in feudal landed property. The serf is the adjunct of the land. Likewise, the lord of an entailed estate, the first-born son, belongs to the land. It inherits him. Indeed, the dominion of private property begins with property in land—that is its basis. But in feudal landed property the lord at least *appears* as the king of the estate. Similarly, there still exists the semblance of a more intimate connection between the proprietor and the land than that of mere *material* wealth. The estate is individualised with its lord: it has his rank, is baronial or ducal with him, has his privileges, his jurisdiction, his political position, etc. It appears as the inorganic body of its lord. Hence the proverb *nulle terre sans maître*, which expresses the fusion of nobility and landed property. Similarly, the rule of landed property does not appear directly as the rule of mere capital. For those belonging to it, the estate is more like their fatherland. It is a constricted sort of nationality.

‖XVIII,2‖ In the same way, feudal landed property gives its name to its lord, as does a kingdom to its king. His family history, the history of his house, etc.—all this individualises the estate for him and makes it literally his house, personifies it. Similarly those working on the estate have not the position of *day-labourers*; but they are in part themselves his property, as are serfs; and in part they are bound to him by ties of respect, allegiance, and duty. His relation to them is therefore directly political, and has likewise a human, *intimate* side. Customs, character, etc., vary from one estate to another and seem to be one with the land to which they belong; whereas later, it is only his purse and not his character, his individuality, which connects a man with an estate. Finally, the feudal lord does not try to extract the utmost advantage from his land. Rather, he consumes what is there and calmly leaves the worry of producing to the serfs and the tenants. Such is *nobility's* relationship to landed property, which casts a romantic glory on its lords.

It is necessary that this appearance be abolished—that landed property, the root of private property, be dragged completely into the movement of private property and that it become a commodity; that the rule of the proprietor appear as the undisguised rule of private property, of capital, freed of all political tincture; that the relationship between proprietor and worker be reduced to the economic relationship of exploiter and exploited; that all [...]^a personal relationship between the proprietor and his property cease, property becoming merely *objective*, material wealth; that the marriage of convenience should take the place of the marriage of honour with the land; and that the land should likewise sink to the status of a commercial value, like man. It is essential that that which is the root of landed property—filthy self-interest—make its appearance, too, in its cynical form. It is essential that the immovable monopoly turn into the mobile and restless monopoly, into competition; and that the idle enjoyment of the products of other people's blood and sweat turn into a bustling commerce in the same commodity. Lastly, it is essential that in this competition landed property, in the form of capital, manifest its dominion over both the working class and the proprietors themselves who are either being ruined or raised by the laws governing the movement of capital. The medieval proverb *nulle terre sans seigneur* is thereby replaced by that other proverb, *l'argent n'a pas de maître*, wherein is expressed the complete domination of dead matter over man.

||XIX,2| (2) Concerning the argument of division or non-division of landed property, the following is to be observed.

The *division of landed property* negates the *large-scale monopoly* of property in land—abolishes it; but only by *generalising* this monopoly. It does not abolish the source of monopoly, private property. It attacks the existing form, but not the essence, of monopoly. The consequence is that it falls victim to the laws of private property. For the division of landed property corresponds to the movement of competition in the sphere of industry. In addition to the economic disadvantages of such a dividing-up of the instruments of labour, and the dispersal of labour (to be clearly distinguished from the division of labour: in separated

---

^a A word in the manuscript cannot be deciphered.— *Ed.*

labour the work is not shared out amongst many, but each carries on the same work by himself, it is a multiplication of the same work), this division [of land], like that competition [in industry], necessarily turns again into accumulation.

Therefore, where the division of landed property takes place, there remains nothing for it but to return to monopoly in a still more malignant form, or to negate, to abolish the division of landed property itself. To do that, however, is not to return to feudal ownership, but to abolish private property in the soil altogether. The first abolition of monopoly is always its generalisation, the broadening of its existence. The abolition of monopoly, once it has come to exist in its utmost breadth and inclusiveness, is its total annihilation. Association, applied to land, shares the economic advantage of large-scale landed property, and first[a] brings to realisation the original tendency inherent in [land] division, namely, equality. In the same way association also re-establishes, now on a rational basis, no longer mediated by serfdom, overlordship and the silly mysticism of property, the intimate ties of man with the earth, since the earth ceases to be an object of huckstering, and through free labour and free enjoyment becomes once more a true personal property of man. A great advantage of the division of landed property is that the masses, which can no longer resign themselves to servitude, perish through property in a different way than in industry.

As for large landed property, its defenders have always, sophistically, identified the economic advantages offered by large-scale agriculture with large-scale landed property, as if it were not precisely as a result of the abolition of property that this advantage, for one thing, would receive its ||XX,2| greatest possible extension, and, for another, only then would be of social benefit. In the same way, they have attacked the huckstering spirit of small landed property, as if large landed property did not contain huckstering latent within it, even in its feudal form—not to speak of the modern English form, which combines the landlord's feudalism with the tenant farmer's huckstering and industry.

Just as large landed property can return the reproach of monopoly levelled against it by partitioned land, since partitioned land is also based on the monopoly of private property, so can partitioned landed property likewise return to large landed property the reproach of partition, since partition also prevails there, though in a rigid and frozen form. Indeed, private property rests

---

[a] In the manuscript the word "first" (*erst*) cannot be clearly deciphered.—*Ed.*

altogether on partitioning. Moreover, just as division of the land leads back to large landed property as a form of capital wealth, so must feudal landed property necessarily lead to partitioning or at least fall into the hands of the capitalists, turn and twist as it may.

For large landed property, as in England, drives the overwhelming majority of the population into the arms of industry and reduces its own workers to utter wretchedness. Thus, it engenders and enlarges the power of its enemy, capital, industry, by throwing poor people and an entire activity of the country on to the other side. It makes the majority of the people of the country industrial and thus opponents of large landed property. Where industry has attained to great power, as in England at the present time, it progressively forces from large landed property its monopoly against foreign countries[a] and throws it into competition with landed property abroad. For under the sway of industry landed property could keep its feudal grandeur secure only by means of monopolies against foreign countries, thereby protecting itself against the general laws of trade, which are incompatible with its feudal character. Once thrown into competition, landed property obeys the laws of competition, like every other commodity subjected to competition. It begins thus to fluctuate, to decrease and to increase, to fly from one hand to another; and no law can keep it any longer in a few predestined hands.||XXI,2| The immediate consequence is the splitting up of the land amongst many hands, and in any case subjection to the power of industrial capitals.

Finally, large landed property which has been forcibly preserved in this way and which has begotten by its side a tremendous industry leads to crisis even more quickly than the partitioning of land, in comparison with which the power of industry remains constantly of second rank.

Large landed property, as we see in England, has already cast off its feudal character and adopted an industrial character insofar as it is aiming to make as much money as possible. To the owner it yields the utmost possible rent, to the tenant farmer the utmost possible profit on his capital. The workers on the land, in consequence, have already been reduced to the minimum, and the class of tenant farmers already represents within landed property the power of industry and capital. As a result of foreign competition, rent in most cases can no longer form an independent income. A large number of landowners are forced to displace

---

[a] Originally it was "against the monopoly of foreign countries", then Marx crossed out "the monopoly of".— *Ed.*

tenant farmers, some of whom in this way [...]ᵃ sink into the proletariat. On the other hand, many tenant farmers will take over landed property; for the big proprietors, who with their comfortable incomes have mostly given themselves over to extravagance and for the most part are not competent to conduct large-scale agriculture, often possess neither the capital nor the ability for the exploitation of the land. Hence a section of this class, too, is completely ruined. Eventually wages, which have already been reduced to a minimum, must be reduced yet further, to meet the new competition. This then necessarily leads to revolution.

Landed property had to develop in each of these two ways so as to experience in both its necessary downfall, just as industry both in the form of monopoly and in that of competition had to ruin itself so as to learn to believe in man. |XXI|

[ESTRANGED LABOUR]

||XXII| We have proceeded from the premises of political economy. We have accepted its language and its laws. We presupposed private property, the separation of labour, capital and land, and of wages, profit of capital and rent of land—likewise division of labour, competition, the concept of exchange-value, etc. On the basis of political economy itself, in its own words, we have shown that the worker sinks to the level of a commodity and becomes indeed the most wretched of commodities; that the wretchedness of the worker is in inverse proportion to the power and magnitude of his production; that the necessary result of competition is the accumulation of capital in a few hands, and thus the restoration of monopoly in a more terrible form; and that finally the distinction between capitalist and land rentier, like that between the tiller of the soil and the factory worker, disappears and that the whole of society must fall apart into the two classes—the *property owners* and the propertyless *workers*.

Political economy starts with the fact of private property; it does not explain it to us. It expresses in general, abstract formulas the *material* process through which private property actually passes, and these formulas it then takes for *laws*. It does not *comprehend* these

---

ᵃ Here one word in the manuscript cannot be deciphered.—*Ed.*

laws, i.e., it does not demonstrate how they arise from the very nature of private property. Political economy throws no light on the cause of the division between labour and capital, and between capital and land. When, for example, it defines the relationship of wages to profit, it takes the interest of the capitalists to be the ultimate cause, i.e., it takes for granted what it is supposed to explain. Similarly, competition comes in everywhere. It is explained from external circumstances. As to how far these external and apparently accidental circumstances are but the expression of a necessary course of development, political economy teaches us nothing. We have seen how exchange itself appears to it as an accidental fact. The only wheels which political economy sets in motion are *greed* and the *war amongst the greedy—competition*.[a]

Precisely because political economy does not grasp the way the movement is connected, it was possible to oppose, for instance, the doctrine of competition to the doctrine of monopoly, the doctrine of the freedom of the crafts to the doctrine of the guild, the doctrine of the division of landed property to the doctrine of the big estate — for competition, freedom of the crafts and the division of landed property were explained and comprehended only as accidental, premeditated and violent consequences of monopoly, of the guild system, and of feudal property, not as their necessary, inevitable and natural consequences.

Now, therefore, we have to grasp the intrinsic connection between private property, avarice, the separation of labour, capital and landed property; the connection of exchange and competition, of value and the devaluation of men, of monopoly and competition, etc.— we have to grasp this whole estrangement connected with the *money* system.

Do not let us go back to a fictitious primordial condition as the political economist does, when he tries to explain. Such a primordial condition explains nothing; it merely pushes the question away into a grey nebulous distance. The economist assumes in the form of a fact, of an event, what he is supposed to deduce—namely, the necessary relationship between two things—between, for example, division of labour and exchange. Thus the theologian explains the origin of evil by the fall of man; that is, he assumes as a fact, in historical form, what has to be explained.

We proceed from an *actual* economic fact.

The worker becomes all the poorer the more wealth he produces,

---

[a] After the paragraph the following sentence is crossed out in the manuscript: "We now have to examine the nature of this *material* movement of property."—*Ed.*

the more his production increases in power and size. The worker becomes an ever cheaper commodity the more commodities he creates. The *devaluation* of the world of men is in direct proportion to the *increasing value* of the world of things. Labour produces not only commodities: it produces itself and the worker as a *commodity*—and this at the same rate at which it produces commodities in general.

This fact expresses merely that the object which labour produces—labour's product—confronts it as *something alien,* as a *power independent* of the producer. The product of labour is labour which has been embodied in an object, which has become material: it is the *objectification* of labour. Labour's realisation is its objectification. Under these economic conditions this realisation of labour appears as *loss of realisation* for the workers[71]; objectification as *loss of the object and bondage to it*; appropriation as *estrangement, as alienation.*[72]

So much does labour's realisation appear as loss of realisation that the worker loses realisation to the point of starving to death. So much does objectification appear as loss of the object that the worker is robbed of the objects most necessary not only for his life but for his work. Indeed, labour itself becomes an object which he can obtain only with the greatest effort and with the most irregular interruptions. So much does the appropriation of the object appear as estrangement that the more objects the worker produces the less he can possess and the more he falls under the sway of his product, capital.

All these consequences are implied in the statement that the worker is related to the *product of his labour* as to an *alien* object. For on this premise it is clear that the more the worker spends himself, the more powerful becomes the alien world of objects which he creates over and against himself, the poorer he himself—his inner world—becomes, the less belongs to him as his own. It is the same in religion. The more man puts into God, the less he retains in himself. The worker puts his life into the object; but now his life no longer belongs to him but to the object. Hence, the greater this activity, the more the worker lacks objects. Whatever the product of his labour is, he is not. Therefore the greater this product, the less is he himself. The *alienation* of the worker in his product means not only that his labour becomes an object, an *external* existence, but that it exists *outside him,* independently, as something alien to him, and that it becomes a power on its own confronting him. It means that the life which he has conferred on the object confronts him as something hostile and alien.

‖XXIII/ Let us now look more closely at the *objectification*, at the production of the worker; and in it at the *estrangement*, the *loss* of the object, of his product.

The worker can create nothing without *nature*, without the *sensuous external world*. It is the material on which his labour is realised, in which it is active, from which and by means of which it produces.

But just as nature provides labour with [the] *means of life* in the sense that labour cannot *live* without objects on which to operate, on the other hand, it also provides the *means of life* in the more restricted sense, i.e., the means for the physical subsistence of the *worker* himself.

Thus the more the worker by his labour *appropriates* the external world, sensuous nature, the more he deprives himself of *means of life* in two respects: first, in that the sensuous external world more and more ceases to be an object belonging to his labour—to be his labour's *means of life*; and secondly, in that it more and more ceases to be *means of life* in the immediate sense, means for the physical subsistence of the worker.

In both respects, therefore, the worker becomes a servant of his object, first, in that he receives an *object of labour*, i.e., in that he receives *work*; and secondly, in that he receives *means of subsistence*. This enables him to exist, first, as a *worker*; and, second, as a *physical subject*. The height of this servitude is that it is only as a *worker* that he can maintain himself as a *physical subject*, and that it is only as a *physical subject* that he is a worker.

(According to the economic laws the estrangement of the worker in his object is expressed thus: the more the worker produces, the less he has to consume; the more values he creates, the more valueless, the more unworthy he becomes; the better formed his product, the more deformed becomes the worker; the more civilised his object, the more barbarous becomes the worker; the more powerful labour becomes, the more powerless becomes the worker; the more ingenious labour becomes, the less ingenious becomes the worker and the more he becomes nature's servant.)

Political economy conceals the estrangement inherent in the nature of labour by not considering the **direct** *relationship between the* **worker** (labour) *and production.* It is true that labour produces wonderful things for the rich—but for the worker it produces privation. It produces palaces—but for the worker, hovels. It produces beauty—but for the worker, deformity. It replaces labour by machines, but it throws one section of the workers back to a barbarous type of labour, and it turns the other section into a machine. It produces intelligence—but for the worker, stupidity, cretinism.

The direct relationship of labour to its products is the relationship of the worker to the objects of his production. The relationship of the man of means to the objects of production and to production itself is only a *consequence* of this first relationship—and confirms it. We shall consider this other aspect later. When we ask, then, what is the essential relationship of labour we are asking about the relationship of the *worker* to production.

Till now we have been considering the estrangement, the alienation of the worker only in one of its aspects, i.e., the worker's *relationship to the products of his labour*. But the estrangement is manifested not only in the result but in the *act of production*, within the *producing activity* itself. How could the worker come to face the product of his activity as a stranger, were it not that in the very act of production he was estranging himself from himself? The product is after all but the summary of the activity, of production. If then the product of labour is alienation, production itself must be active alienation, the alienation of activity, the activity of alienation. In the estrangement of the object of labour is merely summarised the estrangement, the alienation, in the activity of labour itself.

What, then, constitutes the alienation of labour?

First, the fact that labour is *external* to the worker, i.e., it does not belong to his intrinsic nature; that in his work, therefore, he does not affirm himself but denies himself, does not feel content but unhappy, does not develop freely his physical and mental energy but mortifies his body and ruins his mind. The worker therefore only feels himself outside his work, and in his work feels outside himself. He feels at home when he is not working, and when he is working he does not feel at home. His labour is therefore not voluntary, but coerced; it is *forced labour*. It is therefore not the satisfaction of a need; it is merely a *means* to satisfy needs external to it. Its alien character emerges clearly in the fact that as soon as no physical or other compulsion exists, labour is shunned like the plague. External labour, labour in which man alienates himself, is a labour of self-sacrifice, of mortification. Lastly, the external character of labour for the worker appears in the fact that it is not his own, but someone else's, that it does not belong to him, that in it he belongs, not to himself, but to another. Just as in religion the spontaneous activity of the human imagination, of the human brain and the human heart, operates on the individual independently of him—that is, operates as an alien, divine or diabolical activity—so is the worker's activity not his spontaneous activity. It belongs to another; it is the loss of his self.

As a result, therefore, man (the worker) only feels himself freely active in his animal functions — eating, drinking, procreating, or at most in his dwelling and in dressing-up, etc.; and in his human functions he no longer feels himself to be anything but an animal. What is animal becomes human and what is human becomes animal.

Certainly eating, drinking, procreating, etc., are also genuinely human functions. But taken abstractly, separated from the sphere of all other human activity and turned into sole and ultimate ends, they are animal functions.

We have considered the act of estranging practical human activity, labour, in two of its aspects. (1) The relation of the worker to the *product of labour* as an alien object exercising power over him. This relation is at the same time the relation to the sensuous external world, to the objects of nature, as an alien world inimically opposed to him. (2) The relation of labour to the *act of production* within the *labour* process. This relation is the relation of the worker to his own activity as an alien activity not belonging to him; it is activity as suffering, strength as weakness, begetting as emasculating, the worker's *own* physical and mental energy, his personal life—for what is life but activity?—as an activity which is turned against him, independent of him and not belonging to him. Here we have *self-estrangement*, as previously we had the estrangement of the *thing*.

‖XXIV‖ We have still a third aspect of *estranged labour* to deduce from the two already considered.

Man is a species-being,[73] not only because in practice and in theory he adopts the species (his own as well as those of other things) as his object, but—and this is only another way of expressing it—also because he treats himself as the actual, living species; because he treats himself as a *universal* and therefore a free being.

The life of the species, both in man and in animals, consists physically in the fact that man (like the animal) lives on inorganic nature; and the more universal man (or the animal) is, the more universal is the sphere of inorganic nature on which he lives. Just as plants, animals, stones, air, light, etc., constitute theoretically a part of human consciousness, partly as objects of natural science, partly as objects of art—his spiritual inorganic nature, spiritual nourishment which he must first prepare to make palatable and digestible—so also in the realm of practice they constitute a part of human life and human activity. Physically man lives only on these products of nature, whether they appear in the form of food, heating, clothes, a dwelling, etc. The universality of man appears in practice precisely in the universality which makes all nature his *inorganic* body—both inasmuch as nature is (1) his direct means of life, and (2) the material, the object, and the instrument of his life activity. Nature is man's *inorganic body*—nature, that is, insofar as it is not itself human body. Man *lives* on nature—means that nature is his *body*, with which he must remain in continuous interchange if he is not to die. That man's physical and spiritual life is linked to nature means simply that nature is linked to itself, for man is a part of nature.

In estranging from man (1) nature, and (2) himself, his own active functions, his life activity, estranged labour estranges the *species* from man. It changes for him the *life of the species* into a means of individual life. First it estranges the life of the species and individual life, and secondly it makes individual life in its abstract form the purpose of the life of the species, likewise in its abstract and estranged form.

For labour, *life activity, productive life* itself, appears to man in the first place merely as a *means* of satisfying a need—the need to maintain physical existence. Yet the productive life is the life of the species. It is life-engendering life. The whole character of a species—its species-character—is contained in the character of its life activity; and free, conscious activity is man's species-character. Life itself appears only as a *means to life*.

The animal is immediately one with its life activity. It does not distinguish itself from it. It is *its life activity*. Man makes his life activity itself the object of his will and of his consciousness. He has conscious life activity. It is not a determination with which he directly merges. Conscious life activity distinguishes man immediately from animal life activity. It is just because of this that he is a species-being. Or it is only because he is a species-being that he is a conscious being, i.e., that his own life is an object for him. Only because of that is his activity free activity. Estranged labour reverses this relationship, so that it is just because man is a conscious being that he makes his life activity, his *essential being*, a mere means to his *existence*.

In creating a *world of objects* by his practical activity, in his *work upon* inorganic nature, man proves himself a conscious species-being, i.e., as a being that treats the species as its own essential being, or that treats itself as a species-being. Admittedly animals also produce. They build themselves nests, dwellings, like the bees, beavers, ants, etc. But an animal only produces what it immediately needs for itself or its young. It produces one-sidedly, whilst man produces universally. It produces only under the dominion of immediate physical need, whilst man produces even when he is free from physical need and only truly produces in freedom therefrom. An animal produces only itself, whilst man reproduces the whole of nature. An animal's product belongs immediately to its physical body, whilst man freely confronts his product. An animal forms objects only in accordance with the standard and the need of the species to which it belongs, whilst man knows how to produce in accordance with the standard of every species, and knows how to apply everywhere the inherent standard to the object. Man therefore also forms objects in accordance with the laws of beauty.

It is just in his work upon the objective world, therefore, that man really proves himself to be a *species-being*. This production is his active species-life. Through this production, nature appears as *his* work and his reality. The object of labour is, therefore, the *objectification of man's species-life*: for he duplicates himself not only, as in consciousness, intellectually, but also actively, in reality, and therefore he sees himself in a world that he has created. In tearing away from man the object of his production, therefore, estranged labour tears from him his *species-life*, his real objectivity as a member of the species, and transforms his advantage over animals into the disadvantage that his inorganic body, nature, is taken away from him.

Similarly, in degrading spontaneous, free activity to a means, estranged labour makes man's species-life a means to his physical existence.

The consciousness which man has of his species is thus transformed by estrangement in such a way that species[-life] becomes for him a means.

Estranged labour turns thus:

(3) *Man's species-being*, both nature and his spiritual species-property, into a being *alien* to him, into a *means* for his *individual existence*. It estranges from man his own body, as well as external nature and his spiritual aspect, his *human* aspect.

(4) An immediate consequence of the fact that man is estranged from the product of his labour, from his life activity, from his species-being is the *estrangement of man* from *man*. When man confronts himself, he confronts the *other* man. What applies to a man's relation to his work, to the product of his labour and to himself, also holds of a man's relation to the other man, and to the other man's labour and object of labour.

In fact, the proposition that man's species-nature is estranged from him means that one man is estranged from the other, as each of them is from man's essential nature.

The estrangement of man, and in fact every relationship in which man [stands] to himself, is realised and expressed only in the relationship in which a man stands to other men.

Hence within the relationship of estranged labour each man views the other in accordance with the standard and the relationship in which he finds himself as a worker.

||XXV| We took our departure from a fact of political economy—the estrangement of the worker and his product. We have formulated this fact in conceptual terms as *estranged, alienated* labour. We have analysed this concept—hence analysing merely a fact of political economy.

Let us now see, further, how the concept of estranged, alienated labour must express and present itself in real life.

If the product of labour is alien to me, if it confronts me as an alien power, to whom, then, does it belong?

If my own activity does not belong to me, if it is an alien, a coerced activity, to whom, then, does it belong?

To a being *other* than myself.

Who is this being?

The *gods*? To be sure, in the earliest times the principal production (for example, the building of temples, etc., in Egypt, India and Mexico) appears to be in the service of the gods, and the product belongs to the gods. However, the gods on their own were never the lords of labour. No more was *nature*. And what a contradiction it would be if, the more man subjugated nature by his labour and the more the miracles of the gods were rendered superfluous by the miracles of industry, the more man were to renounce the joy of production and the enjoyment of the product to please these powers.

The *alien* being, to whom labour and the product of labour belongs, in whose service labour is done and for whose benefit the product of labour is provided, can only be *man* himself.

If the product of labour does not belong to the worker, if it confronts him as an alien power, then this can only be because it belongs to some *other man than the worker*. If the worker's activity is a torment to him, to another it must give *satisfaction* and pleasure. Not the gods, not nature, but only man himself can be this alien power over man.

We must bear in mind the previous proposition that man's relation to himself only becomes for him *objective* and *actual* through his relation to the other man. Thus, if the product of his labour, his labour objectified, is for him an *alien, hostile*, powerful object independent of him, then his position towards it is such that someone else is master of this object, someone who is alien, hostile, powerful, and independent of him. If he treats his own activity as an unfree activity, then he treats it as an activity performed in the service, under the dominion, the coercion, and the yoke of another man.

Every self-estrangement of man, from himself and from nature, appears in the relation in which he places himself and nature to men other than and differentiated from himself. For this reason religious self-estrangement necessarily appears in the relationship of the layman to the priest, or again to a mediator, etc., since we are here dealing with the intellectual world. In the real practical world self-estrangement can only become manifest through the real practical relationship to other men. The medium through which estrangement takes place is itself *practical*. Thus through estranged labour man not only creates his relationship to the object and to the act of production as to powers[a] that are alien and hostile to him; he also creates the relationship in which other men stand to his production and to his product, and the relationship in which he stands to these other men. Just as he creates his own production as the loss of his reality, as his punishment; his own product as a loss, as a product not belonging to him; so he creates the domination of the person who does not produce over production and over the product. Just as he estranges his own activity from himself, so he confers upon the stranger an activity which is not his own.

We have until now considered this relationship only from the standpoint of the worker and later we shall be considering it also from the standpoint of the non-worker.

Through *estranged, alienated labour*, then, the worker produces the relationship to this labour of a man alien to labour and standing outside it. The relationship of the worker to labour creates the relation to it of the capitalist (or whatever one chooses to call the master of labour). *Private property* is thus the product, the result, the necessary consequence, of *alienated labour*, of the external relation of the worker to nature and to himself.

Private property thus results by analysis from the concept of *alienated labour*, i.e., of *alienated man*, of estranged labour, of estranged life, of *estranged* man.

True, it is as a result of the *movement of private property* that we have obtained the concept of *alienated labour (of alienated life)* in political economy. But analysis of this concept shows that though private property appears to be the reason, the cause of alienated labour, it is rather its consequence, just as the gods are *originally* not

---

[a] In the manuscript *Menschen* (men) instead of *Mächte* (powers).— Ed.

the cause but the effect of man's intellectual confusion. Later this relationship becomes reciprocal.

Only at the culmination of the development of private property does this, its secret, appear again, namely, that on the one hand it is the *product* of alienated labour, and that on the other it is the *means* by which labour alienates itself, the *realisation of this alienation*.

This exposition immediately sheds light on various hitherto unsolved conflicts.

(1) Political economy starts from labour as the real soul of production; yet to labour it gives nothing, and to private property everything. Confronting this contradiction, Proudhon has decided in favour of labour against private property.[74] We understand, however, that this apparent contradiction is the contradiction of *estranged labour* with itself, and that political economy has merely formulated the laws of estranged labour.

We also understand, therefore, that *wages* and *private property* are identical. Indeed, where the product, as the object of labour, pays for labour itself, there the wage is but a necessary consequence of labour's estrangement. Likewise, in the wage of labour, labour does not appear as an end in itself but as the servant of the wage. We shall develop this point later, and meanwhile will only draw some con-||XXVI| clusions.[75]

An enforced *increase of wages* (disregarding all other difficulties, including the fact that it would only be by force, too, that such an increase, being an anomaly, could be maintained) would therefore be nothing but better *payment for the slave,* and would not win either for the worker or for labour their human status and dignity.

Indeed, even the *equality of wages*, as demanded by Proudhon, only transforms the relationship of the present-day worker to his labour into the relationship of all men to labour. Society is then conceived as an abstract capitalist.

Wages are a direct consequence of estranged labour, and estranged labour is the direct cause of private property. The downfall of the one must therefore involve the downfall of the other.

(2) From the relationship of estranged labour to private property it follows further that the emancipation of society from private property, etc., from servitude, is expressed in the *political* form of the *emancipation of the workers*; not that *their* emancipation alone is at stake, but because the emancipation of the workers contains universal human emancipation—and it contains this, because the whole of human servitude is involved in the relation of the worker to production, and all relations of servitude are but modifications and consequences of this relation.

Just as we have derived the concept of *private property* from the concept of *estranged, alienated labour* by *analysis*, so we can develop every *category* of political economy with the help of these two factors; and we shall find again in each category, e.g., trade, competition, capital, money, only a *particular* and *developed expression* of these first elements.

Before considering this phenomenon, however, let us try to solve two other problems.

(1) To define the general *nature of private property*, as it has arisen as a result of estranged labour, in its relation to *truly human* and *social property*.

(2) We have accepted the *estrangement of labour*, its *alienation*, as a fact, and we have analysed this fact. How, we now ask, does *man* come to *alienate*, to estrange, his *labour*? How is this estrangement rooted in the nature of human development? We have already gone a long way to the solution of this problem by *transforming* the question of the *origin of private property* into the question of the relation of *alienated labour* to the course of humanity's development. For when one speaks of *private property*, one thinks of dealing with something external to man. When one speaks of labour, one is directly dealing with man himself. This new formulation of the question already contains its solution.

As to (1): The general nature of private property and its relation to truly human property.

Alienated labour has resolved itself for us into two components which depend on one another, or which are but different expressions of one and the same relationship. *Appropriation* appears as *estrangement*, as *alienation*; and *alienation* appears as *appropriation, estrangement* as truly *becoming a citizen*.[76]

We have considered the one side—*alienated* labour in relation to the worker himself, i.e., the *relation of alienated labour to itself*. The product, the necessary outcome of this relationship, as we have seen, is the *property relation of the non-worker to the worker and to labour*. *Private property*, as the material, summary expression of alienated labour, embraces both relations — the *relation of the worker to labour and to the product of his labour and to the non-worker*, and the relation of the *non-worker to the worker and to the product of his labour*.

Having seen that in relation to the worker who *appropriates* nature by means of his labour, this appropriation appears as estrangement, his own spontaneous activity as activity for another and as activity of another, vitality as a sacrifice of life, production of the object as loss of the object to an alien power, to an *alien* person—we shall now consider the relation to the worker, to labour and its object of this person who is *alien* to labour and the worker.

First it has to be noted that everything which appears in the worker as an *activity of alienation, of estrangement,* appears in the non-worker as a *state of alienation, of estrangement.*

Secondly, that the worker's *real, practical attitude* in production and to the product (as a state of mind) appears in the non-worker confronting him as a *theoretical* attitude.

||XXVII| *Thirdly,* the non-worker does everything against the worker which the worker does against himself; but he does not do against himself what he does against the worker.

Let us look more closely at these three relations.[a] |XXVII||

---

[a] At this point the first manuscript breaks off unfinished.—*Ed.*

[Second Manuscript]

[ANTITHESIS OF CAPITAL AND LABOUR. LANDED PROPERTY AND CAPITAL]

[...] ||XL| forms the interest on his capital.[a] The worker is the subjective manifestation of the fact that capital is man wholly lost to himself, just as capital is the objective manifestation of the fact that labour is man lost to himself. But the *worker* has the misfortune to be a *living* capital, and therefore an *indigent* capital, one which loses its interest, and hence its livelihood, every moment it is not working. The *value* of the worker as capital rises according to demand and supply, and *physically* too his *existence*, his *life*, was and is looked upon as a supply of a *commodity* like any other. The worker produces capital, capital produces him—hence he produces himself, and man as *worker*, as a *commodity*, is the product of this entire cycle. To the man who is nothing more than a *worker*—and to him as a worker—his human qualities only exist insofar as they exist for capital *alien* to him. Because man and capital are alien, foreign to each other, however, and thus stand in an indifferent, external and accidental relationship to each other, it is inevitable that this foreignness should also appear as something *real*. As soon, therefore, as it occurs to capital (whether from necessity or caprice) no longer to be for the worker, he himself is no longer for himself: he has no work, hence no wages, and since he has no existence *as a human being* but only *as a worker*, he can go and bury himself, starve to death, etc. The worker exists as a worker only when he exists *for himself* as capital; and he exists as capital only when some *capital* exists *for him*. The existence of

---

[a] With these words page XL of the second manuscript begins; the preceding pages have not been preserved.— *Ed.*

capital is *his* existence, his *life*; as it determines the tenor of his life in a manner indifferent to him.

Political economy, therefore, does not recognise the unemployed worker, the workingman, insofar as he happens to be outside this labour relationship. The rascal, swindler, beggar, the unemployed, the starving, wretched and criminal workingman—these are *figures* who do not exist *for political economy* but only for other eyes, those of the doctor, the judge, the grave-digger, and bum-bailiff, etc.; such figures are spectres outside its domain. For it, therefore, the worker's needs are but the one *need*—to maintain *him whilst he is working* and insofar as may be necessary to prevent the *race of labourers* from [dying] out. The wages of labour have thus exactly the same significance as the *maintenance* and *servicing* of any other productive instrument, or as the *consumption of capital* in general, required for its reproduction with interest, like the oil which is applied to wheels to keep them turning. Wages, therefore, belong to capital's and the capitalist's necessary *costs*, and must not exceed the bounds of this necessity. It was therefore quite logical for the English factory owners, before the Amendment Bill of 1834,[a] to deduct from the wages of the worker the public charity which he was receiving out of the Poor Rate and to consider this to be an integral part of wages.[77]

Production does not simply produce man as a *commodity*, the *human commodity*, man in the role of *commodity*; it produces him in keeping with this role as a *mentally* and physically *dehumanised* being.— Immorality, deformity, and dulling of the workers and the capitalists.— Its product is the *self-conscious and self-acting commodity* ... the *human* commodity.... Great advance of Ricardo, Mill, etc., on Smith and Say, to declare the *existence* of the human being—the greater or lesser human productivity of the commodity—to be *indifferent* and even *harmful*. Not how many workers are maintained by a given capital, but rather how much interest it brings in, the sum-total of the annual *savings*, is said to be the true purpose of production.

It was likewise a great and consistent advance of modern ||XLI| English political economy, that, whilst elevating *labour* to the position of its *sole* principle, it should at the same time expound with complete clarity the *inverse* relation between wages and interest on capital, and the fact that the capitalist could normally *only* gain by pressing down

---

[a] See this volume, pp. 194-95.—*Ed.*

wages, and vice versa. Not the defrauding of the consumer, but the capitalist and the worker taking advantage of each other, is shown to be the *normal* relationship.

The relations of private property contain latent within them the relation of private property as *labour,* the relation of private property as *capital,* and the *mutual relation* of these two to one another. There is the production of human activity as *labour*—that is, as an activity quite alien to itself, to man and to nature, and therefore to consciousness and the expression of life—the *abstract* existence of man as a mere *workman* who may therefore daily fall from his filled void into the absolute void—into his social, and therefore actual, non-existence. On the other hand, there is the production of the object of human activity as *capital*—in which all the natural and social characteristic of the object is *extinguished*; in which private property has lost its natural and social quality (and therefore every political and social illusion, and is not associated with any *apparently* human relations); in which the *selfsame* capital remains the *same* in the most diverse natural and social manifestations, totally indifferent to its *real* content. This contradiction, driven to the limit, is of necessity the limit, the culmination, and the downfall of the whole private-property relationship.

It is therefore another great achievement of modern English political economy to have declared rent of land to be the difference in the interest yielded by the worst and the best land under cultivation; to have [exposed][a] the landowner's romantic illusions—his alleged social importance and the identity of his interest with the interest of society, a view still maintained by *Adam Smith* after the Physiocrats; and to [have] anticipated and prepared the movement of the real world which will transform the landowner into an ordinary, prosaic capitalist, and thus simplify and sharpen the contradiction [between capital and labour] and hasten its resolution. *Land* as *land,* and *rent* as *rent,* have lost their *distinction of rank* and become insignificant *capital* and *interest*—or rather, *capital* and *interest* that signify only money.

The *distinction* between capital and land, between profit and rent, and between both and wages, and *industry,* and *agriculture,* and *immovable* and *movable* private property—this distinction is not rooted in the nature of things, but is a *historical* distinction, a *fixed* historical moment in the formation and development of the contradiction between capital and labour. In industry, etc., as opposed to immovable landed property, is only expressed the way in which [industry] came into being and the contradiction to agriculture

---

[a] The manuscript is damaged here.—*Ed.*

in which industry developed. This distinction only continues to exist as a *special* sort of work — as an *essential, important* and *life-embracing* distinction — so long as industry (town life) develops *over* and *against* landed property (aristocratic feudal life) and itself continues to bear the feudal character of its opposite in the form of monopoly, craft, guild, corporation, etc., within which labour still has a *seemingly social* significance, still the significance of the *real* community, and has not yet reached the stage of *indifference* to its content, of complete being-for-self,[78] i. e., of abstraction from all other being, and hence has not yet become *liberated* capital.

||XLII|| But liberated *industry,* industry constituted for itself as such, and *liberated capital,* are the necessary *development* of labour. The power of industry over its opposite is at once revealed in the emergence of *agriculture* as a real industry, while previously it left most of the work to the soil and to the *slave* of the soil, through whom the land cultivated itself. With the transformation of the slave into a *free* worker — i. e., into a *hireling* — the landlord himself is transformed into a captain of industry, into a capitalist — a transformation which takes place at first through the intermediacy of the *tenant farmer.* The *tenant farmer,* however, is the landowner's representative—the landowner's revealed *secret:* it is only through him that the landowner has his *economic* existence — his existence as a private proprietor — for the rent of his land only exists due to the competition between the farmers.

Thus, in the person of the *tenant farmer* the landlord *has* already become in essence a *common* capitalist. And this must come to pass, too, in actual fact: the capitalist engaged in agriculture — the tenant — must become a landlord, or vice versa. The tenant's *industrial hucksterism* is the *landowner*'s industrial hucksterism, for the being of the former postulates the being of the latter.

But mindful of their contrasting origin, of their line of descent, the landowner knows the capitalist as his insolent, liberated, enriched slave of yesterday and sees himself as a *capitalist* who is threatened by him. The capitalist knows the landowner as the idle, cruel, egotistical master of yesterday; he knows that he injures him as a capitalist, but that it is to industry that he owes all his present social significance, his possessions and his pleasures; he sees in him a contradiction to *free* industry and to *free* capital — to capital independent of every natural limitation. This contradiction is extremely bitter, and each side tells the truth about the other. One need only read the attacks of immovable on movable property and vice versa to obtain a clear picture of their respective worthlessness. The landowner lays stress on the noble lineage of his property, on feudal souvenirs or reminiscences, the poetry of recollection, on his romantic disposition, on his political importance, etc.; and when he talks economics, it is *only* agriculture that he holds to be productive. At the same time he depicts his adversary as a sly, hawking, carping, deceitful, greedy, mercenary, rebellious, heartless and spiritless person who is estranged from the community and freely trades it away, who breeds, nourishes and cherishes competition, and with it pauperism, crime, and the dissolution of all social bonds, an extorting, pimping, servile, smooth, flattering, fleecing, dried-up *rogue* without honour, principles, poetry, substance, or anything else. (Amongst others see the Physiocrat *Bergasse*, whom Camille Desmoulins flays in his journal, *Révolutions de France et de Brabant*[79]; see von Vincke, Lancizolle, Haller, Leo, Kosegarten* and also *Sismondi*.)

Movable property, for its part, points to the miracles of industry and progress. It is the child of modern times, whose legitimate, native-born son it is. It pities its adversary as a simpleton, *unenlightened* about his own nature (and in this it is completely right), who wants to replace moral capital and free labour by brute, immoral violence and serfdom. It depicts him as a Don Quixote, who under the guise of *bluntness, respectability,* the *general interest,* and *stability,* conceals incapacity for progress, greedy self-indulgence, selfishness, sectional interest, and evil intent. It declares him an artful *monopolist*; it pours cold water on his reminiscences, his poetry, and his romanticism by a historical and sarcastic enumeration of the baseness, cruelty, degradation, prostitution, infamy, anarchy and rebellion, of which romantic castles were the workshops.

||XLIII| It claims to have obtained political freedom for everybody; to have loosed the chains which fettered civil society; to have linked together different worlds; to have created trade promoting friendship between the peoples; to have created pure morality and a pleasant culture; to have given the people civilised needs in place of their crude wants, and the means of satisfying them. Meanwhile,

---

* See on the other hand the garrulous, old-Hegelian theologian *Funke* who tells, after Herr Leo, with tears in his eyes how a slave had refused, when serfdom was abolished, to cease being the *property of the gentry*.[80] See also the *patriotic visions of Justus Möser,* which distinguish themselves by the fact that they never for a moment [...][a] abandon the respectable, petty-bourgeois "*home-baked*", *ordinary,* narrow horizon of the philistine, and which nevertheless remain *pure* fancy. This contradiction has given them such an appeal to the German heart.— *Note by Marx.*

---

[a] A few words cannot be deciphered here.— *Ed.*

it claims, the landowner—this idle, parasitic grain-profiteer—raises the price of the people's basic necessities and so forces the capitalist to raise wages without being able to increase productivity,[a] thus impeding [the growth of] the nation's annual income, the accumulation of capital, and therefore the possibility of providing work for the people and wealth for the country, eventually cancelling it, thus producing a general decline—whilst he parasitically exploits *every* advantage of modern civilisation without doing the least thing for it, and without even abating in the slightest his feudal prejudices. Finally, let him—for whom the cultivation of the land and the land itself exist only as a source of money, which comes to him as a present—let him just take a look at his *tenant farmer* and say whether he himself is not a *downright, fantastic, sly* scoundrel who in his heart and in actual fact has for a long time belonged to *free* industry and to *lovely* trade, however much he may protest and prattle about historical memories and ethical or political goals. Everything which he can really advance to justify himself is true only of the *cultivator of the land* (the capitalist and the labourers), of whom the *landowner* is rather the *enemy*. Thus he gives evidence against himself. [Movable property claims that] *without* capital landed property is dead, worthless matter; that its civilised victory has discovered and made human labour the source of wealth in place of the dead thing. (See Paul Louis Courier, Saint-Simon, Ganilh, Ricardo, Mill, McCulloch and Destutt de Tracy and Michel Chevalier.)

The *real* course of development (to be inserted at this point) results in the necessary victory of the *capitalist* over the *landowner*—that is to say, of developed over undeveloped, immature private property—just as in general, movement must triumph over immobility; open, self-conscious baseness over hidden, unconscious baseness; *cupidity* over *self-indulgence*; the avowedly restless, adroit self-interest of *enlightenment* over the parochial, worldly-wise, respectable, idle and fantastic *self-interest of superstition*; and *money* over the other forms of private property.

Those states which sense something of the danger attaching to fully developed free industry, to fully developed pure morality and to fully developed philanthropic trade, try, but in vain, to hold in check the capitalisation of landed property.

Landed property in its distinction from capital is private property—capital—still afflicted with *local* and political prejudices; it is capital which has not yet extricated itself from its entanglement with the world and found the form proper to itself—capital *not*

---

[a] "Productivity" has been used here to render *Produktionskraft*.—*Ed.*

yet *fully developed*. It must achieve its abstract, that is, its *pure*, expression in the course of its *cosmogony*.

The character of *private property* is expressed by labour, capital, and the relations between these two. The movement through which these constituents have to pass is:

First. *Unmediated* or *mediated unity of the two.*

Capital and labour are at first still united. Then, though separated and estranged, they reciprocally develop and promote each other as *positive* conditions.

[Second.] *The two in opposition,* mutually excluding each other. The worker knows the capitalist as his own non-existence, and vice versa: each tries to rob the other of his existence.

[Third.] *Opposition* of each *to* itself. Capital=stored-up labour=labour. As such it splits into *capital itself* and its *interest,* and this latter again into *interest and profit.* The capitalist is completely sacrificed. He falls into the working class, whilst the worker (but only exceptionally) becomes a capitalist. Labour as a moment of capital—its *costs.* Thus the wages of labour—a sacrifice of capital.

Splitting of labour into *labour itself* and the *wages of labour*. The worker himself a capital, a commodity.

Clash of mutual contradictions. |XLIII||

[Third Manuscript][81]

[PRIVATE PROPERTY AND LABOUR. POLITICAL ECONOMY AS A PRODUCT OF THE MOVEMENT OF PRIVATE PROPERTY]

|I| Re p. XXXVI[a] The *subjective essence* of private property—*private property* as activity for itself,[82] as *subject,* as *person*—is *labour.* It is therefore evident that only the political economy which acknowledged *labour* as its principle—*Adam Smith*—and which therefore no longer looked upon private property as a mere *condition* external to man—that it is this political economy which has to be regarded on the one hand as a product of the real *energy* and the real *movement* of private property (it is a movement of private property become independent for itself in consciousness—the modern industry as Self—as a product of modern *industry*—and on the other hand, as a force which has quickened and glorified the energy and development of modern *industry* and made it a power in the realm of *consciousness.*

To this enlightened political economy, which has discovered—within private property—the *subjective essence* of wealth, the adherents of the monetary and mercantile system, who look upon private property *only as an objective* substance confronting men, seem therefore to be *fetishists, Catholics. Engels* was therefore right to call *Adam Smith* the *Luther of Political Economy.*[b] Just as Luther recognised *religion—faith—*as the substance of the external *world* and in consequence stood opposed to Catholic paganism—just as he superseded *external* religiosity by making religiosity the *inner* substance of man—just as he negated the priests outside the layman because he transplanted the priest into laymen's hearts, just so with

---

[a] This refers to the missing part of the second manuscript.—*Ed.*
[b] Cf. Frederick Engels, "Outlines of a Critique of Political Economy" (see this volume, p. 422).—*Ed.*

wealth: wealth as something outside man and independent of him, and therefore as something to be maintained and asserted only in an external fashion, is done away with; that is, this *external, mindless objectivity* of wealth is done away with, with private property being incorporated in man himself and with man himself being recognised as its essence. But as a result man is brought within the orbit of private property, just as with Luther he is brought within the orbit of religion. Under the semblance of recognising man, the political economy whose principle is labour rather carries to its logical conclusion the denial of man, since man himself no longer stands in an external relation of tension to the external substance of private property, but has himself become this tense essence of private property. What was previously *being external to oneself*—man's actual externalisation—has merely become the act of externalising— the process of alienating. This political economy begins by seeming to acknowledge man (his independence, spontaneity, etc.); then, locating private property in man's own being, it can no longer be conditioned by the local, national or other *characteristics of private property* as of *something existing outside itself*. This political economy, consequently, displays a *cosmopolitan*, universal energy which overthrows every restriction and bond so as to establish itself instead as the *sole* politics, the sole universality, the sole limit and sole bond. Hence it must throw aside this *hypocrisy* in the course of its further development and come out *in its complete cynicism*. And this it does—untroubled by all the apparent contradictions in which it becomes involved as a result of this theory—by developing the idea of *labour* much *more one-sidedly*, and therefore *more sharply* and *more consistently*, as the sole *essence of wealth*; by proving the implications of this theory to be *anti-human* in character, in contrast to the other, original approach. Finally, by dealing the death-blow to *rent*—that last, *individual, natural* mode of private property and source of wealth existing independently of the movement of labour, that expression of feudal property, an expression which has already become wholly economic in character and therefore incapable of resisting political economy. (The *Ricardo* school.) There is not merely a relative growth in the *cynicism* of political economy from Smith through Say to Ricardo, Mill, etc., inasmuch as the implications of *industry* appear more developed and more contradictory in the eyes of the last-named; these later economists also advance in a positive sense constantly and consciously further than their predecessors in their estrangement from man. They do so, however, *only* because their science develops more consistently and truthfully. Because they make private property in its active form the subject, thus simultaneously turning man into the essence — and at the same time turning man as non-essentiality into the essence — the contradiction of reality corresponds completely to the contradictory being which they accept as their principle. Far from refuting it, the ruptured ||II| *world of industry* confirms their *self-ruptured* principle. Their principle is, after all, the principle of this rupture.

The physiocratic doctrine of *Dr. Quesnay* forms the transition from the mercantile system to Adam Smith. *Physiocracy* represents directly the decomposition of feudal property in *economic* terms, but it therefore just as directly represents its *economic metamorphosis* and restoration, save that now its language is no longer feudal but economic. All wealth is resolved into *land* and *cultivation* (agriculture). Land is not yet *capital*: it is still a *special* mode of its existence, the validity of which is supposed to lie in, and to *derive from*, its natural peculiarity. Yet land is a general natural *element*, whilst the mercantile system admits the existence of wealth only in the form of *precious metal*. Thus the *object* of wealth—its matter—has straightway obtained the highest degree of universality within the *bounds of nature*, insofar as even as *nature*, it is immediate objective wealth. And land only exists for *man* through labour, through agriculture.

Thus the subjective essence of wealth has already been transferred to labour. But at the same time agriculture is the *only productive* labour. Hence, labour is not yet grasped in its generality and abstraction: it is still bound to a particular *natural element as its matter*, and it is therefore only recognised in a *particular mode of existence determined by nature*. It is therefore still only a *specific, particular* alienation of man, just as its product is likewise conceived nearly [as] a specific form of wealth—due more to nature than to labour itself. The land is here still recognised as a phenomenon of nature independent of man—not yet as capital, i.e., as an aspect of labour itself. Labour appears, rather, as an aspect of the *land*. But since the fetishism of the old external wealth, of wealth existing only as an object, has been reduced to a very simple natural element, and since its essence — even if only partially and in a particular form — has been recognised within its subjective existence, the necessary step forward has been made in revealing the *general nature* of wealth and hence in the raising up of *labour* in its total absoluteness (i.e., its abstraction) as the *principle*. It is argued against physiocracy that *agriculture*, from the economic point of view—that is to say, from the only valid point of view—does not differ from any other industry; and that the *essence* of wealth, therefore, is not a *specific* form of labour bound to a particular element—a particular expression of labour—but *labour in general*.

Physiocracy denies *particular*, external, merely objective wealth by declaring labour to be the *essence* of wealth. But for physiocracy labour is at first only the *subjective essence* of landed property. (It takes its departure from the type of property which historically appears as the dominant and acknowledged type.) It turns only landed property into *alienated man*. It annuls its feudal character by declaring *industry* (agriculture) as its *essence*. But it disavows the world of industry and acknowledges the feudal system by declaring *agriculture* to be the *only* industry.

It is clear that if the *subjective essence* of industry is now grasped (of industry in opposition to landed property, i.e., of industry constituting itself as industry), this essence includes within itself its opposite. For just as industry incorporates annulled landed property, the *subjective* essence of industry at the same time incorporates the subjective essence of *landed property*.

Just as landed property is the first form of private property, with industry at first confronting it historically merely as a special kind of property—or, rather, as landed property's liberated slave—so this process repeats itself in the scientific analysis of the *subjective* essence of private property, *labour*. Labour appears at first only as *agricultural labour*; but then asserts itself as *labour* in general.

|III| All wealth has become *industrial* wealth, the *wealth* of *labour*; and *industry* is accomplished labour, just as the *factory system* is the perfected essence of *industry*, that is of labour, and just as *industrial capital* is the accomplished objective form of private property.

We can now see how it is only at this point that private property can complete its dominion over man and become, in its most general form, a world-historical power.

[PRIVATE PROPERTY AND COMMUNISM]

Re p. XXXIX.[a] The antithesis between *lack of property* and *property*, so long as it is not comprehended as the antithesis of *labour* and *capital*, still remains an indifferent antithesis, not

---

[a] This refers to the missing part of the second manuscript.— *Ed.*

grasped in its *active connection,* in its *internal* relation, not yet grasped as a *contradiction*. It can find expression in this *first* form even without the advanced development of private property (as in ancient Rome, Turkey, etc.). It does not yet *appear* as having been established by private property itself. But labour, the subjective essence of private property as exclusion of property, and capital, objective labour as exclusion of labour, constitute *private property* as its developed state of contradiction — hence a dynamic relationship driving towards resolution.

Re the same page. The transcendence of self-estrangement follows the same course as self-estrangement. *Private property* is first considered only in its objective aspect—but nevertheless with labour as its essence. Its form of existence is therefore *capital,* which is to be annulled "as such" (Proudhon). Or a *particular form of labour*—labour levelled down, fragmented, and therefore unfree—is conceived as the source of private property's *perniciousness* and of its existence in estrangement from men. For instance, *Fourier,* who, like the Physiocrats, also conceives *agricultural labour* to be at least the *exemplary* type, whereas *Saint-Simon* declares in contrast that *industrial labour* as such is the essence, and accordingly aspires to the *exclusive* rule of the industrialists and the improvement of the workers' condition. Finally, *communism* is the *positive* expression of annulled private property — at first as *universal* private property. By embracing this relation as a *whole,* communism is:

(1) In its first form only a *generalisation* and *consummation* of it [of this relation]. As such it appears in a twofold form: on the one hand, the dominion of *material* property bulks so large that it wants to destroy *everything* which is not capable of being possessed by all as *private property*. It wants to disregard talent, etc., in an *arbitrary* manner. For it the sole purpose of life and existence is direct, physical *possession.* The category of the *worker* is not done away with, but extended to all men. The relationship of private property persists as the relationship of the community to the world of things. Finally, this movement of opposing universal private property to private property finds expression in the brutish form of opposing to *marriage* (certainly a *form of exclusive private property*) the *community of women,* in which a woman becomes a piece of *communal* and *common* property. It may be said that this idea of the *community of women gives away the secret* of this as yet completely crude and thoughtless communism.[83] Just as

woman passes from marriage to general prostitution,* so the entire world of wealth (that is, of man's objective substance) passes from the relationship of exclusive marriage with the owner of private property to a state of universal prostitution with the community. This type of communism—since it negates the *personality* of man in every sphere—is but the logical expression of private property, which is this negation. General *envy* constituting itself as a power is the disguise in which *greed* re-establishes itself and satisfies itself, only in *another* way. The thought of every piece of private property as such is *at least* turned against *wealthier* private property in the form of envy and the urge to reduce things to a common level, so that this envy and urge even constitute the essence of competition. Crude communism[a] is only the culmination of this envy and of this levelling-down proceeding from the *preconceived* minimum. It has a *definite, limited* standard. How little this annulment of private property is really an appropriation is in fact proved by the abstract negation of the entire world of culture and civilisation, the regression to the *unnatural* |IV| simplicity of the *poor* and crude man who has few needs and who has not only failed to go beyond private property, but has not yet even reached it.

The community is only a community of *labour*, and equality of *wages* paid out by communal capital—by the *community* as the universal capitalist. Both sides of the relationship are raised to an *imagined* universality—*labour* as the category in which every person is placed, and *capital* as the acknowledged universality and power of the community.

In the approach to *woman* as the *spoil* and handmaid of communal lust is expressed the infinite degradation in which man exists for himself, for the secret of this approach has its *unambiguous*, decisive, *plain* and undisguised expression in the relation of *man* to *woman* and in the manner in which the *direct* and *natural* species-relationship is conceived. The direct, natural, and necessary relation of person to person is the *relation of man to woman*. In this *natural* species-relationship man's relation to nature is immediately his relation to man, just as his relation to man is immediately his relation to nature—his own *natural* destination. In

---

* Prostitution is only a *specific* expression of the *general* prostitution of the *labourer*, and since it is a relationship in which falls not the prostitute alone, but also the one who prostitutes—and the latter's abomination is still greater—the capitalist, etc., also comes under this head.—*Note by Marx.*[84]

---

[a] The manuscript has "*Kommunist*".—*Ed.*

this relationship, therefore, is *sensuously manifested,* reduced to an observable *fact,* the extent to which the human essence has become nature to man, or to which nature to him has become the human essence of man. From this relationship one can therefore judge man's whole level of development. From the character of this relationship follows how much *man* as a *species-being,* as *man,* has come to be himself and to comprehend himself; the relation of man to woman is the *most natural* relation of human being to human being. It therefore reveals the extent to which man's *natural* behaviour has become *human,* or the extent to which the *human* essence in him has become a *natural* essence—the extent to which his *human nature* has come to be *natural* to him. This relationship also reveals the extent to which man's *need* has become a *human* need; the extent to which, therefore, the *other* person as a person has become for him a need—the extent to which he in his individual existence is at the same time a social being.

The first positive annulment of private property—*crude communism*—is thus merely a *manifestation* of the vileness of private property, which wants to set itself up as the *positive community system.*

(2) Communism (α) still political in nature—democratic or despotic; (β) with the abolition of the state, yet still incomplete, and being still affected by private property, i. e., by the estrangement of man. In both forms communism already is aware of being reintegration or return of man to himself, the transcendence of human self-estrangement; but since it has not yet grasped the positive essence of private property, and just as little the *human* nature of need, it remains captive to it and infected by it. It has, indeed, grasped its concept, but not its essence.

(3) *Communism* as the *positive* transcendence of *private property* as *human self-estrangement,* and therefore as the real *appropriation* of the *human* essence by and for man; communism therefore as the complete return of man to himself as a *social* (i. e., human) being—a return accomplished consciously and embracing the entire wealth of previous development. This communism, as fully developed naturalism, equals humanism, and as fully developed humanism equals naturalism; it is the *genuine* resolution of the conflict between man and nature and between man and man—the true resolution of the strife between existence and essence, between objectification and self-confirmation, between freedom and necessity, between the individual and the species. Communism

is the riddle of history solved, and it knows itself to be this solution.

|V| The entire movement of history, just as its [communism's] *actual* act of genesis—the birth act of its empirical existence—is, therefore, also for its thinking consciousness the *comprehended* and *known* process of its *becoming*. Whereas the still immature communism seeks an *historical* proof for itself—a proof in the realm of what already exists—among disconnected historical phenomena opposed to private property, tearing single phases from the historical process and focusing attention on them as proofs of its historical pedigree (a hobby-horse ridden hard especially by Cabet, Villegardelle, etc.). By so doing it simply makes clear that by far the greater part of this process contradicts its own claim, and that, if it has ever existed, precisely its being in the *past* refutes its pretension to *reality*.

It is easy to see that the entire revolutionary movement necessarily finds both its empirical and its theoretical basis in the movement of *private property*—more precisely, in that of the economy.

This *material*, immediately *perceptible* private property is the material perceptible expression of *estranged human* life. Its movement—production and consumption—is the *perceptible* revelation of the movement of all production until now, i. e., the realisation or the reality of man. Religion, family, state, law, morality, science, art, etc., are only *particular* modes of production, and fall under its general law. The positive transcendence of *private property*, as the appropriation of *human* life, is therefore the positive transcendence of all estrangement—that is to say, the return of man from religion, family, state, etc., to his *human*, i. e., *social*, existence. Religious estrangement as such occurs only in the realm of *consciousness*, of man's inner life, but economic estrangement is that of *real life*; its transcendence therefore embraces both aspects. It is evident that the *initial* stage of the movement amongst the various peoples depends on whether the true *recognised* life of the people manifests itself more in consciousness or in the external world — is more ideal or real. Communism begins from the outset (*Owen*) with atheism; but atheism is at first far from being *communism*; indeed, that atheism is still mostly an abstraction.

The philanthropy of atheism is therefore at first only *philosophical*, abstract philanthropy, and that of communism is at once *real* and directly bent on *action*.

We have seen how on the assumption of positively annulled private property man produces man—himself and the other man;

how the object, being the direct manifestation of his individuality, is simultaneously his own existence for the other man, the existence of the other man, and that existence for him. Likewise, however, both the material of labour and man as the subject, are the point of departure as well as the result of the movement (and precisely in this fact, that they must constitute the *point of departure*, lies the historical *necessity* of private property). Thus the *social* character is the general character of the whole movement: *just as* society itself produces *man as man*, so is society *produced* by him. Activity and enjoyment, both in their content and in their *mode of existence*, are *social*: *social*[a] activity and *social* enjoyment. The *human* aspect of nature exists only for *social* man; for only then does nature exist for him as a *bond* with *man*—as his existence for the other and the other's existence for him—and as the life-element of human reality. Only then does nature exist as the *foundation* of his own *human* existence. Only here has what is to him his *natural* existence become his *human* existence, and nature become man for him. Thus *society* is the complete unity of man with nature—the true resurrection of nature—the accomplished naturalism of man and the accomplished humanism of nature.

‖VII‖ Social activity and social enjoyment exist by no means *only* in the form of some *directly* communal activity and directly *communal* enjoyment, although *communal* activity and *communal* enjoyment—i. e., activity and enjoyment which are manifested and affirmed in *actual* direct *association* with other men—will occur wherever such a *direct* expression of sociability stems from the true character of the activity's content and is appropriate to the nature of the enjoyment.

But also when I am active *scientifically*, etc.—an activity which I can seldom perform in direct community with others—then my activity is *social*, because I perform it as a *man*. Not only is the material of my activity given to me as a social product (as is even the language in which the thinker is active): my *own* existence *is* social activity, and therefore that which I make of myself, I make of myself for society and with the consciousness of myself as a social being.

My *general* consciousness is only the *theoretical* shape of that of which the *living* shape is the *real* community, the social fabric, although at the present day *general* consciousness is an abstraction from real life and as such confronts it with hostility. The *activity* of

---

[a] This word is crossed out in the manuscript.—*Ed.*

my general consciousness, as an activity, is therefore also my *theoretical* existence as a social being.

Above all we must avoid postulating "society" again as an abstraction *vis-à-vis* the individual. The individual *is the social being*. His manifestations of life—even if they may not appear in the direct form of *communal* manifestations of life carried out in association with others—*are* therefore an expression and confirmation of *social life*. Man's individual and species-life are not *different*, however much—and this is inevitable—the mode of existence of the individual is a more *particular* or more *general* mode of the life of the species, or the life of the species is a more *particular* or more *general* individual life.

In his *consciousness of species* man confirms his real *social life* and simply repeats his real existence in thought, just as conversely the being of the species confirms itself in species consciousness and exists for itself in its generality as a thinking being.

Man, much as he may therefore be a *particular* individual (and it is precisely his particularity which makes him an individual, and a real *individual* social being), is just as much the *totality*—the ideal totality—the subjective existence of imagined and experienced society for itself; just as he exists also in the real world both as awareness and real enjoyment of social existence, and as a totality of human manifestation of life.

Thinking and being are thus certainly *distinct*, but at the same time they are in *unity* with each other.

Death seems to be a harsh victory of the species over the *particular* individual and to contradict their unity. But the particular individual is only a *particular species-being*, and as such mortal.

⟨(4)[a] Just as *private property* is only the perceptible expression of the fact that man becomes *objective* for himself and at the same time becomes to himself a strange and inhuman object; just as it expresses the fact that the manifestation of his life is the alienation of his life, that his realisation is his loss of reality, is an *alien* reality: so, the positive transcendence of private property—i. e., the *perceptible* appropriation for and by man of the human essence and of human life, of objective man, of human *achievements*—should not be conceived merely in the sense of *immediate*, one-sided *enjoyment*, merely in the sense of *possessing*, of *having*. Man appropriates his comprehensive essence in a comprehensive manner, that is to say, as a whole man. Each of his *human* relations to the world—seeing, hearing, smelling, tasting, feeling, thinking,

---

[a] In the manuscript: "5".—*Ed.*

observing, experiencing, wanting, acting, loving—in short, all the organs of his individual being, like those organs which are directly social in their form, ||VII| are in their *objective* orientation, or in their *orientation to the object*, the appropriation of the object, the appropriation of *human* reality. Their orientation to the object is the *manifestation of the human reality*,* it is human *activity* and human *suffering*, for suffering, humanly considered, is a kind of self-enjoyment of man.

Private property has made us so stupid and one-sided that an object is only *ours* when we have it—when it exists for us as capital, or when it is directly possessed, eaten, drunk, worn, inhabited, etc.,—in short, when it is *used* by us. Although private property itself again conceives all these direct realisations of possession only as *means of life*, and the life which they serve as means is the *life of private property*—labour and conversion into capital.

In the place of *all* physical and mental senses there has therefore come the sheer estrangement of *all* these senses, the sense of *having*. The human being had to be reduced to this absolute poverty in order that he might yield his inner wealth to the outer world. (On the category of "having", see *Hess*[a] in the *Einundzwanzig Bogen*.)

The abolition of private property is therefore the complete *emancipation* of all human senses and qualities, but it is this emancipation precisely because these senses and attributes have become, subjectively and objectively, *human*. The eye has become a *human* eye, just as its *object* has become a social, *human* object—an object made by man for man. The *senses* have therefore become directly in their practice *theoreticians*. They relate themselves to the *thing* for the sake of the thing, but the thing itself is an *objective human* relation to itself and to man,** and vice versa. Need or enjoyment has consequently lost its *egotistical* nature, and nature has lost its mere *utility* by use becoming *human* use.

In the same way, the senses and enjoyment of other men have become my *own* appropriation. Besides these direct organs, therefore, *social* organs develop in the *form* of society; thus, for

---

* For this reason it is just as highly varied as the *determinations* of human *essence* and *activities*.—*Note by Marx*.

** In practice I can relate myself to a thing humanly only if the thing relates itself humanly to the human being.—*Note by Marx*.

---

[a] Moses Hess, "Philosophie der Tat".—*Ed*.

instance, activity in direct association with others, etc., has become an organ for *expressing* my own *life*, and a mode of appropriating *human* life.

It is obvious that the *human* eye enjoys things in a way different from the crude, non-human eye; the human *ear* different from the crude ear, etc.

We have seen that man does not lose himself in his object only when the object becomes for him a *human* object or objective man. This is possible only when the object becomes for him a *social* object, he himself for himself a social being, just as society becomes a being for him in this object.

On the one hand, therefore, it is only when the objective world becomes everywhere for man in society the world of man's essential powers—human reality, and for that reason the reality of his *own* essential powers—that all *objects* become for him the *objectification* of himself, become objects which confirm and realise his individuality, become *his* objects: that is, *man himself* becomes the object. The *manner* in which they become *his* depends on the *nature of the objects* and on the nature of the *essential power* corresponding to *it*; for it is precisely the *determinate nature* of this relationship which shapes the particular, *real* mode of affirmation. To the *eye* an object comes to be other than it is to the *ear*, and the object of the eye *is* another object than the object of the *ear*. The specific character of each essential power is precisely its *specific essence*, and therefore also the specific mode of its objectification, of its *objectively actual*, living *being*. Thus man is affirmed in the objective world not only in the act of thinking, ||VIII| but with *all* his senses.

On the other hand, let us look at this in its subjective aspect. Just as only music awakens in man the sense of music, and just as the most beautiful music has *no* sense for the unmusical ear—is [no] object for it, because my object can only be the confirmation of one of my essential powers—it can therefore only exist for me insofar as my essential power exists for itself as a subjective capacity; because the meaning of an object for me goes only so far as *my* sense goes (has only a meaning for a sense corresponding to that object)—for this reason the *senses* of the social man *differ from* those of the non-social man. Only through the objectively unfolded richness of man's essential being is the richness of subjective *human* sensibility (a musical ear, an eye for beauty of form—in short, *senses* capable of human gratification, senses affirming themselves as essential powers of *man*) either cultivated or brought into being. For not only the five senses but also the so-called mental senses, the practical senses (will, love, etc.), in a word, *human* sense, the human nature of the senses, comes to be by virtue of *its* object, by virtue of *humanised* nature. The *forming* of the five senses is a labour of the entire history of the world down to the present. The *sense* caught up in crude practical need has only a *restricted* sense.) For the starving man, it is not the human form of food that exists, but only its abstract existence as food. It could just as well be there in its crudest form, and it would be impossible to say wherein this feeding activity differs from that of *animals*. The care-burdened, poverty-stricken man has no *sense* for the finest play; the dealer in minerals sees only the commercial value but not the beauty and the specific character of the mineral: he has no mineralogical sense. Thus, the objectification of the human essence, both in its theoretical and practical aspects, is required to make man's *sense human*, as well as to create the *human sense* corresponding to the entire wealth of human and natural substance.

⟨Just as through the movement of *private property*, of its wealth as well as its poverty—of its material and spiritual wealth and poverty—the budding society finds at hand all the material for this *development*, so *established* society produces man in this entire richness of his being—produces the *rich* man *profoundly endowed with all the senses*—as its enduring reality.⟩

We see how subjectivity and objectivity, spirituality and materiality, activity and suffering, lose their antithetical character, and thus their existence as such antitheses only within the framework of society; ⟨we see how the resolution of the *theoretical* antitheses is *only* possible in a *practical* way, by virtue of the practical energy of man. Their resolution is therefore by no means merely a problem of understanding, but a *real* problem of life, which *philosophy* could not solve precisely because it conceived this problem as *merely* a theoretical one.

We see how the history of *industry* and the established *objective existence* of industry are the *open* book of *man's essential powers*, the perceptibly existing human *psychology*. Hitherto this was not conceived in its connection with man's *essential being*, but only in an external relation of utility, because, moving in the realm of estrangement, people could only think of man's general mode of being—religion or history in its abstract-general character as politics, art, literature, etc.—∥IX∣ as the reality of man's essential powers and *man's species-activity*. We have before us the *objectified essential powers* of man in the form of *sensuous, alien, useful objects*, in the form of estrangement, displayed in *ordinary material industry* (which can be conceived either as a part of that general movement, or that movement can be conceived as a *particular* part of industry, since all human activity hitherto has been labour—that is, industry—activity estranged from itself).

A *psychology* for which this book, the part of history existing in the most perceptible and accessible form, remains a closed book, cannot become a genuine, comprehensive and *real* science.⟩ What indeed are we to think of a science which *airily* abstracts from this large part of human labour and which fails to feel its own incompleteness, while such a wealth of human endeavour, unfolded before it, means nothing more to it than, perhaps, what can be expressed in one word—"*need*", "*vulgar need*"?

The *natural sciences* have developed an enormous activity and have accumulated an ever-growing mass of material. Philosophy, however, has remained just as alien to them as they remain to philosophy. Their momentary unity was only a *chimerical illusion*. The will was there, but the power was lacking. Historiography itself pays regard to natural science only occasionally, as a factor of enlightenment, utility, and of some special great discoveries. But natural science has invaded and transformed human life all the more *practically* through the medium of industry; and has prepared human emancipation, although its immediate effect had to be the furthering of the dehumanisation of man. *Industry* is the *actual*, historical relationship of nature, and therefore of natural science, to man. If, therefore, industry is conceived as the *exoteric* revelation of man's *essential powers*, we also gain an understanding of the *human* essence of nature or the *natural* essence of man. In consequence, natural science will lose its abstractly material—or rather, its idealistic—tendency, and will become the basis of *human* science, as it has already become—albeit in an estranged form—the basis of actual human life, and to assume *one* basis for life and a different basis for *science* is as a matter of course a lie. ⟨The nature which develops in human history—the genesis of human society—is man's *real* nature; hence nature as it develops through industry, even though in an *estranged* form, is true *anthropological* nature.⟩

Sense-perception (see Feuerbach) must be the basis of all science. Only when it proceeds from sense-perception in the twofold form of *sensuous* consciousness and *sensuous* need—that is, only when science proceeds from nature—is it *true* science. All history is the history of preparing and developing "*man*" to become the object of *sensuous* consciousness, and turning the requirements of "man as man" into his needs. History itself is a *real* part of *natural history*—of nature developing into man. Natural science will in time incorporate into itself the science of man, just as the science of man will incorporate into itself natural science: there will be *one* science.

|| X | *Man* is the immediate object of natural science; for immediate, *sensuous nature* for man is, immediately, human sensuousness (the expressions are identical)—presented immediately in the form of the *other* man sensuously present for him. Indeed, his own sense-perception first exists as human sensuousness for himself through the *other* man. But *nature* is the immediate object of the *science of man*: the first object of man—man—is nature, sensuousness; and the particular human sensuous essential powers can only find their self-understanding in the science of the natural world in general, just as they can find their objective realisation only in *natural* objects. The element of thought itself—the element of thought's living expression—*language*—is of a sensuous nature. The *social* reality of nature, and *human* natural science, or the *natural science of man*, are identical terms.

⟨It will be seen how in place of the *wealth* and *poverty* of political economy come the *rich human being* and the rich *human* need. The *rich* human being is simultaneously the human being *in need of* a totality of human manifestations of life—the man in whom his own realisation exists as an inner necessity, as *need*. Not only *wealth*, but likewise the *poverty* of man—under the assumption of socialism[85]—receives in equal measure a *human* and therefore social significance. Poverty is the passive bond which causes the human being to experience the need of the greatest wealth—the *other* human being. The dominion of the objective being in me, the sensuous outburst of my life activity, is *passion*, which thus becomes here the *activity* of my being.⟩

(5) A *being* only considers himself independent when he stands on his own feet; and he only stands on his own feet when he owes his *existence* to himself. A man who lives by the grace of another regards himself as a dependent being. But I live completely by the grace of another if I owe him not only the maintenance of my life, but if he has, moreover, *created* my *life*—if he is the *source* of my life. When it is not of my own creation, my life has necessarily a source of this kind outside of it. The *Creation* is therefore an idea very difficult to dislodge from popular consciousness. The fact that nature and man exist on their own account is *incomprehensible* to it, because it contradicts everything *tangible* in practical life.

The creation of the *earth* has received a mighty blow from *geognosy*—i. e., from the science which presents the formation of the earth, the development of the earth, as a process, as a self-generation. *Generatio aequivoca* is the only practical refutation of the theory of creation.[86]

Now it is certainly easy to say to the single individual what Aristotle has already said: You have been begotten by your father and your mother; therefore in you the mating of two human beings—a species-act of human beings—has produced the human being. You see, therefore, that even physically man owes his existence to man. Therefore you must not only keep sight of the *one* aspect—the *infinite* progression which leads you further to inquire: Who begot my father? Who his grandfather? etc. You must also hold on to the *circular movement* sensuously perceptible in that progress by which man repeats himself in procreation, *man* thus always remaining the subject. You will reply, however: I grant you this circular movement; now grant me the progress which drives me ever further until I ask: Who begot the first man, and nature as a whole? I can only answer you: Your question is itself a product of abstraction. Ask yourself how you arrived at that question. Ask yourself whether your question is not posed from a standpoint to which I cannot reply, because it is wrongly put. Ask yourself whether that progress as such exists for a reasonable mind. When you ask about the creation of nature and man, you are abstracting, in so doing, from man and nature. You postulate them as *non-existent*, and yet you want me to prove them to you as *existing*. Now I say to you: Give up your abstraction and you will also give up your question. Or if you want to hold on to your abstraction, then be consistent, and if you think of man and nature as *non-existent*, ||XI| then think of yourself as non-existent, for you too are surely nature and man. Don't think, don't ask me, for as soon as you think and ask, your *abstraction* from the existence of nature and man has no meaning. Or are you such an egotist that you conceive everything as nothing, and yet want yourself to exist?

You can reply: I do not want to postulate the nothingness of nature, etc. I ask you about its *genesis*, just as I ask the anatomist about the formation of bones, etc.

But since for the socialist man the *entire so-called history of the world* is nothing but the creation of man through human labour, nothing but the emergence of nature for man, so he has the visible, irrefutable proof of his *birth* through himself, of his *genesis*. Since the *real existence* of man and nature has become evident in practice, through sense experience, because man has thus become evident for man as the being of nature, and nature for man as the being of man, the question about an *alien* being, about a being above nature and man—a question which implies the admission of the unreality of nature and of man—has become impossible in practice. *Atheism*, as the denial of this unreality, has no longer any meaning, for atheism is a *negation of God*, and postulates the *existence of man* through this negation; but socialism as socialism no longer stands in any need of such a mediation. It proceeds from the *theoretically and practically sensuous consciousness* of man and of nature as the *essence*. Socialism is man's *positive self-consciousness*, no longer mediated through the abolition of religion, just as *real life* is man's positive reality, no longer mediated through the abolition of private property, through *communism*. Communism is the position as the negation of the negation, and is hence the *actual* phase necessary for the next stage of historical development in the process of human emancipation and rehabilitation. *Communism* is the necessary form and the dynamic principle of the immediate future, but communism as such is not the goal of human development, the form of human society.[87] |XII|

[HUMAN REQUIREMENTS AND DIVISION OF LABOUR UNDER THE RULE OF PRIVATE PROPERTY]

||XIV|[88] (7) We have seen what significance, given socialism, the *wealth* of human needs acquires, and what significance, therefore, both a *new mode of production* and a new *object* of production obtain: a new manifestation of the forces of *human* nature and a new enrichment of *human* nature. Under private property their significance is reversed: every person speculates on creating a *new* need in another, so as to drive him to fresh sacrifice, to place him in a new dependence and to seduce him into a new mode of *enjoyment* and therefore economic ruin. Each tries to establish over the other an *alien* power, so as thereby to find satisfaction of his own selfish need. The increase in the quantity of objects is therefore accompanied by an extension of the realm of the alien powers to which man is subjected, and every new product represents a new *potentiality* of mutual swindling and mutual plundering. Man becomes ever poorer as man, his need for *money* becomes ever greater if he wants to master the hostile power. The power of his *money* declines in inverse proportion to the increase in the volume of production: that is, his neediness grows as the *power* of money increases.

The need for money is therefore the true need produced by the economic system, and it is the only need which the latter produces. The *quantity* of money becomes to an ever greater degree its sole *effective* quality. Just as it reduces everything to its abstract form, so it reduces itself in the course of its own movement to *quantitative* being. *Excess* and *intemperance* come to be its true norm.

Subjectively, this appears partly in the fact that the extension of products and needs becomes a *contriving* and ever-*calculating* subservience to inhuman, sophisticated, unnatural and *imaginary* appetites. Private property does not know how to change crude need into *human* need. Its *idealism* is *fantasy, caprice* and *whim*; and no eunuch flatters his despot more basely or uses more despicable means to stimulate his dulled capacity for pleasure in order to sneak a favour for himself than does the industrial eunuch—the producer—in order to sneak for himself a few pieces of silver, in order to charm the golden birds out of the pockets of his dearly beloved neighbours in Christ. He puts himself at the service of the other's most depraved fancies, plays the pimp between him and his need, excites in him morbid appetites, lies in wait for each of his weaknesses—all so that he can then demand the cash for this service of love. (Every product is a bait with which to seduce away the other's very being, his money; every real and possible need is a weakness which will lead the fly to the glue-pot. General exploitation of communal human nature, just as every imperfection in man, is a bond with heaven—an avenue giving the priest access to his heart; every need is an opportunity to approach one's neighbour under the guise of the utmost amiability and to say to him: Dear friend, I give you what you need, but you know the *conditio sine qua non*; you know the ink in which you have to sign yourself over to me; in providing for your pleasure, I fleece you.)

This estrangement manifests itself in part in that the sophistication of needs and of the means [of their satisfaction] on the one side produces a bestial barbarisation, a complete, crude, abstract simplicity of need, on the other; or rather in that it merely reproduces itself in its opposite. Even the need for fresh air ceases to be a need for the worker. Man returns to a cave dwelling, which is now, however, contaminated with the pestilential breath of civilisation, and which he continues to occupy only *precariously*, it being for him an alien habitation which can be withdrawn from him any day—a place from which, if he does ||XV| not pay, he can be thrown out any day. For this mortuary he has to *pay*. A dwelling in the *light*, which Prometheus in Aeschylus designated as one of the greatest boons, by means of which he made the savage into a human being,[a] ceases to exist for the worker. Light, air, etc.—the simplest *animal* cleanliness—ceases to be a need for man. *Filth*, this stagnation and putrefaction of man—the *sewage* of civilisation (speaking quite literally)—comes to be the *element of life* for him. Utter, *unnatural* depravation, putrefied nature, comes to be his *life-element*. None of his senses exist any longer, and [each has ceased to function] not only in its human fashion, but in an *inhuman* fashion, so that it does not exist even in an animal fashion. The crudest *methods* (and *instruments*) of human labour are coming back: the *treadmill* of the Roman slaves, for instance, is the means of production, the means of existence, of many English workers. It is not only that man has no human needs—even his *animal* needs cease to exist. The Irishman no longer knows any need now but the need to *eat*, and indeed only the need to eat *potatoes*—and *scabby potatoes* at that, the worst kind of potatoes. But in each of their industrial towns England and France have already a *little* Ireland. The savage and the animal have at least the need to hunt, to roam, etc.—the need of companionship. The simplification of the machine, of labour is used to make a worker out of the human being still in the making, the completely immature human being, the *child*—whilst the worker has become a neglected child. The machine accommodates itself to the *weakness* of the human being in order to make the *weak* human being into a machine.

⟨How the multiplication of needs and of the means [of their satisfaction] breeds the absence of needs and of means is demonstrated by the political economist (and by the capitalist: in general it is always *empirical* businessmen we are talking about when we refer to political economists, [who represent] their *scientific* creed and form of existence) as follows:

(1) By reducing the worker's need to the barest and most miserable level of physical subsistence, and by reducing his activity to the most abstract mechanical movement; thus he says: Man has no other need either of activity or of enjoyment. For he declares that this life, *too*, is *human* life and existence.

(2) By *counting* the most *meagre* form of life (existence) as the standard, indeed, as the general standard—general because it is applicable to the mass of men. He turns the worker into an insensible being lacking all needs, just as he changes his activity into a pure abstraction from all activity. To him, therefore, every *luxury* of the worker seems to be reprehensible, and everything that goes beyond the most abstract need—be it in the realm of passive enjoyment, or a

---

[a] Aeschylus, *Prometheus Bound.—Ed.*

manifestation of activity—seems to him a luxury. Political economy, this science of *wealth,* is therefore simultaneously the science of renunciation, of want, of *saving*—and it actually reaches the point where it *spares* man the *need* of either fresh *air* or physical *exercise.* This science of marvellous industry is simultaneously the science of *asceticism,* and its true ideal is the *ascetic* but *extortionate* miser and the *ascetic* but *productive* slave. Its moral ideal is the *worker* who takes part of his wages to the savings-bank, and it has even found ready-made a servile *art* which embodies this pet idea: it has been presented, bathed in sentimentality, on the stage. Thus political economy—despite its wordly and voluptuous appearance—is a true moral science, the most moral of all the sciences. Self-renunciation, the renunciation of life and of all human needs, is its principal thesis. The less you eat, drink and buy books; the less you go to the theatre, the dance hall, the public house; the less you think, love, theorise, sing, paint, fence, etc., the more you *save*—the *greater* becomes your treasure which neither moths nor rust will devour—your *capital.* The less you *are,* the less you express your own life, the more you *have,* i.e., the greater is your *alienated* life, the greater is the store of your estranged being. Everything ||XVI| which the political economist takes from you in life and in humanity, he replaces for you in *money* and in *wealth*; and all the things which you cannot do, your money can do. It can eat and drink, go to the dance hall and the theatre; it can travel, it can appropriate art, learning, the treasures of the past, political power—all this it *can* appropriate for you—it can buy all this: it is true *endowment.* Yet being all this, it *wants* to do nothing but create itself, buy itself; for everything else is after all its servant, and when I have the master I have the servant and do not need his servant. All passions and all activity must therefore be submerged in *avarice.* The worker may only have enough for him to want to live, and may only want to live in order to have that. >

It is true that a controversy now arises in the field of political economy. The one side (Lauderdale, Malthus, etc.) recommends *luxury* and execrates thrift. The other (Say, Ricardo, etc.) recommends thrift and execrates luxury. But the former admits that it wants luxury in order to produce *labour* (i. e., absolute thrift); and the latter admits that it recommends thrift in order to produce *wealth* (i. e., luxury). The Lauderdale-Malthus school has the *romantic* notion that avarice alone ought not to determine the consumption of the rich, and it contradicts its own laws in advancing *extravagance* as a direct means of enrichment. Against it, therefore, the other side very earnestly and circumstantially proves that I do not increase but reduce my *possessions* by being extravagant. The Say-Ricardo school is hypocritical in not admitting that it is precisely whim and caprice which determine production. It forgets the "refined needs"; it forgets that there would be no production without consumption; it forgets that as a result of competition production can only become more extensive and luxurious. It forgets that, according to its views, a thing's value is determined by use, and that use is determined by fashion. It wishes to see only "useful things" produced, but it forgets that production of too many useful things produces too large a *useless* population. Both sides forget that extravagance and thrift, luxury and privation, wealth and poverty are equal.

And you must not only stint the gratification of your immediate senses, as by stinting yourself of food, etc.: you must also spare yourself all sharing of general interests, all sympathy, all trust, etc., if you want to be economical, if you do not want to be ruined by illusions.

⟨ You must make everything that is yours *saleable,* i. e., useful. If I ask the political economist: Do I obey economic laws if I extract money by offering my body for sale, by surrendering it to another's lust? (The factory workers in France call the prostitution of their wives and daughters the nth working hour, which is literally correct.)—Or am I not acting in keeping with political economy if I sell my friend to the Moroccans? (And the direct sale of men in the form of a trade in conscripts, etc., takes place in all civilised countries.)—Then the political economist replies to me: You do not transgress my laws; but see what Cousin Ethics and Cousin Religion have to say about it. My *political economic* ethics and religion have nothing to reproach you with, but— But whom am I now to believe, political economy or ethics?—The ethics of political economy is *acquisition,* work, thrift, sobriety—but political economy promises to satisfy my needs.—The political economy of ethics is the opulence of a good conscience, of virtue, etc.; but how can I live virtuously if I do not live? And how can I have a good conscience if I do not know anything? It stems from the very nature of estrangement that each sphere applies to me a different and opposite yardstick—ethics one and political economy another; for each is a specific estrangement of man and⟩ ‖XVII‖ focuses attention on a particular field of estranged essential activity, and each stands in an estranged relation to the other. Thus M. *Michel Chevalier* reproaches Ricardo with having ignored ethics.[a] But

---

[a] Cf. Michel Chevalier, *Des intérêts matériels en France.—Ed.*

Ricardo is allowing political economy to speak its own language, and if it does not speak ethically, this is not Ricardo's fault. M. Chevalier takes no account of political economy insofar as he moralises, but he really and necessarily ignores ethics insofar as he practises political economy. The relationship of political economy to ethics, if it is other than an arbitrary, contingent and therefore unfounded and unscientific relationship, if it is not being posited for the sake of *appearance* but is meant to be *essential,* can only be the relationship of the laws of political economy to ethics. If there is no such connection, or if the contrary is rather the case, can Ricardo help it? Moreover, the opposition between political economy and ethics is only an *apparent* opposition and just as much no opposition *as it is* an opposition. All that happens is that political economy expresses moral laws *in its own way.*

⟨ Frugality as the principle of political economy is *most brilliantly* shown in its *theory of population.* There are too *many* people. Even the existence of men is a pure luxury; and if the worker is "ethical", he will be *sparing* in procreation. (Mill suggests public acclaim for those who prove themselves continent in their sexual relations, and public rebuke for those who sin against such barrenness of marriage....[a] Is this not ethics, the teaching of asceticism?) The production of people appears as public destitution.⟩

The meaning which production has in relation to the rich is seen *revealed* in the meaning which it has for the poor. Looking upwards the manifestation is always refined, veiled, ambiguous — outward appearance; downwards, it is rough, straightforward, frank — the real thing. The worker's *crude* need is a far greater source of gain than the *refined* need of the rich. The cellar dwellings in London bring more to those who let them than do the palaces; that is to say, with reference to the landlord they constitute *greater wealth,* and thus (to speak the language of political economy) greater *social* wealth.

Industry speculates on the refinement of needs, it speculates however just as much on their *crudeness,* but on their artificially produced crudeness, whose true enjoyment, therefore, is *self-stupefaction* — this *illusory* satisfaction of need — this civilisation contained *within* the crude barbarism of need. The English gin

---

[a] James Mill, *Elements of Political Economy,* London, 1821, p. 44 (Marx quotes from the French edition, *Élémens d'économie politique.* Trad. par. J. T. Parisot, Paris, 1823. p. 59).—*Ed.*

shops are therefore the *symbolical* representations of private property. Their *luxury* reveals the true relation of industrial luxury and wealth to man. They are therefore rightly the only Sunday pleasures of the people which the English police treats at least mildly. |XVII||

||XVIII|[89] We have already seen how the political economist establishes the unity of labour and capital in a variety of ways: (1) Capital is *accumulated labour.* (2) The purpose of capital within production—partly, reproduction of capital with profit, partly, capital as raw material (material of labour), and partly, as an automatically *working instrument* (the machine is capital directly equated with labour)—is *productive labour.* (3) The worker is a capital. (4) Wages belong to costs of capital. (5) In relation to the worker, labour is the reproduction of his life-capital. (6) In relation to the capitalist, labour is an aspect of his capital's activity.

Finally, (7) the political economist postulates the original unity of capital and labour as the unity of the capitalist and the worker; this is the original state of paradise. The way in which these two aspects, ||XIX| as two persons, confront each other is for the political economist an *accidental* event, and hence only to be explained by reference to external factors. (See Mill.[a])

The nations which are still dazzled by the sensuous glitter of precious metals, and are therefore still fetish-worshippers of metal money, are not yet fully developed money-nations. Contrast of France and England.

The extent to which the solution of theoretical riddles is the task of practice and effected through practice, the extent to which true practice is the condition of a real and positive theory, is shown, for example, in *fetishism.* The sensuous consciousness of the fetish-worshipper is different from that of the Greek, because his sensuous existence is different. The abstract enmity between sense and spirit is necessary so long as the human feeling for nature, the human sense of nature, and therefore also the *natural* sense of *man,* are not yet produced by man's own labour.

Equality is nothing but a translation of the German "Ich=Ich"[b][90] into the French, i.e., political, form. Equality as the *basis* of communism is its *political* justification, and it is the same as when the German justifies it by conceiving man as *universal self-consciousness.* Naturally, the transcendence of the estrangement

---

[a] James Mill, *Elements of Political Economy,* p. 45 sqq. (Parisot, p. 60 sqq.).—*Ed.*
[b] The English equivalent of *ich* is "I".—*Ed.*

always proceeds from that form of the estrangement which is the *dominant* power: in Germany, *self-consciousness*; in France, *equality*, because it is politics; in England, real, material, *practical* need taking only itself as its standard. It is from this standpoint that Proudhon is to be criticised and appreciated.

If we characterise *communism* itself because of its character as negation of the negation, as the appropriation of the human essence through the intermediary of the negation of private property—as being not yet the *true*, self-originating position but rather a position originating from private property [...][a] in old-German fashion—in the way of Hegel's phenomenology—[...] finished as a *conquered moment* and [...] one might be satisfied by it, in his consciousness [...] of the human being only by *real* [...] transcendence of his thought now as before [...], since with him[b] therefore the real estrangement of the life of man remains, and remains all the more, the more one is conscious of it as such, hence it [the negation of this estrangement] can be accomplished solely by bringing about communism.

In order to abolish the *idea* of private property, the *idea* of communism is quite sufficient. It takes *actual* communist action to abolish actual private property. History will lead to it; and this movement, which *in theory* we already know to be a self-transcending movement, will constitute in actual fact a very rough and protracted process. But we must regard it as a real advance to have at the outset gained a consciousness of the limited character as well as of the goal of this historical movement—and a consciousness which reaches out beyond it.

When communist *artisans* associate with one another, theory, propaganda, etc., is their first end. But at the same time, as a result of this association, they acquire a new need—the need for society—and what appears as a means becomes an end. In this practical process the most splendid results are to be observed whenever French socialist workers[c] are seen together. Such things as smoking, drinking, eating, etc., are no longer means of contact or means that bring them together. Association, society and conversation, which again has association as its end, are enough for them; the brotherhood of man is no mere phrase with them, but a fact of life, and the nobility of man shines upon us from their work-hardened bodies.

---

[a] A part of this section of the manuscript is torn off.—*Ed.*
[b] Or maybe "it"—the German pronoun *ihm* can be either.—*Ed.*
[c] In the manuscript: *ouvriers.*—*Ed.*

|XX| ⟨When political economy claims that demand and supply always balance each other, it immediately forgets that according to its own claim (theory of population) the supply of *people* always exceeds the demand, and that, therefore, in the essential result of the whole production process—the existence of man—the disparity between demand and supply gets its most striking expression.

The extent to which money, which appears as a means, constitutes true *power* and the sole *end*—the extent to which in general *the means* which turns me into a being, which gives me possession of the alien objective being, is an *end in itself* ... can be clearly seen from the fact that landed property, wherever land is the source of life, and *horse* and *sword,* wherever these are the *true means of life,* are also acknowledged as the true political powers in life. In the Middle Ages a social estate is emancipated as soon as it is allowed to carry the *sword.* Amongst nomadic peoples it is the *horse* which makes me a free man and a participant in the life of the community.

We have said above that man is regressing to the *cave dwelling,* etc.—but he is regressing to it in an estranged, malignant form. The savage in his cave—a natural element which freely offers itself for his use and protection—feels himself no more a stranger, or rather feels as much at home as a *fish* in water. But the cellar dwelling of the poor man is a hostile element, "a dwelling which remains an alien power and only gives itself up to him insofar as he gives up to it his own blood and sweat"—a dwelling which he cannot regard as his own hearth—where he might at last exclaim: "Here I am at home"—but where instead he finds himself in *someone else*'s house, in the house of a *stranger* who always watches him and throws him out if he does not pay his rent. He is also aware of the contrast in quality between his dwelling and a human dwelling that stands in the *other* world, in the heaven of wealth.

Estrangement is manifested not only in the fact that *my* means of life belong to *someone else,* that which *I* desire is the inaccessible possession of *another,* but also in the fact that everything is itself something *different* from itself—that my activity is *something else* and that, finally (and this applies also to the capitalist), all is under [the sway][a] of *inhuman* power.

There is a form of inactive, extravagant wealth given over wholly to pleasure, the enjoyer of which on the one hand *behaves*

---

[a] The manuscript is damaged here.—*Ed.*

as a mere *ephemeral* individual frantically spending himself to no purpose, and also regards the slave-labour of others (human *sweat and blood*) as the prey of his cupidity. He therefore knows man himself, and hence also his own self, as a sacrificed and futile being. With such wealth contempt of man makes its appearance, partly as arrogance and as squandering of what can give sustenance to a hundred human lives, and partly as the infamous illusion that his own unbridled extravagance and ceaseless, unproductive consumption is the condition of the other's *labour* and therefore of his *subsistence*. He regards the realisation of the *essential powers* of man only as the realisation of his own excesses, his whims and capricious, bizarre notions. This wealth which, on the other hand, again knows wealth as a mere means, as something that is good for nothing but to be annihilated and which is therefore at once slave and master, at once magnanimous and base, capricious, presumptuous, conceited, refined, cultured and witty — this wealth has not yet experienced *wealth* as an utterly *alien power* over itself: it sees in it, rather, only its own power, and [not][a] wealth but *enjoyment* [is its final][a] aim.

This [...][b] ||XXI| and the glittering illusion about the nature of wealth, blinded by sensuous appearances, is confronted by the *working, sober, prosaic, economical* industrialist who is quite enlightened about the nature of wealth, and who, while providing a wider sphere for the other's self-indulgence and paying fulsome flatteries to him in his products (for his products are just so many base compliments to the appetites of the spendthrift), knows how to appropriate for himself in the only *useful* way the other's waning power. If, therefore, industrial wealth appears at first to be the result of extravagant, fantastic wealth, yet its motion, the motion inherent in it, ousts the latter also in an active way. For the fall in the *rate of interest* is a necessary consequence and result of industrial development. The extravagant rentier's means therefore dwindle day by day in *inverse* proportion to the increasing possibilities and pitfalls of pleasure. Consequently, he must either consume his capital, thus ruining himself, or must become an industrial capitalist.... On the other hand, there is a direct, constant rise in the *rent of land* as a result of the course of industrial development; nevertheless, as we have already seen, there must come a time when landed property, like every other

---

[a] The manuscript is damaged here.—*Ed.*
[b] A part of this page of the manuscript is ripped off, about three lines are missing.—*Ed.*

kind of property, is bound to fall within the category of profitably self-reproducing capital^a—and this in fact results from the same industrial development. Thus the squandering landowner, too, must either consume his capital, and thus be ruined, or himself become the farmer of his own estate—an agricultural industrialist.

The diminution in the interest on money, which Proudhon regards as the annulling of capital and as a tendency to socialise capital, is therefore in fact rather only a symptom of the total victory of working capital over squandering wealth—i. e., the transformation of all private property into industrial capital. It is a total victory of private property over all those of its qualities which are still in *appearance* human, and the complete subjection of the owner of private property to the essence of private property—*labour*. To be sure, the industrial capitalist also takes his pleasures. He does not by any means return to the unnatural simplicity of need; but his pleasure is only a side-issue—recreation—something subordinated to production; at the same time it is a *calculated* and, therefore, itself an *economical* pleasure. For he debits it to his capital's expense account, and what is squandered on his pleasure must therefore amount to no more than will be replaced with profit through the reproduction of capital. Pleasure is therefore subsumed under capital, and the pleasure-taking individual under the capital-accumulating individual, whilst formerly the contrary was the case. The decrease in the interest rate is therefore a symptom of the annulment of capital only inasmuch as it is a symptom of the growing domination of capital—of the estrangement which is growing and therefore hastening to its annulment. This is indeed the only way in which that which exists affirms its opposite. 〉

The quarrel between the political economists about luxury and thrift is, therefore, only the quarrel between that political economy which has achieved clarity about the nature of wealth, and that political economy which is still afflicted with romantic, anti-industrial memories. Neither side, however, knows how to reduce the subject of the controversy to its simple terms, and neither therefore can make short work of the other. |XXII|

||XXXIV|[91] Moreover, *rent of land qua* rent of land has been overthrown, since, contrary to the argument of the Physiocrats which maintains that the landowner is the only true producer,

---

^a See this volume, pp. 265-70.—*Ed.*

modern political economy has proved that the landowner as such is rather the only completely unproductive rentier. According to this theory, agriculture is the business of the capitalist, who invests his capital in it provided he can expect the usual profit. The claim of the Physiocrats—that landed property, as the sole productive property, should alone pay state taxes and therefore should alone approve them and participate in the affairs of state—is transformed into the opposite position that the tax on the rent of land is the only tax on unproductive income, and is therefore the only tax not detrimental to national production. It goes without saying that from this point of view also the political privilege of landowners no longer follows from their position as principal tax-payers.

Everything which Proudhon conceives as a movement of labour against capital is only the movement of labour in the determination of capital, of *industrial capital*, against capital not consumed *as* capital, i. e., not consumed industrially. And this movement is proceeding along its triumphant road—the road to the victory of *industrial* capital. It is clear, therefore, that only when *labour* is grasped as the essence of private property, can the economic process as such be analysed in its real concreteness.

Society, as it appears to the political economist, is *civil society*[92] in which every individual is a totality of needs and only ||XXXVI| exists for the other person, as the other exists for him, insofar as each becomes a means for the other. The political economist reduces everything (just as does politics in its *Rights of Man*) to man, i. e., to the individual whom he strips of all determinateness so as to class him as capitalist or worker.

The *division of labour* is the economic expression of the *social character of labour* within the estrangement. Or, since *labour* is only an expression of human activity within alienation, of the manifestation of life as the alienation of life, the *division of labour,* too, is therefore nothing else but the *estranged, alienated* positing of human activity as a *real activity of the species* or as *activity of man as a species-being.*

As for the *essence of the division of labour*—and of course the division of labour had to be conceived as a major driving force in the production of wealth as soon as *labour* was recognised as the *essence of private property*—i.e., as for the *estranged and alienated form of human activity as an activity of the species*—the political economists are very vague and self-contradictory about it.

Adam Smith: "This *division of labour* [...] is not originally the effect of any human wisdom [...]. It is the necessary, [...] slow and gradual consequence of [...] the propensity to truck, barter, and exchange one thing for another. [...] This propensity" to trade is probably a "necessary consequence of the use of reason and of speech [...]. It is common to all men, and to be found in no other race of animals." The animal, when it is grown up, is entirely independent. "Man has almost constant occasion for the help of others, and it is in vain for him to expect it from their benevolence only. He will be more likely to prevail if he can appeal to their personal interest, and show them that it·is for their own advantage to do for him what he requires of them. [...] We address ourselves, not to their *humanity* but to their *self-love*, and never talk to them of *our own necessities* but of *their advantages*. [...]

"As it is by treaty, by barter, and by purchase that we obtain from one another the greater part of those mutual good offices which we stand in need of, so it is this same *trucking* disposition which originally gives occasion to the *division of labour*. In a tribe of hunters or shepherds a particular person makes bows and arrows, for example, with more readiness and dexterity than any other. He frequently exchanges them for cattle or for venison with his companions; and he finds at last that he can in this manner get more cattle and venison than if he himself went to the field to catch them. From a regard to his own interest, therefore, the making of bows, etc., grows to be his chief business [....]

"The difference of *natural talents* in different men [...] is not [...] so much the *cause* as the *effect* of the division of labour.... Without the disposition to truck [...] and exchange, every man must have procured to himself every necessary and conveniency of life [....] All must have had [...] the *same work* to do, and there could have been no such *difference of employment* as could alone give occasion to any great difference of talents.

"As it is this disposition which forms that difference of talents [...] among men [...] so it is this same disposition which renders that difference useful. Many tribes of animals [...] of the same species derive from nature a much more remarkable distinction of genius, than what, antecedent to custom and education, appears to take place among men. By nature a philosopher is not in talent and in intelligence half so different from a street porter, as a mastiff is from a greyhound, or a greyhound from a spaniel, or this last from a shepherd's dog. Those different tribes of animals, however, though all of the same species, are of scarce any use to one another. The mastiff cannot add to the advantages of his strength ||XXXVI| by making use of the swiftness of the greyhound, etc. The effects of these different talents or grades of intelligence, for want of the power or disposition to barter and exchange, cannot be brought into a common stock, and do not in the least contribute to the better *accommodation* and *conveniency* of the *species*. Each animal is still obliged to support and defend itself, separately and independently, and derives no sort of advantage from that variety of talents with which nature has distinguished its fellows. Among men, on the contrary, the most dissimilar geniuses are of use to one another; the *different produces* of their respective talents, by the general disposition to truck, barter, and exchange, being brought, as it were, into a common stock, where every man may purchase whatever part of the produce of other men's industry he has occasion for. [...]

"As it is the power of *exchanging* that gives occasion to the *division of labour*, so the *extent of this division* must always be limited by the *extent of that power*, or, in other words, by the *extent of the market*. When the market is very small, no person can have any encouragement to dedicate himself entirely to one employment, for want of the power to exchange all that surplus part of the produce of his own labour, which is over and above his own consumption, for such parts of the produce of other men's labour as he has occasion for...."

In an *advanced* state of society "every man thus lives by exchanging and becomes in some measure a *merchant*, and the *society itself* grows to be what is properly a *commercial* society". (See Destutt de Tracy [,*Élémens d'idéologie*, Paris, 1826, pp. 68 and 78]: "Society is a series of reciprocal exchanges; *commerce* contains the whole essence of society.") ... The accumulation of capitals mounts with the division of labour, and vice versa."

So much for Adam Smith.[a]

"If every family produced all that it consumed, society could keep going although no exchange of any sort took place; *without* being *fundamental*, exchange is indispensable in our advanced state of society. The division of labour is a skilful deployment of man's powers; it increases society's production—its power and its pleasures—but it curtails, reduces the ability of every person taken individually. Production cannot take place without exchange."

Thus J. B. Say.[b]

"The powers inherent in man are his intelligence and his physical capacity for work. Those which arise from the condition of society consist of the capacity to *divide up labour* and to *distribute different jobs amongst different people* ... and the *power* to exchange *mutual services* and the products which constitute these means. The motive which impels a man to give his services to another is self-interest—he requires a reward for the services rendered. The right of exclusive private property is indispensable to the establishment of exchange amongst men." "Exchange and division of labour reciprocally condition each other."

Thus Skarbek.[c]

Mill presents developed exchange—*trade*—as a *consequence of the division of labour.*

"The agency of man can be traced to very simple elements. He can, in fact, do nothing more than produce motion. He can move things towards one another, and he can separate them from one another: ||XXXVII| the properties of matter perform all the rest." "In the employment of labour and machinery, it is often found that the effects can be increased by skilful distribution, by separating all those operations which have any tendency to impede one another, and by bringing together all those operations which can be made in any way to aid one another. As men in general cannot perform many different operations with the same quickness and dexterity with which they can by practice learn to perform a few, it is always an advantage to limit as much as possible the number of operations imposed upon each. For dividing labour, and distributing the powers of men and machinery, to the greatest advantage, it is in most cases necessary to operate upon a large scale; in other words, to produce the commodities in greater masses. It is this advantage which gives existence to the great manufactories; a few of which, placed in the most convenient situations, frequently supply not one country, but many countries, with as much as they desire of the commodity produced."

---

[a] Adam Smith, *Wealth of Nations*, Book I, Chs. II-IV, pp. 12-25. (Garnier, t. 1, l. I, Chs. II-IV, pp. 29-46), quoted with omissions and alterations.—*Ed.*

[b] Jean-Baptiste Say, *Traité d'économie politique*, Paris, 1817, t. I, pp. 300, 76-77; t. II, p. 6.—*Ed.*

[c] Frédéric Skarbek, *Théorie des richesses sociales*, Paris, 1829, t. I, pp. 25-27, 75 and 121-32.—*Ed.*

Thus *Mill*.ᵃ

The whole of modern political economy agrees, however, that division of labour and wealth of production, division of labour and accumulation of capital, mutually determine each other; just as it agrees that only private property which is *at liberty* to follow its own course can produce the most useful and comprehensive division of labour.

Adam Smith's argument can be summarised as follows: Division of labour bestows on labour infinite productive capacity. It stems from the *propensity to exchange* and *barter,* a specifically human propensity which is probably not accidental, but is conditioned by the use of reason and speech. The motive of those who engage in exchange is not *humanity* but *egoism.* The diversity of human talents is more the effect than the cause of the division of labour, i.e., of exchange. Besides, it is only the latter which makes such diversity useful. The particular attributes of the different breeds within a species of animal are by nature much more marked than the degrees of difference in human aptitude and activity. But because animals are unable to engage in *exchange,* no individual animal benefits from the difference in the attributes of animals of the same species but of different breeds. Animals are unable to combine the different attributes of their species, and are unable to contribute anything to the *common* advantage and comfort of the species. It is otherwise with *men,* amongst whom the most dissimilar talents and forms of activity are of use to one another, *because* they can bring their *different* products together into a common stock, from which each can purchase. As the division of labour springs from the propensity to *exchange,* so it grows and is limited by the *extent of exchange*—by the *extent of the market.* In advanced conditions, every man is a *merchant,* and society is a *commercial society.*

Say regards *exchange* as accidental and not fundamental. Society could exist without it. It becomes indispensable in the advanced state of society. Yet *production* cannot take place *without it.* Division of labour is a *convenient, useful* means—a skilful deployment of human powers for social wealth; but it reduces the *ability of each person* taken *individually.* The last remark is a step forward on the part of Say.

Skarbek distinguishes the *individual* powers *inherent in man*—intelligence and the physical capacity for work—from the

---

ᵃ James Mill, *Elements of Political Economy,* pp. 5-6 and 8-9 (Parisot, pp. 7, 11-12).—*Ed.*

powers *derived* from society—*exchange* and *division of labour*, which mutually condition one another. But the necessary premise of exchange is *private property*. Skarbek here expresses in an objective form what Smith, Say, Ricardo, etc., say when they designate *egoism* and *self-interest* as the basis of exchange, and *buying and selling* as the *essential* and *adequate* form of exchange.

Mill presents *trade* as the consequence of the *division of labour*. With him *human* activity is reduced to *mechanical motion*. Division of labour and use of machinery promote wealth of production. Each person must be entrusted with as small a sphere of operations as possible. Division of labour and use of machinery, in their turn, imply large-scale production of wealth, and hence of products. This is the reason for large manufactories.

||XXXVIII| The examination of *division of labour* and *exchange* is of extreme interest, because these are *perceptibly alienated* expressions of human *activity* and *essential power* as a *species* activity and species power.

To assert that *division of labour* and *exchange* rest on *private property* is nothing but asserting that *labour* is the essence of private property—an assertion which the political economist cannot prove and which we wish to prove for him. Precisely in the fact that *division of labour* and *exchange* are aspects of private property lies the twofold proof, on the one hand that *human* life required *private property* for its realisation, and on the other hand that it now requires the supersession of private property.

Division of labour and *exchange* are the two *phenomena* which lead the political economist to boast of the social character of his science, while in the same breath he gives unconscious expression to the contradiction in his science—the motivation of society by unsocial, particular interests.

The factors we have to consider are: Firstly, the *propensity to exchange*—the basis of which is found in egoism—is regarded as the cause or reciprocal effect of the division of labour. Say regards exchange as not *fundamental* to the nature of society. Wealth—production—is explained by division of labour and exchange. The impoverishment of individual activity, and its loss of character as a result of the division of labour, are admitted. Exchange and division of labour are acknowledged as the sources of the great *diversity of human talents*—a diversity which in its turn becomes *useful* as a result of exchange. Skarbek divides man's essential powers of production—or productive powers—into two parts: (1) those which are individual and inherent in him—his intelligence and his special disposition, or capacity, for work; and

(2) those *derived* from society and not from the actual individual—division of labour and exchange.

Furthermore, the division of labour is limited by the *market*. Human labour is simple *mechanical motion*: the main work is done by the material properties of the objects. The fewest possible operations must be apportioned to any one individual. Splitting up of labour and concentration of capital; the insignificance of individual production and the production of wealth in large quantities. Meaning of free private property within the division of labour. |XXXVIII||[a]

[THE POWER OF MONEY]

||XLI|[93] If man's *feelings*, passions, etc., are not merely anthropological phenomena in the [narrower][b] sense, but truly *ontological*[94] affirmations of being (of nature), and if they are only really affirmed because their *object* exists for them as a *sensual* object, then it is clear that:

(1) They have by no means merely one mode of affirmation, but rather that the distinct character of their existence, of their life, is constituted by the distinct mode of their affirmation. In what manner the object exists for them, is the characteristic mode of their *gratification*.

(2) Wherever the sensuous affirmation is the direct annulment of the object in its independent form (as in eating, drinking, working up of the object, etc.), this is the affirmation of the object.

(3) Insofar as man, and hence also his feeling, etc., is *human*, the affirmation of the object by another is likewise his own gratification.

(4) Only through developed industry—i.e., through the medium of private property—does the ontological essence of human passion come into being, in its totality as well as in its humanity; the science of man is therefore itself a product of man's own practical activity.

(5) The meaning of private property—apart from its estrangement—is the *existence of essential objects* for man, both as objects of enjoyment and as objects of activity.

---

[a] That part of the third manuscript which serves as a supplement to p. XXXIX of the second manuscript breaks off at this point on the left side of p. XXXVIII. The right-hand side of p. XXXVIII is empty. Then follows the "Introduction" (pp. XXXIX-XL) and the passage on money (pp. XLI-XLIII).—*Ed.*

[b] This word cannot be clearly deciphered in the manuscript.—*Ed.*

By possessing the *property* of buying everything, by possessing the property of appropriating all objects, *money* is thus the *object* of eminent possession. The universality of its *property* is the omnipotence of its being. It is therefore regarded as omnipotent.... Money is the *procurer* between man's need and the object, between his life and his means of life. But *that which* mediates *my* life for me, also *mediates* the existence of other people for me. For me it is the *other* person.

"What, man! confound it, hands and feet
And head and backside, all are yours!
And what we take while life is sweet,
Is that to be declared not ours?
　　　　Six stallions, say, I can afford,
　　　　Is not their strength my property?
　　　　I tear along, a sporting lord,
　　　　As if their legs belonged to me."

Goethe: *Faust* (Mephistopheles)[a]

Shakespeare in *Timon of Athens*:

"Gold? Yellow, glittering, precious gold? No, Gods,
I am no idle votarist! ...
Thus much of this will make black white, foul fair,
Wrong right, base noble, old young, coward valiant.
... Why, this
Will lug your priests and servants from your sides,
Pluck stout men's pillows from below their heads:
This yellow slave
Will knit and break religions, bless the accursed;
Make the hoar leprosy adored, place thieves
And give them title, knee and approbation
With senators on the bench: This is it
That makes the wappen'd widow wed again;
She, whom the spital-house and ulcerous sores
Would cast the gorge at, this embalms and spices
To the April day again. Come, damned earth,
Thou common whore of mankind, that put'st odds
Among the rout of nations."

And also later:

"O thou sweet king-killer, and dear divorce
'Twixt natural son and sire! thou bright defiler
Of Hymen's purest bed! thou valiant Mars!
Thou ever young, fresh, loved and delicate wooer,
Whose blush doth thaw the consecrated snow
That lies on Dian's lap! Thou *visible God*!

---

[a] Goethe, *Faust*, Part 1, Faust's Study; (the English translation is taken from Goethe's *Faust*, Part 1, translated by Philip Wayne, Penguin, 1949, p. 91).—*Ed.*

> That solder'st *close impossibilities,*
> And makest them kiss! That speak'st with every tongue,
> ||XLII| To every purpose! O thou touch of hearts!
> Think, thy slave man rebels, and by thy virtue
> Set them into confounding odds, that beasts
> May have the world in empire!"[a]

Shakespeare excellently depicts the real nature of *money*. To understand him, let us begin, first of all, by expounding the passage from Goethe.

That which is for me through the medium of *money*—that for which I can pay (i. e., which money can buy)—that am *I myself*, the possessor of the money. The extent of the power of money is the extent of my power. Money's properties are my—the possessor's—properties and essential powers. Thus, what I *am* and *am capable of* is by no means determined by my individuality. I *am* ugly, but I can buy for myself the *most beautiful* of women. Therefore I am not *ugly*, for the effect of *ugliness*—its deterrent power—is nullified by money. I, according to my individual characteristics, am *lame,* but money furnishes me with twenty-four feet. Therefore I am not lame. I am bad, dishonest, unscrupulous, stupid; but money is honoured, and hence its possessor. Money is the supreme good, therefore its possessor is good. Money, besides, saves me the trouble of being dishonest: I am therefore presumed honest. I am *brainless,* but money is the *real brain* of all things and how then should its possessor be brainless? Besides, he can buy clever people for himself, and is he who has[b] power over the clever not more clever than the clever? Do not I, who thanks to money am capable of *all* that the human heart longs for, possess all human capacities? Does not my money, therefore, transform all my incapacities into their contrary?

If *money* is the bond binding me to *human* life, binding society to me, connecting me with nature and man, is not money the bond of all *bonds*? Can it not dissolve and bind all ties? Is it not, therefore, also the universal *agent of separation*? It is the *coin* that really *separates* as well as the real *binding agent*—the [...][c] *chemical* power of society.

Shakespeare stresses especially two properties of money:

(1) It is the visible divinity—the transformation of all human and natural properties into their contraries, the universal confounding and distorting of things: impossibilities are soldered together by it.

(2) It is the common whore, the common procurer of people and nations.

---

[a] Shakespeare, *Timon of Athens*, Act IV, Scene 3. (Marx quotes the Schlegel-Tieck translation.)—*Ed.*

[b] In the manuscript: "is".—*Ed.*

[c] In the manuscript one word cannot be deciphered.—*Ed.*

The distorting and confounding of all human and natural qualities, the fraternisation of impossibilities—the *divine* power of money—lies in its *character* as men's estranged, alienating and self-disposing *species-nature*. Money is the alienated *ability of mankind*.

That which I am unable to do as a *man,* and of which therefore all my individual essential powers are incapable, I am able to do by means of *money.* Money thus turns each of these powers into something which in itself it is not—turns it, that is, into its *contrary.*

If I long for a particular dish or want to take the mail-coach because I am not strong enough to go by foot, money fetches me the dish and the mail-coach: that is, it converts my wishes from something in the realm of imagination, translates them from their meditated, imagined or desired existence into their *sensuous, actual* existence—from imagination to life, from imagined being into real being. In effecting this mediation, [money] is the *truly creative* power.

No doubt the *demand* also exists for him who has no money, but his demand is a mere thing of the imagination without effect or existence for me, for a third party, for the [others], ||XLIII| and which therefore remains even for me *unreal* and *objectless.* The difference between effective demand based on money and ineffective demand based on my need, my passion, my wish, etc., is the difference between *being* and *thinking,* between the idea which merely *exists* within me and the idea which exists as a *real object* outside of me.

If I have no money for travel, I have no *need*—that is, no real and realisable need—to travel. If I have the *vocation* for study but no money for it, I have *no* vocation for study—that is, no *effective,* no *true* vocation. On the other hand, if I have really *no* vocation for study but have the will *and* the money for it, I have an *effective* vocation for it. *Money* as the external, universal *medium* and *faculty* (not springing from man as man or from human society as society) for turning an *image into reality* and *reality into a mere image,* transforms the *real essential powers of man and nature* into what are merely abstract notions and therefore *imperfections* and tormenting chimeras, just as it transforms *real imperfections and chimeras*—essential powers which are really impotent, which exist only in the imagination of the individual—into *real essential powers* and *faculties.* In the light of this characteristic alone, money is thus the general distorting of *individualities* which turns them into their opposite and confers contradictory attributes upon their attributes.

Money, then, appears as this *distorting* power both against the individual and against the bonds of society, etc., which claim to be *entities* in themselves. It transforms fidelity into infidelity, love into hate, hate into love, virtue into vice, vice into virtue, servant into master, master into servant, idiocy into intelligence, and intelligence into idiocy.

Since money, as the existing and active concept of value, confounds and confuses all things, it is the general *confounding* and *confusing* of all things—the world upside-down—the confounding and confusing of all natural and human qualities.

He who can buy bravery is brave, though he be a coward. As money is not exchanged for any one specific quality, for any one specific thing, or for any particular human essential power, but for the entire objective world of man and nature, from the standpoint of its possessor it therefore serves to exchange every quality for every other, even contradictory, quality and object: it is the fraternisation of impossibilities. It makes contradictions embrace.

Assume *man* to be *man* and his relationship to the world to be a human one: then you can exchange love only for love, trust for trust, etc. If you want to enjoy art, you must be an artistically cultivated person; if you want to exercise influence over other people, you must be a person with a stimulating and encouraging effect on other people. Every one of your relations to man and to nature must be a *specific expression,* corresponding to the object of your will, of your *real individual* life. If you love without evoking love in return—that is, if your loving as loving does not produce reciprocal love; if through a *living expression* of yourself as a loving person you do not make yourself a *beloved one,* then your love is impotent—a misfortune. ||XLIII|

[CRITIQUE OF THE HEGELIAN DIALECTIC AND PHILOSOPHY AS A WHOLE]

||XI| (6) This is perhaps the place at which, by way of explanation and justification, we might offer some considerations in regard to the Hegelian dialectic generally and especially its exposition in the *Phänomenologie* and *Logik,*[a] and also, lastly, the relation [to it] of the modern critical movement.[95]

So powerful was modern German criticism's preoccupation with the past—so completely was its development entangled with the

---

[a] Georg Wilhelm Friedrich Hegel, *Phänomenologie des Geistes* and *Wissenschaft der Logik.—Ed.*

subject-matter—that there prevailed a completely uncritical attitude to the method of criticising, together with a complete lack of awareness about the *apparently formal*, but really *vital* question: how do we now stand as regards the Hegelian *dialectic?* This lack of awareness about the relationship of modern criticism to the Hegelian philosophy as a whole and especially to the Hegelian dialectic has been so great that critics like *Strauss* and *Bruno Bauer* still remain within the confines of the Hegelian logic; the former completely so and the latter at least implicitly so in his *Synoptiker*[a] (where, in opposition to Strauss, he replaces the substance of "abstract nature" by the "self-consciousness" of abstract man), and even in *Das entdeckte Christenthum*. Thus in *Das entdeckte Christenthum*, for example, you get:

> "As though in positing the world, self-consciousness does not posit that which is different [from itself] and in what it is creating it does not create itself, since it in turn annuls the difference between what it has created and itself, since it itself has being only in creating[b] and in the movement—as though its purpose were not this movement?" etc.; or again: "They" (the French materialists) "have not yet been able to see that it is only as the movement of self-consciousness that the movement of the universe has actually come to be for itself, and achieved unity with itself." [Pp. 113, 114-15.]

Such expressions do not even show any verbal divergence from the Hegelian approach, but on the contrary repeat it word for word.

||XII| How little consciousness there was in relation to the Hegelian dialectic during the act of criticism (Bauer, the *Synoptiker*), and how little this consciousness came into being even after the act of material criticism, is proved by Bauer when, in his *Die gute Sache der Freiheit,* he dismisses the brash question put by Herr Gruppe—"What about logic now?"—by referring him to future critics.[96]

But even now—now that *Feuerbach* both in his "Thesen" in the *Anekdota*[c] and, in detail, in the *Philosophie der Zukunft* has in principle overthrown the old dialectic and philosophy; now that that school of criticism, on the other hand, which was incapable of accomplishing this, has all the same seen it accomplished and has proclaimed itself pure, resolute, absolute criticism that has come into the clear with itself; now that this criticism, in its spiritual

---

[a] Bruno Bauer, *Kritik der evangelischen Geschichte der Synoptiker.—Ed.*

[b] In the manuscript: "in movement".—*Ed.*

[c] Ludwig Feuerbach, "Vorläufige Thesen zur Reformation der Philosophie" in *Anekdota zur neuesten deutschen Philosophie und Publicistik.—Ed.*

pride, has reduced the whole process of history to the relation between the rest of the world and itself (the rest of the world, in contrast to itself, falling under the category of the "masses") and dissolved all dogmatic antitheses into the *single* dogmatic antithesis of its own cleverness and the stupidity of the world—the antithesis of the critical Christ and Mankind, the *"rabble"*; now that daily and hourly it has demonstrated its own excellence against the dullness of the masses; now, finally, that it has proclaimed the critical *Last Judgment* in the shape of an announcement that the day is approaching when the whole of decadent humanity will assemble before it and be sorted by it into groups, each particular mob receiving its *testimonium paupertatis*[a]; now that it has made known in print[b] its superiority to human feelings as well as its superiority to the world, over which it sits enthroned in sublime solitude, only letting fall from time to time from its sarcastic lips the ringing laughter of the Olympian Gods—even now, after all these delightful antics of idealism (i. e., of Young Hegelianism) expiring in the guise of criticism—even now it has not expressed the suspicion that the time was ripe for a critical settling of accounts with the mother of Young Hegelianism—the Hegelian dialectic—and even had nothing to say about its critical attitude towards the Feuerbachian dialectic. This shows a completely uncritical attitude to itself.

Feuerbach is the only one who has a *serious, critical* attitude to the Hegelian dialectic and who has made genuine discoveries in this field. He is in fact the true conqueror of the old philosophy. The extent of his achievement, and the unpretentious simplicity with which he, Feuerbach, gives it to the world, stand in striking contrast to the opposite attitude [of the others].

Feuerbach's great achievement is:

(1) The proof that philosophy is nothing else but religion rendered into thought and expounded by thought, i. e., another form and manner of existence of the estrangement of the essence of man; hence equally to be condemned;

(2) The establishment of *true materialism* and of *real science,* by making the social relationship of "man to man" the basic principle of the theory;

(3) His opposing to the negation of the negation, which claims to be the absolute positive, the self-supporting positive, positively based on itself.

---

[a] Certificate of poverty.—*Ed.*
[b] This refers to the *Allgemeine Literatur-Zeitung.*—*Ed.*

Feuerbach explains the Hegelian dialectic (and thereby justifies starting out from the positive facts which we know by the senses) as follows:

Hegel sets out from the estrangement of substance (in logic, from the infinite, the abstractly universal)—from the absolute and fixed abstraction; which means, put in a popular way, that he sets out from religion and theology.

Secondly, he annuls the infinite, and posits the actual, sensuous, real, finite, particular (philosophy, annulment of religion and theology).

Thirdly, he again annuls the positive and restores the abstraction, the infinite—restoration of religion and theology.

Feuerbach thus conceives the negation of the negation *only* as a contradiction of philosophy with itself—as the philosophy which affirms theology (the transcendent, etc.) after having denied it, and which it therefore affirms in opposition to itself.

The positive position or self-affirmation and self-confirmation contained in the negation of the negation is taken to be a position which is not yet sure of itself, which is therefore burdened with its opposite, which is doubtful of itself and therefore in need of proof, and which, therefore, is not a position demonstrating itself by its existence—not an acknowledged ||XIII| position; hence it is directly and immediately confronted by the position of sense-certainty based on itself.*

But because Hegel has conceived the negation of the negation, from the point of view of the positive relation inherent in it, as the true and only positive, and from the point of view of the negative relation inherent in it as the only true act and spontaneous activity of all being, he has only found the *abstract, logical, speculative* expression for the movement of history, which is not yet the *real* history of man as a given subject, but only the *act of creation,* the *history of the origin* of man.

We shall explain both the abstract form of this process and the difference between this process as it is in Hegel in contrast to modern criticism, in contrast to the same process in Feuerbach's *Wesen des Christenthums,* or rather the *critical* form of this in Hegel still uncritical process.

Let us take a look at the Hegelian system. One must begin with Hegel's *Phänomenologie,* the true point of origin and the secret of the Hegelian philosophy.

* Feuerbach also defines the negation of the negation, the definite concept, as thinking surpassing itself in thinking and as thinking wanting to be directly awareness, nature, reality.— *Note by Marx.*[97]

Phenomenology.
A. *Self-consciousness.*
I. *Consciousness.*(α) Certainty at the level of sense-experience; or the "this" and "meaning". (β) *Perception*, or the thing with its properties, and *deception*. (γ) Force and understanding, appearance and the supersensible world.
II. *Self-consciousness.* The truth of certainty of self. (a) Independence and dependence of self-consciousness; lordship and bondage. (b) Freedom of self-consciousness. Stoicism, scepticism, the unhappy consciousness.
III. *Reason.* Reason's certainty and reason's truth. (a) Observation as a process of reason. Observation of nature and of self-consciousness. (b) Realisation of rational self-consciousness through its own activity. Pleasure and necessity. The law of the heart and the insanity of self-conceit. Virtue and the course of the world. (c) The individuality which is real in and for itself. The spiritual animal kingdom and the deception or the real fact. Reason as lawgiver. Reason which tests laws.
B. *Mind.*
I. *True* mind; ethics. II. Mind in self-estrangement, culture. III. Mind certain of itself, morality.
C. Religion. *Natural* religion; *religion of art*; *revealed* religion.
D. *Absolute Knowledge.*

Hegel's *Enzyklopädie*,[a] beginning as it does with logic, with *pure speculative thought*, and ending with *absolute knowledge*—with the self-conscious, self-comprehending philosophic or absolute (i. e., superhuman) abstract mind—is in its entirety nothing but the *display*, the self-objectification, of the *essence* of the philosophic mind, and the philosophic mind is nothing but the estranged mind of the world thinking within its self-estrangement—i. e., comprehending itself abstractly.

Logic—mind's *coin of the realm*, the speculative or *mental value* of man and nature—its essence which has grown totally indifferent to all real determinateness, and hence unreal—is *alienated thinking*, and therefore thinking which abstracts from nature and from real man: *abstract* thinking.

Then: *The externality of this abstract thinking ... nature*, as it is for this abstract thinking. Nature is external to it—its self-loss; and it apprehends nature also in an external fashion, as abstract thought, but as alienated abstract thinking. Finally, *mind*, this thinking

---

[a] Georg Wilhelm Friedrich Hegel, *Encyclopädie der philosophischen Wissenschaften im Grundrisse.—Ed.*

returning home to its own point of origin—the thinking which as the anthropological, phenomenological, psychological, ethical, artistic and religious mind is not valid for itself, until ultimately it finds itself, and affirms itself, as *absolute* knowledge and hence absolute, i. e., abstract, mind, thus receiving its conscious embodiment in the mode of existence corresponding to it. For its real mode of existence is *abstraction*.

There is a double error in Hegel.

The first emerges most clearly in the *Phänomenologie,* the birth-place of the Hegelian philosophy. When, for instance, wealth, state power, etc., are understood by Hegel as entities estranged from the *human* being, this only happens in their form as thoughts.... They are thought-entities, and therefore merely an estrangement of *pure,* i. e., abstract, philosophical thinking. The whole process therefore ends with absolute knowledge. It is precisely abstract thought from which these objects are estranged and which they confront with their presumption of reality. The *philosopher*—who is himself an abstract form of estranged man—takes himself as the *criterion* of the estranged world. The whole *history of the alienation process* and the whole *process of the retraction* of the alienation is therefore nothing but the *history of the production* of abstract (i. e., absolute) ||XVII|[98] thought—of logical, speculative thought. The *estrangement,* which therefore forms the real interest of this alienation and of the transcendence of this alienation, is the opposition of *in itself* and *for itself,* of *consciousness and self-consciousness,* of *object and subject*—that is to say, it is the opposition between abstract thinking and sensuous reality or real sensuousness within thought itself. All other oppositions and movements of these oppositions are but the *semblance,* the *cloak,* the *exoteric* shape of these oppositions which alone matter, and which constitute the *meaning* of these other, profane oppositions. It is not the fact that the human being *objectifies himself inhumanly,* in opposition to himself, but the fact that he *objectifies himself* in *distinction* from and in *opposition* to abstract thinking, that constitutes the posited essence of the estrangement and the thing to be superseded.

||XVIII| The appropriation of man's essential powers, which have become objects—indeed, alien objects—is thus in the first place only an *appropriation* occurring in *consciousness,* in *pure thought,* i. e., in *abstraction*: it is the appropriation of these objects as *thoughts* and as *movements of thought.* Consequently, despite its thoroughly negative and critical appearance and despite the genuine criticism contained in it, which often anticipates far later

development, there is already latent in the *Phänomenologie* as a germ, a potentiality, a secret, the uncritical positivism and the equally uncritical idealism of Hegel's later works—that philosophic dissolution and restoration of the existing empirical world.

In the second place: the vindication of the objective world for man—for example, the realisation that *sensuous* consciousness is not an *abstractly* sensuous consciousness but a *humanly* sensuous consciousness, that religion, wealth, etc., are but the estranged world of *human* objectification, of *man's* essential powers put to work and that they are therefore but the *path* to the true *human* world—this appropriation or the insight into this process appears in Hegel therefore in this form, that *sense, religion,* state power, etc., are *spiritual* entities; for only *mind* is the *true* essence of man, and the true form of mind is thinking mind, the logical, speculative mind. The *human character* of nature and of the nature created by history—man's products—appears in the form that they are *products* of abstract mind and as such, therefore, phases of *mind—thought-entities*. The *Phänomenologie* is, therefore, a hidden, mystifying and still uncertain criticism; but inasmuch as it depicts man's *estrangement,* even though man appears only as mind, there lie concealed in it *all* the elements of criticism, already *prepared* and *elaborated* in a manner often rising far above the Hegelian standpoint. The "unhappy consciousness", the "honest consciousness", the struggle of the "noble and base consciousness", etc., etc.—these separate sections contain, but still in an estranged form, the *critical* elements of whole spheres such as religion, the state, civil life, etc. Just as *entities, objects,* appear as thought-entities, so the *subject* is always *consciousness* or *self-consciousness*; or rather the object appears only as *abstract* consciousness, man only as *self-consciousness*: the distinct forms of estrangement which make their appearance are, therefore, only various forms of consciousness and self-consciousness. Just as *in itself* abstract consciousness (the form in which the object is conceived) is merely a moment of distinction of self-consciousness, what appears as the result of the movement is the identity of self-consciousness with consciousness—absolute knowledge—the movement of abstract thought no longer directed outwards but proceeding now only within its own self: that is to say, the dialectic of pure thought is the result. |XVIII||

||XXIII|[99] The outstanding achievement of Hegel's *Phänomenologie* and of its final outcome, the dialectic of negativity as the moving and generating principle, is thus first that Hegel conceives the self-creation of man as a process, conceives objectifi-

cation as loss of the object, as alienation and as transcendence of this alienation; that he thus grasps the essence of *labour* and comprehends objective man—true, because real man—as the outcome of man's *own labour*. The *real, active* orientation of man to himself as a species-being, or his manifestation as a real species-being (i. e., as a human being), is only possible if he really brings out all his *species-powers*—something which in turn is only possible through the co-operative action of all of mankind, only as the result of history—and treats these powers as objects: and this, to begin with, is again only possible in the form of estrangement.

We shall now demonstrate in detail Hegel's one-sidedness and limitations as they are displayed in the final chapter of the *Phänomenologie*, "Absolute Knowledge"—a chapter which contains the condensed spirit of the *Phänomenologie*, the relationship of the *Phänomenologie* to speculative dialectic, and also Hegel's *consciousness* concerning both and their relationship to one another.

Let us provisionally say just this much in advance: Hegel's standpoint is that of modern political economy.[100] He grasps *labour* as the *essence* of man—as man's essence which stands the test: he sees only the positive, not the negative side of labour. Labour is *man's coming-to-be for himself* within *alienation,* or as *alienated* man. The only labour which Hegel knows and recognises is *abstractly mental* labour. Therefore, that which constitutes the *essence* of philosophy—the *alienation of man who knows himself*, or *alienated* science *thinking itself*—Hegel grasps as its essence; and in contradistinction to previous philosophy he is therefore able to combine its separate aspects, and to present his philosophy as *the* philosophy. What the other philosophers did—that they grasped separate phases of nature and of human life as phases of self-consciousness, namely, of abstract self-consciousness—is *known* to Hegel as the *doings* of philosophy. Hence his science is absolute.

Let us now turn to our subject.

"*Absolute Knowledge*". The last chapter of the "*Phänomenologie*".

The main point is that the *object of consciousness* is nothing else but *self-consciousness,* or that the object is only *objectified self-consciousness*—self-consciousness as object. (Positing of man=self-consciousness.)

The issue, therefore, is to surmount the *object of consciousness*. *Objectivity* as such is regarded as an *estranged* human relationship which does not correspond to the *essence of man*, to self-consciousness. The *reappropriation* of the objective essence of man, produced within the orbit of estrangement as something alien, therefore denotes not only the annulment of *estrangement,* but of *objectivity* as well. Man, that is to say, is regarded as a *non-objective, spiritual* being.

The movement of *surmounting the object of consciousness* is now described by Hegel in the following way:

The *object* reveals itself not merely as *returning* into the *self*—this is according to Hegel the *one-sided* way of apprehending this movement, the grasping of only one side. Man is equated with self. The self, however, is only the *abstractly* conceived man—man created by abstraction. Man *is* selfish. His eye, his ear, etc., are *selfish.* In him every one of his essential powers has the quality of *selfhood.* But it is quite false to say on that account "*self-consciousness* has eyes, ears, essential powers". *Self-consciousness* is rather a quality of human nature, of the human eye, etc.; it is not human nature that is a quality of ||XXIV| *self-consciousness.*

The self-abstracted entity, fixed for itself, is man as *abstract egoist*—*egoism* raised in its pure abstraction to the level of thought. (We shall return to this point later.)

For Hegel the *human being*—*man*—equals *self-consciousness.* All estrangement of the human being is therefore *nothing* but *estrangement of self-consciousness.* The estrangement of self-consciousness is not regarded as an *expression*—reflected in the realm of knowledge and thought—of the *real* estrangement of the human being. Instead, the *actual* estrangement—that which appears real—is according to its *innermost,* hidden nature (which is only brought to light by philosophy) nothing but the *manifestation* of the estrangement of the real human essence, of *self-consciousness.* The science which comprehends this is therefore called *phenomenology.* All reappropriation of the estranged objective essence appears, therefore, as incorporation into self-consciousness: The man who takes hold of his essential being is *merely* the self-consciousness which takes hold of objective essences. Return of the object into the self is therefore the reappropriation of the object.

Expressed in *all its aspects,* the *surmounting of the object of consciousness* means:

(1) That the object as such presents itself to consciousness as something vanishing.

(2) That it is the alienation of self-consciousness which posits thinghood.[101]

(3) That this alienation has not merely a *negative* but a *positive* significance.

(4) That it has this meaning not merely *for us* or intrinsically, but *for self-consciousness itself.*

(5) *For self-consciousness*, the negative of the object, or its annulling of itself, has *positive* significance—or it *knows* this futility of the object—because of the fact that it alienates itself, for in this alienation it posits *itself* as object, or, for the sake of the indivisible unity of *being-for-self*, posits the object as itself.

(6) On the other hand, this contains likewise the other moment, that self-consciousness has also just as much superseded this alienation and objectivity and resumed them into itself, being thus *at home* in *its* other-being *as such*.

(7) This is the movement of consciousness and this is therefore the totality of its moments.

(8) Consciousness must similarly be related to the object in the totality of its determinations and have comprehended it in terms of each of them. This totality of its determinations makes the object *intrinsically a spiritual being*; and it becomes so in truth for consciousness through the apprehending of each one of the determinations as *self* or through what was called above the *spiritual* attitude to them.[102]

As to (1): That the object as such presents itself to consciousness as something vanishing—this is the above-mentioned *return of the object into the self*.

As to (2): The *alienation of self-consciousness* posits *thinghood*. Because man equals self-consciousness, his alienated, objective essence, or *thinghood*, equals *alienated self-consciousness*, and *thinghood* is thus posited through this alienation (thinghood being *that* which is an *object for man* and an object for him is really only that which is to him an essential object, therefore his *objective* essence. And since it is not *real man*, nor therefore *nature*—man being *human nature*—who as such is made the subject, but only the abstraction of man, self-consciousness, so thinghood cannot be anything but alienated self-consciousness). It is only to be expected that a living, natural being equipped and endowed with objective (i.e., material) essential powers should of his essence have *real natural objects*; and that his self-alienation should lead to the positing of a *real, objective world*, but within the framework of *externality*, and, therefore, an overwhelming world not belonging to his own essential being. There is nothing incomprehensible or mysterious in this. It would be mysterious, rather, if it were otherwise. But it is equally clear that a *self-consciousness* by its alienation can posit only *thinghood*, i.e., only an abstract thing, a thing of abstraction and not a *real* thing. It is ||XXVI|[103] clear, further, that thinghood is therefore utterly without any *independence*, any *essentiality* vis-à-vis self-consciousness; that on the contrary it is a mere creature—something *posited* by self-consciousness. And what is posited, instead of confirming itself, is but confirmation of the act of positing which for a moment fixes its energy as the product, and gives it the *semblance*—but only for a moment—of an independent, real substance.

Whenever real, corporeal *man*, man with his feet firmly on the solid ground, man exhaling and inhaling all the forces of nature, *posits* his real, objective *essential powers* as alien objects by his externalisation, it is not the *act of positing* which is the subject in this process: it is the subjectivity of *objective* essential powers, whose action, therefore, must also be something *objective*. An objective being acts objectively, and he would not act objectively if the objective did not reside in the very nature of his being. He only creates or posits objects, because he is posited by objects—because at bottom he is *nature*. In the act of positing, therefore, this objective being does not fall from his state of "pure activity" into a *creating of* the *object*; on the contrary, his *objective* product only confirms his *objective* activity, his activity as the activity of an objective, natural being.

Here we see how consistent naturalism or humanism is distinct from both idealism and materialism, and constitutes at the same time the unifying truth of both. We see also how only naturalism is capable of comprehending the action of world history.

⟨*Man* is directly a *natural being*. As a natural being and as a living natural being he is on the one hand endowed with *natural powers, vital powers*—he is an *active* natural being. These forces exist in him as tendencies and abilities—as *instincts*. On the other hand, as a natural, corporeal, sensuous, objective being he is a *suffering*, conditioned and limited creature, like animals and plants. That is to say, the *objects* of his instincts exist outside him, as *objects* independent of him; yet these objects are *objects* that he *needs*—essential *objects*, indispensable to the manifestation and confirmation of his essential powers. To say that man is a *corporeal*, living, real, sensuous, objective being full of natural vigour is to say that he has *real, sensuous objects* as the object of his being or of his life, or that he can only *express* his life in real, sensuous objects. *To be* objective, natural and sensuous, and at the same time to have object, nature and sense outside oneself, or oneself to be object, nature and sense for a third party, is one and the same thing.⟩ *Hunger* is a natural *need*; it therefore needs a *nature* outside itself, an *object* outside itself, in order to satisfy itself, to be stilled. Hunger is an acknowledged need of my body for an *object* existing outside it, indispensable to its integration and to the expression of its essential being. The sun is the *object* of the plant—an indispensable object to it, confirming its life—just as the plant is an object of the sun, being an *expression* of the life-awakening power of the sun, of the sun's *objective* essential power.

A being which does not have its nature outside itself is not a *natural* being, and plays no part in the system of nature. A being which has no object outside itself is not an objective being. A being which is not itself an object for some third being has no being for its *object*; i.e., it is not objectively related. Its being is not objective.

||XXVII| A non-objective being is a *non-being*.

Suppose a being which is neither an object itself, nor has an object. Such a being, in the first place, would be the *unique* being: there would exist no being outside it—it would exist solitary and alone. For as soon as there are objects outside me, as soon as I am not *alone*, I am *another—another reality* than the object outside me. For this third object I am thus a *different reality* than itself; that is, I am *its* object. Thus, to suppose a being which is not the object of another being is to presuppose that *no* objective being exists. As soon as I have an object, this object has me for an object. But a *non-objective* being is an unreal, non-sensuous thing—a product of mere thought (i.e., of mere imagination)—an abstraction. To be *sensuous*, that is, to be really existing, means to be an object of sense, to be a *sensuous* object, and thus to have sensuous objects outside oneself—objects of one's sensuousness. To be sensuous is to *suffer*.

Man as an objective, sensuous being is therefore a *suffering* being—and because he feels that he suffers, a *passionate* being. Passion is the essential power of man energetically bent on its object.

⟨But man is not merely a natural being: he is a *human* natural being. That is to say, he is a being for himself. Therefore he is a *species-being*, and has to confirm and manifest himself as such both in his being and in his knowing. Therefore, *human* objects are not natural objects as they immediately present themselves, and neither is *human sense* as it immediately *is*—as it is objectively—*human* sensibility, human objectivity. Neither nature objectively nor nature subjectively is directly given in a form adequate to the *human* being.⟩ And as everything natural has to *come into being*, man too has his act of origin—*history*—which, however, is for him a known history, and hence as an act of origin it is a conscious self-transcending act of origin. History is the true natural history of man (on which more later).

Thirdly, because this positing of thinghood is itself only an illusion, an act contradicting the nature of pure activity, it has to be cancelled again and thinghood denied.

Re 3, 4, 5 and 6. (3) This externalisation of consciousness has not merely a *negative* but a *positive* significance, and (4) it has this meaning not merely *for us* or intrinsically, but for consciousness itself. (5) *For consciousness* the negative of the object, its annulling of itself, has *positive* significance—i.e., consciousness *knows* this nullity of the object—because it alienates *itself*; for in this alienation it *knows* itself as object, or, for the sake of the indivisible unity of *being-for-itself*, the object as itself. (6) On the other hand, there is also this other moment in the process, that consciousness has also just as much superseded this alienation and objectivity and resumed them into itself, being thus *at home* in its *other-being as such*.

As we have already seen, the appropriation of what is estranged and objective, or the annulling of objectivity in the form of *estrangement* (which has to advance from indifferent strangeness to real, antagonistic estrangement), means likewise or even primarily for Hegel that it is *objectivity* which is to be annulled, because it is not the *determinate* character of the object, but rather its *objective* character that is offensive and constitutes estrangement for self-consciousness. The object is therefore something negative, self-annulling—a *nullity*. This nullity of the object has not only a negative but a *positive* meaning for consciousness, since this *nullity* of the object is precisely the *self-confirmation* of the non-objectivity, of the ||XXVIII| *abstraction* of itself. For *consciousness itself* the nullity of the object has a positive meaning because it *knows* this nullity, the objective being, as its *self-alienation*; because it knows that it exists only as a result of its own self-alienation....

The way in which consciousness is, and in which something is for it, is *knowing*. Knowing is its sole act. Something therefore comes to be for consciousness insofar as the latter *knows* this *something*. Knowing is its sole objective relation.

It [consciousness] then knows the nullity of the object (i.e., knows the non-existence of the distinction between the object and itself, the non-existence of the object for it) because it knows the object as its *self-alienation*; that is, it knows itself—knows knowing as object—because the object is only the *semblance* of an object, a piece of mystification, which in its essence, however, is nothing else but knowing itself, which has confronted itself with itself and hence has confronted itself with a *nullity*—a something which has *no* objectivity outside the knowing. Or: knowing knows that in relating itself to an object it is only *outside* itself—that it only externalises itself; that *it itself* only *appears* to itself as an object—or that that which appears to it as an object is only itself.

On the other hand, says Hegel, there is here at the same time this other moment, that consciousness has just as much annulled and reabsorbed this externalisation and objectivity, being thus *at home* in its *other-being as such*.

In this discussion all the illusions of speculation are brought together.

First of all: consciousness, self-consciousness, is *at home* in *its other-being as such*. It is therefore—or if we here abstract from the Hegelian abstraction and put the self-consciousness of man instead of self-consciousness—it is *at home* in its *other-being as such*. This implies, for one thing, that consciousness (knowing as knowing, thinking as thinking) pretends to be directly the *other* of itself—to be the world of sense, the real world, life—thought surpassing itself in thought (Feuerbach).[104] This aspect is contained herein, inasmuch as consciousness as mere consciousness takes offence not at estranged objectivity, but at *objectivity as such*.

Secondly, this implies that self-conscious man, insofar as he has recognised and superseded the spiritual world (or his world's spiritual, general mode of being) as self-alienation, nevertheless again confirms it in this alienated shape and passes it off as his true mode of being—re-establishes it, and pretends to be *at home in his other-being as such*. Thus, for instance, after superseding religion, after recognising religion to be a product of self-alienation, he yet finds confirmation of himself in *religion as religion*. Here *is* the root of Hegel's *false* positivism, or of his merely *apparent* criticism: this is what Feuerbach designated as the positing, negating and re-establishing of religion or theology—but it has to be expressed in more general terms. Thus reason is at home in unreason as unreason. The man who has recognised that he is leading an alienated life in law, politics, etc., is leading his true human life in this alienated life as such. Self-affirmation, self-confirmation *in contradiction* with itself—in contradiction with both the knowledge and the essential being of the object—is thus true *knowledge* and *life*.

There can therefore no longer be any question about an act of accommodation on Hegel's part vis-à-vis religion, the state, etc., since this lie is the lie of his principle.

‖XXIX‖ If I *know* religion as *alienated* human self-consciousness, then what I know in it as religion is not my self-consciousness, but my alienated self-consciousness confirmed in it. I therefore know my self-consciousness that belongs to itself, to its very nature, confirmed not in *religion* but rather in *annihilated* and *superseded* religion.

In Hegel, therefore, the negation of the negation is not the confirmation of the true essence, effected precisely through negation of the pseudo-essence. With him the negation of the negation is the confirmation of the pseudo-essence, or of the self-estranged essence in its denial; or it is the denial of this pseudo-essence as an objective being dwelling outside man and independent of him, and its transformation into the subject.

A peculiar role, therefore, is played by the act of *superseding* in which denial and preservation, i.e., affirmation, are bound together.

Thus, for example, in Hegel's philosophy of law, *civil law* superseded equals *morality*, morality superseded equals the *family*, the family superseded equals *civil society*, civil society superseded equals the *state*, the state superseded equals *world history*. In the *actual world* civil law, morality, the family, civil society, the state, etc., remain in existence, only they have become *moments*—modes of the existence and being of man—which have no validity in isolation, but dissolve and engender one another, etc. They have become *moments of motion*.

In their actual existence this *mobile* nature of theirs is hidden. It appears and is made manifest only in thought, in philosophy. Hence my true religious existence is my existence in the *philosophy of religion*; my true political existence is my existence in the *philosophy of law*; my true natural existence, existence in the *philosophy of nature*; my true artistic existence, existence in the *philosophy of art*; my true *human* existence, my *existence in philosophy*. Likewise the true existence of religion, the state, nature, art, is the *philosophy* of religion, of nature, of the state and of art. If, however, the philosophy of religion, etc., is for me the sole true existence of religion then, too, it is only as a *philosopher of religion* that I am truly religious, and so I deny *real* religious sentiment and the really *religious* man. But at the same time I *assert* them, in part within my own existence or within the alien existence which I oppose to them—for this *is* only their *philosophic* expression—and in part I assert them in their distinct original shape, since for me they represent merely the *apparent* other-being, allegories, forms of their own true existence (i.e., of my *philosophical* existence) hidden under sensuous disguises.

In just the same way, *quality* superseded equals *quantity*, quantity superseded equals *measure*, measure superseded equals *essence*, essence superseded equals *appearance*, appearance superseded equals *actuality*, actuality superseded equals the *concept*, the concept superseded equals *objectivity*, objectivity superseded equals the *absolute idea*, the absolute idea superseded equals *nature*, nature superseded equals *subjective* mind, subjective mind superseded equals *ethical* objective mind, ethical mind superseded equals *art,* art superseded equals *religion,* religion superseded equals *absolute knowledge.*[105]

On the one hand, this act of superseding is a transcending of a conceptual entity; thus, private property *as a concept* is transcended in the *concept* of morality. And because thought imagines itself to be directly the other of itself, to be *sensuous reality*—and therefore takes its own action for *sensuous, real* action—this superseding in thought, which leaves its object in existence in the real world, believes that it has really overcome it. On the other hand, because the object has now become for it a moment of thought, thought takes it in its reality too to be self-confirmation of itself—of self-consciousness, of abstraction.

||XXX| From the one point of view the entity which Hegel *supersedes* in philosophy is therefore not *real* religion, the *real* state, or *real* nature, but religion itself already as an object of knowledge, i.e., *dogmatics*; the same with *jurisprudence, political science* and *natural science*. From the one point of view, therefore, he stands in opposition both to the *real* thing and to immediate, unphilosophic *science* or the unphilosophic *conceptions* of this thing. He therefore contradicts their conventional conceptions.[a]

On the other hand, the religious, etc., man can find in Hegel his final confirmation.

It is now time to formulate the *positive* aspects of the Hegelian dialectic within the realm of estrangement.

(a) *Supersession* as an objective movement of *retracting* the alienation *into self*. This is the insight, expressed within the estrangement, concerning the *appropriation* of the objective essence through the supersession of its estrangement; it is the estranged insight into the *real objectification* of man, into the real appropriation of his objective essence through the annihilation of the *estranged* character of the objective world, through the supersession of the objective world in its estranged mode of being. In the same way atheism, being the supersession of God, is the advent of theoretical humanism, and communism, as the supersession of private property, is the vindication of real human life as man's possession and thus the advent of practical humanism, or atheism is humanism mediated with itself through the supersession of religion, whilst communism is humanism mediated with itself through the supersession of private property. Only through the supersession of this mediation—which is itself, however, a necessary

---
[a] The conventional conceptions of theology, jurisprudence, political science, natural science, etc.—*Ed.*

premise—does positively self-deriving humanism, *positive* humanism, come into being.

But atheism and communism are no flight, no abstraction, no loss of the objective world created by man—of man's essential powers born to the realm of objectivity; they are not a returning in poverty to unnatural, primitive simplicity. On the contrary, they are but the first real emergence, the actual realisation for man of man's essence and of his essence as something real.

Thus, by grasping the *positive* meaning of self-referred negation (although again in estranged fashion) Hegel grasps man's self-estrangement, the alienation of man's essence, man's loss of objectivity and his loss of realness as self-discovery, manifestation of his nature, objectification and realisation. ⟨In short, within the sphere of abstraction, Hegel conceives labour as man's act of *self-genesis*—conceives man's relation to himself as an alien being and the manifestation of himself as an alien being to be the emergence of *species-consciousness* and *species-life*.⟩

(b) However, apart from, or rather in consequence of, the reversal already described, this act appears in Hegel:

First as a *merely formal*, because abstract, act, because the human being itself is taken to be only an *abstract, thinking being*, conceived merely as self-consciousness. And,

Secondly, because the exposition is *formal* and *abstract*, the supersession of the alienation becomes a confirmation of the alienation; or for Hegel this movement of *self-genesis* and *self-objectification* in the form of *self-alienation and self-estrangement* is the *absolute*, and hence final, *expression of human life*—with itself as its aim, at peace with itself, and in unity with its essence.

This movement, in its abstract ||XXXI| form as dialectic, is therefore regarded as *truly human life*, and because it is nevertheless an abstraction—an estrangement of human life—it is regarded as a *divine process*, but as the divine process of man, a process traversed by man's abstract, pure, absolute essence that is distinct from himself.

Thirdly, this process must have a bearer, a subject. But the subject only comes into being as a result. This result—the subject knowing itself as absolute self-consciousness—is therefore *God, absolute Spirit, the self-knowing and self-manifesting idea*. Real man and real nature become mere predicates—symbols of this hidden, unreal man and of this unreal nature. Subject and predicate are therefore related to each other in absolute reversal—a *mystical subject-object* or a *subjectivity reaching beyond the object*—absolute subject as a *process*, as *subject alienating* itself and returning from alienation into itself, but at the same time retracting this alienation into itself, and the subject as this process; a pure, *incessant* revolving within itself.

First. *Formal and abstract* conception of man's act of self-creation or self-objectification.

Hegel having posited man as equivalent to self-consciousness, the estranged object—the estranged essential reality of man—is nothing but *consciousness*, the thought of estrangement merely—estrangement's *abstract* and therefore empty and unreal expression, *negation*. The supersession of the alienation is therefore likewise nothing but an abstract, empty supersession of that empty abstraction—the *negation of the negation*. The rich, living, sensuous, concrete activity of self-objectification is therefore reduced to its mere abstraction, *absolute negativity*—an abstraction which is again fixed as such and considered as an independent activity—as sheer activity. Because this so-called negativity is nothing but the *abstract, empty* form of that real living act, its content can in consequence be merely a *formal* content produced by abstraction from all content. As a result therefore one gets general, abstract *forms of abstraction* pertaining to every content and on that account indifferent to, and, consequently, valid for, all content—the thought-forms or logical categories torn from *real* mind and from *real* nature. (We shall unfold the *logical* content of absolute negativity further on.)

‖ Hegel's positive achievement here, in his speculative logic, is that the *definite concepts*, the universal *fixed thought-forms* in their independence vis-à-vis nature and mind are a necessary result of the general estrangement of the human being and therefore also of human thought, and that Hegel has therefore brought these together and presented them as moments of the abstraction-process. For example, superseded being is essence, superseded essence is concept, the concept superseded is ... absolute idea. But what, then, is the absolute idea? It supersedes its own self again, if it does not want to perform once more from the beginning the whole act of abstraction, and to satisfy itself with being a totality of abstractions or the self-comprehending abstraction. But abstraction comprehending itself as abstraction knows itself to be nothing: it must abandon itself—abandon abstraction—and so it arrives at an entity which is its exact opposite—at *nature*. Thus, the entire logic is the demonstration that abstract thought is nothing in itself; that the absolute idea is nothing for itself; that only *nature* is something.

‖XXXII‖ The absolute idea, the abstract idea, which

"*considered* with regard to its unity with itself is *intuiting*" (Hegel, *Encyclopädie*,

3rd edition, p. 222 [§244]), and which (loc. cit.) "in its own absolute truth *resolves* to let the moment of its particularity or of initial characterisation and other-being, the *immediate idea*, as its reflection, *go forth* freely *from itself* as *nature*" (loc. cit.), this whole idea which behaves in such a strange and bizarre way, and which has given the Hegelians such terrible headaches, is from beginning to end nothing else but *abstraction* (i.e., the abstract thinker), which, made wise by experience and enlightened concerning its truth, resolves under various (false and themselves still abstract) conditions to *abandon itself* and to replace its self-absorption (nothingness), generality and indeterminateness by its other-being, the particular, and the determinate; resolves to let *nature*, which it held hidden in itself only as an abstraction, as a thought-entity, *go forth freely from itself*: that is to say, this idea resolves to forsake abstraction and to have a look at nature *free* of abstraction. The abstract idea, which without mediation becomes *intuiting*, is indeed nothing else but abstract thinking that gives itself up and resolves on *intuition*. This entire transition from logic to natural philosophy is nothing else but the transition—so difficult to effect for the abstract thinker, who therefore describes it in such a far-fetched way—from *abstracting* to *intuiting*. The *mystical* feeling which drives the philosopher forward from abstract thinking to intuiting is *boredom*—the longing for a content.

(The man estranged from himself is also the thinker estranged from his *essence*—that is, from the natural and human essence. His thoughts are therefore fixed mental forms dwelling outside nature and man. Hegel has locked up all these fixed mental forms together in his logic, interpreting each of them first as negation—that is, as an *alienation* of *human* thought—and then as negation of the negation—that is, as a superseding of this alienation, as a *real* expression of human thought. But as this still takes place within the confines of the estrangement, this negation of the negation is in part the restoring of these fixed forms in their estrangement; in part a stopping at the last act—the act of self-reference in alienation—as the true mode of being of these fixed mental forms*; and in part, to the extent that this abstrac-

* (This means that what Hegel does is to put in place of these fixed abstractions the act of abstraction which revolves in its own circle. We must therefore give him the credit for having indicated the source of all these inappropriate concepts which originally appertained to particular philosophers; for having brought them together; and for having created the entire compass of abstraction as the object of criticism, instead of some specific abstraction.) (Why Hegel separates thought from the *subject* we shall see later; at this stage it is already clear, however, that when man is not, his characteristic expression cannot be human either, and so neither could thought be grasped as an expression of man as a human and natural subject endowed with eyes, ears, etc., and living in society, in the world, and in nature.)—*Note by Marx.*

tion apprehends itself and experiences an infinite weariness with itself, there makes its appearance in Hegel, in the form of the resolution to recognise *nature* as the essential being and to go over to intuition, the abandonment of abstract thought—the abandonment of thought revolving solely within the orbit of thought, of thought sans eyes, sans teeth, sans ears, sans everything.)

‖XXXIII‖ But *nature* too, taken abstractly, for itself—nature fixed in isolation from man—is *nothing* for man. It goes without saying that the abstract thinker who has committed himself to intuiting, intuits nature abstractly. Just as nature lay enclosed in the thinker in the form of the absolute idea, in the form of a thought-entity—in a shape which was obscure and enigmatic even to him—so by letting it emerge from himself he has really let emerge only this *abstract nature*, only nature as a *thought-entity*—but now with the significance that it is the other-being of thought, that it is real, intuited nature—nature distinguished from abstract thought. Or, to talk in human language, the abstract thinker learns in his intuition of nature that the entities which he thought to create from nothing, from pure abstraction—the entities he believed he was producing in the divine dialectic as pure products of the labour of thought, for ever shuttling back and forth in itself and never looking outward into reality—are nothing else but *abstractions* from *characteristics of nature*. To him, therefore, the whole of nature merely repeats the logical abstractions in a sensuous, external form. He once more *resolves* nature into these abstractions. Thus, his intuition of nature is only the act of confirming his abstraction from the intuition of nature[a]—is only the conscious repetition by him of the process of creating his abstraction. Thus, for example, time equals negativity referred to itself (op. cit.,[b] p. 238). To the superseded becoming as being there corresponds, in natural form, superseded movement as matter. Light is *reflection-in-itself,* the *natural* form. Body as *moon* and *comet* is the *natural* form of the *antithesis* which according to logic is on the one side the *positive resting on itself* and on the other side the *negative* resting on itself. The earth is the *natural* form of the logical *ground,* as the negative unity of the antithesis, etc.

---

[a] The following passage is crossed out in the manuscript: "Let us consider for a moment Hegel's characteristics of nature and the transition from nature to the mind. Nature has resulted as the idea in the form of the other-being. Since the id [ea]...."—*Ed.*

[b] Georg Wilhelm Friedrich Hegel, *Encyclopädie der philosophischen Wissenschaften im Grundrisse.*—*Ed.*

Nature as nature—that is to say, insofar as it is still sensuously distinguished from that secret sense hidden within it—nature isolated, distinguished from these abstractions, is *nothing*—a *nothing proving itself to be nothing*—is *devoid of sense*, or has only the sense of being an externality which has to be annulled.

"In the finite-*teleological* position is to be found the correct premise that nature does not contain within itself the absolute purpose." P. 225 [§ 245].

Its purpose is the confirmation of abstraction.

"Nature has shown itself to be the idea in the *form of other-being*. Since the *idea* is in this form the negative of itself or *external to itself,* nature is not just relatively external *vis-à-vis* this idea, but *externality* constitutes the form in which it exists as nature." P. 277 [§ 247].

Externality here is not to be understood as the *world of sense* which *manifests* itself and is accessible to the light, to the man endowed with senses. It is to be taken here in the sense of alienation, of a mistake, a defect, which ought not to be. For what is true is still the idea. Nature is only the *form* of the idea's *other-being*. And since abstract thought is the *essence,* that which is external to it is by its essence something merely *external*. The abstract thinker recognises at the same time that *sensuousness—externality* in contrast to thought shuttling back and forth *within itself*—is the essence of nature. But he expresses this contrast in such a way as to make this *externality of nature,* its *contrast* to thought, its *defect,* so that inasmuch as it is distinguished from abstraction, nature is something defective. ||XXXIV| An entity which is defective not merely for me or in my eyes but in itself—intrinsically—has something outside itself which it lacks. That is, its essence is different from it itself. Nature has therefore to supersede itself for the abstract thinker, for it is already posited by him as a potentially *superseded* being.

"*For us,* mind has *nature* for its *premise,* being nature's *truth* and for that reason its *absolute prius*. In this truth nature *has vanished,* and mind has resulted as the idea arrived at being-for-itself, the *object* of which, as well as the *subject,* is the *concept*. This identity is *absolute negativity,* for whereas in nature the concept has its perfect external objectivity, this its alienation has been superseded, and in this alienation the concept has become identical with itself. But it is this identity, therefore, only in being a return out of nature." P. 392 [§ 381].

"As the *abstract* idea, *revelation* is unmediated transition to, the *coming-to-be* of, nature; as the revelation of the mind, which is free, it is the *positing* of nature as the *mind*'s world—a positing which, being reflection, is at the same time a *presupposing* of the world as independently existing nature. Revelation in conception is the creation of nature as the mind's being, in which the mind procures the *affirmation* and the *truth* of its freedom". "*The absolute is mind*. This is the highest definition of the absolute." [P. 393, § 384.] |XXXIV||

LETTERS

October 1843-August 1844

1843

1
TO LUDWIG FEUERBACH
IN BRUCKBERG[106]

Kreuznach, October 3, 1843

Dear Sir,

A few months ago while passing through [Bruckberg], Dr. Ruge informed you of our plan to publish Franco-German *Jahrbücher* and asked at the same time for your collaboration. It has now been already settled that *Paris* is to be the place for printing and publication and that the first monthly number is to appear by the end of November.

Before I leave for Paris in a few days time I feel obliged to make a brief *epistolary* approach to you since I have not had the privilege of making your personal acquaintance.

You were one of the first writers who expressed the need for a Franco-German scientific alliance. You will, therefore, assuredly be one of the first to support an enterprise aimed at bringing such an alliance into being. For German and French articles are to be published *promiscue*[a] in the *Jahrbücher*. The best Paris writers have agreed to co-operate. Any contribution from you will be most welcome and there is probably something at your disposal that you have already written.

From your preface to the 2nd edition of *Das Wesen des Christenthums,* I am almost led to conclude that you are engaged on a fuller work on *Schelling* or that you have something about this windbag in mind.[107] Now that would be a marvellous beginning.

Schelling, as you know, is the 38th member of the [German] Confederation.[108] The entire German police is at his disposal as I myself once experienced when I was editor of the *Rheinische Zeitung.* That is, a censorship order can prevent anything against

---

[a] Mixed, alternately.— *Ed.*

the holy Schelling [...]ᵃ from getting through. Hence it is almost impossible in Germany to attack Schelling except in books of over 21 sheets, and books of over 21 sheets are not books read by the people.¹⁰⁹ *Kapp*'sᵇ book is very commendable but it is too circumstantial and rather inaptly separates judgment from facts. Moreover, our governments have found a means of making such works ineffective. They must not be mentioned. They are ignored or the few official reviews dismiss them with a few contemptuous words. The great Schelling himself pretends he knows nothing about these attacks and he succeeded in diverting attention from Kapp's book by making a tremendous *fiscal* to-do about old Paulus' soup.ᶜ¹¹⁰ That was a diplomatic master stroke!

But just imagine Schelling exposed in Paris, before the French literary world! His vanity will not be able to restrain itself, this will wound the Prussian Government to the quick, it will be an attack on Schelling's sovereignty abroad, and a *vain* monarch sets much greater store by his *sovereignty abroad* than at home.

How cunningly Herr von Schelling enticed the French, first of all the weak, eclectic *Cousin*, then even the gifted *Leroux*. For Pierre Leroux and his like still regard Schelling as the man who replaced transcendental idealism by rational realism, abstract thought by thought with flesh and blood, specialised philosophy by world philosophy! To the French romantics and mystics he cries: "I, the union of philosophy and theology", to the French materialists: "I, the union of flesh and idea", to the French sceptics: "I, the destroyer of dogmatism", in a word, "I ... Schelling!"

Schelling has not only been able to unite philosophy and theology, but philosophy and diplomacy too. He has turned philosophy into a general diplomatic science, into a diplomacy for all occasions. Thus an attack on Schelling is indirectly an attack on our entire policy, and especially on Prussian policy. Schelling's philosophy is Prussian policy *sub specie philosophiae*.

You would therefore be doing a great service to our enterprise, but even more to truth, if you were to contribute a characterisation of Schelling to the very first issue. You are just the man for this because you are *Schelling in reverse*. The *sincere thought*—we may believe the best of our opponent—of the *young* Schelling for the realisation of which however he did not possess the necessary

---

ᵃ A word here is indecipherable.— *Ed.*
ᵇ [Ch. Kapp,] *Friedrich Wilhelm Joseph von Schelling....*— *Ed.*
ᶜ H. E. G. Paulus, *Die endlich offenbar gewordene positive Philosophie der Offenbarung.*— *Ed.*

qualities except imagination, he had no energy but vanity, no driving force but opium, no organ but the irritability of a feminine perceptivity, this sincere thought of his youth, which in his case remained a fantastic youthful dream, has become truth, reality, manly seriousness in your case. Schelling is therefore an *anticipated caricature* of you, and as soon as reality confronts the caricature the latter must dissolve into thin air. I therefore regard you as the necessary, natural—that is, nominated by Their Majesties Nature and History—opponent of Schelling. Your struggle with him is the struggle of the imagination of philosophy with philosophy itself.

I confidently expect a contribution from you in the form you may find most convenient.[111] My address is: "Herr Mäurer. Rue Vanneau No. 23, Paris, for the attention of Dr. Marx." Although she does not know you, my wife sends greetings. You would not believe how many followers you have among the fair sex.

Yours very truly,
Dr. Marx

First published in part in: K. Grün, *Ludwig Feuerbach in seinem Briefwechsel und Nachlass, sowie in seiner Philosophischen Charakterentwicklung,* Bd. I, Leipzig und Heidelberg, 1874; in full in: Karl Marx and Frederick Engels, *Collected Works,* second Russ. ed., Vol. 27, 1962

Printed according to the original

The full text is published in English for the first time

2

TO JULIUS FRÖBEL[112]

IN ZURICH

Paris, November 21, 1843
rue Vanneau, No. 31, Faub. St. Germain

Dear Friend,

Your letter has just arrived, but with some very strange symptoms.

1) *Everything* which you say you enclosed is missing with the exception of *Engels' article.*[a] This, however, is all in pieces and is therefore useless. It begins with No. 5.

---

[a] Frederick Engels, "Outlines of a Critique of Political Economy" (see this volume, pp. 418-43).— *Ed.*

2) The letters for Mäurer and myself were wrapped up in the enclosed envelope which is post-marked St. Louis. The few pages of Engels' article were in the same wrapper.

3) Mäurer's letter, which, like mine, I found open in the enclosed envelope, is also superscribed in a strange hand. I enclose the page with the writing.

Hence there are only two possibilities.

Either the *French* Government opened and seized your letters and your packet. In which case return the enclosed addresses. We will then not only initiate *proceedings* against the *French Post-Office* but, at the same time, publicise this fact in all the opposition papers. In any event it would be better if you addressed all packets to a *French bookshop*. However, we do not believe that the French Government has perpetrated the kind of *infamy* which so far only the Austrian Government has permitted itself.

There thus remains the *second possibility,* that your *Bluntschli* and associates have played this police-spy trick. If this is so, then (1) You must bring proceedings against the Swiss and (2) Mäurer as a *French citizen* will protest to the Ministry.

As far as the business itself is concerned, it is now necessary:

α) To ask Schüller not to issue the aforesaid document for the time being, as this must be the principal ornament of our first number.[a]

β) Send the whole of the contents to Louis Blanc's address: No. 2 or 3, rue Taitbout.

γ) Ruge is not yet here. I cannot very well begin with the printing until he has arrived. I have had to reject the articles so far sent to me by the local people (Hess, Weill, etc.) after many protracted discussions. But Ruge is probably coming at the end of this month, and if at that time we also have the document you promised, we can begin with the printing. I have written to Feuerbach,[b] Kapp and Hagen. Feuerbach has already replied.[113]

δ) Holland seems to me to be the most suitable place providing that your police spies have not already been in direct touch with the government.

If your Swiss people have perpetrated the infamy I will not only attack them in the *Réforme,* the *National,* the *Démocratie pacifique,* the *Siècle, Courrier, La Presse, Charivari, Commerce* and the *Revue indépendante,* but in the *Times* as well, and, if you wish, in a pamphlet written in French.

---

[a] Of the *Deutsch-Französische Jahrbücher*.— *Ed.*

[b] See previous letter.— *Ed.*

These pseudo-Republicans will have to learn that they are not dealing with young cowhands, or tailors' apprentices.

As to the *office* I will try to acquire one along with the new lodging into which I intend moving. This will be convenient from the business and financial viewpoint.

Please excuse this scraggy letter. I can't write for indignation.

Yours, Marx

In any case, whether the Paris doctrinaires or the Swiss peasant lads were responsible for the trick, we will get *Arago* and *Lamartine* to make an intervention in the Chamber. If these gentlemen want to make a scandal, *ut scandalum fiat*.[a] Reply quickly for the matter is pressing. Since Mäurer is a *French citizen,* the plot on the part of the Zurichers would be a violation of international law, with which the cowhands shall not get away.

First published in German and Russian in the journal *Voprosy istorii KPSS* No. 4, 1958

Printed according to the original
Published in English for the first time

---

[a] Scandal they shall have.— *Ed.*

1844

3
TO LUDWIG FEUERBACH[114]
IN BRUCKBERG

Paris, August 11 [1844]
rue Vanneau 38

Dear Sir,

Since I just have the opportunity, I take the liberty of sending you an article of mine in which some elements of my critical philosophy of law[a] are outlined. I had already finished it once but have since revised it in order to make it more generally comprehensible. I don't attribute any exceptional value to this essay but I am glad to have an opportunity of assuring you of the great respect and—if I may use the word—love, which I feel for you. Your *Philosophie der Zukunft,* and your *Wesen des Glaubens,* in spite of their small size, are certainly of greater weight than the whole of contemporary German literature put together.

In these writings you have provided—I don't know whether intentionally—a philosophical basis for socialism and the Communists have immediately understood them in this way. The unity of man with man, which is based on the real differences between men, the concept of the human species brought down from the heaven of abstraction to the real earth, what is this but the concept of *society!*

Two translations of your *Wesen des Christenthums,* one in English and one in French, are in preparation and almost ready for printing. The first will be published in Manchester (Engels has been supervising it) and the second in Paris[115] (the Frenchman Dr. Guerrier and the German Communist *Ewerbeck* have translated it with the help of a French literary expert).[b]

At present, the French will immediately pounce on the book, for

---

[a] "Contribution to the Critique of Hegel's Philosophy of Law. Introduction" (see this volume, pp. 175-87).—*Ed.*

[b] This paragraph is in square brackets in the original.—*Ed.*

both parties—priests, and Voltairians and materialists—are looking about for help from outside. It is a remarkable phenomenon that, in contrast to the eighteenth century, religiosity has now passed to the middle and upper classes while on the other hand irreligiosity—but an irreligiosity of men regarding themselves as men—has descended to the French proletariat. You would have to attend one of the meetings of the French workers to appreciate the pure freshness, the nobility which burst forth from these toil-worn men. The English proletarian is also advancing with giant strides but he lacks the cultural background of the French. But I must not forget to emphasise the theoretical merits of the German artisans in Switzerland, London and Paris. The German artisan is still however too much of an artisan.

But in any case it is among these "barbarians" of our civilised society that history is preparing the practical element for the emancipation of mankind.

For me the difference between the French character and our German character was never demonstrated so sharply and convincingly as in a Fourierist work which begins with the following sentences:

"It is in his *passions* that *man* reveals himself completely." "Have you ever met a person who *thought in order to think,* who *remembered in order to remember,* who *imagined in order to imagine,* who *wished in order to wish?* Has this ever happened to you?... No, obviously not!"[a]

The main driving force of nature as of society is, therefore, the *magical,* the *passionate,* the non-*reflecting attraction* and

"everything which exists, man, plant, animal or planet, has received an amount of power corresponding to its mission in the system of the universe".[b]

From this there follows: "The *attractive powers* are proportional to the *destinies.*"[c]

Do not all these sentences give the impression that the Frenchman has deliberately set his passion against the pure activity of German thought? One does not think in order to think, etc.

---

[a] "L'homme est tout entier dans ses *passions.*" "Avez-vous jamais rencontré un homme qui *pensât pour penser,* qui se *ressouvint pour se ressouvenir,* qui *imaginât pour imaginer?* qui *voulait pour vouloir?* cela vous est-il jamais arrivé à vous même? non, évidemment non!"

All French passages occurring in this letter are translated in the text and the French original given in footnotes. The quotations are taken from *Exposition de la science sociale, constituée par C. Fourier,* by E de Pompery, Paris, 1840, pp. 13 and 29.— *Ed.*

[b] "Tout être, homme, plante, animal ou globe a reçu une somme des forces en rapport avec sa mission dans l'ordre universel".— *Ed.*

[c] "Les *attractions* sont proportionnelles aux *destinées.*"— *Ed.*

In his critical Berlin *Literatur-Zeitung*,^a *Bruno Bauer*, my friend of many years standing — but now rather estranged — has provided fresh proof of how difficult it is for Germans to extricate themselves from the contrary one-sidedness. I don't know if you have read the journal. It contains much covert polemic against you.

The character of the *Literatur-Zeitung* can be reduced to the following: "Criticism" is transformed into a transcendental being. These Berliners do not regard themselves as *men* who *criticise,* but as *critics* who, *incidentally,* have the misfortune of being men. They therefore acknowledge only one *real* need, the need of *theoretical* criticism. People like Proudhon are therefore accused of having made some *"practical" "need"* their point of departure. This criticism therefore lapses into a sad and supercilious intellectualism. *Consciousness* or *self-consciousness* is regarded as the *only* human quality. Love, for example, is rejected, because the loved one is only an *"object".* Down with the object. This criticism thus regards itself as the only *active* element in history. It is confronted by the whole of humanity as a *mass,* an inert mass, which has value only as the antithesis of intellect. It is therefore regarded as the greatest crime if the critic displays *feeling* or *passion,* he must be an *ironical ice-cold* σοφός.^b

Thus Bauer says literally:

> "The critic should participate neither in the sufferings nor in the joys of society; he should know neither friendship and love, nor hate and envy; he should be enthroned in a solitude, where only the laughter of the Olympian Gods over the topsy-turviness of the world resounds occasionally from his lips."[116]

The tone of Bauer's *Literatur-Zeitung* is therefore one of dispassionate *contempt* and he makes it all the easier for himself by flinging the results of your work and of our time as a whole at other people's heads. He only exposes contradictions and, satisfied with this occupation, he departs with a contemptuous "Hm". He declares that criticism does not *give* anything, it is far too spiritual for that. Indeed, he plainly expresses the hope:

> "the time is not distant when the whole of degenerate mankind will rally against criticism" — and *criticism* means *Bauer* and *company*— "they will then sort out this mass into different groups and distribute the *testimonium paupertatis* to all of them".

It seems that Bauer has fought against *Christ* out of *rivalry.* I am going to publish a small booklet attacking this aberration of criticism. It would be of the *greatest* value to me if *you* would let me know in

---

^a *Allgemeine Literatur-Zeitung.—Ed.*
^b Sage.—*Ed.*
^c Karl Marx and Frederick Engels, *The Holy Family.* See this edition, Vol. 4.—*Ed.*

advance *your* opinion, and in general some speedy sign of life from you would make me happy. The German artisans in Paris, i. e., the Communists amongst them, several hundreds, have been having lectures twice a week throughout this summer on your *Wesen des Christenthums* from their secret leaders,[a] and have been remarkably responsive. The short extract from the letter of a German lady which appeared in the feuilleton of *Vorwärts!* (No. 64)[b] without the knowledge of the writer, is taken from a letter of my wife, who is now visiting her mother[c] in Trier.

With best wishes for your well-being.

Yours,

Karl Marx

First published in the journal *Probleme des Friedens und des Sozialismus* No. 2, 1958

Printed according to the original
Translated from the German and French

---

[a] Of the League of the Just.— *Ed.*
[b] See this volume, p. 580.— *Ed.*
[c] Karoline von Westphalen.— *Ed.*

FROM THE PREPARATORY MATERIALS

FROM THE *MEMOIRES DE R. LEVASSEUR (DE LA SARTHE)*. Paris, 1829, etc. In 4 volumes

Volume 1 [117]

[EXCERPTS]

"So what we today assume to have been the frenzy of a few excited maniacs, was the general feeling of a whole people and in a way its manner of life." P. 21.

"*Later one saw different opinions dividing the nation; but it was not like this in 1788*: all those in France who were not making a living out of abuses were united in a unanimous wish to destroy a rule of the sword; all those who were not devourers of the national wealth wished to see its management entrusted to the representatives of the people; all those who were not members of the privileged castes wished to see the law applied equally to all and to make all citizens liable to the same burdens." P. 27.

"The Constitution was revised" (after the King's flight) "in a less popular way than it had been originally drawn up; the changes made were not very important but they sufficed to make the Assembly lose all its popularity and the Constitution its most desirable sanction, that of the nation." P. 32.

"The session of the Legislative Assembly was nothing but a barely concealed war of the popular power against the royal authority. A war in which each of the two contenders used the Constitution in turn either as a sword or as a shield. An implacable war in which the Constitution, ceaselessly invoked by both sides, was for both sides only an empty word in which nobody believed. For the rest, this impotent Assembly, wrapped by the Constitution in swaddling-clothes, was unable to *do anything useful*... consequently the numerous events which happened *during its lifetime did not originate from this body*. Constitutionally speaking, or according to the limits of their legal powers, the court and the Assembly *could do nothing, and they did nothing*. These two great colossi regarded one another in silence and demanded of *secret conspiracies* what they could not expect from the law." Pp. 37, 38.

"Neither the one nor the other" (party) "was honest.... Hence the crisis in which France had been left by the Constituent Assembly could only be solved in one of two ways: the toppling of the throne or the return to the old regime. Thus for each of the two parties it was a question of their very existence." P. 38.

"This great epoch of 1791 to 1792 which decided France's destiny was not marked by outstanding parliamentary struggles. It was between the *people* and the *rulers* that the battle continued to be waged. June 20, Pétion's triumph on July 14, and the movements which marked the entry of the volunteers from Marseilles into Paris, these events led to important results [118] without the Assembly playing the least part in them.

The deputies acted as *conspirators* and not as *deputies*. Even the declaration of war, the major event of this period, was decided by the Jacobins."[119] P. 39.

La Fayette.[120] P. 40.
August 10.[121] P. 41.

"The *insurrection*, which had *replaced all existing authorities* on August 10, continued ... it was an active force and it crushed the enemies of liberty. P. 43.

"The only force which existed in France during the interregnum which began on August 10[122] was the popular élan, insurrection, anarchy.... The only means of salvation still remaining was, therefore, to make use of the resources offered by anarchy and to direct against our enemies the brutal force which it aroused." Pp. 43, 44.

"The decrees which it" (the Legislative Assembly) "issued had not the slightest authority. The Ministry, product of an impotent Assembly, was not itself a real power.... The government therefore passed into the hands of those who knew how to separate themselves from it, that is, to the *popular societies* and the *municipalities*. But these improvised centres of government, *products of anarchy itself* and having no basis in law or in the Constitution, were simply the leaders of the people, powerful as long as they restricted themselves to directing the line of march of the people and giving effect to its wishes; they would not have been able to enforce obedience had they come into conflict with the people and wished to impose on it the *rule of law*." Pp. 44, 45.

"It is the *Gironde* which has separated itself from us. It is Buzot who left the place he had occupied in the Constituent Assembly; it is Vergniaud who abandoned the seat he had recently occupied in the Legislative Assembly" (i.e., on the left). P. 49. "We were far from seeking *divisions*.... Pétion was nominated President [of the Convention] almost unanimously; the other members of the committee[123] were chosen from amongst the most influential deputies of the previous Assembly[a]" P. 49.

The new deputies (belonging to the Mountain) knew nothing of the internal split. P. 50.

"Thus when we met, the new deputies ... who formed the great majority in the Mountain, did not even know that there were two camps and that the Republicans were not all inspired by the same sentiments and the same aspirations." P. 51.

"The *Centre* was made up of all those who have the constant habit of declaring themselves in favour of the winning side and who, before they show their colours, look for ways of not compromising themselves and without incurring any risk await further developments. This kind of deputy, who first concealed himself in the Centre, later became an ardent Montagnard and then an even more ardent reactionary. There were also ... men of talent: *Barère* ... Sieyès, Dulaure ... Boissy d'Anglas." P. 52.

"The only party which came to the Convention with a complete system and a previously worked-out plan took their place on the seats on the right." (The Girondists.) P. 52. "By swarming on to the seats opposite ours, they declared war on us, before they even knew us." P. 53.

The main speakers for the Girondists [were] lawyers from the Bordeaux Bar; the Girondists [were] all-powerful in the Legislative Assembly where they [had] controlled the majority; they also dominated the Jacobin Club, that is, public opinion; at the time of the insurrection of August 10 [they] believed they had France in their

---

[a] i.e., the Legislative Assembly.— *Ed.*

hands; when the National Convention was convoked they concluded therefore that no majority independent of them could come about. But the forty-two-day interregnum changed the position. The energy which the Legislative Assembly, that is, the Girondists, had displayed in the struggle with the Crown vanished after August 10. "Feeble and irresolute as soon as the helm of the state was indisputably in their hands" ... [In their] speeches, declamations, they divorced themselves from public opinion without being able to prevent disorder, "merely depriving themselves of the means available to them for controlling the torrent. The Jacobin Club then became the thermometer of public opinion. It very rarely happened that the majority of Frenchmen opposed its decisions". For a long time the word of the Girondists had been law in the Jacobin Club; even before the end of the Constituent Assembly they expelled the Lameths and drove the Constitutionals "into the unpopular precincts of the Feuillants".[124] After August 10 they were superseded and went into opposition to the Jacobins. The Provisional Council of Ministers, entrusted with executive power by the Gironde on August 10, was powerless "since the party on which it depended had made itself unpopular", "executive power was in fact exercised by the Communes, especially by the *Commune of Paris*, composed of men of vigour and beloved of the people. *The elections* in the capital took place under the influence of the Commune whose leading members were elected". Pp. 53, 54. Hence the hostile attitude of the Girondists. "On their arrival in Paris all the deputies who were known to have energy and patriotism were admitted to the Jacobin Club in which the Commune had great influence. These deputies sat on the left-hand side, which was sufficient to make the men of the Gironde take their seats on the right. The Jacobins, having spurned their authority, had become their enemies", and also those deputies who sat on the side of the Commune and the deputies of Paris. P. 55.

"Thus at the *beginning* of the session, the Convention was not divided into parties.... But there arose in its midst an ambitious clique which wished to impose its opinions on the assembly and prepared to fight to avenge the wounds which its self-conceit had suffered and to satisfy its particular resentments." P. 55

Danton, pp. 56, 57. *Robespierre, Marat*, pp. 57, 58.[125]

"The majority of the party of the Gironde were by no means traitors but some were concealed in its ranks. No, it did not desire the ruin of the Republic, but its theories led in that direction." P. 59. The Girondists were the aggressors, the Montagnards were at first on the defensive. ibid.

On September 21. 1792, the session of the Convention begins. The President is *Pétion.*

Danton, pp. 60, 61, 62.[a]

The first two decrees passed by the assembly had been proposed by *Danton:* 1) "No Constitution without the approval of the people."[b] 2) "Safety of persons and property to be protected by the nation." Unanimous adoption of *Grégoire's* motion:— 3) Abolition of the monarchy.

The *Girondists* begin the struggle. P. 63.

"On *September 24, Kersaint,* speaking of the dangers facing the Convention in the capital, proposes to surround it [the Convention] with a force drawn from the Departments. P. 63. The Girondists are against the Commune, which has been

---
[a] This refers to a speech of Danton (see this volume, p. 368).—*Ed*
[b] This sentence is in German in the manuscripts.—*Ed.*

effacing them since August 10, as well as against Danton, who dominated the Executive Council. [P. 64.] Before the convocation of the Convention the [members of the] deputation of Paris had nearly all been part of the Commune of August 10. P. 63.

Hence the wrath of the Girondists "against that redoubtable Commune and particularly against the deputation of Paris". Pp. 63, 64.

Thus one sees: the Girondists wanted to avenge themselves for their defeat and insignificance during the interregnum beginning on August 10.

Joseph Egalité [Duke of] Orléans and *Jean Paul Marat.* Pp. 64, 65.[a]

"Such a man" (Marat) "would never have exercised the least influence if the Girondists had not increased his importance by attacking in his person the very principle of energy and provided him with the opportunity at least to display the calmness, the consistency, *sang-froid* and contempt for insults characteristic of real conviction and devotion." P. 65.

September 24. Concealed attack on the Commune and on a number of Paris deputies "for seeking to organise a dictatorship".

September 25. Barbaroux and Rebecqui accuse Robespierre.[b] *Danton* pleads for harmony. Pp. 66, 67. The Girondists continue with their denunciations. Vergniaud against Marat. P. 67.

Marat, pp. 68, 69.[126]

The dissensions continue every day: "the differences between the Ministers Roland and Danton, the offences ascribed to the Commune of Paris, Marat's posters, were the pretexts for these useless struggles". P. 69. Victory seemed almost always to go to the Girondists. P. 70. The majority are as yet not firmly organised and vacillate undecidedly. "Thus for a long time a large number of firm Republicans voted with the Right—they included Philippeaux, Cambon, Cambacérès, etc." P. 70.[c]

September 29. Roland, elected deputy of the Somme Department, announces to the Convention his intention of resigning his position as Minister of the Interior. *Buzot* demands "that the Minister be invited to remain at his post; all the Girondists support him". Philippeaux proposes "to ask Danton to support this invitation". Danton is against this: "the only possible way in which Roland can be retained in his post is to pronounce his election invalid".

Struggle, Roland's letter, etc. Pp. 70, 71[c].
Decree dissolving the Commune of Paris. Pp. 73, 74, 75.[d]

"The mutual accusations were repeated each day with renewed fury. The Right always began the attack, basing itself on facts that occurred prior to the meeting of the Convention, constantly exploiting the kind of repugnance which *Marat* aroused in the assembly as a whole in order to incriminate the entire Mountain." P. 78, cf. p. 79. "... inter-party strife in the course of which the elected representatives of the people wasted precious time and consumed energies which they ought to have directed entirely against the enemies of France." P. 79.

---

[a] Cf. this volume, pp. 368-69.—*Ed.*
[b] Cf. this volume, p. 369.—*Ed.*
[c] Cf. this volume, p. 369.—*Ed.*
[d] Cf. this volume, p. 369.—*Ed.*

October 29. Roland's, Louvet's accusation against Robespierre. P. 80 sqq.

"... he" (*Louvet*) "and *Barbaroux* were, quite undoubtedly, the only *men of action* in their party". P. 81.

"*The long-winded and garrulous eloquence* of the latter" (Robespierre). P. 82.[127]

"The committees of the Convention and the Convention itself dealt with all the branches of administration and performed through decrees numerous and frequent acts of executive authority. On the other hand, the municipalities had also taken over a large section of the administration. Civil power, military power, even judicial power, nothing was properly organised.... As soon as, for any reason whatsoever, a gathering of citizens was called upon to deal with a matter of public concern, it would at the same time interfere in matters quite unconnected with the task it had been given.... If there existed an infinity of *powers in practice*, a single collective entity, the *Convention, legally united in itself all the authority of the social body*, and it frequently used it: it acted as the *legislative authority* through its decrees, as the administration through its committees, and besides it exercised judicial power through the manner in which it extended the right of indictment." P. 85.

"As a transitional state between the monarchy which had been destroyed and the Republic which was being organised, as a weapon of war against the aristocracy, the emigration and foreign invaders, this concentration of all powers was a happy symptom and, I would say, even indispensable." P. 86.

"It is they" (*the Girondists*) "who demanded bills of indictment against their colleagues; it is they who in handing over Marat to the Revolutionary Tribunal violated the immunity of the elected representatives of the people." P. 87.[a]

December 16. Buzot's motion for the expulsion of [the Duke of] Orléans and his sons; Buzot was supported by Louvet and Lanjuinais.[128]

Roland's intrigues. Pp. 88, 89.[b]

"In spite of their prejudices against us, *Louvet, Roland, Guadet, Pétion, Gensonné* were true and sincere Republicans." P. 90.

About the Girondists, pp. 90, 91.[129]

"The dissensions which hampered the deliberations of the National Convention soon manifested themselves in the *Executive Council*. When Servan was compelled to relinquish the Ministry of War on account of ill health, the Convention, on Roland's suggestion, unhesitatingly appointed citizen Pache, then working in the Ministry of the Interior, to take his place. The new Minister did not share the aversions and the views of his patron." P. 91.

"During these interminable quarrels, the *committees* of the Convention were not as inactive as the Convention itself. The Committee of National Defence, under the influence of *Carnot*, assisted our armies and paved the way for our victories; the Committee of Accounts, for which *Cambon* was the regular reporter, created resources with the aid of the paper money, which under the name of assignats was so greatly and so frequently devalued, and by the sale of national property." Pp. 92, 93.

"By the end of January 1793 ... the Montagnards had abandoned the defensive which they had maintained perhaps too long and gone over in their turn to the attack on the Gironde." P. 100.

---

[a] Cf. this volume, p. 373.— *Ed.*
[b] Cf. this volume, p. 370-371.— *Ed.*

After the death of Michel de Le Peletier Saint-Fargeau ... "the Girondists ceased to have an assured majority". P. 101.

Danton, p. 143 sqq.^a

THE STRUGGLE BETWEEN THE MONTAGNARDS AND THE GIRONDISTS

An interregnum begins on *August 10*, 1792. Impotence of the Legislative Assembly, impotence of the Ministry to which it had given rise. Government passes over to the *public meetings* and *municipalities*; improvised centres of government, products of anarchy, they were bound to be the expression of the popular movement, for their power was only the power of popular opinion (pp. 44, 45). From now on division amongst those with influence.

One party wishes to re-establish the order disrupted by August 10 and to ensure the implementation of the existing laws. The principal members of the Ministry and of the Legislative Assembly are the leaders of this party.

The other party sees in anarchy the only mobile d'action[b], in the enthusiasm which it produces the substitute for a ready-made organisation, the only power of resistance externally and internally. These men are the masters of the Commune of Paris and of nearly all other municipalities in France, they possess one voice (Danton) in the Ministry (pp. 45, 46).

The *Girondists* (the first party) do not oppose any effective means to the popular movement. Their theories are limited in practice to speeches and declamations, which make their unpopularity almost universal without having the slightest effect on developments.

"During this period, the Commune of Paris drives the citizens towards the frontiers; the alarm guns, thundering away hour after hour, proclaim the public danger; all citizens enrol in the sections in order to march against the enemy."

During this period occur the *September days*.[130]

Had they been quelled, all public life would have been extinguished (pp. 46, 47).

The provinces detest the September murders but they are grateful to the men who are maintaining the *insurrectionary fever* in order to fill the army camps with citizen soldiers.

The Girondists are despised; lacking the courage to drive the citizens against the foreign troops, they do not even know how to organise an energetic resistance to the crimes which they denounce and which they use as a means of recrimination against their vigorous enemy.

---

[a] Cf. this volume, p. 373-74.—*Ed.*

[b] Driving force.—*Ed.*

The elections took place during this stormy period.

When the Convention opened, Paris was still in the grip of the insurrectionary movement and the Commune was all-powerful.

The Girondists were the first to separate themselves from the Montagnards. The almost unanimous election of *Pétion* as President of the Convention shows how little the newly-arrived men of the Mountain were looking for divisions; the other members of the committee were likewise elected from amongst the most influential members of the previous Assembly.[a] Almost all the newly-arrived deputies knew nothing of the inner dissensions. Robespierre and Pétion, Danton and Guadet equally enjoyed their respect.

The only party which came to the assembly with a complete system and a previously worked-out plan (the Girondists), took their place on the right-hand side. By leaving their former seats (on the left) and rushing *en masse* to the right-hand side, they declared war on the newly-arrived Republicans who surged on to the left as the traditional side of patriotism.

The Girondists had controlled the majority in the *assemblée legislative* as well as in the Jacobin Club. They thought they had France in their hands at the time of August 10. In summoning the National Convention they never suspected for a moment that a majority independent of them could arise. But the forty-two-day interregnum altered the state of affairs and the character of the elections.

"The Legislative Assembly, that is, the Girondists, had displayed some energy in the struggle against the Court. They showed themselves to be weak and irresolute as soon as they obtained undisputed control of the state. They did not know how to restrain the current unleashed by August 10; they were inept enough to oppose it with declamations. They isolated themselves from public opinion without being able to prevent any disorder whatsoever. They only deprived themselves of the means they had to direct events. The *Jacobin Club* was the thermometer of public opinion at that time. [...] The word of the Gironde had been law there for a long time. Even before the dissolution of the Constituent Assembly they had dethroned the Lameths and driven the Constitutionals into the unpopular precincts of the Feuillants. After August 10, they allowed themselves in their turn to be superseded: they lost their popularity, nearly all of them left a society whose merits they had loudly proclaimed as long as it applauded their views but which they regarded as nothing more than a den of rebels as soon as it thought differently than they did.

"The Gironde had, moreover, on August 10 vested executive power in a Provisional Council of Ministers. Without any support in the nation, this Council was powerless as soon as the party to which it belonged became unpopular. The executive power was in fact exercised by the Communes, and especially by the Commune of Paris, composed of vigorous men of the people. The elections in the capital took place under the influence of the Commune. Its leading members were elected [to the Convention]."

---

[a] i.e., the Legislative Assembly.—*Ed.*

Hence the hostile attitude of the Girondists from the very first moments of the Convention.

"All new deputies who were known to have energy or patriotism, were admitted on their arrival to the Jacobin Club, in which the Commune had great influence. These deputies took their seats on the left side. This sufficed to drive the Girondists to the right. The Jacobins [...] had become their enemies [...]; they called their new opponents Jacobins. [...] Originally only enemies of the Commune and of the deputation of Paris, they extended their hatred to include all who sat on the side used by the Jacobins and who were ardent Republicans. Thus at the beginning of the session, the Convention was not divided; a solid mass of Republicans united by a common feeling, in other respects however differing on many points. But an ambitious clique arose in its midst, which wished to impose its opinions on the assembly and prepared to fight to avenge the wounds which its self-conceit had suffered and to satisfy its private resentments."

The majority of the Girondists were not traitors, but there were traitors in their ranks; the ruin of the Republic was not their aim but the consequence of their theories; the few Royalists in the Convention therefore joined forces with them. They were the attackers; the Mountain was on the defensive for a long time; the Girondists were unable to sacrifice their egotism for the public cause (pp. 47-59).

On *September 21*, 1792, opening of the Convention. *Pétion* President. *Danton* resigns his post as Minister of Justice. A conciliatory speech. No Constitution could exist unless it was accepted by a majority of the primary meetings. A declaration regarding security of property ought to be decreed. Both Danton's proposals became decrees (the first decrees promulgated by the Convention). In his speech Danton declared that the popular agitation was temporarily necessary; now, however, the constituted power of the Convention should replace it, excesses should be abandoned.

Unanimous abolition of the monarchy on Grégoire's motion.

The first session of the Convention shows the desire of the Mountain for general reconciliation in the interests of order and of freedom. The Girondists immediately demonstrate their urge to take revenge.

On *September 24, Kersaint,* speaking of the dangers in the capital, proposes to surround it [the Convention] with *force recruited from the Departments.* This is the first declaration of war by the Girondists who are full of anger against the deputation of Paris because the Girondists who had been members of the Legislative Assembly were annihilated as a result of the activities of the Commune and because of Danton's domination in the Executive Council.

Jean Paul Marat and *Joseph Egalité* in particular gave the Girondists the opportunity of making spiteful charges against the

Mountain, charges of blood-thirstiness and anarchy on the one side and of ambition and Royalism on the other.

September 24. Indirect accusations that the Commune of Paris is striving for a dictatorship.

September 25: *Rebecqui and Barbaroux* name Robespierre as the candidate of the dictatorship. Danton again preaches concord and defends the Commune: an extra-legal power had been necessary under the weak leadership of the *assemblée legislative,* now there should be a return to order. Girondists do not pay attention to Danton's admonitions; they keep returning to the past in order to seek continual grounds for recrimination.

Vergniaud and Boileau attack Marat. Marat's courageous reply. The assembly turns to the business of the day. But the hostilities already initiated are continued.

"While [the Assembly] waited for a decisive act and a split between Roland and Danton, the alleged outrages by the Commune of Paris and Marat's posters served as pretexts for these useless conflicts. Victory seemed almost always to favour the side of the Girondists. The majority was not yet organised during these first conflicts, swaying uncertainly this way and that. For a considerable time many firm Republicans, e. g., *Philippeaux, Cambon, Cambacérès,* voted with the Right.

September 29: Roland, elected deputy of the Somme Department, informs the Assembly that he would relinquish his position as Minister of the Interior. Those on the right express their regrets. Buzot proposes to request Roland to remain at his post, Philippeaux would like Danton to support this request; Danton opposes; an invitation is below the dignity of the Convention; the only way to keep Roland at his post is to declare his election null and void. The Girondists insist on an invitation. Valazé declares that Roland's name is holy to him. Louvet, Barbaroux overwhelm him with praise. This time the men of the Centre, Barère, Lacroix, Tureau,[a] who often provided the Right with a majority without actually belonging to them, are against Buzot's proposal.

September 30: Roland writes a letter to the Convention in which he states that he wants to remain Minister, he praises himself a great deal in this letter, lectures his opponents, accuses Danton indirectly; all these reproaches against Danton and the Commune refer to facts which occurred prior to the meeting of the Convention; evidence of the hatred of a vanquished party for the victors.

Each day the Right persecutes the Commune, which is defended by the deputies of Paris. Finally this revolutionary authority is ordered to dissolve; it is requested to give an account of itself. New source of strife emerges. The *comité de surveillance* of the Commune gives notice to the Convention of the seizure of important papers

---

[a] This is evidently a misprint, it refers to Thuriot.—*Ed.*

which will throw light on the treacheries of the Court, in which several deputies will find themselves compromised. It asks that it should not be compelled to part with these documents and to be allowed to continue to function until a favourable moment for their use. [...] The Girondists regard this as an open wish on the part of the Commune to perpetuate its functions; the Montagnards see in their opponents people interested in stifling the truth. The discussion confirms each party in its prejudices. [...] The documents are finally handed over to a commission of 25 representatives, which comprises no members either of the Commune and the deputation of Paris, or of the Constituent and Legislative Assemblies.

Nothing emerges either against the Commune or against the Gironde. Even the report of *Joseph Delaunay* (a Girondist deputy) comes out, in the main, in favour of the Commune.

"The mutual accusations are repeated daily with renewed fury, the Right always initiating the attack, basing themselves on facts which occurred before the convocation of the Convention. [...] Freedom of opinion is always misconstrued when a representative of the Left wishes to speak; Robespierre was driven from the rostrum by uproar and insults."

Marat was only able to make his reply by dint of perseverance.

Up to now the Right has always had a majority; the Mountain votes with it whenever questions of principle, establishment of order, implementation of laws, etc., are involved.

In his reports to the Convention, Roland constantly repeats that the crimes of the interregnum still have to be punished, and introduces indirect accusations against Robespierre and Danton, and also against the deputation of Paris.

Roland is furious because Danton's supremacy in the Council has crushed him.

On *October 29* Roland makes a report to the Convention in which Robespierre is again accused. While on the rostrum seeking to defend himself, Robespierre is interrupted by the clamour of the Girondists and by constant interjections by President *Guadet*.

Louvet's attack on Robespierre.

November 5.[a] Robespierre's reply.

"Return to the order of the day demanded on all sides, even Vergniaud, Guadet and Pétion support this. Only Salles, Barbaroux, Lanjuinais, Larivière stand by Louvet [...]. The return to the agenda is adopted almost unanimously. Barbaroux still demands the floor in order to support the accusations [...] and then goes down to the bar and wants to speak as plaintiff and even as the accused. This unseemly scene is prolonged and, as usual, ends without the assembly having made any decisions whatsoever" (pp. 60-83).

December 16. Thuriot brings about the proclamation of the unity and indivisibility of the Republic. *Buzot* proposes a motion for the expulsion of the Duke of Orléans and his sons and is supported by Louvet and Lanjuinais. In this way the Girondists make the first attempt to decimate the National Assembly. Incidentally, the

---

[a] Marx has: "November 6", apparently a slip of the pen.—*Ed.*

From the *Mémoires de R. Levasseur*

Girondists are on friendly terms with Orléan's creatures—Dumouriez, Sillery, Biron, Valence.

The Ministers showed open bias in favour of the Girondists.

"When Louvet accused Robespierre, the Convention ordered the printing of both the indictment and the defence. Roland had Louvet's speech distributed in large quantities with the words: *Imprimé par ordre de la Convention*,[a] and restricted the distribution of Robespierre's speech to members of the Convention. Thus the impression was to be produced among the public that a kind of censure had been pronounced on Robespierre. A similar knavish trick was repeated over the decree concerning the banishment of the Bourbons. Before the reading of the minutes, which signified its adoption, i.e., before the final wording had been approved by majority decision as was the rule, its printing was speeded up and its dispatch to the 84 Departments carefully arranged by Roland, while the postponement of any decision regarding the fate of Philippe Egalite was not given the same publicity. Thus one could believe that the supporters of Orléans brought about the repeal of a decree which concerned him by a surprise move on the next morning [...]."

The dissensions which interfered with the deliberations of the National Convention soon crept into the *Executive Council* itself. Servan retiring on account of ill health, the Convention on *Roland*'s recommendation appointed *Pache*, then working in the Ministry of the Interior. Pache wanted to be independent, in addition he associated with the Jacobins. Pache was a good patriot but a bad Minister of War. By accusing him of treason, the Girondists caused a redoubling of the recriminations which for a long time had been levelled against Roland.

Assignats, law concerning the practice of worship (cf. p. 93), *decree concerning food,* compare Levasseur's speech, p. 94 sqq.[131]

Shortly after the decree on *means of subsistence,* discussions in connection with the trial of Louis XVI. This occasioned further acrimony.

End of January 1793. Baseless animosities, just as at the beginning of the Convention. But a big change has taken place in the temper of the assembly. The Mountain has now gone over from the defensive to the offensive. The war of the parties is at fever heat.

"There is a feeling that from now on it is impossible to advance towards any organisation of the Republic without the complete destruction of one of the two parties.

"The assassination of Michel de Le Peletier Saint-Fargeau led to an argument and an open breach between the two extremes."

The *Marsh,* tired of the capricious intrigues and the conceit of the Girondists, frequently allies itself with the Mountain against them. Roland's resignation accepted.

January 28: *Buzot* denounces the *comité de sûreté générale*[b] (in

---

[a] Printed by order of the Convention.—*Ed.*

[b] Committee of Public Safety.—*Ed.*

which apart from the Girondists there are several Montagnards—Tallien, Chabot, Bazire) on account of the arrest of a journalist and demands its dissolution.
"The Girondists were in the habit of sacrificing any institution rather than allow it to flourish in the hands of their opponents" (pp. 84-103).

March 8. Great agitation because of the military set-backs in Belgium under Dumouriez. Commissioners are sent to all the sections [of] Paris to call the citizens to arms, and also to the Departments.

March 9. The Commissioners present their reports. Guarantees are demanded against internal conspiracies. Decree for the establishment of an extraordinary criminal court, from whose findings there is no appeal, for the hearing of all cases involving traitors, conspirators and counter-revolutionaries. Great excitement in the capital. The printing-presses belonging to Gorsas are smashed up; he is forced to flee. The people were so worked up that it required a decree of the Convention to get the bakers to return to the bakeries and the Post-Office clerks to the telegraph office.

March 10. Debates about the organisation of the Revolutionary Tribunal.

Great excitement in Paris. Evening session of the Convention at 9 o'clock. The seats on the right almost empty. After midnight the combined crowds in the Champs Elysées assume a rebellious character. They go to the Jacobin and Cordelier Clubs, they preach insurrection against the Convention. These proposals are rejected by the Montagnards.[132]

March 11. Decree relating to the Revolutionary Tribunal.

March 12. Marat speaks against the assaults made on the 10th.

March 13. Complaints and attacks by the Girondists in connection with March 10.
"The rebellious movements of March 10 in Paris were nurtured by all the parties, because all of them took part in the agitation—an agitation stirred up in order to drive the people to the frontiers; the scenes on March 10 were a necessary consequence of this impassioned state. The Mountain, sitting alone in the Chamber, had quietened the threatening disorders in a few hours. Pache and Santerre [...] were praised for their ardour; Marat and Dubois-Crancé pacified both the Jacobin and the Cordelier Clubs and persuaded them to abandon their sinister plans. Marat first of all denounced the March 10 disorders, he initiated a decree of indictment against Fournier l'Américain, one of their instigators; La Source, an impassioned Girondist, addressed eulogies to him during the March 12 session. Finally, [...] a member of the Right who had insulted Marat during the same sitting [...] was censured and it was unanimously decided to enter this in the official record despite the revolting partisanship against the *ami du peuple* which people were in the habit of displaying" [pp. 122-23].

When it was first established, the *comité de sûreté générale* was composed overwhelmingly of Girondists.

A few days after March 10, the Girondists wanted to shift responsibility for it on to the Mountain.

"Stormy sessions became the customary state of affairs in the Convention. Tumultuous scenes. [...] The galleries often participated in these scandalous interruptions. Then the Girondists screamed that they were no longer safe in Paris, they called the Departmental forces to their aid. The Mountain, from their side, accused their opponents of preaching civil war. Sometimes whole days and nights passed in these wretched debates" [p. 127].

Nevertheless the immunity of deputies was still respected on all sides until now. The Right was the first to depart from this rule. On Guadet's motion, Marat was committed for trial. The Legislation Committee prepared a bill of indictment in which his condemnation was anticipated. Marat was unanimously acquitted by the Revolutionary Tribunal, and led back to the Convention by the people in triumph [pp. 127-29].

This event had important results. Party conflicts of the deputies assumed the form of legal proceedings. The persecution of Marat was the immediate prelude to May 31.[133]

March 18. Defeat of Dumouriez near Neerwinden; his letters to the Executive Council contain insults against the Convention (Danton's opinion regarding Dumouriez, p. 133).[134] The Girondists applaud his insolent letters.

March 29. A letter from Dumouriez evokes the greatest indignation. Decree ordering Dumouriez to appear before the bar of the House, etc. The treason of Dumouriez.

April 3. La Source dares to denounce Danton as an accomplice of Dumouriez. (Cf. p. 137.) Danton declares war on the Girondists. Danton's speech makes great impression. Danton had tried to bring about a reconciliation between the two sides of the assembly.

"Although he was sitting on the summit of the Mountain, he was, to some extent, the leader of the Marsh. He had often criticised the passion of the Montagnards, fought against Robespierre's suspicions, maintained that instead of fighting the Girondists one should compel them to support the Mountain in order jointly to save the common cause. Even a few days before La Source's attack, Danton had had a conference with the chief leaders of the Right at which agreement was reached to work together in harmony and to concentrate on the struggle against the foreigners and the aristocrats. The whole of the Mountain loved Danton but the majority thought that he misjudged the situation if he hoped to establish an alliance between the Mountain and the Gironde." [p. 143].

"The discussions assumed a much more serious character toward the end of April and the beginning of May. No more parliamentary bickering but a life and death struggle. Each side began to seek help from outside in order to win. But [...] the Mountain, in spite of this internal discord, paid serious attention to matters concerning France while the Gironde only thought about the destruction of its opponents and abandoned completely the direction of the state. During these two months the question of the *maximum* was dealt with.[135] [...] The Right fought [...] this measure by means of slanders. It made accusations about violation of the right to own property and threats to the life of property owners. These declamations were aimed at turning the *middle classes* against the Mountain. The maximum was adopted" [p. 147, 150].

The Girondists always had the majority when party wrangling was involved, as, for example, when such questions as the impeachment of Marat, the March disorders, the petitions of the sections, the Commission of the Twelve, were being discussed. The Mountain had the majority when big questions of general interest were involved, such as the maximum, means for revolutionary recruitment, the extraordinary tribunal, forced loans, etc.

An incident occurred during the discussion of the maximum. *Ducos* was on the rostrum criticising the proposed measure, counterposing the sansculottes to the middle classes, when a violent uproar broke out in one of the public galleries. Guadet demands the transfer of the Convention to Versailles. Acclamation on the right. Levasseur demands that the rules should be observed and the galleries cleared. Resistance by the Right. Philippeaux, Danton, Lacroix vainly call on the assembly to remember its dignity and its urgent obligations. In vain they demand that matters of the greatest importance should not be interrupted on account of an insignificant incident. The Girondists had to give vent to their rage. Animated discussion, attacks on the Paris authorities, threats that the provinces would take vengeance.

Thus the tocsin of civil war was sounded at the very moment when it was a question of interests which had roused the people. The intention was to incite the two classes of the people against one another. The Mountain went with the party of the popular masses, where the sinewy arms and strong devotion are to be found [pp. 152-53].

Disorders in the Vendée had developed into a real civil war. New enrolments and renewed expenditure of funds became necessary. Danton, Desmoulins, Philippeaux, Couthon tried to find means to make this possible. The only possible means of meeting the urgent expenditure was the mobilisation of the national wealth, an *emprunt force*[a] (cf. p. 161 sqq.), which was derived from superfluous wealth in the hands of citizens.

The Girondists, who denounced the measures of the Mountain, did not even propose an alternative plan. They did nothing at all.

Written at the end of 1843 and the beginning of 1844	Printed according to the manuscript
First published in part in: K. Marx and F. Engels, *Works*, Vol. III, Russ. ed., 1930; in full in: Marx/Engels, *Gesamtausgabe*, Abt. 1, Bd. 3, 1932	Translated from the French and German Published in English for the first time

---

[a] A forced loan.— *Ed.*

SUMMARY OF FREDERICK ENGELS' ARTICLE "OUTLINES OF A CRITIQUE OF POLITICAL ECONOMY" PUBLISHED IN *DEUTSCH-FRANZÖSISCHE JAHRBÜCHER*[136]

Private property. Its immediate consequence — *trade* — like every activity, is a *direct* source of gain for the trader. The next category to which trade gives rise is *value.* Abstract real value and exchange-value. For *Say* utility is the determining feature of real value, for Ricardo and Mill[a] — the *cost of production.* For the Englishmen, competition as against the cost of production represents utility; for Say, it is the cost of production. *Value* is the ratio of the *production costs* to *utility.* Its immediate application: the *decision* whether to produce at all, whether utility outweighs the cost of production. The practical application of the concept of value is limited to the decision about production. The distinction between *real value and exchange-value* is based on the fact that the *equivalent* given in trade is *no equivalent. Price*: the relationship [between] cost of production and competition. Only that which can be monopolised has *price.* Ricardo's definition of *rent of land* is incorrect because it presupposes that a fall in demand instantly reacts on rent and· at once puts out of cultivation a corresponding quantity of the worst cultivated land. This is incorrect. This definition leaves out competition, that of Adam Smith leaves out fertility. *Rent* is the relationship between *productivity of the soil* and *competition.* The *value of land*[b] is to be measured by the productiveness of equal areas using equal amounts of labour.

The separation of capital from labour. The separation of capital and profit. The division of profit into profit and interest.... Profit, the weight that capital puts in the scales when the costs of

---

[a] Engels writes "McCulloch" (see this volume, p. 424).—*Ed.*

[b] Engels stipulates: provided private property is abolished (see this volume, pp. 429-30).—*Ed.*

production are determined, remains inherent in capital, and the latter reverts to labour[a]. The separation of labour and wages. The significance of wages. The significance of labour in determining the production costs. The split between land and the human being. Human labour[b] divided into labour and capital.

Written in the first half of 1844

First published in: Marx/Engels, *Gesamtausgabe*, Abt. 1, Bd. 3, 1932

Printed according to the manuscript

Published in English for the first time

---

[a] Engels discusses the role of profit after the abolition of private property (see this volume, p. 431).—*Ed.*

[b] Engels has: "human activity" (see this volume, p. 432).—*Ed.*

FREDERICK ENGELS

WORKS

May 1843-June 1844

LETTERS FROM LONDON[137]

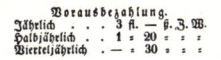

I

[*Schweizerischer Republikaner* No. 39, May 16, 1843]

The democratic party in England is making rapid progress. While Whiggism and Toryism, the moneyed aristocracy and the landed aristocracy are engaged in a boring verbal battle over trifles in the "national talkshop", as the Tory Thomas Carlyle calls it, or in the "House which claims to represent the parishes of England", as the Chartist Feargus O'Connor says, while the Established Church exerts all its influence on the bigoted inclinations of the nation in order to maintain its decaying edifice a little longer, while the Anti-Corn Law League[138] squanders hundreds of thousands in the irrational hope to see in return millions flowing into the pockets of the cotton-manufacturing lords — during this time despised and derided socialism marches forward calmly and confidently and gradually compels the attention of public opinion. During this time, too, a new party of countless numbers has taken shape in a few years under the banner of the People's Charter[139] and has carried out such vigorous agitation that compared with it O'Connell and the League are bunglers and blunderers. It is well known that in England parties coincide with social ranks and classes; that the Tories are identical with the aristocracy and the bigoted, strictly orthodox section of the Church of England; that the Whigs consist of manufacturers, merchants and dissenters, of the upper middle class as a whole; that the lower middle class constitute the so-called "radicals", and that, finally, Chartism has its strength in the working men, the proletarians. Socialism does not form a closed political party, but on the whole it derives its supporters from the lower middle class and the proletarians. Thus, in England, the remarkable fact is seen that the lower the position of a class in society, the more "uneducated" it is in the usual sense of the word, the more closely is it connected with progress, and the greater is its future. In general, this is a feature of every revolutionary epoch, as was seen in particular in the religious revolution of which the outcome was Christianity: "blessed are the poor",[a] "the wisdom of this world is foolishness",[b] etc. But this portent of a great revolution has probably never been so clearly expressed and so sharply delineated as now in England. In Germany, the movement proceeds from the class which is not only educated but even learned; in England, for three hundred years the educated and all the learned people have been deaf and blind to the signs of the times. Well known throughout the world is the pitiful routine of the English universities, compared with which our German colleges are like gold; but on the Continent people cannot even imagine the kind of works produced by the foremost English theologians and even by some of the foremost English natural scientists, and what miserable reactionary publications form the bulk of the weekly "list of new books". England is the homeland of political economy, but what about the level of scholarship among professors and practical politicians? Adam Smith's free trade has been pushed to the insane conclusions of the Malthusian theory of population and has produced nothing but a new, more civilised form of the old monopoly system, a form which finds its representatives among the present-day Tories, and which successfully combated the Malthusian nonsense, but in the end arrived once more at Malthus' conclusions. Everywhere there is inconsistency and hypocrisy, while the striking economic tracts of the Socialists and partly also of the Chartists are thrown aside with contempt and find readers only among the lower classes. Strauss' *Das Leben Jesu* was translated into English. Not a single "respectable" book publisher wanted to print it; finally it appeared in separate parts, 3d. per part, and that was done by the publishing house of a minor but energetic antiquarian.[140] The same thing occurred with translations of Rousseau, Voltaire, Holbach, etc. Byron and Shelley are read almost exclusively by the lower classes; no "respectable" person could have the works of the latter on his desk without his coming into the most terrible disrepute. It remains true: blessed are the poor, for theirs is the kingdom of heaven and, however long it may take, the kingdom of this earth as well.

---

[a] Matthew 5:3.—*Ed.*
[b] 1 Corinthians 1:20.—*Ed.*

Parliament now has before it Sir James Graham's Bill on the education of children working in factories, in accordance with which their hours of work are to be restricted, compulsory education introduced, and the High Church entrusted with supervision of the schools.[141] This Bill has, of course, given rise to general commotion and has provided the parties with a fresh opportunity for testing their strength. The Whigs want to have the Bill rejected completely because it ousts the dissenters from the education of the young and, by restricting the working hours of children, causes difficulties for the manufacturers. Among the Chartists and Socialists, on the other hand, there is considerable agreement with the general humane tendency of the Bill, except for the provisions relating to the High Church. Lancashire, the main factory centre, is also, of course, the main centre of agitation in regard to the Bill. Here, the Tories are quite powerless in the towns; moreover, their meetings in this connection were not held in public. The congregations of the dissenters first of all met in order to put forward a petition against the Bill, and then arranged for town meetings in alliance with the liberal manufacturers. A town meeting of this kind is summoned by the highest urban official, is completely public, and every inhabitant has the right to speak at it. Here, therefore, if the meeting hall is sufficiently large, only the strongest and most energetic party can be victorious. And at all the town meetings so far convened, the Chartists and Socialists have won. The first such meeting was in Stockport, where the resolutions put forward by the Whigs received only one vote, while the entire meeting voted for those of the Chartists, so that the Mayor of Stockport, a Whig, as chairman of the meeting had to sign a Chartist petition and send it to a Chartist M.P. (Duncombe) for presentation to Parliament. The second meeting was in Salford, a sort of suburb of Manchester, with a population of about 100,000; I attended it. The Whigs had taken every precaution to ensure victory for themselves. The borough reeve[a] took the chair and talked a great deal about impartiality; but when a Chartist asked whether a discussion would be allowed, he was given the reply: yes, when the meeting is over! It was intended to have the first resolution smuggled through, but the Chartists were on the alert and prevented this. When one of the Chartists climbed on to the platform, a clergyman dissenter came forward and tried to throw him off! However, everything went well until, finally, a petition on Whig lines was proposed. Then a Chartist

---

[a] Engels uses the English term.—*Ed.*

spoke and proposed an amendment; thereupon the chairman and his whole retinue of Whigs rose and left the hall. But the meeting continued, and the Chartist petition was put to the vote; but police officers, who had already intervened several times on the side of the Whigs, put out the lights just at the right moment and forced the meeting to disperse. Nevertheless, the Whigs caused all their resolutions to be published, as carried, in the next issue of the local newspaper, and the borough reeve[a] was dishonest enough to sign his name "on behalf of and on the instructions of the meeting"! So much for Whig fairness! The third meeting took place two days later in Manchester, and here the radical parties likewise achieved a most brilliant victory. Although the time was so chosen that the majority of the factory workers could not be present, there was nevertheless a considerable majority of Chartists and Socialists in the hall. The Whigs confined themselves solely to the points which they had in common with the Chartists; a Socialist and a Chartist spoke from the platform and bore witness that the Whigs on this occasion had behaved like good Chartists. The Socialist told them frankly that he had come with the intention of creating opposition if there was the slightest occasion for it, but everything had gone according to his wishes. So it has turned out, therefore, that Lancashire, and particularly Manchester, the stronghold of Whiggism, the centre of the Anti-Corn Law League, is able to show a brilliant majority in favour of radical democracy and thereby the power of the "liberals" is completely held in check.

II

[*Schweizerischer Republikaner* No. 41, May 23, 1843]

The Augsburg *Allgemeine Zeitung* has a liberal correspondent (*) in London who writes favourably about the manoeuvres of the Whigs in horribly long and boring articles. "The Anti-Corn Law League is now the power in the land," declares this oracle and thereby utters the greatest lie ever told by a partisan correspondent.[142] The League — the power in the land! Where is this power? In the Ministry? In it are Peel, Graham and Gladstone, the bitterest enemies of the League. In Parliament? But there every one of its proposals is rejected by a majority rarely equalled in the annals of the English Parliament. Where then is this power? In the public, in the nation? This question can only be answered in the affirmative by such an

---

[a] Engels gives this term in English.—*Ed*.

empty-headed, frivolous correspondent, for whom Drury Lane is the public and a drummed-up meeting is public opinion. If this sagacious correspondent is so blind as to be incapable of seeing in broad daylight—this is the legacy of the Whigs—then I will tell him how matters stand with the power of the League. It has been driven out of the Ministry and Parliament by the Tories, and out of public opinion by the Chartists. Feargus O'Connor has triumphantly routed it in all the towns of England, everywhere he has challenged it to a public debate and the League has never picked up the gage. The League cannot call a single public meeting without being most ignominiously trounced by the Chartists. Or does the Augsburg correspondent really not know that the pompous January meetings in Manchester and the meetings now being held in the Drury Lane theatre in London, where the liberal gentlemen tell one another lies and try to deceive themselves about their inner instability—does he really not know these are "whited sepulchres"? Who are admitted to these meetings? *Only members of the League or persons to whom the League gives tickets.* Hence no hostile party can have a chance of successful opposition there, and therefore no one applies for tickets; no matter what cunning it resorted to, it could not manage to smuggle in even a hundred of its supporters. The League has been organising such meetings, which are afterwards called "public", for some years past and at them it congratulates itself on its "progress". It is very becoming that at these "public" ticket meetings, the League rails against the "spectre of Chartism", especially since it knows that at *truly* public meetings O'Connor, Duncombe, Cooper, etc., are giving a straightforward reply to those attacks. Up to now the Chartists have shattered every public meeting of the League by a brilliant majority, but the League has never been able to disrupt a Chartist meeting. Hence the League's hatred of the Chartists, hence the clamour about the "disorder" caused by the Chartists at a meeting—that is to say, the rebellion of the majority against the minority, which from the platform tries to make use of the majority for its own ends. Where then is the power of the League?—In its imagination and—in its purse. The League is wealthy, by the abolition of the Corn Laws it hopes to conjure up a trade boom and therefore throws a sprat to catch a mackerel. Its subscriptions bring in considerable sums of money which cover the expenditure on all the pompous meetings and the rest of the appearance and tawdry finery. But behind this glittering exterior there is nothing real. The National Charter Association[a]—the Chartists' organisation[143]—has

---

[a] Engels gives this name in English.—*Ed.*

a greater number of members, and it will soon be seen that it can also collect more money, although it consists only of poor workers, while the League has all the rich manufacturers and merchants in its ranks. And the reason is that the Chartist Association gets its money—even if only in pennies—from nearly every one of its members, whereas although considerable sums of money are contributed to the League, they come only from certain individuals. The Chartists can easily collect *a million pennies*[144] weekly; it is very questionable whether the League could sustain this. The League opened a subscription list for £50,000 and received about £70,000. Feargus O'Connor is about to open a subscription list of £*125,000* for one project[145] and soon afterwards perhaps another for an equal amount—he will certainly get it—and what does the League then intend to do with its "huge funds"?

Why the Chartists are in opposition to the League will be dealt with on another occasion.[146] For the present only one further remark, viz., that the efforts and work of the League have *one* good side. This is the movement which is being aroused by the Anti-Corn Law agitation in a hitherto entirely stable class of society—the agricultural population. Up to now the latter has taken no interest in public affairs; dependent on the landowners who can put an end to the lease agreement any year, the farmers, phlegmatic and ignorant, have sent only Tories to Parliament year after year—251 out of the 658 members of the House of Commons—and up to now this has been the strong basis of the reactionary party. If an individual farmer wanted to come out against this traditional vote, he found no support among his fellow farmers and the landlord could easily give him notice. Now, however, a considerable alertness among this class of the population is evident; there already exist liberal farmers, and among them there are people who realise that in very many cases the interests of the landlord and those of the tenant are directly opposed. Three years ago, particularly in England herself, no one could have said this to a tenant without being laughed at or even beaten up. Among this class the work of the League will bear fruit, but quite certainly the fruit will be different from what the League expects, for while it is probable that the mass of the tenants will gradually go over to the Whigs, it is still more probable that the mass of the agricultural labourers will be impelled to take the side of the Chartists. One without the other is impossible, and thus here, too, the League will obtain only feeble compensation for the decisive and total withdrawal from it of the working class which the League has suffered during the past five years in the towns and factory districts owing to Chartism. The kingdom of the *juste-milieu* has had its day and the "power in the land" has become divided into two extremes. In view of these undeniable facts, however, I ask the correspondent of the Augsburg *Allgemeine Zeitung*: Where is the "power of the League"?

III

[*Schweizerischer Republikaner* No. 46, June 9, 1843]

The English Socialists are far more principled and practical than the French, which is especially due to the fact that they are engaged in an open struggle against the various churches and do not want to have anything to do with religion. In the larger towns they usually maintain a hall[a] where every Sunday they listen to speeches which are often polemical against Christianity and atheistic, but often also deal with some aspect of the workers' life; of their lecturers (preachers) Watts in Manchester seems at any rate to be an outstanding man, who has written some very talented pamphlets on the existence of God and on political economy. The lecturers have a very good manner of arguing; they always start out from experience and from verifiable or obvious facts and at the same time the exposition is carried out in such a systematic way that it is very difficult to fight them on the ground they have chosen. If anyone tries to carry the argument into a different sphere they laugh in his face. If, for example, I say: For man the existence of God does not depend on facts for its proof, they retort: "What a ridiculous proposition you put forward: if God does not manifest Himself through facts, why should we want to trouble ourselves about Him? From your proposition it follows directly that it is a matter of indifference to people whether God exists or does not exist. And since we have thousands of other things to care about, we leave to you the good God above the clouds, where perhaps He exists, or perhaps does not exist. What we do not know through facts does not concern us at all; we keep to the basis of 'real facts', where there can be no question of such fantastic things as God and religious theories." So the rest of their communist propositions are supported by proof based on facts, in accepting which they are indeed careful. The stubbornness of these people is indescribable, and how the clergy are going to win them over—heaven alone knows. In Manchester, for instance, the communist community has 8,000 members openly registered at

---

[a] This word is in English in the original.—*Ed.*

the hall and paying their subscriptions to it. The assertion that half of the working classes of Manchester share their views on property is no exaggeration; because when Watts says from the platform (for the Communists the platform is what the pulpit is for the Christians): Today I am going to one or other meeting, you can count on it that the motion put by the lecturer will have a majority.

But among the Socialists, too, there are theoreticians or, as the Communists call them, *complete* atheists, while the former are called *practical* atheists. Of these theoreticians the most famous is Charles Southwell in Bristol, who published a polemical journal *The Oracle of Reason* and was punished for that by a year's imprisonment and a fine of about £100. Of course, the fine was quickly covered by subscriptions, for every Englishman subscribes to *his* newspaper, helps *his* leaders to pay fines, pays for *his* chapel or hall, attends *his* meetings. But Charles Southwell is already in prison again; in fact the hall in Bristol had to be sold because there are not so many Socialists in Bristol and among them few are rich, whereas such a hall is a fairly expensive thing. It was bought by a Christian denomination and converted into a chapel. When this new chapel was consecrated, the Socialists and Chartists crowded into it to see and hear the ceremony. But when the clergyman began to praise God that all the wicked doings had been ended, and that where formerly God had been defamed, praises would now be sung to the Almighty, they regarded this as an attack, and since according to English notions every attack demands resistance, they raised a shout of Southwell, Southwell! Let Southwell speak in opposition! Southwell therefore got up and began to make a speech. Now, however, clergymen of the Christian denomination put themselves at the head of the columns of their parishioners and hurled themselves on Southwell; other members of the denomination called in the police, because Southwell was said to have disturbed a Christian religious service; the clergymen laid hold of him, struck him (as often happens in such cases) and handed him over to a policeman. Southwell himself ordered his supporters not to offer physical resistance; when he was led away, some 6,000 people followed him crying "hurrah" and cheering him.

The founder of the socialist movement, Owen, writes in his numerous booklets like a German philosopher, i.e., very badly, but at times he has his lucid moments and then his obscure writings become readable; moreover, his views are comprehensive. According to Owen "marriage, religion and property are the sole causes of all the calamity that has existed since the world began" (!!),[147] all his writings teem with outbursts of rage against the theologians, lawyers and doctors, all of whom he lumps together. "The law-courts are the seat of a class of people which is still completely theological and *therefore prejudiced*; the laws also are imbued with theology and must therefore be abolished together with the jury."

While the Church of England lived in luxury, the Socialists did an incredible amount to educate the working classes in England. At first one cannot get over one's surprise on hearing in the Hall of Science[a] the most ordinary workers speaking with a clear understanding on political, religious and social affairs; but when one comes across the remarkable popular pamphlets and hears the lecturers of the Socialists, for example Watts in Manchester, one ceases to be surprised. The workers now have good, cheap editions of translations of the French philosophical works of the last century, chiefly Rousseau's *Contrat social*, the *Système de la Nature*[148] and various works by Voltaire, and in addition the exposition of communist principles in penny and twopenny pamphlets and in the journals. The workers also have in their hands cheap editions of the writings of Thomas Paine and Shelley. Furthermore, there are also the Sunday lectures, which are very diligently attended; thus during my stay in Manchester I saw the Communist Hall, which holds about 3,000 people, crowded every Sunday, and I heard there speeches which have a direct effect, which are made from the special viewpoint of the people, and in which witty remarks against the clergy occur. It happens frequently that Christianity is directly attacked and Christians are called "our enemies".

In their form, these meetings partly resemble church gatherings; in the gallery a choir accompanied by an orchestra sings social hymns; these consist of semi-religious or wholly religious melodies with communist words, during which the audience stands. Then, quite nonchalantly, without removing his hat, a lecturer comes on to the platform, on which there is a table and chairs; after raising his hat by way of greeting those present, he takes off his overcoat and then sits down and delivers his address, which usually gives much occasion for laughter, for in these speeches the English intellect expresses itself in superabundant humour. In one corner of the hall is a stall where books and pamphlets are sold and in another a booth with oranges and refreshments, where everyone can obtain what he needs or to

---

[a] This term is given in English in the original.—*Ed.*

which he can withdraw if the speech bores him. From time to time tea-parties are arranged on Sunday evenings at which people of both sexes, of all ages and classes, sit together and partake of the usual supper of tea and sandwiches; on working days dances and concerts are often held in the hall, where people have a very jolly time; the hall also has a café.

How does it happen that all this kind of thing is tolerated? Firstly, under the Whig Ministry the Communists secured the passage of an Act of Parliament and in general achieved such a strong position at that time that now, as being a corporation, it is no longer possible to take any steps against them. Secondly, the authorities would very much like to attack prominent individuals, but they know that this would only redound to the advantage of the Socialists by drawing public attention to them, which is what the Socialists want. If they were to become martyrs for their cause (and how many of them would be ready for that at any time), it would give rise to agitation. But agitation is a means of making their cause still more widely known, whereas at present a large part of the nation takes no notice of them, regarding them as a sect like any other. The Whigs knew very well that repressive measures have a stronger effect in favour of a cause than agitation for the cause itself, and hence they gave the Communists an opportunity to exist and take form; but every form is a bond. The Tories, on the other hand, take some action against them when the atheistic publications seem too outrageous, but every time it is to the advantage of the Communists. In December 1840, Southwell and others were punished for blasphemy; immediately three new periodicals appeared: one was *The Atheist,* another *The Atheist and Republican,* and the third, published by the lecturer Watts, *The Blasphemer.* A few issues of *The Blasphemer* caused a great sensation, and the authorities tried in vain to discover how this trend could be suppressed. They left it alone, and lo and behold, all three papers ceased to exist!

Thirdly, the Socialists, like all the other parties, save themselves by circumventing the law and resorting to verbal quibbles, which is the regular practice here.

Thus everything here displays life and cohesion, a solid basis and action; thus everything here is assuming a definite external shape; whereas we imagine that we know something if we have swallowed the dull, miserable contents of Stein's book,[a] or that we

---

[a] Lorenz von Stein, *Der Socialismus und Communismus des heutigen Frankreichs.*—*Ed.*

are of some importance if somewhere or other we utter an opinion perfumed with attar of roses.

In the Socialists, English energy is very clearly evident, but what astonished me more was the good-natured character of these people, I almost called them lads, which, however, is so far removed from weakness that they laugh at the mere Republicans, because a republic would be just as hypocritical, just as theological, just as unjust in its laws, as a monarchy; but for the reform of society they are ready to sacrifice their worldly goods and life itself together with their wives and children.

IV

[*Schweizerischer Republikaner* No. 51, June 27, 1843]

One hears nothing now but talk about O'Connell and the Irish Repeal[a] (abolition of the Union of Ireland and England).[149] O'Connell, the cunning old lawyer, who during the Whig government sat calmly in the House of Commons and helped to pass "liberal" measures in order to be rejected by the House of Lords, O'Connell has suddenly left London and absented himself from the parliamentary debates and is now raising again his old question of repeal. No one was thinking about it any more; and then Old Dan[b] turns up in Dublin and is again raking up the stale obsolete lumber. It is not surprising that the old yeast is now producing remarkable air-bubbles. The cunning old fox is going from town to town, always accompanied by a bodyguard such as no king ever had — two hundred thousand people always surround him! How much could have been done if a sensible man possessed O'Connell's popularity or if O'Connell had a little more understanding and a little less egoism and vanity! Two hundred thousand men — and what men! People who have nothing to lose, two-thirds of whom are clothed in rags, genuine proletarians and sansculottes and, moreover, Irishmen, wild, headstrong, fanatical Gaels. One who has never seen Irishmen cannot know them. Give me two hundred thousand Irishmen and I will overthrow the entire British monarchy. The Irishman is a carefree, cheerful, potato-eating child of nature. From his native heath, where he grew up, under a broken-down roof, on weak tea and meagre food, he is suddenly thrown into our civilisation. Hunger drives

---

[a] Here and later Engels uses the English word "repeal".—*Ed.*
[b] In the original "Old Dan", i.e., Daniel O'Connell.—*Ed.*

him to England. In the mechanical, egoistic, ice-cold hurly-burly of the English factory towns, his passions are aroused. What does this raw young fellow—whose youth was spent playing on moors and begging at the roadside—know of thrift? He squanders what he earns, then he starves until the next pay-day or until he again finds work. He is accustomed to going hungry. Then he goes back, seeks out the members of his family on the road where they had scattered in order to beg, from time to time assembling again around the teapot, which the mother carries with her. But in England the Irishman saw a great deal, he attended public meetings and workers' associations, he knows what Repeal is and what Sir Robert Peel stands for, he quite certainly has often had fights with the police and could tell you a great deal about the heartlessness and disgraceful behaviour of the "Peelers"[a] (the police). He has also heard a lot about Daniel O'Connell. Now he once more returns to his old cottage with its bit of land for potatoes. The potatoes are ready for harvesting, he digs them up, and now he has something to live on during the winter. But here the principal tenant[150] appears, demanding the rent. Good God, where's the money to come from? The principal tenant is responsible to the landowner for the rent, and therefore has his property attached. The Irishman offers resistance and is thrown into gaol. Finally, he is set free again, and soon afterwards the principal tenant or someone else who took part in the attachment of the property is found dead in a ditch.

That is a story from the life of the Irish proletarians which is of daily occurrence. The half-savage upbringing and later the completely civilised environment bring the Irishman into contradiction with himself, into a state of permanent irritation, of continually smouldering fury, which makes him capable of anything. In addition he bears the burden of five centuries of oppression with all its consequences. Is it surprising that, like any other half-savage, he strikes out blindly and furiously on every opportunity, that his eyes burn with a perpetual thirst for revenge, a destructive fury, for which it is altogether a matter of indifference what it is directed against, so long as it can strike out and destroy? But that is not all. The violent national hatred of the Gaels against the Saxons, the orthodox Catholic fanaticism fostered by the clergy against Protestant-episcopal arrogance—with these elements anything can be accomplished. And all these elements are in O'Connell's hands. And what a multitude of people are at his disposal!

---

[a] This word is in English in the original.—*Ed.*

The day before yesterday in Cork—150,000 men, yesterday in Nenaph—200,000, today in Kilkenny—400,000, and so it goes on. A triumphal procession lasting a fortnight, a triumphal procession such as no Roman emperor ever had. And if O'Connell really had the welfare of the people in view, if he were really concerned to abolish poverty—if his miserable, petty *juste-milieu* aims were not behind all the clamour and the agitation for Repeal—I should truly like to know what Sir Robert Peel could refuse him if he demanded it while at the head of such a force as he now has. But what does he achieve with all his power and his millions of valiant and desperate Irishmen? He is unable to accomplish even the wretched Repeal of the Union; of course solely because he is not serious about it, because he is misusing the impoverished, oppressed Irish people in order to embarrass the Tory Ministers and to put back into office his *juste-milieu* friends. Sir Robert Peel, too, knows this well enough, and hence 25,000 soldiers are quite enough to keep all Ireland in check. If O'Connell were really the man of the people, if he had sufficient courage *and were not himself afraid of the people,* i.e., if he were not a double-faced Whig, but an upright, consistent democrat, then the last English soldier would have left Ireland long since, there would no longer be any idle Protestant priest in purely Catholic districts, or any Old-Norman baron in his castle. But there is the rub. If the people were to be set free even for a moment, then Daniel O'Connell and his moneyed aristocrats would soon be just as much left high and dry as he wants to leave the Tories high and dry. That is the reason for Daniel's close association with the Catholic clergy, that is why he warns his Irishmen against dangerous socialism, that is why he rejects the support offered by the Chartists,[151] although for appearances sake he now and again talks about democracy—just as Louis Philippe in his day talked about Republican institutions—and that is why he will never succeed in achieving anything but the political education of the Irish people, which in the long run is to no one more dangerous than to himself.

Written in May-June 1843

First published in *Schweizerischer Republikaner* Nos. 39, 41, 46 and 51, May 16 and 23 and June 9 and 27, 1843

Printed according to the journal

The full text is published in English for the first time

THE
NEW MORAL WORLD:
AND
GAZETTE OF THE RATIONAL SOCIETY.

Enrolled under Acts of Parliament, 10 Geo. IV. c. 56, and 4, 5, Will. IV. c. 40.

"ANY GENERAL CHARACTER, FROM THE BEST TO THE WORST, FROM THE MOST IGNORANT TO THE MOST ENLIGHTENED, MAY BE GIVEN TO ANY COMMUNITY, EVEN TO THE WORLD AT LARGE, BY THE APPLICATION OF PROPER MEANS, WHICH MEANS ARE TO A GREAT EXTENT AT THE COMMAND AND UNDER THE CONTROL OF THOSE WHO HAVE INFLUENCE IN THE AFFAIRS OF MEN."—ROBERT OWEN.

W. JOHNSTON, PRINTER, LITTLE RED LION COURT, CHARTERHOUSE LANE, LONDON.

No. 19. Vol. V. *Third Series.*   SATURDAY, NOVEMBER 4, 1843.   PRICE 2d.

PROGRESS OF SOCIAL REFORM ON THE CONTINENT [152]

[*The New Moral World* No. 19, November 4, 1843]

It has always been in some degree surprising to me, ever since I met with English Socialists, to find that most of them are very little acquainted with the social movement going on in different parts of the continent. And yet there are more than half a million of Communists in France, not taking into account the Fourierists, and other less radical Social reformers; there are Communist associations in every part of Switzerland, sending forth missionaries to Italy, Germany, and even Hungary; and German philosophy, after a long and troublesome circuit, has at last settled upon Communism.

Thus, the three great and civilised countries of Europe— England, France, and Germany, have all come to the conclusion, that a thorough revolution of social arrangements, based on community of property, has now become an urgent and unavoidable necessity. This result is the more striking, as it was arrived at by each of the above nations independently of the others; a fact, than which there can be no stronger proof, that Communism is not the consequence of the particular position of the English, or any other nation, but that it is a necessary conclusion, which cannot be avoided to be drawn from the premises given in the general facts of modern civilisation.

It must, therefore, appear desirable, that the three nations should understand each other, should know how far they agree, and how far they disagree; because there must be disagreement also, owing to the different origin of the doctrine of Community in each of the three countries. The English came to the conclusion *practically*, by the rapid increase of misery, demoralisation, and pauperism in their own country: the French *politically*, by first asking for political liberty and equality; and, finding this insufficient, joining social liberty, and social equality to their political claims: the Germans became Communists *philosophically*, by reasoning upon first principles. This being the origin of Socialism in the three countries, there must exist differences upon minor points; but I think I shall be able to show that these differences are very insignificant, and quite consistent with the best feeling on the part of the Social reformers of each country towards those of the other. The thing wanted is, that they should know each other; this being obtained, I am certain, they all will have the best wishes for the success of their foreign brother Communists.

I

FRANCE

France is, since the Revolution, the exclusively political country of Europe. No improvement, no doctrine can obtain national importance in France, unless embodied in some political shape. It seems to be the part the French nation have to perform in the present stage of the history of mankind, to go through all the forms of political development, and to arrive, from a merely political beginning, at the point where all nations, all different paths, must meet at Communism. The development of the public mind in France shows this clearly, and shows at the same time, what the future history of the English Chartists must be.

The French Revolution was the rise of democracy in Europe. Democracy is, as I take all forms of government to be, a contradiction in itself, an untruth, nothing but hypocrisy (theology, as we Germans call it), at the bottom. Political liberty is sham-liberty, the worst possible slavery; the appearance of liberty, and therefore the reality of servitude. Political equality is the same; therefore democracy, as well as every other form of government, must ultimately break to pieces: hypocrisy cannot subsist, the contradiction hidden in it must come out; we must have either a regular slavery—that is, an undisguised despotism, or real liberty, and real equality—that is, Communism. Both these consequences were brought out in the French Revolution; Napoleon established the first, and Babeuf the second. I think I may be short upon the subject of Babouvism, as the history of his conspiracy, [written] by Buonarroti,[a] has been translated into the English language.[153] The Communist plot did not succeed, because

---

[a] Ph. Buonarroti, *Conspiration pour l'égalité dite de Babeuf, suivie du procès auquel elle donna lieu, et des pièces justificatives, etc.*—*Ed.*

the then Communism itself was of a very rough and superficial kind; and because, on the other hand, the public mind was not yet far enough advanced.

The next French Social reformer was Count de Saint-Simon. He succeeded in getting up a sect, and even some establishments; none of which succeeded. The general spirit of the Saint-Simonian doctrines is very much like that of the Ham-Common Socialists, in England[154]; although, in the *detail* of the arrangements and ideas, there is a great difference. The singularities and eccentricities of the Saint-Simonians very soon became the victims of French wit and satire; and everything once made ridiculous is inevitably lost in France. But, besides this, there were other causes for the failure of the Saint-Simonian establishments; all the doctrines of this party were enveloped in the clouds of an unintelligible mysticism, which, perhaps, in the beginning, attract the attention of the people; but, at last, must leave their expectations disappointed. Their economical principles, too, were not unexceptionable; the share of each of the members of their communities in the distribution of produce was to be regulated, firstly, by the amount of work he had done; and, secondly, the amount of talent he displayed. A German Republican, Boerne, justly replied to this principle, that talent, instead of being rewarded, ought rather to be considered as a natural preference; and, therefore, a deduction ought to be made from the share of the talented, in order to restore equality.

Saint-Simonism, after having excited, like a brilliant meteor, the attention of the thinking, disappeared from the Social horizon. Nobody now thinks of it, or speaks of it; its time is past.

Nearly at the same time with Saint-Simon, another man directed the activity of his mighty intellect to the social state of mankind—*Fourier*. Although Fourier's writings do not display those bright sparks of genius which we find in Saint-Simon's and some of his disciples; although his style is hard, and shows, to a considerable extent, the toil with which the author is always labouring to bring out his ideas, and to speak out things for which no words are provided in the French language—nevertheless, we read his works with greater pleasure; and find more real value in them, than in those of the preceding school. There is mysticism, too, and as extravagant as any, but this you may cut off and throw it aside, and there will remain something not to be found among the Saint-Simonians—scientific research, cool, unbiassed, systematic thought; in short, *social philosophy*; whilst Saint-Simonism can only be called *social poetry*. It was Fourier, who, for the first time, established the great axiom of social philosophy, that every individual having an inclination or predilection for some particular kind of work, the sum of all these inclinations of all individuals must be, upon the whole, an adequate power for providing for the wants of all. From this principle, it follows, that if every individual is left to his own inclination, to do and to leave what he pleases, the wants of all will be provided for, without the forcible means used by the present system of society. This assertion looks bold, and yet, after Fourier's mode of establishing it, is quite unassailable, almost self-evident—the egg of Columbus. Fourier proves, that every one is born with an inclination for some kind of work, that *absolute idleness* is nonsense, a thing which never existed, and cannot exist: that the essence of the human mind is to be active itself, and to bring the body into activity; and that, therefore, there is no necessity for making the people active by force, as in the now existing state of society, but only to give their natural activity the right direction. He goes on proving the identity of labour and enjoyment, and shows the irrationality of the present social system, which separates them, making labour a toil, and placing enjoyment above the reach of the majority of the labourers; he shows further, how, under rational arrangements, labour may be made, what it is intended to be, an enjoyment, leaving every one to follow his own inclinations. I cannot, of course, follow Fourier through the whole of his theory of *free labour*, and I think this will be sufficient to show the English Socialists that Fourierism is a subject well worthy of their attention.[155]

Another of the merits of Fourier is to have shown the advantages—nay, the necessity of association. It will be sufficient only to mention this subject, as I know the English to be fully aware of its importance.

There is one inconsistency, however, in Fourierism, and a very important one too, and that is, his nonabolition of private property. In his *Phalanstères* or associative establishments, there are rich and poor, capitalists and working men. The property of all members is placed into a joint stock, the establishment carries on commerce, agricultural and manufacturing industry, and the proceeds are divided among the members; one part as wages of labour, another as reward for skill and talent, and a third as profits of capital. Thus, after all the beautiful theories of association and free labour; after a good deal of indignant declamation against commerce, selfishness, and competition, we have in practice the old competitive system upon an improved plan, a poor-law bastile on more liberal principles! Certainly, here we cannot stop; and the French, too, have not stopped here.

The progress of Fourierism in France was slow, but regular. There are not a great many Fourierists, but they count among their numbers a considerable portion of the intellect now active in France. Victor Considérant is one of their cleverest writers. They have a newspaper, too, the *Phalange*, published formerly three times a week, now daily.[156]

As the Fourierists are now represented in England also by Mr. Doherty, I think I may have said enough concerning them, and now pass to the most important and most radical party in France, the *Communists*.

I said before, that everything claiming national importance in France must be of a political nature, or it will not succeed. Saint-Simon and Fourier did not touch politics at all, and their schemes, therefore, became not the common property of the nation, but only subjects of private discussion. We have seen how Babeuf's Communism arose out of the democracy of the first revolution. The second revolution, of 1830, gave rise to another and more powerful Communism. The "great week" of 1830[a] was accomplished by the union of the middle and working classes, the liberals and the republicans. After the work was done, the working classes were dismissed, and the fruits of the revolution were taken possession of by the middle classes only. The working men got up several insurrections, for the abolition of political monopoly, and the establishment of a republic,[157] but were always defeated; the middle class having not only the army on their side, but forming themselves the national guard besides. During this time (1834 or 1835) a new doctrine sprang up among the republican working men. They saw that even after having succeeded in their democratic plans, they would continue [to be] the dupes of their more gifted and better educated leaders, and that their social condition, the cause of their political discontent, would not be bettered by any political change whatsoever. They referred to the history of the great revolution, and eagerly seized upon Babeuf's Communism. This is all that can, with safety, be asserted concerning the origin of modern Communism in France; the subject was first discussed in the dark lanes and crowded alleys of the Parisian suburb, Saint-Antoine, and soon after in the secret assemblies of conspirators. Those who know more about its origin are very careful to keep their knowledge to themselves, in order to avoid the "strong arm of the law". However, Communism spread rapidly over Paris, Lyons, Toulouse, and the other large and

---

[a] That is, from July 27 to August 20, the peak of the July revolution.—*Ed.*

manufacturing towns of the realm; various secret associations followed each other, among which the "Travailleurs Egalitaires", or Equalitarian Working Men, and the Humanitarians,[158] were the most considerable. The Equalitarians were rather a "rough set", like the Babouvists of the great revolution; they purposed making the world a working-man's community, putting down every refinement of civilisation, science, the fine arts, etc., as useless, dangerous, and aristocratic luxuries, a prejudice necessarily arising from their total ignorance of history and political economy. The Humanitarians were known particularly for their attacks on marriage, family, and other similar institutions. Both these, as well as two or three other parties, were very short-lived, and the great bulk of the French working classes adopted, very soon, the tenets propounded by M. Cabet, "Père Cabet" (Father C.), as he is called, and which are known on the continent under the name of Icarian Communism.

This sketch of the History of Communism in France shows, in some measure, what the difference of French and English Communism must be. The origin of Social reform, in France, is a political one; it is found, that democracy cannot give real equality, and therefore the Community scheme is called to its aid. The bulk of the French Communists are, therefore, republicans besides; they want a community state of society, under a republican form of government. Now, I do not think that the English Socialists would have serious objections to this; because, though they are more favourable to an elective monarchy, I know them to be too enlightened to force their kind of government upon a people totally opposed to it. It is evident, that to try this would involve this people in far greater disorders and difficulties than would arise from their own democratic mode of government, even supposing this to be bad.

But there are other objections that could be made to the French Communists. They intend overthrowing the present government of their country by force, and have shown this by their continual policy of secret associations. This is true. Even the Icarians, though they declare in their publications that they abhor physical revolutions and secret societies, even they are associated in this manner, and would gladly seize upon any opportunity to establish a republic by force.[159] This will be objected to, I dare say, and rightly, because, at any rate, secret associations are always contrary to common prudence, inasmuch as they make the parties liable to unnecessary legal persecutions. I am not inclined to defend such a line of policy, but it has to be explained, to be accounted for; and it is fully done so by the difference of the French and English national character and government. The English constitution has now been, for about one hundred and fifty years, uninterruptedly, the law of the land; every change has been made by legal means, by constitutional forms; therefore the English must have a strong respect for their laws. But, in France, during the last fifty years, one forced alteration has followed the other; all constitutions, from radical democracy to open despotism, all kinds of laws were, after a short existence, thrown away and replaced by others; how can the people then respect their laws? And the result of all these convulsions, as now established in the French constitution and laws, is the oppression of the poor by the rich, an oppression kept up by force—how can it be expected that the oppressed should love their public institutions, that they should not resort to the old tricks of 1792? They know that, if they are anything, they are it by meeting force by force, and having, at present, no other means, why should they hesitate a moment to apply this? It will be said further: why do not the French Communists establish communities, as the English have done? My reply is, because they *dare* not. If they did, the first experiment would be put down by soldiers. And if they were suffered to do so, it would be of no use to them. I always understood the Harmony Establishment to be only an experiment, to show the possibility of Mr. Owen's plans,[160] if put into practice, to force public opinion to a more favourable idea of the Socialist schemes for relieving public distress. Well, if that be the case, such an experiment would be of no avail in France. Show the French, not that your plans are practical, because that would leave them cool and indifferent. Show them that your communities will not place mankind under an "ironbound despotism", as Mr. Bairstow the Chartist said, in his late discussion with Mr. Watts.[161] Show them that real liberty and real equality will be only possible under Community arrangements, show them that *justice* demands such arrangements, and then you will have them all on your side.

But to return to the social doctrines of the Icarian Communists. Their "holy book" is the *Voyage en Icarie* (Travels in Icaria) of Father Cabet, who, by-the-by, was formerly Attorney-General, and Member of the Chamber of Deputies. The general arrangements for their Communities are very little different to those of Mr. Owen. They have embodied in their plans everything rational they found in Saint-Simon and Fourier; and, therefore, are very much superior to the old French Communists. As to marriage, they perfectly agree with the English. Everything possible is done to secure the liberty of the individual. Punishments are to be abolished, and to be replaced by education of the young, and rational mental treatment of the old.

It is, however, curious, that whilst the English Socialists are generally opposed to Christianity, and have to suffer all the religious prejudices of a really Christian people, the French Communists, being a part of a nation celebrated for its infidelity, are themselves Christians. One of their favourite axioms is, that Christianity *is* Communism, "*le Christianisme c'est le Communisme*". This they try to prove by the bible, the state of community in which the first Christians are said to have lived, etc. But all this shows only, that these good people are not the best Christians, although they style themselves so; because if they were, they would know the bible better, and find that, if some few passages of the bible may be favourable to Communism, the general spirit of its doctrines is, nevertheless, totally opposed to it, as well as to every rational measure.

The rise of Communism has been hailed by most of the eminent minds in France; Pierre Leroux, the metaphysician; George Sand, the courageous defender of the rights of her sex; Abbé de Lamennais, author of the *Words of a Believer*,[a] and a great many others, are, more or less, inclined towards the Communist doctrines. The most important writer, however, in this line is Proudhon, a young man, who published two or three years ago his work: *What is Property? (Qu'est ce que la Propriété?)* where he gave the answer: "*La propriété c'est le vol*", Property is robbery. This is the most philosophical work, on the part of the Communists, in the French language; and, if I wish to see any French book translated into the English language, it is this. The right of private property, the consequences of this institution, competition, immorality, misery, are here developed with a power of intellect, and real scientific research, which I never since found united in a single volume. Besides this, he gives very important remarks on government, and having proved that every kind of government is alike objectionable, no matter whether it be democracy, aristocracy, or monarchy, that all govern by force; and that, in the best of all possible cases, the force of the majority oppresses the weakness of the minority, he comes, at last, to the conclusion: "*Nous voulons l'anarchie!*" What we want is anarchy; the rule of nobody, the responsibility of every one to nobody but himself.

---

[a] F. R. de Lamennais, *Paroles d'un croyant*, 1833.—*Ed.*

Upon this subject I shall have to speak more, when I come to the German Communists. I have now only to add, that the French Icarian Communists are estimated at about half a million in number, women and children not taken into account. A pretty respectable phalanx, isn't it? They have a monthly paper, the *Populaire*, edited by Father Cabet; and, besides this, P. Leroux publishes a periodical, the *Independent Review*,[a] in which the tenets of Communism are philosophically advocated.

Manchester, Oct. 23, 1843

II
GERMANY AND SWITZERLAND

[*The New Moral World* No. 21, November 18, 1843]

Germany had her Social Reformers as early as the Reformation. Soon after Luther had begun to proclaim church reform and to agitate the people against spiritual authority, the peasantry of Southern and Middle Germany rose in a general insurrection against their temporal lords. Luther always stated his object to be, to return to original christianity in doctrine and practice; the peasantry took exactly the same standing, and demanded, therefore, not only the ecclesiastical, but also the social practice of primitive christianity. They conceived a state of villainy and servitude, such as they lived under, to be inconsistent with the doctrines of the Bible; they were oppressed by a set of haughty barons and earls, robbed and treated like their cattle every day, they had no law to protect them, and if they had, they found nobody to enforce it. Such a state contrasted very much with the communities of early christians and the doctrines of Christ, as laid down in the Bible. Therefore they arose and began a war against their lords, which could only be a war of extermination. Thomas Münzer, a preacher, whom they placed at their head, issued a proclamation,[162] full, of course, of the religious and superstitious nonsense of the age, but containing also among others, principles like these: That according to the Bible, no christian is entitled to hold any property whatever exclusively for himself; that community of property is the only proper state for a society of christians; that it is not allowed to any good christian to have any authority or command over other christians, nor to hold any office of government or hereditary power, but on the contrary, that, as all men

---

[a] *La Revue indépendante.*— Ed.

are equal before God, so they ought to be on earth also. These doctrines were nothing but conclusions drawn from the Bible and from Luther's own writings; but the Reformer was not prepared to go as far as the people did; notwithstanding the courage he displayed against the spiritual authorities, he had not freed himself from the political and social prejudices of his age; he believed as firmly in the right divine of princes and landlords to trample upon the people, as he did in the Bible. Besides this, he wanted the protection of the aristocracy and the protestant princes, and thus he wrote a tract against the rioters,[a] disclaiming not only every connection with them, but also exhorting the aristocracy to put them down with the utmost severity, as rebels against the laws of God. "Kill them like dogs!" he exclaimed. The whole tract is written with such an animosity, nay, fury and fanaticism against the people, that it will ever form a blot upon Luther's character; it shows that, if he began his career as a man of the people, he was now entirely in the service of their oppressors. The insurrection, after a most bloody civil war, was suppressed, and the peasants reduced to their former servitude.

If we except some solitary instances, of which no notice was taken by the public, there has been no party of Social Reformers in Germany, since the peasants' war, up to a very recent date. The public mind during the last fifty years was too much occupied with questions of either a merely political or merely metaphysical nature—questions, which had to be answered, before the social question could be discussed with the necessary calmness and knowledge. Men, who would have been decidedly opposed to a system of community, if such had been proposed to them, were nevertheless paving the way for its introduction.

It was among the working class of Germany that Social Reform has been of late made again a topic of discussion. Germany having comparatively little manufacturing industry, the mass of the working classes is made up by handicraftsmen, who previous to their establishing themselves as little masters, travel for some years over Germany, Switzerland, and very often over France also. A great number of German workmen is thus continually going to and from Paris, and must of course there become acquainted with the political and social movements of the French working classes. One of these men, William Weitling, a native of Magdeburg in

---

[a] This is a reference to Luther's *Wyder die mördische unnd reubischenn Rottenn der Paurenn.—Ed.*

Prussia, and a simple journeyman-tailor, resolved to establish communities in his own country.

This man, who is to be considered as the founder of German Communism, after a few years' stay in Paris, went to Switzerland, and, whilst he was working in some tailor's shop in Geneva, preached his new gospel to his fellow-workmen. He formed Communist Associations in all the towns and cities on the Swiss side of the lake of Geneva, most of the Germans who worked there becoming favourable to his views. Having thus prepared the public mind, he issued a periodical, the *Young Generation*,[a] for a more extensive agitation of the country. This paper, although written for working men only, and by a working man, has from its beginning been superior to most of the French Communist publications, even to Father Cabet's *Populaire*. It shows that its editor must have worked very hard to obtain that knowledge of history and politics which a public writer cannot do without, and which a neglected education had left him deprived of. It shows, at the same time, that Weitling was always struggling to unite his various ideas and thoughts on society into a complete system of Communism. The *Young Generation* was first published in 1841; in the following year, Weitling published a work: *Guarantees of Harmony and Liberty*,[b] in which he gave a review of the old social system and the outlines of a new one. I shall, perhaps, some time give a few extracts from this book.

Having thus established the nucleus of a Communist party in Geneva and its neighbourhood, he went to Zurich, where, as in other towns of Northern Switzerland, some of his friends had already commenced to operate upon the minds of the working men. He now began to organise his party in these towns. Under the name of Singing Clubs, associations were formed for the discussion of Social reorganisation. At the same time Weitling advertised his intention to publish a book,— *The Gospel of the Poor Sinners*.[163] But here the police interfered with his proceedings.

In June last, Weitling was taken into custody, his papers and his book were seized, before it left the press. The Executive of the Republic appointed a committee to investigate the matter, and to report to the Grand Council, the representatives of the people. This report has been printed a few months since.[c] It appears from it, that

---

[a] *Die junge Generation.—Ed.*
[b] Wilhelm Weitling, *Garantien der Harmonie und Freiheit.—Ed.*
[c] [J. C. Bluntschli,] *Die Kommunisten in der Schweiz nach den bei Weitling vorgefundenen Papieren.—Ed.*

a great many Communist associations existed in every part of Switzerland, consisting mostly of German working men; that Weitling was considered as the leader of the party, and received from time to time reports of progress; that he was in correspondence with similar associations of Germans in Paris and London, and that all these societies, being composed of men who very often changed their residence, were so many seminaries of these "dangerous and Utopian doctrines", sending out their elder members to Germany, Hungary, and Italy, and imbuing with their spirit every workman who came within their reach. The report was drawn up by Dr. Bluntschli, a man of aristocratic and fanatically christian opinions, and the whole of it therefore is written more like a party denunciation, than like a calm, official report. Communism is denounced as a doctrine dangerous in the extreme, subversive of all existing order, and destroying all the sacred bonds of society. The pious doctor, besides, is at a loss for words sufficiently strong to express his feelings as to the frivolous blasphemy with which these infamous and ignorant people try to justify their wicked and revolutionary doctrines, by passages from the Holy Scriptures. Weitling and his party are, in this respect, just like the Icarians in France, and contend that christianity is Communism.

The result of Weitling's trial did very little to satisfy the anticipations of the Zurich government. Although Weitling and his friends were sometimes very incautious in their expressions, yet the charge of high treason and conspiracy against him could not be maintained; the criminal court sentenced him to six months' imprisonment, and eternal banishment from Switzerland; the members of the Zurich associations were expelled the Canton; the report was communicated to the governments of the other Cantons and to the foreign embassies, but the Communists in other parts of Switzerland were very little interfered with. The prosecution came too late, and was too little assisted by the other Cantons; it did nothing at all for the destruction of Communism, and was even favourable to it, by the great interest it produced in all countries of the German tongue. Communism was almost unknown in Germany, but became by this an object of general attention.

Besides this party there exists another in Germany, which advocates Communism. The former, being thoroughly a popular party, will no doubt very soon unite all the working classes of Germany; that party which I now refer to is a philosophical one, unconnected in its origin with either French or English Communists, and arising from that philosophy which, since the last fifty years, Germany has been so proud of.

The political revolution of France was accompanied by a philosophical revolution in Germany. Kant began it by overthrowing the old system of Leibnitzian metaphysics, which at the end of last century was introduced in all Universities of the Continent. Fichte and Schelling commenced rebuilding, and Hegel completed the new system. There has never been, ever since man began to think, a system of philosophy as comprehensive as that of Hegel. Logic, metaphysics, natural philosophy, the philosophy of mind, the philosophy of law, of religion, of history, all are united in one system, reduced to one fundamental principle. The system appeared quite unassailable from without, and so it was; it has been overthrown from *within* only, by those who were Hegelians themselves. I cannot, of course, give here a complete development either of the system or of its history, and therefore must restrain myself to the following remarks. The progress of German philosophy from Kant to Hegel was so consistent, so logical, so necessary, if I may say so, that no other systems besides those I have named could subsist. There are two or three of them, but they found no attention; they were so neglected, that nobody would even do them the honour to overthrow them. Hegel, notwithstanding his enormous learning and his deep thought, was so much occupied with abstract questions, that he neglected to free himself from the prejudices of his age—an age of restoration for old systems of government and religion. But his disciples had very different views on these subjects. Hegel died in 1831, and as early as 1835 appeared Strauss' *Life of Jesus*, the first work showing some progress beyond the limits of orthodox Hegelianism. Others followed; and in 1837 the Christians rose against what they called the New Hegelians, denouncing them as Atheists, and calling for the interference of the state. The state, however, did not interfere, and the controversy went on. At that time, the New, or Young Hegelians, were so little conscious of the consequences of their own reasoning, that they all denied the charge of Atheism, and called themselves Christians and Protestants, although they denied the existence of a God who was not man, and declared the history of the gospels to be a pure mythology. It was not until last year, in a pamphlet,[a] by the writer of these lines, that the charge of Atheism was allowed to be just. But the development went

---

[a] Frederick Engels, *Schelling and Revelation* (see this edition, Vol. 2).—*Ed.*

on. The Young Hegelians of 1842 were declared Atheists and Republicans; the periodical of the party, the *German Annals*,[a] was more radical and open than ever before; a political paper[b] was established, and very soon the whole of the German liberal press was entirely in our hands. We had friends in almost every considerable town of Germany; we provided all the liberal papers with the necessary matter, and by this means made them our organs; we inundated the country with pamphlets, and soon governed public opinion upon every question. A temporary relaxation of the censorship of the press added a great deal to the energy of this movement, quite novel to a considerable part of the German public. Papers, published under the authorisation of a government censor, contained things which, even in France, would have been punished as high treason, and other things which could not have been pronounced in England, without a trial for blasphemy being the consequence of it. The movement was so sudden, so rapid, so energetically pursued, that the government as well as the public were dragged along with it for some time. But this violent character of the agitation proved that it was not founded upon a strong party among the public, and that its power was produced by the surprise and consternation only of its opponents. The governments, recovering their senses, put a stop to it by a most despotic oppression of the liberty of speech. Pamphlets, newspapers, periodicals, scientific works were suppressed by dozens, and the agitated state of the country soon subsided. It is a matter of course that such a tyrannical interference will not check the progress of public opinion, nor quench the principles defended by the agitators; the entire persecution has been of no use whatever to the ruling powers; because, if *they* had not put down the movement, it would have been checked by the apathy of the public at large, a public as little prepared for radical changes as that of every other country; and, if even this had not been the case, the republican agitation would have been abandoned by the agitators themselves, who now, by developing farther and farther the consequences of their philosophy, became Communists. The princes and rulers of Germany, at the very moment when they believed to have put down for ever republicanism, saw the rise of Communism from the ashes of political agitation; and this new doctrine appears to them even more dangerous and formidable than that in whose apparent destruction they rejoiced.

---

[a] *Deutsche Jahrbücher für Wissenschaft und Kunst*.—*Ed*.
[b] *Rheinische Zeitung für Politik, Handel und Gewerbe*.—*Ed*.

As early as autumn, 1842, some of the party contended for the insufficiency of political change, and declared their opinion to be, that a *Social* revolution based upon common property, was the only state of mankind agreeing with their abstract principles. But even the leaders of the party, such as Dr. Bruno Bauer, Dr. Feuerbach, and Dr. Ruge, were not then prepared for this decided step. The political paper of the party, the *Rhenish Gazette*,[a] published some papers advocating Communism, but without the wished-for effect. Communism, however, was such a *necessary* consequence of New Hegelian philosophy, that no opposition could keep it down, and, in the course of this present year, the originators of it had the satisfaction of seeing one republican after the other join their ranks. Besides Dr. Hess, one of the editors of the now suppressed *Rhenish Gazette*, and who was, in fact, the first Communist of the party, there are now a great many others; as Dr. Ruge, editor of the *German Annals*, the scientific periodical of the Young Hegelians, which has been suppressed by resolution of the German Diet[164]; Dr. Marx, another of the editors of the *Rhenish Gazette*; George Herwegh, the poet whose letter to the King of Prussia was translated, last winter, by most of the English papers,[165] and others: and we hope that the remainder of the republican party will, by-and-by, come over too.

Thus, philosophical Communism may be considered for ever established in Germany, notwithstanding the efforts of the governments to keep it down. They have annihilated the press in their dominions, but to no effect; the progress parties profit by the free press of Switzerland and France, and their publications are as extensively circulated in Germany, as if they were printed in that country itself. All persecutions and prohibitions have proved ineffectual, and will ever do so; the Germans are a philosophical nation, and will not, cannot abandon Communism, as soon as it is founded upon sound philosophical principles: chiefly if it is derived as an unavoidable conclusion from their *own* philosophy. And this is the part we have to perform now. Our party has to prove that either all the philosophical efforts of the German nation, from Kant to Hegel, have been useless—worse than useless; or, that they must end in Communism; that the Germans must either reject their great philosophers, whose names they hold up as the glory of their nation, or that they must adopt Communism. And this *will* be proved; this dilemma the Germans *will* be forced into, and there can scarcely be any doubt as to which side of the question the people will adopt.

---

[a] *Rheinische Zeitung.—Ed.*

There is a greater chance in Germany for the establishment of a Communist party among the educated classes of society, than anywhere else. The Germans are a very disinterested nation; if in Germany principle comes into collision with interest, principle will almost always silence the claims of interest. The same love of abstract principle, the same disregard of reality and self-interest, which have brought the Germans to a state of political nonentity, these very same qualities guarantee the success of philosophical Communism in that country. It will appear very singular to Englishmen, that a party which aims at the destruction of private property is chiefly made up by those who have property; and yet this is the case in Germany. We can recruit our ranks from those classes only which have enjoyed a pretty good education; that is, from the universities and from the commercial class; and in either we have not hitherto met with any considerable difficulty.

As to the particular doctrines of our party, we agree much more with the English Socialists than with any other party. Their system, like ours, is founded upon philosophical principle; they struggle, as we do, against religious prejudices whilst the French reject philosophy and perpetuate religion by dragging it over with themselves into the projected new state of society. The French Communists could assist us in the first stages only of our development, and we soon found that we knew more than our teachers; but we shall have to learn a great deal yet from the English Socialists. Although our fundamental principles give us a broader base, inasmuch as we received them from a system of philosophy embracing every part of human knowledge; yet in everything bearing upon practice, upon the *facts* of the present state of society, we find that the English Socialists are a long way before us, and have left very little to be done. I may say, besides, that I have met with English Socialists with whom I agree upon almost every question.

I cannot now give an exposition of this Communist system without adding too much to the length of this paper; but I intend to do so some time soon, if the Editor of the *New Moral World*[a] will allow me the space for it.[166] I therefore conclude by stating that, notwithstanding the persecutions of the German governments (I understand that, in Berlin, Mr. Edgar Bauer is being prosecuted for a Communist publication[167]; and in Stuttgart another gentleman has

---

[a] G. A. Fleming.—*Ed.*

been committed for the novel crime of "Communist correspondence"!), notwithstanding this, I say, every necessary step is taken to bring about a successful agitation for Social Reform, to establish a new periodical, and to secure the circulation of all publications advocating Communism.

Written on October 23 and at the beginning of November 1843

Printed according to the newspaper

First published in *The New Moral World*, Third Series, Nos. 19 and 21, November 4 and 18, 1843

Signed: *F. Engels*

PROGRESS OF COMMUNISM IN GERMANY. PERSECUTION OF THE COMMUNISTS IN SWITZERLAND [168]

Frankfort, November 26. The associations of the working classes for the purpose of introducing practically the ideas of socialism, or rather communism, by means of revolutionary reform, become daily more frequent and more dangerous. The governments are daily issuing decrees against the wandering customs of artisans and apprentices; they especially prohibited their visiting Switzerland, which is considered as the home of these revolutionary ideas. Several apostles of socialism have been arrested.[a]

* * *

The *Basle Gazette* of the 29th states the Supreme Tribunal of Zurich has passed judgment on the appeal of M. Weitling, who was found guilty in the first instance of disaffection, and sentenced to several months' imprisonment[b] and five years' banishment; first, for having excited the people to revolt; and, secondly, for having entered into secret associations[169] notwithstanding the laws of the country concerning refugees. He was acquitted of the charges brought against him of bringing religion into contempt.

First published in *The Northern Star* No. 317, December 9, 1843 and in *The New Moral World*, December 16, 1843

Printed according to the newspaper *The Northern Star*

---

[a] In *The New Moral World* the following paragraph was added: "Several apostles of Socialism have been arrested; but a better means than those of compulsion has been thought of; it consists in the organisation of a great association for the purpose of bestowing sound instruction to the working classes by propagating useful lectures among them. A reading company (*Leseverein*) has been established here in Frankfort, and several hundreds of the working classes are already enrolled in it."

[b] See this volume, p. 403.—*Ed.*

THE *TIMES* ON GERMAN COMMUNISM

To the Editor of the New Moral World

Sir.—Seeing the paper from the *Times* on the Communists in Germany, republished in *The New Moral World*,[170] I thought it better not to let it pass without some commentatory remarks, which you perhaps will find worth inserting.

The *Times* hitherto enjoyed on the continent the reputation of a well-informed newspaper, but a few more articles like that on German Communism must very soon destroy that opinion. Every one who has the slightest knowledge of the social movements in France and Germany, must at once perceive that the author of the paper alluded to speaks of a subject of which he is thoroughly ignorant. He knows not even so much about it as would enable him to expose the weaker parts of the party he attacks. If he wanted to decry Weitling, he could have found in his writings passages much more fitted for his purpose than those he translates. If he only would have given himself the trouble to read the report of the Zurich committee,[a] which he professes to have read, but evidently has not, he would have found plenty of matter for slander, lots of garbled passages collected expressly for the purpose. It is very curious, after all, that the Communists themselves must furnish their opponents with arms for the combat; but, standing upon the broad base of philosophical argument, they can afford to do so.

The correspondent of the *Times* begins by describing the Communist party as very weak in France, and doubts whether the insurrection of 1839, in Paris,[171] was got up by them, or, which he

---

[a] [J. C. Bluntschli,] *Die Kommunisten in der Schweiz nach den bei Weitling vorgefundenen Papieren* (see also this volume, pp. 402-03).—*Ed.*

thinks very likely, by the "powerful" republican party. My well-informed informer of the English public, do you consider a party very weak which numbers about half a million of adult males? Do you know that the "powerful" republican party in France is, and has been these last nine years, in a state of utter dissolution and increasing decay? Do you know that the *National* newspaper, the organ of this "powerful" party, has a more limited circulation than any other Paris paper? Must I, a foreigner, remind you of the republican subscription for the Irish repeal fund, got up by the *National* last summer, and amounting to less than one hundred pounds, although the republicans affected considerable sympathy for the Irish repealers?[172] Do you not know that the mass of the republican party, the working classes, have seceded from their richer partisans long since, and not joined, no, *established* the Communist party, long before Cabet commenced to advocate Communism? Do you not know that all the "power" of the French republicans consists in the reliance they have in the Communists, who wish to see a republic established before they begin putting Communism into practice? It seems you are ignorant of all these things, and yet you ought to know them, in order to form a correct opinion of continental Socialism.

As to the insurrection of 1839, I do not consider such things creditable to any party; but I have it from parties actively engaged in this *émeute*, that it was plotted and executed by the Communists.[173]

The well-informed correspondent goes on to state that

"Fourier's and Cabet's doctrines seemed more to occupy the minds of some literary and scientific characters, than to gain general favour with the people".

Of Fourier this is true, as I had occasion to show in a former number of this paper[a]; but Cabet! Cabet, the author of almost nothing but small pamphlets,—Cabet, who is always called Father Cabet, a name not likely to be given by "literary and scientific characters",—Cabet, whose greatest fault is superficiality and want of regard for the just claims of scientific research,—Cabet, the editor of a paper[b] calculated for the information of those who are able to *read* only—that this man's doctrines should occupy the mind of a professor of the Parisian university, like Michelet, or Quinet, whose boast is a deepness deeper than mysticism? It is too ludicrous.

---

[a] See this volume, pp. 394-96.—*Ed.*
[b] *Le Populaire de 1841.*—*Ed.*

The correspondent then speaks of the celebrated German nocturnal meeting at Hambach and Steinholzli,[174] and expresses his opinion

"that this bore rather a political than a social revolutionary character".

I hardly know where to begin in exposing the blunders of this sentence. Firstly, "nocturnal meetings" are quite unknown on the continent: we have no torch-light Chartists' or nocturnal Rebeccaite assemblages.[175] The Hambach meeting was held in open day, under the eyes of the authorities. Secondly, Hambach is a place in Bavaria, and Steinholzli in Switzerland, some hundred miles from Hambach; yet our correspondent speaks of the "Hambach *and* Steinholzli meeting". Thirdly, these two meetings were separated by a considerable extent, not only of space, but of time also. The Steinholzli meeting took place several years after the other. Fourthly, these meetings not only *seemed*, but in reality did bear a merely political character; they were held before the Communists appeared in the field.

The sources from which our correspondent got his invaluable information, were "the report of the (Zurich) Commission, the published and unpublished Communist writings discovered at the arrest of Weitling, and personal inquiry". Now it is evident, from the ignorance of our correspondent, that he never read the report; it is evident that "*published* communistical writings" could not be *"discovered"* at the arrest of anybody, as the very fact of their "publication" destroys every possibility of a "discovery". The attorney-general of Zurich certainly would not boast of the "discovery" of books which every bookseller could have furnished him with! As to the "unpublished" writings, for the suppression of which the prosecution was commenced, the Zurich senators would have been inconsistent indeed, had they, as our correspondent appears to believe, afterwards published them themselves! They did no such thing. In fact, in all the report of our correspondent, there is nothing produced, which he could have procured from this source and from that of personal inquiry, if it be not the two novel facts, that the German Communists got their doctrine chiefly from Cabet and Fourier, whom they attack; as our correspondent could have read in the same book from which he so extensively quotes (Weitling's *Guarantees*,[a] p. 228); and that "they consider as their four evangelists, Cabet, Proudhon, Weitling, and—and—Constant"! Benjamin Constant, the friend of Madame de Staël, died long ago, and never thought of anything connected with

---

[a] Wilhelm Weitling, *Garantien der Harmonie und Freiheit.—Ed.*

social reform. Evidently our correspondent means Considérant, the Fourierist, editor of the *Phalange*, now the *Démocratie Pacifique*, who is not at all connected with the Communists.

"The Communist doctrine is at present more negative than positive" and immediately after this assertion is given, our correspondent cuts its throat by laying down, in twelve paragraphs, an outline of Weitling's proposed arrangements for a new social state, which arrangements are altogether positive, and do not even mention the destruction of the present social system.

These extracts, however, are given in a very confused manner, showing that our correspondent did in several cases fail to hit upon the vital point of the question, and gave in its stead some rather insignificant details. Thus he omits to state the chief point in which Weitling is superior to Cabet, namely, the abolition of all government by force and by majority, and the establishment in its stead of a mere administration, organising the different branches of labour, and distributing its produce; he omits the proposal to nominate all officers of this administration, and in every particular Branch, not by a majority of the community at large, but by those only who have a knowledge of the particular kind of work the future officer has to perform; and, one of the most important features of the plan, that the nominators are to select the fittest person, by means of some kind of prize essays, without knowing the author of any of these essays; the names to be sealed up, and that paper only to be opened which contains the name of the successful competitor; obviating by this all personal motives which could bias the minds of the electors.

As to the remainder of the extracts from Weitling, I leave it to the readers of this periodical to judge, whether they contain such contemptible stuff as our correspondent thinks them to be; or whether they do not advocate in most, if not in all cases, the same principles and proposals, for the propagation of which this paper was established. At any rate, if the *Times* should wish to comment again on German Communism, it would do well to provide another correspondent.

I am, Sir, yours truly,
F. Engels

Written on January 13, 1844
First published in *The New Moral World*, Third Series, No. 30, January 20, 1844

Printed according to the newspaper

FRENCH COMMUNISM

To the Editor of the New Moral World

Manchester, January 28, 1844

DEAR SIR,—In my letter to you in the *New Moral World* of the 13th instant I committed an error. I considered the correspondent of the *Times* wrong in naming a M. Constant as a Communist[a]; but since I wrote, I have received some French Communist publications, in which an Abbé Constant is named as a partisan of the Community System. At the same time, Mr. Goodwyn Barmby had the kindness to give me some further information about the Abbé Constant, who, he says, has been imprisoned for his principles, and is the author of several Communist works. His creed is thus expressed in his own words: I am a christian and I take christianity to be community only.

Requesting you, therefore, to correct the above error in your next number,

I am, dear Sir, yours respectfully,

F. Engels

Written on January 28, 1844

First published in *The New Moral World*, Third Series, No. 32, February 3, 1844

Printed according to the newspaper

---

[a] See this volume, pp. 412-13.—*Ed.*

CONTINENTAL MOVEMENTS

The well-known novel of Eugène Sue, *The Mysteries of Paris*, has made a deep impression upon the public mind, especially in Germany; the forcible manner in which this book depicts the misery and demoralisation falling to the share of the "lower orders" in great cities, could not fail to direct public attention to the state of the poor in general. The Germans begin to discover, as the *Allgemeine Zeitung*, the *Times* of Germany, says, that the style of novel writing has undergone a complete revolution during these last ten years; that instead of kings and princes, who formerly were the heroes of similar tales, it is now the poor, the despised class, whose fates and fortunes, joys and sufferings, are made the topic of romance; they are finding out at last that this new class of novel writers, such as G. Sand, E. Sue, and Boz,[a] is indeed a sign of the times. The good Germans always thought, that misery and destitution existed in Paris and Lyons, London and Manchester only, and that Germany was entirely free from such excrescences of over-civilisation and of excessive manufacturing industry. Now, however, they begin to see that they also may muster a considerable amount of social disease; the Berlin papers confess, that the "Voigtland" of that town is not inferior in this respect to St. Giles'[176] or any other abode of the pariahs of civilisation; they confess, that, although trades' unions and strikes have hitherto been unknown in Germany, yet help is much needed, in order to avoid the occurrence of similar things among their own countrymen. Dr. Mundt, a lecturer at the Berlin university, has commenced a course of public lectures on the different systems of Social Re-organisation; and although he is not

---

[a] Charles Dickens.—*Ed.*

the man to form a correct and impartial judgment upon such things, yet these lectures must do a great deal of good. It may easily be conceived, how favourable this moment is for the commencement of a more extensive social agitation in Germany, and what will be the effect of a new periodical advocating a thorough social reform. Such a periodical has been established in Paris under the title of *German and French Annals*[a]; its editors, Dr. Ruge and Dr. Marx, as well as its other contributors, belong to the "learned Communists" of Germany, and are supported by the most distinguished Socialist authors of France. The periodical, which is to be published in monthly numbers, and to contain French as well as German articles, could not, indeed, commence at a more favourable moment, and its success may be considered as certain, even before the first number is issued.[177]

F. E.

Written late in January 1844

First published in *The New Moral World*, Third Series, No. 32, February 3, 1844

Printed according to the newspaper

---

[a] *Deutsch-Französische Jahrbücher*.—*Ed.*

THE PRESS AND THE GERMAN DESPOTS

Our readers are aware of the rapid progress in Germany of Republican and Communist principles, which progress has of late excited unusual terror amongst the crowned brigands and their advisers of that great confederation of nations.[a] Additional measures of repression are, therefore, being called into operation to check the growth of these "dangerous doctrines", particularly in Prussia. It appears that in the year 1834, a secret Conference of Plenipotentiaries was held at Vienna, when a Protocol was agreed to, but which has only recently been published, imposing most absolute restrictions upon the press, and proclaiming and enforcing the "right divine" of Princes over all legislative and other popular bodies whatsoever. As a specimen of the "Holy Alliance" principle of this atrocious Protocol, we may state that the eighteenth article provides that

"Princes who are menaced on the part of their states by any infringement of the orders laid down by the decree of the Diet of 1832, are to dissolve these states, and to obtain military aid in support from the rest of the confederation." [178]

We may add, as a proof of how the fairness and freedom of the press is understood in Prussia, that strict orders have been given to the censors at Cologne, Münster, and other Catholic towns, not to permit the republication of any parts of the Irish trials now in progress.[179] One German journal wished to send a reporter or correspondent to Dublin; but there was no hope of being allowed to publish even his letter. No matter, liberty shall yet be triumphant, despite their dungeons and bayonets.

Written at the end of January and the beginning of February 1844

First published in *The Northern Star* No. 325, February 3, 1844

Printed according to the newspaper

---

[a] i.e., the German Confederation.—*Ed.*

OUTLINES OF A CRITIQUE
OF POLITICAL ECONOMY[180]

Political economy came into being as a natural result of the expansion of trade, and with its appearance elementary, unscientific huckstering was replaced by a developed system of licensed fraud, an entire science of enrichment.

This political economy or science of enrichment born of the merchants' mutual envy and greed, bears on its brow the mark of the most detestable selfishness. People still lived in the naive belief that gold and silver were wealth, and therefore considered nothing more urgent than the prohibition everywhere of the export of the "precious" metals. The nations faced each other like misers, each clasping to himself with both arms his precious money-bag, eyeing his neighbours with envy and distrust. Every conceivable means was employed to lure from the nations with whom one had commerce as much ready cash as possible, and to retain snugly within the customs-boundary all which had happily been gathered in.

If this principle had been rigorously carried through trade would have been killed. People therefore began to go beyond this first stage. They came to appreciate that capital locked up in a chest was dead capital, while capital in circulation increased continuously. They then became more sociable, sent off their ducats as call-birds to bring others back with them, and realised that there is no harm in paying A too much for his commodity so long as it can be disposed of to B at a higher price.

On this basis the *mercantile system* was built. The avaricious character of trade was to some extent already beginning to be hidden. The nations drew slightly nearer to one another, concluded trade and friendship agreements, did business with one another and, for the sake of larger profits, treated one another with all possible love and kindness. But in fact there was still the old avarice and selfishness and from time to time this erupted in wars, which in that day were all based on trade jealousy. In these wars it also became evident that trade, like robbery, is based on the law of the strong hand. No scruples whatever were felt about exacting by cunning or violence such treaties as were held to be the most advantageous.

The cardinal point in the whole mercantile system is the theory of the balance of trade. For as it still subscribed to the dictum that gold and silver constitute wealth, only such transactions as would finally bring ready cash into the country were considered profitable. To ascertain this, exports were compared with imports. When more had been exported than imported, it was believed that the difference had come into the country in ready cash, and that the country was richer by that difference. The art of the economists, therefore, consisted in ensuring that at the end of each year exports should show a favourable balance over imports; and for the sake of this ridiculous illusion thousands of men have been slaughtered! Trade, too, has had its crusades and inquisitions.

The eighteenth century, the century of revolution, also revolutionised economics. But just as all the revolutions of this century were one-sided and bogged down in antitheses — just as abstract materialism was set in opposition to abstract spiritualism, the republic to monarchy, the social contract to divine right — likewise the economic revolution did not get beyond antithesis. The premises remained everywhere in force: materialism did not attack the Christian contempt for and humiliation of Man, and merely posited Nature instead of the Christian God as the Absolute confronting Man. In politics no one dreamt of examining the premises of the state as such. It did not occur to economics to question the *validity of private property*. Therefore, the new economics was only half an advance. It was obliged to betray and to disavow its own premises, to have recourse to sophistry and hypocrisy so as to cover up the contradictions in which it became entangled, so as to reach the conclusions to which it was driven not by its premises but by the humane spirit of the century. Thus economics took on a philanthropic character. It withdrew its favour from the producers and bestowed it on the consumers. It affected a solemn abhorrence of the bloody terror of the mercantile system, and proclaimed trade to be a bond of friendship and union among nations as among individuals. All was pure splendour and magnificence — yet the premises reasserted themselves soon enough, and in contrast to this sham philanthropy produced the Malthusian population theory—the crudest, most barbarous theory that ever existed, a system of despair which struck down all those beautiful phrases about philanthropy and world citizenship. The premises begot and reared the factory system and modern slavery, which yields nothing in inhumanity and cruelty to ancient slavery. Modern economics—the system of free trade based on Adam Smith's *Wealth of Nations*—reveals itself to be that same hypocrisy, inconsistency and immorality which now confront free humanity in every sphere.

But was Smith's system, then, not an advance? Of course it was, and a necessary advance at that. It was necessary to overthrow the mercantile system with its monopolies and hindrances to trade, so that the true consequences of private property could come to light. It was necessary for all these petty, local and national considerations to recede into the background, so that the struggle of our time could become a universal human struggle. It was necessary for the theory of private property to leave the purely empirical path of merely objective inquiry and to acquire a more scientific character which would also make it responsible for the consequences, and thus transfer the matter to a universally human sphere. It was necessary to carry the immorality contained in the old economics to its highest pitch, by attempting to deny it and by the hypocrisy introduced (a necessary result of that attempt). All this lay in the nature of the case. We gladly concede that it is only the justification and accomplishment of free trade that has enabled us to go beyond the economics of private property; but we must at the same time have the right to expose the utter theoretical and practical nullity of this free trade.

The nearer to our time the economists whom we have to judge, the more severe must our judgment become. For while Smith and Malthus found only scattered fragments, the modern economists had the whole system complete before them: the consequences had all been drawn; the contradictions came clearly enough to light; yet they did not come to examining the premises, and still accepted the responsibility for the whole system. The nearer the economists come to the present time, the further they depart from honesty. With every advance of time, sophistry necessarily increases, so as to prevent economics from lagging behind the times. This is why *Ricardo*, for instance, is more guilty than *Adam Smith*, and *McCulloch* and *Mill* more guilty than *Ricardo*.

Even the mercantile system cannot be correctly judged by modern economics since the latter is itself one-sided and as yet burdened with that very system's premises. Only that view which rises above the opposition of the two systems, which criticises the premises common to both and proceeds from a purely human, universal basis, can assign to both their proper position. It will become evident that the protagonists of free trade are more inveterate monopolists than the old mercantilists themselves. It will become evident that the sham humanity of the modern economists hides a barbarism of which their predecessors knew nothing; that the older economists' conceptual confusion is simple and consistent compared with the double-tongued logic of their attackers, and that neither of the two factions can reproach the other with anything which would not recoil upon themselves.

This is why modern liberal economics cannot comprehend the restoration of the mercantile system by List, whilst for us the matter is quite simple. The inconsistency and ambiguity of liberal economics must of necessity dissolve again into its basic components. Just as theology must either regress to blind faith or progress towards free philosophy, free trade must produce the restoration of monopolies on the one hand and the abolition of private property on the other.

The only *positive* advance which liberal economics has made is the elaboration of the laws of private property. These are contained in it, at any rate, although not yet fully elaborated and clearly expressed. It follows that on all points where it is a question of deciding which is the shortest road to wealth—i. e., in all strictly economic controversies—the protagonists of free trade have right on their side. That is, needless to say, in controversies with the monopolists—not with the opponents of private property, for the English Socialists have long since proved both practically and theoretically that the latter are in a position to settle economic questions more correctly even from an economic point of view.

In the critique of political economy, therefore, we shall examine the basic categories, uncover the contradiction introduced by the free-trade system, and bring out the consequences of both sides of the contradiction.

———

The term national wealth has only arisen as a result of the liberal economists' passion for generalisation. As long as private property exists, this term has no meaning. The "national wealth" of the English is very great and yet they are the poorest people under the sun. One must either discard this term completely, or accept such premises as give it meaning. Similarly with the terms national economy and political or public economy. In the present circumstances that science ought to be called *private* economy, for its public connections exist only for the sake of private property.

The immediate consequence of private property is *trade*—exchange of reciprocal requirements—buying and selling. This trade, like every activity, must under the dominion of private property become a direct source of gain for the trader; i. e., each must seek to sell as dear as possible and buy as cheap as possible. In every purchase and sale, therefore, two men with diametrically opposed interests confront each other. The confrontation is decidedly antagonistic, for each knows the intentions of the other—knows that they are opposed to his own. Therefore, the first consequence is mutual mistrust, on the one hand, and the justification of this mistrust—the application of immoral means to attain an immoral end—on the other. Thus, the first maxim in trade is secretiveness—the concealment of everything which might reduce the value of the article in question. The result is that in trade it is permitted to take the utmost advantage of the ignorance, the trust, of the opposing party, and likewise to impute qualities to one's commodity which it does not possess. In a word, trade is legalised fraud. Any merchant who wants to give truth its due can bear me witness that actual practice conforms with this theory.

The mercantile system still had a certain artless Catholic candour and did not in the least conceal the immoral nature of trade. We have seen how it openly paraded its mean avarice. The mutually hostile attitude of the nations in the eighteenth century, loathsome envy and trade jealousy, were the logical consequences of trade as such. Public opinion had not yet become humanised. Why, therefore, conceal things which resulted from the inhuman, hostile nature of trade itself?

But when the *economic Luther*,[a] Adam Smith, criticised past economics things had changed considerably. The century had been humanised; reason had asserted itself; morality began to claim its eternal right. The extorted trade treaties, the commercial wars, the strict isolation of the nations, offended too greatly against advanced consciousness. Protestant hypocrisy took the place of Catholic candour. Smith proved that humanity, too, was

---

[a] Cf. Karl Marx, *Economic and Philosophic Manuscripts of 1844*, p. 290 of this volume.—*Ed.*

rooted in the nature of commerce; that commerce must become "among nations, as among individuals, a bond of union and friendship" instead of being "the most fertile source of discord and animosity" (cf. *Wealth of Nations*, Bk. 4, Ch. 3, § 2); that after all it lay in the nature of things for trade, taken overall, to be advantageous to *all* parties concerned.

Smith was right to eulogise trade as humane. There is nothing absolutely immoral in the world. Trade, too, has an aspect wherein it pays homage to morality and humanity. But what homage! The law of the strong hand, the open highway robbery of the Middle Ages, became humanised when it passed over into trade; and trade became humanised when its first stage characterised by the prohibition of the export of money passed over into the mercantile system. Then the mercantile system itself was humanised. Naturally, it is in the interest of the trader to be on good terms with the one from whom he buys cheap as well as with the other to whom he sells dear. A nation therefore acts very imprudently if it fosters feelings of animosity in its suppliers and customers. The more friendly, the more advantageous. Such is the humanity of trade. And this hypocritical way of misusing morality for immoral purposes is the pride of the free-trade system. "Have we not overthrown the barbarism of the monopolies?" exclaim the hypocrites. "Have we not carried civilisation to distant parts of the world? Have we not brought about the fraternisation of the peoples, and reduced the number of wars?" Yes, all this you have done—but *how*! You have destroyed the small monopolies so that the *one* great basic monopoly, property, may function the more freely and unrestrictedly. You have civilised the ends of the earth to win new terrain for the deployment of your vile avarice. You have brought about the fraternisation of the peoples—but the fraternity is the fraternity of thieves. You have reduced the number of wars—to earn all the bigger profits in peace, to intensify to the utmost the enmity between individuals, the ignominious war of competition! When have you done anything out of pure humanity, from consciousness of the futility of the opposition between the general and the individual interest? When have you been moral without being interested, without harbouring at the back of your mind immoral, egoistical motives?

By dissolving nationalities, the liberal economic system had done its best to universalise enmity, to transform mankind into a horde of ravenous beasts (for what else are competitors?) who devour one another just *because* each has identical interests with all the others—after this preparatory work there remained but one step to take before the goal was reached, the dissolution of the family. To accomplish this, economy's own beautiful invention, the factory system, came to its aid. The last vestige of common interests, the community of goods in the possession of the family, has been undermined by the factory system and—at least here in England—is already in the process of dissolution. It is a common practice for children, as soon as they are capable of work (i. e., as soon as they reach the age of nine), to spend their wages themselves, to look upon their parental home as a mere boarding-house, and hand over to their parents a fixed amount for food and lodging. How can it be otherwise? What else can result from the separation of interests, such as forms the basis of the free-trade system? Once a principle is set in motion, it works by its own impetus through all its consequences, whether the economists like it or not.

But the economist does not know himself what cause he serves. He does not know that with all his egoistical reasoning he nevertheless forms but a link in the chain of mankind's universal progress. He does not know that by his dissolution of all sectional interests he merely paves the way for the great transformation to which the century is moving—the reconciliation of mankind with nature and with itself.

The next category established by trade is *value*. There is no dispute between the old and the modern economists over this category, just as there is none over all the others, since the monopolists in their obsessive mania for getting rich had no time left to concern themselves with categories. All controversies over such points stem from the modern economists.

The economist who lives by antitheses has also of course a *double value*—abstract or real value and exchange-value. There was a protracted quarrel over the nature of real value between the English, who defined the costs of production as the expression of real value, and the Frenchman Say, who claimed to measure this value by the utility of an object. The quarrel hung in doubt from the beginning of the century, then became dormant without a decision having been reached. The economists cannot decide anything.

The English—McCulloch and Ricardo in particular—thus assert that the abstract value of a thing is determined by the costs of production. *Nota bene* the abstract value, not the exchange-value, the *exchangeable value*,[a] value in exchange—that, they say, is something quite different. Why are the costs of production the measure of value? Because—listen to this!—because no one in ordinary conditions and leaving aside the circumstance of competition would sell an object for less than it costs him to produce it. Would sell? What have we to do with "selling" here, where it is not a question of value in *exchange*? So we find trade again, which we are specifically supposed to leave aside—and what trade! A trade in which the cardinal factor, the circumstance of competition, is not to be taken into account! First, an abstract value; now also an abstract trade—a trade without competition, i. e., a man without a body, a thought without a brain to produce thoughts. And does the economist never stop to think that as soon as competition is left out of account there is no guarantee at all that the producer will sell his commodity just at the cost of production? What confusion!

Furthermore: Let us concede for a moment that everything is as the economist says. Supposing someone were to make with tremendous exertion and at enormous cost something utterly useless, something which no one desires—is that also worth its production costs? Certainly not, says the economist: Who will want to buy it? So we suddenly have not only Say's much decried utility but alongside it—with "buying"—the circumstance of competition. It can't be done—the economist cannot for one moment hold on to his abstraction. Not only what he painfully seeks to remove—competition—but also what he attacks—utility—crops up at every moment. Abstract value and its determination by the costs of production are, after all, only abstractions, nonentities.

But let us suppose once more for a moment that the economist is correct—how then will he determine the costs of production without taking account of competition? When examining the costs of production we shall see that this category too is based on competition, and here once more it becomes evident how little the economist is able to substantiate his claims.

If we turn to Say, we find the same abstraction. The utility of an object is something purely subjective, something which cannot be decided absolutely, and certainly something which cannot be decided at least as long as one still roams about in antitheses. According to this theory, the necessities of life ought to possess more value than luxury articles. The only possible way to arrive at a more or less objective, *apparently* general decision on the greater

---

[a] English term quoted by Engels.—*Ed.*

or lesser utility of an object is, under the dominion of private property, by competition; and yet it is precisely that circumstance which is to be left aside. But if competition is admitted production costs come in as well; for no one will sell for less than what he has himself invested in production. Thus, here, too, the one side of the opposition passes over involuntarily into the other.

Let us try to introduce clarity into this confusion. The value of an object includes both factors, which the contending parties arbitrarily separate—and, as we have seen, unsuccessfully. Value is the relation of production costs to utility. The first application of value is the decision as to whether a thing ought to be produced at all; i.e., as to whether utility counterbalances production costs. Only then can one talk of the application of value to exchange. The production costs of two objects being equal, the deciding factor determining their comparative value will be utility.

This basis is the only just basis of exchange. But if one proceeds from this basis, who is to decide the utility of the object? The mere opinion of the parties concerned? Then in any event *one* will be cheated. Or are we to assume a determination grounded in the inherent utility of the object independent of the parties concerned, and not apparent to them? If so, the exchange can only be effected by *coercion*, and each party considers itself cheated. The contradiction between the real inherent utility of the thing and the determination of that utility, between the determination of utility and the freedom of those who exchange, cannot be superseded without superseding private property; and once this is superseded, there can no longer be any question of exchange as it exists at present. The practical application of the concept of value will then be increasingly confined to the decision about production, and that is its proper sphere.

But how do matters stand at present? We have seen that the concept of value is violently torn asunder, and that each of the separate sides is declared to be the whole. Production costs, distorted from the outset by competition, are supposed to be value itself. So is mere subjective utility—since no other kind of utility can exist at present. To help these lame definitions on to their feet, it is in both cases necessary to have recourse to competition; and the best of it is that with the English competition represents utility, in contrast to the costs of production, whilst inversely with Say it introduces the costs of production in contrast to utility. But what kind of utility, what kind of production costs, does it introduce? Its utility depends on chance, on fashion, on the whim of the rich; its production costs fluctuate with the fortuitous relationship of demand and supply.

The difference between real value and exchange-value is based on a fact—namely, that the value of a thing differs from the so-called equivalent given for it in trade; i.e., that this equivalent is not an equivalent. This so-called equivalent is the *price* of the thing, and if the economist were honest, he would employ this term for "value in exchange". But he has still to keep up some sort of pretence that price is somehow bound up with value, lest the immorality of trade become too obvious. It is, however, quite correct, and a fundamental law of private property, that *price* is determined by the reciprocal action of production costs and competition. This purely empirical law was the first to be discovered by the economist; and from this law he then abstracted his "real value", i.e., the price at the time when competition is in a state of equilibrium, when demand and supply cover each other. Then, of course, what remains over are the costs of production and it is these which the economist proceeds to call "real value", whereas it is merely a definite aspect of price. Thus everything in economics stands on its head. Value, the primary factor, the source of price, is made dependent on price, its own product. As is well known, this inversion is the essence of abstraction; on which see Feuerbach.

According to the economists, the production costs of a commodity consist of three elements: the rent for the piece of land required to produce the raw material; the capital with its profit, and the wages for the labour required for production and manufacture. But it becomes immediately evident that capital and labour are identical, since the economists themselves confess that capital is "stored-up labour". We are therefore left with only two sides—the natural, objective side, land; and the human, subjective side, labour, which includes capital and, besides capital, a third factor which the economist does not think about—I mean the mental element of invention, of thought, alongside the physical element of sheer labour. What has the economist to do with inventiveness? Have not all inventions fallen into his lap without any effort on his part? Has *one* of them cost him anything? Why then should he bother about them in the calculation of production costs? Land, capital and labour are for him the conditions of wealth, and he requires nothing else. Science is no concern of his.

What does it matter to him that he has received its gifts through Berthollet, Davy, Liebig, Watt, Cartwright, etc.—gifts which have benefited him and his production immeasurably? He does not know how to calculate such things; the advances of science go beyond his figures. But in a rational order which has gone beyond the division of interests as it is found with the economist, the mental element certainly belongs among the elements of production and will find its place, too, in economics among the costs of production. And here it is certainly gratifying to know that the promotion of science also brings its material reward; to know that a single achievement of science like James Watt's steam-engine has brought in more for the world in the first fifty years of its existence than the world has spent on the promotion of science since the beginning of time.

We have, then, two elements of production in operation—nature and man, with man again active physically and mentally, and can now return to the economist and his production costs.

What cannot be monopolised has no value, says the economist—a proposition which we shall examine more closely later on. If we say "has no *price*", then the proposition is valid for the order which rests on private property. If land could be had as easily as air, no one would pay rent. Since this is not the case, but since, rather, the extent of a piece of land to be appropriated is limited in any particular case, one pays rent for the appropriated, i.e., the monopolised land, or one pays down a purchase price for it. After this enlightenment about the origin of the value of land it is, however, very strange to have to hear from the economist that the rent of land is the difference between the yield from the land for which rent is paid and from the worst land worth cultivating at all. As is well known, this is the definition of rent fully developed for the first time by Ricardo. This definition is indeed correct in practice if one presupposes that a fall in demand reacts *instantaneously* on rent, and at once puts a corresponding amount of the worst cultivated land out of cultivation. This, however, is not the case, and the definition is therefore inadequate. Moreover, it does not cover the causation of rent, and is therefore even for that reason untenable. In opposition to this definition, Col. T. P. Thompson, the champion of the Anti-Corn Law League,[181] revived Adam Smith's definition, and substantiated it. According to him, rent is the relation between the competition of those striving for the use of the land and the limited quantity of available land.

Here at least is a return to the origin of rent; but this explanation does not take into account the varying fertility of the soil, just as the previous explanation leaves out competition.

Once more, therefore, we have two one-sided and hence only partial definitions of a single object. As in the case of the concept of value, we shall again have to combine these two definitions so as to find the correct definition which follows from the development of the thing itself and thus embraces all practice. Rent is the relation between the productivity of the land, the natural side (which in turn consists of *natural* fertility and *human* cultivation—labour applied to effect improvement), and the human side, competition. The economists may shake their heads over this "definition"; they will discover to their horror that it embraces everything relevant to this matter.

The *landowner* has nothing with which to reproach the merchant.

He practises robbery in monopolising the land. He practises robbery in exploiting for his own benefit the increase in population which increases competition and thus the value of his estate; in turning into a source of personal advantage that which has not been his own doing—that which is his by sheer accident. He practises robbery in *leasing his land,* when he eventually seizes for himself the improvements effected by his tenant. This is the secret of the ever-increasing wealth of the big landowners.

The axioms which qualify as robbery the landowner's method of deriving an income—namely, that each has a right to the product of his labour, or that no one shall reap where he has not sown—are not advanced by us. The first excludes the duty of feeding children; the second deprives each generation of the right to live, since each generation starts with what it inherits from the preceding generation. These axioms are, rather, consequences of private property. One should either put into effect the consequences or abandon private property as a premise.

Indeed, the original act of appropriation itself is justified by the assertion of the still earlier existence of *common* property rights. Thus, wherever we turn, private property leads us into contradictions.

To make land an object of huckstering—the land which is our one and all, the first condition of our existence—was the last step towards making oneself an object of huckstering. It was and is to this very day an immorality surpassed only by the immorality of self-alienation. And the original appropriation—the monopolisation of the land by a few, the exclusion of the rest from that which is the condition of their life—yields nothing in immorality to the subsequent huckstering of the land.

If here again we abandon private property, rent is reduced to its truth, to the rational notion which essentially lies at its root. The value of the land divorced from it as rent then reverts to the land itself. This value, to be measured by the productivity of equal areas of land subjected to equal applications of labour, is indeed taken into account as part of the production costs when determining the value of products; and like rent, it is the relation of productivity to competition—but to *true* competition, such as will be developed when its time comes.

We have seen that capital and labour are initially identical; we see further from the explanations of the economist himself that, in the process of production, capital, the result of labour, is immediately transformed again into the substratum, into the material of labour; and that therefore the momentarily postulated separation of capital from labour is immediately superseded by the unity of both. And yet the economist separates capital from labour, and yet clings to the division without giving any other recognition to their unity than by his definition of capital as "stored-up labour". The split between capital and labour resulting from private property is nothing but the inner dichotomy of labour corresponding to this divided condition and arising out of it. And after this separation is accomplished, capital is divided once more into the original capital and profit—the increment of capital, which it receives in the process of production; although in practice profit is immediately lumped together with capital and set into motion with it. Indeed, even profit is in its turn split into interest and profit proper. In the case of interest, the absurdity of these splits is carried to the extreme. The immorality of lending at interest, of receiving without working, merely for making a loan, though already implied in private property, is only too obvious, and has long ago been recognised for what it is by unprejudiced popular consciousness, which in such matters is usually right. All these subtle splits and divisions stem from the original separation of capital from labour and from the culmination of this separation—the division of mankind into capitalists and workers—a division which daily becomes ever more acute, and which, as we shall see, is *bound* to deepen. This separation, however, like the separation already considered of land from capital and labour, is in the final analysis an impossible separation. What share land, capital and labour each have in any particular product cannot be determined. The three magnitudes are incommensurable. The land produces the raw material, but not without capital and labour. Capital presupposes land and labour. And labour presupposes *at least* land, and usually also capital. The functions of these three elements are completely different, and are not to be measured by a fourth common standard. Therefore, when it comes to dividing the proceeds among the three elements under existing conditions, there is no inherent standard; it is an entirely alien and with regard to them fortuitous standard that decides—competition, the cunning right of the stronger. Rent implies competition; profit on capital is solely determined by competition; and the position with regard to wages we shall see presently.

If we abandon private property, then all these unnatural divisions disappear. The difference between interest and profit disappears; capital is nothing without labour, without movement. The significance of profit is reduced to the weight which capital carries in the determination of the costs of production; and profit thus remains inherent in capital, in the same way as capital itself reverts to its original unity with labour.

Labour—the main factor in production, the "source of wealth", free human activity—comes off badly with the economist. Just as capital has already been separated from labour, so labour is now in turn split for a second time: the product of labour confronts labour as wages, is separated from it, and is in its turn as usual determined by competition—there being, as we have seen, no firm standard determining labour's share in production. If we do away with private property, this unnatural separation also disappears. Labour becomes its own reward, and the true significance of the wages of labour, hitherto alienated, comes to light—namely, the significance of labour for the determination of the production costs of a thing.

We have seen that in the end everything comes down to competition, so long as private property exists. It is the economist's principal category—his most beloved daughter, whom he ceaselessly caresses—and look out for the Medusa's head which she will show you!

The immediate consequence of private property was the split of production into two opposing sides—the natural and the human sides, the soil which without fertilisation by man is dead and sterile, and human activity, the first condition of which is that very soil. Furthermore we have seen how human activity in its turn was dissolved into labour and capital, and how these two sides antagonistically confronted each other. Thus we already had the struggle of the three elements against one another, instead of their mutual support; now we have to add that private property brings in its wake the fragmentation of each of these elements. One piece of land stands confronted by another, one capital by another, one labourer by another. In other words, because private property isolates everyone in his own crude solitariness, and because, nevertheless, everyone has the same interest as his neighbour, one landowner stands antagonistically confronted by another, one capitalist by another, one worker by another. In this discord of identical interests resulting precisely from this identity is consummated the immorality of mankind's condition hitherto; and this consummation is competition.

The opposite of *competition* is *monopoly*. Monopoly was the war-cry of the Mercantilists; competition the battle-cry of the liberal economists. It is easy to see that this antithesis is again a quite hollow antithesis. Every competitor *cannot but* desire to have the monopoly, be he worker, capitalist or landowner. Each smaller group of competitors cannot but desire to have the monopoly for itself against all others. Competition is based on self-interest, and self-interest in turn breeds monopoly. In short, competition passes over into monopoly. On the other hand, monopoly cannot stem the tide of competition—indeed, it itself breeds competition; just as a prohibition of imports, for instance, or high tariffs positively breed the competition of smuggling. The contradiction of competition is exactly the same as that of private property. It is in the interest of each to possess everything, but in the interest of the whole that each possess an equal amount. Thus, the general and the individual interest are diametrically opposed to each other. The contradiction of competition is that each cannot but desire the monopoly, whilst the whole as such is bound to lose by monopoly and must therefore remove it. Moreover, competition already presupposes monopoly—namely, the monopoly of property (and here the hypocrisy of the liberals comes once more to light); and so long as the monopoly of property exists, for so long the possession of monopoly is equally justified—for monopoly, once it exists, is also property. What a pitiful half-measure, therefore, to attack the small monopolies, and to leave untouched the basic monopoly! And if we add to this the economist's proposition mentioned above, that nothing has value which cannot be monopolised—that nothing, therefore, which does not permit of such monopolisation can enter this arena of competition—then our assertion that competition presupposes monopoly is completely justified.

———

The law of competition is that demand and supply always strive to complement each other, and therefore never do so. The two sides are torn apart again and transformed into flat opposition. Supply always follows close on demand without ever quite covering it. It is either too big or too small, never corresponding to demand; because in this unconscious condition of mankind no one knows how big supply or demand is. If demand is greater than supply the price rises and, as a result, supply is to a certain degree stimulated. As soon as it comes on to the market, prices fall; and if it becomes greater than demand, then the fall in prices is so significant that demand is once again stimulated. So it goes on unendingly—a permanently unhealthy state of affairs—a constant alternation of over-stimulation and flagging which precludes all advance—a state of perpetual fluctuation without ever reaching its goal. This law with its constant adjustment, in which whatever is lost here is gained there, is regarded as something excellent by the economist. It is his chief glory—he cannot see enough of it, and considers it in all its possible and impossible applications. Yet it is obvious that this law is purely a law of nature and not a law of the mind. It is a law which produces revolution. The economist comes along with his lovely theory of demand and supply, proves to you that "one can never produce too much", and practice replies with trade crises, which reappear as regularly as the comets, and of which we have now on the average one every five to seven years. For the last eighty years these trade crises have arrived just as regularly as the great plagues did in the past—and they have brought in their train more misery and more immorality than the latter. (Compare Wade: *History of the Middle and Working Classes,* London, 1835, p. 211.) Of course, these commercial upheavals confirm the law, confirm it exhaustively—but in a manner different from that which the economist would have us believe to be the case. What are we to think of a law which can only assert itself through periodic upheavals? It is certainly a natural law based on the unconsciousness of the participants. If the producers as such knew how much the consumers required, if they were to organise production, if they were to share it out amongst themselves, then the fluctuations of competition and its tendency to crisis would be impossible. Carry on production consciously as human beings—not as dispersed atoms without consciousness of your species—and you have overcome all these artificial and untenable antitheses. But as long as you continue to produce in the present unconscious, thoughtless manner, at the mercy of chance—for just so long trade crises will remain; and each successive crisis is bound to become more universal and therefore worse than the preceding one; is bound to impoverish a larger body of small capitalists, and to augment in increasing proportion the numbers of the class who live by labour alone, thus considerably enlarging the mass of labour to be employed (the major problem of our economists) and finally causing a social revolution such as has never been dreamt of in the philosophy[a] of the economists.

The perpetual fluctuation of prices such as is created by the condition of competition completely deprives trade of its last vestige of morality. It is no longer a question of *value*; the same system which appears to attach such importance to value, which confers on the abstraction of value in money form the honour of having an existence of its own—this very system destroys by means of competition the inherent value of all things, and daily and hourly changes the value-relationship of all things to one another. Where is there any possibility remaining in this whirlpool of an exchange based on a moral foundation? In this continuous up-and-down, everyone *must* seek to hit upon the most favourable moment for purchase and sale; everyone must become a speculator—that is to say, must reap where he has not sown; must enrich himself at the expense of others, must calculate on the misfortune of others, or let chance win for him. The speculator always counts on disasters, particularly on bad harvests. He utilises everything—for instance, the New York fire in its time[182]—and immorality's culminating point is the speculation on the Stock Exchange, where history, and with it mankind, is demoted to a means of gratifying the avarice of the calculating or gambling speculator. And let not the honest "respectable" merchant rise above the gambling on the Stock Exchange with a Pharisaic "I

---

[a] Cf. Shakespeare, *Hamlet*, Act I, Scene 5, lines 166-67.—*Ed.*

thank thee, O Lord...", etc. He is as bad as the speculators in stocks and shares. He speculates just as much as they do. He has to: competition compels him to. And his trading activity therefore implies the same immorality as theirs. The truth of the relation of competition is the relation of consumption to productivity. In a world worthy of mankind there will be no other competition than this. The community will have to calculate what it can produce with the means at its disposal; and in accordance with the relationship of this productive power to the mass of consumers it will determine how far it has to raise or lower production, how far it has to give way to, or curtail, luxury. But so that they may be able to pass a correct judgment on this relationship and on the increase in productive power to be expected from a rational state of affairs within the community, I invite my readers to consult the writings of the English Socialists, and partly also those of Fourier.

Subjective competition—the contest of capital against capital, of labour against labour, etc.—will under these conditions be reduced to the spirit of emulation grounded in human nature (a concept tolerably set forth so far only by Fourier), which after the transcendence of opposing interests will be confined to its proper and rational sphere.

The struggle of capital against capital, of labour against labour, of land against land, drives production to a fever-pitch at which production turns all natural and rational relations upside-down. No capital can stand the competition of another if it is not brought to the highest pitch of activity. No piece of land can be profitably cultivated if it does not continuously increase its productivity. No worker can hold his own against his competitors if he does not devote all his energy to labour. No one at all who enters into the struggle of competition can weather it without the utmost exertion of his energy, without renouncing every truly human purpose. The consequence of this over-exertion on the one side is, inevitably, slackening on the other. When the fluctuation of competition is small, when demand and supply, consumption and production, are almost equal, a stage must be reached in the development of production where there is so much superfluous productive power that the great mass of the nation has nothing to live on, that the people starve from sheer abundance. For some considerable time England has found herself in this crazy position, in this living absurdity. When production is subject to greater fluctuations, as it is bound to be in consequence of such a situation, then the alternation of boom and crisis, over-production and slump, sets in. The economist has never been able to find an explanation for this mad situation. In order to explain it, he invented the population theory, which is just as senseless—indeed even more senseless than the contradiction of coexisting wealth and poverty. The economist *could not afford* to see the truth; he could not afford to admit that this contradiction is a simple consequence of competition; for in that case his entire system would have fallen to bits.

For us the matter is easy to explain. The productive power at mankind's disposal is immeasurable. The productivity of the soil can be increased *ad infinitum* by the application of capital, labour and science. According to the most able economists and statisticians (cf. Alison's *Principles of Population,* Vol. I, Chs. 1 and 2), "over-populated" Great Britain can be brought within ten years to produce a corn yield sufficient for a population six times its present size. Capital increases daily; labour power grows with population; and day by day science increasingly makes the forces of nature subject to man. This immeasurable productive capacity, handled consciously and in the interest of all, would soon reduce to a minimum the labour falling to the share of mankind. Left to competition, it does the same, but within a context of antitheses. One part of the land is cultivated in the best possible manner, whilst another part—in Great Britain and Ireland thirty million acres of good land—lies barren. One part of capital circulates with colossal speed; another lies dead in the chest. One part of the workers works fourteen or sixteen hours a day, whilst another part stands idle and inactive, and starves. Or the partition leaves this realm of simultaneity: today trade is good; demand is very considerable; everyone works; capital is turned over with miraculous speed; farming flourishes; the workers work themselves sick. Tomorrow stagnation sets in. The cultivation of the land is not worth the effort; entire stretches of land remain untilled; the flow of capital suddenly freezes; the workers have no employment, and the whole country labours under surplus wealth and surplus population.

The economist cannot afford to accept this exposition of the subject as correct; otherwise, as has been said, he would have to give up his whole system of competition. He would have to recognise the hollowness of his antithesis of production and consumption, of surplus population and surplus wealth. To bring fact and theory into conformity with each other—since this fact simply could not be denied—the population theory was invented.

Malthus, the originator of this doctrine, maintains that population is always pressing on the means of subsistence; that as soon as production increases, population increases in the same proportion; and that the inherent tendency of the population to multiply in excess of the available means of subsistence is the root of all misery and all vice. For, when there are too many people, they have to be disposed of in one way or another: either they must be killed by violence or they must starve. But when this has happened, there is once more a gap which other multipliers of the population immediately start to fill up once more: and so the old misery begins all over again. What is more, this is the case in all circumstances—not only in civilised, but also in primitive conditions. In New Holland,[a] with a population density of *one* per square mile, the savages suffer just as much from over-population as England. In short, if we want to be consistent, we must admit *that the earth was already over-populated when only one man existed*. The implications of this line of thought are that since it is precisely the poor who are the surplus, nothing should be done for them except to make their dying of starvation as easy as possible, and to convince them that it cannot be helped and that there is no other salvation for their whole class than keeping propagation down to the absolute minimum. Or if this proves impossible, then it is after all better to establish a state institution for the painless killing of the children of the poor, such as "Marcus"[183] has suggested, whereby each working-class family would be allowed to have two and a half children, any excess being painlessly killed. Charity is to be considered a crime, since it supports the augmentation of the surplus population. Indeed, it will be very advantageous to declare poverty a crime and to turn poor-houses into prisons, as has already happened in England as a result of the new "liberal" Poor Law.[184] Admittedly it is true that this theory ill conforms with the Bible's doctrine of the perfection of God and of His creation; but "it is a poor refutation to enlist the Bible against facts".

Am I to go on any longer elaborating this vile, infamous theory, this hideous blasphemy against nature and mankind? Am I to pursue its consequences any further? Here at last we have the immorality of the economist brought to its highest pitch. What are all the wars and horrors of the monopoly system compared with this theory! And it is just this theory which is the keystone of the liberal system of free trade, whose fall entails the downfall of the entire edifice. For if here competition is proved to be the cause of

---

[a] The old name for Australia.—*Ed.*

misery, poverty and crime, who then will still dare to speak up for it?

In his above-mentioned work, Alison has shaken the Malthusian theory by bringing in the productive power of the land, and by opposing to the Malthusian principle the fact that each adult can produce more than he himself needs—a fact without which mankind could not multiply, indeed could not even exist; if it were not so how could those still growing up live? But Alison does not go to the root of the matter, and therefore in the end reaches the same conclusion as Malthus. True enough, he proves that Malthus' principle is incorrect, but cannot gainsay the facts which have impelled Malthus to his principle.

If Malthus had not considered the matter so one-sidedly, he could not have failed to see that surplus population or labour-power is invariably tied up with surplus wealth, surplus capital and surplus landed property. The population is only too large where the productive power as a whole is too large. The condition of every over-populated country, particularly England, since the time when Malthus wrote, makes this abundantly clear. These were the facts which Malthus ought to have considered in their totality, and whose consideration was bound to have led to the correct conclusion. Instead, he selected one fact, gave no consideration to the others, and therefore arrived at his crazy conclusion. The second error he committed was to confuse means of subsistence with [means of] employment. That population is always pressing on the means of employment—that the number of people produced depends on the number of people who can be employed—in short, that the production of labour-power has been regulated so far by the law of competition and is therefore also exposed to periodic crises and fluctuations—this is a fact whose establishment constitutes Malthus' merit. But the means of employment are not the means of subsistence. Only in their end-result are the means of employment increased by the increase in machine-power and capital. The means of subsistence increase as soon as productive power increases even slightly. Here a new contradiction in economics comes to light. The economist's "demand" is not the real demand; his "consumption" is an artificial consumption. For the economist, only that person really demands, only that person is a real consumer, who has an equivalent to offer for what he receives. But if it is a fact that every adult produces more than he himself can consume, that children are like trees which give superabundant returns on the outlays invested in them—and these certainly are facts, are they not?—then it must be assumed that each worker ought to be able to produce far more than he needs and that the community, therefore, ought to be very glad to provide him with everything he needs; one must consider a large family to be a very welcome gift for the community. But the economist, with his crude outlook, knows no other equivalent than that which is paid to him in tangible ready cash. He is so firmly set in his antitheses that the most striking facts are of as little concern to him as the most scientific principles.

We destroy the contradiction simply by transcending it. With the fusion of the interests now opposed to each other there disappears the contradiction between excess population here and excess wealth there; there disappears the miraculous fact (more miraculous than all the miracles of all the religions put together) that a nation has to starve from sheer wealth and plenty; and there disappears the crazy assertion that the earth lacks the power to feed men. This assertion is the pinnacle of Christian economics—and that our economics is essentially Christian I could have proved from every proposition, from every category, and shall in fact do so in due course.[185] The Malthusian theory is but the economic expression of the religious dogma of the contradiction of spirit and nature and the resulting corruption of both. As regards religion, and together with religion, this contradiction was resolved long ago, and I hope that in the sphere of economics I have likewise demonstrated the utter emptiness of this contradiction. Moreover, I shall not accept as competent any defence of the Malthusian theory which does not explain to me on the basis of its own principles how a people can starve from sheer plenty and bring this into harmony with reason and fact.

At the same time, the Malthusian theory has certainly been a necessary point of transition which has taken us an immense step further. Thanks to this theory, as to economics as a whole, our attention has been drawn to the productive power of the earth and of mankind; and after overcoming this economic despair we have been made for ever secure against the fear of over-population. We derive from it the most powerful economic arguments for a social transformation. For even if Malthus were completely right, this transformation would have to be undertaken straight away; for only this transformation, only the education of the masses which it provides, makes possible that moral restraint of the propagative instinct which Malthus himself presents as the most effective and easiest remedy for over-population. Through this theory we have come to know the deepest degradation of mankind, their dependence on the conditions of competition. It has shown us how in the last instance private property has turned man into a commodity whose production and destruction also depend solely on demand; how the system of competition has thus slaughtered, and daily continues to slaughter, millions of men. All this we have seen, and all this drives us to the abolition of this degradation of mankind through the abolition of private property, competition and the opposing interests.

Yet, so as to deprive the universal fear of over-population of any possible basis, let us once more return to the relationship of productive power to population. Malthus establishes a formula on which he bases his entire system: population is said to increase in a geometrical progression—$1+2+4+8+16+32$, etc.; the productive power of the land in an arithmetical progression—$1+2+3+4+5+6$. The difference is obvious, is terrifying; but is it correct? Where has it been proved that the productivity of the land increases in an arithmetical progression? The extent of land is limited. All right! The labour-power to be employed on this land-surface increases with population. Even if we assume that the increase in yield due to increase in labour does not always rise in proportion to the labour, there still remains a third element which, admittedly, never means anything to the economist—science—whose progress is as unlimited and at least as rapid as that of population. What progress does the agriculture of this century owe to chemistry alone—indeed, to two men alone, Sir Humphry Davy and Justus Liebig! But science increases at least as much as population. The latter increases in proportion to the size of the previous generation, science advances in proportion to the knowledge bequeathed to it by the previous generation, and thus under the most ordinary conditions also in a geometrical progression. And what is impossible to science? But it is absurd to talk of over-population so long as "there is enough waste land in the valley of the Mississippi for the whole population of Europe to be transplanted there"[a]; so long as no more than one-third of the earth can be considered cultivated, and so long as the production of this third itself can be raised sixfold and more by the application of improvements already known.

Thus, competition sets capital against capital, labour against labour, landed property against landed property; and likewise each of these elements against the other two. In the struggle the stronger wins; and in order to predict the outcome of the struggle,

---

[a] A. Alison, loc. cit., p. 548.—Ed.

we shall have to investigate the strength of the contestants. First of all, labour is weaker than either landed property or capital, for the worker must work to live, whilst the landowner can live on his rent, and the capitalist on his interest, or, if the need arises, on his capital or on capitalised property in land. The result is that only the very barest necessities, the mere means of subsistence, fall to the lot of labour; whilst the largest part of the products is shared between capital and landed property. Moreover, the stronger worker drives the weaker out of the market, just as larger capital drives out smaller capital, and larger landed property drives out smaller landed property. Practice confirms this conclusion. The advantages which the larger manufacturer and merchant enjoy over the smaller, and the big landowner over the owner of a single acre, are well known. The result is that already under ordinary conditions, in accordance with the law of the stronger, large capital and large landed property swallow small capital and small landed property—i.e., centralisation of property. In crises of trade and agriculture, this centralisation proceeds much more rapidly.

In general large property increases much more rapidly than small property, since a much smaller portion is deducted from its proceeds as property-expenses. This law of the centralisation of private property is as immanent in private property as all the others. The middle classes must increasingly disappear until the world is divided into millionaires and paupers, into large landowners and poor farm labourers. All the laws, all the dividing of landed property, all the possible splitting-up of capital, are of no avail: this result must and will come, unless it is anticipated by a total transformation of social conditions, a fusion of opposed interests, an abolition of private property.

Free competition, the key-word of our present-day economists, is an impossibility. Monopoly at least intended to protect the consumer against fraud, even if it could not in fact do so. The abolition of monopoly, however, opens the door wide to fraud. You say that competition carries with it the remedy for fraud, since no one will buy bad articles. But that means that everyone has to be an expert in every article, which is impossible. Hence the necessity for monopoly, which many articles in fact reveal. Pharmacies, etc., *must* have a monopoly. And the most important article—money—requires a monopoly most of all. Whenever the circulating medium has ceased to be a state monopoly it has invariably produced a trade crisis; and the English economists, Dr. Wade among them, do concede in this case the necessity for monopoly. But monopoly is no protection against counterfeit money. One can take one's stand on either side of the question: the one is as difficult as the other. Monopoly produces free competition, and the latter, in turn, produces monopoly. Therefore, both must fall, and these difficulties must be resolved through the transcendence of the principle which gives rise to them.

Competition has penetrated all the relationships of our life and completed the reciprocal bondage in which men now hold themselves. Competition is the great mainspring which again and again jerks into activity our aging and withering social order, or rather disorder; but with each new exertion it also saps a part of this order's waning strength. Competition governs the numerical advance of mankind; it likewise governs its moral advance. Anyone who has any knowledge of the statistics of crime must have been struck by the peculiar regularity with which crime advances year by year, and with which certain causes produce certain crimes. The extension of the factory system is followed everywhere by an increase in crime. The number of arrests, of criminal cases—indeed, the number of murders, burglaries, petty thefts, etc., for a large town or for a district—can be predicted year by year with unfailing precision, as has been done often enough in England. This regularity proves that crime, too, is governed by competition; that society creates a *demand* for crime which is met by a corresponding *supply*; that the gap created by the arrest, transportation or execution of a certain number is at once filled by others, just as every gap in population is at once filled by new arrivals; in other words, that crime presses on the means of punishment just as the people press on the means of employment. How just it is to punish criminals under these circumstances, quite apart from any other considerations, I leave to the judgment of my readers. Here I am merely concerned in demonstrating the extension of competition into the moral sphere, and in showing to what deep degradation private property has brought man.

In the struggle of capital and land against labour, the first two elements enjoy yet another special advantage over labour—the assistance of science; for in present conditions science, too, is directed against labour. Almost all mechanical inventions, for instance, have been occasioned by the lack of labour-power; in particular Hargreaves', Crompton's and Arkwright's cotton-spinning machines. There has never been an intense demand for labour which did not result in an invention that increased labour productivity considerably, thus diverting demand away from human labour. The history of England from 1770 until now is a continuous demonstration of this. The last great invention in cotton-spinning, the self-acting mule, was occasioned solely by the demand for labour, and rising wages. It doubled machine-labour, and thereby cut down hand-labour by half; it threw half the workers out of employment, and thereby reduced the wages of the others by half; it crushed a plot of the workers against the factory owners, and destroyed the last vestige of strength with which labour had still held out in the unequal struggle against capital. (Cf. Dr. Ure, *Philosophy of Manufactures,* Vol. 2.) The economist now says, however, that in its final result machinery is favourable to the workers, since it makes production cheaper and thereby creates a new and larger market for its products, and thus ultimately re-employs the workers put out of work. Quite right. But is the economist forgetting, then, that the production of labour-power is regulated by competition; that labour-power is always pressing on the means of employment, and that, therefore, when these advantages are due to become operative, a surplus of competitors for work is already waiting for them, and will thus render these advantages illusory; whilst the disadvantages—the sudden withdrawal of the means of subsistence from one half of the workers and the fall in wages for the other half—are not illusory? Is the economist forgetting that the progress of invention never stands still, and that these disadvantages, therefore, perpetuate themselves? Is he forgetting that with the division of labour, developed to such a high degree by our civilisation, a worker can only live if he can be used at this particular machine for this particular detailed operation; that the change-over from one type of employment to another, newer type is almost invariably an absolute impossibility for the adult worker?

In turning my attention to the effects of machinery, I am brought to another subject less directly relevant—the factory system, and I have neither the inclination nor the time to treat this here. Besides, I hope to have an early opportunity to expound in detail the despicable immorality of this system, and to expose mercilessly the economist's hypocrisy which here appears in all its brazenness.[186]

Written in October and November 1843 Printed according to the journal
First published in the *Deutsch-Französische Jahrbücher,* 1844
Signed: **Frederick Engels in Manchester**

THE CONDITION OF ENGLAND[187]
Past and Present by Thomas Carlyle, London, 1843

Of all the fat books and thin pamphlets which have appeared in England in the past year for the entertainment or edification of "educated society", the above work is the only one which is worth reading. All the multi-volume novels with their sad and amusing intricacies, all the edifying and meditative, scholarly and unscholarly Bible commentaries—and novels and books of edification are the two staples of English literature—all these you may with an easy conscience leave unread. Perhaps you will find some books on geology, economics, history or mathematics which contain a small grain of novelty—however these are matters which one studies, but does not *read*, they represent dry, specialised branches of science, arid botanising, plants whose roots were long ago torn out of the general soil of humanity from which they derived their nourishment. Search as you will, Carlyle's book is the only one which strikes a human chord, presents human relations and shows traces of a human point of view.

It is remarkable how greatly the upper classes of society, such as the Englishman calls *"respectable people"*, or *"the better sort of people"*,[a] etc., have intellectually declined and lost their vigour in England. All energy, all activity, all substance are gone; the landed aristocracy goes hunting, the moneyed aristocracy makes entries in the ledger and at best dabbles in literature which is equally empty and insipid. Political and religious prejudices are inherited from one generation to another; everything is now made easy and there is no longer any need to worry about principles as one had to formerly; they are now picked up already in the cradle, ready-

---

[a] The words in inverted commas are given by Engels in English.— *Ed.*

made, one has no notion where they come from. What more does one need? One has enjoyed a good education, that is, one has been tormented to no avail with the Romans and Greeks at school, for the rest one is "respectable", that is, one has so many thousand pounds to one's name and thus does not have to bother about anything except marrying, if one does not already have a wife.

And now, to cap it all, this bugbear which people call "intellect"! Where should intellect come from, in such a life, and if it did come, where might it find a home with them? Everything there is as fixed and formalised as in China—woe be to the man who oversteps the narrow bounds, woe, thrice woe to the man who offends against a time-honoured prejudice, nine times woe to him if it is a religious prejudice. For all questions they have just two answers, a Whig answer and a Tory answer; and these answers were long ago prescribed by the sage supreme masters of ceremony of both parties, you have no need of deliberation and circumstantiality, everything is cut and dried, Dicky Cobden or Lord John Russell has said this, and Bobby Peel or *the* Duke, that is, the Duke of Wellington, has said that, and that is an end of the matter.

You good Germans are told year in, year out by the liberal journalists and parliamentarians what wonderful people, what independent men the English are, and all on account of their free institutions, and from a distance it all looks quite impressive. The debates in the Houses of Parliament, the free press, the tumultuous popular meetings, the elections, the jury system—these cannot fail to impress the timid spirit of the average German, and in his astonishment he takes all these splendid appearances for true coin. But ultimately the position of the liberal journalist and parliamentarian is really far from being elevated enough to provide a comprehensive view, whether it be of the development of mankind or just that of a single nation. The English Constitution was quite good in its day and has achieved a fair number of good things, indeed since 1828 it has set to work on its greatest achievement—that is to say, on its own destruction[188]—but it has not achieved what the liberal attributes to it. It has not made independent men of the English. The English, that is, the educated English, according to whom the national character is judged on the Continent, these English are the most despicable slaves under the sun. Only that part of the English nation which is unknown on the Continent, only the workers, the pariahs of England, the poor, are really respectable, for all their roughness and for all their moral degradation. It is from them that England's salvation will come, they still comprise flexible material; they have no education, but no prejudices either, they still have the strength for a great national deed—they still have a future. The aristocracy—and nowadays that also includes the middle classes—has exhausted itself; such ideas as it had, have been worked out and utilised to their ultimate logical limit, and its rule is approaching its end with giant strides. The Constitution is its work, and the immediate consequence of this work was that it entangled its creators in a mesh of institutions in which any free intellectual movement has been made impossible. The rule of public prejudice is everywhere the first consequence of so-called free political institutions, and in England, the politically freest country in Europe, this rule is stronger than anywhere else—except for North America, where public prejudice is legally acknowledged as a power in the state by lynch law. The Englishman crawls before public prejudice, he immolates himself to it daily—and the more liberal he is, the more humbly does he grovel in the dust before his idol. Public prejudice in "educated society" is however either of Tory or of Whig persuasion, or at best radical—and even that no longer has quite the odour of propriety. If you should go amongst educated Englishmen and say that you are Chartists or democrats—the balance of your mind will be doubted and your company fled. Or declare you do not believe in the divinity of Christ, and you are done for; if moreover you confess that you are atheists, the next day people will pretend not to know you. And when the independent Englishman for once—and this happens rarely enough—really begins to think and shakes off the fetters of prejudice he has absorbed with his mother's milk, even then he has not the courage to speak out his convictions openly, even then he feigns an opinion before society that is at least tolerated, and is quite content if occasionally he can discuss his views with some like-minded person in private.

Thus the minds of the educated classes in England are closed to all progress and only kept to some degree in movement by the pressure of the working class. It cannot be expected that the literary diet of their decrepit culture should be different from these classes themselves. The whole of fashionable literature moves in a never-ending circle and is just as boring and sterile as this blasé and effete fashionable society.

When Strauss' *Das Leben Jesu* and its fame crossed the Channel, no respectable man dared to translate the book, nor any bookseller of repute to print it. Finally it was translated by a socialist "lecturer" (there is no German word for this propagandist term)—a man, therefore, in one of the world's least fashionable situations—a small socialist printer printed it in instalments at a penny each,[189] and the workers of Manchester, Birmingham and London were the only readers Strauss had in England.

If, by the way, either of the two parties into which the educated section of the English people is split deserves any preference, it is the Tories. In the social circumstances of England the Whig is himself too much of an interested party to be able to judge; industry, that focal point of English society, is in his hands and makes him rich; he can find no fault in it and considers its expansion the only purpose of all legislation, for it has given him his wealth and his power. The Tory on the other hand, whose power and unchallenged dominance have been broken by industry and whose principles have been shaken by it, hates it and sees in it at best a necessary evil. This is the reason for the formation of that group of philanthropic Tories whose chief leaders are Lord Ashley, Ferrand, Walter, Oastler, etc., and who have made it their duty to take the part of the factory workers against the manufacturers. Thomas Carlyle too was originally a Tory and still stands closer to that party than to the Whigs. This much is certain: a Whig would never have been able to write a book that was half so humane as *Past and Present*.

Thomas Carlyle has become known in Germany through his efforts to make German literature accessible to the English. For several years he has been mainly occupied with the social conditions of England—the only educated man of his country to do so!—and as early as 1838 he wrote a brief work entitled *Chartism*. At that time the Whigs were in office and proclaimed with much trumpeting that the "spectre" of Chartism, which had arisen round 1835, was now destroyed. Chartism was the natural successor to the old radicalism which had been appeased for a few years by the Reform Bill[190] and reappeared in 1835-36 with new strength and with its ranks more solid than ever before. The Whigs thought they had suppressed this Chartism, and Thomas Carlyle took this as his cue to expound the real causes of Chartism and the impossibility of eradicating it before these causes were eradicated. It is true that as a whole the position taken by that book is the same as in *Past and Present*, though with rather stronger Tory colouring, but this is perhaps merely a result of the fact that the Whigs as the ruling party were the most open to criticism. At all events, everything that is in the smaller book is to be found in *Past and Present*, with greater clarity, with the argument further developed, and with an explicit description of the consequences, and therefore makes a critical analysis of *Chartism* on our part superfluous.

Past and Present is a parallel between England in the twelfth and in the nineteenth centuries and consists of four sections, entitled "Proem", "The Ancient Monk", "The Modern Worker" and "Horoscope". Let us consider these sections in turn; I cannot resist the temptation to translate the finest of the book's often marvellously fine passages.—Criticism will no doubt take care of itself.

The first chapter of the "Proem" is called "Midas".

"The condition of England ... is justly regarded as one of the most ominous, and withal one of the strangest, ever seen in this world. England is full of wealth [...] in every kind; yet England is dying of inanition. With unabated bounty the land of England blooms and grows; waving with yellow harvests; thick-studded with workshops, industrial implements, with fifteen millions of workers, understood to be the strongest, the cunningest and the willingest our Earth ever had; these men are here; the work they have done, the fruit they have realised is here, abundant, exuberant on every hand of us: and behold, some baleful fiat as of Enchantment has gone forth, saying, 'Touch it not, ye workers, ye master-workers, ye master-idlers; none of you can touch it, no man of you shall be the better for it; this is enchanted fruit!'"[a]

This fiat falls on the workers first. In 1842 England and Wales counted 1,430,000 paupers, of whom 222,000 were incarcerated in workhouses—Poor-law Bastilles the common people call them.—Thanks to the humanity of the Whigs! Scotland has no poor law, but poor people in plenty. Ireland, incidentally, can boast of the gigantic number of 2,300,000 paupers.

"At Stockport Assizes" (Cheshire) "a Mother and a Father are arraigned and found guilty of poisoning three of their children, to defraud a 'burial-society' of some 3l. 8s. due on the death of each child: [...] and the official authorities, it is whispered, hint that perhaps the case is not solitary, that perhaps you had better not probe farther into that department of things.... Such instances are like the highest mountain apex emerged into view; under which lies a whole mountain region and land, not yet emerged. A human Mother and Father had said to themselves, What shall we do to escape starvation? We are deep sunk here, in our dark cellar; and help is far.—Yes, in the Ugolino Hunger-tower stern things happen; best-loved little Gaddo fallen dead on his Father's knees!—The Stockport Mother and Father think and hint: Our poor little starveling *Tom*, who cries all day for victuals, who will see only evil and not good in this world: if he were out of misery at once; ... and the rest of us perhaps kept alive? It is thought, and hinted; at last it is done. And now Tom being killed, and all spent and eaten, Is it poor little starveling Jack that must go, or poor little starveling Will?—What an inquiry of ways and means!

"In starved sieged cities, in the uttermost doomed ruin of old Jerusalem fallen under the wrath of God, it was prophesied and said, 'The hands of the pitiful

---

[a] *Past and Present*, London, 1843, p. 1.—*Ed.*

women have sodden their own children.' The stern Hebrew imagination could conceive no blacker gulf of wretchedness; that was the ultimatum of degraded god-punished man. And we here, in modern England, exuberant with supply of all kinds, [...] are *we* reaching that?—How come these things? Wherefore are they, wherefore should they be?"[a]

This happened in 1841. I would add that five months ago Betty Eules of Bolton was hanged in Liverpool; she had poisoned three children of her own and two stepchildren for the same reason. So much for the poor. How do things stand with the rich?

"This successful industry of England, with its plethoric wealth, has as yet made nobody rich; it is an enchanted wealth, and belongs yet to nobody. [...] We can spend thousands where we once spent hundreds; but can purchase nothing good with them. [...] Many men eat finer cookery, drink dearer liquors, [...] what increase of blessedness is there? Are they better, beautifuller, stronger, braver? Are they even what they call 'happier'?"[b]

The master-worker is not happier, the master-idler—that is, the aristocratic landowner—is not happier.

"To whom, then, is this wealth of England wealth? Who is it that it blesses; makes happier, wiser, beautifuller, [...] better? [...] As yet no one. [...] Our successful industry is hitherto unsuccessful; [...] In the midst of plethoric plenty, the people perish; with gold walls, and full barns, no man feels himself safe or satisfied. [...]

"Midas longed for gold, and insulted the Olympians. He got gold, so that whatsoever he touched became gold,—and he, with his long ears, was little the better for it. Midas had misjudged the celestial music-tones; Midas had insulted Apollo and the gods: the gods gave him his wish, and a pair of long ears, which also were a good appendage to it. What a truth in these old Fables!"[c]

"How true," he continues in the second chapter, "is that other old Fable of the Sphinx [....] Nature, like the Sphinx, [...] is a goddess, but one not yet disimprisoned", still half encased in brutishness, in the inarticulate—there is order and wisdom on the one hand, but also darkness, ferocity and fatality.[d]

Sphinx-like nature—German mysticism, say the English, when they read this chapter—has a question to put to every man and every age—happy is the man who answers it aright; he who does not answer it or answers wrongly, falls a prey to that part of the Sphinx which is brutish and ferocious, instead of the beautiful bride he finds a devouring lioness. And so it is with nations too: can you solve the riddle of destiny? And all unfortunate peoples, like all unfortunate individuals, have answered the question wrongly, have taken the semblance for the truth, have abandoned the eternal inner facts of the universe in favour of transient outer appearances, and England too has done this. England, as Carlyle

---

[a] Thomas Carlyle, *Past and Present*, London, 1843, pp. 4, 5, 6.—*Ed.*
[b] op. cit., p. 6.—*Ed.*
[c] op. cit., pp. 7-8.—*Ed.*
[d] op. cit., p. 9.—*Ed.*

later puts it, has fallen a prey to atheism and its present condition is the necessary consequence of that. We shall have occasion to speak of this later, for the present let us simply observe that the parable of the Sphinx, if it is to be accepted in the above pantheistic sense reminiscent of the older Schelling, could well have been developed somewhat further by Carlyle—the answer to the riddle today is, as it was in the myth: man; indeed he is the answer in the widest possible sense. That too will be settled.

The next chapter gives us the following description of the Manchester insurrection of August 1842.[191]

"A million of hungry operative men [...] rose all up, came all out into the streets, and—stood there. What other could they do? Their wrongs and griefs were bitter, insupportable, their rage against the same was just: but who are they that cause these wrongs, who that will [...] make effort to redress them? Our enemies are we know not who or what; our friends are we know not where! How shall we attack any one, shoot or be shot by any one? O, if the accursed invisible Nightmare, that is crushing out the life of us and ours, would take a shape; approach us like the Hyrcanian[a] tiger, the Behemoth of Chaos, the Archfiend himself; in any shape that we could see, and fasten on!"[b]

But the misfortune of the workers in the summer insurrection of 1842 was precisely that they did not know whom to fight against. The evil they suffered was social—and social evils cannot be abolished as the monarchy or privileges are abolished. Social evils cannot be cured by People's Charters,[192] and the people sensed this—otherwise the People's Charter would be today the basic law of England. Social evils need to be studied and understood, and this the mass of the workers has not yet done up till now. The great achievement of the uprising was that England's most vital question, the question of the final destiny of the working class, was, as Carlyle says, raised in a manner audible to every thinking ear in England. The question can now no longer be evaded. England must answer it or perish.

Let us pass over the final chapters of this section, and for the moment too the whole of that which follows, and let us straightaway take the third section which treats of *"The Modern Worker"*, so that we may have before us all of a piece the description of the condition of England which was begun in the "Proem".

We have abandoned, Carlyle continues, the piety of the Middle Ages and acquired nothing in its place: we have

"forgotten God [....] We have quietly closed our eyes to the eternal Substance of things, and opened them only to the Shews and Shams of things. We quietly believe this Universe to be intrinsically a great unintelligible Perhaps; extrinsically,

---

[a] In the original: *syrkanisch.—Ed.*
[b] Carlyle, op. cit., p. 20.—*Ed.*

clear enough, it is a great, most extensive Cattlefold and Workhouse, with most extensive Kitchen-ranges,[a] Dining-tables,—whereat he is wise who can find a place! All the Truth of this Universe is uncertain; only the profit and loss of it, the pudding and praise of it, are and remain very visible to the practical man.

"There is no longer any God for us! God's Laws are become a Greatest-Happiness Principle, a Parliamentary Expediency: the Heavens overarch us only as an Astronomical Time-keeper; a butt for Herschel-telescopes to shoot science at, to shoot sentimentalities at[b]:—in our and old Jonson's dialect, man has lost the soul out of him; and now [...] begins to find the want of it! This is verily the plague-spot; centre of the universal Social Gangrene [....] There is no religion; there is no God; man has lost his soul, and vainly seeks antiseptic salt. Vainly: in killing Kings, in [passing] Reform Bills,[c] in French Revolutions, Manchester Insurrections, is found no remedy. The foul [...] leprosy, alleviated for an hour, reappears in new force and desperateness next hour."[d]

Since however the place of the old religion could not remain entirely vacant, we have acquired a new gospel in its stead, a gospel that accords with the hollowness and lack of substance of the age—the gospel of Mammon. The Christian heaven and the Christian hell have been abandoned, the former as doubtful, and the latter as absurd—and you have acquired a new hell; the hell of modern England is the consciousness of "not succeeding, of not making money".

"True [...] we [...] with our Mammon-Gospel, have come to strange conclusions. We call it a *Society*; and go about professing[e] openly the totalest separation, isolation. Our life is not a mutual helpfulness; but rather, cloaked under due laws-of-war, named 'fair competition' and so forth, it is a mutual hostility. We have profoundly forgotten [...] that Cash-payment is not the sole relation of human beings; [...] 'My starving workers?' answers the rich Mill-owner: 'Did not I hire them fairly in the market? Did I not pay them, to the last sixpence, the sum covenanted for? What have I to do with them more?'—Verily Mammon-worship is a melancholy creed."[f]

"A poor Irish Widow [...] of Edinburgh, went forth with her three children [...] to solicit help from the Charitable Establishments of that City." At every establishment "she was refused; [...] her strength and heart failed her: she sank down in typhus-fever; died, and infected her Lane with fever, so that 'seventeen other persons' died of fever there in consequence. The humane Physician" who tells this story—Dr. W. P. Alison—"asks thereupon [...] Would it not have been *economy* to help this poor Widow? She took typhus-fever, and killed seventeen of you!—Very curious. The forlorn Irish Widow applies to her fellow-creatures [...] 'Behold I am sinking, bare of help: ye must help me! I am your sister, bone of your bone; *one* God made us; ye must help me!' They answer, 'No; impossible: thou art no sister of ours.' But she proves her

---

[a] Engels has: "Kitchen-buildings".—*Ed.*
[b] Engels has: "the heaven is an astronomical clock, a hunting-ground for Herschel-telescopes, where one hunts scientific results and sentimentalities".—*Ed.*
[c] Engels has: "in French Revolutions, in Reform Bills".—*Ed.*
[d] Carlyle, op. cit., pp. 185-86.—*Ed.*
[e] Engels has: "establishing".—*Ed.*
[f] Carlyle, op. cit., p. 198.—*Ed.*

sisterhood; her typhus-fever kills *them*: they actually were her brothers, though denying it! Had man ever to go lower for a proof?"[a]

Carlyle, incidentally, is in error here, as is Alison. The rich have no sympathy, no interest in the death of the "seventeen". Is it not a public blessing that the "surplus population" should be reduced by seventeen? If only it were a few million instead of a miserly "seventeen", it would be by so much the better.—This is the reasoning of wealthy English Malthusians.

And then there is the other, even worse gospel of dilettantism which has produced a government which does not govern; this gospel has deprived people of all seriousness and impels them to want to appear that which they are not—the striving for "happiness", that is, for good food and drink; this gospel has lifted crude matter on to the throne and destroyed all spiritual substance; what shall be the consequence of all this?

"But what will reflective readers say of a Governing Class[b] such as ours, addressing its Workers with an indictment of 'Over-production'! Over-production: runs it not so? 'Ye miscellaneous [...] manufacturing individuals, ye have produced too much! We accuse you of making above two-hundred thousand shirts for the bare backs of mankind. Your trousers too, which you have made, of fustian, of cassimere, of Scotch-plaid, of [...] nankeen and woollen broadcloth, are they not manifold? Of hats [...], of shoes [...], of stools to sit on, spoons to eat with—Nay [....] You produce gold-watches, jewelleries, silver-forks [...], commodes, chiffoniers, stuffed sofas—Heavens, the Commercial Bazaar and multitudinous Howel-and-Jameses cannot contain you. You have produced, produced;—he that seeks your indictment, let him look around. Millions of shirts, and empty pairs of breeches, hang there in judgment against you. We accuse you of over-producing: you are criminally guilty of producing shirts, breeches, hats, shoes and commodities, in a frightful over-abundance. And now there is a glut, and your operatives cannot be fed!'"[c]

My lords and gentlemen, of what do you accuse those poor workers? "My lords and gentlemen,—why, it was you that were appointed [...] to guard against 'gluts' [....] you were appointed to preside over the Distribution and Apportionment of the Wages of Work done; and to see well that there went no labourer without his hire, were it of money-coins, were it of hemp gallows-ropes: that function was yours, and from immemorial time has been [...].These poor shirt-spinners have forgotten much, which by the virtual unwritten law of their position they should have remembered: but by any *written* recognised law of their position, what have they forgotten? They were set to make shirts. The Community [...] commanded them, saying, 'Make shirts';—and there the shirts are! Too many shirts? Well, that is a novelty, in this intemperate Earth, with its nine-hundred millions of bare backs! But the Community commanded you", my lords and gentlemen, "saying, 'See that the shirts are well apportioned [...]';—and where is the apportionment? Two million shirtless or ill-shirted workers sit [...] in Workhouse Bastilles, five million more [...] in Ugolino Hunger-cellars; and for remedy, you say [...] 'Raise *our* rents!' [...] You continue [...] in [...] a [...] triumphant

---

[a] Carlyle, op. cit., pp. 201-02.—*Ed.*
[b] Engels has: "And what are we to say to a government".—*Ed.*
[c] Carlyle, op. cit., p. 230.—*Ed.*

manner: 'Will you bandy[a] accusations, will you accuse *us* of over-production? We take the Heavens and the Earth to witness that we have produced nothing at all. [...] In the wide domains of created Nature, circulates no shirt or thing of our producing. [...] We are innocent of producing;—ye ungrateful, what mountains of things have we not, on the contrary, had to "consume", and make away with! [...] have they not disappeared before us; as if we had the talent of ostriches [...] and a kind of divine faculty to eat? Ye ungrateful!—and did you not grow under the shadow of our wings? Are not your filthy mills built on these fields of *ours* [...]? And we shall not offer you our own wheat at the price that pleases us [...]? What would become of you, if we'" who own the soil of England "'chose [...] to decide on growing no wheat more?'"[b]

This attitude of the aristocracy, this barbaric question, what would become of you if we did not deign to allow corn to grow, has produced the "mad and miserable Corn Laws"[193]; the Corn Laws which are so insane that no arguments can be brought against them but such as "must needs make an Angel in Heaven and an Ass on Earth weep". The Corn Laws prove that the aristocracy has not yet learned to do no mischief, to sit still and do nothing, to say nothing of doing good, and yet this, according to Carlyle, is their duty:

"You are bound to furnish guidance and governance to England! That is the law of your position." And every worker in the workhouse has the right to ask *them* above all, "'Why am I here?' His appeal is audible in Heaven; and will become audible enough on Earth too, if it remain unheeded here. His appeal is against you", my lords and gentlemen; "you stand in the front-rank of the accused; you, by the very place you hold, have first of all to answer him [...]"[c]

"The fate of the Idle Aristocracy, as one reads its horoscope hitherto in Corn-Laws and such like, is an abyss that fills one with despair. Yes, my rosy fox-hunting brothers [...] through those fresh buxom countenances of yours, through your Corn-Law Majorities, *Sliding-Scales*,[d] Protecting-Duties, Bribery-Elections and triumphant Kentish-fire, a thinking eye discerns ghastly images of ruin, too ghastly for words; a handwriting as of Mene, Mene.[e] [...] Good God! did not a French Donothing Aristocracy, hardly above half a century ago, declare in like manner [...] 'We cannot exist, and continue to dress and parade ourselves, on the [...] rent of the soil [...] we must have farther payment than rent of the soil, we must be exempted from taxes too,'—we must have a Corn-Law to extend our rent? This was in 1789; in four years more"—have you heard of "the Tanneries of Meudon, and the long-naked making for themselves breeches of human skins! May the merciful Heavens avert the omen; may we be wiser, that so we be less wretched."[f]

And the working aristocracy is caught in the partridge nets of the idle aristocracy and with its "Mammonism" eventually finds itself in dire straits too.

---

[a] Engels has: "concoct".—*Ed.*
[b] Carlyle, op. cit., pp. 231-32.—*Ed.*
[c] op. cit., p. 238.—*Ed.*
[d] Engels gives this term in English.—*Ed.*
[e] A phantom handwriting proclaiming imminent doom.—*Ed.*
[f] Carlyle, op. cit., pp. 240-41.—*Ed.*

"The Continental people it would seem, are 'exporting our machinery, beginning to spin cotton and manufacture for themselves, to cut us out of this market and then out of that!' Sad news indeed; [...]—by no means the saddest news. The saddest news is, that we should find our National Existence, as I sometimes hear it said, depend on selling manufactured cotton at a farthing an ell cheaper than any other People. A most narrow stand for a great Nation to base itself on! A stand which, with all the Corn-Law Abrogations conceivable, I do not think will be capable of enduring."[a]

"No great Nation can stand on the apex of such a pyramid; screwing itself higher and higher; balancing itself on its great-toe!"[b] "In brief, all this Mammon-Gospel", with its Hell of "failing to make money", "of Supply-and-demand, Competition", free-trade, "*Laissez-faire*,[194] and Devil take the hindmost, begins to be [...] the shabbiest Gospel ever preached on Earth".[c]

"Yes, were the Corn-Laws ended tomorrow, there is nothing yet ended; there is only room made for all manner of things beginning. The Corn-Laws gone, and Trade made free, it is [...] certain this paralysis of industry will pass away. We shall have another period of commercial enterprise, of victory and prosperity [...]. The strangling band of Famine will be loosened from our necks; we shall have room again to breathe; time to bethink ourselves, to repent and consider! A [...] thrice-precious space of years; wherein to struggle as for life in reforming our foul ways; in alleviating, instructing, regulating our people [...] that something like spiritual food be imparted them, some real governance and guidance be provided them! It will be a priceless time. For our new period [...] of commercial prosperity will and can,[d] on the old methods of 'Competition and Devil take the hindmost', prove but a paroxysm: [...] likely enough, [...] our last. [...] If our Trade in twenty years [...] double itself; yet then also [...] our Population is doubled: we shall then be as we are, only twice as many of us, twice and ten times as unmanageable!"[e]

"Ah me, into what [...] latitudes, in this Time-Voyage, have we wandered; [...]—where the men go about as if by galvanism,[f] with meaningless glaring eyes, and have no soul, but only a beaver-faculty and stomach! The haggard despair of Cotton-factory, Coal-mine [operatives], Chandos Farm-labourers, in these days, is painful to behold; but not so painful [...] to the inner sense, as that brutish godforgetting Profit-and-Loss Philosophy, and Life-theory, which we hear jangled on all hands of us, in senate-houses, spouting-clubs, leading-articles, pulpits and platforms, everywhere as the Ultimate Gospel and candid Plain-English of Man's Life."[g]

"And yet I will venture to believe that in no time, since the beginnings of Society, was the lot of those same dumb millions of toilers so entirely unbearable as it is [...] now [...]. It is not to die, or even to die of hunger, that makes a man wretched [...] all men must die,—the last exit of us all is in a Fire-Chariot of Pain. But it is to live miserable we know not why; to work sore and yet gain nothing; to be heart-worn, weary, yet isolated, unrelated, girt in with a cold universal *Laissez-faire*: it is to die slowly all our life long, imprisoned in a deaf, dead, Infinite Injustice, as in the accursed [iron] belly of a Phalaris' Bull! This is and remains forever intolerable to all men whom God has

---

[a] Carlyle, op. cit., pp. 246-47.—*Ed.*
[b] op. cit., p. 248.—*Ed.*
[c] op. cit., pp. 247-48 (Engels has summarised this passage).—*Ed.*
[d] Engels has: "must".—*Ed.*
[e] Carlyle, op. cit., pp. 249-50.—*Ed.*
[f] Engels has: "like galvanised corpses".—*Ed.*
[g] Carlyle, op. cit., pp. 251-52.—*Ed.*

made. Do we wonder at French Revolutions, Chartisms, Revolts of Three Days[a]? The times, if we will consider them, are really unexampled."[b]

If in such unexampled times the aristocracy shows itself incapable of guiding public affairs, it is necessary to expel it. Hence democracy.

"To what extent Democracy has now reached, how it advances irresistible with ominous, ever-increasing speed, he that will open his eyes on any province of human affairs may discern. [...] From the thunder of Napoleon battles, to the jabbering of Open-vestry in St. Mary Axe, all things announce Democracy."[c]

But what, after all, is democracy?

Nothing but the absence of masters who could govern you, and the acceptance of this unavoidable absence, the attempt to manage without them. "No man oppresses thee, O free and independent Franchiser: but does not this stupid Porter-pot oppress thee? No Son of Adam can bid thee come or go; but this absurd Pot of *Heavy-wet*,[d] this can and does! Thou art the thrall not of Cedric the Saxon, but of thy own brutal appetites [....] And thou pratest of thy 'liberty'? Thou entire blockhead!"[e]

"The notion that a man's liberty consists in giving his vote at election-hustings, and saying, 'Behold now I too have my twenty-thousandth part of a Talker in our National Palaver; will not all the gods be good to me?'—is one of the pleasantest! [...] The liberty especially which has to purchase itself by social isolation, and each man standing separate from the other, having 'no business with him' but a cash account. [...] This liberty turns out, before it have long continued in action, [...] to be, for the Working Millions a liberty to die by want of food; for the Idle Thousands and Units [...] a [...] liberty to *live in want of work*[f] [....] Brethren, we know but imperfectly yet, after ages of Constitutional Government, what Liberty is and Slavery is. Democracy [...] shall go its full course [...]. The Toiling Millions [...], in most vital need and passionate instinctive desire of Guidance, shall cast away False-Guidance; and hope, for an hour, that No-Guidance will suffice them: but it can be for an hour only. [...] The oppression of man by his Mock-Superiors [...] let him shake off [...]; I blame him not, I pity and commend him. But oppression by your Mock-Superiors well shaken off, the grand problem yet remains to solve: That of finding government by your Real-Superiors!"[g]

The leadership, as it now exists, is, to be sure, wretched enough. "In the case of the late Bribery Committee" of Parliament "it seemed to be the conclusion of the soundest practical minds that Bribery could not be put down; that Pure Election was a thing we had seen the last of, and must now go on without, as we best could."

"A Parliament, [...] which proclaims itself elected and eligible by bribery [....] What Legislating can you get out of" that? [...] "Bribery means not only length of purse, [...] but it means dishonesty, and even impudent dishonesty;—brazen insensibility to lying and to making others lie [.,..] What an improvement, were there once fairly,

---

[a] Engels has: "a French Revolution, a 'great week',[195] an English Chartism".—*Ed.*
[b] Carlyle, op. cit., p. 283.—*Ed.*
[c] op. cit., p. 289.—*Ed.*
[d] Engels gives "Heavy-wet" in English.—*Ed.*
[e] Carlyle, op. cit., p. 292.—*Ed.*
[f] In the original a pun: *Freiheit des Verfaulens* (liberty of rotting) *für die faulen* (for the idle).—*Ed.*
[g] Carlyle, op. cit., pp. 293-95.—*Ed.*

in Downing-street, an Election-Office opened,[a] with a Tariff of Boroughs! Such and such a population, amount of property-tax, ground-rental [...] returns two Members, returns one Member, for so much money down: Ipswich so many thousands, Nottingham so many,—[...] now at least you have it fairly by length of purse, and leave the dishonesty, the impudence, the unveracity all handsomely aside."[b]

"Our [...] Parliament announces itself elected and eligible in this manner [....] What is to become of a Parliament elected or eligible in this manner? Unless Belial and Beelzebub have got possession of the throne of this Universe, such Parliament is preparing itself for new Reform-bills. We shall have to try it by Chartism, or any conceivable *ism,* rather than put up with this! [...] A Parliament working with a lie in its mouth, will have to take itself away. [...] At all hours of the day and night, some Chartism[c] is advancing, some armed Cromwell is advancing, to apprise such Parliament: 'Ye are no Parliament. In the name of God,—go!'"[d]

This is the condition of England, according to Carlyle. An idle landowning aristocracy which "have not yet learned even to sit still and do no mischief", a working aristocracy submerged in Mammonism, who, when they ought to be collectively the leaders of labour, "captains of industry", are just a gang of industrial buccaneers and pirates. A Parliament elected by bribery, a philosophy of simply looking on, of doing nothing, of *laissez-faire,* a worn-out, crumbling religion, a total disappearance of all general human interests, a universal despair of truth and humanity, and in consequence a universal isolation of men in their own "brute individuality", a chaotic, savage confusion of all aspects of life, a war of all against all, a general death of the spirit, a dearth of "soul", that is, of truly human consciousness: a disproportionately strong working class, in intolerable oppression and wretchedness, in furious discontent and rebellion against the old social order, and hence a threatening, irresistibly advancing democracy—everywhere chaos, disorder, anarchy, dissolution of the old ties of society, everywhere intellectual insipidity, frivolity, and debility.—That is the condition of England. Thus far, if we discount a few expressions that have derived from Carlyle's particular standpoint, we must allow the truth of all he says. He, alone of the "respectable" class, has kept his eyes open at least towards the facts, he has at least correctly apprehended the immediate present, and that is indeed a very great deal for an "educated" Englishman.

How does the future appear? Matters will not and cannot remain as they are now. We have seen that Carlyle has, as he himself admits, no "Morison's pill",[196] no panacea for curing the

---

[a] Engels has: "Be honest, open an election office in Downing-street".—*Ed.*
[b] Carlyle, op. cit., pp. 338-39.—*Ed.*
[c] Engels has: "Chartist".—*Ed.*
[d] Carlyle, op. cit., p. 340.—*Ed.*

ills of society. In that too he is right. All social philosophy, as long as it still propounds a few principles as its final conclusion, as long as it continues to administer Morison's pills, remains very imperfect; it is not the bare conclusions of which we are in such need, but rather *study*; the conclusions are nothing without the reasoning that has led up to them; this we have known since Hegel; and the conclusions are worse than useless if they are final in themselves, if they are not turned into premises for further deductions. But the conclusions must also assume a distinct form for a time, they must in the course of development evolve from vague imprecision into clear ideas, and then of course, in the case of such an exclusively empirical nation as the English are, they cannot avoid becoming "Morison's pills". Carlyle himself, although he has absorbed much that is German and is quite far removed from crass empiricism, would probably have a few pills to hand if he were less vague and hazy about the future.

Meanwhile he declares everything to be useless and unprofitable as long as mankind persists in atheism, as long as it has not recovered its "soul". Not that traditional Catholicism can be restored in its vigour and vitality, nor that today's religion can be maintained—he knows very well that rituals, dogmas, litanies and Sinai thunder cannot help, that all the thunder of Sinai does not make the truth any truer, nor does it frighten any sensible person, that we are far beyond the religion of fear, but religion itself must be restored, we ourselves see where "two centuries of Atheist Government"—since the "blessed" restoration of Charles II—have brought us, and we shall gradually also be obliged to recognise that this atheism is beginning to show signs of wear and tear. But we have seen what Carlyle calls atheism: it is not so much disbelief in a personal God, as disbelief in the inner essence, in the infinity of the universe, disbelief in reason, despair of the intellect and the truth; his struggle is not against disbelief in the revelation of the Bible, but against the most frightful disbelief, the disbelief in the "Bible of Universal History". That is the eternal book of God in which every man, while his spirit and the light of his eyes are yet with him, may see God's finger write. To make mockery of this is disbelief like none other, a disbelief you would punish, not by burning at the stake, but nevertheless with the most imperative command to keep one's silence until one has something better to say. Why should blissful silence be broken by loud noise, just to proclaim such stuff? If there is no divine reason in the past, but merely diabolic unreason, it will pass away for ever, speak no more of it; we whose fathers were all hanged, should not talk of ropes!

"But modern England cannot believe in history." The eye sees of all things only so much as it can see by its own inherent capacity. A godless century cannot comprehend epochs filled with God. It sees in the past (the Middle Ages) only empty strife, the universal rule of brute force, it does not see that in the last analysis might and right coincide, it just sees stupidity, savage unreason, more fitting to Bedlam than to a human world. From this it naturally follows that the same qualities should continue to prevail in our own time. Millions held in Bastille workhouses; Irish widows who prove that they are human beings by typhus-fever: what would you have? It was ever so, or worse. Has history not always been the exploitation of obdurate stupidity by successful mountebanks? There was no God in the past; nothing but mechanisms and chaotic brute-gods:—how shall the poor "philosophic historian", to whom his own century is all godless, "see any God in other centuries"?

And yet our age is not so utterly forsaken.

"Nay, in our poor distracted[a] Europe itself, in these newest times, have there not religious voices risen,—with a religion new and yet the oldest; entirely indisputable to all hearts of men? Some I do know, who did not call or think themselves 'Prophets' [...]; but who were, in very truth, melodious Voices from the eternal Heart of Nature once again; souls forever venerable to all that have a soul. A French Revolution is one phenomenon; as complement and spiritual exponent thereof, a Poet Goethe and German Literature is to me another. The old Secular or Practical World [...] having gone up in fire, is not here the prophecy and dawn of a new Spiritual World, parent of far nobler, wider, new Practical Worlds? A Life of Antique devoutness, Antique veracity and heroism, has again become possible, is again seen actual there, for the most modern man. A phenomenon, as quiet as it is, comparable for greatness to no other! [...] Touches there are [...] of new Sphere-melody; audible once more, in the infinite jargoning discords [...] of the thing called Literature."[b]

Goethe is the prophet of the "religion of the future", and its cult is work.

"For there is a perennial nobleness, and even sacredness, in Work. Were he never so benighted, forgetful of his high calling, there is always hope in a man that actually and earnestly works: in Idleness alone is there perpetual despair. Work, never so Mammonish, mean, is in communication with Nature; the real desire to get Work done will itself lead one more and more to truth, to Nature's appointments and regulations....

"An endless significance lies in Work; a man perfects himself by working. Foul jungles are cleared away, fair seedfields rise instead, and stately cities; and withal the man himself first ceases to be a jungle and foul unwholesome desert thereby. Consider how, even in the meanest sorts of Labour, the whole soul of a man is composed into a kind of real harmony, the instant he sets himself to work! Doubt,

---

[a] Engels has "fragmented".—*Ed.*
[b] Carlyle, op. cit., pp. 316-17.—*Ed.*

Desire, Sorrow, Remorse,[a] Indignation, Despair itself, all these like helldogs lie beleaguering the soul of the poor dayworker, as of every man: but he bends himself with free valour against his task, and [...] all these shrink murmuring far off into their caves. The man is now a man. The blessed glow of Labour in him, is it not as purifying fire, wherein all poison is burnt up, and of sour smoke itself there is made bright blessed flame!"[b]

"Blessed is he who has found his work; let him ask no other blessedness. He has a work, a life-purpose; he has found it, and will follow it! How, as a free-flowing channel, dug [...] through the sour mud-swamp of one's existence, [...] it[c] runs and flows;—draining off the sour festering water, gradually from the root of the remotest grass-blade; making, instead of pestilential swamp, a green fruitful meadow [....] Labour is Life [....] Properly thou hast no other knowledge but what thou hast got by working: the rest is yet all a hypothesis [...] a thing to be argued of in schools, a thing floating in the clouds, in endless logic-vortices, till we try it and fix it. 'Doubt, of whatever kind, can be ended by Action alone.'"[d]

"Admirable was that saying[e] of the old Monks, '*Laborare est Orare*, Work is Worship.' Older than all preached Gospels was this unpreached, inarticulate, but ineradicable, forever-enduring Gospel: Work, and therein have wellbeing. Man [...] lies there not, in the innermost heart of thee, a Spirit of active Method, a Force for Work;—and burns like a painfully smouldering fire, giving thee no rest till thou unfold it, till thou write it down in beneficent Facts around thee! What is immethodic, waste, thou shalt make methodic, regulated, arable; obedient and productive to thee. Wheresoever thou findest Disorder, there is thy eternal enemy; attack him swiftly, subdue him; make Order of him, the subject not of Chaos, but of Intelligence, Divinity and Thee! [...] But above all, where thou findest Ignorance, Stupidity, Brute-mindedness [...] attack it, I say; smite it wisely, unweariedly, and rest not while thou livest and it lives; but smite, smite, in the name of God! [....] Thou [...] shalt work while it is called Today. For the Night cometh, wherein no man can work.

"All true Work is sacred [....] Sweat of the brow; [...] sweat of the brain, sweat of the heart; which includes all Kepler calculations, Newton meditations, all Sciences, all spoken Epics, all acted Heroisms, Martyrdoms,—up to that 'Agony of bloody sweat', which all men have called divine! [...] If this is not 'worship' [...] the more pity for worship [...]. Who art thou that complainest of thy life of toil? Complain not. [...] To thee Heaven, though severe, is not unkind; Heaven is kind,—as a noble Mother; as that Spartan Mother, saying while she gave her son his shield, 'With it, my son, or upon it!' [...] Complain not; the very Spartans did not complain."

"*One* monster there is in the world: the idle man. What is his 'Religion'? That Nature is a Phantasm [ ]. That God is a lie; and that Man and his Life are a lie."[f]

But work too has been dragged into the furious vortex of disorder and chaos, the principle which was to cleanse, enlighten, evolve, has succumbed to involution, confusion and obscurity. This really leads to the main issue, the future of work.

---

[a] Engels has *Unruhe*—"disquiet", "anxiety".—*Ed.*
[b] Carlyle, op. cit., pp. 264-65.—*Ed.*
[c] Engels has "his life" instead of "it".—*Ed.*
[d] Carlyle, op. cit., p. 266.—*Ed.*
[e] Carlyle has just "that" instead of "that saying", and means "that religion".—*Ed.*
[f] Carlyle, op. cit., pp. 270-73.—*Ed.*

"What a business will this be, which our Continental friends, groping this long while somewhat absurdly about it and about it, call 'Organisation of Labour';—which must be taken out of the hands of absurd windy persons, and put into the hands of wise, laborious [...] and valiant men,[a] to begin with it straightway; to proceed with it, and succeed in it more and more, if Europe, at any rate if England, is to continue habitable much longer. Looking at the kind of most noble Corn-Law Dukes [or Practical Duces] we have, and also of right reverend Soul-Overseers, Christian Spiritual Duces 'on a minimum of four thousand five hundred', one's hopes are a little chilled. Courage, nevertheless; there are many brave men in England! My indomitable Plugson,[b]—nay is there not even in thee some hope? Thou art hitherto a Bucanier [...] but in that grim brow, in that indomitable heart which can conquer Cotton, do there not perhaps lie other ten times nobler conquests?"[c]

"Look around you. Your world-hosts are all in mutiny, in confusion, destitution; on the eve of fiery wreck and madness! They will not march farther for you, on the sixpence a day and supply-and-demand principle: they will not; nor ought they, nor can they.[d] [...] Their souls are driven nigh mad; let yours be [...] saner. Not as a bewildered bewildering mob; but as a firm regimented mass, with real captains over them, will these men march any more. All human interests, combined human endeavours [...] have, at a certain stage of their development, required organising: and Work, the grandest of human interests, does now require it."[e]

In order to effect this organisation, in order to put true guidance and true government in the place of false guidance, Carlyle longs for a "true aristocracy", a "hero-worship", and puts forward the second great problem to discover the ἄριϛτοι, the best, whose task it is to combine "with inevitable Democracy indispensable Sovereignty".

From these excerpts Carlyle's position emerges fairly clearly. His whole outlook is essentially pantheistic, and, more specifically, pantheistic with German overtones. The English have no pantheism but merely scepticism; the conclusion of all English philosophising is the despair of reason, the confessed inability to solve the contradictions with which one is ultimately faced, and consequently on the one hand a relapse into faith and on the other devotion to pure practice, without a further thought for metaphysics, etc. Carlyle with his pantheism derived from German literature is therefore a "phenomenon" in England, and for the practical and sceptical English a pretty incomprehensible one. People gape at him, speak of "German mysticism" and distorted English; others claim there is at bottom something in it, his

---

[a] Engels has: "valiant, wise, laborious men".—*Ed.*
[b] Engels has: "you indomitable factory-lord".—*Ed.*
[c] Carlyle, op. cit., pp. 262-63.—*Ed.*
[d] Engels has: "they will not and that is their right".—*Ed.*
[e] Carlyle, op. cit., p. 368.—*Ed.*

English, though unusual, is very fine, he is a prophet, etc.—but nobody really knows what to make of it all.

For us Germans, who know the antecedents of Carlyle's position, the matter is clear enough. On the one hand vestiges of Tory romanticism and humane attitudes originating with Goethe, and on the other sceptical-empirical England, these factors are sufficient for one to deduce the whole of Carlyle's view of the world from them. Like all pantheists, Carlyle has not yet resolved the contradiction, and Carlyle's dualism is aggravated by the fact that though he is acquainted with German literature, he is not acquainted with its necessary corollary, German philosophy, and all his views are in consequence ingenuous, intuitive, more like Schelling than Hegel. With Schelling—that is to say, with the old Schelling, not the Schelling of the philosophy of revelation [197]—Carlyle really has a great deal in common; with Strauss, whose outlook is similarly pantheistic, he is on common ground in his "hero-worship" or "cult of genius".

The critique of pantheism has recently been so exhaustively set forth in Germany that little more remains to be said. Feuerbach's "Theses" in the *Anekdota*[a] and Bruno Bauer's works contain all the relevant material. We will therefore be able to confine ourselves simply to following up the implications of Carlyle's position and showing that it is basically only a first step towards the position adopted by this journal.

Carlyle complains about the emptiness and hollowness of the age, about the inner rottenness of all social institutions. The complaint is fair; but by simply complaining one does not dispose of the matter; in order to redress the evil, its cause must be discovered; and if Carlyle had done this, he would have found that this desultoriness and hollowness, this "soullessness", this irreligion and this "atheism" have their roots in religion itself. Religion by its very essence drains man and nature of substance, and transfers this substance to the phantom of an other-worldly God, who in turn then graciously permits man and nature to receive some of his superfluity. Now as long as faith in this other-worldly phantom is vigorous and alive, thus long man will acquire in this roundabout way at least some substance. The strong faith of the Middle Ages did indeed give the whole epoch considerable energy in this way, but it was energy that did not come from without but was already present within human nature,

---

[a] Ludwig Feuerbach, "Vorläufige Thesen zur Reformation der Philosophie" in *Anekdota zur neuesten deutschen Philosophie und Publicistik.*—*Ed.*

though as yet unperceived and undeveloped. Faith gradually weakened, religion crumbled in the face of the rising level of civilisation, but still man did not perceive that he had worshipped and deified his own being in the guise of a being outside himself. Lacking awareness and at the same time faith, man can have no substance, he is *bound* to despair of truth, reason and nature, and this hollowness and lack of substance, the despair of the eternal facts of the universe will last until mankind perceives that the being it has worshipped as God was its own, as yet unknown being, until—but why should I copy Feuerbach.

The hollowness has long been there, for religion represents man's action of making himself hollow; and you are surprised that now, when the purple that concealed it has faded, when the fog that enveloped it has passed away, that now, to your consternation, it emerges in the full light of day?

Carlyle accuses the age furthermore—this is the immediate consequence of the foregoing—of hypocrisy and lying. Naturally the hollowness and enervation must be decently concealed and kept upright by accessories, padded clothes and whalebone stays! We too attack the hypocrisy of the present Christian state of the world; the struggle against it, our liberation from it and the liberation of the world from it are ultimately our sole occupation; but because through the development of philosophy we are able to discern this hypocrisy, and because we are waging the struggle scientifically, the nature of this hypocrisy is no longer so strange and incomprehensible to us as it admittedly still is to Carlyle. This hypocrisy is traced back by us to religion, the first word of which is a lie—or does religion not begin by showing us something human and claiming it is something superhuman, something divine? But because we know that all this lying and immorality follows from religion, that religious hypocrisy, theology, is the archetype of all other lies and hypocrisy, we are justified in extending the term "theology" to the whole untruth and hypocrisy of the present, as was originally done by Feuerbach and Bruno Bauer. Carlyle should read their works if he wishes to know the origin of the immorality that plagues our whole society.

A new religion, a pantheistic hero-worship, a cult of work, ought to be set up or is to be expected; but this is impossible; all the possibilities of religion are exhausted; after Christianity, after absolute, i.e., abstract, religion, after "religion as such", no other form of religion can arise. Carlyle himself realises that Catholic, Protestant or any other kind of Christianity is irresistibly moving towards its downfall; if he knew the nature of Christianity, he would realise that after it no other religion is possible. Not even pantheism! Pantheism itself is another consequence of Christianity and cannot be divorced from its antecedent, at least that is true of modern pantheism, of Spinoza's, Schelling's, Hegel's and also Carlyle's pantheism. Once more, Feuerbach relieves me of the trouble of providing proof of this.

As I have said, we too are concerned with combating the lack of principle, the inner emptiness, the spiritual deadness, the untruthfulness of the age; we are waging a war to the death against all these things, just as Carlyle is, and there is a much greater probability that we shall succeed than that he will, because we know what we want. We want to put an end to atheism, as Carlyle portrays it, by giving back to man the substance he has lost through religion; not as divine but as human substance, and this whole process of giving back is no more than simply the awakening of self-consciousness. We want to sweep away everything that claims to be supernatural and superhuman, and thereby get rid of untruthfulness, for the root of all untruth and lying is the pretension of the human and the natural to be superhuman and supernatural. For that reason we have once and for all declared war on religion and religious ideas and care little whether we are called atheists or anything else. If however Carlyle's pantheistic definition of atheism were correct, it is not we but our Christian opponents who would be the true atheists. We have no intention of attacking the "eternal inner Facts of the universe", on the contrary, we have for the first time truly substantiated them by proving their perpetuity and rescuing them from the omnipotent arbitrariness of an inherently self-contradictory God. We have no intention of pronouncing "the world, man and his life a lie"; on the contrary, our Christian opponents are guilty of this act of immorality when they make the world and man dependent on the grace of a God who in reality was only created from the reflected image of man in the crude *hyle* of his own undeveloped consciousness. We have no intention whatever of doubting or despising the "revelation of history", for history is all and everything to us and we hold it more highly than any other previous philosophical trend, more highly than Hegel even, who after all used it only as a case against which to test his logical problem.

It is the other side that scorns history and disregards the development of mankind; it is the Christians again who, by putting forward a separate "History of the Kingdom of God" deny that real history has any inner substantiality and claim that this substantiality belongs exclusively to their other-worldly, abstract and, what is more, fictitious history; who, by asserting that the culmination of the human species is their Christ, make history attain an imaginary goal, interrupt it in mid-course and are now obliged, if only for the sake of consistency, to declare the following eighteen hundred years to be totally nonsensical and utterly meaningless. *We* lay claim to the meaning of history; but we see in history not the revelation of "God" but of man and only of man. We have no need, in order to see the splendour of the human character, in order to recognise the development of the human species through history, its irresistible progress, its ever-certain victory over the unreason of the individual, its overcoming of all that is apparently supernatural, its hard but successful struggle against nature until the final achievement of free, human self-consciousness, the discernment of the unity of man and nature, and the independent creation—voluntarily and by its own effort—of a new world based on purely human and moral social relationships—in order to recognise all that in its greatness, we have no need first to summon up the abstraction of a "God" and to attribute to it everything beautiful, great, sublime and truly human; we do not need to follow this roundabout path, we do not need first to imprint the stamp of the "divine" on what is truly human, in order to be sure of its greatness and splendour. On the contrary, the "more divine", in other words, the more inhuman, something is, the less we shall be able to admire it. Only the *human* origin of the content of all religions still preserves for them here and there some claim to respect; only the consciousness that even the wildest superstition nevertheless has within it at bottom the eternal determinants of human nature, in however dislocated and distorted a form, only this awareness saves the history of religion, and particularly of the Middle Ages, from total rejection and *eternal* oblivion, which would otherwise certainly be the fate of these "godly" histories. The more "godly" they are, the more inhuman, the more bestial, and the "godly" Middle Ages did indeed produce the culmination of human bestiality, serfdom, *jus primae noctis*, etc. The god*lessness* of our age, of which Carlyle so much complains, is precisely its *saturation* with God. From this it also becomes clear why, above, I gave man as the solution to the riddle of the Sphinx. The question has previously always been: what is God? and German philosophy has answered the question in this sense: God is man. Man has only to understand himself, to take himself as the measure of all aspects of life, to judge according to his being, to organise the world in a truly human manner according to the demands of his own nature, and he will have solved the riddle of our time. Not in other-worldly, non-existent regions, not beyond time and space, not with a "God" immanent in or opposed to the world, is the truth to be found, but much nearer, in man's own breast. Man's own substance is far more splendid and sublime than the imaginary substance of any conceivable "God", who is after all only the more or less indistinct and distorted image of man himself. So when Carlyle follows Ben Jonson in saying, man has lost his soul and is only now beginning to notice the want of it, the right formulation would be: in religion man has lost his own substance, has alienated his humanity, and now that religion, through the progress of history, has begun to totter, he notices his emptiness and instability. But there is no other salvation for him, he cannot regain his humanity, his substance, other than by thoroughly overcoming all religious ideas and returning firmly and honestly, not to "God", but to himself.

All of this may also be found in Goethe, the "prophet", and anyone who has his eyes open can read this between the lines. Goethe did not like to be concerned with "God"; the word made him uncomfortable, he felt at home only in human matters, and this humanity, this emancipation of art from the fetters of religion is precisely what constitutes Goethe's greatness. Neither the ancients nor Shakespeare can measure up to him in this respect. But this consummate humanity, this overcoming of the religious dualism can only be apprehended in its full historical significance by those who are not strangers to that other aspect of German national development, philosophy. What Goethe could only express spontaneously, and therefore, it is true, in a certain sense "prophetically", has been developed and substantiated in contemporary German philosophy. Carlyle too embodies assumptions which, logically, must lead to the position set forth above. Pantheism itself is but the last, preliminary step towards a free and human point of view. History, which Carlyle presents as the real "revelation", contains only what is human, and only by an arbitrary act can its content be taken away from humanity and credited to the account of a "God". Work, free activity, in which Carlyle similarly sees a "cult", is again a purely human matter and can only be linked with "God" in an arbitrary manner. What is the point of continually pushing to the fore a word which *at best* only expresses the boundlessness of indetermination and, what is more, maintains the illusion of dualism, a word which in itself is the denial of nature and humanity?

So much for the inward, religious aspect of Carlyle's standpoint. It serves as a point of departure for the assessment of the outward, politico-social aspect; Carlyle has still enough religion to remain in a state of unfreedom; pantheism still recognises something higher than man himself. Hence his longing for a "true aristocracy", for "heroes"; as if these heroes could at best be more than *men*. If he had understood man as man in all his infinite complexity, he would not have conceived the idea of once more dividing mankind into two lots, sheep and goats, rulers and ruled, aristocrats and the rabble, lords and dolts, he would have seen the proper social function of talent not in ruling by force but in acting as a stimulant and taking the lead. The role of talent is to convince the masses of the truth of its ideas, and it will then have no need further to worry about their application, which will follow entirely of its own accord. Mankind is surely not passing through democracy to arrive back eventually at the point of departure.—What Carlyle says about democracy, incidentally, leaves little to be desired, if we discount what we have just been referring to, his lack of clarity about the goal, the purpose of modern democracy. Democracy, true enough, is only a transitional stage, though not towards a new, improved aristocracy, but towards real human freedom; just as the irreligiousness of the age will eventually lead to complete emancipation from everything that is religious, superhuman and supernatural, and not to its restoration.

Carlyle recognises the inadequacy of "competition, demand" and "supply, Mammonism", etc., and is far removed from asserting the absolute justification of landownership. So why has he not drawn the straightforward conclusion from all these assumptions and rejected the whole concept of property? How does he think he will destroy "competition", "supply and demand", Mammonism, etc., as long as the root of all these things, private property, exists? "Organisation of labour" cannot help in this respect, it cannot even be applied without a certain identity of interests. Why then does he not act consistently and decisively, proclaiming the identity of interests the only truly human state of affairs, and thereby putting an end to all difficulties, all imprecision and lack of clarity?

In all Carlyle's rhapsodies, there is not a syllable mentioning the English Socialists. As long as he adheres to his present point of view, which is admittedly infinitely far in advance of that of the mass of educated people in England but still abstract and theoretical, he will indeed not be able to view their efforts with particular sympathy. The English Socialists are purely practical and therefore also propose remedies, home-colonies,[198] etc., rather in the manner of Morison's pills; their philosophy is truly English, sceptical, in other words they despair of theory, and for all practical purposes they cling to the materialism upon which their whole social system is based; all this will have little appeal for Carlyle, but he is as one-sided as they. Both have only overcome the contradiction *within* the contradiction; the Socialists within the sphere of practice, Carlyle within the sphere of theory, and even there only spontaneously, whereas the Socialists, by means of reasoning, have definitely overcome the practical aspect of the contradiction. The Socialists are still Englishmen, when they ought to be simply men, of philosophical developments on the Continent they are only acquainted with materialism but not with German philosophy, that is their only shortcoming, and they are directly engaged on the rectification of this deficiency by working for the removal of national differences. We have no need to be very hasty in forcing German philosophy on them, they will come to it of their own accord and it could be of little use to them now. But in any case they are the only party in England which has a future, relatively weak though they may be. Democracy, Chartism must soon be victorious, and then the mass of the English workers will have the choice only between starvation and socialism.

For Carlyle and his standpoint, ignorance of German philosophy is not a matter of such indifference. He is himself a theoretician of the German type, and yet at the same time his nationality leads him to empiricism; he is beset by a flagrant contradiction which can only be resolved if he continues to develop his German-theoretical viewpoint to its final conclusion, until it is totally reconciled with empiricism. To surmount the contradiction in which he is working, Carlyle has only *one* more step to take, but as all experience in Germany has shown, it is a difficult one. Let us hope that he will take it, and although he is no longer young, he will still probably be capable of it, for the progress shown in his last book[a] proves that his views are still developing.[199]

All this shows that Carlyle's book is ten thousand times more worth translating into German than all the legions of English novels which every day and every hour are imported into Germany, and I can only advocate such a translation. But let our hack translators just keep their hands off it! Carlyle writes a very particular English, and a translator who does not thoroughly understand English and references to English conditions would make the most absurd howlers.

---

[a] Thomas Carlyle, *Past and Present*.—*Ed.*

Following this somewhat general introduction, I shall examine in greater detail in the following numbers of this journal the condition of England and the essential part of it, the condition of the working class. The condition of England is of immense importance for history and for all other countries; for as regards social matters England is of course far in advance of all other countries.

Written in January 1844

First published in the *Deutsch-Französische Jahrbücher*, 1844

Signed: *Frederick Engels in Manchester*

Printed according to the journal

Published in English for the first time

THE CONDITION OF ENGLAND [200]

I.

THE EIGHTEENTH CENTURY

[*Vorwärts!* No. 70, August 31, 1844]

The century of revolution has to all appearances passed England by, causing little change. While on the Continent an entire old world was shattered, while a twenty-five-year war [201] cleared the air, in England everything remained calm, neither state nor church were in any way threatened. And yet since the middle of the last century England has experienced a greater upheaval than any other country—an upheaval which is all the more momentous the more quietly it is brought about, and it will therefore in all probability attain its goal more readily in practice than the political revolution in France or the philosophical revolution in Germany. The revolution in England is a social one and therefore more comprehensive and far-reaching than any other. There are no fields—however remote—of human knowledge and no conditions of life which have not contributed to it and which in turn have not been affected by it. The only true revolution is a social revolution, to which political and philosophical revolution must lead; and this social revolution has already been in progress in England for seventy or eighty years and is rapidly approaching its crisis at this very time.

The eighteenth century was the assembling, the gathering of mankind from the fragmentation and isolation into which it had been driven by Christianity; it was the penultimate step towards the self-understanding and self-liberation of mankind, but just because it was the penultimate step it was still partial and remained within the contradictions. The eighteenth century collated the results of the past, which had previously been scattered and appeared to be fortuitous, and laid bare their necessity and inner connection. The jumble of countless scientific discoveries was put in order, classified and the causal connections shown; knowledge became science, and the sciences approached their perfection, that is to say, they took philosophy on the one hand and practice on the other as their point of departure. Before the eighteenth century science did not exist; the study of nature assumed its scientific form only in the eighteenth century or, in some fields, a few years earlier. Newton created scientific astronomy with the law of gravitation, scientific optics with the decomposition of light, scientific mathematics with the binomial theorem and the theory of infinity, and scientific mechanics with the analysis of the nature of forces. Physics likewise acquired its scientific character in the eighteenth century; chemistry was only brought into being by Black, Lavoisier and Priestley; geography became a science with the establishment of the form of the earth and the many voyages which only now were of benefit to science; with Buffon and Linné natural history too became a science; even geology gradually began to struggle free from the whirl of fantastic hypotheses which threatened to engulf it. The concept of the Encyclopaedia was typical of the eighteenth century; it was based on the awareness that all these sciences were interconnected but it was not yet able to show these connections, so that only a simple juxtaposition could be achieved. History was in a similar position; now for the first time we find voluminous compilations of world history, as yet without any critical comment, and entirely without a philosophical approach, but nevertheless universal history instead of the previous historical fragments limited both in time and place. Politics was given a human foundation, and political economy was reformed by Adam Smith. The culmination of science in the eighteenth century was materialism, the first system of natural philosophy and the consequence of this development of the natural sciences. The struggle against the abstract subjectivity of Christianity forced the philosophy of the eighteenth century to the other extreme; it opposed subjectivity with objectivity, the mind with nature, spiritualism with materialism, the abstract individual with the abstract universal or substance. The eighteenth century represents the revival of the spirit of antiquity as against that of Christianity. Materialism and the republic; the philosophy and politics of the ancient world, arose anew, and the French, the exponents of the ethos of antiquity *within* Christianity, assumed the historical initiative for a time.

The eighteenth century thus did not resolve the great antithesis which has been the concern of history from the beginning and whose development constitutes history, the antithesis of substance and subject, nature and mind, necessity and freedom; but it set the two sides against each other, fully developed and in all their sharpness, and thereby made it necessary to overcome the antithesis. The consequence of this clear final evolution of the antithesis was general revolution which spread over various nations and whose imminent completion will at the same time resolve the antithesis of history up to the present. The Germans, the nation of Christian spiritualism, experienced a philosophical revolution; the French, the nation of classical materialism and hence of politics, had to go through a political revolution; the English, a nation that is a mixture of German and French elements, who therefore embody both sides of the antithesis and are for that reason more universal than either of the two factors taken separately, were for that reason drawn into a more universal, a social revolution.

This will need to be elaborated in greater detail, for the position of nations, at least with regard to recent times, has in our philosophy of history so far been dealt with very inadequately, or rather not at all.

That Germany, France and England are the three foremost countries at the present moment in history, I can doubtless take for granted; that the Germans represent the Christian spiritual principle, the French that of classical materialism, in other words, that the former represent religion and the church and the latter politics and the state, is equally obvious or will be made so in due course; the significance of the English in recent history is less conspicuous and yet for our present purpose it is the most important. The English nation was formed from Germanic and Romance people at a time when the two nations had only just separated from one another and their development towards the two sides of the antithesis had scarcely begun. The Germanic and Romance elements developed alongside one another and eventually formed one nation which contains the two unmediated sides. Germanic idealism retained abundant scope so that it was even able to turn into its opposite, abstract externalism; the fact that women and children may still be legally sold, and indeed the whole mercantile spirit of the English, must definitely be attributed to the Germanic element. In a similar fashion, Romance materialism turned into abstract idealism, inwardness and piety; hence the phenomenon of Romance Catholicism persisting *within* Germanic Protestantism, the Established Church, the papacy of the sovereign and the thoroughly Catholic manner of disposing of religion with mere formalities. The English nation is characterised by this unresolved contradiction and the mingling of the sharpest contrasts. The English are the most religious nation on earth and at the same time the most irreligious; they worry more about the next world than any other nation, and at the same time they live as though this world were all that mattered to them; their expectation of heaven does not hinder them in the slightest from believing equally firmly in the "hell of making no money". Hence the everlasting inner restlessness of the English, which is caused by the sense of being unable to resolve the contradiction and which drives them out of themselves and into activity. The sense of contradiction is the source of energy, but merely externalised energy, and this sense of contradiction was the source of colonisation, seafaring, industry and the immense practical activity of the English in general. The inability to resolve the contradiction runs like a thread through the whole of English philosophy and forces it into empiricism and scepticism. Because Bacon could not resolve the contradiction between idealism and realism with *his* intellect, the intellect as such had to be incapable of solving it, idealism was simply discarded and empiricism regarded as the only remedy. From the same source derives the critical analysis of cognition and the whole psychological tendency within whose bounds English philosophy has moved from the outset, and in the end, after many unsuccessful attempts at resolving the contradiction, philosophy declares it to be insoluble and the intellect to be inadequate, and seeks a way out either in religious faith or in empiricism. Humean scepticism is still the form all irreligious philosophising takes in England today. We cannot know, this viewpoint argues, whether a God exists; if one exists, he is incapable of any communication with us, and we have therefore so to arrange our practical affairs as if he did not exist. We cannot know whether the mind is distinct from the body and immortal; we therefore live as if this life were the only one we have and do not bother about things that go beyond our understanding. In short, this scepticism is in practice exactly the same as French materialism, but in metaphysical theory it never advances beyond the inability of arriving at any definitive conclusion.

However because the English embodied within them both the elements which were responsible for historical progress on the Continent, they were therefore able, even without having much contact with the Continent, to keep abreast of development there and at times even to be ahead of it. The English revolution of the seventeenth century provides the exact model for the French one of 1789. In the "Long Parliament" the three stages which in

France took the form of Constituent and Legislative Assembly and National Convention, are easy to distinguish; the transition from constitutional monarchy to democracy, military despotism, restoration and *juste-milieu* revolution[a] is sharply delineated in the English revolution. Cromwell is Robespierre and Napoleon rolled into one; the Presbyterians, Independents and Levellers correspond to the Gironde, the Montagnards and the Hébertists and Babouvists; in both cases the political outcome is rather pitiable, and the whole parallel, which could be elaborated in much greater detail, incidentally also proves that a religious and an irreligious revolution, as long as they remain political, will in the final analysis amount to the *same* thing. Admittedly, this lead the English had over the Continent was only temporary and was gradually evened out again; the English revolution ended in *juste-milieu* and the creation of two national parties, whilst the French one is not yet complete and cannot be so until it achieves the result which the German philosophical and the English social revolutions have to achieve as well.

The English national character is thus substantially different both from the German and from the French character; the despair of overcoming the contradiction and the consequent total surrender to empiricism are its peculiar characteristics. The pure Germanic element converted its abstract inwardness into abstract outwardness, but this outwardness never lost the mark of its origin and always remained subordinate to inwardness and spiritualism. The French too are to be found on the side of materialism and empiricism; but because this empiricism is the primary national tendency and not a secondary consequence of a national consciousness divided within itself, it asserts itself nationally, generally and finds expression in political activity. The Germans asserted the absolute justification of spiritualism and hence sought to set forth the universal interests of mankind in religious and later in philosophic terms. The French opposed this spiritualism with materialism as something absolutely justified and consequently considered that the state was the eternal manifestation of these interests. The English however *have* no universal interests, they cannot mention them without touching that sore spot, the contradiction, they despair of them and have only individual interests. This absolute subjectivity, the fragmentation of the universal into the many individual parts, is admittedly of Germanic origin, but, as we have said, it is cut off from its roots and

---

[a] The French revolution of July 1830.—*Ed.*

therefore only takes effect *empirically,* which is precisely what distinguishes English social empiricism from French political empiricism. France's actions were always national, conscious of their entireness and universality from the start; England's actions were the work of independent coexisting individuals—the movement of disconnected atoms—who rarely acted together as one whole, and even then only from *individual* motives, and whose lack of unity is at this very time exposed to the light of day in the universal misery and complete fragmentation of society.

In other words, only England has a *social* history. Only in England have individuals as such, without consciously standing for universal principles, furthered national development and brought it near to its conclusion. Only here have the masses acted as masses, for the sake of their interests as individuals; only here have principles been turned into interests before they were able to influence history. The French and the Germans are gradually attaining a social history too, but they have not got one yet. On the Continent too there have been poverty, misery and social oppression, this however has had no effect on national development; but the misery and poverty of the working class in present-day England has national and even world-historical importance. On the Continent the social aspect is still completely hidden by the political aspect and has not yet become detached from it, whilst in England the social aspect has gradually prevailed over the political one and has made it subservient. The whole of English politics is fundamentally social in nature, and social questions are expressed in a political way only because England has not yet advanced beyond the state, and because politics is a necessary expedient there.

As long as church and state are the only forms in which the universal characteristics of human nature are realised, there can be no question of social history. Antiquity and the Middle Ages were also therefore without social development; only the Reformation, the first, as yet biassed and blundering attempt at a reaction against the Middle Ages, brought about a major social change, the transformation of serfs into "free" workers. But even this change remained without much enduring effect on the Continent, indeed it really took root there only after the revolution of the eighteenth century; whereas in England the category of serfs was transformed during the Reformation into villeins, bordars and cottars[a] and thus into a class of workers enjoying personal freedom,[202] and as

---

[a] Engels gives the words "villeins", "bordars" and "cottars" in English.—*Ed.*

early as the eighteenth century the consequences of this revolution became evident there. Why this happened only in England is explained above.

[*Vorwärts!* No. 71, September 4, 1844]

Antiquity, which as yet knew nothing of the rights of the individual, whose whole outlook was essentially abstract, universal and material, could therefore not exist without slavery. The Christian-Germanic view of the world, by contrast with antiquity, set up abstract subjectivity, and hence arbitrariness, inwardness and spiritualism, as the basic principle. However this subjectivity, precisely because it was abstract and one-sided, was bound to turn at once into its opposite and to engender, not the freedom of the individual, but the enslavement of the individual. Abstract inwardness became abstract outwardness, the rejection and alienation of man, and the first consequence of the new principle was the restoration of slavery in another form, that of serfdom, which was less offensive but for that reason hypocritical and more inhuman. The dissolution of the feudal system, the political Reformation, in other words, the *apparent* acknowledgement of reason, and hence really the culmination of unreason, *appeared* to abolish this serfdom, but in reality only made it more inhuman and more universal. It was the first to declare that mankind should no longer be held together by force, that is, by *political* means, but by self-interest, that is, by *social* means, and through this new principle it laid the foundation for social advance. But although it thus negated the state, on the other hand it actually revived the state by restoring to it the content which had previously been usurped by the church, and thus gave the state, which in the Middle Ages had been an empty form of little consequence, the strength for further development. The Christian state, the culmination of the political aspect of the Christian world order, arose from the ruins of feudalism; another aspect of the Christian world order attained its culmination by elevating interestedness to a general principle. For interest is essentially subjective and egoistical, it is the interest of the individual, and as such the highest point of the Germanic and Christian principle of subjectivity and particularisation. The consequence of elevating interest to the nexus of man to man—that is as long as interest remains directly subjective and purely egoistical—is bound to be universal fragmentation, the concentration of each individual upon himself, isolation, the transformation of mankind into a collection of mutually repelling atoms; and this particularisation is again the ultimate consequence of the Christian principle of subjectivity, the culmination of the Christian world order.

Moreover, as long as private property, the basic form of alienation, exists, interest must necessarily be the interest of the individual and its domination will be the domination of property. The abolition of feudal servitude has made "cash-payment the sole relation of human beings".[a] Property, a natural, spiritless principle, as opposed to the human and spiritual principle, is thus enthroned, and ultimately, to complete this alienation, money—the alienated, empty abstraction of property—is made master of the world. Man has ceased to be the slave of men and has become the slave of *things*; the perversion of the human condition is complete; the servitude of the modern commercial world, this highly developed, total, universal venality, is more inhuman and more all-embracing than the serfdom of the feudal era; prostitution is more immoral and more bestial than the *jus primae noctis*.

The Christian world order cannot be taken any further than this; it must collapse under its own weight and make way for a humane, rational order. The Christian state is merely the last possible manifestation of the state as such; its demise will necessarily mean the demise of the state as such. The disintegration of mankind into a mass of isolated, mutually repelling atoms in itself means the destruction of all corporate, national and indeed of any particular interests and is the last necessary step towards the free and spontaneous association of men. The supremacy of money as the culmination of the process of alienation is an inevitable stage which has to be passed through, if man is to return to himself, as he is now on the verge of doing.

These consequences of the abolition of the feudal system have been taken to such lengths by the social revolution in England that the crisis which will destroy the Christian world order can no longer be far away, and indeed that the time of this crisis can be predicted with certainty, even if not quantitatively, in years, at least qualitatively; for this crisis must begin when the Corn Laws are repealed and the People's Charter introduced,[203] in other words, when the aristocracy of birth has been politically overcome by the money aristocracy and the latter in turn by working-class democracy.

The sixteenth and seventeenth centuries had brought into being all the preconditions for social revolution, they had destroyed the

---

[a] Thomas Carlyle, *Past and Present*, p. 198.—*Ed.*

Middle Ages, established social, political and religious Protestantism, created England's colonies, sea-power and trade, and set up alongside the aristocracy a growing and already quite powerful middle class. Social conditions gradually settled down after the disturbances of the seventeenth century and acquired a stable form which they retained until about 1780 or 1790.

There were at that time three classes of landowners, the aristocratical landlords, still the only, and unchallenged, nobility of the kingdom, who leased their estates in parcels and consumed the income in London or while travelling; the non-aristocratical landlords or country gentlemen (usually called squires[a]), who lived at their country-seats, put out their land on lease and enjoyed among their tenants and other local inhabitants the aristocratic esteem which was denied to them in the town on account of their humble origin, lack of education and unpolished country manners. This class has now totally disappeared. The old squires who ruled with patriarchal authority the countryfolk of the district and acted as advisers, arbiters and everything rolled into one, are quite extinct; their descendants call themselves the untitled aristocracy of England, as regards education and fine manners, luxury and aristocratic demeanour they vie with the aristocracy, which has little advantage left over them, and all they have in common with their rude and unpolished forefathers are their estates.

The third class of landowners was that of the yeomen,[b] who owned small plots of land which they worked themselves, usually in the good old careless manner of their forebears; this class too has disappeared from the face of England, the social revolution has expropriated it and brought about the curious situation, that at the same time as in France the large landed estates were being forcibly parcelled out, in England the parcels were being attracted by the large landed estates and swallowed up by them. Alongside the yeomen there were small tenant farmers who were usually engaged in weaving as well as farming; they too are no longer to be found in modern England; almost all the land belongs now to a small number of large estates and is thus let on lease. The competition of the large tenant farmers drove the small tenant farmers and yeomen out of the market and impoverished them; they became agricultural day-labourers and weavers dependent on wages and supplied the masses whose influx caused the towns to grow with such amazing rapidity.

---

[a] Engels gives the words "country gentlemen" and "squires" in English.—*Ed.*
[b] Engels gives this word in English.—*Ed.*

The farmers of those days led a quiet and placid life of godliness and propriety, they lived with few cares, but also without any changes, without general interests, without culture and mental activity; they were still at the prehistoric stage. The position in the towns was not very different. Only London was an important centre of trade; Liverpool, Hull, Bristol, Manchester, Birmingham, Leeds and Glasgow were still insignificant. The main industries, spinning and weaving, were carried on chiefly in the country or at least not within the towns, but in their vicinity; the production of metal and pottery wares was still at the handicraft stage of development; not much was therefore likely to happen in the towns. The extreme simplicity of the electoral system relieved the townsfolk of any political cares, they were nominally Whig or Tory, but knew very well that it really made no difference, for they did not have the vote; small merchants, shopkeepers and craftsmen made up the whole urban population and led that familiar life of the small provincial town which is so totally incomprehensible to the English today. Little use was as yet made of the mines; iron, copper and tin lay more or less undisturbed below ground, and coal was only used for domestic purposes. In short, the situation in England was then similar to that which, alas, still exists in most of France and particularly in Germany, that is, a state of antediluvian apathy towards all general and intellectual interests, a state of social infancy, in which society does not as yet exist, where there is as yet no life, no consciousness, no activity. This state is in fact a continuation of feudalism and of medieval thoughtlessness, and will only be overcome with the arrival of modern feudalism, with the division of society into owners of property and non-owners. We on the Continent, as we have said, are still deeply immersed in this state; the English fought against it for eighty years and overcame it forty years ago. If civilisation is a matter of practice, a social quality, then the English are indeed the most civilised people in the world.

I mentioned above that the sciences had assumed their scientific form in the eighteenth century and were consequently connected on the one hand with philosophy and on the other with practice. The result of taking philosophy as the point of departure was materialism (for which Newton was just as much a prerequisite as Locke), the Enlightenment and the French political revolution. The result of taking practice as the point of departure was the English social revolution.

In 1760 George III began his reign, drove out the Whigs—who had held office almost uninterruptedly since the reign of George I

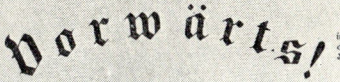

A page from issue No. 70 of *Vorwärts!*. carrying Engels' article "The Condition of England. The Eighteenth Century"

but had of course governed in a thoroughly conservative manner—and laid the foundation of the Tory monopoly which lasted until 1830. The government thereby regained its inner truth; in a politically conservative period in England, it was quite appropriate that the conservative party should rule. From then on social developments absorbed the energies of the nation and ousted political interests, indeed destroyed them, for all domestic politics is from then on just concealed socialism, the form that social issues take to succeed in asserting themselves generally and nationally.

In 1763 Dr. James Watt of Greenock began working on the design of the steam-engine, and completed it in 1768.

In 1763 Josiah Wedgwood laid the foundations of the English pottery industry by the introduction of scientific principles. By his efforts a desolate area of Staffordshire has been turned into an industrial region—the Potteries—which now employs 60,000 people and has played a very important part in the social and political movement of recent years.

In 1764 in Lancashire James Hargreaves invented the spinning-jenny, a machine operated by one worker, which enabled him to spin sixteen times as much yarn as on the old spinning-wheel.[a]

In 1768 Richard Arkwright, a barber from Preston in Lancashire, invented the spinning-throstle, the first spinning-machine which was designed from the outset for mechanical power. It produced water-twist, that is, yarn used for warps in weaving.

In 1776 in Bolton, Lancashire, Samuel Crompton invented the spinning-mule by combining the mechanical principles applied in the jenny and the throstle. The mule, like the jenny, spins the mule-twist, that is, the weaver's weft; all three machines are designed for the working-up of cotton.

In 1787 Dr. Cartwright invented the power-loom, which however still had to undergo a number of improvements and could not be used in practice until 1801.

These inventions stimulated social development. Their most immediate consequence was the rise of English industry, or more specifically of cotton manufacture in the first instance. The jenny had, it is true, made the production of yarn cheaper, and by the expansion of the market that followed from this, it had given the first impetus to industry; but it left the social aspect, the character of the industrial enterprise, more or less unaffected. It was Ark-

---

[a] Engels gives most of the technical terms in this and the following two paragraphs in English.—*Ed.*

wright's and Crompton's machines and Watt's steam engine that first set the movement going, by creating the factory system. Smaller factories, driven by horses or water-power, arose first, but were soon displaced by the larger factories driven by water or steam. The first steam spinning-mill was set up by Watt in Nottinghamshire in 1785; others followed it, and soon the new system became general. The spread of the steam spinning-mill, like all the other industrial improvements introduced simultaneously or later, proceeded with enormous speed. The import of raw cotton, which in 1770 was still less than five million pounds a year, rose to 54 million pounds (1800) and 360 million pounds (1836). Then the steam-loom was actually introduced and gave a new impetus to industrial progress; all the machines underwent countless small but, when taken together, very significant improvements, and each new improvement encouraged the spread of the industrial system as a whole. All branches of the cotton industry were revolutionised; printing was immensely improved by the introduction of mechanical aids and simultaneously by the advances made in chemistry, by which dyeing and bleaching profited as well. Hosiery manufacture too was carried along by this current; and since 1809 machines were used to manufacture fine cotton goods, tulle, lace, etc. I have not the space here to pursue the progress of cotton manufacture through all the details of its history; I can only indicate the outcome, and that, when compared with the antediluvian cotton industry with its four million pounds of imported cotton, with its spinning-wheel, hand-carding and hand-loom, cannot fail to impress.

In 1833, 10,264 million skeins of yarn were spun in Britain, their length amounting to over 5,000 million miles, and 350 million ells of cotton fabric were printed; 1,300 cotton mills were in operation, which employed 237,000 spinners and weavers; over 9 million spindles, 100,000 steam-looms and 240,000 hand-looms, 33,000 hosiery looms and 3,500 bobbinet machines were in operation; cotton-manufacturing machinery used 33,000 h.p. of steam-power and 11,000 h.p. of water-power, and one and a half million people lived directly or indirectly from this industry. Lancashire derives its subsistence solely and Lanarkshire largely from the spinning and weaving of cotton; the subsidiary branches of the cotton industry are chiefly located in Nottinghamshire, Derbyshire and Leicestershire. The quantity of exported cotton goods has increased eightfold since 1801; the amount consumed in the country itself has increased a great deal more.

[*Vorwärts!* No. 72, September 7, 1844]

The impetus given to cotton manufacturing was soon communicated to other branches of industry. The *woollen* industry had until then been the most important branch of industry; it was now displaced by cotton, but instead of declining, it also grew. In 1785 the whole wool crop of three preceding years lay unused; the spinners could not work it up as long as they had no alternative to their crude spinning-wheel. Then people began to apply the machines for spinning cotton to wool, and this, after a few modifications, was entirely successful; then the wool industry experienced the same rapid growth as we have already observed in the case of cotton manufacture. The import of raw wool rose from 7 million pounds (1801) to 42 million pounds (1835); in the latter year 1,300 woollen mills employing 71,300 workers were in operation, not counting a host of hand-weavers who worked at home, and printers, dyers, bleachers, etc., etc., who also live indirectly from the wool industry. This industry is chiefly located in the West Riding of Yorkshire and the west of England (especially Somerset, Wiltshire, etc.).

The *linen* industry was formerly located chiefly in Ireland. The first factories for the processing of flax were built towards the end of the last century in Scotland. The machinery was however still very far from perfect; the material gave rise to difficulties which necessitated significant modifications in the machines. They were first improved by the Frenchman Girard (1810); but these improvements acquired practical importance first of all in England. The introduction of steam-looms into the linen industry took place even later; and from this point on linen manufacture expanded at immense speed, although it suffered from the competition of cotton. In England Leeds became the centre of the linen industry, in Scotland Dundee and in Ireland Belfast. Dundee alone imported 3,000 tons of flax in 1814 and 19,000 tons in 1834. The export of linen from Ireland, where hand-weaving continued to exist alongside power-weaving, rose by 20 million yards from 1800 to 1825, almost all of which went to England, and from there some of it was re-exported. Exports from the whole of Britain to foreign countries rose by 27 million yards between 1820 and 1833; in 1835 there were 347 flax mills in operation, 170 of these in Scotland; 33,000 workers were employed in these mills, not counting the many Irish artisans.

The *silk* industry only became important after 1824 with the abolition of the heavy customs duties; since then the import of raw silk has doubled and the number of factories increased to 266, employing 30,000 workers. This industry is chiefly located in Cheshire (Macclesfield, Congleton and district), then follow Manchester, and Paisley in Scotland. The centre of ribbon-making is Coventry in Warwickshire.

These four industries which produce yarn and fabrics were thus totally revolutionised. Domestic industry was replaced by collective labour in large buildings; manual labour was supplanted by steam-power and the use of machinery. With the aid of the machine a child of eight was now able to produce more than twenty grown men before. Six hundred thousand factory workers, of whom half are children and more than half female, are doing the work of one hundred and fifty million people.

But that is only the beginning of the industrial revolution. We have seen that dyeing, printing and bleaching expanded as a result of the advance in spinning and weaving and consequently sought the assistance of engineering and chemistry. Since the application of the steam-engine and of metal cylinders in printing, one man does the work of two hundred; the use of chlorine instead of oxygen in bleaching has reduced the time required for this operation from a few months to a few hours. While the industrial revolution thus affected the processes to which the product was subjected *after* spinning and weaving, its repercussions on the materials used by the new industry were even more significant. It was only through the steam-engine that the inexhaustible coal fields beneath the surface of England acquired their great importance; new coal mines were opened in large numbers and the old ones worked with redoubled energy. The manufacture of spinning-machines and looms also began to constitute a separate branch of industry and reached a degree of perfection unattained by any other nation. The machines were made by machines, and by a division of labour extending to the minutest detail, it was possible to achieve the precision and exactitude which distinguish English machines. The machine-building industry in its turn influenced iron and copper mining, which however received their chief impetus from another direction, but this too was caused by the original revolution effected by Watt and Arkwright.

The consequences of an industrial impetus, once given, are endless. The progress made in one industry is communicated to all the others. The newly-created forces demand nourishment, as we have just seen; the newly-created working population brings in its wake new conditions of life and new needs. The mechanical advantages of factory production reduce the price of manufactured articles, and therefore make the necessities of life and in consequence wages in general cheaper; all other products can be sold more cheaply and thereby reach a wider market in proportion to their cheapness. Once the advantageous application of mechanical devices has been demonstrated, it is gradually imitated throughout industry; the advance in civilisation, which is the inevitable consequence of all industrial improvements, generates new needs, new industries and thus again new improvements. The consequence of the revolution in cotton-spinning was necessarily a revolution in the whole of industry; and if we cannot always trace how the motive forces are imparted to the more remote branches of the industrial system, only the absence of statistical and historical information is to blame. But we shall see everywhere that the introduction of mechanical devices and of scientific principles in general has been the mainspring of progress.

After spinning and weaving, *metal*-working is the most important industry in England. It is chiefly located in Warwickshire (Birmingham) and Staffordshire (Wolverhampton). Steam-power was very soon employed in this industry and this, together with division of labour, cut the production costs of metal goods by three-quarters. On the other hand, exports multiplied fourfold from 1800 to 1835. In the former year 86,000 cwt. of iron goods and the same quantity of copper goods were exported, in the latter year 320,000 cwt. of iron and 210,000 cwt. of copper and brass goods. The export of bar-iron and pig-iron became significant at the same time; in 1800, 4,600 tons of bar-iron were exported, in 1835, 92,000 tons of bar-iron and 14,000 tons of pig-iron.

English cutlery is made exclusively in Sheffield. The use of steam-power, especially for grinding and polishing blades, the conversion of iron into steel, which only then became important, and the newly-invented method of casting steel, brought about a complete revolution here too. Sheffield alone consumes annually 500,000 tons of coal and 12,000 tons of iron, of which 10,000 tons come from abroad (particularly from Sweden).

The use of cast-iron goods also dates from the second half of the last century and has attained its present importance only in the last few years. Gas-lighting (introduced, in effect, since 1804) created an enormous demand for cast-iron pipes; the railways, suspension bridges, etc., machinery, etc., increased this demand still more. In 1780 puddling was invented, that is, the conversion of cast into wrought iron by heating and removing the carbon, and this gave new importance to the English iron-ore mines. For lack of charcoal the English had until then to obtain all their wrought iron from abroad. Since 1790 nails have been made by machine, and screws since 1810; in Sheffield Huntsman invented crucible steel-making in 1760; wire was drawn by machinery, and generally a host of new machines was introduced throughout the iron and brass industry, manual labour was ousted and, insofar as the nature of the business permitted, the factory system was established.

The increase in mining was only the necessary consequence of this. Until 1788 all iron-ore had been smelted with charcoal and iron extraction had therefore been limited by the small quantity of fuel available. After 1788 coke (coked coal) began to be used instead of charcoal and the amount produced annually was as a result multiplied by six in six years. In 1740, the annual output was 17,000 tons, in 1835, 553,000 tons. Extraction from the tin and copper mines has trebled since 1770. But along with the iron mines the coal mines are the most important in England. The growth of coal production since the middle of the last century cannot be assessed. The vast quantity of coal which is now consumed by the countless steam-engines working in the factories and mines, by the forges, by the smelting-furnaces and casting-works and by the domestic heating of a population that has doubled, bears no relation whatever to the amount consumed one hundred or eighty years ago. The smelting of pig-iron alone devours over three million tons a year (at twenty cwt. a ton).

The most immediate consequence of the creation of industry was the improvement of the means of communication. In the last century the roads in England were just as bad as elsewhere and remained so until the celebrated McAdam based road-building on scientific principles and thereby gave a new impetus to the advance of civilisation. From 1818 to 1829 new highways with a total length of 1,000 English miles were laid down in England and Wales, not counting smaller country lanes, and almost all the old roads were reconstructed according to McAdam's principles. In Scotland the public works authorities have built over 1,000 bridges since 1803. In Ireland, the wide, desolate bogs of the south, inhabited by half-wild robbers, were traversed by roads. By these means the remotest localities in the country, which had previously had no contact with the outside world, were now made accessible; in particular the Celtic-speaking areas of Wales, the Scottish Highlands and the south of Ireland were thereby compelled to make acquaintance with the outside world and accept the civilisation imposed upon them.

In 1755 the first canal of any note was constructed in Lancashire; in 1759 the Duke of Bridgewater started to build a canal from Worsley to Manchester. Since then canals have been constructed to a total length of 2,200 miles; in addition England has another 1,800 miles of navigable rivers, which for the most part have also been opened up only recently.

Since 1807, steam-power has been used for the propulsion of ships, and since the construction of the first British steamship (1811), 600 others have been built. In 1835 there were some 550 steamships sailing from British ports.

The first public railway was built in Surrey in 1801; but only with the opening of the Liverpool-Manchester railway (1830) did the new form of transport become important. Six years later, 680 miles of railway had been constructed and four major lines—from London to Birmingham, Bristol and Southampton, and from Birmingham to Manchester and Liverpool—were in operation. Since then the network has been extended over the whole of England; London is the junction of nine railways, and Manchester of five.*

This revolution through which British industry has passed is the foundation of every aspect of modern English life, the driving force behind all social development. Its first consequence was, as we have already indicated, the elevation of self-interest to a position of dominance over man. Self-interest seized the newly-created industrial powers and exploited them for its own purposes; these powers, which by right belong to mankind, became, owing to the influence of private property, the monopoly of a few rich capitalists and the means to the enslavement of the masses. Commerce absorbed industry into itself and thereby became omnipotent, it became the nexus of mankind; all personal and national intercourse was reduced to commercial intercourse, and—which amounts to the same thing—property, things, became master of the world.

[*Vorwärts!* No. 73, September 11, 1844]

The domination of property was bound to turn first against the state and to destroy it, or, at least, as it cannot do without it, to undermine it. Adam Smith began this undermining at the very time of the industrial revolution by publishing in 1776 his *Inquiry into the Nature and Causes of the Wealth of Nations* and thereby

---

* The above statistical data are mainly drawn from *The Progress of the Nation* by G. Porter, a Board of Trade official under the Whig Ministry, that is, from official sources.—*Note by Engels.*[204]

created the science of finance. Up to now all finance had been entirely national; the economy had been regarded as a mere branch of affairs of the state as a whole and subordinated to the state as such; Adam Smith subordinated cosmopolitanism to national aims and raised the economy of the state to the very essence and purpose of the state. He reduced politics, parties, religion, indeed everything, to economic categories and thereby recognised property as the essence of the state and enrichment as its purpose. On the other hand, William Godwin (*Political Justice*, 1793 [a]) supported the republican political system, propounded, at the same time as J. Bentham, the principle of utility, whereby the republican *salus publica suprema lex* [b] was taken to its legitimate conclusions, and attacked the very essence of the state itself with his aphorism that the state is an evil. Godwin still defines the principle of utility quite generally as the duty of the citizen to live only for the general good without regard to his individual interest; Bentham, on the contrary, takes the essentially social nature of this principle further and in accordance with the national trend of that time makes the individual interest the basis of the general interest: he recognises that the two are identical in the proposition, which his pupil Mill in particular developed, that charity is nothing but enlightened egoism, and he substitutes the greatest happiness of the greatest number for the "general good". Bentham here makes the same error in his empiricism as Hegel made in his theory; he does not seriously try to overcome the contradictions, he turns the subject into the predicate, subordinates the whole to the part and in so doing stands everything on its head. First he says that the general and individual interests are inseparable and then he stays unilaterally at the crudest individual interest. His proposition is only the empirical expression of another one, namely, that man is mankind, but because it is expressed empirically it grants the rights of the species not to the free, self-conscious, creative man, but to the crude and blind man who remains within the confines of the contradictions. Bentham makes free competition the essence of morality, regulates human relations according to the laws of property, of things, according to the laws of nature, and thus represents the culmination of the old, naturally evolved Christian world order, the highest point of alienation, and not the beginning of a new order to be created by self-conscious man in full freedom. He does not advance beyond the state, but strips it of all

---

[a] *An Enquiry Concerning Political Justice.*—*Ed.*
[b] The public good is the supreme law.—*Ed.*

meaning, substitutes social principles for political ones, turns the political organisation into the form of the social content and thus carries the contradiction to its extreme limit.

The democratic party originated at the same time as the industrial revolution. In 1769 J. Horne Tooke founded the Society of the Bill of Rights, in which, for the first time since the republic,[a] democratic principles were discussed again. As in France, the democrats were exclusively men with a philosophical education, but they soon found that the upper and middle classes were opposed to them and only the working class lent a ready ear to their principles. Amongst the latter class they soon founded a party, which by 1794 was already fairly strong[205] and yet still only strong enough to act by fits and starts. From 1797 to 1816 it disappeared from view; in the turbulent years from 1816 to 1823 it was again very active but then subsided once more into inactivity until the July revolution. From then on it has maintained its importance alongside the old parties and is making steady progress, as we shall later see.

The most important effect of the eighteenth century for England was the creation of the proletariat by the industrial revolution. The new industry demanded a constantly available mass of workers for the countless new branches of production, and moreover workers such as had previously not existed. Up to 1780 England had few proletarians, a fact which emerges inevitably from the social condition of the nation as described above. Industry concentrated work in factories and towns; it became impossible to combine manufacturing and agricultural activity, and the new working class was reduced to complete dependence on its labour. What had hitherto been the exception became the rule and spread gradually outside the towns too. Small-scale farming was ousted by the large tenant farmers and thus a new class of agricultural labourers was created. The population of the towns trebled and quadrupled and almost the whole of this increase consisted solely of workers. The expansion of mining likewise required a large number of new workers, and these too lived solely from their daily wage.

On the other hand, the middle class rose to become definitely aristocratic. During the industrial advance manufacturers multiplied their capital in an amazingly rapid fashion; the merchants likewise received their share, and the capital created by this rev-

---

[a] Of 1649-60.—*Ed.*

olution was the means by which the English aristocracy fought the French Revolution.

The result of this whole development was that England is now split into three parties, the landed aristocracy, the monied aristocracy, and working-class democracy. These are the only parties in England, they alone act as driving forces, and *how* they act we will perhaps try to describe in a later article.

Written in February 1844
First published in *Vorwärts!* (Paris) Nos. 70, 71, 72 and 73, August 31 and September 4, 7 and 11, 1844

Printed according to the newspaper

THE CONDITION OF ENGLAND

II

THE ENGLISH CONSTITUTION[206]

[*Vorwärts!* No. 75, September 18, 1844]

In the previous article we elaborated the criteria for assessing the present position of the British Empire in the history of civilisation, and gave the relevant facts concerning the development of the English nation insofar as they are indispensable to this purpose but are little known on the Continent; having thus justified our initial assumptions, we can now proceed without more ado to the object of our investigation.

The position of England has hitherto seemed enviable to all other nations of Europe, and indeed so it is to anyone who dwells on the surface and observes simply with the eyes of a politician. Britain is an empire of such a kind as is possible today, and such as all other empires in essence were as well; for the empires of Alexander and Caesar too represented, like the British, the rule of civilised nations over barbarians and colonies. No other country in the world can measure up to England in terms of power and wealth, and this power and wealth do not lie in the hands of a single despot, as was the case in Rome, but belong to the educated part of the nation. The fear of despotism and the struggle against the power of the Crown came to an end a hundred years ago; England is undeniably the freest, in other words, the least unfree, country in the world, not excepting North America, and the educated Englishman consequently has about him a degree of innate independence such as no Frenchman, to say nothing of German, can boast of. The political activity, the free press, the maritime supremacy and the colossal industry of England have so fully developed the energy inherent in the national character, the combination of the most resolute force and the calmest deliberation, in almost every individual that in this respect too the continental nations trail infinitely far behind the English. The history of the British Army and Navy is a series of brilliant victories, whilst England has scarcely seen an enemy on its shores for the past eight hundred years; the stature of its literature can only be rivalled by the literature of ancient Greece and Germany; England has produced at least two great names—Bacon and Locke—in philosophy, and innumerable ones in the empirical sciences, and if it is a question of which nation has *done* most, no one can deny that the English are that nation.

These are the things of which England can be proud, in which she surpasses the Germans and the French, and which I have listed here at the outset, so that the good Germans may convince themselves of my "impartiality" at the very start; for I know full well that in Germany it is much more acceptable to make inconsiderate statements about the Germans than about any other nation. And, broadly speaking, the things I have just listed form the subject-matter of that whole literature, so voluminous and yet so very unproductive and unnecessary, which has been churned out about England on the Continent. It has not occurred to anyone to investigate the nature of English history and of the English national character, and just how paltry all the literature about England is, is revealed by the simple fact that Herr von Raumer's paltry work about England[a] is still, as far as I know, held to be the best on the subject in Germany.

Since England has hitherto only been considered from the political angle, let us begin with that. Let us examine the English Constitution, which, as the Tories put it, is "the most perfect product of English reason", and let us, as another favour to the politician, for the present proceed quite empirically.

The *juste-milieu* esteem it a particular beauty of the English Constitution that it has developed "historically"; that means, in plain German, that the old basis created by the revolution of 1688 has been preserved, and this foundation, as they call it, further built on. We shall soon see what characteristics the English Constitution has acquired in consequence; for the moment a simple comparison of the Englishman of 1688 with the Englishman of 1844 will suffice to prove that an identical constitutional foundation for both of them is an absurdity and an impossibility. Even disregarding the general progress of civilisation, the political character of the nation alone is quite different from what it was

---

[a] *England im Jahre 1835.*— Ed.

then. The Test Act, the Habeas Corpus Act and the Bill of Rights[a] were Whig measures which arose from the weakness and defeat of the Tories at that time and were directed against these Tories, in other words, against absolute monarchy and open or concealed Catholicism.[207] But within the next fifty years the old Tories disappeared and their descendants adopted the principles which were hitherto the property of the Whigs; since George I ascended the throne, the monarchical, Catholic Tories have become an aristocratic, High-Church party, and since the French Revolution, which first woke them up, the positive precepts of Toryism have evaporated increasingly into abstract "conservatism", the undisguised, unthinking defence of the *status quo*—indeed even this stage has already been left behind. Through Sir Robert Peel Toryism has decided to acknowledge change, it has realised that the English Constitution cannot be defended, and is making concessions simply to maintain that tottering structure as long as possible.

The Whigs have undergone an equally important development, a new democratic party has arisen, and yet the foundation of 1688 is still supposed to be adequate for 1844! Now the inevitable consequence of this "historical development" is that the inner contradictions which are characteristic features of constitutional monarchy and which were sufficiently exposed even at the time when modern German philosophy still upheld a republican viewpoint—that these contradictions attain their most extreme form in the modern English monarchy. In fact the English constitutional monarchy is the culmination of constitutional monarchy as such, it is the only state where, insofar as this is still possible at the present time, a *real* aristocracy of birth has held its position alongside a comparatively highly developed public consciousness, and consequently where that trinity of legislative power really exists which on the Continent has been artificially restored and is maintained only with difficulty.

If the essence of the state, as of religion, is mankind's fear of itself, this fear reaches its highest pitch in constitutional, and particularly in the English, monarchy. The experience of three millennia has not made men wiser but on the contrary more confused and more prejudiced, it has made them mad, and the result of this madness is the political condition of present-day Europe. The pure monarchy arouses terror—people think of

---

[a] Engels uses the English term "Bill of Rights".—*Ed.*

Oriental and Roman despotism. Pure aristocracy is no less frightening—the patricians of Rome and the feudalism of the Middle Ages, the nobili of Venice and Genoa have not been in vain. Democracy is more dreadful than either; Marius and Sulla, Cromwell and Robespierre, the bloody heads of two kings, proscription lists and dictatorship speak loudly enough of the "horrors" of democracy. What is more, it is generally known that none of these forms has ever been able to survive for long. What then was to be done? Instead of proceeding on a straight course, instead of concluding from the imperfection or rather inhumanity of all forms of the state that the state itself is the cause of all these inhumanities and is itself inhuman, instead of that people took comfort in the view that immorality only adheres to particular *forms* of the state, they deduced from the above premises that the result of three immoral factors can be a moral product, and created the constitutional monarchy.

The first axiom of constitutional monarchy is that of the balance of powers, and this axiom is the most perfect expression of mankind's fear of itself. It is not my intention to comment on the absurd irrationality and total impracticability of this axiom, I will merely examine whether it is applied in the English Constitution; as I promised, I shall stick exclusively to empirical facts, so much so indeed that it will perhaps be too much even for our political empiricists. I shall therefore not take the English Constitution as it figures in Blackstone's *Commentaries*,[a] in de Lolme's fantasies[b] or in the long series of constituent statutes from "Magna Carta" to the Reform Bill, but as it is in reality.[208]

First, the monarchic element. Everyone knows the real significance of the sovereign king of England, whether male or female. The power of the Crown is reduced in practice to nil, and if this situation, notorious the world over, needed any further proof, the fact that the whole struggle against the Crown ceased over a hundred years ago and that even the radical democratic Chartists know their time is better spent on other things than on this struggle, should be sufficient proof. What then becomes of that third part of the legislative power which in theory is assigned to the Crown? Nevertheless—and in this, fear reaches its climax—the English Constitution cannot exist without the monarchy. Remove the Crown, the "subjective apex", and the whole artificial structure comes tumbling down. The English Constitution

---

[a] W. Blackstone, *Commentaries on the Laws and Constitution of England.—Ed.*
[b] J. L. Delolme, *La Constitution de l'Angleterre.—Ed.*

is an inverted pyramid; the apex is at the same time the base. And the less important the monarchic element became in reality, the more important did it become for the Englishman. Nowhere, as we all know, is a non-ruling personage more revered than in England. The English press surpasses the German by far in slavish servility. But this loathsome cult of the king as such, the veneration of an empty idea — or rather not an idea but the *word* "king" — stripped of all content, is the culmination of monarchy, just as the veneration of the mere *word* "God" is the culmination of religion. The word "king" is the essence of the state, just as the word "God" is the essence of religion, even though neither word has any meaning at all. The essential thing about both of them is to make sure that the essential thing, that is, man, who is behind these words, is not discussed.

Then, the aristocratic element. At least in the sphere assigned to it by the Constitution, it fares little better than the Crown. If the mockery which has continuously been heaped on the House of Lords for more than a hundred years has gradually become so much a part of public opinion that this branch of the legislature is generally regarded as a home for superannuated statesmen and the offer of a peerage as an insult by any not yet totally worn-out member of the House of Commons, it may easily be imagined in what esteem the second of the political powers established by the Constitution is held. In fact the activity of the Lords in the Upper House has been reduced to a mere empty formality, rising only rarely to a kind of force of inertia such as was displayed during the Whig Ministry of 1830 to 1840 — and even then the Lords are not strong in themselves but through the Tories, the party whose most genuine representatives they are; and the House of Lords, whose main advantage in constitutional theory is supposed to be the fact that it is equally independent of the Crown and of the people, is in reality dependent on a party, that is, on the state of public opinion, and also on the Crown, because of its right to create peers. But the weaker the Upper House was, the firmer was its position in public opinion. The constitutional parties, the Tories, Whigs and Radicals, shrink with equal horror from the idea of abolishing this empty formality, and the Radicals go no further than to observe that the Lords, as the only power in the Constitution that is answerable to no one, are an anomaly and that therefore the hereditary peerage should be replaced by an elected peerage. Once more it is the fear of humanity which maintains this empty form, and the Radicals, who are demanding a purely democratic basis for the House of Commons, take this fear even further than the other two parties by attempting to breathe new life into the worn-out, antiquated House of Lords by an infusion of popular blood, so as to avoid abandoning it altogether. The Chartists have a better idea of what they must do; they know that before the assault of a democratic House of Commons, the whole rotten structure, Crown, Lords and so forth, must collapse of its own accord, and unlike the Radicals they therefore do not worry about the reform of the peerage.

And just as the veneration for the Crown has grown in proportion as the power of the Crown diminished, so the aristocracy has risen all the higher in popular esteem the more the political influence of the House of Lords declined. It is not just that the most humiliating formalities of the feudal era have been retained, that the members of the House of Commons, when they appear in an official capacity before the Lords, have to stand cap in hand before the seated and behatted Lords and that the official mode of addressing a nobleman is "may it please your lordship",[a] etc.; the worst of it is that all these formalities really are the expression of public opinion, which regards a Lord as a being of a superior kind and harbours a respect for pedigrees, sonorous titles, old family mementoes, etc., which is as repugnant and nauseating to us continentals as the cult of the Crown. In this aspect of the English character too we have again the same veneration for an empty, meaningless word, the utterly insane, fixed idea that a great nation, that the human race and the universe, could not exist without the word "aristocracy".

For all that, the aristocracy nevertheless has an important influence in reality; but just as the power of the Crown is the power of the Ministers, in other words, of the representatives of the majority of the House of Commons, and has thus taken quite a different turn from that intended by the Constitution, so the power of the aristocracy consists in something quite other than its right to an hereditary seat in the legislature. The aristocracy is strong because of its vast estates, its wealth in general, and it therefore shares this strength with all other, non-aristocratic men of wealth; the power of the Lords is effective not in the House of Lords but in the House of Commons, and this brings us to that component of the legislature which according to the Constitution is supposed to represent the democratic element.

---

[a] Engels gives this phrase both in German and in English.— *Ed.*

[*Vorwärts!* No. 76, September 21, 1844]

If the Crown and the House of Lords are powerless, it follows that all power must necessarily be concentrated in the House of Commons, and this is the case. In reality the House of Commons makes the laws and administers them through the Ministers, who are but a committee of the House. The House of Commons being thus omnipotent, England ought to be a pure democracy, even if nominally the other two branches of the legislature continue to exist, provided the democratic element itself were truly democratic. But there is no question of this. The local organisations were quite unaffected by the constitutional settlement after the revolution of 1688; the cities, boroughs and constituencies which had previously had the right to send a member retained it; and this right was by no means one of the democratic "universal human rights", but an entirely feudal privilege, which as late as Elizabeth's reign was conferred quite arbitrarily by the grace and favour of the Crown on many towns which had not previously been represented. Even the representative character which the elections to the House of Commons at least originally had, was soon lost through "historical development". The composition of the old House of Commons is well known. In the towns the return of a member was either in the hands of an individual or of an exclusive corporation co-opting its own members; only a few boroughs were open, in other words, had a fairly large electorate, and here the most brazen bribery put paid to the last vestiges of true representation. The closed boroughs were mostly in the pocket of one individual, usually a lord; and in the rural constituencies the all-powerful big landowners suppressed any free, spontaneous stirring there might be among the people, who were moreover politically inert. The old House of Commons was no more than an exclusive medieval corporation independent of the people, the culmination of the "historical" right, incapable of adducing even a single genuinely or apparently rational argument for its existence, existing in defiance of all reason and hence denying in 1794 through its committee that it was an assembly of representatives and that England was a representative state.* In comparison with such a Constitution, the theory of representative government, even of an ordinary constitutional monarchy with a chamber of deputies, must have appeared thoroughly revolutionary and reprehensible,

---

* Second Report of the Committee of Secrecy, to whom the Papers referred to in His Majesty's Message on the 12 May 1794, were delivered (Report on the London Revolutionary Societies, London, 1794). Page 68 ff.— *Note by Engels.*

and the Tories were therefore quite right when they described the Reform Bill as a measure diametrically opposed to the spirit and the letter of the Constitution and which undermined the Constitution. The Reform Bill, however, went through, and it is now our task to see what it has made of the English Constitution and particularly of the House of Commons. In the first place, the conditions for the election of members in the countryside have remained exactly the same. The electors are here almost exclusively tenant farmers, and they are utterly dependent on their landlord since the latter, who has no contractual relationship with them, may at any time terminate the lease. The members for the counties (as opposed to the towns) remain, as they were before, deputies of the landowners, since it is only at times of the greatest unrest, as in 1831,[209] that the tenant farmers dare to vote against the landowners. Indeed, the Reform Bill only aggravated the evil, since it increased the number of county members. Of the 252 county members, the Tories can consequently always count on at least 200, except when there is general unrest among the tenant farmers which would make any intervention by the landowners unwise. In the towns representation was introduced, at least formally, and every man occupying a house of at least ten pounds sterling annual rental value and paying direct taxes (poor-rate, etc.) received the vote. By this means the enormous majority of the working classes is excluded; for in the first place it is naturally only the married who live in separate houses, and even if a significant number of these houses have an annual rent of ten pounds, almost all the occupiers avoid the payment of direct taxes and are therefore not electors. Universal suffrage as advocated by the Chartists would at least treble the number of persons entitled to vote. The towns are thus in the hands of the middle class, and this in its turn is in the smaller towns very frequently—directly or indirectly—dependent on the landlords, via the tenant farmers, who are the main customers of the tradesmen and craftsmen. Only in the large towns does the middle class really achieve supremacy, and in the smaller factory towns, especially in Lancashire, where the middle class lacks significant numbers and the country people significant influence, where therefore even a minority of the working class has a decisive effect on the outcome, the illusory representation approaches true representation in some measure. These towns, e.g., Ashton, Oldham, Rochdale, Bolton, etc., consequently send almost exclusively Radicals to Parliament. In these places, as in all factory towns generally, an extension of the franchise on Chartist principles would enable this party to gain a majority of votes. Apart from these various and in practice very complex influences, various local interests also make themselves felt, and finally, a very significant influence—bribery. In the first article of the present series,[a] we already mentioned that the House of Commons, through its Bribery Committee, declared that it was elected by bribery, and Thomas Duncombe, the only thoroughgoing Chartist member, long ago told the House of Commons plainly that not a single member of the whole assembly, not even he himself, could say that he had secured his seat by the free vote of his constituents without bribery.[210] Last summer, Richard Cobden, member for Stockport and leader of the Anti-Corn Law League, declared at a public meeting in Manchester that bribery had reached greater proportions than ever, that in the Tory Carlton Club and the Liberal Reform Club in London the representation of towns was positively auctioned to the highest bidder, and that these clubs acted as contractors—for so many pounds we guarantee you a certain position, etc.—And on top of all this we must not forget the fine manner in which the elections are held, the general drunkenness amid which the votes are cast, the public houses where the electors become intoxicated at the candidates' expense, the disorder, the brawling, the howling of the crowds at the voting-booths; thus putting the finishing touches to the hollowness of representation which is valid for *seven* years.

[*Vorwärts!* No. 77, September 25, 1844]

We have seen that the Crown and the House of Lords have lost their importance; we have seen how the all-powerful House of Commons is recruited; the question is now: who then actually rules in England? Property rules. Property enables the aristocracy to control the election of deputies for rural areas and small towns; property enables the merchants and manufacturers to choose the members for the large and to some extent also for the small towns; property enables both to increase their influence by bribery. The rule of property is explicitly recognised in the Reform Bill by the property qualification incorporated in it. And to the extent that property and the influence conferred by property constitute the essence of the middle class, to the extent therefore that the aristocracy brings its property to bear in the elections and thus does not act as an aristocracy but puts itself on

---

[a] See this volume, pp. 455-56.— *Ed.*

a level with the middle class, to the extent that the influence of the actual middle class is on the whole much greater than that of the aristocracy, to that extent the middle class does indeed rule. But how and why does it rule? Because the people do not as yet really understand the nature of property, because they are in general—at least in the countryside—still intellectually dead and therefore tolerate the tyranny of property. England is admittedly a democracy, but in the same way as Russia is a democracy; as the people unwittingly rules everywhere, and the government in every state is but another expression for the level of education of the people.

It will be difficult to retrace our steps from the practice of the English Constitution to the theory of it. There is the most flagrant contradiction between the theory and the practice; the two are so estranged from one another that they no longer have any similarity. On the one hand the trinity of the legislature—on the other the tyranny of the middle class; on the one hand a two-chamber system—on the other the all-powerful House of Commons; on the one hand the royal prerogative—on the other a government chosen by the Commons; on the one hand an independent House of Lords with hereditary legislators—on the other a home for antiquated members of the Commons. Each of the three components of the legislature has had to surrender its power to another element: the Crown to the Ministers, in other words to the majority of the House of Commons, the Lords to the Tory party, that is, to a popular element, and to the Ministers who create the peers, in other words, basically to a popular element too, and the Commons to the middle class, or, which amounts to the same thing, to the people that has not yet come of age politically. In reality the English Constitution has ceased to exist at all, the whole wearisome process of legislation is a mere farce; the contradiction between theory and practice has become so glaring that it cannot possibly persist for long, and even if the vitality of this ailing Constitution appears to have been somewhat increased by the emancipation of the Catholics,[211] of which we shall have cause to speak further,[a] and by the parliamentary and municipal reform, these measures—which in themselves are an admission that hope of preserving the Constitution has been given up—introduce into it elements which unquestionably contradict the fundamental principles of the Constitution and thus further intensify the conflict by making the theory contradict itself.

---

[a] See this volume, pp. 501-03.—*Ed.*

We have seen that the organisation of powers in the English Constitution depends entirely on fear. This fear is even more evident in the rules by which legislation proceeds, the so-called Standing Orders.[a] Every Bill must pass three readings in each of the two Houses, at stated intervals; after the second reading it is referred to a Committee which discusses it in detail; in cases of some importance, the House becomes a Committee of the whole House to discuss the Bill and appoints a reporter, who afterwards with great solemnity presents a report on the discussion to the very House that discussed the Bill. Incidentally, is this not the most splendid example of "the transcendent within the immanent and the immanent within the transcendent" that a Hegelian could possibly wish for? "The knowledge the House of Commons has of the committee is the knowledge the committee has of itself", and the reporter is "the absolute personification of the intermediary, in whom the two are identical". Every Bill is thus discussed eight times before it can receive the royal assent. Once more it is of course fear of humanity that underlies this absurd procedure. They realise that progress is the essence of humanity but have not the courage to proclaim progress openly; they pass laws which are supposed to have absolute validity and which therefore put barriers in the way of progress; and by reserving the right to amend laws, the progress which they have just denied is allowed in again through the backdoor. But care must be taken not to proceed too fast, not to be over-hasty! Progress is revolutionary, it is dangerous, and there must therefore be a powerful brake on it; before they decide to acknowledge it, they must ponder the matter eight times. But this fear, which is futile in itself, and only proves that those who are filled with it are themselves not yet real, free men, is bound to lead to the introduction of inappropriate measures. Instead of ensuring a comprehensive examination of the Bills, the repeated reading of them becomes quite superfluous in practice and a mere formality. The main argument is usually concentrated in the first or second reading, sometimes also in the debates in committee, according to what suits the opposition best. The whole futility of this multiplication of debates becomes evident when one considers that the fate of each Bill is already decided at the outset, and where it is *not* decided, the debate concerns not the particular Bill but the existence of a Cabinet. The outcome of all these antics, which are repeated eight times, is thus not a calmer discussion in the House itself, but something quite

---

[a] Here and below Engels gives this term in English.— *Ed.*

different which was by no means the intention of those who introduced these antics. The protracted nature of the deliberations gives public opinion time to form an opinion about the proposed measure and if need be to oppose it by means of meetings and petitions, and often—as last year in the case of Sir James Graham's Education Bill[a]—successfully. But this, as we have said, was not the original purpose and could be achieved far more simply.

While we are now on the subject of the Standing Orders, we may mention a few more points which betray the fear that is part of the English Constitution and the original corporate character of the House of Commons. The debates in the House of Commons are not public; admission is a privilege and is usually secured only by written order of a member. During divisions the galleries are cleared; despite this absurd secretiveness, the abolition of which the House has always vigorously opposed, the names of the members who have voted for and against are in all the newspapers on the following day. The Radical members have never been able to get approval for an authentic publication of the minutes—a fortnight ago a motion to this end failed[212]— and as a consequence the printer of the parliamentary reports that appear in the papers is solely responsible for their content and can be sued, according to the law even by the government, for the publication of defamatory statements by anyone who feels insulted by a remark by a Member of Parliament, while the author of the defamation is protected from any prosecution by his parliamentary privilege. These and a host of other points in the Standing Orders show the exclusive, anti-popular character of the reformed Parliament; and the tenacity with which the House of Commons holds to these customs shows clearly enough that it has no desire to transform itself from a privileged, corporative body into an assembly of representatives of the people.

[*Vorwärts!* No. 78, September 28, 1844]

Another proof of this is the privilege enjoyed by Parliament, the exceptional position of its members *vis-à-vis* the courts and the right of the House of Commons to have anyone it wishes arrested. Originally aimed against infringements by the Crown, which has since that time been deprived of all its power, this privilege has in recent times only been used against the people. In 1771 the House was angered by the insolence of the newspapers which had

---

[a] See this volume, p. 381.—*Ed.*

published its debates, a thing which after all only the House itself was entitled to do, and tried to put a stop to this insolence by arresting the printers and then the officials who had released these printers. Of course this was unsuccessful; but the attempt shows the nature of the privileges Parliament enjoys, and its failure shows that even the House of Commons, despite its being exalted over the people, is nevertheless dependent on the latter, in other words, that the House of Commons does not rule either.

In a country where "Christianity is part and parcel of the laws of the land"[a] the *Established Church* is necessarily part of the Constitution. According to her Constitution, England is essentially a Christian state, indeed a fully developed and powerful Christian state; state and church merge entirely with one another and are inseparable. This unity of church and state can however only exist in *one* Christian denomination, to the exclusion of all others, and these excluded sects are of course thereby branded as heretical and are victims of religious and political persecution. So it is in England. These sects were thus all along thrown together as one class, excluded, as nonconformists or dissenters, from all participation in the state, harassed and hampered in their worship and prosecuted by penal laws. The more fervently they declared themselves against the unity of church and state, the more violently was this unity defended by the ruling party and exalted to a vital concern of the state. When the Christian state in England was still in its heyday, the persecution of the dissenters and more especially of the Catholics was therefore a daily occurrence, a persecution which was admittedly less violent but more universal and persistent than that of the Middle Ages. The disease ceased to be acute and became chronic, the sudden, blood-thirsty outbursts of anti-Catholic fury were transformed into cold political calculation which sought to exterminate heterodoxy by gentler but sustained pressure. Persecution was transferred to the secular sphere and thereby made harder to bear. Disbelief in the Thirty-Nine Articles[213] ceased to be blasphemy, instead it was made a crime against the state.

But the progress of history was not to be halted; the discrepancy between the legislation of 1688 and public opinion as it existed in 1828 was so great that in the latter year even the House of Commons found itself obliged to revoke the most oppressive laws against the dissenters. The Test Act and the religious clauses of the Corporation Act[214] were abolished; the emancipation of the

---

[a] Engels gives this phrase both in German and in English.— *Ed.*

Catholics[215] followed in the next year, despite the furious opposition of the Tories. The Tories, the exponents of the Constitution, were perfectly correct in their opposition, as not one of the liberal parties, not even the Radicals, attacked the Constitution itself. The Constitution was to remain the foundation for them too, and on the basis of the Constitution only the Tories were consistent. They realised, and said so, that the above measures would inevitably bring about the downfall of the Anglican Church and necessarily that of the Constitution too; that to give the dissenters the civil rights would mean the *de facto* destruction of the Anglican Church and the sanctioning of the attacks on the Anglican Church; that it is a dangerous inconsistency towards the state itself to allow a Catholic a share in administration and legislation since he recognises the authority of the Pope over the power of the state. Their arguments could not be answered by the Liberals; nevertheless, the emancipation went through and the prophecies of the Tories are already beginning to be fulfilled.

So in this way the Anglican Church has become an empty name and now only differs from the other denominations by virtue of the three million pounds it draws annually, and a few small privileges which are just sufficient to sustain the struggle against it. Amongst these are the ecclesiastical courts in which the Anglican bishop exercises sole but quite unimportant jurisdiction and whose oppressiveness consists particularly in the law costs; and then there are also the local church rates which are used for the maintenance of the buildings available for the use of the Established Church; the dissenters come under the jurisdiction of these courts and are equally liable for payment of these rates.

But it is not just the legislation *against* the church but also the legislation *for* it which has contributed towards making the Established Church an empty name. The Church of Ireland has always been a mere name, a perfect established or government church, a complete hierarchy from the archbishop down to the vicar, lacking nothing except a congregation, and whose occupation consists in preaching, praying and singing off litanies to the empty pews. The Church of England has an audience, it is true, although it too, especially in Wales and the factory districts, has been to a considerable degree dislodged by the dissenters, but then the well-paid pastors trouble themselves little about their sheep. If you wish to bring a caste of priests into disrepute and cause its downfall, then pay it well, says Bentham, and the English and Irish churches testify to the truth of this statement. In the countryside and in the towns of England nothing is more hateful and more contemptible to the people than a Church of England parson.ᵃ And in the case of as pious a people as the English, that is really saying something.

It is self-evident that the emptier and more meaningless the name of the Anglican Church becomes, the more firmly does the conservative party and indeed the confirmed constitutional party become attached to it; the separation of church and state might draw tears even from Lord John Russell; it is equally self-evident that the emptier the name becomes, the harsher and the more strongly felt does its oppressiveness become. The Irish Church particularly, because it is the most insignificant, is the most hated; it has no other purpose than to embitter the people, than to remind them that they are a subjugated people upon whom the conqueror forces his religion and his institutions.

Hence England is now at a stage of transition from a determinate to an indeterminate Christian state, to a state which bases itself not on one determinate denomination but on an indeterminate Christianity, a mean of all existing denominations. Naturally the old, determinate, Christian state defended itself against unbelief, and the Apostasy Act of 1699 punishes it with the loss even of the passive civil rights and with imprisonment; this Act has never been annulled, but is no longer ever applied. Another law, originating in Elizabeth's times, lays down that anyone who fails to attend church on Sunday without a proper excuse (if I am not mistaken, even the episcopal church is laid down, because Elizabeth acknowledged no dissenting chapels) is to be made to attend it by a fine or imprisonment. In the countryside this law is still frequently applied; even here, in civilised Lancashire, a few hours travel from Manchester, there are some bigoted Justices of the Peace who — as Mr. Gibson, member for Manchester, alleged a fortnight ago in the House of Commons[216]— have sentenced a large number of people, sometimes to six weeks imprisonment, for failing to attend church. However the main laws against unbelief are those which disqualify from taking an oath anyone who does not believe in a God or in any reward or punishment in the afterlife, and make blasphemy a punishable offence. Blasphemy is everything which aims to bring the Bible or the Christian religion into contempt, and equally the direct denial of the existence of God; the penalty for this is imprisonment — usually one year, and a fine.

ᵃ The words "Church of England parson" are in English in the original.— *Ed.*

[*Vorwärts!* No. 80, October 5, 1844]

But the indeterminate Christian state too is moving towards its downfall, even before it has been officially recognised by legislation. The Apostasy Act is, as we have said, entirely obsolete; the requirement of church attendance is likewise rather antiquated and it is only enforced in exceptional cases; the blasphemy law is likewise beginning—thanks to the fearlessness of the English Socialists and particularly of Richard Carlile—to become antiquated and is only applied here and there in particularly bigoted localities such as Edinburgh, and even a refusal of the oath is avoided where possible. The Christian party has become so weak that it realises itself that a strict operation of these laws would bring about their repeal before long, and it therefore prefers to remain passive so that the Damocles sword of Christian legislation may at least remain suspended over the heads of the unbelievers and perhaps continue to be effective as a threat and deterrent.

Apart from the political institutions proper which we have so far considered, there are several other matters which may be included in the sphere of the Constitution. There has so far been scarcely any mention of the rights of the citizen; within the Constitution strictly speaking, the individual has no rights in England. These rights exist either through custom or by virtue of individual statutes which are quite unconnected with the Constitution. We shall see how this strange separation has arisen; for the moment we move on to a critique of these rights.

The first is the right that any man may publish his opinion without hindrance and without the previous permission of the government—the freedom of the press. Taken as a whole it is true that nowhere is the freedom of the press more extensive than in England; and yet this freedom is still very limited here. The law of libel, the law of high treason and the law of blasphemy weigh heavily on the press, and if the press is rarely prosecuted, *that is not due to the law* but to the government's fear of the inevitable unpopularity which would follow measures taken against the press. English newspapers of all parties commit press offences every day, both against the government and against individuals, but they are allowed to pass with impunity, until it is possible to launch a political trial, and then the occasion is used to deal with the press as well. That is how it turned out with the Chartists in 1842 and just recently with the Irish Repealers.[217] The freedom of the press in England has been living just as much on grace and favour for the past hundred years as it did in Prussia from 1842.

The second "birthright"ᵃ of the Englishman is the right of popular assembly, a right which no other nation in Europe has enjoyed to date. This right, although very ancient, was subsequently made explicit in a statute as the right of the people to assemble for the purpose of discussing grievances and petitioning the legislature for their remedy. This wording contains a limitation. If no petition results from a meeting, the latter thereby acquires if not precisely an illegal character, then at least a very ambiguous one. In O'Connell's trial the Crown particularly emphasised that the meetings which were described as illegal were not convened for the deliberation of petitions. The main limitation however is imposed by the police; the central or local government can prohibit any meeting in advance, or interrupt and dissolve it, and it has done this often enough, not just at Clontarf but actually in England in the case of Chartist and Socialist meetings.[218] This however is not considered an attack on the Englishman's birthrights because the Chartists and Socialists are poor devils and thus have no rights; no one cares two hoots about it except the *Northern Star* and the *New Moral World,* and therefore one hears nothing about it on the Continent.

Then the right of association. All associations which pursue lawful aims by lawful means are permitted; but in any given case, only one big society is allowed, and this may not include branch associations. The formation of societies divided into local branches, each with its own organisation, is only permitted for charitable, or pecuniary purposes in general, and may only be embarked upon in England on the issue of a certificate by an official appointed for this purpose. The Socialists obtained such a certificate for their organisation by declaring their purpose was of this nature; it was denied to the Chartists, although they copied the statutes of the socialist society word for word in their own. They are now forced to circumvent the law and are thus put in a position where a single slip of the pen by a single member of the Chartist association[219] may entangle the whole society in the snares of the law. But even apart from that, the right of association, in its full extent, is a privilege of the rich; an association needs money first of all, and it is easier for the rich Anti-Corn Law League[220] to raise hundreds of thousands than for the poor Chartist society or the Union of British Miners to meet the bare expenses of association. And an association which has no funds at its disposal is not likely to have much effect and cannot conduct any agitation.

ᵃ Engels gives this term both in German and in English.— *Ed.*

[*Vorwärts!* No. 83, October 16, 1844]

The right of Habeas Corpus, that is, the right of any accused person (high treason constitutes an exception) to be released on bail pending the start of the trial, this much-praised right is once more a privilege of the rich. The poor man cannot offer surety and therefore must go to prison.

The last of these rights of the individual is the right of each man to be tried only by his peers, and that too is a privilege of the rich man. The poor man is not tried by his peers, he is without exception tried by his born enemies, for in England the rich and the poor are openly at war with one another. The jury must have certain qualifications, and their nature is evident from the fact that the jury list in Dublin, a city of 250,000 inhabitants, contains only 800 qualified persons. At the most recent Chartist trials at Lancaster, Warwick and Stafford,[221] the workers were tried by landlords and tenant farmers, who are mostly Tories, and by manufacturers or merchants, who are mostly Whigs, but in any case they are the enemies of the Chartists and the workers. But that is not all. A so-called impartial jury does not exist. When O'Connell was tried four weeks ago in Dublin, every member of the jury, being a Protestant and Tory, was his enemy. "His peers" would have been Catholics and Repealers—and not even they, for they were his friends. A Catholic in the jury would have prevented the verdict, he would have made any verdict impossible, except an acquittal. This case is a particularly blatant example; but fundamentally it is the same in any case. Trial by jury is in essence a political and not a legal institution; but because all law is essentially political in origin, the *reality* of legal practice is revealed in it, and the English trial by jury, because it is the most highly developed, is the consummation of juridical mendacity and immorality. The starting point is the fiction of the "impartial juryman"; it is impressed upon the jury that they must forget everything relating to the current case that they may have heard before the trial, and judge only by the evidence brought before the Court—as though such a thing were possible. The second fiction is that of the "impartial judge", whose task is to expound the law and bring together the arguments presented by both sides, without partiality, quite "objectively"—as though that were possible! It is moreover required of the judge that he should especially and in spite of everything exert no influence on the verdict of the jury and should not put the verdict into their mouths—in other words, he must present the premises as they need to be presented for the conclusion to be drawn; but he should not draw the conclusion himself, he may not even draw it for himself, for that would have an effect on his presentation of the premises—all these and a hundred other impossibilities, inhumanities and stupidities are demanded, simply so as decently to conceal the original stupidity and inhumanity. But there is no deceiving actual practice, in practice all this rubbish is ignored, the judge gives the jury clearly enough to understand what sort of verdict it is to pronounce, and that verdict is then regularly brought in by the obedient jury.

But next! The defendant must be protected in every way, the defendant, like the king, is sacred and inviolable and can do no wrong, in other words, he can do nothing at all, and if he does do anything, it has no validity. The defendant may confess his crime, it will avail him not at all. The law decides that he is not trustworthy; I believe it was in 1819 that a man arraigned his wife for adultery after she had confessed to her husband, during an illness she thought would prove fatal, that she had committed adultery—but the defence counsel for the wife objected that the defendant's confession was no evidence, and the charge was dismissed.* The sanctity of the defendant is furthermore sustained in the legal formalities which surround the English jury, and which offer such a very fertile field to the cavilling wiles of the barristers. That a trivial technical blunder can upset a whole trial verges on the incredible. In 1800 a man was found guilty of forgery but released because his defence counsel discovered before the sentence was pronounced that on the forged banknote the name was written in the abbreviated form Bartw, while in the bill of indictment Bartholomew was written in full. The judge, as I have said, accepted the objection as adequate and released the convicted man.** In 1827 a woman was charged with infanticide in Winchester but acquitted because in the verdict of the coroner's jury the latter declared "upon their oath" (The jurors of our Lord the King upon their oath present that, etc.ᵃ) that such and such had happened, whereas this jury of thirteen men had sworn not one oath but thirteen oaths and the verdict therefore ought to have read "upon their oaths".*** A year ago in Liverpool a boy who stole a handkerchief out of someone's pocket one Sunday evening was caught in the act and arrested. His father objected that the

---

* Wade, *British History*, London, 1838.— *Note by Engels.*
** Ibid.— *Note by Engels.*
*** Ibid.— *Note by Engels.*

ᵃ Given by Engels in English.— *Ed.*

police officer had arrested him unlawfully because there is a law which says no one may perform on Sunday the work by which he earns his living; the police, therefore, may not arrest anyone on Sunday. The judge agreed with this, but continued to examine the boy, and when the latter confessed he was a thief by profession, he was fined five shillings because he had followed his profession on a Sunday. For each of these examples I could give a hundred more, but they speak for themselves well enough. English law sanctifies the defendant and is applied against the society for whose protection it really exists. As in Sparta, it is not the crime but the stupidity with which it is committed that is punished. Any form of protection is turned against the person whom it is intended to protect; the law is intended to protect society and attacks it; it is intended to protect the defendant and injures him—for it is obvious that any man who is too poor to oppose the official pettifogging with a counsel equally skilled in pettifogging has against him all the forms which were created for his protection. Any man who is too poor to provide a defence counsel or an appropriate number of witnesses has no hope in any suit that is in the least degree doubtful. Before the trial he can read only the indictment and the statements originally made to the magistrate and therefore does not know the details of what is to be brought against him (and this is most dangerous precisely for the man who is innocent); he must answer at once when the prosecutor has concluded his case and may only speak once; if he does not deal with everything, or if a witness whom he had not regarded as necessary is absent, then he is lost.

[*Vorwärts!* No. 84, October 19, 1844]

But the culmination of the whole system is the rule that the twelve jurors must be unanimous in their verdict.

They are locked in a room and are not let out until they are agreed or the judge realises that they cannot be brought to unanimity. It is however thoroughly inhuman and to such an extent contrary to human nature that it is quite ridiculous to demand that twelve people should be of exactly the same opinion on a particular issue. But it is consistent. The procedure of the Inquisition is to torture the accused physically or mentally; the jury system declares the accused sacred and tortures the witnesses with a cross-examination in no way less formidable than that of the Inquisition; it even tortures the jury; it must have a verdict, though the heavens should fall in the process; the jury is punished by imprisonment until it produces a verdict; and if it should be so capricious as to wish to adhere to its oath, a new jury is appointed, there is a retrial, and so on until either the prosecution or the jury becomes weary of the struggle and surrenders unconditionally. Proof enough that the whole legal system cannot exist without torture and is in any case barbaric. But there is no other possibility; if one wants to have mathematical certainty in matters which do not admit of such certainty, one cannot but end up in absurdity and barbarism. Practice once again brings to light what lies behind all these things; in practice the jury takes the easy way out and, there being no alternative, breaks its oath with perfect composure. In 1824, a jury in Oxford could not agree. One man said: guilty; eleven: not guilty. Finally they reached a settlement; the one dissenter wrote "guilty" on the bill of indictment and withdrew; then came the foreman with the other jurors, picked up the paper and wrote "not" in front of the word "guilty" (Wade, *British History*).

Another case is recounted by Fonblanque, editor of the *Examiner*, in his work *England under Seven Administrations*. In this instance too a jury could not reach a decision, and eventually the jurors had recourse to the drawing of lots; they took two straws and drew; the opinion of the party which drew the longer straw was adopted.

While we are concerned with the legal institutions, we may examine the matter a little more closely in order to complete our survey of the legal situation in England. It is well known that the English Penal Code is the most severe in Europe. As recently as 1810 it was in no way inferior in barbarity to that of the Carolina [222]; burning, breaking on the wheel, quartering, disembowelment while the person was still alive, etc., were widely used types of punishment. Since then, it is true, the most outrageous atrocities have been abolished, but there still remain numerous instances of brutality and infamy unamended on the statute-book. The death penalty applies to seven crimes (murder, high treason, rape, sodomy, breaking and entering, robbery with violence and arson with intent to kill); only in 1837 was the formerly much more widely applicable death penalty limited to this number; and in addition, English penal law knows two forms of punishment of particularly choice barbarity—transportation, or debasement through association, and solitary confinement, or debasement through isolation. Neither could be more cruelly or more vilely chosen to ruin systematically and consistently the victims of the law physically, intellectually and morally and to reduce them to below the level of beasts. The criminal who is transported finds himself in such an abyss of degradation and loathsome bestiality that the best of men cannot but succumb there in six months; anyone who wishes to read the reports of eyewitnesses about New South Wales and Norfolk Island will agree when I maintain that everything I have said earlier falls far short of the actual truth. The prisoner in solitary confinement is driven insane; the model gaol in London, after only three months of existence, had already three lunatics to transfer to Bedlam, to say nothing of the religious mania which is still usually regarded as sanity.

The penal laws against political crimes are drawn up in almost exactly the same terms as in Prussia; particularly "exciting discontent"[a] and "seditious language" are phrased in the same vague way which gives so much latitude to the judge and jury. In this field too the penalties are harsher than elsewhere; transportation is the main form.

If these severe penalties and these ill-defined political crimes are less significant in practice than it might seem according to the law, this is, on the one hand, a failing in the law itself, which is so confused and unclear that a clever barrister can raise objections in the defendant's favour at every turn. English law is either common law, in other words, unwritten law such as existed at the time when statutes were first gathered and later collated by legal authorities; on the most important points this law is naturally uncertain and ambiguous; or else it is statute law, which consists of an infinite number of individual acts of Parliament gathered over five hundred years, which contradict each other and represent not a "state of law", but a state of complete lawlessness. The barrister is everything here; anyone who has wasted a lot of his time on this legal jungle, on this chaos of contradictions is all-powerful in an English law-court. The uncertainty of the law naturally led to belief in the authority of decisions taken by past judges in similar cases, and this only aggravates the uncertainty, since these decisions also contradict one another, and the outcome of the proceedings depends again on the learning and presence of mind of the barrister. On the other hand, lack of importance of English penal law is however just a matter of clemency, etc., and regard for public opinion, which the law by no means obliges the government to have; and the vigorous opposition to all law-reforms shows that the legislature is by no means inclined to

---

[a] Engels gives some of the legal terms in this and the following paragraph both in German and in English.— *Ed.*

change this state of affairs. But it should never be forgotten that property rules and that in consequence this clemency is only practised towards "respectable" criminals; it is on the poor man, on the pariah, on the proletarian that the full force of the law's barbarity descends, and no one cares a brass farthing about it.

This favouritism towards the rich is moreover explicitly stated in the law. While all serious crimes are liable to the severest penalties, fines are stipulated for almost all minor[a] offences, fines which are of course the same for the poor and the rich but which affect the rich man little or not at all, while in nine cases out of ten the poor man cannot pay them and is then committed without more ado to the treadmill for a few months "in default of payment".[b] One only needs to read the police reports in the first English newspaper that comes to hand to be convinced of the truth of this statement. The maltreatment of the poor and the preferential treatment of the rich in all the courts of law is so universal, is practised so openly and brazenly, and is reported so shamelessly by the newspapers that one can rarely read a paper without being filled with indignation. Such a rich man is always treated with uncommon courtesy, and however brutal his offence may have been, "the judges are always very sorry" that they have to sentence him to what is usually a quite paltry fine. The administration of the law is in this respect still more inhuman than the law itself; "law grinds the poor and rich men rule the law"[b] and "there is one law for the poor and another for the rich"[b] are completely true sayings that have long since become proverbial. But how can it be otherwise? The magistrates and the jury alike are themselves rich, are chosen from the middle class and are thus biassed towards their own kind and are born enemies of the poor. And if the social effect of property, which we cannot go into now, is taken into account, then indeed nobody can be surprised at such a barbaric state of affairs.

The question of *direct* social legislation in which this infamy culminates, will be dealt with later.[223] In any case it could not be described in its full significance at this point.

Let us summarise the conclusions of this critique of the law in England. Whatever objections may be raised to it from the viewpoint of the "constitutional state" are a matter of supreme indifference. The fact that England is not officially a democracy

---

[a] *Vorwärts!* has: "more oppressive".—*Ed.*
[b] Given by Engels in English.— *Ed.*

cannot prejudice *us* against her institutions. For us there is only *one* matter of importance: that we have found everywhere theory and practice in flagrant contradiction with each other. All the powers of the Constitution, the Crown, the House of Lords and the House of Commons, have dissolved before our eyes; we have seen that the Established Church and all the so-called birthrights of the British are empty names, that even trial by jury is in reality only an outward show, that even the law has no existence, in short, that a state, which has given itself a clearly defined legal foundation, denies and abuses this foundation. The Englishman is not free on account of the law but despite the law, if one can say at all that he is free.

We have seen furthermore what a jungle of lies and immorality follows from this state of affairs; people prostrate themselves before empty names and deny reality, they do not want to know anything about it and are reluctant to acknowledge what really exists, what they have themselves created; they deceive themselves and invent a language of conventions with artificial concepts, each of which is a parody of reality, and cling fearfully to these hollow abstractions, so as to avoid having to own to themselves that what matters in real life, in practice, are quite different things. The whole English Constitution and the whole of constitutional public opinion is nothing but a big lie which is constantly supported and concealed by a number of small lies whenever at one point or another its true nature appears a little too openly in the light of day. And even if a person comes to the realisation that the whole of this construction is but untruth and fiction, even then he still adheres to it, indeed more tenaciously than ever, so that the empty words, the few meaninglessly assembled letters, should not fall apart, for these words are after all the pivot on which the world turns, and with them the world and mankind would of necessity plunge into the darkness of chaos! One cannot but turn away in deep disgust from this tissue of blatant and concealed lies, of hypocrisy and self-deception.

Can such a state of affairs last long? There is no chance of that. The struggle of practice against theory, of reality against abstraction, of life against hollow words devoid of meaning, in short, of man against inhumanity, must be decided, and there is no question as to which side will be victorious.

The struggle is already on. The Constitution is shaken to its foundations. What form the immediate future will take emerges from what has just been said. The new, alien elements in the Constitution are democratic in nature; it will become evident that public opinion too is developing in a democratic direction; the immediate future of England will be democracy.

But what a democracy! Not that of the French Revolution, whose antithesis was the monarchy and feudalism, but *the* democracy whose antithesis is the middle class and property. The whole of the preceding development shows this. The middle class and property are dominant; the poor man has no rights, is oppressed and fleeced, the Constitution repudiates him and the law mistreats him; the struggle of democracy against the aristocracy in England is the struggle of the poor against the rich. The democracy towards which England is moving is a *social* democracy.

But democracy by itself is not capable of curing social ills. Democratic equality is a chimera, the fight of the poor against the rich cannot be fought out on a basis of democracy or indeed of politics as a whole. This stage too is thus only a transition, the last purely political remedy which has still to be tried and from which a new element is bound to develop at once, a principle transcending everything of a political nature.

This principle is the principle of socialism.

Written in March 1844

First published in *Vorwärts!* (Paris) Nos. 75, 76, 77, 78, 80, 83 and 84, September 18, 21, 25 and 28, and October 5, 16 and 19, 1844

Printed according to the newspaper

LETTER TO THE EDITOR OF THE *NORTHERN STAR*[224]

I propose furnishing you with reports concerning the progress of the movement party on the Continent for the *Star*, extracts from the German papers, and of my correspondence with well-informed men in Paris and Germany. I see with pleasure, that your paper contains more and better information about the state of public opinion in France than all other English papers together; and I should like to place you in the same position as far as regards Germany. The political state of Germany is becoming more important every day. We shall have a revolution there very shortly, which cannot but end in establishment of a Federal Republic.[225] At the same time, I shall not confine myself to Germany, but report to you everything about Switzerland, Austria, Italy, Russia, &c., which will be likely to prove interesting to your readers; and I shall leave it entirely to yourself to make what use you think proper of the materials furnished by me.

Written late in April 1844

First published in *The Northern Star*
No. 338, May 4, 1844

Printed according to the newspaper

[THE SITUATION IN PRUSSIA]

When Frederick William IV ascended the throne there was not a more popular monarch in all Europe. Now, there is none more unpopular; not one, not even Nicholas of Russia, who is at least worshipped by the dumb beastly stupidity of his degraded serfs. The Prussian King, who calls himself emphatically "the Christian King", and has made his court a most ludicrous assemblage of whining saints and piety-feigning courtiers, has done everything in his power to open the eyes of the nation, and not in vain. He commenced with a show of liberality, then passed over to feudality; and ended in establishing the government of the police-spy. The press is laid down by a rigorous censorship, and by prosecutions in courts of law, before judges, paid by the king, and removable by the king, who conduct trials without juries, and with closed doors. Oppression is very rife. The students at Berlin commenced holding meetings and discussing political subjects; these meetings were stopped by the police, the speakers arrested, prosecuted, and several of them expelled the University. Dr. Nauwerck, lecturer at the University, who lectured on modern politics, and hesitated not to proclaim his Republican opinions, had his lectures visited by the minister's spies, and at last stopped by the illegal interference of the minister, about a month ago. The University protested against such an obstruction, and some of their members published the protest; for this heinous crime they are now under prosecution. At some public demonstrations of the students, which happened in February, cheers were given for Professor Hoffman, who had been dismissed for his having published some satirical poetry. The consequence of this was, that again half-a-dozen students were expelled, and by this disabled to take any Government office, or to exercise the medical profession. At Dusseldorf, on the Rhine, the annual public masquerade during the Carnival was stopped by the police, on account of some political allusions, and the poor Dusseldorfians were even hindered from going to Cologne, and partaking in the procession there. These are only a few of the oppressive measures by which the Government has shown its mind; and they have had a miraculous effect on the development of public opinion. They have awakened the nation from a state of political lethargy, and thrown them into such an excitement that even the oldest and most loyal supporters of the "Christian King" begin to entertain fears for the stability of the present order of things. Dissatisfaction is increasing everywhere, and has become almost universal in the Rhenish provinces, in Eastern Prussia, Posen, Berlin, and all the large towns. The people are resolved to have a free press and constitution to begin with. But there is so much combustible matter heaped up in all Germany, and the shades of opinion are so various, that it is impossible to predict where the movement, if once fairly commenced, may stop. However, it will be in the direction towards democracy; thus much is evident.

Written late in April 1844

First published in *The Northern Star* No. 338, May 4, 1844, with an editorial note: "From our own Correspondent"

Printed according to the newspaper

[NEWS FROM GERMANY]

In the Chamber of Deputies of the Grand Duchy of Baden, Mr. Welcker, a liberal member and the Lord John Russell of that country, implored the government to do something in order to satisfy the discontented feelings of the people:

"for", said he, "I have been travelling much in all parts of Germany, and have been visited there by a great number of men of all ranks and from all parts of the country; and I should lie, I should fail in my duty as a representative of the people, if I did not state that everywhere the principle of monarchical government is daily losing its ground more and more in the minds of all classes of the German nation. I therefore implore the ministers to oppose no longer the current of public opinion; for if something is not done soon; if the breach between the governments of our fatherland and the people is allowed to become wider, then nobody can doubt for a moment what the consequence will be."

And Mr. Welcker's evidence, as to the spread of Republicanism in Germany, may be admitted as the most unquestionable that can be given, because this progress frightens him even more than it does the government; and because it is quite contrary to his own expectations.

M. Frederic Steinmann who has for some time been under prosecution for a book he published, in which he assailed the Austrian government,[a] has been condemned to eight months imprisonment in a fortress, though he lives in Prussia, and published his book there. He was not prosecuted by the Austrian, but by the Prussian government, and in a Prussian court of law.

Dr. Strauss, the author of the *Life of Jesus*,[b] is occupied with a similar work, on the *Acts of the Apostles*,[226] which book he, of

---

[a] F. A. Steinmann, *Caricaturen und Silhouetten des neunzehnten Jahrhunderts.—Ed.*
[b] D. F. Strauss, *Das Leben Jesu.—Ed.*

course, will treat in the same manner as he did the gospels in his former work.

The Russian Diplomacy is very active at present at the different courts of Germany, in order to effect some measures against the violence with which the German press treats the policy of the Czar. The anti-Russian feeling, which is now quite universal in Germany, has vented itself for some time past in all newspapers, and in a great many pamphlets, which makes the autocrat uneasy. But, fortunately, he will not be able to stop these publications.

Serious riots at Munich.— There were riots at Munich on the 3rd inst., on account of a rise in the price of beer. The tumult was serious, and was not quelled without a somewhat sanguinary use of the soldiery, who by express orders of the King,[a] fired on the unarmed people, killing several, and wounding others. The following later particulars show the people have triumphed, and the King succumbed; the cause being that the royal man-slayer *feared that his own tools, the troops, would turn against him!*

"Munich, May 5.—Tranquillity has been re-established in our town, but it cannot be denied that the royal authority has suffered a good deal in the transaction. The King, after having shown himself greatly opposed to any sort of conciliation or compromise, after having himself ordered the soldiery to charge the people, and that in his own presence, ended by requiring of the brewers that they should yield to the popular demands. This morning notice was stuck up at the corners of all the streets, that the increase in the price of beer would not take place, and the people appeared satisfied, but they at the same time retain a secret animosity against the King for having ordered them to be fired upon—an order which cost the lives of several of the people of this town. It appears that the King yielded principally on account of the small degree of devotion shown towards him by the troops, who did not appear at all willing to fire upon the people."

Written in the first half of May 1844

First published in *The Northern Star* No. 340, May 18, 1844, with an editorial note: "From our own Correspondent"

Printed according to the newspaper

---

[a] Ludwig I of Bavaria.—*Ed.*

FATE OF A TRAITOR

Count Adam Gurowski, who took an active part in the revolution of 1830, afterwards deserted his party, was allowed to return to his country, and became notorious in a very unenviable manner by some publications,[227] in which he advised his countrymen to consider the annihilation of their independence as a judgment of God, to which they must humbly submit, and seek shelter at the throne of the mighty Czar, in whose hands God had laid their fates. He told them that Poland could not have met with a better luck than it had done by being subdued under the Russian yoke; that it was their duty to abandon all hopes of independence; and that, *in fine*, the Czar's government was the very best that could be found on the face of the earth. He expected, of course, to be rewarded by Nicholas, but the autocrat was too prudent to trust a traitor. He used him and abandoned him; he gave him a subordinate office, which Gurowski resigned, when he saw that he had no hope of being promoted; he could not even get the rights of a nation which, by his participation in the insurrection, were forfeited; and at last he has chosen to leave Poland again to take shelter in Prussia, and to go to Breslau, where he has requested the authorities to be treated as a military deserter. Despised by his countrymen, whose cause he deserted, scorned by all parties in Europe, abandoned by the Czar, he intends going to America, hoping, perhaps, that his reputation will not follow him across the ocean.

The iron sway with which Russian despotism rules Poland, is at present as unrelenting as ever. Every thing is done to remind the unfortunate Pole at every step that he is a slave. Even the fingerposts on the road sides must have inscriptions in Russian language and characters; not a word of Polish is allowed. The Polish language is banished from all courts of law. A German song, "the gipsy-boy in the North", containing not the slightest allusion to either Russia or Poland, but expressing only a strong desire to return to their native country, was translated into Polish, but suppressed by the Russian censor, as a patriotic, and therefore, of course, criminal song. No wonder, then, that Nicholas should wish to have the German press silenced, the only channel through which the world becomes acquainted with such facts as those. I must, however, not forget one fact: six Poles, soldiers of a Russian regiment at the frontier, deserted, but were caught before they reached Prussia. They were condemned to fifteen hundred lashes each; the punishment was inflicted; their relations were forced to assist at it; three only of the six survived the flogging.

Written in the first half of May 1844

First published in *The Northern Star* No. 340, May 18, 1844, with an editorial note: "From our own Correspondent"

Printed according to the newspaper

BEER RIOTS IN BAVARIA

The Bavarian Beer is the most celebrated of all kinds of this drink brewed in Germany, and, of course, the Bavarians are much addicted to its consumption in rather large quantities. The government laid a new duty of about 100s. *ad valorem* on beer, and in consequence of this an outbreak occurred, which lasted more than four days. The working men assembled in large masses, paraded through the streets, assailed the public houses, smashing the windows, breaking the furniture, and destroying everything in their reach, in order to take revenge for the enhanced price of their favourite drink. The military was called in, but a regiment of horse-guards, when commanded to mount on horseback, *refused to do so.* The police, being, as everywhere, obnoxious to the people, were severely beaten and ill-treated by the rioters, and every station formerly occupied by police-officers had to be occupied by soldiers, who, being upon good terms with the people, were considered less hostile and showed *an evident reluctance to interfere.* They only did interfere when the palace of the King was attacked, and then they merely took up such a position as was sufficient to keep the rioters back. On the second evening (the 2nd of May) the King, in whose family a marriage had just been celebrated, and who for this reason had many illustrious visitors at his court, visited the theatre; but when, after the first act, a crowd assembled before the theatre and threatened to attack it, every one left the house to see what the matter was, and His Majesty, with his illustrious visitors, was obliged to follow them, or else he would have been left alone in his place. The French papers assert that the King on this occasion ordered the military stationed before the theatre to fire upon the people, *and that the soldiers refused.* The

German papers do not mention this, as may be expected from their being published under censorship; but as the French papers are sometimes rather ill-informed about foreign matters, we cannot vouch for the truth of their assertion. From all this, however, it appears, that the Poet King (Ludwig, King of Bavaria, is the author of three volumes of unreadable Poems, of a Traveller's Guide to one of his public buildings,[228] &c. &c.) has been in a very awkward position during these outbreaks. In Munich, a town full of soldiers and police, the seat of a royal court, a riot lasts four days, notwithstanding all the array of the military,—and at last the rioters force their object. The King restored tranquillity by an ordinance, reducing the price of the quart of beer from ten kreutzers ($3^1/_4$d) to nine kreutzers (3d). If the people once know that they can frighten the government out of their taxing system, they will soon learn that it will be as easy to frighten them as far as regards more serious affairs.

Written in mid-May 1844

First published in *The Northern Star* No. 341, May 25, 1844, with an editorial note: "From our own Correspondent"

Printed according to the newspaper

[PARSONOCRACY IN PRUSSIA]

The parsonocracy of this country, enjoying the peculiar protection and favour of the present government, assume every day a more haughty position. It has, for instance, lately occurred in Berlin, that one parson after the other refused to perform marriage ceremonies on a Saturday, alleging as his reason for this refusal, that the parties would in all probability not rise on Sunday morning in a fit state of mind for the celebration of the Lord's day, if they were married on the previous day! Of course the Berliners, who care very little about a due celebration of the Sunday, and on the contrary make it the merriest day of the week, are crying out that the governing party was going to introduce among them *"the English Sunday"*, than which they know nothing more formidable. Indeed, the English Sunday is most repugnant to the feelings and habits of all continental nations.

Written in mid-May 1844
First published in *The Northern Star* No. 341, May 25, 1844, with an editorial note: "From our own Correspondent"

Printed according to the newspaper

[NEWS FROM St. PETERSBURG]

Considerable ministerial changes have occurred in St. Petersburg. The Minister of Finance, M. Cancrin, has fallen into disgrace, and the same is reported concerning the Police Minister, the well-known Count Benkendorff. Nicholas is evidently struggling to keep up a system which is rapidly ruining itself. The anti-Russian feeling in Germany and the other continental states is upon the increase, notwithstanding all the efforts of Nicholas's paid literary army. The financial state of the government is one great difficulty; the pomp of the court, the innumerable army of policemen and spies, the expenses of diplomatists, spies, reporters, of secret intrigues, and bribery all over Europe, the army and navy, and the endless wars against the Circassians,[229] have eaten up everything that taxes and loans could bring together. The restrictive commercial policy of M. Cancrin has made foreign trade in some parts of the empire almost impossible, and has failed to establish a system of national industry at home. Among the nobility, three parties are to be traced distinctly—the court, the old country nobility, and the officers of the army. They are intriguing constantly against each other, their object of course being nothing else but exclusive dominion over the person of the Emperor, who, as all despots, is, after all, only the tool of his favourites.

Written in mid-May 1844

First published in *The Northern Star* No. 341, May 25, 1844, with an editorial note: "From our own Correspondent"

Printed according to the newspaper

THE CIVIL WAR IN THE VALAIS

The valley of the River Rhone, from its source at the foot of the *glacier du Rhone* to the Lake Leman,[a] is one of the finest countries in the world. On its sides are the highest mountains of Europe, two uninterrupted chains of a mean height of 12,000 feet, covered with eternal snow, from which spring the numberless rivulets which feed the Rhone and fertilise the meadows and fields of the valley. Here, within a few hours' walk from eternal winter, the chestnut and the vine are found thriving under a sun as powerful almost in its warmth as that of the evergreen plains of Lombardy. This valley is called the Valais,[b] and inhabited partly by Germans, partly by Frenchmen. The Germans, entering the country from the north-east, occupy the higher and more mountainous part of the valley, where the country is unfavourable to agriculture, but excellent for the breeding of cattle; consequently this part of the population remains up to this time in almost the same state of nature in which their forefathers occupied the Upper Valais. Political and religious education is left entirely in the hands of a few aristocratic families and of the priesthood, who, of course, keep the people as stupid and superstitious as possible. On the contrary, the French settled in the Lower Valais, where the widening of the valley admits of introducing agriculture and other pursuits of industry. The French have founded the more considerable towns of the Valais, are educated and civilised, and by their bordering on the lake and the Radical canton of Vaud,[230] are brought into connection with the outer world, and enabled to keep

---

[a] Lake of Geneva.— *Ed.*
[b] The German name for it is Wallis.— *Ed.*

up with the progress of their neighbour's ideas. Nevertheless, the rough mountaineers of the Upper Valais had, I know not how, many hundred years ago, subdued the French Lower Valais, and continued to consider this part of the country as a conquered province, and to exclude its inhabitants from any participation in government. In 1798, when the French overthrew the old aristocratic system of Swiss patrician despotism,[231] the Lower Valais got its share of government, but not to the full extent it was entitled to. In 1830, when the democratic party in all Switzerland was in the ascendant, the constitution was re-modelled upon fair and democratic principles[232]; but the priest-ridden cow-herds of Upper Valais, and the sovereign rulers of their minds, the parsons, have ever since tried to bring about a change in favour of the old system of injustice. The Radical party, in order to guard against this, formed an association called *Young Switzerland — la jeune Suisse* — among themselves and the Radicals of Vaud. They were most violently assailed and calumniated by the priesthood, and usually attacked upon the ground of being infidels, which, however, on the continent is a charge more laughed at than shuddered at. In 1840 the first outbreak against *Young Switzerland* took place, but, finding the democrats well prepared, the dupes of superstition and ignorance retreated to their unassailable mountain passes, in order to break forth again in March, 1844. They have now succeeded in taking the Radicals by surprise, in profiting by the general reaction in favour of Conservative principles; and of the leading canton (the seat of the federal Government for the time being) Luzern, being a Conservative Canton. The democratic party in Valais is for the moment overwhelmed. The interference of the federal Government will be required; it remains to be seen what profit the priests, who accompanied the Conservative army and headed it, will make of their victory; but at any rate there is no chance, even now, to re-establish anything like the old system, or to keep the Lower Valais and its spirited inhabitants in a state of subjection. A few years, nay, months, may bring back the ascendancy of the democratic party.[233]

Written in the first half of June 1844

First published in *The Northern Star* No. 344, June 15, 1844, with an editorial note: "From our own Correspondent"

Printed according to the newspaper

[NEWS FROM FRANCE]

There has been a serious turn-out of colliers at Rive de Jier, near Lyons, for wages and other grievances. This affair offered upon the whole the same features as the English strikes: processions with banners, meetings, molesting of knobsticks, &c. The strike lasted about six weeks; several of the men were imprisoned for conspiracy, though no serious disturbance appears to have occurred. At last the men are reported to have returned to their pits, though it is not stated whether the object of the strike was accomplished.

Republican Demonstration.— The following account of the gathering of the Republican forces upon the occasion of the funeral of the deceased M. Laffitte from the pen of the correspondent of the *Weekly Dispatch* will be found interesting, as showing the great strength of the Republicans in Paris, and the certainty of a speedy revolution in that country.

"Although no disturbance occurred at the funeral of the celebrated Jacques Laffitte, on the 30th ult.,[a] the Republican party nevertheless made a powerful demonstration of its strength. Five thousand students belonging to the schools of law and medicine, assembled to do honour to a man whose whole life (with one fatal exception) had been devoted to the cause of political liberty. For that one error — viz., conferring the Crown upon Louis Philippe,[234] he partially atoned in the Chamber of Deputies, by imploring pardon of God and of man for the grievous injury he had been instrumental in inflicting upon France and the civilised world. The five thousand students who followed him to his last home, are all staunch Republican spirits — all glowing for political liberty. These noble-minded young men, together with the military students of the Polytechnic Schools, are the hope of young France. Let them eradicate from their breasts that absurd animosity towards England, which would lead them to plunge into war, for the mere purpose of settling the question of national rivalry over again — let them

---

[a] May 30, 1844.— *Ed.*

learn to respect their island-ally as a power advancing with them hand-in-hand in the road of civilisation—and those young men—the rising generation whom the Conservative press of both nations affect to despise—will one day be called upon to decide the destinies of France. In the Revolution of 1830, military students of sixteen and eighteen years of age became the generals of the people in that dreadful struggle with the royal troops. At the death of Louis Philippe the Republicans will no doubt proclaim their principles to be those alone adapted to France and French interests; and the young students of Paris must co-operate with, and advise the people in the political arena, as readily and faithfully as they led them on to victory fourteen years ago. But the demonstration of Republican strength on the occasion of the funeral of M. Laffitte, was not confined to the law and medical students. The Secret Societies were not idle. The members of those formidable political combinations assembled in immense numbers. They are for the most part respectable tradesmen, mechanics, and artisans, and are by no means the despicable rabble and low character which *The Times* and *Journal des Débats* have on various occasions represented them to be. They formed a column four deep, and marched immediately in front of the students. A third section of the Republican party also followed Laffitte to the cemetery of Père La Chaise. This was composed of operatives, all neatly attired, respectable in appearance, and exemplary in behaviour. The friends of liberty, therefore, mustered strong upon this occasion. Indeed, it is absurd for the Conservative press to deny the fact that the numerical strength, and the moral influences of the French Republican party are immense. Ranking amongst its numbers some of the most exalted names in France—names respectively famous in the spheres of war, literature, art, science, and policy—gaining strength daily by the acquisition of those whom the tyranny of the King alienates from the Orleans cause, and professing principles which accord with the new interests and new wants of civilisation, the Republican party is the one to which all eyes will be turned the moment any unforeseen accident or natural occurrence disturbs the reign of the Orleans dynasty."

The "Holy War".— The Emperor of Morocco[a] has declared a "holy war" against France and Frenchmen, and is rousing the various peoples and tribes within and contiguous to his dominions to arms [in] defence of the one faith, and for the extermination of the "Infidels". Abd-el-Kader, the African Wallace, is the leader of this national enterprise for the overthrow and expulsion of the French conquerors.[235] The latest accounts represent the advanced section of the Moorish army as being within sight of the French forces.

From accounts received from Constantine, it appears that the Duke d'Aumale has met with some reverses, which seem to have been the result of his own imprudence and want of experience. It will be seen from the subjoined extracts, that a small body of troops, left in charge of Biskra, has been surprised, the French garrison killed, and the whole of the baggage, ammunition, and stores, carried away by the natives.

A Toulon letter of the 3rd says:—

---

[a] Abd ur-Rahman II.—*Ed.*

"We have received most afflicting news from the province of Constantine, dated the 20th ult. The Duke d'Aumale had left at Biskra a very small garrison, composed only of Lieutenant Petitgand, commandant, Sub-Lieutenant Crochard, and Aide-Surgeon Major Arcelin, with about forty men, from the battalion of the Constantine Fusileers. This small corps was intended to form the nucleus of a new battalion, to be raised from among the tribes in the environs of Biskra. Of all these, only a serjeant-major, named Pelisse, escaped. The new recruits opened the gates of the Casbah during the night to Mahommed Seghir, the Calif[236] of Abd-el-Kader, and his followers, who surprised our men in their sleep, and killed them all. Plunder became general, and 70,000 fr. left with the commandant to pay his men, and all the cannon, muskets, ammunition, and other stores, were carried off. This unfortunate affair is said to have encouraged the surrounding tribes to take up arms. The fatal news having reached the Prince[a] while in the mountains of the Ouled Sultau, he instantly marched to Biskra with a column of 3,000 men. He arrived on the 18th, but the Calif had left on the preceding day. The third battalion of the African Light Infantry marched from Constantine on the 24th for Biskra, to form its garrison."

On Friday, the Chamber of Deputies voted by a majority of 190 to 53 a sum of 7,500,000 f. to defray the expense of increasing the present military force of France in Algeria (96,000, by 15,000 more; thus raising the number of bayonets in Algeria to 111,000).

Written in the first half of June 1844

First published in *The Northern Star* No. 344, June 15, 1844, with an editorial note: "From our own Correspondent"

Printed according to the newspaper

---

[a] Duke d'Aumale.— *Ed.*

[NEWS FROM PRUSSIA]

The people have achieved a great triumph; they have by their steady and protracted opposition forced the King[a] to abandon his pet measure, the proposed new law of divorce.[237] The present law in this respect is very liberal, and, of course, never pleased the Christian King. Ever since his accession to the throne, he was big with an amended law, by which a divorce was to be granted in very few cases only. The holiness of the marriage bond was to be enforced as strictly as possible, and another door to be opened to the parsons to meddle with the family affairs of other people. The spirit of the nation, however, arose against such a law; the press opposed it, and when a democratic paper[b] succeeded in getting and publishing an authentic abstract of the proposed law, a general outcry was raised against it from one end of the country to the other.[238] Nevertheless, the King persisted in his intention. The bill was laid before the Privy Council, in order to be prepared for the provincial Parliaments,[239] the advice of which is necessary, according to the Prussian constitution. Whether there was already a strong opposition in the Privy Council, or whether the King saw that this measure would never pass the provincial Parliaments, may be difficult to decide; it is enough, that an ordinance dated the 11th instant has been directed to the Council, withdrawing the bill, abandoning entirely its principle, and declaring that the King will be satisfied with the alteration of a few formalities of the present law. This most important triumph of the opposition must strengthen permanently the popular party, and will be received

---

[a] Frederick William IV.—*Ed.*
[b] *Rheinische Zeitung.*—*Ed.*

with cheers in every hamlet of the realm. It will show the people that they are strong, and that if united, they may defeat any measure they do not like; nay that by merely using their strength, they may frighten the government into any thing they please. In the manufacturing district of Silesia very serious riots have occurred[a]; the workpeople of the neighbourhood, depending almost entirely upon the linen-manufacture and suffering great distress, not being able to stand the competition against the English machine-made article, have for some time been in a condition similar to that of the English hand-loom weavers. Oppressed by competition, machinery, and greedy manufacturers, they at last arose in Peterswalden (Silesia), demolished the house of a manufacturer, and were only dispersed by the appearance of the military. In Langenbielau, outrages of a similar nature were committed; the military were repelled by the people, and could only restore the peace after having received reinforcements and fired on the rioters, of whom several were killed. In other districts tumultuous assemblages took place, and even in the capital of the province (Breslau), the peace was disturbed. Thus it is evident that the consequences of the factory system, of the progress of machinery, &c., for the working classes are quite the same on the continent as they are in England: oppression and toil for the many, riches and wealth for the few; insecurity of fortune, discontent, and riot exist among the hills of Silesia, as well as in the crowded cities of Lancashire and Yorkshire.[240]

Written in mid-June 1844

First published in *The Northern Star* No. 346, June 29, 1844, with an editorial note: "From our own Correspondent"

Printed according to the newspaper

---

[a] See this volume, p. 201.—*Ed.*

FURTHER PARTICULARS OF THE SILESIAN RIOTS

The riots commenced, as stated in my last,[a] at Peterswalden, in the District of Reichenbach, the centre of the manufacturing part of Silesia. The weavers assembled before the house of one of the most respectable manufacturers, of the name of Zwanziger, singing a song, in which the behaviour of this individual towards his workmen was animadverted upon, and which seems to have been manufactured for the occasion.[241] Mr. Zwanziger sent for the police, and got several of the ringleaders arrested; the people assembled in growing numbers before his door, threatened to rescue them, and, the prisoners not being liberated, they immediately commenced the work of destruction. The doors were forced, the windows smashed, the crowd entered the house, and destroyed every thing within their reach. Zwanziger's family had hardly time to save themselves, and the throwing of stones at them was so incessant that it was found necessary to wrap up in bedding the female part of the family, and have them carried in a coach to Schweidnitz. To this place messengers also were sent to call in the aid of the military, but the commanding officer replied he could do nothing without orders from the provincial authorities at Breslau. The people, in the meantime, entirely demolished the dwelling house of Mr. Zwanziger, and proceeded then to the warehouse, where they destroyed all books, bills of exchange and other documents, and threw the cash they found, amounting to upwards of £1,000, upon the street, where it was picked up by a lot of Bohemian smugglers, who had passed the frontier to see whether they could not profit by the riots. The bales of cotton and

---

[a] See previous article.— *Ed.*

bags, as well as all the manufactured yarn and goods, were, as far as possible, destroyed or made useless, and the machinery in the adjoining factory, entirely broke. Having finished up here, they left the ruins of the demolished buildings and proceeded to Langenbielau, the men of which town joined them immediately, and where Mr. Dierig's factory and warehouse was attacked. Mr. Dierig first tried to buy them off, but after having paid part of his bargain, he was informed that the military were on the road, and he immediately refused to pay the remainder. The crowd immediately forced their way to the premises, and demolished them in the same way as they had done at Peterswalden; while they were engaged in this, a detachment of about 160 foot soldiers arrived, with the civil authorities; the Riot Act was read, the people replied by throwing stones at the military, then the word to fire was given, and twelve of the rioters were killed and many wounded. But the enraged crowd rushed on against the soldiers, and wounded such a number of them by stones, that the commanding officer, who had been dragged from his horse and severely beaten, retreated with them, to await reinforcements, while the destruction of property continued going on. At last two battalions of infantry, a company of rifles, some cavalry and artillery appeared, and dispersed the rioters. Further attempts at similar proceedings were stifled by the military keeping the town and surrounding places occupied, and, as usual, when everything was over, the proper authorities came forward with proclamations and such like, declaring the district in a state of siege, and threatened the most horrible punishments for every breach of the peace. The riots were not confined to these two towns; in Alt-Friedland and Leutmansdorf similar scenes took place, though not characterised by such a violent manifestation of feeling towards the manufacturers; some arms were broke and some windows were smashed before the military could restore tranquility. The people throughout the district profited on this occasion by giving to the manufacturers such a display of their feelings as could not be mistaken. The causes of these affrays were the incredible sufferings of these poor weavers, produced by low wages, machinery, and the avarice and greediness of the manufacturers. It will scarcely be believed that the wages of this oppressed class, in a family where father, mother, and children worked, all of them at the loom, amounted to a sum which would buy no more than six shillings would in England. Besides, they were all in debt, which is not at all a matter of surprise, when wages are so low; and the manufacturers gladly advanced them small sums, which the men could never pay, but which were sufficient to give the masters an absolute sovereignty over them, and to make them the slaves of the manufacturers. Then there was, besides that, the competition of the English article, which had an advantage over them from the superior machinery of the English factories and the low wages there, and which tended to bring down their wages too. In short, it was the factory system with all its consequences that pressed upon the Silesian weavers in the same manner as it has done, and now does, upon the English factory workers and hand-loom weavers and which has occasioned more dissatisfaction and riotous outbreaks within this country than anything else. It is to be noticed, that during all these disturbances, according to the statements of all German papers, not one single robbery has been committed by the starving weavers. They threw the money on the street; they did not convert it to their own use. They left the stealing and plunder to the Bohemian smugglers and poachers.

Written in the latter half of June 1844
First published in *The Northern Star* No. 346, June 29, 1844, with an editorial note: "From our own Correspondent"

Printed according to the newspaper

SUPPLEMENT

Frederick Engels

COLA DI RIENZI[242]

ACT ONE

Scene One

The Forum in Rome, with the Capitol in the background. Enter Colonna with other Patricians, and, soon after, the people, led by Battista.

PATRICIANS

Away, Colonna, the people crowd us.
Come, flee from the wrath of the howling mob!

COLONNA

Flee? A Colonna flee the dregs
Of the people whose necks he so often trod
And trampled on?
Flee, cowardlings, flee! I'll brave their fury!

PATRICIANS

See you them surging along the street?
Can you not hear them raging? Come!

The people, with Battista at their head, crowd onto the stage.

BATTISTA

How are you, fine sirs, today?
Must you make such haste to go?
Surely you'd be glad to stay?

COLONNA (*to the Patricians*)

Can you let them mock you so?

BATTISTA

See their faces, how they plead!
Stay with us, we humbly pray!

COLONNA AND PATRICIANS

Hence, you insolent ones, away!

BATTISTA

Just to serve you is our need!

COLONNA (*to the Patricians*)

Draw, Patricians!

BATTISTA

We would treat you as our parents,
We would never mutiny,
We would never speak too free,
Leave our families in your care.
All our goods you need not spare;
You may torture, thrash or flail us,
Crush, bait, shackle us and gaol us,
For our sins you may impale us,
All we ask you is, please stay!

COLONNA (*to the Patricians*)

Well, my lords, what do you say?

PATRICIANS

Hence, you insolent ones, away!

COLONNA

Hence, you insolent, filthy rabble!
Know you not this voice's thunder
That has rent you oft asunder?
Know you not how this foot treads
When it walks upon your heads?
Know you not your lord and master?

Scene One revised

*Colonna, Orsini, Orlando Orsini. The people in the background.
Enter Patricians; they remain standing on one side.*

ORSINI

Come, Colonna, let us hurry,
For the mob approaches, see!

COLONNA

I shall stand and face their fury.
Never was I known to flee!

ORSINI

Yield, just once, or we'll pay dear.
We were mad to tarry longer.

ORLANDO

We must go, or else I fear
We shall not escape their anger.

COLONNA

No! I'll walk, though I die here,
Through their midst, defying danger!

BATTISTA

(*He comes out from among the people.
The people draw nearer.*)

How are you, fine sirs, today?
Must you make such haste to go?
Surely you'd be glad to stay?

ORSINI

Can you let them mock you so?

BATTISTA

See their faces, how they plead.
Stay with us, we humbly pray!

COLONNA, ORSINI, ORLANDO
Hence, you insolent ones, away!

BATTISTA
Just to serve you is our need!

COLONNA (*to the Patricians*)
Draw, Patricians!

BATTISTA
We would treat you as our parents,
We would never mutiny,
Never speak too evilly,
Leave our families in your care.
All our goods you need not spare;
You may torture, thrash or flail us,
Crush, bait, shackle us and gaol us,
For our sins you may impale us,
All we ask you is, please stay!

COLONNA (*to the Patricians*)
Well, my lords, what do you say?

COLONNA, ORSINI, ORLANDO
Hence, you insolent ones, away!

COLONNA
Hence, you insolent, filthy rabble!
Know you not this voice's thunder
That has rent you oft asunder?
Know you not how this foot treads
When it walks upon your heads?
Know you not your lord and master?

PEOPLE
Down with you!

COLONNA (*to the Patricians*)
Draw your swords! Our lives are at stake!

PEOPLE

Down with you! We are free!

BATTISTA

Do stay with us, we beg you!

PATRICIANS

Away! Just let us flee their rage
Until revenge's hour shall strike!

COLONNA

Let us give in for now.
Rave, you rabble, rave on!
One day we shall return,
Then tremble before our wrath!

PEOPLE

Down with you!

(Exeunt Colonna and Patricians. The people gradually divide into two choruses, the first of which is bigger than the second.)

BATTISTA

See, they quail, those noble lords,
Cowering back with unsheathed swords,
Count and Baron, Marquis and Prince,
Needs must hastily hie them hence!
But what use, if ten small devils
Leave us, and the worst of evils—
Yes, the Prince of Hell, none other—
Comes and takes the whole place over?
Granted those ones are a curse,
Still the Tribune plagues us worse!

FIRST CHORUS

Hail to the Tribune, the people's liberator!
Who dares to revile him?

SECOND CHORUS

Down with him!

BATTISTA

He is as evil and as good
As yonder lords of noble blood.
He ever speaks words passing fair,
Yet to the people shuts his ear.
Tyrants out, a despot in—
'Twill end as it did first begin.

FIRST CHORUS

Silence, slanderer!

SECOND CHORUS

No, say on!

BATTISTA

He is as evil and as good
As yonder lords of noble blood.

FIRST CHORUS

Traitor! Defame not the liberator! Hail to the Tribune!
Hail to Rienzi! Traitor! Away with you!
Beat him, beat him!

SECOND CHORUS

Down with him, the tyrant! Curse Rienzi!
Death to the Tribune! We will protect
you!

BATTISTA

To you he speaks, etc.
Tyrants out, etc.

(*Confusion. The music of a triumphal procession is heard in the distance. Cannon-fire. All are startled.*)

BOTH CHORUSES

He comes! Let us meet him!

FIRST CHORUS

Hail to the liberator.

SECOND CHORUS

He'll fall to our revenge
Soon, as did those others,
However firm he stands.

BOTH CHORUSES

To meet him!

(*Exeunt omnes.*)

Scene Two

Colonna's palace, Camilla's chamber.

CAMILLA

Why that turmoil? What's the meaning
Of that roaring mob out there;
All that raving, running, screaming,
Bloody flags waved in the air?
And I hear a wild throng gathered
At the palace steps: they're crying
Out the name of my own father,
Threatening and vilifying.

Will you escape, father, safe and sound
From the crazed people that riot and swarm?
Will Holy Mary, Protectress, look down
Like a good star and preserve you from harm?
Fear is upon me, black and ineffable,
Father, all for your sake!
Spare me this suffering, dreadful, unbearable,
Father, oh please come back!

All the servants, in their terror,
Leaving me, have run away,
And I stand here white with horror
In the palace on my own.
But—Oh God! for here comes Walter—
Heart, O heart, be still, I pray!—
Now he sees me quail and falter,
Through the gates he runs alone!

Enter Montreal.

CAMILLA

By all the Saints in Heaven, Montreal, you dare—

MONTREAL (*going down on his knees*)

O Camilla! My Camilla!

CAMILLA

You dare set foot inside this house
Denied to you forever by my father?
Let him but meet you here, and from his sword
Your life's in danger!

MONTREAL

Sweet lady, do you mind no more
The love that bound us lastingly,
The vows that by the stars we swore,
The tears you used to shed for me?

CAMILLA

Leave me! O Saints, my poor heart
Is bursting in my breast!

MONTREAL

Beloved, see the hectic fever
That drives the blood into my face.
Am I now strange to you forever
Who on your breast once found my peace?

CAMILLA

I must not look you in the eye,
Being beholden to forswear you.
My wretched heart will break, but I,
Alas, I must not dare come near you.

MONTREAL

O see me begging at your feet,
My only dearest love are you!
But lock your heart against me, sweet,
And Heaven locks its portals too!

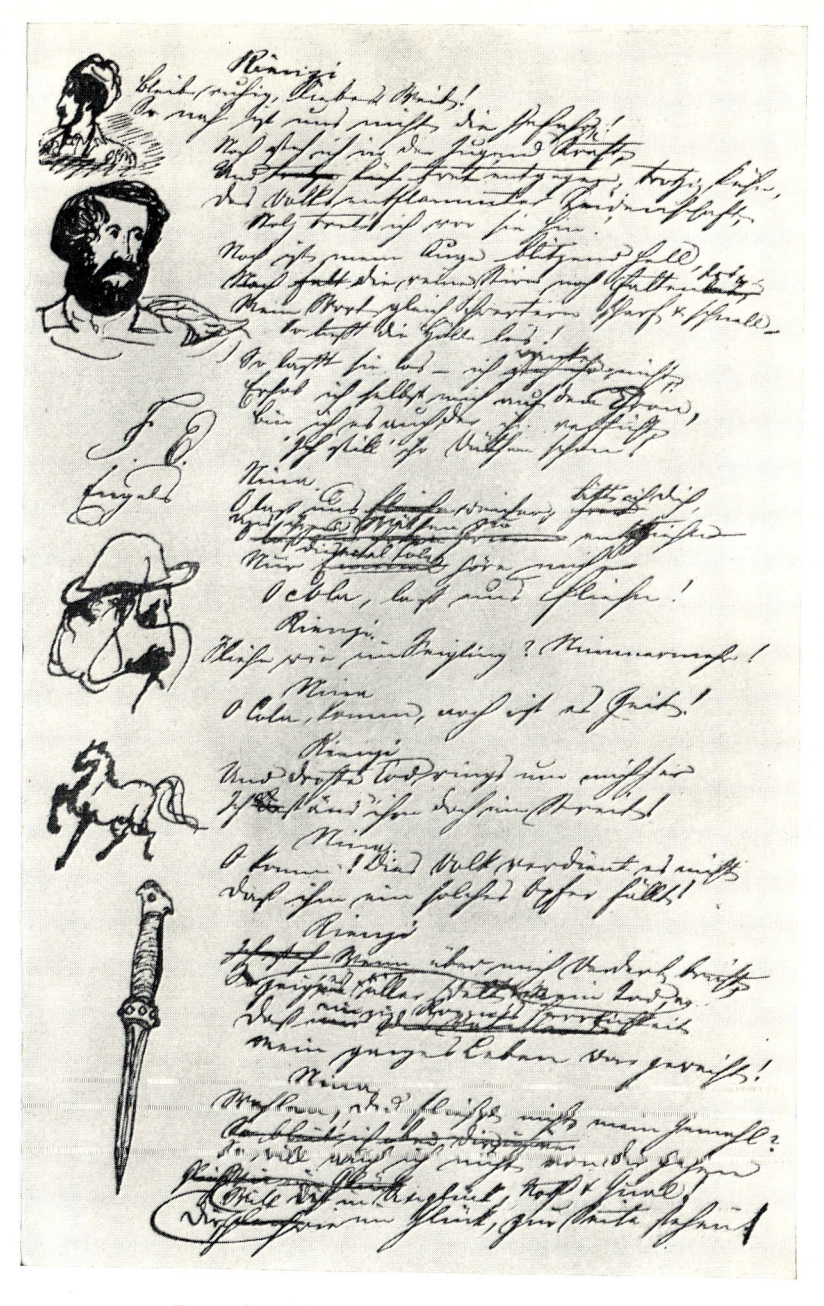

Pages from the manuscript of *Cola di Rienzi*

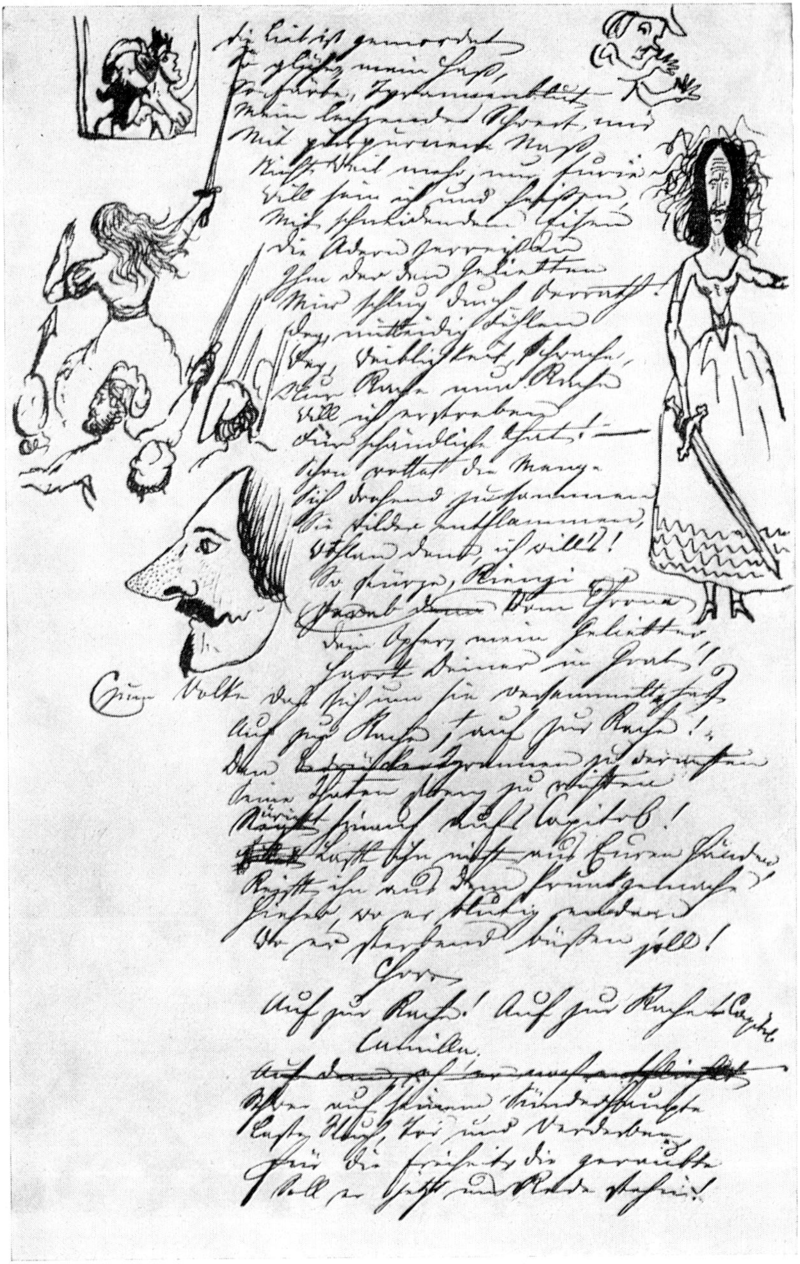

CAMILLA

My breast is heaving up and down,
From him I cannot stay apart.
Once more in true love's toils I'm bound.
Walter—forever yours my heart!

BOTH

O true love's blessed victory!
No matter what else may conspire
Against us, what can mar our sky
When each belongs to each entire?
Though we be shunned the whole world over,
Our bond disparaged as a bane,
If we do not desert each other,
Indeed our star can never wane!

CAMILLA

But tell me, Walter, what arouses
The mob on the streets to such violent rage?
And, above all, my father, my father—
Where is he?

MONTREAL

Fear not! Your father is in safety,
Debating flight with the city nobles
In the Orsinis' palace.
The Tribune approached; rejoicing, the people
All went to meet him. Like lightning he moved,
And, ere the nobles could guess what was happening,
He stood at the gates of the city.
Your father will soon be here with his trusted friends,
To lead you from here to a place of safety.
But look! his suite comes over there,
With trumpets sounding, banners waving!
Yes, I can see his silver hair!
He comes, and so I must be leaving.

CAMILLA

My Walter, go away from me,
But for my love you need not fear.
I shall yearn for you constantly,
My heart shall ever hold you dear!

WALTER

My joy—until we meet again!
The Saints be with you—I will come
Back to you, love, a nobler man,
To carry you, my Princess, home!

Great things to do some day I mean.
My life on it: the time will come,
I'll raise you to the throne as queen
And you shall reign with me in Rome.

CAMILLA

My loving heart content would be
If I were simply your poor wife.
It were the height of bliss for me
To serve you, body and soul, for life!

BOTH

O true love's blessed victory!
etc.

Scene Three

The people swarm onto the stage and range themselves in the background, while Battista [stands] in front with the chorus of malcontents. Triumphal procession.

CHORUS OF PEOPLE

Hail to the Tribune, the people's liberator!
Hail to Rienzi, Father of the Fatherland!

The procession grows.

BATTISTA

With mercenaries he moves in,
The people's freedom claims to win!
He's scared of his own countrymen.
This joke will soon come to an end!

Chorus as above. **BATTISTA**

They fill the air with joyful cries.
Suffering soon will make them wise!

CHORUS OF MALCONTENTS

Down with the foreign mercenaries!
Down with the Tribune!
Curse you, the people's oppressor,
Curse you, desecrator of holy places!
Away with the foreigners, away!

CHORUS OF PEOPLE

Hail to the Tribune on high!
Long live the Father of the Fatherland!

BATTISTA

See, he looks arrogant enough,
Now that his clever trick's come off.
See how defiant he goes there,
Now that he's caught us in his snare.
He will not long remain so proud
When common sense dawns on the crowd.

Chorus of people as above.

RIENZI (*on the rostrum*)

So stand I once again amongst you,
O noble Romans! Again I see
All Rome's holy places—the Capitol,
The eternal Forum! You are welcoming me,
And so my gratitude shall not be wanting.
I swear before God's countenance
To consecrate my whole life to your freedom,
That Ancient Rome shall rise again
As great and free as ever from her ruins!
I shall not rest, nor tarry,
Till Rome in all her ancient splendour,
And in her ancient majesty,
Shines before all the peoples of this Earth!
Even as the phoenix, prouder, more magnificent,
Soars up aloft from its own funeral pyre,
So may the bygone age of world conquest
Return once more, new and imperishable!

CHORUS OF PEOPLE (*as above*)

Curtain

ACT TWO

Scene One

Palestrina. A chamber in Colonna's house. At the beginning, shots are heard from time to time.
Colonna, Camilla.

CAMILLA

Father, for Jesus' sake, what is afoot?
With anxious faces your friends are leaving,
Deserting you; the besiegers' cannon
Are thundering closer and fiercer than ever—
Are we then lost, my father, oh tell me!

COLONNA

Camilla, be calm and listen.
The ambitious Orsini wanted
No more to obey me, the chosen leader,
But stand beside me, give orders like me!
I stuck to my rights;
The rift between us was irremediably wide.
His son stepped forward. Fathers, said he,
Be not divided in danger's hour,
When unity is our foremost need.
I want to reunite you!
Give me, Colonna, your daughter in marriage.
Long have I loved her, the fair Camilla.
If, through your children, you are united
By holy bonds,
Strife no longer shall split you asunder
Over the power in the land.
Then his father spoke up as follows:
So be it! But if you refuse, Colonna,
Tomorrow I shall withdraw my troops
And come to terms with the Tribune.
Then try and hold the fortress alone!
Those were his words. And so, my daughter,
Even before the sun goes down
You'll go—as I told him—to young Orsini
And join him in wedlock. So make you ready.

CAMILLA
Oh God, what shall I do?

COLONNA
You seem unwilling to give in.
I'd long intended that you should win
A better thing on your brow to set
Than Count Orsini's coronet.
Whoever might your hand in marriage merit
At least a princedom should inherit—
Or so I thought. Things worked out differently.
What choice have we?

CAMILLA
So it is settled, then:
I'll be the sacrifice.
For peace between you men,
My own peace I must lose.
Am I so much alone
That he I most despise
Must be my husband—one
I would not freely choose?
Father, I beg you, spare me your fury!
Just for you, I
Would gladly die,
But Count Orsini I never shall marry!

COLONNA
What evil spirit has made you so wild?
You even choose
My wish to refuse?
I, I command you, iniquitous child!

CAMILLA
Command of me whatever you will,
But the vow that I swore
To the man I adore,
I honour it still!

COLONNA
To Montreal I'm to give you away?
I thought the hope of his winning your hand

Had long, long since been gone from your mind.
A fine son-in-law for me, I must say!
Since when have plunderers,
Robbers and murderers
Won the Colonnas' womenfolk, pray?

CAMILLA

Ere I should prove
False to my vow,
Let the Earth now
Swallow me up, or the blackness of night.
Walter, our love
Nothing can blight,
True ones in woe
Live to the day when their darkness turns bright!

COLONNA

Can you not see the threat that surrounds us?
Iron balls
Pound down the walls,
The enemy stranglehold tightens around us.
Think of what's going to happen to you
At the dread hour
When turret and tower
Fall, and foeman comes swarming through.
Who will protect you and save you from force
When the wild soldiers clutch you with their claws?

CAMILLA

My Walter will shield me, he surely will come!
If he comes not, a dagger will save me
From shame!

COLONNA

Did not this Montreal of yours
First put us in this sorry plight,
Sending the Tribune his own force
To harass us by day and night?
Yet this same Montreal
You'd choose before them all?

CAMILLA

I shall stay true to him forever!

COLONNA
Will you not think and have some sense?

CAMILLA
What I've said I won't gainsay.

COLONNA
Intractable one, then get you hence,
I'll tame this obduracy!

CAMILLA
What I've sworn I should forswear?

COLONNA
Yes. Before this day is through—

CAMILLA
Empty then my promise were!

COLONNA
I will see you change your view.

CAMILLA
These my passions—

COLONNA
           I'll suppress!

CAMILLA
This my love—

COLONNA
           cannot survive.

CAMILLA
Such devotion to repress—

COLONNA
                      that will be child's play to me!

CAMILLA
I shall not betray him, never!

COLONNA, CAMILLA

$\begin{cases} \text{Ha,} \\ \text{Yes,} \end{cases}$ it may cost $\begin{cases} \text{you your} \\ \text{me my} \end{cases}$ life.

CAMILLA

I'll be true to him forever.
His I am and e'er shall be!

CAMILLA, COLONNA

All upon it I would stake,
Though it may cost $\begin{cases} \text{you your} \\ \text{me my} \end{cases}$ life.

$\begin{cases} \text{This your vow you must forsake} \\ \text{This my vow I'll not forsake} \end{cases}$

And obey $\begin{cases} \text{me} \\ \text{him} \end{cases}$ constantly!

A SERVANT (*entering*)

My Lord, a stranger waits outside.
He has important news to bring you,
But only to you he'll give his name.

COLONNA

Let him come in!

(*Exit servant. Enter Montreal in cloak and hat. He doffs his hat and flings back his cloak.*)

CAMILLA

Oh Heavens! Walter!

COLONNA

Montreal! You dare to enter my house,
You, whose soldiers besiege us now,
You, that have taken the enemy's side,
You, that have stolen my daughter's heart
From me? What is your purpose here?

MONTREAL

Softly, dear sir, and listen to me!
Do you remember, you turned me away
When I was seeking Camilla's hand?

Now I revenge myself, as befits a knight.
My soldiers have you completely surrounded,
Their guns rock Palestrina's towers.
A sign from me, and the whole wild horde streams in,
And then you are lost. For who will save you?
Well, I will save you, if you so wish!
Palestrina need not fall, and I shall lead you
In pomp and ceremony back to Rome!

COLONNA

So you would treacherously leave the Tribune?
That is hardly a knightly deed —
I'll have no part in it at all.

MONTREAL

What treachery's here? My brothers, not I,
Sent the troops to join the Tribune.
I never sanctioned the deed at all.
Who's to prevent me withdrawing my soldiers?
That I'll do. This only I ask:
Give me what I could anyway win for myself!

COLONNA

What do you want of me?

MONTREAL

In Romagna, in the March of Ancona
Are thousands obedient to my word.
I have no land, and yet I am
The most powerful man in Italy.
I come to you, and I demand:
Agree to let me assume the title
Of Roman *Podestà* and take your daughter
As wife beside me on the Throne!

(*Colonna paces up and down in thought.*)

CAMILLA

Did I not say he'd rescue us,
Hearing that I was in distress?
Did I not know he'd think of me
In times of danger or of stress?

MONTREAL

How could I ever desert my beloved
Or my beloved's father in need?

COLONNA

So be it! I'll sacrifice Orsini.
He always envied me, being vain.
He and his house may fall, but I shall rise!
My son, here is my daughter! She's yours!
Be *Podestà* of Rome with her beside you!

Camilla, past returning
Are hate and enmity.
I have appeased your yearning,
Look up, look up at me!

CAMILLA

Flowers of love's joy so tender
From harsh adversity
Have blossomed in their splendour—
O wondrous Destiny!

MONTREAL

And now what do we care
That once we burned so long,
Wrestling with despair,
And grief, and pain, and wrong!

CAMILLA

O day of joy for lovers!

MONTREAL

O gift of love so true!

CAMILLA

O bliss when suffering's over!

COLONNA

Now take you each the other,
May life be good to you!

ALL THREE

We'll go unhesitating
To meet our destiny,
The Future contemplating
Serene, and gay, and free,
Through harsh pain sanctified,
After long strife together—
Love's flames thus purified
Shall burn and burn forever!

Scene Two

A room in Rienzi's home.

RIENZI (*paper in hand*)

Curse the traitors! For turning the people
Away from me, for reviling me.
As if I'd fatten myself on the poor!
Curse them! If only the people stay loyal,
The future shall see me gloriously vindicated.
My people all, for whom I've gladly
Been cursed, reviled, imprisoned, banned,
For whom I've braved the Tyrants, loudly
Crying amongst them: Hold your hand!
My people, you will not go under
Shamed and abused, like cowards base;
You shall arise in all your grandeur,
A proud and a victorious race!

You know not the many trials,
Cares and anguish I went through;
You know not the many perils
That I faced because of you!
Long years, hesitating never,
Through the thorns I struggled on,
Yet you may not thank me ever
For the good that I have done!

But no! I wanted Rome to free
That fell, a victim to dissension.
Restore her ancient dignity—
Is that no fine and great intention?

O Ancient Rome, do but once show
Yourself to me in your past might,
And I have lived enough, can go
Happy into the grave's dark night!

NINA (*entering*)

Oh Cola, tell me, is it true
That foes are plotting against you?
Is danger hanging over
The head so dear to me?

RIENZI

Calm yourself, my dearest wife.
A few power-seeking, envious ones,
And Walter von Montreal, that traitor,
Are stirring up the people against me,
Hoping to bring about my downfall.
Helped by God and a loyal people,
I shall outwit the treacherous ones.
Before they even sense the danger,
Their heads will roll for their own crimes.
How could these schemes of theirs unnerve me?
Are they as strong as I am here,
With my true-loving wife to serve me,
And with my senses calm and clear?

NINA

Cola, why can't I put to flight
The fears with which I am consumed?
In dreams I've seen your face all white
Since you the purple robe assumed.

RIENZI

My dearest wife, come, fear no more!
We are not in the slightest danger;
Untroubled can the eagle soar
Clear of the snakes that hiss with anger.

NINA

I cannot think what I would do,
If I should lose you, love, one day.

Whoever left me without you,
Would steal my very life away.

COLA

Oh, put aside all fear and care,
For what inspires me is sublime.
I can't go under — do not dare —
Until I have achieved my aim,

Until Rome's might triumphantly
Is born again, and Freedom shakes
The dust off, and the world can see
In trembling how the lion wakes.

If, in the heat of battle, I stood
Alone, in peril of my life,
Deserted and abandoned, would
You not stay by me, dearest wife?

NINA

Dearest, as some God may decree,
So let it be, then, for us two.
I cannot, and I will not, flee,
In need and death I'll stand by you!

BOTH

Firmly together, on our own,
We shall face treachery and lies.
Though in this world we stood alone,
Our true love ever would suffice!

Scene Three

A hall in the Colonnas' palace, festively arrayed for a banquet.

Montreal, Battista, Chorus of guests.

MONTREAL

Your health, good sirs! Let gaiety
And the wine goblet reign this night!
Think not how late the hour may be,
While the wine laughs in beaker bright.

Let song resound
These halls around
Till the dawn breaks with radiant light!

CHORUS

Drink all the brimming cup may hold,
Quaff merrily the flowing wine;
The goblet filled with liquid gold
Revives man's heart at any time.
Let song resound
These halls around
Until the light of dawn doth shine!

BATTISTA

Ho, there! A song, who'll sing a song?

MONTREAL

Hey, boy, hand me that lute of yours.
Let me sing you a song of Provence
After the fashion of my native land—
The song of a high-born troubadour.

(*Here follows a love-song, to be inserted later.*)

BATTISTA

Long life to all the ladies!

CHORUS

Long life to the ladies! In sparkling wine
We think about them all the time!
Long life to all the ladies!

MONTREAL

Ho, butler, fill the glasses!
Lachrymae Christi, Monte Falerno,
Bring us the best Falernian wine!
Now let us drink and let us sing!

CHORUS

Drink all the brimming cup, etc.

(*The Capitol bell sounds.*)

BATTISTA

What is happening? Hear you the Capitol bell?

MONTREAL

What could it be? Nothing to trouble us!
Let us be merry! It's nothing to alarm us!

BATTISTA

I drink this, noble sir, to you,
And to your gallant following too!
That the Tribune by you may be
Relieved of his authority!
Loudly I cry to one and all:
Long live Walter von Montreal!

CHORUS

Loud ring our voices one and all:
Long live our gracious host!
Long live Walter von Montreal!

CHOIR OF MONKS (*off*)

Requiem aeternam dona eis,
Domine! Et lux perpetua
luceat eis!

MONTREAL

What has come over you, friends?
Let the priests whine of graves and of death,
Life is red-blooded while we draw breath!

(CHOIR OF MONKS *in the background*: Dies irae, dies illa.)

I thank you all, my friends!
Let us drown out those wailing monks
With joyous cries!
Long live Rome, the eternal city!

CHORUS

Long live Rome, the eternal city!
Drink all the brimming cup, etc.

(CHOIR, *off*: Ne me perdas illa die! quia pius es!)

MONTREAL

And here's a toast to the Tribune's downfall,
The traitor who, on the people's sweat,
Carouses there in the Capitol!
Revenge will be on him before he knows it.
Down with him!

CHORUS

Down with the Tribune, be our word—
Let him reap his treason's reward!

(*Three bangs on the door. Confusion.*)

MONTREAL

Enter, you uninvited guests!

(*Enter the Tribune in purple and ermine, followed by men-at-arms.*)

Pause.

RIENZI

Are you so gay, then, Montreal,
When the Capitol bell outside
And the chanting priests tell you the tidings
That your brothers are being led to execution?
Let you and the rest all know this!

CHOIR

Judex ergo nunc tedebit
etc.

[RIENZI]

At last your hour has struck,
And your traitor's reward is settled!

(*Montreal and Battista are led off.*)

Curtain

ACT THREE

Scene One

A room in Rienzi's home.

NINA (*hastening in, breathless*)

Help, Holy Mary!
Help, Father in Heaven!
Oh, what a rabble
Comes down the streets tearing,
Roaring, rampaging,
Many-voiced, raging;
They're bursting through breaches
And soon they will reach us.
Our palace they're nearing!
In wild agitation
They threaten destruction
And grim devastation;
In savage eruption
The rabble draws nigh!

Our deliverance please send,
Ye most blessed ones on high;
Let the angels' wings extend
Over us protectingly.
Hear, oh hear my anguished plea,
Come to us, shield us from danger.
Please, oh please let us not be
Victims of the mob's blind anger!

Nearer and nearer
The rabble is teeming,
Higher and higher
The flood is streaming
Swords are glittering,
Spear-points flickering,
Flashing bright!

Ever nearer and more mighty,
Death enfolds us with his arm.
Help, O Mary! Help, Almighty!
Do not let us come to harm!

RIENZI (*entering*)

It's happened—something I never feared!
The maddened people have risen against me,
Howling vengeance for Montreal's death
And for Battista's too.

NINA

O dearest Cola!
Danger is pressing nearer and nearer,
O save us both!

RIENZI

Keep calm, beloved wife!
Danger is not so very near.
Still in the flush of youth am I,
And with a face unyielding, proud,
I shall go out there to defy
The fury of the crowd!

My eye is swift as lightning blast,
My brow unmarred by life's abuse,
Like swords, my words are keen and fast—
So let all Hell break loose!

Let Hell break loose—still I shall brave it.
I raised myself up to the throne,
Now I must stand my ground and save it.
I'll calm their anger down!

NINA

Oh, let us yield, I humbly pray,
Let us seek refuge from their fury.
Cola, just once, hear what I say,
O Cola, let us hurry!

RIENZI

In cowardice? Not while I draw breath!

NINA

Cola, while still there's time—decide!

RIENZI

I'll stand and face it out with death,
Though he press in from every side!

NINA

Oh, come! The mob does not deserve
So great a sacrifice—oh, no!

RIENZI

If ruin strikes, my death shall serve
Before the whole wide world to show
I did not shrink to dedicate
My life that Rome once more be great.

NINA

So, husband, you'll not run away?
Then from your side I shall not go,
As in good times, likewise in woe
And wretched fortune, I shall stay.

RIENZI

Come to my breast, O marvellous wife!
The reward of striving constantly
Blooms in your love, God's joy, for me,
Though reached I not my goal in life!

NINA

So big, so strong you are, my mate!
Held in your warm embrace, to fall
With you, most wonderful of all—
Oh what a high and blissful fate!

COLA, NINA

And so we go forth joyously,
Embracing one another tight,
Bathed in the glow of true love's light,
To meet whate'er our fate may be!
Though death outside await us twain,
Through fire and sword, both unaffrighted
We go, together and united,
To face what Fortune may ordain!

Scene Two

Before the Capitol.

CAMILLA (*hair unbound, sword in hand*)

So it has come, then,
For what I so languish,
The hour of revenge
For my sorrow and anguish.
The hour of revenge!
His blood shall be shed
In atonement for yours,
My murdered, my dear one,
Though I strike him dead
With this, my own hand.
True love has been murdered,
Burn hatred, burn more,
And stain, blood of tyrants,
My thirsting sword-blade
With purple-red gore.
Not woman, but Fury
Henceforth be my name;
With steel I shall sever
The veins of that same
Vile traitor who sent
My love to his grave!
Away with compassion
And womanly weakness!
Vengeance, ay, vengeance
For that shameful crime
Is all that I crave!
The crowds are all swarming
And gathering together,
More frenzied than ever
I'm going to make them.
Fall, then, Rienzi,
From the throne to your doom—
Your victim, my lover,
Awaits you in the tomb!

(*To the people, who have gathered round her.*)

Vengeance I cry! Vengeance I cry!
For the tyrant's execution,

For the grimmest retribution,
Storm into the Capitol!
From his rooms in all their glory
Drag him hither bodily,
To his end so grim and gory;
Dying, he'll atone for all!

CHORUS

Vengeance! Vengeance!—To the Capitol.

CAMILLA

On his guilty head let roll
Curses, death, calamity.
Liberty from us he stole,
Now it is his reckoning time.
At our feet in terror, he
Shall like any traitor die.
Red his blood shall flow and free
For his most perfidious crime.

CHORUS

At our feet in terror, etc.

Enter Rienzi, Nina following him.

RIENZI

Citizens of Rome! Why do you gather here
In milling crowds, with spear and sword
Before the Capitol?
Do you not trust me now, whom you elected
And on whose shoulders you it was that laid
This purple? What have I done to harm you?
Let me finish my task.
Let me restore our ancient glory
And you'll be lords of the Earth
And free, with laws of your own making.
Listen not to the voice of slander,
Judge me by deeds alone!

CAMILLA

Do not listen to him speaking,
Let yourselves be not misled.

Be intent alone on wreaking
Vengeance for lost liberty!

CHORUS

By your flattery, by your speaking,
We'll no longer be misled.
Now we only think of wreaking
Vengeance for lost liberty!

They press towards him.

NINA

God!

RIENZI

Hence, insolent ones, away!

NINA

See you not the tears I shed?

CAMILLA

Ha, Triumph! Now the vengeance-seeking
Flames I've kindled, as I see.

CHORUS

Now we only think of wreaking
Vengeance for lost liberty!

NINA

Would you spill the blood of him
Whom you owe your fortune to?
If it's blood you want, take mine:
I'll atone for every sin.

CAMILLA

Only vengeance for his crime,
Push compassion far from you!

NINA

Hear my weeping and lamenting,
He did good—give that a thought!

CAMILLA

Think, you Romans, unrelenting,
Of the suffering he brought!

CHORUS

Yes, we're mindful, unrelenting,
Of the suffering he brought.

NINA

Please have mercy!

CAMILLA

Think of vengeance!

NINA

Spare this noble man, I say.

CAMILLA

On the tyrant wreak your vengeance
For your freedom snatched away.

CHORUS

Vengeance on the tyrant, vengeance,
For our freedom snatched away!

NINA

Do not let yourselves be blinded
By your fury's raging fire!

CAMILLA

Ha! Now shall his life be ended
By the people's burning ire!

NINA

Show us mercy!

CAMILLA

Think of vengeance.

NINA

Please have mercy.

CAMILLA

Hear her not.

CHORUS

Ha, you traitor, this our vengeance
And our wrath escape you not!

Written at the end of 1840 and the beginning of 1841

First published in the book: Michael Knieriem, *Friedrich Engels: Cola di Rienzi. Ein unbekannter dramatischer Entwurf*, Trier, 1974

Printed according to the manuscript

Published in English for the first time

APPENDICES

MARRIAGE CONTRACT
between
Herr Carl Marx, Doctor of Philosophy,
resident in Cologne,
and Fräulein Johanna Bertha Julie Jenny von Westphalen,
without occupation, resident in Kreuznach,
June 12, 1843

No. 715

We, Frederick William,
by the Grace of God
King of Prussia,

Grand Duke of Lower Rhine, etc., etc.,

herewith give notice and let it be known that:

Before the Undersigned Wilhelm Christian Heinrich *Burger*, royal Prussian notary in the residence of the town of *Kreuznach*, in the provincial-court district of *Coblenz*, and in the presence of the two witnesses named below, there appeared Herr *Karl Marx*, Doctor of Philosophy, resident in *Cologne*, on the one hand, and Fräulein *Johanna Bertha Julie Jenny von Westphalen*, without occupation, resident in *Kreuznach*, on the other hand.

The declarants stated that they intended to marry and in view of their future marriage, the celebration of which is to take place as soon as possible, they have mutually agreed and laid down the clauses and conditions and the consequences in civil law as follows:

Firstly. Legal common ownership of property shall be established between the future marriage partners insofar as this is not specially amended by the following articles.

Secondly. This common ownership shall also apply to all future fixed assets of the spouses by the future spouses hereby declaring all fixed assets which they will inherit in the future, or which will later fall to the lot of one or other of them, to be movable property, and putting these future fixed assets, which they give wholly into common ownership, on a par with movable property, whereby in accordance with Article fifteen hundred and five of the Civil Code their transformation into movable assets (:*ameublissement*:) takes place.

Thirdly. Each spouse shall for his or her own part pay the debts he or she has made or contracted, inherited or otherwise incurred before marriage; in consequence whereof these debts shall be excluded from the common ownership of property.

Thus everything has been agreed and settled between the future spouses. Concerning which the present marriage contract was adopted, which has been clearly read out to the interested parties.

Done at *Kreuznach* in the dwelling of the widow Frau *von Westphalen, June* twelfth of the year one thousand eight hundred and forty-three, in the presence of the attendant witnesses, personally known to the notary, Johann Anton *Rickes*, private gentleman, and Peter *Beltz*, tailor, both resident in *Kreuznach*. And in witness thereof the present document has been signed first by the above-mentioned declarants, the name, position and residence of whom is known to the notary, and after them by the above-mentioned witnesses and the notary.

The original, which has remained in the possession of the notary, and on which a stamp of two talers has been affixed, has been signed by:

"*Dr. Karl Marx, Jenny von Westphalen, J. A. Rickes, Peter Beltz*, and *Burger*, notary."

At the same time We order and instruct all executors of courts of justice on request to put into operation the present act; Our Procurators-General and Our Procurators at provincial courts of justice to administer the same; all officers and commandants of the armed forces or their representatives to lend a powerful helping hand if legally requested to do so.

In confirmation thereof the present main copy has been signed by the notary and furnished with his seal of office.

Vouching for the correctness of this main copy

Burger, notary[a]

First published in: Marx/Engels, *Gesamtausgabe,* Abt. 1, Bd. 1, Hb. 2, 1929

Printed according to a copy of the document
Published in English for the first time

---

[a] The notary's round seal is attached to the document and also a receipt for 6 talers and 15 groschen.— *Ed.*

EXTRACT FROM THE REGISTER OF MARRIAGES
OF THE REGISTRY OFFICE OF BAD KREUZNACH
FOR THE YEAR 1843

*Municipality: Kreuznach. District: Kreuznach.
Administrative district: Coblenz*

No. 51

In the year one thousand eight hundred and forty-three, on the nineteenth of the month of June, at 10 a.m., there appeared before me, Franz Buss, Chief Burgomaster of Kreuznach, Registrar for Births, Deaths and Marriages, Karl *Marx*, aged twenty-five, born in Trier, administrative district of Trier, Doctor of Philosophy, resident in Cologne, administrative district of Cologne, major son of Heinrich Marx, deceased, in his lifetime King's Counsel, resident in Trier, administrative district of Trier, and of Henriette Pressburg, of no profession, resident in Trier, administrative district of Trier.

And Johanna Bertha Julie Jenny von Westphalen, aged twenty-nine, born at Salzwedel, administrative district of Magdeburg, of no particular occupation, resident in Kreuznach, administrative district of Coblenz, major daughter of Johann Ludwig von Westphalen, deceased, in his lifetime Privy Councillor, resident in Trier, administrative district of Trier, and of Carolina Heubel, of no profession, resident in Kreuznach, administrative district of Coblenz.

The bridegroom's mother consents to the intended marriage by the deed of consent quoted below and the bride's mother by her personal presence. In the deed of consent of the bridegroom's mother the Christian name of the bride's father is given as Ferdinand, but it is Johann Ludwig, as follows from the sworn declaration made before us by the bride and the four witnesses present, after they had previously declared that they knew him closely and well.

The same requested me to perform legally the marriage agreed upon between them. As the prescribed public announcements of this marriage were actually read twice before the main door of the Kreuznach Town Hall, namely, the first on Sunday, the twenty-first of May, and the second on the following Sunday, the twenty-eighth of May, one thousand eight hundred and forty-three, and as the documents of the announcement were duly posted up publicly and no objection to the marriage was lodged, I, in order to comply with the said request, read out the following documents:

a) the birth certificate of the bridegroom, and

b) the death certificate of his father, both certificates drawn up by Chief Burgomaster Görtz and Assistant Thanisch in Trier under the date of the thirtieth and twenty-eighth of January this year;

c) the deed of consent of his mother, recorded by Notary Funck in Trier under the date of the twenty-eighth of January this year;

d) the birth certificate of the bride, furnished by the Royal Consistorial Councillor and Pastor of the Church of Saint Mary at Salzwedel under the date of the eleventh of February this year;

e) the death certificate of her father, furnished by Assistant Thanisch in Trier under the date of the twenty-third of February this year;

f) the attestation of the announcement in Cologne, furnished by the Registrar for Births, Deaths and Marriages Schenk in that city under the date of the fourteenth of June this year;

g) the attestation of the announcement in Bonn, furnished by the Registrar for Births, Deaths and Marriages Gerhard in that city under the date of the sixteenth of the current month and year, and read out aloud Chapter Six of the part dealing with marriage in the Civil Code of Law and thereupon asked the above-named bridegroom and bride whether they wished to be joined in wedlock.

As each of them separately answered this question affirmatively, I declared in the name of the law that Karl Marx and Johanna Bertha Julie Jenny von Westphalen were legally married.

Of this I drew up the present document in the presence of Dr. Karl Engelmann, aged thirty-five, a physician, resident in Kreuznach, a friend of the newly married couple; of Heinrich Balthasar Christian Clevens, aged thirty, a probationer notary, resident in Kreuznach, a friend of the newly married couple; of Elias Mayer, aged sixty-four, man of private means, resident in Kreuznach, a friend of the newly married couple; and of Valentin Keller, aged fifty-six, innkeeper, resident in Kreuznach, a friend of the newly married couple. Then the persons present signed the document with me after it had been read out to them.

Dr. Karl Marx.——— Jenny von Westphalen.———
Caroline von Westphalen. Dr. Carl Engelmann. H. Clevens.
Valentin Keller.——— E. Mayer. ——— Buss.———

Published for the first time

Printed according to a copy of the document

JENNY MARX TO KARL MARX

IN PARIS [243]

[Trier, about June 21, 1844]

You see, dear heart, that I don't deal with you according to the law and demand an eye for an eye, a tooth for a tooth, and a letter for a letter; I am generous and magnanimous, but I hope that my twofold appearance before you will soon yield me golden fruit, a few lines in return, for which my heart is yearning, a few words to tell me that you are well and are longing for me a little. I should so like to know that you miss me and to hear you say you want me. But now quickly, before the holding of the daily court begins again, a bulletin about our little one,[a] for after all she is now the chief person in our alliance and, being at once yours and mine, is the most intimate bond of our love. The poor little doll was quite miserable and ill after the journey, and turned out to be suffering not only from constipation but downright overfeeding. We had to call in the fat pig,[b] and his decision was that it was essential to have a wet-nurse since with artificial feeding she would not easily recover. You can imagine my anxiety. But that is all over now, the dear little Clever Eyes is being fed magnificently by a healthy young wet-nurse, a girl from Barbeln,[c] the daughter of the boatman with whom dear Papa[d] so often sailed. In better times, Mother[e] once provided a complete outfit of clothes for this girl, when she was still a child, and what a coincidence — this poor child, to whom Papa used to give a kreutzer every day, is now giving life and health to our baby. It was not easy to save her life, but she is now almost out of any danger. In spite of all her

---

[a] Their daughter Jenny.— *Ed.*
[b] Schleicher.— *Ed.*
[c] Gretchen.— *Ed.*
[d] Ludwig von Westphalen.— *Ed.*
[e] Caroline von Westphalen.— *Ed.*

sufferings, she looks remarkably pretty and is as flower-white, delicate and transparent as a little princess. In Paris we would never have got her through the illness, so this trip has already been well worth while. Besides, I am now again with my good, poor mother, who only with the greatest struggle can put up with our being separated.

She has had a very bad time at the Wettendorfs'.[244] They are rather coarse people. Ah, if I had only known how things were with poor Mother on many occasions during the winter! But I often wept and was miserable when thinking of her, and you were always so considerate and patient. Another good thing about this wet-nurse is that she is also very useful as a maid, is willing to accompany [us] and, as it happens, served three years in Metz and therefore also speaks French. Hence my return journey is fully assured. What a stroke of luck it is, is it not? Only at present poor Mother has to bear too many expenses and is after all very poor. Edgar[a] robs her of all she has and then writes one nonsensical letter after another, rejoices over the approaching revolutions and the overthrow of all existing conditions, instead of beginning by revolutionising his own conditions, which then always evokes unpleasant discussions and indirect attacks on the mad revolutionary youth. In general, nowhere does a longing for a transformation of the existing state of things arise more strongly than when one sees the surface looking so drearily flat and even, and yet knows what a commotion and ferment is taking place in the depths of mankind.

But let us leave the revolution and come back to our wet-nurse. I shall pay the monthly sum of four talers from the remainder of the journey money, from which I will pay also for the medicine and doctor. True, Mother does not want me to do so, but for food alone she has to bear more than she can. In spite of poverty, she keeps everything about her in decent condition. People in Trier are really behaving excellently towards her and that placates me a little. Moreover, I do not need to visit anyone, for they all come to me and I hold court from morning to night. I cannot give you the names of all of them. Today I also disposed of the patriot Lehmann, who is very well disposed by the way, and is only afraid that your thorough scientific studies might suffer over there. Incidentally, I behave towards everyone in a lordly fashion and my external appearance fully justifies this. For once I am more elegant than any of them and never in my life have I looked better and more blooming than I do now. Everyone is unanimous

---

[a] Edgar von Westphalen, Jenny's brother.—*Ed.*

Jenny von Westphalen in the early 1840s

Pages from the Register of Marriages showing the official entry of the marriage between Karl Marx and Jenny von Westphalen

und das sechste Kapitel des vom Ehestande handelnden Teils des bürgerlichen Gesetzbuches dem vorgelesen, sodann den vorgenannten Bräutigam und die vorgenannte Braut gefragt: ob sie einander ehelichen wollen? Da nun jeder von beiden insbesondere diese Frage bejahend beantwortet hat; so erkläre ich im Namen des Gesetzes, daß

Carl Marx und Johanna Bertha Julie Jenny von Westphalen

mit einander gesetzlich verheirathet sind.

Hierüber habe ich gegenwärtige Urkunde errichtet in Gegenwart des Herrn Carl Engelmann, fünfund dreißig Jahre alt, Standesgeprüften Arzt, wohnhaft zu Creuznach welcher ein Freund der neuen Ehegatten des Heinrich Balthasar Christian Clasens dreißig Jahre alt, Standes Kaplan reichs Landrath wohnhaft zu Creuznach welcher ein Freund der neuen Ehegatten, des Eliäs Jäger, vier und fünfzig Jahre alt, Standes Kaufmann wohnhaft zu Creuznach welcher ein Freund der neuen Ehegatten, und des Valentin Heller, fünf und fünfzig Jahre alt, Standes Gastwirth wohnhaft zu Creuznach welcher ein Freund der neuen Ehegatten zu sein, erklären; und haben die erschienenen Personen die Urkunde, nachdem dieselbe ihnen vorgelesen worden, mit mir unterschrieben.

ss. Karl Marx Jenny v Westphalen

Ludwig v Westphalen

D. Engelmann D. Clasens Valentin Heller

Emmig

about that. And people constantly repeat Herwegh's compliment asking me "when my confirmation has taken place". I think to myself, too, what would be the good of behaving humbly; it does not help anyone out of a difficulty, and people are so happy if they can express their regret. Despite the fact that my whole being expresses satisfaction and *affluence*, everyone still hopes that you will decide after all to obtain a permanent post. O, you asses, as if all of you were standing on firm ground. I know that we are not exactly standing on rock, but where is there any firm foundation now? Can one not see everywhere signs of earthquake and the undermining of the foundations on which society has erected its temples and shops? I think that time, the old mole, will soon stop burrowing underground—indeed in Breslau there have been thunderstorms again.[245] If we can only hold out for a time, until our little one has grown big. As to that, you'll put my mind at ease, won't you, my dear sweet angel, my one and only heart's beloved? How my heart went out to you on June 19![a] How strongly and intimately it beat out of love for you.

But to return to the account of events. It was not until our wedding-day that our dear little baby was well again and sucked healthily and lustily. Then I set out on my difficult journey—you know where to. I wore my nice Paris frock and my face glowed with anxiety and excitement. When I rang, my heart was beating almost audibly. Everything went through my mind. The door opened and Jettchen[b] appeared. She embraced and kissed me and led me into the drawing-room where your mother[c] and Sophie[d] were sitting. Both immediately embraced me, your mother called me "thou", and Sophie sat me on the sofa beside her. She has been terribly ravaged by illness, looks like C×C, and is hardly likely to get well again. And yet Jettchen is in an almost worse state. Only your mother looks well and flourishing, and is cheerfulness itself, almost gay and frolicsome. Alas, this gaiety seems somehow sinister. All the girls were equally affectionate, especially little Caroline.[e] Next morning your mother came already at 9 o'clock to see the baby. In the afternoon Sophie came, and this morning little Caroline also paid a visit to our little angel. Can you imagine such a change?[246] I am very glad about it and Mother as well, but how has it come about so suddenly? What a difference

---

[a] The anniversary of their marriage.— *Ed.*
[b] Marx's sister Henriette.— *Ed.*
[c] Henriette Marx.— *Ed.*
[d] Marx's sister.— *Ed.*
[e] Marx's sister.— *Ed.*

success makes, or in our case rather the *appearance* of success, which by the subtlest tactics I know how to maintain.

That's strange news, isn't it? Just think, how the time runs and even the fattest pigs as well; Schleicher, too, is no longer a politician, and a Socialist, that is to say, like Schmiriaks from the organism of labour, etc. It is enough to make one sick, as the Frankenthaler says. He partly considers that your clique is mad, but he thinks it is high time you attacked Bauer.[a] Ah, Karl, what you are going to do, do it soon.[247] And also do give me soon some sign of your life. I am being treated with great tenderness by the most gentle loving mother, my little one is being properly looked after and cared for, the whole of Trier gapes, stares, admires, and pays court, and yet my heart and soul are turned towards you. Ah, if only I could see you now and again, and ask you: what is that for? Or sing for you: "Do you know also when it will be the day after tomorrow?" Dear heart of mine, how I should like to kiss you, for such cold collations are no good, isn't that true, my dearest one? However, you should read the *Trier'sche Zeitung*, it is quite good now. How do things look with you? It is now already eight days I have been away from you. Even here, with better-quality milk, it would not have been possible to get our baby over her illness without a wet-nurse. Her whole stomach was upset. Today Schleicher has assured me that she is now saved. O, if only poor Mother did not have so many worries, and particularly because of Edgar, who makes use of all the great signs of the times, and all the sufferings of society, in order to cover up and whitewash his own worthlessness. Now the vacation is coming again and then once again nothing will come of the examination. All his essays are ready. It is unpardonable. Mother must deny herself everything, while he has a good time in Cologne going to all the operas, as he himself writes. He speaks with the utmost tenderness of his little sister, his little Jenny, but I find it impossible to be tender towards the scatterbrain.

Dearest heart, I am often greatly worried about our future, both that near at hand and later on, and I think I am going to be punished for my exuberance and cockiness here. If you can, do set my mind at rest about this. There is too much talk on all sides about a *steady* income. I reply then merely by means of my rosy cheeks, my clear skin, my velvet cloak, feather hat and smart coiffure. That has the best and deepest effect, and if as a result I become depressed, nobody sees it. Our baby has such a beautiful

---

[a] Bruno Bauer.— *Ed.*

white colour that everyone wonders at it, and she is so fine and delicate. Schleicher is very solicitous and very nice to the child. Today he did not want to go away at all, then there came God's Wrath, and then Reverchon, then Lehmann, and then Poppey, and so it goes on all the time. Yesterday the Tree-frog,[a] too, was here with his parchment better half. I did not see them. The members of your family have just paid a call in passing, including Sophie in full fig. But how ill she looks!!! — Give greetings from me to Siebenkäs and the Heines, if you see them. I shall have news of you soon, isn't that so? And are you bravely singing the postillion of Longjumeau?

Only don't write with too much rancour and irritation. You know how much more effect your other articles have had. Write either in a matter-of-fact and subtle way or humorously and lightly. Please, dear heart of mine, let your pen run over the paper, even if it should on occasion stumble and fall, and the sentence with it. Your thoughts all the same stand erect like the grenadiers of the old guard, so honourably firm and courageous, and they could say like the old guard: *elle meurt mais elle ne se rend pas.*[b] What does it matter if occasionally the uniform hangs a bit loosely and is not so tightly buttoned up? What is so very nice about the French soldiers is their free and easy appearance. When you think of our stilted Prussians, doesn't it make you shudder? — Just slacken the strappings and remove the cravat and helmet — let the participles take their course and set down the words just as they come of themselves. Such an army does not have to march in such strict order. And your troops are taking the field, are they not? Good luck to the general, my dusky master! Good-bye, dearest heart, my beloved, my entire life. For the present I am in my little Germany, with everything around me, including my little one and my mother, and yet my heart is sad because you are absent; it yearns for you, and it hopes for you and your black messengers.

Good-bye,

Your *Schipp* and *Schribb*

First published in Marx/Engels, *Werke*, Ergänzungsband, Teil 1, Berlin, 1968

Printed according to the original

Published in English for the first time

---

[a] An illegible word follows in the original.— *Ed.*

[b] It dies, but does not surrender.— *Ed.*

JENNY MARX TO KARL MARX

IN PARIS[248]

[Trier, between August 4 and 10, 1844]

My dearest,

I received your letter at the very moment when all the bells were ringing, the guns firing, and the pious crowd flocking into the temples to convey their hallelujahs to the heavenly Lord for having so miraculously saved their earthly Lord.[a] You can imagine with what peculiar feeling I read Heine's poems during the celebration and also chimed in with my hosannas. Did not your Prussian heart also quiver with horror at the news of that crime, that shocking, unthinkable crime? Alas, for the *lost virginity*, the lost honour! Such are the Prussian catchwords. When I heard the little green grasshopper, cavalry captain X., declaiming about the lost virginity, I could only believe that he meant the holy immaculate virginity of Mother Mary, for that after all is the only one officially confirmed. But as for the virginity of the Prussian state! No, I lost any belief in that long ago. As regards the terrible event, one consolation remains for the pure Prussian people, viz., that the motive for the deed was not any political fanaticism, but a purely personal desire for revenge. They console themselves with that—lucky for them—but it is precisely a new proof that a political revolution is impossible in Germany, whereas all the seeds of a social revolution are present. While there has never been a political fanatic there who dared to go to the extreme, the first one to risk an attempt at assassination[b] was driven to it by want, dire want. For three days the man had been begging in vain in Berlin in constant danger of death from starvation—hence it was a social attempt at assassination! If something does break out, it will start from this direction—that is the most sensitive spot, and in this respect a German heart also is vulnerable!

First published in *Vorwärts!* No. 64, August 10, 1844

Printed according to the newspaper

Published in English for the first time

---

[a] Frederick William IV.— *Ed.*

[b] H. L. Tshech — *Ed.*

JENNY MARX TO KARL MARX

IN PARIS

[Trier, between August 11 and 18, 1844]

My dearest, unique Karl,

You cannot believe, darling of my heart, how very happy you make me by your letters,[249] and how your last pastoral letter, you high priest and bishop of my heart, has once again restored soothing calm and peace to your poor lamb. It is certainly wrong and silly to torture oneself with all sorts of cares and glimpses of dark distant perspectives. I am very well aware of that myself in those self-tormenting moments — but although the spirit is willing, the flesh is weak, and so it is always only with your help that I am able to exorcise those demons. Your latest news truly brought me such real and tangible solace that it would be quite wrong to start brooding again. I expect now that it is going to happen as in a game of cards, and I hope that some external circumstance will determine the time of my return home. Perhaps Edgar's[a] arrival or some similar [external][b] occasion. I touch on this painful [point][b] very unwillingly, and it is only in Edgar's presence that I shall return to this matter for a decision. In any case I shall be coming before the winter, how could I indeed resist such dear, heart-warming friendliness as that which shines on me from your lines. And then in the background are dark feelings of anxiety and fear, the real menace of unfaithfulness, the seductions and attractions of a capital city — all those are powers and forces whose effect on me is more powerful than anything else. How I am looking forward after such a long time to rest comfortably and happily once more close to your heart, in your arms. What a lot I shall have to chatter with you about, and what trouble you will have to bring me again *à la hauteur des principes* for in partitioned Germany it is not easy to remain *au courant*.

How glad you will be to see the little creature.[c] I am convinced that you will not be able to recognise our child, unless her little eyes and black crest of hair reveal the secret to you. Everything else is really quite different now, only the resemblance to you becomes ever more obvious. During the last few days she has begun to eat a little broth made from the herbs which I have

---

[a] Edgar von Westphalen.— *Ed.*
[b] Part of the word is covered by an inkspot.— *Ed.*
[c] Their daughter Jenny.— *Ed.*

brought with me, and she relishes it greatly. In the bath she splashes with her little hands so much that the whole room is flooded, and then she dips her tiny finger in the water and afterwards licks it hastily. Her little thumb, which she has always kept bent and then made to peep out between her fingers, has become so unusually supple and flexible owing to this habit that one cannot help being astonished by it. She can become a little piano player—I believe she can do magic tricks with her little thumb. When she cries, we quickly draw her attention to the flowers in the wall-paper, and then she becomes quiet as a mouse and gazes so long that tears come into her eyes. We must not talk to her for too long because it makes her over-exert herself. She wants to imitate every sound and answer it, and the fact that her forehead swells and reddens is a sign of excessive strain. Incidentally, she is the acme of cheerfulness. Every kind of look you give her makes her laugh. You ought to see what a darling little creature I shall bring with me. When she hears anyone speaking she at once looks in that direction and goes on looking until something fresh happens. You can't have any idea of the liveliness of the child. For whole nights through her little eyes refuse to close in sleep, and if one looks at her she laughs out loud. She is happiest when she sees a light or the fire. By that means one can allay her heaviest storm. Karl dear, how long will our little doll play a solo part? I fear, I fear, that when her papa and mama are together once again, and live in common ownership, the performance will soon become a duet. Or should we set about it in the good Parisian style? Usually one finds the greatest number of children where the means are smallest. Recently a poor man with ten children asked for relief from Chief Burgomaster Görtz. When he was reproached for having produced so many children, his only reply was to say: there is a parish fête once a year even in the tiniest and most insignificant village. Then he was given assistance, and no doubt he will be celebrating the eleventh parish fête.

We have not seen your relatives for a long time. First the great illustrious visit and now the important arrangements for the marriage,[a] so that one's presence is inopportune, one does not receive any calls and is oneself modest enough not to visit them again. The marriage is on August 28. On Sunday the banns were called for the first time. In spite of all the magnificence, Jettchen's health becomes worse every day, her cough and hoarseness are increasing. She can hardly walk any longer. She goes about like a

---

[a] Marriage of Marx's sister Henriette (Jettchen) and Theodor Simons.—*Ed.*

ghost, but married she must be. It is generally regarded as terrible and unscrupulous. Rocholl, however, is said to be in favour of it in order to secure something for his nephew.[a] I don't know whether that can turn out well. If at least they were going to live in a town—but in a miserable village, and in winter at that. I can't imagine how your relatives can be cheerful and happy about it. If fate did not somewhat dampen their spirits, there could be no escape from their haughtiness. And the boasting about grand parties and brooches, ear-rings and shawls! I cannot understand your mother. She herself has told us that she thinks Jettchen is consumptive, and yet she lets her marry. But Jettchen is said to want it very strongly. I am curious to know how it will all turn out.

In Trier there is already such a stir and bustle as I have never seen. There is activity everywhere.[250] All the shops have been newly smartened up, everyone is arranging rooms for lodging. We, too, have got a room ready. The whole of Coblenz is coming here and the cream of society is joining in the procession. All the hotels are already full up. 210 new pubs have been established, as well as circuses, theatres, menageries, dioramas, international theatres, in short, everything one could think of is already announcing its presence. The entire palace square is covered with tents. Entire wooden houses have been erected outside the gates. Trier marches on Sunday. Everyone has to join a procession and then come the villages. Every day some 16,000 people. Frau Stein has already sold 400 talers' worth of tiny copies of the sacred linen cloth, made out of old strips of ribbon. Rosaries, worth from six pfennigs to one hundred talers, are displayed at every house. I, too, have bought a little medallion for my little one, and yesterday she herself obtained a small rosary. You cannot imagine the bustling activity that is going on here. Next week half Luxemburg is coming; cousin Michel has also announced his arrival. All the people seem to be mad. What is one to think about it? Is it a good sign of the times that everything has to go to extremes, or are we still a long way from our goal?

Where you are, too, all hell is being let loose. Will things be patched up once more? And tell me, what did the blockhead[b] say about your article?[c] Has he given tit for tat, replied or kept silent? Jung really is an exceptionally noble characher.[251]

---

[a] Theodor Simons.— *Ed.*
[b] Arnold Ruge.— *Ed.*
[c] "Critical Marginal Notes on the Article 'The King of Prussia and Social Reform. By a Prussian'" (see this volume, pp. 189-206).— *Ed.*

What a good thing it is that you are now a little bit in funds again. Only always bear in mind, when the purse is full, how quickly it becomes empty again, and how difficult it is to fill it. You dear good Karl, darling of my heart. How I love you, how my heart yearns for you. I should like so very much that Edgar could still see his charming niece. If only he became an uncle barrister — then I could earlier talk to Mother about my departure. Our little doll is just eating her soup. Just think, she does not want to lie down at all any more, she wants to sit upright all the time. She is then better able to look around her. Tell me, dear heart, for some time past I have noticed that you no longer mention Guerrier. Has anything happened in connection with the worthy cousin? And is there no news of the divine Georg[a]?

I am very eager to know what the Pomeranian[b] is going to do now. Will he keep silent or will he make a row? It is peculiar that from Cologne there never comes anything unpleasant, but always the best. After all, how loyal our friends are, how solicitous, tactful and considerate. Even if it is painful to have to ask for money, in relation to these people it surely ceases to be at all unpleasant and onerous. I can hardly go on writing, the baby keeps distracting my attention with her delicious chuckles and attempts at speech. You cannot have any idea of the beauty of her forehead, the transparency of her skin and the wonderful delicacy of her tiny hands.

Dear good heart of my heart. Do write to me again quite soon. I am so very happy when I see your handwriting. You dear, good, sweet, little wild boar. You dear father of my little doll.

Adieu, heart of my heart.

First published in: Marx/Engels, *Werke*, Ergänzungsband, Teil 1, Berlin, 1968

Printed according to the original

Published in English for the first time

---

[a] Georg Herwegh.— *Ed.*
[b] Arnold Ruge.— *Ed.*

NOTES AND INDEXES

NOTES

[1] Marx mentions his intention of critically analysing Hegel's views on the state and law as far back as in the spring of 1842. In a letter to Arnold Ruge of March 5 he writes that he is preparing an article on Hegel's legal and political views in which he intends first of all to criticise Hegel's apology on behalf of the constitutional monarchy (see this edition, Vol. 1). The above-mentioned article is not extant and it is unknown whether he actually wrote it, but the subject-matter continued to attract his attention. As Marx's theoretical views developed and he gradually adopted a materialist standpoint, largely due to Feuerbach's influence, his plans of writing a critique of Hegel's philosophy became more extensive and profound and finally he conceived the idea of counterposing the materialist conception of social phenomena to their idealist interpretation. For Marx the basic problem was the interdependence of material social relations, property relations and so on — which Hegel called "civil society"— and the political system of society, the state.

Marx began to work on his plan during his stay from May to October 1843 in Kreuznach (where his bride Jenny von Westphalen, whom he married in June 1843, lived with her mother). Here, apparently, he wrote the original version of the work. In the process of writing it he felt the need for greater concrete historical material, and with this aim in view he began to study problems related not only to the theory and history of the state as a whole but to the history of individual countries (England, France, Germany, the United States, Italy, Sweden) and major world-historical events, in particular the Great French Revolution, as can be seen from his five notebooks containing excerpts (the Kreuznach Notebooks). Later on, he wrote an introduction to that work which was published in February 1844 in the *Deutsch-Französische Jahrbücher*. But Marx did not manage to prepare the main sections of his work for publication because he turned to other studies and conceived other literary plans (economic studies, preparation of a book against the Young Hegelians, work on the history of the Convention and so on). However, his work on the manuscript dealing with the criticism of the Hegelian philosophy of law played a major role in his spiritual development and was an important stage in the formation of his materialist views. Marx himself pointed to this in 1859 in the Preface to *A Contribution to the Critique of Political Economy*. Engels, for his part, in his article "Karl Marx" (1869) described the conclusions arrived at by his friend as a result of the critical analysis of

Hegel's views in the following way: "Proceeding from the Hegelian philosophy of law, Marx came to the conclusion that it was not the state which Hegel had described as the 'top of the edifice' but 'the civil society' which Hegel had regarded with disdain that was the sphere in which a key to the understanding of the process of historical development of mankind should be looked for."

The extant manuscript consists of 39 big sheets numbered in Roman figures by the author (II-XL), apparently after the work had been finished. The first sheet is missing. Each sheet is folded in two to form four pages, which are numbered in Arabic figures from sheet I-XXII. The manuscript contains a critical analysis of paragraphs 261-313 of G. W. F. Hegel's *Grundlinien der Philosophie des Rechts*. These paragraphs comprise the subsection "Internal State Law" in the third part of Hegel's work. The missing first sheet apparently dealt with §§ 257-260 as can be seen from the extant text. The manuscript bears the imprint of an unfinished work. Some problems which the author promises to deal with below have not been treated by him in the extant part. The title of the work given by the author, which is missing in the manuscript, is reproduced from the above-mentioned introduction published in the *Deutsch-Französische Jahrbücher*. In one of the notebooks written by Marx in Bonn in 1842 there are some notes connected with this manuscript. The date of writing the notes is not established. The notes contain some subheadings, the first of which refers to the non-extant part of the manuscript and contains references to the sheets and pages of the manuscript of the *Contribution to the Critique of Hegel's Philosophy of Law*. The content of the notes is as follows: "Duplication of the Development System. I. 3,4. *Logical Mysticism*. II, 8. III, 9 [see this volume, pp. 7, 8].

"Mystical way of presentation.

"Ibid. Example, § 267. IV, pp. 13, 14 [see this volume, pp. 10, 11].

"*Idea as Subject*. IV, pp. 15, 16 [see this volume, pp. 11-13]. (Real subjects become mere names.) P. 17, p. 18, pp. 20, 21, pp. 24, 26, 27, p. 28, p. 40, p. 57, pp. 75, 78 [see this volume, pp. 13, 14-15, 16-18, 20-21, 22-24, 33-34, 48-49, 60, 62-63]. XXVI, 2. XXVIII. XXX, 3. XXXI, 3. XXXII, 2. XXXIV, 2, 3, 4. P. XXXVII, 2 [see this volume p. 82-83, 89-90, 98-99, 101-02, 109-10, 114-15]. Opposites. XXXIX [see this volume, p. 121-24]."

Marx's manuscript was first published in Moscow by the Institute of Marxism-Leninism.

This work was first published in English in part in the book *Writings of the Young Marx on Philosophy and Society*, New York, 1967, and in full as a separate edition entitled *Critique of Hegel's 'Philosophy of Right'* by Karl Marx. Translated from the German by Annette Jolin and Joseph O'Malley, Cambridge, 1970.

In translating the term "Hegelsche Rechtsphilosophie", the translators and editors, being aware of the difficulty of its rendering into English, proceeded from the interpretation of this and similar concepts in the works of Marx and Engels written in English. Thus, in the English authorised edition of Engels' work *Socialism: Utopian and Scientific*, Hegel's expression "Begriff des Rechts" is translated in one of the notes as "concept of law" (see Karl Marx and Frederick Engels, *Selected Works*, Vol. 3, Moscow, 1970, p. 115).

In this manuscript as in the other works published in this volume Marx frequently uses two similar German terms, "Entäusserung" and "Entfremdung", to express the notion of "alienation". In the present edition the former is generally translated as "alienation", the latter as "estrangement", because in the later economic works (*Theories of Surplus-Value*) Marx himself used the word "alienation" as the English equivalent of the term "Entäusserung". p. 3

[2] Here and below Marx quotes Hegel, *Grundlinien der Philosophie des Rechts oder Naturrecht und Staatswissenschaft im Grundrisse*, according to the edition *Georg*

Wilhelm Friedrich Hegel's Werke, Bd. 8, hrsg. von Dr. Eduard Gans, Berlin, 1833. Sometimes Marx quotes with omissions which he does not always indicate with dots. Similarly, he does not always reproduce italics, frequently italicising instead other words and passages in the quotations. In the present edition emphasis in the quotations from Hegel's work reproduced by Marx is rendered by italics, whereas passages emphasised by Marx are printed in bold italics. In individual cases where there are no indications in the manuscript, the editors give in square brackets references to the corresponding paragraphs of Hegel's work. p. 5

[3] Marx did not return to this question anywhere else in the extant manuscript. p. 15

[4] Apparently this refers to G. W. F. Hegel, *Encyclopädie der philosophischen Wissenschaften im Grundrisse*, Erster Theil, Die Wissenschaft der Logik. p. 18

[5] This possibly refers to Saint-Simon and his followers, who considered that in the future society the state would turn from an instrument for administering people into an instrument for administering things, i.e., would lose its political character. p. 30

[6] In the extant manuscript an analysis of the Addition to § 290 of Hegel's work is missing. p. 42

[7] The *Prussian Common Law* (Preussische Landrecht)—the laws of the provinces in the kingdom of Prussia codified in 1794. It reflected the backwardness of feudal Prussia in the sphere of law and court procedure. p. 44

[8] The extant manuscript does not deal with this question. p. 59

[9] This section is from the third, concluding part of Hegel's *Grundlinien der Philosophie des Rechts*, comprising §§ 182-256. It precedes the section "Der Staat", the paragraphs of which (§§ 261-313) are analysed in this manuscript. There is no special analysis of this section in the extant part of the manuscript though Marx repeatedly touches on Hegel's views on civil society when examining § 308 (see, in particular, pp. 111-15 of this volume). p. 81

[10] This refers to *la Charte bâclée* (the Constitutional Charter) introduced after the July 1830 revolution in France. p. 113

[11] This problem is not dealt with in the extant part of the manuscript. p. 121

[12] This apparently refers to the same problem which Marx mentioned above, on page 121, as a problem to be analysed later on (see Note 11). p. 123

[13] This note was written by Marx in connection with his reading and summarising of the journal *Historisch-politische Zeitschrift*, edited by Leopold Ranke. Hamburg, 1832, Bd. 1, Heft 1. Marx was interested, in particular, in Ranke's article, "Über die Restauration in Frankreich". This note is to be found in the fourth Kreuznach Notebook which contains Marx's historical excerpts relating to July-August 1843 (see Note 1). The thoughts expressed in it on the inconsistency of the Hegelian idealist conception of the relation between the abstract idea of the state and its concrete historical forms, etc., are directly connected with Marx's work *Contribution to the Critique of Hegel's Philosophy of Law* (see pp. 75-80 and 82-83 of this volume). p. 130

[14] This refers to the Constitutional Charter of 1814, the basic law of the Bourbons returned to power, and the Charter published on August 14, 1830, after the bourgeois revolution in France. The Constitutional Charter of 1830 was the basic law of the July monarchy. It repeated the main principles of the 1814

Charter but the preamble of the 1814 Charter, speaking of the constitution being granted (*octroyée*) by the king, was omitted from the 1830 Constitution and the rights of the Upper and Lower Chambers were extended at the expense of some of the monarch's prerogatives. Under the new constitution the monarch was regarded only as the head of the executive and was deprived of the right to repeal or suspend laws. p. 130

[15] Early in the spring of 1843 Marx conceived the idea of launching a new journal as the organ of the German and French democrats. He intended to publish it in collaboration with the Young Hegelian Arnold Ruge, editor of the journal *Deutsche Jahrbücher*, which had been suppressed by the government (see Marx's letter to Ruge of March 13, 1843, this edition, Vol. 1). At the end of May 1843 Marx went to Dresden to see Ruge on this question. In the course of the preliminary talks, two tendencies became apparent in respect of the line of the future journal. Ruge pursued chiefly educational goals and planned to turn the journal into a means for an exchange of ideas in the sphere of philosophy (primarily German philosophy) and social and political sciences (above all, French), whereas Marx sought to link the theoretical tasks of the journal as closely as possible with the actual revolutionary struggle against the feudal-absolutist order in Germany, to use the journal as an ideological weapon in the struggle for restructuring society. The different approaches to the journal's programme were reflected in the materials prepared for it and in the correspondence between its prospective editors. Marx's intention to turn the journal into a more radical and militant organ is felt also in the given draft programme of the *Deutsch-Französische Jahrbücher*, which Marx wrote after he had received Ruge's programmes in German and French in August 1843. Marx used these programmes but changed some formulations, especially those of the second and partly of the third point which in Ruge's programmes read as follows:

French Text of Ruge's Programme

"2) Reviews of the newspapers, which will give a calm but just and strict appraisal of the periodicals of our day, the spirit inspiring them, their actions and tendencies and also their impact on public opinion.

"3) Critical reviews of books published on both sides of the Rhine."

German Text of Ruge's Programme

"2) Reviews of the newspapers and journals which express their attitude to the problems of the day.

"3) Reviews of old-time writings and *belles-lettres* in Germany as well as reviews of books published in the two countries which open or continue the new epoch."

In elaborating the final text of the programme, Ruge was to take into account the draft written by Marx and reproduce, wholly or in part, some of his formulations. For the sake of comparison we quote below the text printed in issue No. 1-2 of the *Deutsch-Französische Jahrbücher*, Paris, 1844:

"This journal is a critical publication, but it is not a German literary newspaper. We shall publish excerpts from French and German sources:

"1. On men and systems which are of significance and enjoy influence, on topical questions, on the constitution, legislation, political economy, morals and institutions. Instead of the divine policy of the heavenly kingdom it will reflect the true science of human affairs.

"2. Reviews of newspapers and journals which express their attitude to the problems of our day.

"3. Reviews of old-time writings and *belles-lettres* in Germany which of necessity will subject to criticism the old German spirit in its transcendent, now moribund existence; as well as reviews of books of the two countries which open or continue the new epoch which we are entering." p. 131

[16] The journal *Deutsch-Französische Jahrbücher* was to contribute to rallying various representatives of progressive democratic and socialist thought in France and Germany, and to become the organ of "a Franco-German scientific alliance" as Marx wrote in a letter to Ludwig Feuerbach on October 3, 1843 (see p. 349 of this volume). Invitations to contribute to the journal were extended to Frederick Engels, Ludwig Feuerbach, Heinrich Heine, Moses Hess, Karl Bernays, Julius Fröbel, Pierre Joseph Proudhon, Félicité de Lamennais, Alphonse de Lamartine, Louis Blanc, Pierre Leroux, Étienne Cabet and others. This letter of the editorial board of the future journal, which was signed by Marx and Ruge, was published in the Fourierist newspaper *Démocratie pacifique* in reply to an unsigned item, written by Lamartine, which appeared on December 10, 1843, in the newspaper *Bien Public*. p. 132

[17] This refers to a letter of November 16, from Leipzig, which was published in the *Kölnische Zeitung* on November 20, 1843. p. 132

[18] These letters written by Marx form part of his correspondence with Ruge at the time of their preparations for publishing the journal *Deutsch-Französische Jahrbücher*; they were published in the journal in the section "From the Correspondence of 1843", where letters by Ruge, Bakunin and Feuerbach were also printed. In these letters Marx in fact formulated his revolutionary views on the programme of the journal which went further than the tasks of disseminating abstract philosophical ideas and bourgeois-democratic political views, set by its other editor, Ruge.

Marx's letters to Ruge from the *Deutsch-Französische Jahrbücher* were first published in English in the book *Writings of the Young Marx on Philosophy and Society*, New York, 1967.

Despite considerable organisational and material difficulties (the journal was edited in Paris and printed in Zurich) the editorial board managed to put out the first double issue (No. 1-2) of the *Deutsch-Französische Jahrbücher* at the end of February 1844. The main trend of the journal was determined by Marx's letters and articles ("On the Jewish Question", "Contribution to the Critique of Hegel's Philosophy of Law. Introduction") and Engels' articles ("Outlines of a Critique of Political Economy", "The Condition of England. *Past and Present* by Thomas Carlyle"), which were published in it and were imbued with revolutionary-communist spirit. However, the publication of the journal was discontinued (for the reason see this volume, p. 188, and Note 36).

By its sharp political presentation of material the *Deutsch-Französische Jahrbücher* attracted the attention of the progressive sections of society in Germany, France and other countries but at the same time evoked indignation of the conservative press. On March 10, 1844, the Augsburg *Allgemeine Zeitung* wrote: "The criticism to which the new Paris journal resorts knows no mercy, in its polemics it disregards all aesthetic standards, and its satirical tone, though it does not stab like a dagger, punches like a huge fist." The Prussian Government considered the political line of the journal extremely "dangerous", banned its import to Germany and issued warrants for the arrest of Marx, Ruge, Heine and the other contributors in the event of their coming to Prussia. About two-thirds out of the total of three thousand copies fell into the hands of the police. p. 133

[19] This figure of speech was used by analogy with the satirical poem of the German humanist Sebastian Brant, *Das Narrenschiff* (The Ship of Fools), published in 1494. In a letter to Ruge in May 1843 Marx repeated this metaphor (see p. 139 of this volume). p. 134

[20] In a letter to Marx written from Berlin in March 1843, Ruge complained about the absence of any signs of revolutionary ferment in Germany, about the spirit of servility, submission to despotism and allegiance that had been prevalent in the country for many years. This letter was published in the section "From the Correspondence of 1843" in the *Deutsch-Französische Jahrbücher*. p. 134

[21] Marx alludes to the patronage and support which Frederick William IV, while still Crown Prince, extended to the journal *Berliner politisches Wochenblatt* (1831-41) which was the mouthpiece for the ideas of feudal reaction and conservative romanticism.

The coronation of Frederick William IV, which took place on June 7, 1840, in Königsberg, was surrounded with the pageantry of medieval knighthood.
p. 139

[22] In a letter to Marx in August 1843 (published in the *Deutsch-Französische Jahrbücher*) Ruge informed him of the final decision to have the journal published in Paris. Earlier there had been no unanimity on this point, besides Paris other places had been suggested, in particular Switzerland and Strasbourg.
p. 142

[23] Marx's departure for Paris was delayed. He arrived there with Jenny at the end of October 1843. p. 142

[24] This article was written in reply to the Young Hegelian Bruno Bauer, who in his works on this subject reduced the problem of the emancipation of the Jews to their emancipation from Judaism. Being an idealist, Bauer considered the overcoming of religious prejudices as the decisive means for eliminating national contradictions. Polemics with him over this question provided Marx with an occasion for considering from the materialist point of view the broader problem of emancipating not only the Jews but the whole of mankind from economic, political and religious fetters.

When quoting from the works of Bruno Bauer and others Marx sometimes slightly departs from the text of the source; the emphasis, as a rule, is Marx's, but in quoting from Hegel's book *Grundlinien der Philosophie des Rechts* he reproduces also the author's emphasis. Quotations from books and documents in French are given by Marx in the French language. In the present work these are given in French in the text, and the corresponding English texts are given in the footnotes.

The first English translation of this article was published in the book: Karl Marx, *Selected Essays*; London, Parsons, 1926. p. 146

[25] The text of the French Constitution of 1791 (which was preceded by the Declaration of the Rights of Man and of the Citizen) is quoted by Marx from the book: W. Wachsmuth, *Geschichte Frankreichs im Revolutionszeitalter*, Bd. 1, Hamburg, 1840 (documents in the book are cited in French). Excerpts from the Constitution of 1793 are quoted from the documentary publication in many volumes by P. J. B. Buchez and P. C. Roux entitled *Histoire parlementaire de la Révolution française*, Vol. 31, Paris, 1837. Below, when quoting constitutional documents of the period of the French Revolution, Marx uses the same sources, mainly the work of Buchez and Roux. p. 161

[26] The quotation from the Constitution of 1795 is taken from Vol. 36 of the *Histoire parlementaire de la Révolution française* by P. J. B. Buchez and P. C. Roux.
p. 163

[27] The first quotation is taken from the book: W. Wachsmuth, *Geschichte Frankreichs im Revolutionszeitalter*, the second from Vol. 31 of the *Histoire parlementaire de la Révolution française* by P. J. B. Buchez and P. C. Roux. p. 164

[28] Quoted from Thomas Münzer's pamphlet directed against Martin Luther: *Hoch verursachte Schutzrede und Antwort wider das geistlose, sanftlebende Fleisch zu Wittenberg, welches mit verkehrter Weise durch den Diebstahl der heiligen Schrift die erbärmliche Christenheit also ganz jämmerlich besudelt hat.* The pamphlet was published in 1524. Marx quotes it from Leopold Ranke, *Deutsche Geschichte im Zeitalter der Reformation*, Berlin, 1839. p. 172

[29] According to Marx's intention, this article was to serve as an introductory section to a detailed work in which he planned to make a critical analysis of Hegel's idealist philosophy and political views (see Note 1). While working on the "Introduction" Marx did not confine himself to the criticism of Hegel's philosophy; he set himself the task of defining his attitude not only to the existing ideological trends but also to the actual revolutionary processes.

The first English translation of this work was published in the book: Karl Marx, *Selected Essays*, London, Parsons, 1926. p. 175

[30] This remark testifies to Marx's intention to complete his criticism of the Hegelian philosophy of law which he had begun earlier, to finish and prepare for publication the rough draft of the manuscript of 1843 on this subject. However, after the publication of the *Deutsch-Französische Jahrbücher* had been discontinued, Marx gradually abandoned his plan because he was busy with other work, primarily, the study of economic relations. Marx also had other reasons, which he mentioned in the Preface to the *Economic and Philosophic Manuscripts of 1844*, namely, his dissatisfaction with the chosen form of combining a criticism of Hegel's views on different subjects with a critical analysis of these subjects as such, his growing conviction that in this form his work would give "the impression of arbitrary systematism" (see p. 231 of this volume).

Proceeding from these considerations, Marx arrived at the conclusion that it would be better to give a critical analysis of law, ethics, politics, etc., in separate booklets and to crown it all with a critical work summing up his views on the idealist, speculative philosophy. Soon, however, the need arose of first coming out against the Young Hegelians and Marx's plans again underwent a change. He began to connect his elaboration of the principles of a new, revolutionary-materialist world outlook primarily with a criticism of the idealist world outlook of the Young Hegelians and other representatives of German bourgeois and petty-bourgeois ideology. This task was fulfilled by Marx and Engels in their joint works: *The Holy Family* and *The German Ideology*. p. 176

[31] The *historical school of law* — a trend in the historical and legal science which arose in Germany at the end of the 18th century. The representatives of this school (Gustav Hugo, Friedrich Karl von Savigny and others) attempted to justify the privileges of the nobility and feudal institutions on the grounds of stability of historical traditions. For a description of this school see Marx's article "The Philosophical Manifesto of the Historical School of Law" (this edition, Vol. 1). p. 177

[32] This refers to the liberal circles of Germany, representatives of the liberal opposition in the Landtags, liberal publicists of various descriptions, and others, who demanded constitutional reforms. p. 180

[33] This refers to the Young Hegelians. They drew radical atheistic conclusions from Hegel's philosophy but at the same time detached philosophy from reality and turned it into a self-contained and determining force. In fact the Young Hegelians were withdrawing more and more from the practical revolutionary struggle.

p. 181

[34] The *September laws* promulgated by the French Government in September 1835 restricted the rights of the jury and introduced severe measures against the press. They provided for increased money deposits for periodical publications and introduced imprisonment and large fines for publishing statements against private property and the existing state system. The enactment of these laws in conditions of the July constitutional monarchy, which formally proclaimed freedom of the press, emphasised the anti-democratic nature and hypocrisy of the bourgeois system.

p. 184

[35] The *Holy Roman Empire of the German nation* (962-1806) comprised at different times German, Italian, Austrian, Hungarian and Czech lands, Switzerland and the Netherlands and was a loose confederation of feudal kingdoms and principalities, church domains and free cities with different political systems, laws and traditions.

p. 184

[36] The printing of the journal was carried out in Zurich by the publishing house Das literarische Comptoir founded by Julius Fröbel in 1842. Besides the reason mentioned in the letter, disagreements between Marx and Arnold Ruge were largely responsible for the journal ceasing to be published. These disagreements boiled down to the fact that the bourgeois radical Ruge opposed Marx's revolutionary-communist world outlook. The final break between Marx and Ruge took place in March 1844. Ruge's hostile attitude towards the revolutionary struggle of the masses, which became evident at the time of the Silesian uprising of June 1844, induced Marx to come out in the press against his former co-editor.

p. 188

[37] This article was written in reply to Ruge's article signed "Ein Preusse", which was published in the newspaper *Vorwärts!* on July 27, 1844, under the title "Der König von Preussen und die Sozialreform". In his article Ruge represented the Silesian weavers' uprising (June 4-6, 1844) as a futile revolt of the helpless poor people driven to despair. Unlike Ruge, Marx saw it as the first big battle of the German proletariat against the bourgeoisie, as the manifestation of the growth of class-consciousness of the German workers.

With the publication of this article, Marx began to contribute to the newspaper *Vorwärts!*, which prior to that, during the initial period of its publication—from early 1844 to the summer of the same year—was of a moderate liberal trend due to the influence of its publisher, the German businessman Heinrich Börnstein, and its editor Adalbert von Bornstedt. However, when a friend of Marx, Karl Bernays, a revolutionary-minded radical, became its editor in the summer of 1844, the newspaper began to assume a democratic character. Having become a contributor to the newspaper, Marx began to influence its editorial policy and in September became one of its editors. On his proposal Engels, who had published in it two articles in the series "The Condition of England", was also included on the editorial board. Among its other contributors were Heine, Herwegh, Ewerbeck and Bakunin. Under Marx's influence the newspaper began to express communist views. It sharply criticised Prussian absolutism and moderate German liberalism. To comply with the demand of the Prussian Government, the Guizot ministry took repressive measures against its editors and contributors in January 1845 and its publication ceased.

In the quotations from the article by Ruge the emphasis is Marx's. Works of other authors—French and English (in their publications in French)—were quoted by Marx in German, apparently in his own translation.

This article was first published in English in the book: Karl Marx, *Selected Essays*, London, Parsons, 1926. p. 189

[38] The editorial of the French democratic newspaper *La Réforme* of July 20, 1844, dealt with the Cabinet order of the Prussian King Frederick William IV to display concern for the poor. This Cabinet order was prompted by the fear caused by the Silesian weavers' uprising. The author of the article was inclined to take the Prussian King's demagogy for a serious intention to carry out social reforms.
p. 189

[39] Marx refers to the Cabinet order of the Prussian King Frederick William IV of July 18, 1843, issued in connection with the participation of government officials in a banquet arranged in Düsseldorf by the liberals to mark the seventh Rhenish Landtag; the order prohibited the government officials to take part in manifestations of this kind. p. 190

[40] This refers to the *Corn Laws*—a series of laws in England (the first of which dated back to the 15th century) which imposed high duties on imported corn with the aim of maintaining high prices on it on the home market. In the first third of the 19th century several laws were passed (in 1815, 1822 and later) changing the conditions of corn imports, and in 1828 a sliding-scale was introduced, which raised import duties on corn when prices fell on the home market and, vice versa, lowered import duties when prices rose.

In 1838 the Manchester factory owners Cobden and Bright founded the Anti-Corn Law League, which widely exploited the popular discontent at rising corn prices. While agitating for the abolition of the corn duties and demanding complete freedom of trade, the League strove to weaken the economic and political positions of the landed aristocracy and to lower workers' wages.

The struggle between the industrial bourgeoisie and the landed aristocracy over the Corn Laws ended in their repeal in 1846. p. 192

[41] Marx quotes Francis Bacon according to the French translation of McCulloch's book *A Discourse on the Rise, Progress, Peculiar Objects, and Importance, of Political Economy* (J. R. MacCulloch, *Discours sur l'origine, les progrès, les objets particuliers, et l'importance de l'économie politique*, Genève-Paris, 1825, pp. 131-32). p. 193

[42] This quotation from Dr. Kay's pamphlet published anonymously in 1839 is cited by Marx in his own free translation with omissions from the two-volume edition of Eugène Buret, *De la misère des classes laborieuses en Angleterre et en France...*, T. 1, pp. 396, 398, 401. p. 193

[43] The decree of the National Convention of May 11 (22 Floréal), 1794, ordered the compilation of a *Livre de la bienfaisance nationale* (Book of National Charity) in which were to be entered invalids, orphans, the incapacitated and so forth, who were entitled to certain grants. It was one of the palliative measures for fighting the misery of the popular masses, introduced by the Jacobin government before its fall on July 27 (9 Thermidor), 1794.

The irruption of a crowd of hungry women into the building of the National Convention on May 20 (1 Prairial), 1795, marked the beginning of an uprising by the plebeian and proletarian masses of Paris against the Thermidor reaction; they put forward the slogan, "Bread and the Constitution of 1793!" Like the preceding uprising in Germinal (April) of the same year, the Prairial uprising was suppressed by military force. p. 197

[44] Marx refers to the revolutionary song *Das Blutgericht* which was popular among the Silesian weavers on the eve of the revolt. p. 201

[45] This refers to the revolts of the Lyons weavers in November 1831 and April 1834. p. 204

[46] The Cabinet order of Frederick William IV quoted here and below was published on August 9, 1844, in the *Allgemeine Preussische Zeitung*. It was caused by an abortive attempt on the life of the king on July 26, 1844, in Berlin, by the former burgomaster of the town of Storkow, H. L. Tschech, acting on personal grounds. p. 207

[47] This refers to the proposals submitted by the Prussian diplomat Bunsen to Frederick William IV in the spring and summer of 1844 concerning the proposed reform of the Prussian political system. According to Bunsen, his project was drawn up in "the monarchical and conservative spirit" and provided for the institution of an English-type bicameral Prussian parliament (Landtag) with an aristocratic upper chamber and a lower chamber elected on the estates principle. p. 210

[48] These comments are made by Marx in his conspectus of James Mill's book *Elements of Political Economy* (Marx used the French translation published in 1823 under the title *Élémens d'économie politique*), which forms part of the fourth and fifth of the nine notebooks of excerpts made by Marx during his stay in Paris from the end of 1843 till January 1845. The Paris Notebooks reflect Marx's intense work on political economy. The books summarised by Marx include works by J. B. Say, Adam Smith, David Ricardo, McCulloch, James Mill, Destutt de Tracy, Sismondi, Jeremy Bentham, Boisguillebert, Lauderdale, Schütz, List, Skarbek and Buret. At the time Marx used mainly French translations of the English authors. In a number of his conspectuses Marx added his own comments to the excerpts or to his summaries of passages from the books he was studying. However, most of these comments are of a fragmentary nature. Many ideas set forth in them are reproduced in one form or another, and frequently in a more developed form, in the extant sections of the *Economic and Philosophic Manuscripts of 1844*. The most detailed and systematised comments are those from his conspectus of Mill's book, which form two lengthy digressions from the text he was summarising. In their ideas they are close to the *Economic and Philosophic Manuscripts of 1844* and it is possible that they anticipated the thoughts expounded in the missing pages of the second manuscript of this work.

The first author's digression in the conspectus follows a considerable number of excerpts from Mill's book, which, like the other excerpts or summaries of passages in the concluding part of the conspectus, are not given in this edition. The full text of the conspectus was published in: Marx/Engels, *Gesamtausgabe*, Erste Abteilung, Band 3, Berlin, 1932. However, the excerpts from Mill' book made by Marx in between these two digressions, which by their content constitute a link between these comments, are published in full. Marx quotes excerpts from Mill's book and from other French publications partly in French, but mainly in his own translation into German, alternating German text with French. In the present edition the texts quoted or paraphrased by Marx are given in English, exact quotations are reproduced from the original edition:

James Mill, *Elements of Political Economy*, London, 1821. The emphasis in the quotations is Marx's.

The first English translation of this article was published, in part, in the book: *Writings of the Young Marx on Philosophy and Society*, New York, 1967.

p. 211

[49] The text of this comment in the conspectus is immediately preceded by the following excerpts from James Mill's book:

"...A medium of exchange ... is some one commodity, which, in order to effect an exchange between two other commodities, is first received in exchange for the one, and is then given in exchange for the other." (P. 93.) Gold, silver, *money*.

"By *value of money*, is here to be understood the proportion in which it exchanges for other commodities, or the quantity of it which exchanges for a certain quantity of other things."

"This proportion is determined by the *total* amount of money existing in a given country." (P. 95.)

"What regulates the quantity of money?"

"Money is made under two sets of circumstances: Government either leaves the increase or diminution of it free; or it controls the quantity, making it greater or smaller as it pleases.

"When the increase or diminution of money is left free, government opens the mint to the public, making bullion into money for as many as require it. Individuals possessed of bullion will desire to convert it into money only when it is their interest to do so; that is, when their bullion, converted into money, will be more valuable than in its original form. This can only happen when money is peculiarly valuable, and when the same quantity of metal, in the state of coin, will exchange for a greater quantity of other articles than in the state of bullion. As the value of money depends upon the quantity of it, it has a greater value when it is in short supply. It is then that bullion is made into coin. But precisely because of this conversion, the old ratio is restored. Therefore, if the value of money rises above that of the metal of which it is made, the interest of individuals operates immediately, in a state of freedom, to restore the balance by augmenting the quantity of money." (Pp. 99-101.)

"Whenever the coining of money, therefore, is free, its quantity is regulated by the value of the metal, it being the interest of individuals to increase or diminish the quantity, in proportion as the value of the metal in coins is greater or less than its value in bullion.

"But if the *quantity of money* is determined by the *value of the metal*, it is still necessary to inquire what it is which determines the value of the metal.... Gold and silver are in reality commodities. They are commodities for the attaining of which labour and capital must be employed. It is cost of production, therefore, which determines the value of these, as of other ordinary productions." (P. 101.)

p. 211

[50] The *monetary system* — an early type of mercantilism. Its adherents believed that wealth consisted in money, in amassing bullion reserves, hence the prohibition of gold and silver exports, the policy of securing an active trade balance.

p. 213

[51] This passage (which in the original reads as follows: "Durch die wechselseitige Entäusserung oder Entfremdung des Privateigentums ist das *Privateigentum* selbst in die Bestimmung des *entäusserten* Privateigentums geraten") shows that when using the terms "Entäusserung" and "Entfremdung" to denote alienation

Marx imparted to them an identical or nearly identical meaning. On the translation of these terms in this edition see Note 1. p. 219

[52] This refers primarily to James Mill, who divided his system of political economy into four independent sections: Production, Distribution, Exchange and Consumption. p. 221

[53] The rest of the conspectus contains further excerpts from Mill's book. Concerning his excerpts from pages 261-66, on which Mill examines the question of the rent of land, profit on capital and wages as sources of taxation and the state revenue, Marx made the following brief comment:
"Es versteht sich, dass Mill wie Ricardo dagegen protestiert, irgend einem Gouvernement den Gedanken einflössen zu wollen, die Grundrente zur einzigen Quelle der Steuern zu machen, da sie parteiisch ungerechte Belastung einer besonder Klasse von Individuen. *Aber*—und dies ist ein gewichtiges heimtückisches *Aber*—aber die Steuer auf die Grundrente ist die einzige, vom nationalökonomischen Standpunkt aus nicht *schädliche*, also die einzig *nationalökonomisch gerechte Steuer*. Ja, das einzige Bedenken, was die Nationalökonomie aufstellt, ist mehr anlockend als abschreckend, nämlich: dass in einem selbst nur gewöhnlich bevölkerten und ausgedehnten Lande, die Höhe der Grundrente das Bedürfnis der Regierung übersteigen würde." ("Needless to say, Mill, like Ricardo, denies that he wishes to impress on any government the idea that land rent should be made the sole source of taxes, since this would be a partisan measure placing an unfair burden on a particular class of individuals. *But*—and this is a momentous, insidious but—but the tax on land rent is the only tax that is not *harmful* from the standpoint of political economy, hence the only *just tax from the point of view of political economy*. Indeed, the one doubt raised by political economy is rather an attraction than a cause for apprehension, namely, that even in a country with an ordinary number of population and of ordinary size the amount yielded by land rent would exceed the needs of the government.") p. 228

[54] The *Economic and Philosophic Manuscripts of 1844* is the first work in which Marx tried to systematically elaborate problems of political economy from the standpoint of his maturing dialectical-materialist and communist views and also to synthesise the results of his critical review of prevailing philosophic and economic theories. Apparently, Marx began to write it in order to clarify the problems for himself. But in the process of working on it he conceived the idea of publishing a work analysing the economic system of bourgeois society in his time and its ideological trends. Towards the end of his stay in Paris, on February 1, 1845, Marx signed a contract with Carl Leske, a Darmstadt publisher, concerning the publication of his work entitled *A Critique of Politics and of Political Economy*. It was to be based on his *Economic and Philosophic Manuscripts of 1844* and perhaps also on his earlier manuscript *Contribution to the Critique of Hegel's Philosophy of Law*. This plan did not materialise in the 1840s because Marx was busy writing other works and, to some extent, because the contract with the publisher was cancelled in September 1846, the latter being afraid to have transactions with such a revolutionary-minded author. However, in the early 1850s Marx returned to the idea of writing a book on economics. Thus, the manuscripts of 1844 are connected with the conception of a plan which led many years later to the writing of *Capital*.

The *Economic and Philosophic Manuscripts* is an unfinished work and in part a rough draft. A considerable part of the text has not been preserved. What remains comprises three manuscripts, each of which has its own pagination (in Roman figures). The first manuscript contains 27 pages, of which pages I-XII and XVII-XXVII are divided by two vertical lines into three columns supplied with headings written in beforehand: "Wages of Labour", "Profit of Capital" (this section has also subheadings supplied by the author) and "Rent of Land". It is difficult to tell the order in which Marx filled these columns. All the three columns on p. VII contain the text relating to the section "Wages of Labour". Pages XIII to XVI are divided into two columns and contain texts of the sections "Wages of Labour" (pp. XIII-XV), "Profit of Capital" (pp. XIII-XVI) and "Rent of Land" (p. XVI). On pages XVII to XXI, only the column headed "Rent of Land" is filled in. From page XXII to page XXVII, on which the first manuscript breaks off, Marx wrote across the three columns disregarding the headings. The text of these pages is published as a separate section entitled by the editors according to its content "Estranged Labour".

Of the second manuscript only the last four pages have survived (pp. XL-XLIII).

The third manuscript contains 41 pages (not counting blank ones) divided into two columns and numbered by Marx himself from I to XLIII (in doing so he omitted two numbers, XXII and XXV). Like the extant part of the second manuscript, the third manuscript has no author's headings; the text has been arranged and supplied with the headings by the editors.

Sometimes Marx departed from the subject-matter and interrupted his elucidation of one question to analyse another. Pages XXXIX-XL contain the Preface to the whole work which is given in the present volume before the text of the first manuscript. The text of the section dealing with the critical analysis of Hegel's dialectic, to which Marx referred in the Preface as the concluding chapter and which was scattered on various pages, is arranged in one section and put at the end in accordance with Marx's indications.

In order to give the reader a better visual idea of the structure of the work, the text reproduces in vertical lines the Roman numbers of the sheets of the manuscripts, and the Arabic numbers of the columns in the first manuscript. The notes indicate where the text has been rearranged. Passages crossed out by Marx with a vertical line are enclosed in pointed brackets; separate words or phrases crossed out by the author are given in footnotes only when they supplement the text. The general title and the headings of the various parts of the manuscripts enclosed in square brackets are supplied by the editors on the basis of the author's formulations. In some places the text has been broken up into paragraphs by the editors. Quotations from the French sources cited by Marx in French or in his own translation into German, are given in English in both cases and the French texts as quoted by Marx are given in the footnotes. Here and elsewhere Marx's rendering of the quotations or free translation is given in small type but without quotation marks. Emphasis in quotations, belonging, as a rule, to Marx, as well as that of the quoted authors, is indicated everywhere by italics.

The *Economic and Philosophic Manuscripts of 1844* was first published by the Institute of Marxism-Leninism in Moscow in the language of the original: Marx/Engels, *Gesamtausgabe*, Abt. 1, Bd. 3, 1932.

In English this work was first published in 1959 by the Foreign Languages Publishing House (now Progress Publishers), Moscow, translated by Martin Milligan.
p. 229

[55] This refers to Bruno Bauer's reviews of books, articles and pamphlets on the Jewish question, including Marx's article on the subject in the *Deutsch-Französische Jahrbücher*, which were published in the monthly *Allgemeine Literatur-Zeitung*

(issue No. I, December 1843, and issue No. IV, March 1844) under the title "Von den neuesten Schriften über die Judenfrage". Most of the expressions quoted are taken from these reviews. The expressions "utopian phrase" and "compact mass" can be found in Bruno Bauer's unsigned article, "Was ist jetzt der Gegenstand der Kritik?", published in the *Allgemeine Literatur-Zeitung*, issue No. VIII, July 1844. A detailed critical appraisal of this monthly was later on given by Marx and Engels in the book *Die heilige Familie, oder Kritik der kritischen Kritik* (see this edition, Vol. 4, *The Holy Family, or Critique of Critical Criticism*). p. 232

[56] Marx apparently refers to Weitling's works: *Die Menschheit, wie sie ist und wie sie sein sollte*, 1838, and *Garantien der Harmonie und Freiheit*, Vivis, 1842.

Moses Hess published three articles in the collection *Einundzwanzig Bogen aus der Schweiz* (Twenty-One Sheets from Switzerland), Erster Teil (Zürich und Winterthur, 1843), issued by Georg Herwegh. These articles, entitled "Sozialismus und Kommunismus", "Philosophie der Tat" and "Die Eine und die ganze Freiheit", were published anonymously. The first two of them had a note — "Written by the author of 'Europäische Triarchie'". p. 232

[57] The term "element" in the Hegelian philosophy means a vital element of thought. It is used to stress that thought is a process, and that therefore elements in a system of thought are also phases in a movement. The term "feeling" (Empfindung) denotes relatively low forms of mental life in which no distinction is made between the subjective and objective. p. 233

[58] Shortly after writing this Preface Marx fulfilled his intention in *The Holy Family, or Critique of Critical Criticism*, written in collaboration with Engels (see this edition, Vol. 4). p. 234

[59] The expression "common humanity" (in the manuscript in French, "simple humanité") was borrowed by Marx from the first volume (Chapter VIII) of Adam Smith's *Wealth of Nations*, which he used in Garnier's French translation (*Recherches sur la nature et les causes de la richesse des nations*, Paris, 1802, t. I, p. 138). All the subsequent references were given by Marx to this publication, the synopsis of which is contained in his Paris Notebooks with excerpts on political economy. In the present volume wherever there are references to or quotations from this work by Adam Smith the corresponding pages of the English edition are given and references to Garnier's edition are reproduced in square brackets, e.g., Adam Smith, *Wealth of Nations*, Everyman's Library edition, Vol. I, pp. 58-60 [Garnier, t. I, pp. 132-36]. p. 235

[60] Marx uses the German term "Nationalökonomie" to denote both the economic system in the sense of science or theory, and the economic system itself. p. 239

[61] Loudon's work was a translation into French of an English manuscript apparently never published in the original. The author did publish in English a short pamphlet — *The Equilibrium of Population and Sustenance Demonstrated*, Leamington, 1836. p. 244

[62] Unlike the quotations from a number of other French writers such as Constantin Pecqueur and Eugène Buret, which Marx gives in French in this work, the excerpts from J. B. Say's book are given in his German translation. p. 247

[63] From this page of the manuscript quotations from Adam Smith's book (in the French translation), which Marx cited so far sometimes in French and sometimes

in German, are, as a rule, given in German. In this volume the corresponding pages of the English edition are substituted for the French by the editors and Marx's references are given in square brackets (see Note 59). p. 247

[64] The text published in small type here and below is not an exact quotation from Smith but a summary of the corresponding passages from his work. Such passages are subsequently given in small type but without quotation marks. p. 247

[65] The preceding page (VII) of the first manuscript does not contain any text relating to the sections "Profit of Capital" and "Rent of Land" (see Note 54). p. 251

[66] The whole paragraph, including the quotation from Ricardo's book in the French translation by Francisco Solano Constancio: *Des principes de l'économie politique, et de l'impôt*, 2-e éd., Paris, 1835, T. II, pp. 194-95 (see the corresponding English edition *On the Principles of Political Economy, and Taxation*, London, 1817), and from Sismondi's *Nouveaux principes d'économie politique...*, Paris, 1819, T. II, p. 331, is an excerpt from Eugène Buret's book *De la misère des classes laborieuses en Angleterre et en France...*, Paris, 1840, T. I, pp. 6-7, note. p. 257

[67] The allusion is to the following passage: "In a perfectly fair lottery, those who draw the prizes ought to gain all that is lost by those who draw the blanks. In a profession where twenty fail for one that succeeds, that one ought to gain all that should have been gained by the unsuccessful twenty." (Smith, *Wealth of Nations*, Vol. I, Bk. I, p. 94.) p. 258

[68] See Note 65. p. 262

[69] The *Corn Laws*—see Note 40. p. 263

[70] Pages XIII to XV are divided into two columns and not three like the other pages of the first manuscript; they contain no text relating to the section "Rent of Land". On page XVI, which also has two columns, this text is in the first column, while on the following pages it is in the second. p. 264

[71] Marx, still using Hegel's terminology and his approach to the unity of the opposites, counterposes the term "Verwirklichung" (realisation) to "Entwirklichung" (loss of realisation). p. 272

[72] Re the translation of the terms "Entfremdung" and "Entäusserung" which express the concept of alienation see Note 1. p. 272

[73] The term "species-being" (Gattungswesen) is derived from Ludwig Feuerbach's philosophy where it is applied to man and mankind as a whole. p. 275

[74] Apparently Marx refers to Proudhon's book *Qu'est-ce que la propriété?*, Paris, 1841. p. 280

[75] This passage shows that Marx here uses the category of wages in a broad sense, as an expression of antagonistic relations between the classes of capitalists and of wage-workers. Under "the wages" he understands "the wage-labour", the capitalist system as such. This idea was apparently elaborated in detail in that part of the manuscript which is not extant. p. 280

[76] This apparently refers to the conversion of individuals into members of civil society which is considered as the sphere of property, of material relations that determine all other relations. In this case Marx refers to the material rela-

tions of society based on private property and the antagonism of different classes. p. 281

[77] The Poor Law Amendment Act of 1834 deprived poor people considered able to work (including children) of any public relief except a place in the workhouse, where they were compelled to work. p. 284

[78] In the manuscript "sein für sich selbst" which is an expression of Hegel's term "für sich" (for itself) as opposed to "an sich" (in itself). In the Hegelian philosophy the former means roughly explicit, conscious or defined in contrast to "an sich", a synonym for immature, implicit or unconscious. p. 286

[79] This refers to *Révolutions de France et de Brabant*, par Camille Desmoulins. Second Trimestre, contenant mars, avril et mai, Paris, l'an 1^{ier} ,1790, N. 16, p. 139 sq.; N. 23, p. 425 sqq.; N. 26, p. 580 sqq. p. 287

[80] This refers to Georg Ludwig Wilhelm Funke, *Die aus der unbeschränkten Theilbarkeit des Grundeigenthums hervorgehenden Nachtheile*, Hamburg und Gotha, 1839, p. 56, in which there is a reference to Heinrich Leo, *Studien und Skizzen zu einer Naturlehre des Staates*, Halle, 1833, p. 102. p. 287

[81] The third manuscript is a thick notebook the last few pages of which are blank. The pages are divided into two columns by a vertical line, not for the purpose of dividing the text according to the headings but for purely technical reasons. The text of the first three sections comprises pp. I-XI, XIV-XXI, XXXIV-XXXVIII and was written as a supplement to the missing pages of the second manuscript. Pages XI-XIII, XVII, XVIII, XXIII, XXIV, XXVI-XXXIV contain the text of the concluding chapter dealing with the criticism of Hegel's dialectic (on some pages it is written alongside the text of other sections). In some places the manuscript contains the author's remarks testifying to his intention to unite into a single whole various passages of this section separated from each other by the text of other sections. Pages XXIX-XL comprise the draft Preface. Finally, the text on the last pages (XLI-XLIII), is a self-contained essay on the power of money in bourgeois society. p. 290

[82] The manuscript has "als für sich seiende Tätigkeit". For the meaning of the terms "für sich" and "an sich" in Hegel's philosophy see Note 78. p. 290

[83] Marx refers to the rise of the primitive, crude equalitarian tendencies among the representatives of utopian communism at the early stages of its development. Among the medieval religious communistic communities, in particular, there was current a notion of the common possession of women as a feature of the future society depicted in the spirit of consumer communism ideals. In 1534-35 the German Anabaptists, who seized power in Münster, tried to introduce polygamy in accordance with this view. Tommaso Campanella, the author of *Civitas Solis* (early 17th century), rejected monogamy in his ideal society. The primitive communistic communities were also characterised by asceticism and a hostile attitude to science and works of art. Some of these primitive equalitarian features, the negative attitude to the arts in particular, were inherited by the communist trends of the first half of the 19th century, for example, by the members of the French secret societies of the 1830s and 1840s ("worker-egalitarians", "humanitarians", and so on) comprising the followers of Babeuf (for a characterisation of these see Engels, "Progress of Social Reform on the Continent", pp. 396-97 of this volume). p. 294

[84] This note is given by Marx on page V of the manuscript where it is separated by a horizontal line from the main text, but according to its meaning it refers to this sentence. p. 295

[85] This part of the manuscript shows clearly the peculiarity of the terminology used by Marx in his works. At the time he had not worked out terms adequately expressing the conceptions of scientific communism he was then evolving and was still under the influence of Feuerbach in that respect. Hence the difference in the use of words in his early and subsequent, mature writings. In the *Economic and Philosophic Manuscripts of 1844* the word "socialism" is used to denote the stage of society at which it has carried out a revolutionary transformation, abolished private property, class antagonisms, alienation and so on. In the same sense Marx used the expression "communism equals humanism". At that time he understood the term "communism as such" not as the final goal of revolutionary transformation but as the process of this transformation, development leading up to that goal, a lower stage of the process.   p. 304

[86] This expression apparently refers to the theory of the English geologist Sir Charles Lyell who, in his three-volume work *The Principles of Geology* (1830-33), proved the evolution of the earth's crust and refuted the popular theory of cataclysms. Lyell used the term "historical geology" for his theory. The term "geognosy" was introduced by the 18th-century German scientist Abraham Werner, a specialist in mineralogy, and it was used also by Alexander Humboldt.
p. 305

[87] This statement is interpreted differently by researchers. Many of them maintain that Marx here meant crude equalitarian communism, such as that propounded by Babeuf and his followers. While recognising the historic role of that communism, he thought it impossible to ignore its weak points. It seems more justifiable, however, to interpret this passage proceeding from the peculiarity of terms used in the manuscript (see Note 85). Marx here used the term "communism" to mean not the higher phase of classless society (which he at the time denoted as "socialism" or "communism equalling humanism") but movement (in various forms, including primitive forms of equalitarian communism at the early stage) directed at its achievement, a revolutionary transformation process of transition to it. Marx emphasised that this process should not be considered as an end in itself, but that it is a necessary, though a transitional, stage in attaining the future social system, which will be characterised by new features distinct from those proper to this stage.   p. 306

[88] Page XI (in part) and pages XII and XIII are taken up by a text relating to the concluding chapter (see Note 81).   p. 306

[89] The greater part of this page as well as part of the preceding page (XVII) comprises a text relating to the concluding chapter (see Note 81).   p. 312

[90] Apparently Marx refers to a formula of the German philosopher Fichte, an adherent of subjective idealism.   p. 312

[91] The preceding pages starting from p. XXI, which is partly taken up by a text relating to this section, contain the text of the concluding chapter.   p. 316

[92] In some of his early writings Marx already uses the term "bürgerliche Gesellschaft" to mean two things: (1) in a broader sense, the economic system of society regardless of the historical stage of its development, the sum total of material relations which determine political institutions and ideology, and (2) in the narrow sense, the material relations of bourgeois society (later on, that society as a whole), of capitalism. Hence, the term has been translated according

to its concrete meaning in the context as "civil society" in the first case and "bourgeois society" in the second. p. 317

[93] The two previous pages of the manuscript contain the draft Preface to the whole work, which is published on pages 231-34. p. 322

[94] *Ontology*—in some philosophical systems a theory about being, about the nature of things. p. 322

[95] Originally the section on the Hegelian dialectic was apparently conceived by Marx as a philosophical digression in the section of the third manuscript which is published under the heading "Private Property and Communism" and was written together with other sections as an addition to separate pages of the second manuscript (see pp. 293-306 of this volume). Therefore Marx marked the beginning of this section (p. XI in the manuscript) as point 6, considering it to be the continuation of the five points of the preceding section. He marked as point 7 the beginning of the following section, headed "Human Requirements and Division of Labour Under the Rule of Private Property", on page XIV of the manuscript. However, when dealing with this subject on subsequent pages of his manuscript, Marx decided to collect the whole material into a separate, concluding chapter and mentioned this in his draft Preface. The chapter, like a number of other sections of the manuscript, was not finished. While writing it, Marx made special excerpts from the last chapter ("Absolute Knowledge") of Hegel's *Phänomenologie des Geistes*, which are in the same notebook as the third manuscript (these excerpts are not reproduced in this edition). p. 326

[96] The reference is not quite accurate. On page 193 of the work mentioned, Bruno Bauer polemises not against the anti-Hegelian Herr Gruppe but against the Right Hegelian Marheineke. p. 327

[97] Marx here refers to Feuerbach's critical observations on Hegel in §§ 29-30 of his *Grundsätze der Philosophie der Zukunft*.
This note is given at the bottom of page XIII of the third manuscript without any indication what it refers to. The asterisk after the sentence to which it seems to refer is given by the editors. p. 329

[98] Here on page XVII of the third manuscript (part of which comprises a text relating to the section "Human Requirements and Division of Labour Under the Rule of Private Property") Marx gave the note: "see p. XIII", which proves that this text is the continuation of the section dealing with the critical analysis of the Hegelian dialectic begun on pp. XI-XIII. p. 331

[99] At the end of page XVIII of the third manuscript there is a note by Marx: "continued on p. XXII". However number XXII was omitted by Marx in paging (see Note 54). The text of the given chapter is continued on the page marked by the author as XXIII, which is also confirmed by his remark on it: "see p. XVIII". p. 332

[100] Marx apparently refers here not only to the identity of Hegel's views on labour and some other categories of political economy with those of the English classical economists but also to his profound knowledge of economic writings.

In lectures he delivered at Jena University in 1803-04 Hegel cited Adam Smith's work. In his *Philosophie des Rechts* (§ 189) he mentions Smith, Say and Ricardo and notes the rapid development of economic thought.   p. 333

[101] Hegel uses the term "thinghood" (Dingheit) in his work *Phänomenologie des Geistes* to denote an abstract, universal, mediating link in the process of cognition; "thinghood" reveals the generality of the specific properties of individual things. The synonym for it is "pure essence" (das reine Wesen).
p. 334

[102] These eight points of the "surmounting of the object of consciousness", expressed "in all its aspects", are copied nearly word for word from §§ 1 and 3 of the last chapter ("Absolute Knowledge") of Hegel's *Phänomenologie des Geistes*.   p. 335

[103] Number XXV was omitted by Marx in paging the third manuscript.   p. 335

[104] Marx refers to § 30 of Feuerbach's *Grundsätze der Philosophie der Zukunft*, which says: "Hegel is a thinker who *surpasses* himself in thinking".   p. 339

[105] This enumeration gives the major categories of Hegel's *Encyclopädie der philosophischen Wissenschaften* in the order in which they are examined by Hegel. Similarly, the categories reproduced by Marx above (on p. 340) from "civil law" to "world history", are given in the order in which they appear in Hegel's *Philosophie des Rechts*.   p. 341

[106] This letter was written soon after the termination of the talks which Marx had with Arnold Ruge from March to September 1843, on the question of publishing the *Deutsch-Französische Jahrbücher* (see Note 15). The letter was connected with Marx's intention to enlist advanced German and French intellectuals to contribute to the journal. At the end of October 1843 Marx went from Kreuznach to Paris, where the journal was to be published.

This letter was first published in English in abridged form in the book *Karl Marx. Early Texts*, translated and edited by David McLellan, Oxford, 1971.
p. 349

[107] As follows from Feuerbach's reply to Marx on October 25, 1843, Feuerbach when mentioning a book against Schelling, which was soon to appear, referred not to his own work, but to that of his friend and follower Kapp: *Friedrich Wilhelm Joseph von Schelling*, Leipzig, 1843.   p. 349

[108] Marx ironically calls Schelling the 38th member of the German Confederation. The Confederation uniting 33 German states and 4 free cities was established at the 1815 Congress of Vienna with a view to ending feudal disunity in Germany.   p. 349

[109] According to the Prussian censorship instructions all publications of 21 signatures and more were not subject to preliminary censorship.   p. 350

[110] The reference is to German public opinion on the controversy over the book of the German theologian Paulus about Schelling's philosophy of revelation. After this book was published in 1843 Schelling brought in several law-suits against the author demanding that dues should be paid to him for quotations from his lectures. The proceedings were widely commented in the press. This incident prompted Heinrich Heine to write his satirical poem *Kirchenrat Prometheus*.
p. 350

[111] Although in his letter of October 25, 1843, Feuerbach fully agreed with the appraisal of the political tendencies of Schelling's philosophy given by Marx in his letter, he nevertheless refused to send an article on Schelling for the *Deutsch-Französische Jahrbücher* on the plea that he was occupied with other plans. p. 351

[112] This letter concerns the circumstances of publication of the *Deutsch-Französische Jahrbücher* which was printed in the printshop of the publisher Fröbel. Apparently some of the manuscripts were forwarded directly to Fröbel.
p. 351

[113] See Note 111. p. 352

[114] This letter was first published in English in the book: *Karl Marx. Early Texts*, translated and edited by David McLellan, Oxford, 1971. p. 354

[115] The English translation of Feuerbach's *Wesen des Christenthums* was apparently never published. The French translation was published in the book: A. H. Ewerbeck, *Qu'est-ce que la religion d'après la nouvelle philosophie allemande*, Paris, 1850. p. 354

[116] The statements quoted here and some lines below were taken by Marx from articles published in the *Allgemeine Literatur-Zeitung*, issues V and VI, 1844. Marx criticised them in chapters seven and nine of *The Holy Family* (see this edition, Vol. 4). p. 356

[117] The summary of the first volume of the Jacobin Levasseur's *Memoirs* was compiled by Marx in connection with his plans to write a work on the history of the French Revolution. Marx began to be interested in the revolutionary events in France at the end of the eighteenth century as early as the summer of 1843, as can be seen from his excerpts from special works on this subject by the German historians Wachsmuth and Ludwig contained in the Kreuznach Notebooks. As evidenced by A. Ruge (Ruge's letters to Feuerbach of May 15, 1844, to Fleischer of May 20 and July 9, 1844—see *A. Ruges Briefwechsel und Tagebuchblätter*, Bd. I, Berlin, 1886), after he had moved to Paris in the autumn of 1843, Marx planned to write a work on the history of the French Convention. He worked on it during several months of 1844, reading a lot of material, including the press of the time, memoirs of contemporaries, etc. In 1845 the radical *Trier'sche Zeitung* also wrote about these plans of Marx, which were never realised, in connection with Marx's banishment from France. Excerpts from Levasseur's *Memoirs* were published in the newspaper *Vorwärts!* in 1844, evidently on Marx's advice.

The time when this conspectus was compiled apparently coincided with the beginning of Marx's economic research: it is contained in the third notebook of the series with excerpts from the works of economists which Marx made since his arrival in Paris to August 1844. Besides the summary of Levasseur's *Memoirs*, the notebook contains the end of the excerpts from the French translation of Adam Smith's *Wealth of Nations* begun in the second notebook.

The pages of the notebook are divided into two columns by a vertical line. On the left-hand side Marx wrote direct quotations from the book in French (only one quotation is in German) or gave brief rendering in German of separate passages. Marx's own text consists of laconic comments and references which are typed in long primer in this edition. On the right-hand side there is more coherent rendering of the book's contents to which Marx gave the title: "The Struggle Between the Montagnards and the Girondists". The whole text is in

German with the exception of some French terms and expressions which are given in the original in this edition. In some cases, especially when assessing events and public figures, Marx also quotes from Levasseur's text word for word or almost word for word in German. These passages are typed in small type (the quotation marks being the editors').

In this edition we publish first the text of the left columns under the subheading "Excerpts", and then the text of the summary proper, written in the right columns. The italics are Marx's. p. 361

[118] On June 20, 1792, a mass manifestation took place in Paris in front of the Legislative Assembly and the royal palace of the Tuileries. The participants demanded cancellation of the royal veto on the decree of the establishment of a camp of Marseilles volunteers (fédérés) near Paris and restoration to their ministerial posts of the Girondist leaders dismissed by the king. The actual refusal to meet these demands made the atmosphere still more tense. The Mayor of Paris, the Girondist Pétion, dismissed from his post for supporting the manifestation, was recalled under the pressure of the Parisian sections in mid-July 1792. During the month of July 1792, despite the royal veto, detachments of fédérés continued to arrive in Paris from Marseilles and other towns. This strengthened the movement for the abolition of the monarchy and made for an energetic rebuff to the external enemies of the revolution.
p. 361

[119] On April 20, 1792, the Legislative Assembly voted the decree on the declaration of war on Austria, which marked the beginning of revolutionary France's prolonged armed struggle against the coalition of counter-revolutionary states. This act was preceded by intense war propaganda on the part of the Jacobin Club (Appeals of February 15 and 17, 1792) conducted under the influence of Girondists. Representatives of the Left wing of the Club (Robespierre and others), on the contrary, considered it necessary to put off as long as possible the inevitable military conflict with the aim of gaining time for strengthening revolutionary order.

The *Jacobin Club* ("Société des amis de la constitution") founded in October 1789, initially united the representatives of different political trends in the anti-absolutist camp. In July 1791, following the internal struggle, the moderate constitutionalists left the Club, and after the uprising of August 10, 1792, the Girondists followed suit. The influence of the revolutionary-democratic circles (Jacobins) then prevailed entirely. Having become their party centre, the Club, with its branches in the provinces, played an outstanding part in making revolutionary transformations.
p. 362

[120] On the page mentioned Levasseur writes about the ambiguous position of General Lafayette, one of the leaders of the moderate liberal constitutionalists, on the eve of the uprising of August 10, 1792. He enjoyed the confidence neither of the royal court nor of the revolutionary-patriotic camp. p. 362

[121] *August 10, 1792*—the day of the overthrow of the monarchy in France as a result of a popular uprising.
p. 362

[122] *Interregnum*—the period between the uprising of August 10, 1792, and the convocation of the Convention on September 20, 1792, lasting 42 days (the first open session was held on the 21st of September). It was marked by acute struggle between the Legislative Assembly and the revolutionary Paris Commune, which was formed instead of the former municipal council during the uprising of August 10 and directed the actions of the insurgents. p. 362

[123] The *Convention Committee* consisted of a President to be re-elected every fortnight and six secretaries. p. 362

[124] *Feuillants* — moderate liberal constitutionalists whose representatives (the Lameth brothers and others) left the Jacobin Club on July 16, 1791, after it adopted a petition for the dethroning of the king (see Note 119), and formed their own political club (they met in a house formerly occupied by the religious order bearing the name of the Feuillants, which was abolished in 1789). Having a considerable influence among the members of the Legislative Assembly, they strove in the interests of the big bourgeoisie and the liberal nobility to prevent the development of the revolution. p. 363

[125] On these pages Levasseur refutes the Girondists' accusations against the leaders of the Montagnards that they had been bribed by the émigrés and foreign agents. He characterises Danton, Robespierre and Marat (the latter with the reservation that he does not agree with his "wild" theories) as unselfish leaders devoted to the revolution. p. 363

[126] On these pages Levasseur cites Marat's speech in his self-defence in the Convention on September 25, 1792. In this speech Marat succeeded in proving the groundlessness of the Girondist accusation of incitement to revolt against the Convention and in defeating the proposal that his activity should be censured. Although Levasseur disliked Marat, he was compelled to admit the courage and composure with which he fought this campaign of slander and hatred launched by his opponents. p. 364

[127] In Levasseur's book: "It was difficult for the long-winded and garrulous eloquence of the latter to compete with the empty trumpery of Louvet." Further Levasseur speaks about the unsubstantiated accusations that Robespierre aimed at dictatorship and instigated reprisals against royalist prisoners in September 1792. In his speech in the Convention on November 5, 1792, Robespierre fully disproved these Girondist insinuations. p. 365

[128] The discussion of Buzot's proposal which envisaged that the decree on the expatriation of the dethroned Bourbons should apply to the secondary branch of the dynasty as well — the family of the Duke of Orléans — was postponed by a majority vote. Levasseur states that many members of the Convention feared that expatriation of the former Duke of Orléans, Philippe Égalité, would be a dangerous precedent of violating a deputy's immunity. p. 365

[129] On these pages Levasseur characterises the Girondists as a party whose activity objectively played into the hands of counter-revolutionary forces. "Though they were ardent republicans, they, unfortunately, fought on the side of the royalists, and, what is worse, concealed some of the royalists amidst themselves." p. 365

[130] On *September 2-5, 1792*, when the enemy armies were launching an offensive, in an atmosphere of disturbing rumours of counter-revolutionary conspiracies and preparations of reprisals against the families of patriots who fought the foreign enemies, the popular masses of Paris stormed the prisons, organised improvised courts and executed about a thousand prisoners who were supporters of the monarchy. These spontaneous terroristic actions of the people were used by the Girondists to accuse the Jacobins of organising the September massacres. p. 366

[131] The question of *performance of religious rites* arose in the Convention in connection with the discussion of the report on the primary education on December 12 and 14, 1792. The proposal to introduce religious education in the primary schools was rejected during the debate, but at the same time prominent Montagnard leaders (Robespierre, Danton) came out against some deputies who proposed the general prohibition of religious rites.

Under the *Decree on Means of Subsistence* is meant the repeal of the corn trade restrictions and the decision on the armed suppression of the movement for fixed prices adopted by the Convention under pressure of the Girondists in December 1792. These measures strongly infringed the interests of the masses who were suffering from shortage of food and the soaring prices. During this period the Montagnards did not support the popular demands for fixed prices on bread and other products but at the same time they rejected the principle of unrestricted freedom of trade upheld by the Girondists. Thus, speaking on the food question on December 2, 1792, Levasseur advocated the necessity of compulsory measures against sabotage by the farmers and grain merchants.

p. 371

[132] On *March 10, 1793*, representatives of the most radical plebeian trend in the revolutionary camp, called "les enragés", who wanted fixed prices, social measures against poverty, punishment of profiteers, etc., attempted to stir up a rebellion. Participants in the rebellion, during which two Girondist printshops were smashed up, wrote a petition in which they demanded the expulsion of the Girondists from the Convention. However, not being supported by the Jacobins, who were afraid to oppose the Girondists openly, "les enragés" did not attain their goal.

The *Cordelier Club* ("Société des amis droits de l'homme et du citoyen")—one of the most radical democratic organisations during the French Revolution, founded in 1790. The Left-wing Jacobins had a majority in the Club. Despite the fact that "les enragés" took part in its activities, it did not support their action of March 10, 1793.

p. 372

[133] On *May 31* and *June 2, 1793*, a popular uprising took place in Paris resulting in the expulsion of the Girondists from the Convention. A revolutionary-democratic dictatorship of the Jacobins supported by the masses was established. The success of the uprising was achieved through the unity of the revolutionary forces (Jacobins, "les enragés") in their struggle against the political supremacy of the Girondist Party which became an exponent of the counter-revolutionary tendencies of the big bourgeoisie.

p. 373

[134] According to Levasseur's statement Danton described Dumouriez as an extremely talented general, but having political convictions which were doubtful from the point of view of the republicans. Danton pointed to Dumouriez' extreme ambition, his obvious reluctance to submit to the Convention's control and his tendency to surround himself with flatterers and plotters.

p. 373

[135] The aggravation of the food crisis, the growing discontent of the masses and the agitation of "les enragés" for fixed prices compelled the Convention to discuss the food question again in the spring of 1793. Taking into consideration the sentiments of the people, the Jacobins this time spoke in favour of fixing the *maximum* prices on corn. Despite the Girondists' resistance the decree on maximum corn prices was adopted on May 4, 1793.

p. 373

[136] The summary of Engels' article "Outlines of a Critique of Political Economy" is in the fifth notebook of excerpts from the works of economists made by Marx when he was in Paris (concerning the Paris Notebooks see Note 48). The conspectuses and excerpts in the fifth notebook were probably made in the first half of 1844. p. 375

[137] *Letters from London*—a series of articles written by Engels and printed in May-June 1843 in the progressive journal *Schweizerischer Republikaner* published by German emigrants (Fröbel and others) in Zurich. They were actually the continuation of Engels' reports on the social and political conflicts in England which he published in the *Rheinische Zeitung* at the end of 1842, soon after his arrival in that country (see this edition, Vol. 2). In early 1843 Engels temporarily interrupted his activity as a journalist owing, on the one hand, to his intensive study of social conditions in England, the English labour movement and English socialist literature and, on the other, to the closure of the *Rheinische Zeitung* in the spring of 1843. Later, especially from the autumn of 1843, Engels began to contribute to the labour and socialist newspapers in England and on the Continent.

Only the fourth article from the series *Letters from London* was published in English, in the collection: Marx and Engels, *Ireland and the Irish Question*, Moscow, 1971. p. 379

[138] The *Anti-Corn Law League*—see Note 40. p. 379

[139] The *People's Charter*, containing the demands of the Chartists, was published on May 8, 1838, in the form of a bill to be submitted to Parliament. It consisted of six points: universal suffrage (for men over 21), annual parliaments, vote by ballot, equal electoral districts, abolition of the property qualifications for M. P.s, and remuneration of M.P.s. p. 379

[140] The English edition of Strauss' book *Das Leben Jesu* was put out by Hetherington Publishers in 1842 in weekly instalments. p. 380

[141] Graham's Bill "For Regulating the Employment of Children and Young Persons in Factories, and for the Better Education of Children in Factory Districts" was submitted to the House of Commons on March 7, 1843 (see *Hansard's Parliamentary Debates*: Third series, Vol. LXVII, Second Volume of the Session, London, 1843, p. 422 sqq.). p. 381

[142] Engels quotes from an article in the *Allgemeine Zeitung* No. 110, April 20, 1843, datelined: "London, 13 April". p. 382

[143] The *National Charter Association*, founded in July 1840, was the first mass workers' party in the history of the labour movement, numbering up to 50 thousand members in the years of the rise of the Chartist movement. The lack of ideological and tactical unity among its members and the petty-bourgeois ideology of the majority of the Chartist leaders affected the activities of the Association. After the defeat of Chartism in 1848, the Association declined and it ceased its activity in the 1850s. p. 383

[144] The editorial board of the *Schweizerische Republikaner* gave the following note to this passage: "This comprises 1,767,500 Rhenish Fl., a sum which, according to our continental notions of 'the poor' is scarcely probable." p. 384

[145] The reference is apparently to the project to establish a special fund for buying plots of land and distributing them among workers. This plan was proposed by

the Chartist leader Feargus O'Connor as early as 1838; he tried more than once to put it into effect; in 1845, with this aim in view, he founded the Chartist Land Co-operative Society, which was also a failure. p. 384

[146] No article by Engels on this subject was published in the *Schweizerische Republikaner*. Later Engels wrote about the Chartists' attitude towards the Anti-Corn Law League in his book *The Condition of the Working-Class in England* (Chapter "Labour Movements", see this edition, Vol. 4). p. 384

[147] The reference is to the following passage from Robert Owen's work *The Marriage System of the New Moral World*, Leeds, 1838: "I resume the subject of marriage because it is the source of more demoralisation, crime, and misery than any other single cause, with the exception of religion and private property; and these three together form the great trinity of causes of crime and immorality among mankind." (P. 54.) p. 387

[148] An apparent reference to the following editions: J. J. Rousseau, *An Inquiry into the Nature of the Social Contract, or Principles of Political Right*, 184 [...]; [Holbach,] *System of Nature*, London, 1817. Announcements of popular and cheap editions of the classics of French philosophy were published in Owen's weekly *The New Moral World*. p. 387

[149] The *Act of Union* with England was imposed on Ireland by the English Government after the suppression of the Irish rebellion in 1798. The Union, which came into force on January 1, 1801, abolished an autonomous Irish Parliament and made Ireland still more dependent on England. The demand for the repeal of the Union became a most popular watchword in Ireland after the 1820s. However, the Irish liberals who were at the head of the national liberation movement (O'Connell and others) considered the agitation for the repeal of the Union only as a means of obtaining concessions for the Irish bourgeoisie and landowners from the English Government. In 1835 O'Connell came to an agreement with the English Whigs and stopped agitation altogether. Under the impact of the mass movement, however, the Irish liberals were compelled in 1840 to found an Association of Repealers, which they tried to direct onto the path of compromise with the English ruling classes. p. 389

[150] The *principal tenant*—a middleman who leased land directly from the landowner and then let it in small plots to subtenants, who in their turn often parcelled out these plots and let them too. p. 390

[151] The second Chartist petition demanding the adoption of the People's Charter was written by the Executive Committee of the National Charter Association and submitted to Parliament in May 1842. It also demanded for Ireland the right to annul the forced Act of Union of 1801. Despite this, the Irish liberals, far from supporting the Chartists' agitation, took a hostile attitude towards the Chartists. p. 391

[152] With the article "Progress of Social Reform on the Continent" Engels started contributing to the London socialist weekly *The New Moral World: and Gazette of the Rational Society* founded by Robert Owen. The article was supplied with notes (reproduced at the end of this volume). Almost at the same time the article was published in an abridged form in the Chartist newspaper *The Northern Star* Nos. 313 and 315, November 11 and 25, 1843.

The article was welcomed in English proletarian and socialist circles. The editor of the weekly, Fleming, noted in 1844 that the English readers had got to know some representatives of continental socialism, in particular Wilhelm Weitling, thanks to the appearance at the end of the previous year of a series of articles ably written by a German living in England (*The New Moral World*, 1844, No. 14, p. 110). The editorial board of *The Northern Star* assessed Engels' article as "an interesting ... exposition of '*Continental Communism*' from the pen of one who was master of his subject, because he knew the facts with which he made the public acquainted" (*The Northern Star* No. 386, May 4, 1844).

Engels continued to contribute to the organ of the English Owenists after he left England in August 1844 up to May 1845. p. 392

[153] The English translation of Buonarroti's book was published in London in 1836 under the title *Buonarroti's History of Babeuf's Conspiracy for Equality; with the Author's Reflections on the Causes and Character of the French Revolution, and His Estimate of the Leading Men and Events of that Epoch*. The translation was made by Bronterre O'Brien, one of the leaders and theoreticians of Chartism.
p. 393

[154] The reference is to the group of English Utopian Socialists who in 1842 founded the colony-commune Concordium in Ham Common near London; followers of the English mystic J. P. Greaves, the Ham Common Socialists preached moral self-perfection and an ascetic way of life. The colony did not survive long. p. 394

[155] The editors of *The New Moral World* supplied the following note to this passage: "A few years since we gave a complete exposition of the system in a series of articles in this Journal." The author of the note meant two large series of articles: "Socialism in France. Charles Fourier" and "Fourierism"; the first was published in *The New Moral World* in 1839 (Nos. 45-46, 48, 49), the second in 1839-40 (Nos. 53, 55, 57, 61-63, 71, 73-75). p. 395

[156] The editors of *The New Moral World* gave the following note to this passage: "Now entitled *Démocratie Pacifique*." Besides the daily newspaper *La Démocratie Pacifique*, published since August 1843, the Fourierists continued to publish *La Phalange* as a theoretical journal. p. 396

[157] Engels refers here to a series of armed actions by the French proletariat directed against the regime of the bourgeois July monarchy and also to the workers' active participation in the uprisings led by the republican secret societies. The major events in the 1830s were: the uprisings of Lyons workers at the end of November 1831 and in April 1834, and also republican revolts in Paris on June 5, 1832, April 13-14, 1834, and May 12, 1839, the main participants in which were workers. p. 396

[158] "*Travailleurs Égalitaires*"—a secret society of the French Communists-Babouvists, which sprang up in 1840 and consisted mainly of workers. *Humanitarians*—a secret society of Communists-Babouvists, who in 1841 rallied around the newspaper *L'Humanitaire*. These two societies were under the ideological influence of Théodore Dézamy and belonged to the revolutionary and materialist trend in French utopian communism. p. 397

[159] The editors of *The New Moral World* gave the following note to this sentence: "It is proper to reiterate that the Icarian Communists, in their organ, the *Populaire*, have, in the strongest manner, disowned all participation in secret societies, and affixed the names of their leaders to public documents, expositions of their principles and objects." p. 397

160 *Harmony*—the name of a communistic colony founded by the followers of Robert Owen in Hampshire in 1841; the colony survived till the beginning of 1846.
p. 398

161 The public debate between J. Watts, who was at that time an active proponent of Owenism, and the Chartist speaker J. Bairstow took place in Manchester on October 11, 12 and 13, 1843. Engels apparently attended it.
p. 398

162 Münzer's communist revolutionary ideas, which are mentioned below, were expounded in a series of pamphlets issued by him on the eve and during the Peasant War in Germany (1524-25), in particular in the proclamation: "Ausgedrückte Entblössung des falschen Glaubens der ungetreuen Welt durchs Zeugnis des Evangelions Lucae, vorgetragen der elenden erbärmlichen Christenheit zur Erinnerung ihres Irrsals", published in the autumn of 1524 in Mülhausen. Later Engels called this pamphlet "a highly inciting paper" (see F. Engels, *The Peasant War in Germany*, Ch. II; this edition, Vol. 10).
p. 400

163 Engels' statement is based on the prospectus of Wilhelm Weitling's book *Das Evangelium der armen Sünder* which was published at that time. The book itself was published only in 1845 in Berne under the title *Das Evangelium eines armen Sünders*.
p. 402

164 The *Federal Diet*—the supreme body of the German Confederation (1815-66) consisting of representatives of the German states; it defended the conservative monarchical regime in Germany.
p. 406

165 The reference is to a letter written by the democratic poet Georg Herwegh to Frederick William IV in which he accused the king of breaking his promise to introduce the freedom of the press and, in particular, of banning the radical monthly *Der deutsche Bote aus der Schweiz*, which was being prepared for printing at the time. Herwegh's letter appeared in the *Leipziger Allgemeine Zeitung* on December 24, 1842; this led to the banning of the newspaper and Herwegh's banishment from Paris. In England the letter was published in *The Times* on January 16, 1843, in *The Morning Herald* on January 17, 1843, and in other newspapers.
p. 406

166 Engels' article on this subject did not appear in *The New Moral World*.   p. 407

167 Edgar Bauer was sentenced to four years' imprisonment for his book *Der Streit der Kritik mit Kirche und Staat*, Charlottenburg, 1843, confiscated by the Prussian Government.
p. 407

168 During his stay in England Engels attended meetings organised by members of the Chartist movement and tried to establish personal contacts with its leaders. In the autumn of 1843 he visited Leeds, where the central Chartist organ, *The Northern Star*, was published at the time, and got acquainted with its editor George Julian Harney, a prominent figure in the revolutionary wing of the Chartist Party. Engels introduced himself, Harney recalled, as a permanent reader of *The Northern Star*, who was very much interested in the Chartist movement. As a result of this meeting Engels started contributing to the Chartist press, but at first only incidentally. On November 11 and 25, 1843, *The Northern Star* reprinted with some abridgements Engels' article "Progress of Social Reform on the Continent" immediately after its first publication in the weekly *The New Moral World*. Two weeks later these notes connected with the above-mentioned article appeared in the Chartist paper. They also appeared in

The New Moral World. In this volume they are published as one article. Closely connected with these is the short report "The Press and the German Despots" published in *The Northern Star* on February 3, 1844 (see this volume, p. 417). Later Engels proposed to the editors that he would systematically contribute to the paper reports about events on the Continent (see his letter to the editor of *The Northern Star*, p. 514 of this volume). From that time on Engels' articles and reports were regularly published in the newspaper. After his departure from England in August 1844 his reports ceased to appear in the paper but were resumed in the autumn of 1845. (In the summer of that year Engels visited England once more and again met Harney.) He contributed to *The Northern Star* till 1850. p. 409

[169] The reference is to the *League of the Just*, a secret revolutionary organisation founded in 1836 by German proletarianised emigrant craftsmen in Paris. Besides France, League branches existed in Germany, England and Switzerland. A great role in their organisation was played by Weitling. Various theories of utopian communism and socialism, in particular Weitlingism, formed the ideological foundation of the League. The emigrant workers of other nationalities also participated in the League's activities. The internationalisation of the League and the evolution of its members' views under the influence of the ideas of Marx and Engels led to its reorganisation into the Communist League in 1847.

By the time of the publication of this article the final verdict of the Weitling case was not yet pronounced. At the end of December 1843, the Supreme Court of Appeal of the Swiss Bund sentenced Weitling to 10 months of imprisonment and 5-year exile from Switzerland on the basis of the appeal of the prosecutor who protested the decision of the court of the Zurich canton.
p. 409

[170] The reference is to the anonymous article *The Communists in Germany* published in *The Times* on December 29, 1843, and reprinted in *The New Moral World* No. 28 on January 6, 1844. Engels cites from this article below. p. 410

[171] The reference is to the Paris uprising of May 12, 1839, prepared by the secret republican socialist *Société des Saisons* headed by Louis Auguste Blanqui and Armand Barbès; the uprising was suppressed by troops and the National Guard. p. 410

[172] *Repealers*—see Note 149. p. 411

[173] Engels alludes to prominent members of the League of the Just: the type-setter Karl Schapper, the watchmaker Joseph Moll and others, connected with the Blanquist secret *Société des Saisons* which organised the Paris uprising of May 12, 1839. Schapper and Moll took part in the uprising, were prosecuted by the French authorities and compelled to leave for England, where they headed local branches of the League. Engels made their acquaintance in the spring of 1843 in London, as he wrote later in his article "On the History of the Communist League". p. 411

[174] On May 27, 1832, a political manifestation took place near the castle of Hambach in Bavarian Pfalz, which was organised by representatives of the German liberal and radical bourgeoisie. Participants of the "Hambach festival" launched an appeal to fight for the unification of Germany, for the bourgeois freedoms and constitutional reforms.

On July 27, 1834, on the occasion of the anniversary of the July revolution in France a large meeting in defence of the idea of German unification was held in Steinhölzli near Berne (Switzerland) on the initiative of the German emigrants. p. 412

[175] *Rebeccaites*—members of the peasant movement in South Wales in 1843-44 demanding the removal of tollgates. The leader of the movement acted under the assumed name of Rebecca, a personage from the Bible. The Rebeccaites acted at night dressed in women's clothes. p. 412

[176] *Voigtland*—the name given to one of the working-class districts in Berlin. *Saint Giles'*—a district of London populated by poor people. p. 415

[177] The double issue of the *Deutsch-Französische Jahrbücher* (No. 1-2) was put out at the end of February 1844. p. 416

[178] The Final Protocol of the 1834 Vienna Conference of the ministers of the states of the German Confederation envisaged measures for suppressing the liberal and democratic movement in Germany, stricter censorship and mutual support of the states in the struggle against the liberal and radical opposition. This Protocol as well as the decisions of the Federal Diet (the supreme body of the German Confederation) issued in June-July 1832 on the prohibition of popular societies and meetings and also on rendering military aid to those German states which were in danger of an uprising of their subjects was the answer of the ruling circles of Germany to the unrest in the country caused by the July revolution of 1830 in France. The chief inspirer of these police measures was the Austrian Chancellor Metternich.

The Protocol of the Vienna Conference and the reactionary decision of the 1819 Karlsbad Conference of the representatives of the German states, which had been kept secret, were published by the German liberal publicist and historian K. G. Welcker in his book *Wichtige Urkunden für den Rechtszustand der deutschen Nation*, Mannheim, 1844. Even before the book was put out the contents of the Protocol had been known to democratic circles and published in the German emigrant press, in particular in the Paris *Vorwärts!* in January 1844. The text was also reprinted in the *Deutsch-Französische Jahrbücher* at the end of February 1844. p. 417

[179] The reference is to the trial of O'Connell and eight other leaders of the Repeal movement which started in January 1844. Taking advantage of the waverings among the Irish liberal leaders fearing the scope of the movement, the Tory government wanted to deal a smashing blow at the movement by staging this trial. In February 1844 O'Connell and his followers were sentenced to various terms of imprisonment up to twelve months. However, under the impact of mass protest the House of Lords soon quashed the sentence. p. 417

[180] The *Outlines of a Critique of Political Economy* is the first economic work written by Engels. It was one of the principal works published in the *Deutsch-Französische Jahrbücher*, and together with the programme articles written by Marx it determined the journal's communist trend. Marx was very much interested in this work of Engels and wrote a summary of it (see pp. 375-76 of this volume). Later on he mentioned this work more than once in his writings. In the Preface to the first edition of *A Contribution to the Critique of Political Economy* (1859) Marx called it a "brilliant essay on the critique of economic categories". Despite the fact that the work contained some traits of immaturity which are inevitable at the earlier stage of the formation of ideas: the influence

of Feuerbach's abstract humanism which had not yet been completely overcome, a one-sided appraisal of the labour theory of value, etc.— shortcomings about which Engels wrote in a general way in his letter to Wilhelm Liebknecht on April 13, 1876—the work contained profound anticipation of some propositions in the new, materialist economic teaching.

The work also produced a strong impression on other representatives of progressive circles. For example, the Berlin physician Julius Waldeck, stressing in his letter to Johann Jacoby the maturity and boldness of the ideas expounded in this work, exclaimed: "Engels has worked a real miracle!" (G. Mayer, *Friedrich Engels. Eine Biographie*, Bd. 1, S. 171.)

In English the *Outlines of a Critique of Political Economy* was first published as an appendix to the book: Karl Marx, *Economic and Philosophic Manuscripts of 1844*, Foreign Languages Publishing House, Moscow, 1959. p. 418

[181] The *Anti-Corn Law League*—see Note 40. p. 428

[182] The reference is to the New York fire of December 16, 1835. p. 434

[183] Several pamphlets signed "Marcus" appeared in England, in particular: *On the Possibility of Limiting Populousness*, printed by John Hill, Black Horse Court, Fleet Street, 1838, and *The Theory of Painless Extinction*, the publication of which was announced in *The New Moral World* on August 29, 1840. They expounded the Malthusian misanthropic theory of population. The principal ideas of "Marcus" were also summed up in the anonymous pamphlet: *An Essay on Populousness, printed for private circulation; printed for the author*, 1838. p. 437

[184] The reference is to the Poor Law Amendment act of 1834, under which the poor were placed in workhouses named by the people "Poor Law Bastilles". The repeal of this law was one of the main demands of the Chartists.

A characterisation of this law is given in Marx's work "Critical Marginal Notes on the Article 'The King of Prussia and Social Reform. By a Prussian'" (see pp. 194-95 of this volume). p. 437

[185] It is difficult to judge by the available material to which literary plan this statement refers. Possibly Engels had in mind a work on English social history which he intended to write and which he mentions at the end of this work (see p. 443 of this volume). In his series of articles, *The Condition of England*, which is a brief preliminary outline of this work, Engels characterises the economic teaching of Adam Smith and the utilitarianism of Jeremy Bentham and James Mill as a theoretical expression of the domination of private property, egoism, alienation of man, which represent the consummation of the principles following from the Christian world outlook and world order (see pp. 485-87 of this volume). It is probable, however, that he had in mind a plan of some special work on economics. A year later, in particular, Engels worked on a pamphlet about the German economist List (see his letter to Marx of November 19, 1844). p. 439

[186] Engels has in mind a work on English social history which he planned to write and for which he collected material during his stay in England (November 1842-August 1844). He intended to devote a whole chapter of this work to the condition of the working class in England. Later he changed his plans and decided to write a special work on the English proletariat, which he did upon his return to Germany. His book *The Condition of the Working-Class in England* was published in Leipzig in 1845 (see this edition, Vol. 4). p. 443

[187] Engels intended to write *The Condition of England* as a series of articles for the *Deutsch-Französische Jahrbücher*. The critical analysis of Carlyle's book *Past and Present* was the beginning of it, a sort of introduction, which was to be followed, according to the author's plans, by the main sections under the same general title (see p. 468 of this volume). However, two other articles written by Engels on the same subject for the *Deutsch-Französische Jahrbücher* were never printed in the journal as its publication ceased. These articles were published in two parts in the Paris *Vorwärts!* some months later, after Engels met Marx in Paris at the end of August 1844 and with the help of his friend became an editor of and a contributor to the newspaper.

The part of the work published in the *Deutsch-Französische Jahrbücher* aroused considerable interest, as Engels himself stated, among the readers in Germany (see Engels' letter to Marx of early October 1844).

Engels cites from Thomas Carlyle's book in his own translation into German. In so doing he often abridges the text and does not always mark the omissions by leaders. In some cases he merely renders the contents of some passage or another; the italics in quotations as a rule belong to Engels. Engels gives no references to page numbers; for the readers' convenience page numbers are given in footnotes in this edition. p. 444

[188] The reference is to the repeal in 1828 of the Test Act of 1673 and some other acts under which only members of the Church of England could occupy governmental or elective posts, and also to the subsequent abolition of some religious restrictions and of the privileges of the top aristocracy (the Act of Emancipation of 1829, which granted Catholics the right to be elected to Parliament; the Reform Act of 1832). Engels wrote about this in greater detail in the last of the series of his articles *The Condition of England* (see pp. 490-91 of this volume). p. 445

[189] Concerning the English translation of David Strauss' book see Note 140. p. 447

[190] The *Reform Act* passed by the British Parliament in June 1832 was directed against the political monopoly of the landed and financial aristocracy and made membership of Parliament open to representatives of the industrial bourgeoisie. The proletariat and the petty bourgeoisie, which formed the main force in the struggle for the reform, did not get any electoral rights. p. 447

[191] In August 1842 Manchester was the centre of Chartist agitation and of a powerful strike movement. p. 450

[192] The *People's Charter*—see Note 139. p. 450

[193] The *Corn Laws*—see Note 40. p. 453

[194] *Laissez-faire, laissez-aller*—the formula of the economists who advocated free trade and non intervention by the state in the sphere of economic relations. p. 454

[195] By the "*great week*" is meant the bourgeois July revolution of 1830 in France. The major events took place between July 27 and August 2. p. 455

[196] *Morison's pills*—pills invented by the English quack James Morison and widely advertised by him in the mid-twenties of the nineteenth century as a remedy for all ailments. They were prepared from the juice of certain tropical plants. p. 456

[197] Engels has in mind the last period of Schelling's life and activity when, having renounced many of his progressive ideas, he started preaching a mystical philosophy of open irrationalism. At that time Schelling was invited to Berlin University to oppose the influence of the Hegelian school (end of 1841-42). For more detail see Engels' *Schelling and Revelation* (this edition, Vol. 2). p. 461

[198] *Home-colonies*—the name Robert Owen gave to his communist societies.
p. 466

[199] Engels expressed the same hope for subsequent evolution of Carlyle's views in the radical direction in his note to the concluding chapter of his book: *The Condition of the Working-Class in England* (1845) (see this edition, Vol. 4). However, his hopes were not justified and he decided to make the following addition to this note in the second German edition (1892): "But the February Revolution made him [Carlyle] an out-and-out reactionary. His righteous wrath against the Philistines turned into sullen Philistine grumbling at the tide of history that cast him ashore." p. 467

[200] This and the following article are the continuation of *The Condition of England* published in the *Deutsch-Französische Jahrbücher* (see Note 187). Both articles were evidently written not later than February-March 1844, as can be judged by their contents and, in particular, the references to some facts (rejection of the motion to publish parliamentary minutes, O'Connell's trial) as events that had taken place several weeks before (see pp. 500 and 506 of this volume). It is possible that Engels ceased writing this series because of the closure of the *Deutsch-Französische Jahrbücher*. From the last lines of the preceding article we see that the central theme of this series was to be the condition of the working class in England.

In English the article was first published in the book: Karl Marx and Frederick Engels, *Articles on Britain*, Progress Publishers, Moscow, 1971.
p. 469

[201] The reference is to the coalition wars of European states against revolutionary and Napoleonic France lasting from 1792 till 1815. England was an active member of these coalitions. p. 469

[202] According to later historical investigations, in the 15th-17th centuries copyholders (a category of peasants holding land by copy, life and hereditary tenants who paid feudal rent) comprised the majority of the English peasants who had freed themselves from serf bondage. Modern science uses the terms *villeins, bordars* and *cottars* to denote the various categories of serf peasants in medieval England. p. 474

[203] The *People's Charter*—see Note 139. p. 476

[204] In the Introduction to the second German edition (1892) of his book *The Condition of the Working-Class in England* (see this edition, Vol. 4), Engels made the following addition to the analogous note: "The historical outline of the industrial revolution given above is not exact in certain details; but in 1843-44 no better sources were available." The more precise information gained from later investigations includes, in particular, the fact that Arkwright was not the inventor of the spinning-jenny but used a number of inventions made by others. Judging by the corresponding passages in *The Condition of the Working-Class in England*, Engels here made use of other books besides Porter's work: E. Baines, *History of the Cotton Manufacture of Great Britain*, London, 1835; A. Ure,

The Cotton Manufacture of Great Britain, Systematically Investigated and Illustrated, Vols. 1-2, London, 1836. p. 485

[205] The reference is to the democratic correspondence societies organised in various English towns in the 90s of the eighteenth century under the influence of the French revolution. The first—the London Correspondence Society—was founded in 1792. In the autumn of 1793 an attempt was made to unite these organisations by convening a congress in Edinburgh which assumed the name of the Convention. The government answered with reprisals; some members of the Convention were condemned to penal servitude. In 1794 the leaders of the London Correspondence Society (Thomas Hardy, Horne Tooke and others) were arrested. By the end of the 90s the activity of the correspondence societies ceased; however, their ideas and traditions had a great influence on the further development of the radical movement in England, especially in the period of intensive agitation for the democratic reorganisation of its political system in 1816-23. p. 487

[206] In English this article was published in the book: Karl Marx and Frederick Engels, *Articles on Britain,* Progress Publishers, Moscow, 1971. p. 489

[207] The *Test Act* of 1673 demanded recognition of the dogmas of the Church of England by persons occupying governmental posts. At first directed against attempts to re-establish Catholicism, this Act was subsequently applied against various religious sects and trends which deviated from the dogmas of the Established Church.

The *Habeas Corpus Act* was passed by the English Parliament in 1679. Concerning this Act see p. 506 of this volume.

The *Bill of Rights,* passed by the English Parliament in 1689, restricted the rights of the King in Parliament and confirmed the compromise between the landed aristocracy and the top financial and commercial bourgeoisie which had been achieved as a result of the "Glorious Revolution" of 1688. p. 491

[208] The *Magna Carta Libertatum*—a document signed by the English King John Lackland on June 15, 1215, under pressure from the rebellious barons. It restricted the rights of the King, mainly in the interests of the big feudal lords, and contained some concessions to the knights and to the towns.

The *Reform Act*—see Note 190. p. 492

[209] The reference is to the mass campaign for the electoral reform, the peak year being 1831. The Reform Act was passed as a result of this campaign. (Concerning the Reform Act see Note 190.) p. 496

[210] The reference is to Thomas Duncombe's speech in the House of Commons on August 9, 1832 (see *Hansard's Parliamentary Debates,* 1832, Vol. XIV, pp. 1159-1161). p. 497

[211] The *Act of Emancipation*—see Note 188. p. 498

[212] The reference is to the rejection by the House of Commons on February 12, 1844, of the motion by the radical M.P.s, Christie, Duncombe and others, concerning publication of minutes of the parliamentary debates (see *Hansard's Parliamentary Debates,* 1844, Vol. LXXII, pp. 580-600). p. 500

[213] The *Thirty-Nine Articles*—the symbol of faith of the Church of England passed by the English Parliament in 1571. p. 501

²¹⁴ The *Corporation Act,* passed in 1661, demanded recognition of the dogmas of the Church of England by persons holding elective posts (mostly in municipal administration). It was repealed in 1828.
Concerning the repeal of the Test Act see Note 188. p. 501

²¹⁵ See Note 188. p. 502

²¹⁶ The reference is to Thomas Gibson's speech in the House of Commons on February 14, 1844 (see *Hansard's Parliamentary Debates,* 1844, Vol. LXXII, p. 798). p. 503

²¹⁷ *Repealers*—see Note 149. p. 504

²¹⁸ The reference is to the banning by the English authorities of the mass meeting in Clontarf fixed by the Irish Repealers for October 5, 1843. The government concentrated troops in the region to prevent the protest demonstration. In these circumstances O'Connell and his followers decided to cancel the meeting; this encouraged the English authorities, who regarded it as a sign of weakness, and they decided to bring the Irish leaders to trial. The trial took place in January-February 1844 (concerning the trial see Note 179). p. 505

²¹⁹ The reference is to the National Charter Association, concerning which see Note 143. p. 505

²²⁰ The *Anti-Corn Law League*—see Note 40. p. 505

²²¹ The reference is to the trials of the leaders of the National Charter Association and the participants in the strike movement of August 1842, ordered by the authorities in various towns of England after the suppression of the movement. There were mass reprisals. Out of more than 1,500 persons (mostly workers) arrested more than a half were put on trial. Sentences as a rule were very severe. Thus in Stafford (October 1842) fifty accused were sentenced to transportation (many of them for life) and 180 to various terms of imprisonment. A large group of Chartist leaders headed by Feargus O'Connor were also sentenced, their trial being held in March 1843 in Lancaster (later the sentence was quashed owing to mass pressure). Besides the towns mentioned by Engels trials were held in Chester, Liverpool and some other places in the autumn of 1842. p. 506

²²² *Carolina*—the criminal code of the Emperor Charles V (*Constitutio criminalis Carolina*) passed by the Reichstag in Regensburg in 1532; it was marked by the extreme severity of the penalties which it prescribed. p. 509

²²³ This passage proves that Engels intended to continue the series *The Condition of England* (see Note 200). He evidently planned to describe the condition of the English working class and examine the social, including labour, legislation that existed in England. p. 511

²²⁴ This letter written by Engels to the editor of *The Northern Star* is incomplete: only the part of it which was published in the newspaper's editorial article on May 4, 1844, "The 'Movement', at Home and Abroad", has survived. Without mentioning the author's name, the editor of *The Northern Star* introduced him to the readers as the author of an essay on "Continental Communism" (they had in mind Engels' article: "Progress of Social Reform on the Continent" which had been reprinted in the newspaper). Engels' offer to contribute to the newspaper met the intentions of its editor Harney, who wanted to impart an international character to the newspaper by extending information on foreign

affairs, as the editorial article mentioned above stated. From that moment Engels worked as an official reporter of the Chartist newspaper. The same issue carried Engels' note on the situation in Prussia marked: "From our own Correspondent", which (sometimes with slight alterations) was used in respect of all the material he sent to *The Northern Star*. Articles written by Engels were printed in the section: "Movements Abroad" under the editorial headings denoting the country the information referred to ("Germany", "Prussia", "Bavaria", "Poland", "Russia", "Switzerland", "France", etc.). Sometimes several articles by Engels were printed in the same issue under different headings (e. g., on May 18 and 25, 1844). It is possible that in such cases the editors themselves divided the material of a single report into several parts. p. 514

225 In the course of his further study of the position in Germany Engels came to the conclusion that in the historical conditions obtaining the establishment of a centralised and not of a federal republic would meet the aims of the consistent struggle against political disunion and the remnants of medieval particularism in all spheres of social life. During the revolution of 1848-49 Marx and Engels, in contraposition to the petty-bourgeois republicans, who adhered to the principle of federalism, upheld the demand of transforming Germany into a single democratic republic. p. 514

226 The work under this title was not published by David Strauss. p. 517

227 The reference is apparently to the following pamphlets by Adam Gurowski: *La vérité sur la Russie*, 1834 and *La civilisation et la Russie*, 1840. p. 519

228 One of the public buildings of Ludwig of Bavaria, built in 1841 near Regensburg, was named by him "Walhalla" after the legendary posthumous abode of the German mythological heroes. The palace contained a collection of sculptures of famous men in Germany. The King himself wrote a guide book for it: *Walhalla's Genossen, geschildert durch König Ludwig den Ersten von Bayern, dem Gründer Walhalla's*, München, 1842. Poems written by Ludwig of Bavaria provide a sample of meaningless and pretentious poetry; they were published in 1842. p. 522

229 The reference is to the wars waged by the tsarist government against the peoples of the North Caucasus (Adyghei, Chechens, Avars, Lezghins, etc.) fighting for their independence. In the 1820s the liberation struggle of these peoples against the tsarist colonisers and the arbitrary rule of the local feudal lords was headed by Shamil, who was proclaimed Imam of Daghestan in 1834. The movement reached its peak in the 40s of the nineteenth century and was suppressed in 1859. p. 524

230 The canton of Vaud (German: Waadt) was known for its democratic traditions. p. 525

231 Prior to 1798 Switzerland was a union of small autonomous cantons in which political sway was exercised by the mountain patriarchal cantons headed by an aristocratic oligarchy. In 1798 a Helvetic Republic dependent on France was set up in Switzerland which was at the time occupied by the troops of the French Directory. Political privileges of the old cantons were abolished. However, the Treaty of Alliance of 1814 was approved by the Congress of Vienna, 1814-15, which restored the former sovereignty of the cantons; in the majority of them the clerical aristocratic elements again came to the fore. p. 526

232 In 1830 the movement for democratic reforms in Switzerland became more widespread under the influence of the July revolution in France. In the twelve

north-western cantons, which were more advanced, the power went to the bourgeoisie, but its aspirations for the unification of the country encountered resistance from the backward mountain cantons. p. 526

[233] This prevision of Engels came true in three years. In November 1847 a civil war broke out in Switzerland between the aristocratic cantons united into a separate confederation known as the Sonderbund (the treaty was concluded at the end of 1845) and the north-western bourgeois cantons, in the course of which the Sonderbund was defeated. Bourgeois reforms were carried out in the Swiss cantons. Under the Constitution of 1848 Switzerland became a confederation.

In 1844, under the influence of the ruling clerical aristocratic circles the canton of Valais entered the Sonderbund. Radicals in Valais again came to power after the Sonderbund broke up.

Engels' article "The Civil War in Switzerland" was a response to the events of 1847 (see this edition, Vol. 6). p. 526

[234] During the July revolution of 1830, which led to the downfall of the Bourbon dynasty, Jacques Laffitte, a representative of moderate liberal circles of the financial bourgeoisie and a member of the Chamber, which assumed power in Paris, helped to secure the accession to the throne of Louis Philippe, the Duke of Orléans. p. 527

[235] The liberation struggle of the Algerians led by Emir Abd-el-Kader against the French colonisers lasted with interruptions from 1832 to 1847. Taking advantage of their military superiority, the French conquered Abd-el-Kader's state in Western Algeria in the period between 1839 and 1844. However, Abd-el-Kader continued the struggle, resorting to guerrilla warfare and relying on the help of the Sultan of Morocco. When the latter was defeated in the Franco-Moroccan war in 1844, Abd-el-Kader hid in the oases of the Sahara. An uprising in Western Algeria in 1845-47, which was suppressed by the French colonisers, was the last stage of this struggle. p. 528

[236] *Caliphs*—local rulers in Abd-el-Kader's state, subject to the central government. p. 529

[237] The reference is to the Divorce Bill drafted in 1842 by Friedrich Savigny, one of the founders of the reactionary historical school of law, who from 1842 to 1848 was High Chancellor of Prussia. p. 530

[238] Although the Divorce Bill was kept secret, the *Rheinische Zeitung* edited by Marx published the Bill on October 20, 1842, thus initiating a broad discussion on the subject. On December 19, Marx's article "The Divorce Bill" (see this edition, Vol. 1), in which he criticised the Bill, was published. The publication of the Bill in the *Rheinische Zeitung* was one of the reasons for the persecution of the paper, which finally led to its banning in March 1843. p. 530

[239] *Landtags*— provincial and local assemblies of estates established in Prussia in 1823; they consisted in the main of representatives of the nobility; urban and village communities had very small representation. Landtags were convened by the King and their functions were restricted to discussion of bills and to questions of local economy and administration. p. 530

[240] This report had the following paragraph added to it by the editors: "In addition to the above, we give the following paragraph from the *Sun*:

"'We learn from Breslau on the 9th inst. that the weavers have returned to their work after having obtained an increase of wages. They burst in, during their excursions, the doors of several wood-rangers' houses, and carried off the fowling-pieces and ammunition, but without touching anything else.'" p. 531

[241] On the song of Silesian weavers, sung by the participants of the uprising of June 4-6, 1844, see Note 44. p. 532

[242] This draft of the young Engels' verse drama *Cola di Rienzi* only became known after Volume 2, containing his early works, letters and literary experiments, had already gone to press. This draft is therefore being published in the present volume as a supplement, although chronologically it belongs to Volume 2.

The draft manuscript was discovered among the posthumous papers of the German poet Adolf Schults, a native of Elberfeld, by Michael Knieriem, director of Frederick Engels House in Wuppertal. Schults belonged to a group of Wuppertal writers and art-lovers which included many of Engels' fellow pupils from the Elberfeld high school who kept in touch with him during his residence (from July 1838 to March 1841) in Bremen, where he was gaining practical experience with a commercial firm and was also engaged in literary activities. Knieriem arranged the first publication of this drama in co-operation with Hans Pelger, director of Karl Marx House in Trier (see Michael Knieriem, *Friedrich Engels: Cola di Rienzi. Ein unbekannter dramatischer Entwurf. Herausgegeben vom Friedrich-Engels-Haus, Wuppertal, und Karl-Marx-Haus, Trier*, Trier, 1974). The draft was evidently intended for an opera libretto, as may be gathered from a letter of September 30, 1840, sent by Engels' schoolfriend Carl de Haas to Schults and other Elberfeld writers in which there is a reference to Engels' intention of writing the text of an opera at the request of one of his Elberfeld friends. This is also borne out by the style of the work, parts of which are specially adapted for performance (duets, trios, and settings for chorus), and in which provision is made for the insertion of musical episodes. The draft was in all probability written between the end of 1840 and the beginning of 1841, since one page of the manuscript bears a short passage in Hebrew from the Old Testament which was also quoted in a letter of February 22, 1841, from Engels to Friedrich Graeber (see present edition, Vol. 2, p. 526).

Engels took the plot for his drama from events in Rome in the middle of the 14th century—the struggle which developed between the feudal aristocracy on the one hand and the merchant and artisan population on the other. In May 1347, as a result of a popular uprising, a republic was proclaimed in Rome with "people's tribune" Cola di Rienzi at its head. With Rienzi, firm measures against the nobility and a desire to affirm the principle of popular sovereignty and achieve the unification of Italy were combined with fantastic notions about the restoration of ancient Rome's grandeur and world domination. Banished from Rome at the end of 1347 as a result of intrigues by the feudal magnates, Rienzi was reinstated in August 1354 with the aid of mercenary troops commanded by foreign *condottieri*. The people rose against Rienzi, however, resenting his despotic behaviour, his ambitiousness, and the increased tax burden, a measure which was forced on him by the costs of paying the mercenaries and conducting the war with the aristocrats. On October 8, 1354, an insurrection flared up against him and he was killed. The action in Engels' drama deals with the second period of Rienzi's rule.

The manuscript is a rough draft. In several places, there are author's corrections, erasures and additions in the margin. On one page, the initials "F. E." and Engels' signature are to be seen in the margin. Some drawings made by the author on several pages refer to the plot of the drama, while others are unconnected with it (there are also some cartoons). The last pages contain a variant of the beginning of Act One, Scene One (in the present edition, this has been printed after the corresponding first version and has been separated from it, as from the continuation, by a horizontal line). p. 537

[243] In mid-June 1844 Jenny Marx with her baby girl Jenny born on May 1 left Paris, where she had lived with her husband since October 1843, for Trier to visit her mother Caroline von Westphalen. Jenny with her daughter and a wet-nurse returned to Paris in September 1844. p. 575

[244] At the end of 1843 Caroline von Westphalen left Kreuznach, where she had lived after the death of her husband, Ludwig von Westphalen, for Trier. Apparently, she lived in Trier for a time in the house of the tax-collector Wettendorf. p. 576

[245] An allusion to the reverberations of the Silesian uprising of weavers of June 4-6, 1844. In Breslau, the capital of Silesia (Polish: Wrocław), new popular disturbances took place on June 6 and 7. p. 577

[246] Jenny had in mind the strained relations between Marx and his mother caused by Marx's refusal to enter the civil service and his choice, after graduating from the University, of a type of activity which from his mother's point of view could bring neither material welfare nor a stable social position. The fame brought to Marx by the publication of the *Deutsch-Französische Jahrbücher* and a certain improvement in his material condition made Henriette Marx slightly change her attitude towards Marx and his family. p. 577

[247] An apparent reference to the work Marx was planning to write on Bruno Bauer and other Young Hegelians (see Note 30). This plan was realised later, when together with Engels he wrote *The Holy Family, or Critique of Critical Criticism* (see this edition, Vol. 4). p. 578

[248] Only that part of this letter has survived which Marx decided to publish in the Paris newspaper *Vorwärts!*, without mentioning the author's name, under the title "From the Letter of a German Lady". In his letter to Ludwig Feuerbach of August 11, 1844, he wrote that the excerpt had been taken from his wife's letter (see this volume, p. 357). The publication of this letter was prompted by an attempt made on King Frederick William IV on July 26, 1844, by H. L. Tschech (see Note 46). p. 580

[249] Marx's letters to his wife mentioned here have not been found. p. 581

[250] The reference is to the traditional religious rites connected with the cult of the so-called Holy Coat of Trier (supposedly stripped off Christ before his crucifixion) kept in Trier Catholic Cathedral. This cult attracted many pilgrims from other German towns. p. 583

[251] The German radical publicist Georg Jung and other friends of Marx in Cologne took upon themselves to sell a certain number of copies of the *Deutsch-Französische Jahrbücher* which Marx had received instead of author's emoluments and instead of wages for his work as an editor. Some of the copies sent from Switzerland by boat were confiscated by the Baden authorities. On July 31, 1844, Jung wrote to Marx that he had posted Marx 800 francs in compensation of the confiscated copies. p. 583

NAME INDEX

A

Abd-el-Kader (c. 1808-1883) — Emir of Algeria, one of the Arab leaders in the national liberation wars of 1832-47 in Morocco and Algeria against the French conquerors.— 528, 529
Abd ur-Rahman II (c. 1790-1859) — Emperor of Morocco (1822-59).— 528
Aeschylus (525-456 B.C.) — Greek dramatist.— 179, 307
Alexander of Macedon (Alexander the Great) (356-323 B.C.) — soldier and statesman of the ancient world.— 489
Alison, Sir Archibald (1792-1867) — Scottish historian and economist, Tory.— 436, 438, 440, 452
Alison, William Pulteney (1790-1859) — professor of medicine at Edinburgh University, Tory.— 451
Anacharsis (c. 600 B.C.) — Greek philosopher, Scythian by birth.— 180
Arago, Dominique François (1786-1853) — French astronomer, physicist and mathematician; politician, Republican.— 353
Arcelin — military surgeon, served in the French army in Algeria (1841-43).— 529
Aristotle (384-322 B.C.) — Greek philosopher.— 137, 305
Arkwright, Sir Richard (1732-1792) — English industrialist, introduced spinning-looms in production that were later named after him.— 442, 479, 480, 482
Ashley (Cooper, Anthony Ashley, 7th Earl of Shaftesbury) (1801-1885) — English politician, Tory philanthropist.— 447
Aumale, Henri Eugène Philippe Louis d'Orléans, Duc d' (1822-1897) — son of King of the French Louis Philippe; took part in the conquest of Algeria in the forties, one of the commanders in the French army.— 528, 529

B

Babeuf, François Noel (Gracchus) (1760-1797) — French revolutionary, advocate of utopian equalitarian communism, organiser of the conspiracy of "equals".— 393, 396, 397
Bacon, Francis, Baron Verulam, Viscount St. Albans (1561-1626) — English philosopher, naturalist and historian.— 193, 472, 490
Bairstow, Jonathan (born c. 1819) — participant in the Chartist movement, delegate to the Chartist Convention (1842).— 398
Barbaroux, Charles Jean Marie (1767-1794) — leading figure in the French

Revolution, deputy to the Convention, Girondist.— 364, 365, 369, 370

Barère de Vieuzac, Bertrand (1755-1841)— French lawyer, leading figure in the French Revolution, deputy to the Convention, supported the Jacobins; subsequently took part in the Thermidorian coup.— 197, 362, 369

Barmby, John Goodwyn (1820-1881)— English publicist, Christian Socialist, founder of the Communist Propaganda Society.— 414

Bauer, Bruno (1809-1882)—German philosopher, one of the Young Hegelians.— 146-50, 152, 154, 157, 160, 168-72, 231, 232, 327, 356, 406, 462, 578

Bauer, Edgar (1820-1886)—German philosopher and publicist, Young Hegelian, brother and supporter of Bruno Bauer.— 407

Bazire, Claude (1764-1794)—leading figure in the French Revolution, deputy to the Convention, Danton's supporter.— 372

Beaumont de la Bonninière, Gustave Auguste de (1802-1866)—French liberal publicist and politician, author of a number of works on slavery in the United States of America.— 150, 151, 159, 161, 171

Beltz, Peter—Kreuznach tailor, witness to the signing of the marriage contract between Karl Marx and Jenny von Westphalen.— 572

Benkendorff, Alexander Christoforovich (1783-1844)—Count, closest assistant of Emperor of Russia Nicholas I, organiser of the secret police in Russia.— 524

Bentham, Jeremy (1748-1832)—English sociologist, theoretician of utilitarianism.— 486, 502

Bergasse, Nicolas (1750-1832)—French lawyer and politician, monarchist. — 287

Berthollet, Claude Louis, Comte de (1748-1822)—French chemist.— 428

Biron, Armand Louis de Gontaut, Duc de (1747-1793)—leading figure in the French Revolution, general, La Fayette's follower.— 370

Black, Joseph (1728-1799)—Scottish physicist and chemist.— 470

Blackstone, Sir William (1723-1780)— English lawyer, advocate of constitutional monarchy.— 492

Blanc, Jean Joseph Louis (1811-1882)— French petty-bourgeois Socialist, historian.— 352

Bluntschli, Johann Caspar (1808-1881)— Swiss lawyer and conservative politician.— 352, 403, 410

Boileau, Jacques (1752-1793)—leading figure in the French Revolution, deputy to the Convention, Girondist.— 369

Boissy d'Anglas, François Antoine, Comte de (1756-1826)—leading figure in the French Revolution, lawyer and writer, deputy to the Convention, representative of the Marsh.— 362

Börne, Ludwig (1786-1837)—German critic and publicist.— 394

Bourbons—French royal dynasty (1589-1792, 1814-15 and 1815-30).— 134, 371

Boz—see *Dickens, Charles*

Bridgewater, Francis Egerton, Duke of (1736-1803)—powerful English landowner, builder of canals.— 485

Brougham and Vaux, Henry Peter, 1st Baron (1778-1868)—British statesman, lawyer and writer, Whig.— 243

Buchez, Philippe Joseph Benjamin (1796-1865)—French politician, historian, Christian Socialist.— 165

Buffon, Georges Louis Leclerc, Comte de (1707-1788)—French naturalist.— 470

Bunsen, Christian Karl Josias, Baron von (1791-1860)—Prussian diplomat, publicist and theologian.— 210

Buonarroti, Filippo Michele (1761-1837)— Italian revolutionary, Utopian Communist; a leader of the revolutionary movement in France in the late 18th and early 19th centuries, Babeuf's comrade-in-arms.— 393

Buret, Eugène (1811-1842)—French economist, petty-bourgeois Socialist.— 194, 196, 244, 245, 257

Name Index

Burger, Wilhelm Christian Heinrich—Kreuznach notary.—571, 572
Buss, Franz—Oberbürgermeister of Kreuznach in 1843.—573, 574
Buzot, François Léonard Nicolas (1760-1793)—leading figure in the French Revolution, deputy to the Convention, Girondist.—362, 364, 365, 369, 370, 371
Byron, George Gordon Noel, Lord (1788-1824)—English romantic poet.—380

C

Cabet, Etienne (1788-1856)—French publicist, advocate of utopian communism, author of *Voyage en Icarie*.—143, 297, 397, 398, 400, 402, 411-13
Caesar, Gaius Julius (c. 100-44 B.C.)—Roman soldier and statesman.—208, 489
Cambacérès, Jean Jacques Régis de (1753-1824)—took part in the French Revolution, lawyer, deputy to the Convention, Girondist; subsequently a statesman under Napoleon's rule.—364, 369
Cambon, Pierre Joseph (1756-1820)—leading figure in the French Revolution, deputy to the Convention, Montagnard.—364, 365, 369
Cancrin, Yegor Frantsevich (1774-1845)—Russian statesman, Minister of Finance under Nicholas I.—524
Carlile, Richard (1790-1843)—English radical publicist.—504
Carlyle, Thomas (1795-1881)—British writer, historian and philosopher, supported the Tories; preached views bordering on feudal socialism up to 1848; later a relentless opponent of the working-class movement.—379, 444, 447, 449, 450, 452, 453, 455, 456, 457, 460-67, 476
Carnot, Lazare Nicolas Marguerite (1753-1823)—leading figure in the French Revolution, deputy to the Convention, an organiser of the revolutionary army.—365

Cartwright, Edmund (1743-1823)—English inventor.—428, 479
Chabot, François (1759-1794)—clergyman, took part in the French Revolution, deputy to the Convention, Jacobin.—372
Charles II (1630-1685)—King of Great Britain and Ireland (1660-85).—457
Chevalier, Michel (1806-1879)—French engineer, economist and publicist, Saint-Simonist in the thirties, later a free trader.—203, 288, 310-11
Clevens, Heinrich Balthasar Christian—petty official from Kreuznach, witness at the marriage of Karl Marx and Jenny von Westphalen.—574
Cobden, Richard (1804-1865)—English manufacturer and politician, a leader of the free traders and founder of the Anti-Corn Law League.—445, 497
Colonna, Stefano (Stephen) (d. 1379)—member of the princely Roman family, senator, leader of the Ghibelline party; was in constant rivalry with the Orsini family; one of the opposition leaders against Cola di Rienzi; friend of Petrarch.—537-41, 543, 548-55, 557
Columbus, Christopher (1451-1506)—Italian navigator, discoverer of America.—395
Considérant, Victor Prosper (1808-1893)—French publicist, Utopian Socialist, disciple and follower of Fourier.—396, 413
Constant, Alphonse Louis (1816-1875)—French writer, abbot, Christian Socialist.—414
Constant de Rebecque, Henri Benjamin (1767-1830)—French liberal politician, publicist and writer.—412, 414
Cooper, Thomas (1805-1892)—English poet and journalist; at the beginning of the forties was active in the Chartist movement; later propagated Christianity.—383
Courier, Paul Louis (1773-1825)—French philologist and publicist, democrat.—288
Cousin, Victor (1792-1867)—French philosopher.—350

Couthon, Georges (1755-1794) — leading figure in the French Revolution, deputy to the Convention, Jacobin, supporter of Robespierre.— 374

Crétet, Emmanuel (1747-1809) — French politician, Minister of Internal Affairs under Napoleon.— 196

Crochard — sub-lieutenant of the French army in Algeria (1841-43).— 529

Crompton, Samuel (1753-1827) — English inventor.— 442, 479, 480

Cromwell, Oliver (1599-1658) — one of the leaders of the English revolution; became Lord Protector of England, Scotland and Ireland in 1653.— 456, 473, 492

D

Danton, Georges Jacques (1759-1794) — leading figure in the French Revolution, leader of the Jacobin Right wing.— 363, 364, 366-70, 373, 374

Davy, Sir Humphry (1778-1829) — English chemist and physicist.— 428, 440

Delaunay d'Angers, Joseph (1746-1794) — leading figure in the French Revolution, deputy to the Convention, Girondist.— 370

Delolme, Jean Louis (1741-1806) — Swiss statesman, lawyer, advocate of constitutional monarchy.— 492

Desmoulins, Lucie Simplice Camille Benoît (1760-1794) — French publicist, leading figure in the French Revolution, deputy to the Convention, belonged to the Jacobin Right wing.— 287, 374

Destutt de Tracy, Antoine Louis Claude, Comte de (1754-1836) — French economist, philosopher, advocate of constitutional monarchy.— 217, 288, 319

Dézamy, Théodore (1803-1850) — French publicist, advocate of utopian communism.— 143

Dickens, Charles John Huffam (1812-1870) — English writer.— 415

Dierig — manufacturer in Langenbielau (Silesia).— 533

Doherty, Hugh — Irish philologist and philosopher, follower of Fourier.— 396

Dubois-Crancé, Edmond Louis Alexis (1747-1814) — leading figure in the French Revolution, deputy to the Convention, Montagnard.— 372

Ducos, Roger (1747-1816) — leading figure in the French Revolution, chairman of the Jacobin Club (1794); subsequently took part in the Bonapartist coup (1799).— 374

Dulaure, Jacques Antoine (1755-1835) — leading figure in the French Revolution, deputy to the Convention, representative of the Marsh.— 362

Dumouriez, Charles François du Périer (1739-1823) — leading figure in the French Revolution, general, closely associated with the Girondists, betrayed revolutionary France in 1793. — 371, 372, 373

Duncombe, Thomas Slingsby (1796-1861) — English politician, radical, active in the Chartist movement in the forties.— 381, 383, 497

E

Edward III (1312-1377) — King of England (1327-77).— 194

Elizabeth I (1533-1603) — Queen of England (1558-1603).— 194, 495, 503

Elizabeth (1801-1873) — wife of Frederick William IV.— 207

Engelmann, Karl — Kreuznach doctor, witness at the marriage of Karl Marx and Jenny von Westphalen.— 574

Engels, Frederick (1820-1895) — 232, 290, 351-52, 354, 375, 381, 387, 392, 397, 398, 404, 407, 410-13, 414, 446, 448, 449, 455, 456, 458, 459, 460, 490, 492, 514, 532

Eules, Betty — sentenced to death for murdering her children to save them from dire poverty and starvation.— 449

Ewerbeck, August Hermann (1816-1860) — German doctor and man of letters, leader of the Paris communities of the League of the Just, later member of the Communist League.— 354

F

Ferrand, William Bushfield — English landowner, Tory supporter, member of the Young England group.— 447

Feuerbach, Ludwig Andreas von (1804-1872) — German philosopher.— 144, 232-34, 303, 327-29, 339, 349-52, 354-57, 406, 427, 461, 462, 463

Fichte, Johann Gottlieb (1762-1814) — German philosopher.— 404

Fleming, George Alexander — editor of the Owenist journal *The New Moral World* (1837-44); in 1845 founded the journal *The Moral World* which appeared for a few months.— 407

Fonblanque, Albany William (1793-1872) — English liberal journalist.— 509

Fourier, François Marie Charles (1772-1837) — French Utopian Socialist.— 143, 294, 355, 392, 394-96, 398, 412, 413, 435

Fournier-Lhéritier, Claude (called Fournier l'Américain) (1745-1825) — leading figure in the French Revolution, Cordelier.— 372

Frankenthaler — friend of Marx's family in Trier.— 578

Frederick William III (1770-1840) — King of Prussia (1797-1840).— 139-40

Frederick William IV (1795-1861) — King of Prussia (1840-61).— 134, 138-40, 184, 189-91, 193, 195-97, 199, 207-10, 406, 515, 516, 530, 571, 580

Fröbel, Julius (1805-1893) — German radical publicist and publisher of progressive literature.— 351-53

Funck — Trier notary.— 574

Funke, Georg Ludwig Wilhelm — German theologian, Right-wing Hegelian.— 287

G

Ganilh, Charles (1758-1836) — French economist and politician, epigone of mercantilism.— 288

Gensonné, Armand (1758-1793) — leading figure in the French Revolution, deputy to the Convention, a Girondist leader.— 365

George I (1660-1727) — King of Great Britain and Ireland (1714-27).— 478, 491

George III (1738-1820) — King of Great Britain and Ireland (1760-1820).— 478

Gerhard — Bonn official.— 574

Gibson, Thomas Milner (1806-1884) — English politician and statesman, free trader.— 503

Girard, Philippe Henri de (1775-1845) — French engineer, inventor.— 481

Gladstone, William Ewart (1809-1898) — British politician and statesman, Tory and later Peelite, leader of the Liberal Party and head of a number of Liberal cabinets in the latter half of the 19th century.— 382

Godwin, William (1756-1836) — English writer and publicist, one of the founders of anarchism.— 486

Goethe, Johann Wolfgang von (1749-1832) — German poet.— 134, 323, 324, 458, 461, 465

Gorsas, Antoine Joseph (1751-1793) — leading figure in the French Revolution, publicist, publisher of the newspaper *Courrier de Versailles à Paris et de Paris à Versailles*, deputy to the Convention, Girondist.— 372

Görtz — Oberbürgermeister of Trier in 1844.— 574, 582

Graham, Sir James Robert George (1792-1861) — English statesman, Home Secretary in Peel's Cabinet (1841-46).— 381, 382, 500

Grégoire, Henri (1750-1831) — priest, took part in the French Revolution, deputy to the Convention, Jacobin.— 363, 368

Gruppe, Otto Friedrich (1804-1876) — German publicist and philosopher, opponent of the Young Hegelians, attacked Bruno Bauer in 1842.— 327

Guadet, Marguerite Élie (1758-1794) — leading figure in the French Revolution, deputy to the Convention, Girondist.— 365, 367, 370, 373, 374

Guerrier — French Socialist, close associate of Karl Marx and Frederick Engels in the 1840s. — 354, 584

Gurowski, Adam (1805-1866) — Polish publicist, took part in the Polish uprising (1830-31); subsequently betrayed the national liberation movement and emigrated to the United States in 1849. — 519

H

Hagen, Karl (1810-1868) — German historian and politician, Privatdocent at Heidelberg University. — 352

Haller, Karl Ludwig von (1768-1854) — Swiss lawyer and historian, supporter of absolutism. — 287

Hamilton, Thomas (1789-1842) — English writer, author of *Men and Manners in North America*. — 151, 153, 170

Hargreaves, James (d. 1778) — English inventor. — 442, 479

Hegel, Georg Wilhelm Friedrich (1770-1831) — German philosopher. — 4-16, 19-39, 41, 42, 44-57, 58-74, 75-80, 82-104, 107, 108, 111-17, 121-25, 128-29, 130, 153, 155, 163, 175, 181, 231-33, 313, 326-34, 338-45, 404-06, 457, 461, 463, 486

Heine, Heinrich (1797-1856) — German revolutionary poet. — 579, 580

Heine, Mathilde (1815-1883) — Heinrich Heine's wife. — 579

Herwegh, Georg (1817-1875) — German democratic poet. — 146, 406, 577, 584

Hess, Moses (1812-1875) — German radical publicist, one of the chief representatives of "true socialism" in the mid-forties. — 232, 300, 352, 406

Heubel, Carolina — see *Westphalen, Caroline von*

Hoffmann von Fallersleben, August Heinrich (1798-1874) — German poet and philologist. — 515

Holbach, Paul Henri Dietrich, Baron d' (1723-1789) — French philosopher, Enlightener. — 380

Hume, David (1711-1776) — British philosopher, historian and economist. — 472

Huntsman, Benjamin (1704-1776) — English inventor. — 484

J

Jettchen — see *Simons, Henriette*

Jonson, Benjamin (c. 1573-1637) — English dramatist. — 451, 465

Joseph Égalité — see *d'Orléans, Louis Philippe Joseph*

Jung, Georg Gottlob (1814-1886) — German publicist, Young Hegelian, one of the managers of the *Rheinische Zeitung*. — 583

K

Kant, Immanuel (1724-1804) — German philosopher. — 404, 406

Kapp, Christian (1790-1874) — German philosopher, Young Hegelian, friend of Ludwig Feuerbach. — 350, 352

Kay-Shuttleworth, Sir James Phillips (1804-1877) — English physician, public figure. — 193

Keller, Valentin — witness at the marriage of Karl Marx and Jenny von Westphalen. — 574

Kepler, Johann (1571-1630) — German mathematician and astronomer. — 459

Kersaint, Armand Gui Simon de Coetnempren, Comte de (1742-1793) — leading figure in the French Revolution, deputy to the Convention, Girondist. — 363, 368

Kosegarten, Wilhelm (1792-1868) — German publicist. — 287

L

Lacroix, Jean François (1754-1794) — leading figure in the French Revolution, deputy to the Convention,

one of Danton's supporters.— 369, 374
La Fayette, Marie Joseph Paul Yves Roch Gilbert du Motier, Marquis de (1757-1834)—leading figure in the French Revolution, one of the leaders of the moderate constitutionalists (Feuillants); fled to Holland in 1793.— 362
Laffitte, Jacques (1767-1844)—French banker and liberal politician, headed the government in the early period of the July monarchy (1830-31).— 527, 528
Lamartine, Alphonse Marie Louis de (1790-1869)—French poet, historian and politician, one of the leaders of the moderate Republicans in the forties.— 132, 353
Lamennais, Hugues Félicité Robert de (1782-1854) — French abbot, publicist, Christian Socialist.— 132, 399
Lameth, Alexander, Comte de (1760-1829)—leading figure in the French Revolution, deputy to the Constituent Assembly, one of the leaders of the moderate constitutionalists (Feuillants); fled to Austria in 1793.— 363, 367
Lameth, Charles, Comte de (1757-1832)—leading figure in the French Revolution, brother of Alexander Lameth, deputy to the Constituent Assembly, Feuillant; fled to Germany after August 10, 1792.— 363, 367
Lancizolle, Karl Wilhelm von Deleuze de (1796-1871)—German lawyer, author of works on the history of the German states.— 287
Lanjuinais, Jean Denis, Comte (1753-1827)—leading figure in the French Revolution, deputy to the Convention, Girondist.— 365, 370
Larivière, Pierre François Joachim Henri de (1761-1838)—leading figure in the French Revolution, deputy to the Convention, Girondist, after 9 Thermidor supporter of the restoration of monarchy.— 370
La Source, Marie David Albin (1762-1793)—leading figure in the French Revolution, deputy to the Convention, Girondist.— 372, 373

Lauderdale, James Maitland, 8th Earl of (1759-1839)—British politician and economist, criticised Adam Smith's theories.— 309
Lavoisier, Antoine Laurent (1743-1794)—French chemist.— 470
Lehmann—friend of Heinrich Marx's and Ludwig von Westphalen's families in Trier.— 576, 579
Leibniz, Gottfried Wilhelm, Baron von (1646-1716)—German philosopher and mathematician.— 404
Leo, Heinrich (1799-1878)—German historian and publicist, ideologist of Junkerdom.— 287
Le Peletier (or *Lepelletier*), *de Saint-Fargeau, Louis Michel* (1760-1793)—leading figure in the French Revolution, deputy to the Convention, Jacobin.— 366, 371
Leroux, Pierre (1797-1871)—French publicist, Utopian Socialist.— 350, 399, 400
Levasseur de la Sarthe, René (1747-1834)—physician, leading figure in the French Revolution, deputy to the Convention, Jacobin, author of the memoirs on the French Revolution.— 361, 371, 374
Liebig, Justus von, Baron (1803-1873)—German chemist.— 428, 440
Linné, Carl von (1707-1778)—Swedish naturalist, first devised the classification systems for plants and animals.— 470
List, Friedrich (1789-1846)—German vulgar economist, advocated protectionism.— 179, 421
Locke, John (1632-1704)—English dualist philosopher and economist.— 478, 490
Lolme, de—see *Delolme, Jean Louis*
Loudon, Charles (1801-1844)—English doctor, member of the Commission for Investigating Factory Labour.— 244
Louis XVI (1754-1793)—King of France (1774-92).— 361, 371
Louis XVIII (*Louis le Désiré*) (1755-1824)—King of France (1814-15, 1815-24).— 130

Louis Philippe I (1773-1850) — Duke of Orleans, King of the French (1830-48).— 130, 255, 391, 527, 528

Louvet de Couvrai, Jean Baptiste (1760-1797) — French writer, political figure in the French Revolution, deputy to the Convention, Girondist. — 365, 369, 370, 371

Lucian (c. 120-c. 180) — Greek satirist.— 179

Ludwig I Karl August (1786-1868) — King of Bavaria (1825-48).— 518, 521, 522

Luther, Martin (1483-1546) — outstanding figure of the Reformation, founder of Protestantism (Lutheranism) in Germany, German burghers' ideologist.— 182, 290, 291, 400, 401, 422

M

McAdam, John Loudon (1756-1836) — Scottish inventor, who revolutionised road-building.— 484

McCulloch, John Ramsay (1789-1864) — British economist who vulgarised David Ricardo's theories.— 192, 288, 375, 420, 424

Malthus, Thomas Robert (1766-1834) — English clergyman and economist, founder of the misanthropic theory of population.— 194, 309, 380, 420, 437-40, 452

Marat, Jean Paul (1743-1793) — leading figure in the French Revolution, prominent Jacobin.— 363-65, 368-70, 372-74

Marcus — pseudonym used by an author of pamphlets propagating Malthus' theory, published in England in the 1830s.— 437

Marius, Gaius (c. 156-86 B. C.) — Roman soldier and statesman, consul (107, 104-100, 86).— 492

Marshall, John (1783-1841) — British economist and statistician.— 254

Martin du Nord, Nicolas Ferdinand Marie Louis Joseph (1790-1847) — French lawyer and politician, Minister of Justice and Cults during the July monarchy (since 1840).— 149

Marx, Caroline (1824-1847) — sister of Karl Marx.— 577

Marx, Heinrich (1777-1838) — father of Karl Marx.— 573

Marx, Henriette (née Pressburg) (1787-1863) — mother of Karl Marx.— 573, 577, 583

Marx, Henriette — see Simons, Henriette

Marx, Jenny (née von Westphalen) (1814-1881) — wife of Karl Marx.— 351, 357, 571-84

Marx, Jenny (1844-1883) — daughter of Karl Marx.— 576, 577, 579, 581, 582, 584

Marx, Karl (1818-1883).— 132, 133, 134, 139, 141-43, 188, 189, 202, 231, 232, 349-57, 406, 416, 571-84

Marx, Sophie — see Schmalhausen, Sophie

Mäurer, Friedrich Wilhelm German (1813-c. 1882) — German writer, democrat, member of the League of Outlaws, later of the League of the Just.— 351-53

Mayer, Elias — witness at the marriage of Karl Marx and Jenny von Westphalen.— 574

Metternich-Winneburg, Clemens Wenzel Lothar, Fürst von (1773-1859) — Austrian statesman and diplomat, Minister for Foreign Affairs (1809-21), Chancellor (1821-48), one of the organisers of the Holy Alliance.— 209

Michel — cousin of Jenny Marx.— 583

Michelet, Jules (1798-1874) — French historian.— 411

Mill, James (1773-1836) — British economist, and philosopher.— 211, 224, 284, 288, 291, 311, 312, 319, 321, 375, 420, 486

Mohammed Seghir — Caliph of Algeria, who headed Abd-el-Kader's troops in the 1840s.— 529

Montesquieu, Charles Louis de Secondat, Baron de la Brede et de (1689-1755) — French philosopher and sociologist, Enlightener.— 5, 138

Morison, James (1770-1840) — English entrepreneur who amassed his wealth through the sale of so-called Morison's pills.— 456, 457, 466

Möser, Justus (1720-1794) — German historian and politician, one of the founders of the conservative-romanticist trend in historiography.— 287
Mundt, Theodor (1808-1861) — German writer, belonging to the Young Germany literary group, professor of literature in Breslau and Berlin.— 415
Münzer, Thomas (c. 1490-1525) — leader of the urban mob and the poor peasants during the Reformation and the Peasant War in Germany, preached utopian equalitarian communism.— 172, 400

N

Napoleon I Bonaparte (1769-1821) — Emperor of the French (1804-14 and 1815).— 138, 196, 199, 393, 473
Nauwerck, Karl Ludwig Theodor (1810-1891) — German publicist, Young Hegelian.— 515
Newton, Sir Isaac (1642-1727) — English physicist, astronomer and mathematician.— 459, 470, 478
Nicholas I (1796-1855) — Emperor of Russia (1825-55).— 140, 210, 515, 519, 520, 524
Noailles du Gard, Jacques Barthélemy (1758-1828) — French politician, member of the Legislative Corps (1807-15).— 196

O

Oastler, Richard (1789-1861) — English politician, Tory, philanthropist.— 447
O'Connell, Daniel (1775-1847) — Irish lawyer and politician, leader of the Liberal wing of the national liberation movement.— 379, 389-91, 505, 506
O'Connor, Feargus Edward (1794-1855) — a leader of the Chartist Left, editor-in-chief of *The Northern Star*.— 379, 383, 384

d'Orléans, Louis Philippe Joseph, Duc (called *Philippe Égalité*) (1747-1793) — cousin of the King of France Louis XVI, sided with the Revolution in 1789, deputy to the Convention.— 364, 365, 368, 370, 371
Orsini — member of the princely Roman family which was in constant rivalry with the Colonna family; leader of the Guelph party.— 539-40, 545, 548, 549, 554
Owen, Robert (1771-1858) — British Utopian Socialist.— 297, 386, 387, 398

P

Pache, Jean Nicolas (1746-1823) — leading figure in the French Revolution, Jacobin, Minister of War and Mayor of Paris (October 1792-May 1794).— 365, 371, 372
Paine, Thomas (1737-1809) — English publicist, Republican, took part in the American War of Independence and in the French Revolution.— 387
Parisot, Jacques Théodore — translator of James Mill's *Elements of Political Economy* into French.— 211
Paulus, Heinrich Eberhard Gottlob (1761-1851) — German Protestant theologian, supporter of the rationalist trend in Lutheranism.— 350
Pecqueur, Constantin (1801-1887) — French economist, Utopian Socialist. — 243, 254
Peel, Sir Robert (1788-1850) — English statesman, Tory, Prime Minister (1841-46), repealed the Corn Laws in 1846.— 382, 390-91, 445, 491
Pelisse — sergeant of the French army in Algeria during the campaign in the 1840s.— 529
Pétion de Villeneuve, Jérôme (1753-1794) — leading figure in the French Revolution, Mayor of Paris in 1792, deputy to the Convention, Girondist.— 362, 363, 365, 367, 368, 370
Petitgand — lieutenant of the French Army in Algeria, Commandant of Biskra in 1844.— 529

Phalaris (c. 571-555 B.C.)—tyrant of Agrigentum in ancient Sicily; according to legend, burned his opponents in a brazen bull.—454

Philippeaux, Pierre Nicolas (1754-1794)—leading figure in the French Revolution, deputy to the Convention, Right Jacobin, one of Danton's supporters.—364, 369, 374

Plato (c. 427-c. 347 B.C.)—Greek philosopher.—59

Pompery, Edouard de (1812-1895)—French writer and publicist, follower of Fourier whose ideas he propagated in the thirties and forties.—355

Poppey—friend of Heinrich Marx's and Ludwig von Westphalen's families in Trier.—579

Porter, George Richardson (1792-1852)—English economist and statistician.—485

Pressburg, Henriette—see *Marx, Henriette*

Priestley, Joseph (1733-1804)—English chemist and materialist philosopher, public figure.—470

Proudhon, Pierre Joseph (1809-1865)—French publicist, economist and sociologist, one of the founders of anarchism.—143, 201, 241, 280, 294, 313, 316, 317, 356, 399, 412

Q

Quesnay, François (1694-1774)—French economist, doctor, founder of the physiocratic school.—292

Quinet, Edgar (1803-1875)—French historian, attacked Strauss' *Das Leben Jesu*.—411

R

Raumer, Friedrich Ludwig Georg von (1781-1873)—German historian and politician, professor at the universities of Berlin and Breslau.—490

Rebecqui, François Trophime (1760-1794)—leading figure in the French Revolution, deputy to the Convention, Girondist.—364, 369

Reverchon—friend of Heinrich Marx's and Ludwig von Westphalen's families in Trier.—579

Ricardo, David (1772-1823)—English economist.—192, 211, 256, 284, 288, 291, 309-11, 321, 375, 420, 424, 428

Rickes, Johann Anton—witness to the signing of the marriage contract between Karl Marx and Jenny von Westphalen in Kreuznach.—572

Rienzi, Cola di (more correctly, *Rienzo*) (1313-1354)—Italian statesman and leader (people's tribune) of the Roman Republic (1347) and ruler (senator) of Rome (1354); looked for support from the masses in the struggle with the feudal aristocracy.—537, 541, 542, 546-48, 550, 553, 555-57, 559-65

Robespierre, Augustin Bon Joseph (1763-1794)—leading figure in the French Revolution, Jacobin, brother of Maximilien Robespierre.—165

Robespierre, Maximilien François Marie Isidore de (1758-1794)—leading figure in the French Revolution, leader of the Jacobins, head of the revolutionary government (1793-94).—199, 363-65, 367, 369, 370, 371, 373, 473, 492

Rocholl—uncle of Theodor Simons.—583

Roland de la Platière, Jean Marien (1734-1793)—leading figure in the French Revolution, deputy to the Convention, Minister of the Interior, a leader of the Girondists.—364, 365, 369, 370, 371

Rousseau, Jean Jacques (1712-1778)—French philosopher and writer of the Enlightenment.—167, 380, 387

Roux-Lavergne, Pierre Célestin (1802-1874)—French historian and philosopher. —165

Ruge, Arnold (1802-1880)—German radical publicist and philosopher, Young Hegelian.—132, 133, 134, 141, 189-93, 195, 196, 199-206, 349, 352, 406, 416, 583

Name Index

Russell, John Russell, 1st Earl (1792-1878)—British statesman, Whig leader, Prime Minister (1846-52 and 1865-66), Foreign Secretary (1852-53 and 1859-65).—445, 503, 517

S

Saint-Simon, Claude Henri de Rouvroy, Comte de (1760-1825)—French Utopian Socialist.—214, 288, 294, 394, 396, 398
Salles, Jean Baptiste (1760-1794)—leading figure in the French Revolution, deputy to the Convention, Girondist.—370
Sand, George (pseudonym of *Aurore Dupin, Baronne Dudevant*) (1804-1876)—French writer, representative of the democratic trend in romanticism.—399, 415
Santerre, Antoine Joseph (1752-1809)—leading figure in the French Revolution, Commander of the Paris National Guard (1792-93), Girondist supporter.—372
Say, Jean Baptiste (1767-1832)—French economist, one of the founders of the "three production factors" theory.—247, 250, 259-61, 284, 291, 310, 319-21, 375, 424-26
Schelling, Friedrich Wilhelm Joseph von (1775-1854)—German philosopher. —349-51, 404, 450, 461, 463
Schenk—Cologne official.—574
Schleicher, Robert—Trier doctor, friend of Karl Marx's family.—571, 578, 579
Schmalhausen, Sophie (1816-1883)—sister of Karl Marx.—577, 579
Schüller—Düsseldorf publisher.—352
Schulz-Bodmer, Wilhelm (1797-1860)—German publicist, democrat.—242, 254, 258
Servan de Gerbey, Joseph (1741-1808)—leading figure in the French Revolution, general, Minister of War in 1792, Girondist.—365, 371
Shakespeare, William (1564-1616)—English poet and dramatist.—87, 180, 323, 324, 465

Shelley, Percy Bysshe (1792-1822)—English poet, revolutionary romantic.—380, 387
Siebenkäs—friend of Karl Marx's family in Paris.—579
Sieyès, Emmanuel Joseph (1748-1836)—leading figure in the French Revolution, abbot, deputy to the Convention, moderate constitutionalist (Feuillant).—362
Sillery, Charles Alexis Pierre Brulart, Comte de Genlis, Marquis de (1737-1793)—leading figure in the French Revolution, general, deputy to the Convention, Girondist.—371
Simons, Henriette (1820-c. 1856)—sister of Karl Marx.—577, 582, 583
Simons, Theodor (b. 1813)—architect, husband of Henriette Marx.—582
Sismondi, Jean Charles Léonard Simonde de (1773-1842)—Swiss economist, representative of economic romanticism.—257, 287
Skarbek, Frédéric Florian (1792-1866)—Polish economist and writer, follower of Adam Smith.—319-21
Smith, Adam (1723-1790)—British economist.—217, 235, 237, 239, 247, 252, 257-65, 284, 285, 290-92, 317, 319, 320, 375, 380, 420, 422, 428, 470, 485-86
Southwell, Charles (1814-1860)—English Utopian Socialist, follower of Robert Owen.—386, 388
Spinoza, Baruch (or *Benedict*) (1632-1677)—Dutch philosopher.—463
Staël, Madame de (*Anne Louise Germaine, Baronne de Staël-Holstein*, née *Necker*) (1766-1817)—French romantic writer.—412
Stein, Lorenz von (1815-1890)—German lawyer and historian, author of works on the socialist movement, supporter of "social monarchy".—388
Steinmann, Friedrich (1801-1875)—German publicist and man of letters.—517
Strauss, David Friedrich (1808-1874)—German philosopher and publicist, Young Hegelian.—169, 327, 380, 404, 446, 447, 461, 517

Name Index

Stuarts — royal dynasty in Scotland (1371-1714) and in England (1603-1714).— 134
Sue, Eugène Marie Joseph (1804-1857) — French writer, author of sentimental social novels.— 415
Sulla, Lucius Cornelius (138-78 B.C.) — Roman soldier, dictator.— 492

T

Tallien, Jean Lambert (1767-1820) — leading figure in the French Revolution, deputy to the Convention, representative of the Marsh, one of the chief participants in the Thermidorian coup.— 372
Thanisch — Trier official.— 574
Thompson, Thomas Perronet (1783-1869) — English politician and economist, free trader.— 428
Thuriot de La Rosière, Jacques Alexandre (1753-1829) — leading figure in the French Revolution, deputy to the Convention, for a time supported the Jacobins.— 369
Tocqueville, Alexis Charles Henri Maurice Clérel de (1805-1859) — French liberal historian and politician.— 151
Tooke, John Horne (1736-1812) — English radical politician.— 487
Tschech, Heinrich Ludwig (1789-1844) — Prussian official, democrat, burgomaster of Storkow in 1832-41; executed for an attempt on the life of Frederick William IV.— 580

U

Ure, Andrew (1778-1857) — English chemist and economist, free trader.— 443

V

Valazé, Eléonor Bernard Anne Christophe Zoa du Friche, Baron de (1751-1793) — leading figure in the French Revolution, deputy to the Convention, Girondist.— 369

Valence, Cyrus Marie Alexandre de Timburne-Timbronne, Comte de (1757-1822) — leading figure in the French Revolution, general, Dumouriez's comrade-in-arms.— 370
Vergniaud, Pierre Victurnien (1753-1793) — leading figure in the French Revolution, deputy to the Convention, one of the Girondist leaders.— 362, 364, 369, 371
Villegardelle, François (1810-1856) — French publicist, follower of Fourier. — 297
Vincke, Friedrich Wilhelm Ludwig, Baron von (1774-1844) — Prussian statesman.— 287
Voltaire, François Marie Arouet de (1694-1778) — French philosopher, writer and historian of the Enlightenment. — 380, 387

W

Wade, John (1788-1875) — English publicist, economist and historian.— 433, 441, 507, 509
Wallace, Sir William (c. 1270-1305) — leader of the Scottish uprising against British domination.— 528
Walter, John (1776-1847) — English politician, associated with the Tories.— 447
Watt, James (1736-1819) — Scottish engineer, inventor of the steam-engine.— 428, 479, 480, 482
Watts, John (1818-1887) — English Utopian Socialist, follower of Robert Owen.— 385-88, 398
Wedgwood, Josiah (1730-1795) — English pottery manufacturer, who devised improved pottery techniques. — 479
Weill, Alexandre (Abraham) (1811-1899) — German journalist, democrat, lived as an émigré in France in the forties.— 352
Weitling, Wilhelm Christian (1808-1871) — one of the early leaders of the working-class movement in Germany, tailor by trade, one of the theoreticians of utopian equalitarian commu-

Name Index 637

nism.—143, 201, 232, 401-03, 409, 410, 412
Welcker, Karl Theodor (1790-1869)—German lawyer, liberal publicist, Landtag deputy in Baden.—517
Wellington, Arthur Wellesley, Duke of (1769-1852)—British general and statesman, Tory, Prime Minister (1828-30).—445
Westphalen, Caroline von (d. 1856)—mother of Jenny Marx.—357, 572-78
Westphalen, Edgar von (1819-c. 1890)—brother of Jenny Marx.—576, 578, 581, 584

Westphalen, Jenny—see Marx, Jenny
Westphalen, Johann Ludwig von (1770-1842)—father of Jenny Marx, Privy Councillor in Trier.—573, 574, 575
Wettendorf—friend of Marx's family in Trier.—576

Z

Zöpfl, Heinrich (1807-1877)—German lawyer.—137
Zwanziger—German textile manufacturer, owner of a factory in Peterswalden (Silesia).—532

INDEX OF LITERARY
AND MYTHOLOGICAL NAMES

Adam (Bib.).—455
Apollo—the god of the arts (Gr. Relig.).—449

Battista—a character in Frederick Engels' drama Cola di Rienzi.—537-42, 546, 557-60, 562
Beelzebub—a biblical name for the Devil, the spirit of evil.—456
Belial—the Hebrew name for the spirit of evil, one of the biblical names of the Devil.—456

Camilla—a character in Frederick Engels' drama Cola di Rienzi; daughter of Stefano Colonna.—543-46, 548-55, 564-68
Cedric the Saxon—a character in Walter Scott's Ivanhoe.—455
Christ, Jesus (Bib.).—85, 152, 212, 328, 356, 400, 446, 463, 548
Cinderella—the heroine of a popular European tale.—202
Cronus—a Titan, father of Zeus (Gr. Myth.).—242

Diana—the goddess of hunting (Rom. Relig.).—323
Don Quixote—the title and hero of a Spanish romance written by Cervantes.—287

Faust—the title and hero of a tragedy by Goethe.—323

Janus—an ancient Roman deity represented with two opposite faces.—86

Laocoön—Trojan priest of Apollo who incensed the gods and was destroyed with his two sons by two huge serpents (Class. Myth.).—170

Mars—the god of war (Rom. Relig.).—324
Mary—the mother of Jesus (Bib.).—33, 543, 561, 562, 580
Medusa—one of the three snake-haired Gorgons, whose terrifying aspect turned the beholder to stone (Gr. Myth.).—432
Mephistopheles—a character in Goethe's Faust.—323
Midas—a king of Phrygia who turned to gold everything he touched, insulted by him, Apollo changed his ears into ass's ears (Gr. Myth.).—448, 449
Montreal, Walter—a character in Frederick Engels' drama Cola di Rienzi.—543-50, 553, 555-57, 559-65
Moses (Bib.).—177

Nemesis—the goddess of retributive justice (Gr. Relig.).—234

Nina—a character in Frederick Engels' drama *Cola di Rienzi*; wife of *Cola di Rienzi*.—556, 557, 561-63, 565-67

Orlando—a character in Frederick Engels' drama *Cola di Rienzi*; son of Orsini.—539, 540

Prometheus—a Titan who stole fire from Olympus and gave it to man (Gr. Relig.).—179, 307

Shylock—a character in Shakespeare's *The Merchant of Venice*.—177, 214

Snug—a character in Shakespeare's *A Midsummer Night's Dream*.—86

INDEX OF QUOTED
AND MENTIONED LITERATURE

WORKS BY KARL MARX AND FREDERICK ENGELS

Marx, Karl. *Contribution to the Critique of Hegel's Philosophy of Law. Introduction*
— Zur Kritik der Hegelschen Rechtsphilosophie. Einleitung. In: *Deutsch-Französische Jahrbücher*, Paris, 1844.—202, 231, 354

Marx, Karl. *Critical Marginal Notes on the Article "The King of Prussia and Social Reform. By a Prussian"*
— Kritische Randglossen zu dem Artikel "Der König von Preussen und die Sozialreform. Von einem Preussen". In: *Vorwärts!* Nos. 63 and 64, August 7 and 10, Paris, 1844.—583

Marx, Karl. *The Philosophical Manifesto of the Historical School of Law*
— Das philosophische Manifest der historischen Rechtsschule. In: *Rheinische Zeitung* No. 221, August 9, 1842.—175

Engels, Frederick. *Outlines of a Critique of Political Economy*
— Umrisse zu einer Kritik der Nationalökonomie. In: *Deutsch-Französische Jahrbücher*, 1-2. Lfg., Paris, 1844.—232, 290, 351, 375

Engels, Frederick. *Schelling and Revelation. Critique of the Latest Attempt of Reaction Against the Free Philosophy*
— Schelling und die Offenbarung. Kritik des neuesten Reaktionsversuchs gegen die freie Philosophie, Leipzig, 1842.—404

WORKS BY DIFFERENT AUTHORS

Aeschylus. *Prometheus Bound*.—179, 307-08
Alison, A. *The Principles of Population, and their Connection with Human Happiness*, Vols. 1-2, London, 1840.—436, 440
Aristoteles. *De republica libri VIII*. In: *Aristoteles opera ex recensione*, I. Bekkeri, Tomus X, Oxonii, 1837.—137

Baines, E. *History of the Cotton Manufacture in Great Britain...*, London [1835].—479-80
Bauer, B. *Das entdeckte Christenthum. Eine Erinnerung an das achtzehnte Jahrhundert und ein Beitrag zur Krisis des neunzehnten*, Zürich und Winterthur, 1843.—327

Bauer, B. *Die Fähigkeit der heutigen Juden und Christen, frei zu werden.* In: *Einundzwanzig Bogen aus der Schweiz,* hrsg. von Georg Herwegh. Erster Theil, Zürich und Winterthur, 1843.—146, 148-49, 154, 168
— *Die gute Sache der Freiheit und meine eigene Angelegenheit,* Zürich und Winterthur, 1842.—327
— *Die Judenfrage,* Braunschweig, 1843.—146, 148, 149, 152, 155, 157, 160, 168-71
— *Kritik der evangelischen Geschichte der Synoptiker,* Bd. 1-2, Leipzig, 1841; Bd. 3, Braunschweig, 1842.—169, 327
Bauer, E. *Der Streit der Kritik mit Kirche und Staat,* Charlottenburg, 1843.—407-08
Beaumont, G. de. *Marie ou l'esclavage aux États-Unis, tableau de moeurs Américaines,* T. 1-2, Bruxelles, 1835.—150, 159, 161, 171
Bible
— Matthew 5:3.—380
— 1 Corinthians 1:20.—380
[Blackstone, W.] *Commentaries on the Laws of England.* In four books, London, 1765-69.—492
[Bluntschli, J. C.] *Die Kommunisten in der Schweiz nach den bei Weitling vorgefundenen Papieren. Wörtlicher Abdruck des Kommissionalberichtes an die H. Regierung des Standes Zürich,* Zürich, 1843.—403, 410
Buchez, P. J. B. et Roux, P. C. *Histoire parlementaire de la Révolution française ou Journal des Assemblées Nationales, depuis 1789 jusqu'en 1815...,* Tomes 1-40, Paris, 1834-38. Tome 28, 1836.—165
Buonarroti, Ph. *History of Babeuf's Conspiracy for Equality; with the Author's Reflections on the Causes and Character of the French Revolution and his Estimate of the leading Men and Events of that Epoch. Also, his Views of democratic Government, Community of Property, and political and social Equality.* Translated from the French language, London, 1836.—393
Buret, E. *De la misère des classes laborieuses en Angleterre et en France; de la nature de la misère, de son existence, de ses effets, de ses causes, et de l'insuffisance des remèdes qu'on lui a opposés jusqu'ici; avec l'indication des moyens propres à en affranchir les sociétés,* T. 1, Paris, 1840.—192, 193, 196, 244, 245, 257

Cabet, E. *Voyage en Icarie, Roman philosophique et social.* Deuxième édition, Paris, 1842.—143, 398
Carlyle, Th. *Chartism,* London, 1840.—447-48, 467
— *Past and Present,* London, 1843.—444, 447-56, 458-60, 476
Chevalier, M. *Des intérêts matériels en France.* Travaux publics, Paris-Bruxelles, 1838.—203, 311

Delolme, J. L. *La Constitution de l'Angleterre,* Amsterdam, 1771.—492
Destutt de Tracy [,A.-L.-C.]. *Élémens d'idéologie.* IV-e et V-e parties. Traité de la volonté et de ses effets, Paris, 1826.—217, 318

Einundzwanzig Bogen aus der Schweiz. Hrsg. von Georg Herwegh, Zürich und Winterthur, 1843.—146, 232, 300
Ewerbeck, A. H. *Qu'est-ce que la religion d'après la nouvelle philosophie allemande,* Paris, 1850.—354

Index of Quoted and Mentioned Literature 641

Feuerbach, L. *Grundsätze der Philosophie der Zukunft,* Zürich und Winterthur, 1843.—232, 327, 354
— *Vorläufige Thesen zur Reformation der Philosophie.* In: *Anekdota zur neuesten deutschen Philosophie und Publicistik* von Bruno Bauer, Ludwig Feuerbach, Friedrich Köppen, Karl Nauwerck, Arnold Ruge und einigen Ungenannten; hrsg. von Arnold Ruge, Bd. I-II, Zürich und Winterthur, 1843.—232, 327, 461
— *Das Wesen des Christenthums,* Leipzig, 1841.—330, 340, 354, 357
— *Das Wesen des Glaubens im Sinne Luther's. Ein Beitrag zum "Wesen des Christenthums",* Leipzig, 1844.—354
Fonblanque, A. *England under Seven Administrations,* Vols. I-III, London, 1837.—509
Funke, G. L. W. *Die aus der unbeschränkten Theilbarkeit des Grundeigenthums hervorgehenden Nachtheile hinsichtlich der Cultur des Bodens und der Bevölkerung und die hierdurch bewirkte Auflösung der historischen Elemente des Staates und somit des ständisch-organischen Staates selbst,* Hamburg und Gotha, 1839.—287

Godwin, W. *An Enquiry Concerning Political Justice, and its Influence on General Virtue and Happiness,* Vols. I-II, London, 1793.—486
Goethe, J. W. von. *Faust. Der Tragödie. Erster Teil.*—323
Graham, J. *Factories' Education.* In: *Hansard's Parliamentary Debates; Third Series; Commencing with the Accession of William IV. Vol. LXVII. Comprising the Period from the twenty-eighth Day of February, to the twenty-fourth Day of March 1843,* London, 1843.—381, 504
Gurowski, A. *La vérité sur la Russie,* Paris, 1834.—519
— *La civilisation et la Russie,* St. Pétersbourg, 1840.—519

Hamilton [,Th.]. *Die Menschen und die Sitten in den Vereinigten Staaten von Nordamerika.* Nach der 3. engl. Aufl. übersetzt, Mannheim, 1834.—151, 153, 170-71
Hegel, G. W. F. *Werke,* Berlin, 1831-45:
— *Grundlinien der Philosophie des Rechts, oder Naturrecht und Staatswissenschaft im Grundrisse,* Bd. 8, 1833.—5-29, 32-38, 40-44, 49-56, 58-60, 62, 65-71, 74-76, 78, 79, 81, 82, 85, 91, 93, 95-98, 100-03, 107, 111, 113-18, 121-25, 128, 129, 153, 163
— *Phänomenologie des Geistes,* Bd. 2, 1832.—232, 327, 330-33
— *Wissenschaft der Logik,* Bd. 3-5, 1833-34.—18, 232, 327, 345, 346
— *Encyclopädie der philosophischen Wissenschaften im Grundrisse,* 3. Ausg., Heidelberg, 1830.—330, 344-46
Hess, M. *Philosophie der Tat.* In: *Einundzwanzig Bogen aus der Schweiz.* Hrsg. von Georg Herwegh, Zürich und Winterthur, 1843.—300
[Holbach, P. H.] *Nature, and her Laws; as Applicable to the Happiness of Man, Living in Society; Contrasted with Superstition and Imaginary Systems.* From the French of de Mirabaud, Vols. 1-2, London, 1834.—380, 387

[Kapp, C.] *Friedrich Wilhelm Joseph von Schelling,* Leipzig, 1843.—350
[Kay, J. P.] *Recent Measures for the Promotion of Education in England.* In: Eugène Buret, *De la misère des classes laborieuses en Angleterre et en France; de la nature de*

la misère, de son existence, de ses effets, de ses causes, et de l'insuffisance des remèdes qu'on lui a opposés jusqu'ici; avec l'indication des moyens propres à en affranchir les sociétés, T. 1, Paris, 1840.—193

Lamartine, Alph.[-M.-L. de] *Histoire des Girondins*, T. 1-4, Bruxelles, 1847.—131
Lamennais [,F.-R.] de. *Paroles d'un croyant, 1833*, Bruxelles, 1834.—399
Leo, H. *Studien und Skizzen zu einer Naturlehre des Staates*, Halle, 1833.—287
[Levasseur, R.] *Mémoires de R. Levasseur (de la Sarthe), ex-conventionnel*, T. 1-4, Paris, 1829-31. Tome 1.—361-74
List, F. *Das nationale System der politischen Oekonomie*, Stuttgart und Tübingen, 1841.—179
Loudon, Ch. *Solution du problème de la population et de la subsistance, soumise à un médecin dans une série des lettres*, Paris, 1842.—244
Lucianus. *Theon dialogoi.*—179
Ludwig von Bayern. *Walhalla's Genossen, geschildert durch König Ludwig den Ersten von Bayern, dem Gründer Walhalla's*, München, 1842.—522
Luther, M. *Wyder die mördische unnd reubischenn Rottenn der Paurenn*, Wittenberg, 1525.—401

MacCulloch, J. R. *Discours sur l'origine, les progrès, les objets particuliers, et l'importance de l'économie politique. Traduit de l'anglais par G. Prévost*, Genève-Paris, 1825.—193
Marcus. *An Essay on Populousness ... printed for the Author*, 1838.—437
— *On the Possibility of Limiting Populousness*. Printed by John Hill, Black Horse Court, Fleet Street, 1838.—437
— *The Theory of Painless Extinction*. Cf. *The New Moral World*: Advertisements, 29. VIII. 1840.—437
[Marx, J.] *Aus dem Briefe einer deutschen Dame*. In: *Vorwärts!* No. 64, August 10, 1844.—357
Mill, J. *Élémens d'économie politique; traduits de l'anglais par J. T. Parisot*, Paris, 1823.—211, 222-24, 311, 312, 319-20
Montesquieu, Ch.-L. de. *De l'esprit des loix*, T. 1-2, Genève, 1748.—138
Möser, J. *Patriotische Phantasien. Hrsg. von seiner Tochter J. W. J. v. Voigt, geb. Möser*, 4 Teile, Berlin, 1775-86.—287
Münzer, Th. *Hoch verursachte Schutzrede und Antwort wider das geistlose, sanftlebende Fleisch zu Wittenberg, welches mit verkehrter Weise durch den Diebstahl der heiligen Schrift die erbärmliche Christenheit also ganz jämmerlich besudelt hat*. In: Leopold Ranke, *Deutsche Geschichte im Zeitalter der Reformation*, Bd. 1-2, Berlin, 1839.—172
— *Ausgedrückte Entblössung des falschen Glaubens der ungetreuen Welt durchs Zeugnis des Evangelions Lucae, vorgetragen der elenden erbärmlichen Christenheit zur Erinnerung ihres Irrsals*. In: W. Zimmermann, *Allgemeine Geschichte des grossen Bauern Krieges*, Th. 1-3, Stuttgart, 1841-43.—400

Owen, R. *The Marriage System of the New Moral World; with a Faint Outline of the Present very Irrational System; as Developed in a Course of Ten Lectures*, Leeds, 1838.—387

Paulus, H. E. G. *Die endlich offenbar gewordene positive Philosophie der Offenbarung oder Entstehungsgeschichte, wörtlicher Text, Beurtheilung und Berichtigung der v. Schellingischen Entdeckungen über Philosophie überhaupt, Mythologie und Offenbarung des dogmatischen Christenthums im Berliner Wintercursus von 1841-42*, Darmstadt, 1843.—350

Pecqueur, C. *Théorie nouvelle d'économie sociale et politique, ou études sur l'organisation des sociétés*, Paris, 1842.—243-44, 254-55

Pompery, É. de. *Exposition de la science sociale, constituée par C. Fourier*. Deuxième édition, revuée et augmentée, Paris, 1840.—355

Porter, G. R. *The Progress of the Nation, in its Various Social and Economical Relations, from the Beginning of the 19th Century to the Present Time*, Vols. 1-2, London, 1836-38.—485

Proudhon, P.-J. *Qu'est-ce que la propriété? Ou recherches sur le principe du droit et du gouvernement*. Premier mémoire, Paris, 1841.—316, 317, 399

Raumer, F. L. G. von. *England im Jahre 1835*, T. 1-2, Leipzig, 1836.—490

Ricardo, D. *Des principes de l'économie politique, et de l'impôt. Traduit de l'anglais par F. S. Constancio. D. M. etc.; avec des notes explicatives et critiques, par M. Jean-Baptiste Say*, T. 2, 2-e éd., Paris, 1835.—256

Rousseau, J.-J. *Du contrat social; ou principes du droit politique*, Londres, 1782.—167, 387

— *An Inquiry into the Nature of the Social Contract or Principles of Political Right*, London, 1840.—380

[Ruge, A.] *Der König von Preussen und die Sozialreform*. In: *Vorwärts!* No. 60, July 27, Paris, 1844.—189, 192, 195, 199, 200, 202-05

Say, J.-B. *Traité d'économie politique, ou Simple exposition de la manière dont se forment, se distribuent, et se consomment les richesses*. Troisième édition, T. 1-2, Paris, 1817.—247, 250, 259, 262-63, 319

Schiller, J. C. F. von. *Don Carlos.*—15

Schulz, W. *Die Bewegung der Production. Eine geschichtlich-statistische Abhandlung zur Grundlegung einer neuen Wissenschaft des Staats und der Gesellschaft*, Zürich und Winterthur, 1843.—242-44, 254-56, 258

Shakespeare, W. *Hamlet.*—180

— *A Midsummer Night's Dream.*—86

— *Timon of Athens.*—323-24

Sismondi, J.-C.-L. S. de. *Nouveaux principes d'économie politique ou de la richesse dans ses rapports avec la population*, T. I-II, Paris, 1819.—256-57, 287

Skarbek, F. *Théorie des richesses sociales. Suivie d'une bibliographie de l'économie politique*, T. 1-2, Paris, 1839.—319

Smith, A. *An Inquiry into the Nature and Causes of the Wealth of Nations*, Vols. I-II, London, 1776; Vol. III, Dublin, 1776.—420, 423, 485

— *Recherches sur la nature et les causes de la richesse des nations. Traduction nouvelle, avec des notes et observation; par Germain Garnier*, T. 1-2, Paris, 1802.—217, 237, 239, 247-53, 256, 257, 259, 262, 264, 265, 317-19

Stein, L. von. *Der Socialismus und Communismus des heutigen Frankreichs. Ein Beitrag zur Zeitgeschichte*, Leipzig, 1842.—388

[Steinmann, F. A.] *Caricaturen und Silhouetten des neunzehnten Jahrhunderts. Vom Verfasser des Mefistofeles*, Coesfeld, 1843.—517

Strauss, D. F. *Das Leben Jesu,* Bd. 1-2, Tübingen, 1835-36.—169, 380, 404, 446, 517
Sue, E. *Les mystères de Paris,* Bruxelles, 1843.—415

Tocqueville, A. de. *De la démocratie en Amérique,* Paris, 1836.—151
T[reskow], A. von. *Der bergmännische Distrikt zwischen Birmingham und Wolverhampton, mit besonderer Bezugnahme auf die Gewinnung des Eisens.* In: *Deutsche Vierteljahrs Schrift,* 3. Heft, Stuttgart und Tübingen [1838].—258

Ure, A. *The Philosophy of Manufactures: or, an Exposition of the Scientific, Moral, and Commercial Economy of the Factory System of Great Britain,* London, 1835.—443

Wade, J. *British History...,* London, 1838.—507, 509
— *History of the Middle and Working Classes; with a Popular Exposition of the Economical and Political Principles...,* third edition, London, 1835.—433
Weitling, W. *Das Evangelium eines armen Sünders,* Bern, 1845.—201, 232, 402
— *Garantien der Harmonie und Freiheit,* Vivis, 1842.—201, 232, 402, 412
— *Die Menschheit, wie sie ist und wie sie sein sollte,* 1838.—232, 402

Zöpfl, H. *Grundsätze des Allgemeinen und Constitutionell-Monarchistischen Staatsrechts, mit Rücksicht auf das gemeingültige Recht in Deutschland...,* 2. unveränd. Abdruck, Heidelberg, 1841.—137

DOCUMENTS

Constitutio criminalis Carolina.—509

Déclaration des droits de l'homme et du citoyen. 1791. In: W. Wachsmuth, *Geschichte Frankreichs im Revolutionszeitalter,* T. 1, Hamburg, 1840.—161, 162, 164
Déclaration des droits de l'homme et du citoyen. 1793. In: P. J. B. Buchez et P.C. Roux, *Histoire parlementaire de la Révolution française ou Journal des Assemblées Nationales, depuis 1789 jusqu'en 1815...,* T. 31, Paris, 1837.—161-64
Déclaration des droits de l'homme et du citoyen. 1795. In: P. J. B. Buchez et P. C. Roux, *Histoire parlementaire de la Révolution française ou Journal des Assemblées Nationales, depuis 1789 jusqu'en 1815...,* T. 36, Paris, 1838.—161, 164

Extraits des Enquêtes publiées en Angleterre sur l'Irlande, Vienne, 1840.—244

Königliche Cabinetsordre vom 18. Juli 1843. In: *Allgemeine Preussische Staats-Zeitung* No. 29, July 26, 1843.—189-91

Magna Charta Libertatum.—492

Das Schlussprotokoll der Wiener Ministerial-Konferenz vom 12. Juni 1834. In: *Vorwärts!* No. 7, January 24, 1844, Supplement; *Deutsch-Französische Jahrbücher,* 1ste und 2te Lieferung, Paris, 1844; Welcker, C., *Wichtige Urkunden für den Rechtszustand der deutschen Nation,* Mannheim, 1844.—417

ANONYMOUS ARTICLES AND REPORTS PUBLISHED
IN PERIODIC EDITIONS

Allgemeine Zeitung (Augsburg) No. 110, April 20, 1843: *London, 13. April.*—382, 385

The Times (London) No. 492, December 29, 1843: *The Communists in Germany.*—410, 412, 413

INDEX OF PERIODICALS

Allgemeine Literatur-Zeitung—a democratic monthly published in Charlottenburg from December 1843 to October 1844; it was edited by Bruno Bauer.—356

Allgemeine Zeitung—a conservative daily founded in 1798; from 1810 to 1882 it was published in Augsburg.—188, 382, 385, 415

Anekdota zur neuesten deutschen Philosophie und Publicistik—a collection published in Switzerland (Zurich and Winterthur) in 1843; it was edited by Arnold Ruge. Among its contributors were Karl Marx, Bruno Bauer and Ludwig Feuerbach. Only two volumes appeared.—232, 328, 461

Atheist—a publication issued in Manchester at the end of 1840.—388

Atheist and Republican—a newspaper published in England at the end of 1840.—388

Berliner politisches Wochenblatt—a conservative weekly published from 1831 to 1841 with the participation of Karl Ludwig von Haller, Heinrich Leo, Friedrich von Raumer and others; it was patronised by King Frederick William IV.—139

Le Bien Public—a moderate republican newspaper published from 1843 to 1848 in Mâcon, and from May 1848 in Paris; Lamartine was one of its founders.—132

Le Charivari—a republican satirical newspaper published in Paris from 1832 to 1934.—352

Le Commerce—a liberal daily; under this title it was published in Paris from 1837 to 1848.—352

Le Courrier Suisse—a conservative newspaper published in Lausanne from 1840 to 1853.—352

La Démocratie pacifique—a daily newspaper of the Fourierists published in Paris from 1843 to 1851 under the editorship of Victor Considérant.—132, 352, 413

Deutsche Jahrbücher für Wissenschaft und Kunst—a Young Hegelian literary and philosophical journal published in Leipzig from July 1841 under the editorship of Arnold Ruge. In January 1843 it was closed down by the Saxon government and prohibited throughout Germany by order of the Federal Diet.—132, 405, 406

Deutsche Vierteljahrs Schrift—a newspaper published in Stuttgart and Tübingen from 1838 to 1870.—258

Deutsch-Französische Jahrbücher—a yearly edited by Arnold Ruge and Karl Marx and published in German in Paris; only the first issue, a double one, appeared in February 1844.—131, 133, 188, 202, 231, 232, 349, 352, 375, 416

The Examiner—a weekly, organ of the Liberals, published in London from 1808 to 1881.—509

Journal des Débats politiques et littéraires—a daily founded in Paris in 1789; organ of the government during the July monarchy.—528

Die junge Generation—a monthly published by Wilhelm Weitling in Switzerland from 1841 to 1843; it propagated utopian egalitarian communism.—402

Kölnische Zeitung—a daily, organ of the liberal bourgeoisie, published under this title from 1802 to 1945.—132

Le National—a newspaper published in Paris from 1830 to 1851; in the forties, organ of the moderate republicans.—352, 411

The New Moral World: and Gazette of the Rational Society—a weekly founded by Robert Owen; it was the organ of the Utopian Socialists and appeared from 1834 to 1846, at first in Leeds, and then in London. Engels contributed to it from November 1843 to May 1845.—392, 400, 408, 410, 414, 505

The Northern Star—a weekly, central organ of the Chartists, published from 1837 to 1852, at first in Leeds, and then in London; it was founded and edited by Feargus O'Connor; George Harney was one of the editors. Engels contributed to it from 1843 to 1850.—505, 514

The Oracle of Reason: Or, Philosophy Vindicated—an atheistic weekly published from 1841 to 1843, at first in Bristol, and then in Sheffield and London.—386

La Phalange. Revue de la science sociale—a Fourierist organ published in Paris from 1832 to 1849; it changed its title, frequency of publication, volume and size several times.—396, 413

Le Populaire de 1841—a newspaper published in Paris from 1841 to 1852; it propagated peaceful utopian communism; up to 1849 it was edited by Étienne Cabet.—400, 402, 411

La Presse—a daily published in Paris from 1836; in the 1840s, organ of the opposition.—352

La Réforme—a daily, organ of the republican democrats and petty-bourgeois Socialists, published in Paris from 1843 to 1850.—189, 191, 352

Révolutions de France et de Brabant—a weekly published by the Jacobin Camille Desmoulins in Paris from 1789 to July 1792.—287

La Revue indépendante—a monthly propagating the ideas of utopian socialism; it was published in Paris from 1841 to 1848 under the editorship of Pierre Leroux, George Sand and Louis Viardot.—352, 400

Rheinische Zeitung für Politik, Handel und Gewerbe—a daily founded on January 1, 1842, as the organ of the Rhenish bourgeois opposition. It was published in Cologne till March 31, 1843. When edited by Marx (from October 15, 1842, to March 17, 1843), the paper became a mouthpiece of revolutionary-democratic ideas, which caused its suppression.—132, 349, 405, 406, 530

Schweizerischer Republikaner—a radical weekly published in Zurich from 1830 to 1851. In 1843 Engels contributed to it.—379, 382, 385, 389

Le Siècle—a daily published in Paris from 1836 to 1939. In the 1840s it was an organ of the opposition demanding electoral and other reforms.—352

The Times—a daily founded in London in 1785.—352, 410, 413, 414, 415, 528

Trier'sche Zeitung—a daily founded in 1757; appeared under this title from 1815; in the early 1840s it became a radical organ, later coming under the influence of "true socialism".—578

Vorwärts!—a German newspaper which appeared in Paris twice a week from January to December 1844; at first the organ of the moderate and from May 1844 of the radical-democratic representatives of the German emigrants; Marx and Engels took part in its publication, thus strengthening its revolutionary trend.—189, 201, 357, 469, 475, 481, 485, 489, 497, 500, 504, 506, 508

Weekly Dispatch—a radical weekly published under this title in London from 1801 to 1928.—527

SUBJECT INDEX

A

Absolutism—79, 190
Abstract and concrete—28, 78, 325, 331-32
Abstraction—15, 61, 64, 79, 89, 235, 270, 275-76, 286, 298-99, 305, 307, 327, 329, 334, 338-39, 342-46, 424-25, 427, 464, 475
  See also *Person, Thinking, Abstract and concrete*
Activity—80, 236-37, 272, 274-75, 276-78, 302, 304, 308, 317, 348
  — social—298, 303
  — objective—336
  — abstract—183, 238, 308
  — human—432
  See also *Labour, Man*
Administration—44, 49-50
  See also *Bureaucracy*
Aesthetics—273, 277
Agriculture—263-65, 286-87, 292, 294, 429, 436, 440
  — and industry—285-88, 293
  See also *Fertility, Science*
Aim—166-67, 286
Algeria—528-29
Alienation—309, 310, 314, 324-26, 339-40
  — of species-activity of man—212, 217-18, 219, 226, 227, 275-76, 277-78, 279-80, 302-03, 307, 317, 321, 324-25, 328-29

  — of the product of labour—216, 219, 238, 272, 274, 277-80, 292, 302, 306
  — as the domination of the world of things over man—272, 306
  — under the rule of private property—173-74, 212, 217-19, 237-38, 266, 271, 278-80, 281-82, 291-93, 297, 309, 314, 317, 322-23, 476
  — and objectification—271-72, 281, 303
  — Hegel's conception of alienation—329-35, 338-46
  See also *Christianity, Consciousness, Estranged labour, Estrangement, Landed property, Man, Nature, Private property, Production, Profit, Science, Self-estrangement, State, Value, Wages, Worker*
America—see *United States of America*
Animal—12, 81, 104, 117, 275-77, 308
  See also *Man*
Antagonism—see *Contradiction and Opposites*
Anti-Corn Law League, the—380, 382-84, 428, 505
  See also *Corn Laws*
Antiquity—110, 180, 470, 474, 475
  See also *Greece, People, Rome, Slavery, State*
Anthropologism (philos.)—322
Appearance—56, 311
Appropriation—281, 322, 331, 341

Arbitrariness, caprice— 20, 25, 36, 57, 68, 100
See also *Violence*
Aristocracy— 32, 399, 455, 491-92
— landed— 265-70, 379, 444-46, 449, 453, 456, 476-77, 488, 497-98
— moneyed— 266, 379, 444-46, 449, 453, 456, 476-77, 488
— in England— 379, 444-46, 449, 453, 456, 476-77, 493-94, 497-98
See also *Nobility*
Aristotle's philosophy— 137, 305
Art— 275, 297, 302, 309, 326, 340-41
Artisans, handicraftsmen— 32, 264, 355, 357, 401
Asceticism— 311
Atheism, atheists— 152, 190, 297, 305-06, 341-42, 385-86, 388, 404, 450, 457, 463
See also *Communism, Religion*
Austria— 183, 352
Authority— 47, 232

B

Babouvism— 393, 396
Banking— 214, 216
Being, existence— 27
— and consciousness— 290, 298-99, 301, 312, 325, 329-32, 342-43, 344-45
See also *Thinking*
Bible, the— 158, 171
Bill of exchange— 213
Bourgeoisie— 185, 199-202, 497-98, 513
See also *Bourgeoisie in England, Bourgeoisie in France, Bourgeoisie in Germany, Capitalist, Classes, Middle class, Working class*
Bourgeoisie in England— 192-95, 200, 379-80, 444-46, 456, 477, 487, 496-98, 513
Bourgeoisie in France— 185, 200, 396
Bourgeoisie in Germany— 185-86, 190, 191, 193, 199-200, 202
Bourgeois political economy— 217-18, 221, 231-32, 240-46, 248-55, 257-58, 270-73, 280-81, 284, 304, 307, 308-11, 313-14, 316-17, 418, 419, 433-37, 438-39, 443

— classical (Adam Smith, David Ricardo)— 192-93, 211, 217-18, 235, 239-40, 246-54, 255-65, 285, 290-92, 309-11, 317-21, 333, 375, 418-21, 422-31, 485-86
— petty-bourgeois political economy — 316
— in England— 211-28, 291, 309-12, 319-20, 420-21, 424-25, 485-87
— in France— 246-47, 291, 309-11, 318-19, 320-21, 375, 424-26
— in Poland— 319-21
See also *Capitalist, Competition, Industry, Landed property, Law, Malthusianism, Mercantilism, Money, Physiocrats, Private property, Production, Value, Wages, Wealth*
Bourgeois society— 117, 185-86, 188, 197-98, 212, 214-15, 219, 237-41, 250, 260, 262-64, 270, 280-81, 285, 302, 317, 321-22, 324-26, 477-78
See also *Capitalist, Industry, Interest, interests, Money, Private property, Production*
Bureaucracy— 44-48, 50-54, 60, 63, 66, 76-77, 79, 119, 122-24
See also *Administration*

C

Capital
— as a form of estrangement— 215, 221, 300, 316
— as accumulated labour— 237, 239, 240, 247, 250, 289, 312, 427, 430
— conditions for private property becoming capital— 293, 315-16
— as private property in products of other men's labour— 247, 285
— as governing power over labour and its products— 241, 246-47, 272-73, 283
— as dominating power in bourgeois society— 266, 267, 269-70
— its separation from labour— 213-14, 221, 235, 270-72, 285-86, 288-89, 312, 375-76, 430-32
— its separation from landed property— 221, 235, 270-71, 286-89
— and capitalist competition— 238, 250-52, 255, 435-36, 440

— conditions for accumulation of—
238-40, 250-51, 253-54, 258, 268,
270, 287-88
— concentration of—238, 251, 253,
268, 321
— and interest on—239-52, 263-
64, 283, 284, 289, 316, 317, 430
— profit on—250-52, 375, 430
— costs of—289, 312, 316
— fixed and circulating—253-54
— advanced—248
— industrial—293, 315-17
— and crude egalitarian communism—296
See also *Capitalist, Competition, Labour, Landed property, Private property*
Capitalist, capitalists
— economic prerequisites for domination of—235-36, 239, 246-47
— as owner of means of subsistence for worker—235-37, 240, 279-80, 283-84
— competition among capitalists and ruin of small capitalists—237-38, 250-53, 263-64, 288-89, 432, 433-34
— and landlord—263-64, 265, 267-68, 269-70, 286-89, 315
— bourgeois classical economists on—247-49, 250-52, 270, 284, 285, 308, 312, 316
— and crude egalitarian communism—296
See also *Capital, Competition, Labour, Landed property, Private property, Profit, Worker, Working class*
Categories—343, 424
Catholicism—48, 50-51, 183, 190, 290, 422, 457, 471
Censorship—184, 340
Chance—see *Necessity and chance*
Chartism—190, 379-85, 386, 391, 393, 447-48, 467, 492-94, 496, 497, 504-05
— People's Charter—373, 450, 476
Chemistry—440
Child labour—308, 424
Christianity
— and essence of religion—30, 462
— as a form of man's estrangement—79, 137, 156-57, 158-59, 173-74, 463

— its dogmas—33, 91, 152, 439
— and man—419
— and Judaism—147, 149-50, 168, 171-74
— and communism—385, 399, 403, 407
— Hegel on—88-89
See also *Bible, Catholicism, Church, Clergy, Communism, Judaism, Lutheranism, Protestantism, State*
Church—158, 474
— and the state—474-75
— and socialism—385-87
Civilisation—81, 295, 308, 478
See also *Culture*
Civil society
— opposition and contradiction between the state and civil society—7-9, 40, 70-71, 72-73, 78-79, 81, 90, 159-60, 162, 172-74, 182-83, 197, 198
— under feudalism—111, 164-65
— under the bourgeois mode of production—163-64, 166-67, 171-72, 184-85, 287-88, 316-17
— Hegel's idealist conception of—5-11, 30, 40-42, 44, 46, 48-50, 51-53, 65-66, 71-73, 75-77, 78-79, 83, 84-86, 89-90, 95-96, 99, 102, 111-12, 116-17, 118-20, 121, 122-23, 340
— and the citizen—8, 21, 40-42, 50-51, 76-77, 80, 90, 104, 111, 114-15, 121, 123-24, 128-29, 154, 155-56, 159-62, 164, 166-68
— civil life and civil organisation—76-77, 78-79, 231
See also *Community, Emancipation, Hegel's teaching on the state, State*
Classes, the
— and revolution—184-86, 204
— in bourgeois society—89-90, 238-40, 265, 269-70
— in England—379-80, 384
— in France—186
— in Germany—185-86, 380
See also *Bourgeoisie, Capitalist, Estates, Peasantry, People, Working class*
Class struggle, the—185-86, 235, 260
— in England—379, 380, 415
— in France—186

654   Subject Index

— in Germany—186, 415-16
See also *Interest, interests, People, Politics, Revolution, Working class*
Clergy, the—50, 108, 171, 185
Commodity—213-14, 251, 263-64, 267, 269, 270-72, 283-84, 422, 440, 441
See also *Capital, Worker*
Communal being, community—78-80, 164, 204-05, 286, 295-96
Communism (theory)
— scientific—294-98, 313-14, 342, 405-07, 415-16
— premises for the rise of scientific communism—312-13, 392-93, 403-06
— and atheism—190, 297, 342
— crude egalitarian—295, 296
— utopian—142-44, 294-97, 399-400, 401-02, 403-04
— Icarian—142-43, 396-400, 403-04, 411-13
— artisans'—409, 410, 413
— and Christianity—385-86, 399, 404, 408
— as actual humanism—296-98, 302-04, 336, 342
See also *Interest, interests, Labour, Man, Politics, Property, Science, Weitling's communism*
Communist movement, the
— in England—312-13, 385, 392-93, 406-07
— in France—312-13, 392-94, 395-400, 403-04, 407-08
— in Germany—312-13, 392-93, 400-04, 406-07
Communist society—297-98, 305-06, 312-13, 398-99, 433-35, 438-39
See also *Interest, interests, Labour, Man, Science*
Community—48, 67
— primitive—313-14
Competition
— private property as the basis of capitalist competition—294-95, 431-32
— law of—432-34
— its influence on development of productive forces—255, 310, 434-35
— its influence on market prices—252, 263-64, 375, 426-27, 430

— its influence on production of labour-power—438
— contradictions of capitalist competition—431-33
— among capitalists—250, 440
— and advantage of big capitalists over small capitalists—252-53
— among landlords—263-65, 267-70, 440, 441
— among workers—235, 238, 240, 435-36, 440
— and economic crises—433-37
— and monopoly—431-33
— bourgeois economists on—213, 221, 248, 251, 258, 270-71, 424-26
— transformation of competition into emulation in future society—434-35
See also *Capital, Capitalist, Landed property, Worker*
Concept—25-26, 341, 343
Concrete—see *Abstract and concrete*
Consciousness
— its role in social progress—56
— its role in man's activity—275-77
— and being—290, 298-99, 301, 312-13, 329-32, 343, 344-45
— estranged—297-99, 463
— Hegel's conception of—19, 56, 332-34, 338, 355-56
See also *Ratiocination, Reason, Self-consciousness, Thinking*
Constitution—55, 56-57, 130, 163-64, 221
— in England—397-98, 445-46, 489-513
— in France—113-14, 130, 161-65, 397-98
See also *Hegel's teaching on the state, Law, Legislative power*
Consumption—80-81, 220, 221, 224, 225, 226, 273, 300, 310, 315, 316, 435, 438
See also *Production*
Contract—30
— social—419
Contradiction—294, 326, 435-36
— in essence and in fact—91, 291-92
— affirmation through contradiction—339
— determination through contradiction—421, 429, 432-33
— in society—321

See also *Sense organs*
Fertility—260, 264-65
See also *Agriculture, Science*
Fetishism—290, 292, 312
Feudalism—165-66, 178-79, 181, 183-84, 185, 266-69, 286-87, 290, 477-78
See also *Corporations, Estate-representative system, Estates, Feudal rule, Industry, Landed property, Middle Ages, Monarchy, People, Primogeniture, Serfdom, Trade*
Feudal rule—109
Feuerbach's philosophy—144-45, 187, 232-34, 303-04, 327-30, 339, 350-51, 354-55, 427, 462-63
Form and content—62, 63-65
Fourier's socialism—142-43, 294, 392, 394-96, 398-99, 411-12, 434-35
France
— in the epoch of absolutism—109, 130
— during Consulate and Empire—195-96, 199, 393-94, 397-98
— during the July revolution of 1830 and July monarchy—30, 49, 55, 113-14, 119-20, 130, 150-51, 183-84, 194, 214-15, 351-52, 395-96, 527-29
— economy and industry of—312, 478
— class struggle in—186
— poor laws—196-97
— public and political thought of—312-13, 393-400
— French, the—354-56, 397-98, 471, 472-74
See also *Bourgeoisie in France, Classes, Class struggle, Clergy, Communist movement, Constitution, French philosophy, Humanitarians, Liberalism, Lyons weavers' uprisings of 1831 and 1834, Napoleonic wars, Nobility, Paris, Parliament, Peasantry, Religion, Republicans, Socialism, Vendée, Voltairians, Workers' movement*
Freedom
— its determination by the history of society—313-14, 466
— and necessity—296-97
— social—393-94, 398-99
— in bourgeois society—103, 105-07, 152-53, 162, 167, 237

— Hegel's conception of—5, 56, 62, 65-66, 99-100, 101-03, 105-06, 108
See also *Free trade, Law, Religion, Rights, political*
Free trade—179-80, 269, 420-22, 423-24
See also *Protectionism*
French bourgeois revolution of the end of the 18th century—363-74, 469-513
— prerequisites of—204-05, 471, 472-73, 478-79
— ideologists of—199, 396-97
— Convention—196-97, 199, 397-98, 472-73
— dissolution of estates and formation of classes—79-80
— contradictions between its theory and practice—164-65
— its influence on other European states—133-37, 139-40, 393-94, 404, 474-75, 487
See also *Girondists, Jacobins, Montagnards*
French philosophy—349-51, 387, 399-400, 419, 470-71, 472-74, 478-79
See also *Encyclopaedists, Voltairians*

G

General—see *Individual, particular and general*
Geognosy—304
German Confederation, the—349
Germanomaniacs—177, 179
German philosophy—106-07, 108, 110, 175-76, 179-81, 187, 233, 313, 392, 403-07, 460, 461, 465, 467, 471-74
See also *Feuerbach's philosophy, Hegel's philosophy, Kant's philosophy, Schelling's philosophy, Young Hegelians*
Germans—38, 137, 180-81, 354-55, 445, 460, 471, 472-74
Germany
— constitution of—109, 110, 146-47, 149-51, 156-58, 178-79, 183-84
— in Middle Ages—56, 109
— during Reformation—182-83, 399-402
— industry and trade of—109, 140-42, 178-80, 187, 401-02, 415, 478

— home policy and conditions—
133-39, 140-42, 180-81, 190, 192, 193-94, 380, 417, 514, 517-18, 521, 522
— and Russia—140-41, 517-18
— prospects of revolution—133-36, 139-40, 182-87, 205-06, 392
See also *Artisans, Austria, Bourgeoisie in Germany, Classes, Class struggle, German Confederation, German philosophy, Peasant War in Germany (1524-25), Prussia, Socialism, Working class in Germany, Workers' movement*
Girondists, the—362-74
God, gods—28, 272, 278, 306, 463-65
Greece—32, 38, 51, 72, 136, 178-79, 312-13
Guilds, medieval—286
See also *Corporations, medieval*

H

Hegel's philosophy—5-28, 29-46, 47-56, 57-59, 60-76, 77-80, 81-86, 87-105, 106-08, 110-16, 121-30, 181, 232, 234, 329-35, 337-42, 343-44, 403-05, 456-57, 463
— dialectic—232-34, 327-29, 332-33, 341-42
— logic—327, 329-31, 343-44, 403-04
— philosophy of law—61, 63, 340, 403-04
— abstract historism—329-31
See also *Alienation, Christianity, Consciousness, Essence and phenomenon, Estrangement, Freedom, Hegel's teaching on the state, Labour, Law, Nature, Private property, Property, Young Hegelians*
Hegel's teaching on the state
— idealist conception of the state—7-13, 14-15, 18-19, 20-21, 23, 29-33, 38-40, 61-63, 67, 115-16, 130, 330-31
— constitution—10, 11-15, 18-20, 24-25, 37, 54-59, 97-98
— political conviction—10-11, 13-14, 19-20, 96-97, 98, 102, 124-125
— the state and civil society—5-11, 30, 41-42, 44-45, 46, 48-50, 52-53, 65-66, 71-73, 75-79, 81, 83, 84-86, 89-90, 99, 102, 111-15, 116, 119-20, 121-23
— various authorities—11-17, 18-19, 58-59, 73
— monarch—18-21, 23-29, 32-38, 40-41, 42-43, 44, 51-52, 59-60, 68, 83, 84-87, 95-96, 107-10
— executive power—18-20, 35-37, 41, 42-54, 57, 58-60, 62-64, 65-70, 76-77, 83-87, 89-92, 95-96, 102, 119-20, 124-25
— legislative power—18-20, 24-25, 53-60, 68-69, 72-73, 77, 85, 89-90, 92, 95, 106-07, 116, 118-20
— estates' deputation—43, 59-64, 65-73, 77-78, 83-85, 87, 89, 92-93, 95, 96, 115, 117, 119, 121, 125
— sovereignty—21, 25, 28-29, 32-33, 37, 42-43, 51-53, 72-73
— constitutional state of affairs—22, 30, 37
— primogeniture—97-103, 105-08, 111, 130
— election—120-21
— and morals—107, 122
— and civil law—5-7, 30
— and individual—7-10, 19-20, 21-22, 24-26, 29-35, 38-39, 41-43, 51, 58-59, 63-64, 76-77, 79, 118
— and family—5-11, 30, 38, 41-42, 94, 99, 104
— and the people—19-20, 29-30, 38, 53-54, 61, 63-67, 69, 83, 85, 102
Heraldry—105
Historical and logical—179-80, 285-86, 297-98, 329
Historical school of law, the—177
Historiography—303
History—147-48, 151-52, 176, 178-79, 296-98, 303-04, 313, 327-28, 332-33, 337, 463-65, 470, 474-75
— world history—305-06, 336, 340, 457-58
— modern history—32, 54, 81, 198, 286-87, 419, 422-23, 458, 464, 469-71, 475, 478-79
See also *Historiography, Middle Ages*
Holland—133

English bourgeois revolution of the 17th century, English philosophy, Industrial revolution (in England), Ireland, Lancashire, Liberalism, Literature, Monarchy, Parliament, Pauperism, Peasantry, Reformation, Religion, Scotland, Socialism, Tories, Trade unions, Whigs, Workers' movement, Workhouses, Working class in England
English bourgeois revolution of the 17th century—472-73, 476, 478-79, 490-91, 495
English philosophy—460, 471-74, 478-79, 490
Enjoyment—315-16, 322
Equality—79, 163-64, 268, 313, 393-94, 398-99
Essence and phenomenon—21, 311
— dialectical conception of development of essence—87-89, 90, 91-93
— contradictions between essence and phenomenon—55-56
— essential distinctions—286
— and existence—87-89, 296-97, 305-06
— and general—23-24, 26
— abstract essence—306-07
— criticism of Hegel's idealist conception of essence and phenomenon—7-8, 9, 90, 332-33, 337, 341
See also *Opposites*
Estate-representative system—75, 79, 80-81, 84-85, 118-20, 128, 143-44
See also *Estates, Hegel's teaching on the state*
Estates
— in feudal society—62-63, 65-72, 76-78, 79-80, 81, 83, 84, 89-90, 114-15, 313-14
— general estate—50, 70-71, 103
— middle estate—53, 186-87
— and individual in the epoch of feudalism—79-80, 81, 146-47, 153, 167
— dissolution of estates and formation of classes—78-80, 165-66, 186-87
— Hegel's theory of—59-60, 65-73, 75-76, 78, 82, 83-85, 89-98, 102, 111-12, 121-22
See also *Classes, Clergy, Corporations, Estate-representative system, Hegel's*

teaching on the state, Middle Ages, Nobility, Peasantry, State
Estranged labour—219-20, 228, 237, 240-42, 271, 275-82, 294, 296-97, 300, 303, 317, 442-43
Estrangement
— in the process of labour—213, 217, 220, 270-71, 273-74, 275-76, 277-79, 281, 291, 303
— political—31-32, 100-01
— religious—158, 212, 272, 278-79, 291, 297-98, 331-33, 339, 340, 465
— ways of transcendence of—296-300, 303-04, 312-13, 316, 338-42
See also *Alienation, Christianity, Consciousness, Estranged labour, Landed property, Man, Nature, Private property, Production, Profit, Science, Self-estrangement, State, Value, Wages, Worker*
Ethics, morality—94, 100, 107, 133, 215, 231, 287-89, 297-98, 309-11, 341, 421-22, 423-24, 430, 432, 434-35, 442
Europe—183, 393
Exchange—215, 217, 219-21, 224-27, 270-71, 320-21, 426-27
Exchange-value—211, 213, 219-20, 424-27
See also *Value*
Executive, the
— under the rule of private property—41, 57, 76-77, 79-80
— contradiction between executive and legislative power under rule of private property—57, 58-60, 64-65, 120
See also *Hegel's teaching on the state, Legislative power, State*
Exploitation—140-42, 267
See also *Capitalist, Private property, Working class*

F

Factory system—424, 442-43
Family—5-11, 38-40, 78, 93-94, 96, 98-100, 104, 165, 297, 340, 424
See also *Hegel's teaching on the state, Marriage, State*
Feeling—322

— apparent—280, 439
See also *Essence and phenomenon, Interest, interests*
Corn Laws, the—263, 383-84, 453, 476
See also *Anti-Corn Law League*
Corporations, medieval—32, 44-46, 48-49, 52, 68, 81, 89-90, 93, 102, 109, 112, 115, 122, 165-66, 286
Counter-revolution—176
Credit system—214-17
Crime—442
Criticism, critique—91, 142-45, 175-78, 181-82, 231-34, 327, 328, 329-30, 331-33, 356
Culture—295
See also *Civilisation*

D

Definition, determination—426, 428, 429
Demand and supply—211, 213, 226, 235-37, 262, 313-14, 325, 411-12, 433, 435-36, 438
Democracy—29-32, 115-16, 139-40, 159, 393, 454-55, 466, 491-92
— bourgeois—393, 396-97, 399-400
— working-class—476
— and people—28-30
— as a political form of social emancipation—29-30
See also *Freedom, Rights, political*
Dependence—102, 225
Despotism—32, 138, 140, 165-66
See also *Absolutism, Monarchy*
Dissenters—379-81
Division of labour—220, 236-40, 249, 264, 267, 271, 272, 317, 319-21, 443
Doctrinairism—144
Dogmatism—91

E

Economic crisis—237, 239-41, 263-64
— commercial crisis—433-34, 441
— and capitalist competition—269-70, 433-37
Education—80, 152, 193, 195
Egalitarianism—397
Egoism—172, 174, 185, 217, 288, 300, 321

Election—120-21
See also *Suffrage*
Emancipation—146-47, 168, 170-71, 174, 182-83, 184-85, 186, 187, 201
— political—146, 147-48, 149-52, 155-56, 159-60, 162, 164-66, 168, 182-83, 280-81, 306
— of mankind—146, 149-50, 151-52, 155, 160, 168, 170, 174, 184-85, 186, 280-81, 300, 303, 305-06, 354
See also *Revolution, Revolution, bourgeois, Revolution, proletarian*
Empiricism—8, 9, 33, 39
Encyclopaedists—470
England
— political and social system of—113, 120, 180, 192, 195, 445-46, 498, 503
— as a leading capitalist power—471, 477-78, 489
— economy, industry and trade of—179-80, 192-94, 201, 423-24, 435-37, 446-47, 476-78, 485-86
— landed property of—268-69
— home conditions of—179-80, 192-94, 435-37, 467-68, 473-74, 476-77, 478-79
— legislation of—191-94, 386, 498-99, 501-02, 505-13
— Poor Laws—193-95, 197, 284, 437-38, 496
— struggle for electoral reform in the 1840s—486-87, 496-98
— political parties of ruling classes—486-88
— culture of—380, 387, 444-47
— press, journalism of—444-45, 446-47, 493, 500-01, 504
— education, schools of—380-81, 443
— church of—379, 381, 385-87, 473-75, 501-04, 512
— and Ireland—389-91
— prospects of proletarian revolution—182, 200, 312-13, 380, 467, 469, 472-73, 476-77, 512-13
— English, the—445-46, 471-74, 489-90, 493
See also *Anti-Corn Law League, Aristocracy, Bourgeoisie in England, Classes, Class struggle, Communist movement, Constitution, Corn Laws, Dissenters,*

Subject Index 659

Holy Roman Empire, the—184
Housing question, the (under capitalism)
—257-58, 263, 307, 312, 313-15
See also Worker
Humanism—143, 232, 296, 298, 302-04, 336, 342, 460
Humanitarians, the (secret society in France)—397

I

Idea—11, 183, 466
Idealism—328, 336
Imagination—27
Individual, particular and general—23-25, 26, 39-40, 83-84, 90
See also Essence and phenomenon, Interest, interests, Opposites
Individual, personality, the
— social essence of—21, 38, 76, 77, 80, 217
— role of individual in history—466
— and the people—164, 355-56
— role of individual in science—64
— in bourgeois society—263, 274-75
— and Christianity—419
— Hegel's abstract and mystical conception of personality—23, 26-27, 100, 106-07
See also Estates, Man, Nature, Science, Society
Individuality—77, 228
See also Hegel's teaching on the state, Law, State
Industrial revolution, the (in England)—443, 469, 478-88, 513
See also Progress
Industry
— under feudalism—108
— in bourgeois society—198, 263-64, 269-70, 307, 322
— and economic policy—178-79, 269
— and landed property—269, 285-87, 293
— as a condition for the rise of proletariat—186, 269
— bourgeois economists on—263, 290-92
See also Agriculture, Capital, Economic crisis, Production

Instruments of labour—254, 264, 267-68
Interest, interests
— relations between individual, private interests and general interest under the estates system—5, 6, 41-42, 49, 56, 63-65, 68, 103, 123, 128
— separation of interests under the rule of private property—47-49, 423-25, 466, 475-76
— opposition of private interest and the interest of society under the capitalist mode of production—41-42, 239, 250-51, 263, 285, 287, 321, 433
— opposition of interests of workers and capitalists—240-41, 263-64
— opposition between interests of landlords and interests of tenants and farm labourers—260, 263-64
— struggle of interests under capitalist competition—422, 432-33
— political and social interests in the bourgeois state—479
— intellectual—478
— and principles—407
— transcendence of opposing interests in communist society—428, 434-37, 438-39, 441, 475
— criticism of Hegel's idealist views of—15, 47-48, 56
Interest (financial)—285, 375, 430, 431
— rate of—252, 315
— compound—239, 250
— simple—239
— on capital—239, 252, 264, 283-84, 289, 316
— on money—240, 253, 265, 316
Ireland, Irish, the—308, 389-91, 417, 436
Italy—514

J

Jacobins 100, 367
Jews—146-50, 154, 155, 160, 162, 169-74
See also Judaism
Journalism—444-45
See also Press

Subject Index

Judaism— 147-51, 155, 161, 167-68, 169-73
— and Christianity— 146, 148, 167-68, 169, 172
See also *Jews*
Judiciary— 41, 50, 108
Justice (social)— 398

K

Kant's philosophy— 404
Knowledge— 335, 338-39
See also *Progress, Science*

L

Labour, work
— its social significance— 79-80, 236
— man as a product of labour— 305, 333, 342
— as an inner need of man— 228, 236, 275, 277, 465
— and private property— 315-16, 320-21
— and capital— 221, 249, 312, 425, 428, 430
— its separation from capital— 214, 226, 235, 270-71, 430
— contradiction between labour and capital— 285-86, 289, 294, 432, 435-36
— its separation from wages— 376, 431
— advance made by human labour on the natural product— 249, 305, 312
— object of— 273-74
— mode of— 165, 308, 312
— abstract— 235, 240-41, 292-93
— industrial— 247, 253, 286, 293
— under communism— 435-37
— Fourier on— 395-96
— Hegel on— 332-33, 342
See also *Activity, Agriculture, Alienation, Capital, Child labour, Estranged labour, Estrangement, Instruments of labour, Man, Nature, Needs, Private property, Production, Wages*

Labour time— 239-40
Lancashire— 381
Land— 375-76, 428, 440
Landed property
— as a form of alienation under the rule of private property— 221, 235, 441
— under feudalism— 97-103, 266-68, 314
— non-productive character of landlords in bourgeois society— 262-64, 271, 316-17, 429, 440
— capitalisation of— 263-64, 265, 267-68, 269-70, 286-89, 315-16
— and industry— 286-89, 293
— and technical progress— 264-65
— its division under capitalism— 267-69
— competition among landed proprietors— 264-66, 267-70, 440, 441
— and class of tenants— 268-70, 286, 288, 429
— necessity for abolition of— 267-69
— bourgeois economists on— 240, 258-59, 260, 261-64, 286-89
— Physiocrats on— 293, 316-17
— Hegel on— 98, 100, 104, 107
See also *Agriculture, Aristocracy, Capitalist, Competition, Interest, interests, Primogeniture, Rent of land, Trade*
Language— 226, 298, 304
See also *Consciousness, Thinking*
Law
— as a form of estrangement— 297, 339-41
— civil— 26, 101, 105-06, 107, 110, 111, 166, 340
— criminal— 241
— constitutional— 101, 107, 110, 115, 124
— Roman— 107, 110-11
— abstract— 101, 107, 110
— and proletariat— 186-87
— and religion— 176
— and bourgeois political economy— 231
— in Germany— 111
See also *Hegel's teaching on the state, Judiciary, Law* (juridical), *Person, Privacy of correspondence, Rights, political, Suffrage*

Law (economic)—211, 270, 273, 310-11, 432-33
Law (juridical)—30, 37, 54, 56, 57-59, 76, 115, 119
Lease, tenant farmers—286-88, 384, 390, 429, 477
See also *Landed property*
Legislative power—65, 68, 72, 73, 75, 77, 92-93, 106, 112, 113, 116, 118-21
— social basis of—104-05, 118-19
— elements of—60, 83-87, 99
— inner contradictions of—89-90, 95
— contradictions between legislative power and constitution—54, 55, 57-58
See also *Executive, Hegel's teaching on the state, Parliament, State*
Legitimism—190
Liberalism—133, 190, 192, 421-22, 423, 432, 445
— in England—381, 383-84
— in France—396
— in Germany—133
Literature—302
— belles-lettres—415
— English—380, 444-45, 446, 465, 467, 490
— German—458, 460-61, 465
Logic—10, 17-18, 330
See also *Concept, Definition, Object, Predicate, Subject*
Love—11, 98, 100, 295-96, 300, 301, 326, 356
Lutheranism—182, 290, 291, 400-02
See also *Protestantism, Reformation*
Luxury—see *Wealth*
Lynch law—446
Lyons weavers' uprisings of 1831 and 1834—203

M

Machine, machines—201, 238-39, 240, 308, 312, 443
See also *Worker*
Malthusianism—194, 197, 311, 314, 380, 420-21, 435-40, 452
Man, human being
— as species-being—154, 162, 164, 182, 204-05, 217, 275-78, 295-99, 302-03, 307, 313-14, 320, 325, 328-29, 337
— as determined by social relations—30, 38-40, 78-81, 474-75
— as the motive force and the object of social progress—19, 21, 25-26, 29, 57, 82
— as individual—77, 104-05, 115-16, 167, 217, 298-99, 320, 322, 326, 336-37
— and animal—81, 302, 319-20
— needs of—225-26, 276-77, 306-07, 336
— objectification of his nature—225-26, 228, 276-77
— in bourgeois society—101, 162, 263, 316-17, 322-24, 326, 442
— estranged under the rule of private property—32, 81, 158, 173-74, 212, 213-14, 215, 217, 220-24, 278-80, 281, 285, 291-92, 293, 296-97, 301, 306, 310-11, 325, 328-29, 333-34, 335-36, 339, 341, 342, 343-45
— his self-estrangement in religion—29, 152, 175-76, 290-91, 303, 461, 464-65
— criticism of the idealist conception of man—82, 116, 167, 327, 330-35, 339-40, 342-45, 466
See also *Consciousness, Hegel's teaching on the state, Individual, Labour, Private property, State, Worker*
Mankind—430, 437-39, 442, 462, 465-66, 473-76
Manufacture—248
Marriage—30, 295, 311
See also *Family*
Materialism—105, 302, 336, 355, 419, 478
Mathematics—48
Means of production—376
See also *Instruments of labour, Production*
Measure—341
Mercantile system, the—213-14, 290, 292, 418-19, 420, 421, 422-23, 432
Middle Ages, the—32, 72, 79-81, 108, 113, 187, 263, 314, 458, 461, 464, 474, 475

See also *Corporations, Estates, Feudalism, Guilds, Politics, State, Trade*
Middle class, the— 93-94, 187
  See also *Bourgeoisie*
Mind— 7, 17, 89, 108
Monarchy— 68, 83-85, 86-87, 89, 92-93, 94, 95, 399, 419
  — absolute— 79, 138-39, 158, 185
  — constitutional— 25, 29-30, 36-37, 83, 94, 113, 492
  — and democracy— 28-32, 399
  — in England— 388, 492-93, 497
  — in Germany— 137-38, 183-84, 190
  See also *Absolutism, Estate-representative system, Hegel's teaching on the state, Princes, Prussia, Russia, Sovereignty*
Monetary system— see *Mercantile system*
Money— 171-72, 212-14, 322
  — as a form of estrangement under the rule of private property— 220-21, 271, 306-07, 309, 324-26, 476
  — as an expression of value— 214, 326, 434-35
  — power of money under the rule of private property— 170-72, 213-14, 309, 310, 322-26, 450-52
  — money fetishism— 312
  — as a state monopoly— 441
  — paper— 214, 250
  — metal— 312
  — and credit— 214-16
  — and banks— 216
  — possibility of abolishing money— 170
  — bourgeois economists on— 211, 213-14
  — Saint-Simonists on— 214
  See also *Banking, Bill of exchange, Credit system, Interest, Politics, State, Value*
Monopoly— 65, 221, 236, 263, 268-71, 286, 421, 423, 432-33, 441-42
Monotheism— 171
Montagnards— 362, 363, 365-74
Morocco— 528-29
Music— 301
Mysticism— 7, 9, 12, 14, 17, 19, 23-24, 34, 39-40, 52, 58, 61, 62, 83, 107, 332, 343-45, 394-95, 411
Myths— 180

N

Napoleonic wars— 138, 469
Naturalism— 232, 298-99, 336
  See also *Communism, Humanism*
Natural science— 275-79, 303, 304, 341-49, 380
  See also *Chemistry, Mathematics*
Nature
  — as an object of cognition— 337, 341
  — as man's inorganic body— 275-76, 277, 305-06
  — as element of production— 248-50, 272-73, 428
  — and society and individual— 64, 104-05, 301-06, 312-13, 324, 335-37
  — its estrangement from man under the rule of private property— 275-77, 278-79, 281, 285, 296-97, 303-04, 326
  — French Enlighteners on— 419
  — Hegel's idealist conception of— 343-49
  See also *Humanism, Labour, Man, Naturalism, Science, Society*
Necessity and chance— 6, 21, 56, 79-80, 211, 270-71, 433-34
Needs, requirements
  — as the motive force of social and scientific progress— 178, 295-96, 303-04, 313-14
  — in the sphere of economic relations— 219-20, 224-28, 303, 313
  — labour as an inner need of man— 228, 395
  — physical— 241-42, 276-77, 284, 336
  — social— 56, 79-80, 120, 313-14
  — and their estrangement under the rule of private property— 296-97, 306-12, 316-17, 322
Negation of the negation (philos.)— 268, 305-06, 313, 328-30, 337-38, 340-43, 344-45, 346
Nobility, landed aristocracy— 105, 113, 185-86, 266-67

O

Object — 100
See also *Subject*
Objectification — 224-25, 228, 271-73, 277, 281-82, 296-97, 301-03, 329-30, 331-33, 342
See also *Alienation, Estrangement, Labour*
Officialdom — see *Bureaucracy*
Opposites, antitheses
— conditions of their existence — 325-26
— struggle of opposites — 88, 288-89
— transformation of opposites into each other — 316-17, 424-25
— fusion and separation of — 88, 432-33
— supersession of antitheses — 316-17, 426-27, 433-34, 438-39
— opposition between generality and singularity — 84
— opposition of essences and opposites within one essence — 87-89, 293, 325
— abstract antitheses — 88, 294
— Hegel's conception of — 331-32, 346
See also *Interest, interests*
Owen's socialism — 297, 386, 398

P

Pantheism — 450, 457, 460, 462-63, 465-66
Paris — 142
Parliament — 92, 112-14, 123-24
— in England — 120, 194, 197, 381, 445, 456, 493-501
— in France — 120
See also *Legislative power*
Part and whole — 231
Parties, political — 113, 114, 180, 181, 190-91, 192-93, 197, 379
Party, proletarian — 144, 314, 379-80, 406-07, 411
See also *Revolution, proletarian, Working class*
Patriotism — 11, 133, 179

Pauperism — 191-97, 200, 287
— in England — 192-95, 197, 200, 392-93, 448, 449
See also *Workhouses*
Peasantry — 94-95, 98, 99, 270
— in England — 384, 474-78, 487
Peasant War in Germany, the (1524-25) — 182-83, 399-402
People, nation — 28-30, 53-54, 57
— in ancient times — 180
— in the epoch of feudalism and absolute monarchies — 28-30, 31-33, 61, 63-67, 69, 78-79, 83, 92, 165-66, 186-87
— in bourgeois society — 498
— as the motive force of historic progress — 57, 133-36, 433-34, 435-36, 439
— and individual — 164, 355-56
— its significance and role in revolution — 57, 184-86, 365-66
— as a political force — 53-54, 57-58, 61, 63-64, 65-69, 78-79, 83, 92, 119, 127-28, 166, 498, 501
— and development of its political consciousness — 57, 63-64, 177-78, 182, 495, 498
— preconditions for its free development — 182-83
— and property — 498
— and proletariat as its vanguard — 202, 204
— and bourgeoisie — 185-86
— and the state — 28-33, 53-54, 57, 64-65, 78
— sovereignty of — 28-33, 38, 53-54, 57, 65, 69, 83, 153
— and officials — 53-54, 63, 124-25
— and religion — 176, 179-80
— interests of — 64-65, 391
See also *Classes, Class struggle, Democracy, Hegel's teaching on the state, Population, State*
Person, individual — 22-23, 24, 26-27, 117, 119
— abstract — 38, 40
— private — 40, 77, 80, 103
— juridical — 38
See also *Individual, personality*
Phenomenon — see *Essence and phenomenon*
Philistines — 136-37, 139-41, 185

Philosophy
— and changing of reality—142-44, 176, 179-82, 187, 302
— and science—478-79
— and natural science—303
— and the state—97, 181-82
— and religion—89, 144-45, 175, 232-34, 328-29, 340
— of history—471
— social—394, 456
— of law—101, 179-81, 231
See also Aesthetics, Alienation, Categories, Contradiction, English philosophy, Essence and phenomenon, Estrangement, Form and content, French philosophy, German philosophy, Idealism, Logic, Materialism, Necessity and chance, Negation of the negation, Opposites, Part and whole, Quality and quantity
Physiocrats—285, 292-94, 298, 316-17
Poland—519-20
Police—41, 49, 163
Political economy—see Bourgeois political economy
Politics
— as a form of estrangement—31-32, 100-01, 302-03, 339
— its determination by social and economic relations—94, 155-56, 178-79, 185, 199
— in the Middle Ages—31-32, 70-71, 79, 81-82, 84, 95, 105-06, 112-13, 165
— in bourgeois society—79, 113-14, 118, 121, 164-66, 199
— and class struggle—190-91, 204
— of parties—143-44, 190-91
— and religion—156-57, 159, 176
— political consciousness—10-11, 97-98, 102, 204
— and money—170-72, 309
— and bourgeois political economy—241
— and theory of scientific communism—313
See also Parties, political
Population—261-62, 311, 313-14, 435-38, 440, 442
See also Malthusianism
Poverty—302, 304
Practice—see Theory and Practice

Precious metals—213, 312
Predicate—10, 23, 26, 343
Press—131, 404-06, 413, 417
See also Journalism
Price—211, 219, 235-36, 238-39, 240, 248, 250-51, 263, 375, 426-28, 433-34
Primogeniture—40, 97, 98-108, 111-12, 130
Princes, sovereigns—72, 108, 185
Principles—406-07, 424
Privacy of correspondence—164, 351-52
Private life—80, 197
Private property
— as a product of estranged labour—211-14, 217-22, 224, 226, 228, 237, 271, 279-80, 290-91, 294, 315-17, 320-21, 322, 476
— in ancient times—107, 110-11, 294
— feudal—40, 49, 97-101, 103-11, 124, 165, 292
— formation of bourgeois property—293, 315-16, 423-24
— bourgeois—140-41, 143-44, 246-47, 251, 267, 285-86, 288-89, 294, 302, 375, 421-22, 427-28, 432-33, 441, 466, 485
— and the bourgeois state—152, 153-56, 165, 198
— as the basis of capitalist competition—294-95, 432
— as a factor restricting political freedom in bourgeois society—162-64, 167
— man and his needs under the rule of private property—300, 307, 311-12, 322, 442
— its abolition—187, 280-81, 296-97, 300, 305-06, 312-13, 342, 406-07, 420-21, 426, 429-30, 439, 441, 466
— as a prerequisite of bourgeois political economy—217-18, 270, 419-20, 421-22
— bourgeois classical political economy on—262-63, 290-92, 319-21
— Hegel on—98-101, 103-10, 124
— Utopian Communists on—142-43, 294-96

Subject Index   665

See also *Capital, Labour, Landed property, Value*
Privileges—72, 81, 108, 114, 160, 162, 166
Production
— as social human activity—225, 276-77, 302-03, 306, 313-14
— in ancient times—278-79
— as estrangement of labour under the rule of private property—225, 240, 274-77, 281-84, 296-98, 432
— anarchy of production in bourgeois society—263-64, 433-34, 435-36
— and consumption—220, 224-26, 310
— and division of labour—220
— and exchange—225
— and distribution—221
— costs of production—201, 375, 426-27
— object of production in classless society—228, 306, 433-35
— science as an element of production under communism—427-28, 435-36
— bourgeois economists on—280-81, 312, 313-14, 316-17, 321
See also *Consumption, Division of labour, Labour*
Productive power, productivity—240, 287-88, 434-36
Product of labour—220, 238-41, 246-47, 270, 273-75, 280-82, 431
Profession—153
Profit
— as a form of estrangement—221, 270, 375-76, 430
— as a result of human labour—249-50
— and market price—236
— of capitalist—235, 240, 246-47, 252, 258, 315-16, 431
— and rent of land—285-86
— bourgeois economists on—241, 247-48, 250-51, 312
See also *Capital, Revenue, Wages*
Progress—304-05, 499
— historical—57, 134, 296-97, 423-24, 433-34, 435-36, 439, 463-64
— prerequisites for social progress—19-20, 57, 111

— social consequences of economic progress in bourgeois society—238-40
— scientific and technical—427-28, 435-37, 440, 442-43, 482-83
See also *Industrial revolution (in England), Science*
Proletariat, the—see *Working class*
Property
— feudal—30, 32, 103-04, 267, 291, 292
— public—109, 392, 405-06
— Hegel's conception of—97, 165
See also *Landed property, Private property*
Prostitution—244, 258, 287, 294, 310
Protectionism—178-79, 192-93, 269, 524
See also *Trade*
Protestantism—155, 182, 190, 422, 462, 471, 477
See also *Lutheranism*
Proudhonism—143, 241, 280, 294, 316, 356, 399
Prussia—31, 51, 133-36, 137-42, 183, 189, 191-92, 207-10, 515-16, 525-26, 530-31
See also *Absolutism, Censorship, Despotism, Germany, Monarchy, Prussianism*
Prussianism—133
Psychology—302-03
Public opinion—379
— and the press—404-06
— and literature—415

Q

Quality and quantity—306-07, 341
Quantity—see *Quality and quantity*

R

Radicalism
— in England—379, 301-02, 115, 46, 447-48, 493, 496-97, 500
— in France—395
Ratiocination—27, 30
Raw material—262, 312, 427
Reality—9, 183, 299, 341

Reason—457, 460, 462
Reformation—182-83, 399-401, 470, 474
See also *Lutheranism*
Religion
— origin and essence of—30, 152, 155, 175-76, 461-62, 491, 493
— as a fantastic reflection of reality—279-80, 461-62
— its social and gnosiological roots—155-56, 173-74, 280, 305, 307, 461-62, 463-65
— as a product of estrangement—155, 158, 173-74, 212, 272, 274, 277-79, 291, 297-98, 302-03, 331-32, 339-40, 465
— as a form of social consciousness—29, 143, 151, 175-76
— its social role—175-76, 182-83
— religious consciousness—159, 190
— religious myths—180
— history of—463-64
— significance of criticism of religion—175-76
— "religion is the opium of the people"—175-76
— supersession of religion, its conditions—147-49, 151, 155-56, 175-76, 182, 297-98, 305-06, 339-42
— in slave-owning society—184
— and the state—146-162, 167, 191, 501-04
— and politics—156, 159, 175-76
— and philosophy—89, 144, 175-76
— and morality—310, 462-63
— and freedom of conscience—161-62
— in Egypt—278-79
— in England—471-74, 485-86, 501-04
— in France—354, 471-74
— in Germany—471-74
— in India—278-79
— in Mexico—278-79
— in the U.S.A.—150, 155
See also *Atheism, Catholicism, Christianity, Clergy, God, Law, Lutheranism, Man, Monotheism, Myths, People, Politics, Protestantism, Reformation, State, Superstition, Theology*
Rentiers—252, 315

Rent of land—221, 235-36, 240-41, 259-65, 269-70, 285, 291, 315-16, 375, 427-31
See also *Capital, Landed property, Wages*
Representative bodies—53-54, 111-12, 116, 118-19, 121-24, 125-26
See also *Hegel's teaching on the state, Parliament, State*
Republic—30-31, 140, 151-52, 388, 419
Republicans
— in England—388
— in France—395-96, 411
— in Germany—405, 406, 417
Revenue—235
See also *Profit*
Revolution—56, 57, 90, 130, 133-34, 380
See also *Emancipation, English bourgeois revolution of the 17th century, French bourgeois revolution of the end of the 18th century, Revolution, bourgeois, Revolution, proletarian*
Revolution, bourgeois, the—164-67, 176-77, 184-85, 205-06, 419, 469, 471, 472, 476-77, 513
Revolution, proletarian, the
— as social revolution—182-85, 473-74, 476-77
— inevitability of and prerequisites for—140, 182, 269-70, 296-97, 434, 476-77
— historical significance of—182-85, 205-06, 392, 469, 471, 472-73, 513
— as permanent revolution—156
— proletariat as the motive force of—184-87, 202, 204, 205
— and importance of its scientific theory—182, 186-87, 202, 204, 296-97, 405-06
— and petty-bourgeois and utopian theories—241-42, 397-98
See also *Class struggle, Emancipation, English bourgeois revolution of the 17th century, French bourgeois revolution of the end of the 18th century, Revolution, Revolution, bourgeois, Working class*
Rights, innate human—105, 164-65
Rights, political—160-65, 287-88, 393, 417, 504-06
Romanticism—287, 350, 461

Rome—38, 51, 107, 110, 111, 184, 294, 308, 489
See also *Law*
Russia—53, 140, 514, 519-20, 524
See also *Despotism, Serfdom*

S

Saint-Simon's socialism—214, 294, 394-96, 398
Scepticism—460, 466, 472
Science
— as a form of social consciousness—142-43, 297-98
— and reality—47, 303
— in bourgeois society—427, 442, 443
— as a form of superseding man's estrangement—304
— role of individual in science—64, 298
— as a productive force under communism—428, 435-37
— its role in technical progress—427-28, 440, 482
— Hegel's idealist conception of—11, 25, 27, 148
See also *Chemistry, Mathematics, Natural science, Philosophy, Production*
Schelling's philosophy—349-51, 404, 461-62
Scholars, learned people—32, 380
Scotland—448
Scythians—180
Self-consciousness—19, 100, 306, 312-14, 327, 332-35, 340-41, 343, 356
See also *Consciousness*
Self-estrangement, alienation—169-70, 173-74, 176, 214, 221, 272-75, 281, 291, 294, 296, 317, 333, 338-39, 342
See also *Alienation, Estrangement*
Sense organs—299-300
See also *Feeling*
Serfdom—32, 105-06, 187, 269, 266, 267, 268, 287-88, 464, 476
Slavery—110, 198, 263, 475
Socialism (theory)—142-43, 146, 202, 204, 205-06, 304, 305-06, 354, 512-13
— in England—379-82, 385-86, 388-89, 392, 393, 397-99, 407, 421, 446-47, 466, 467, 505

— in France—232, 385, 392-94, 395-400, 407, 410-11, 414
— in Germany—232, 392-93, 400, 403-04, 405-10, 417
— in Ireland—391
— in Switzerland—392-403
See also *Communism, Communist movement, Communist society, Fourier's socialism, Owen's socialism, Saint-Simon's socialism, Workers' movement*
Social relations—219, 226, 260, 278-79, 286-87, 324, 329-30, 421-22, 441
Society—321, 325
— in the Middle Ages—80-81
— and the state—104-05, 198
— and individual—38, 64, 80-81, 101, 104-05, 163-65, 175, 217, 300-01, 324
— and humanism—297-98, 302-04
See also *Bourgeois society, Civil society, Communist society, Individual, Social relations*
Sophistry—154, 233, 268, 419, 420
Sovereignty—23-24, 28-29, 33, 38, 73, 108
— of monarch—27-28, 34, 96
— of the people—28, 153
Spirituality—302, 419, 473
State, the—29-33, 37-42, 57, 58, 63, 78, 143-44, 156-58, 160-61, 198-99, 297-98, 340
— and civil society—7-11, 39-40, 70-71, 72-73, 78, 81, 90, 153-56, 159, 160, 162, 167, 171-72, 173-74, 183, 197-98
— as an expression of estrangement—31-32, 473-74
— prerequisites of—7-9, 10-11
— of antiquity—30-33, 51, 72, 198
— in the Middle Ages—30-32, 37, 72, 81
— Christian state—146-48, 149-51, 155-58, 160, 168-69, 476
— modern—30-33, 63, 64-65, 80, 82, 83-84, 91, 181, 183, 198-99, 419
— and the people—28-33, 53-54, 57-58, 64-65, 78, 117-18
— and family—7-11, 38-40, 78, 137-38
— and individual—38-40, 80-81, 168, 175

— and economic relations—231, 297-98
— and legislative power—56, 58, 64-65, 84, 90
— and suffrage—153
— and money—216
— and primogeniture—99
— and religion—31, 148-50, 153, 154-57, 158-59, 174, 473
— and bourgeois revolution—135, 165
— its abolition under communism—295-96, 476
See also *Absolutism, Church, Civil society, Democracy, Executive, Hegel's teaching on the state, Legislative power, Monarchy, Republic*
Stock Exchange, the—434
Subject—271-72, 277, 301, 322, 325, 332-34, 335-39
Substance—62
Suffrage—152-53
See also *Election*
Superstition—151, 464
Switzerland—402-03, 514, 525
See also *Socialism*

T

Taxes—58-60, 72, 316-17
Terrorism—156
Theology—150-51, 156, 232-34, 271, 329, 389, 462
Theory and practice—164-65, 181, 183-84, 239, 241, 275-76, 282, 300, 302, 312-13, 422-23, 429, 478-79
Thinking, thought—304-05, 328-29, 333-34, 339, 341, 344, 345-46
— abstract—330-31
— and being—299, 301, 343, 344-45
— and language—304
See also *Consciousness, Knowledge, Self-consciousness*
Tories—192, 379-81, 388, 391, 441, 491, 493
Town and country—79
Trade—375, 421-22
— in the Middle Ages—32, 80, 108, 418-20, 422-23
— in bourgeois society—198, 238, 251, 281, 288, 321, 418, 419-20, 422-23, 485
— in land—265-66, 268, 269, 288, 429-30
See also *Economic crisis, Free trade, Protectionism*
Trade unions—415
Truth—430, 435, 436, 457
Turkey—294

U

Unemployment—see *Working class*
United States of America—31, 150, 153, 155, 160, 170, 175, 446
Unity—90, 92
See also *Interest, interests, Essence and phenomenon*
Universities—380
Uprising of Silesian weavers in 1844—189-90, 200-04, 530-34
Utility—300, 302, 375, 425-26

V

Value—427, 429
— as abstract expression of social relations—212-13, 226-27
— as a form of alienation of private property—212-13, 221
— determination of—211, 240, 310, 375, 425-26, 430, 433-35
— and costs of production—211, 375, 424-27
— and exchange-value—211, 213, 219-20, 375, 424-25
— bourgeois economists on—211, 375, 424-27
— influence of fashion on—310
See also *Exchange-value, Money*
Vendée—374
Violence, force—68, 218
— as an instrument of class rule—398, 399
Voltairians—355

W

Wages
— as expression of alienated labour under the rule of private proper-

ty—219-21, 225, 238, 376, 431-32
— their essence under capitalism—235, 241, 285-86
— level of—235
— and intensification of labour—237
— and demand for labour—236, 239
— and competition among workers—235
— as a constituent part of market price—235-36, 263-64
— and capital—289
— and rent of land—264-65
— bourgeois political economy on—235, 240-42, 247-48, 252, 270, 288, 312, 427, 443
— and crude egalitarian communism—296
— Proudhon on—241-42, 280
See also *Labour, Worker*
Wars—419, 423
See also *Violence*
Wealth
— labour as a source of—237, 291, 293, 431
— under capitalism—267, 304, 311-12, 314-16
— capitalists amass riches, causing the impoverishment of the working class—237-40, 241, 271, 421-22
— under socialism—304
— bourgeois classical political economy on—240-41, 250-52, 290-91, 309-10, 316, 320-21, 421-22
— Mercantilists on—292
— Physiocrats on—292-93
— Hegel on—332
— Proudhon on—316
Weitling's communism—143, 201, 292, 402-03, 412-13
Whigs—379, 381-82, 384, 388-89, 391, 447, 491, 493
Will—8, 58, 64, 91, 100-01, 102, 104, 119, 198-99, 225, 301, 326
Women's question—172, 295
Worker
— his estrangement under the capitalist mode of production—204, 238-39, 241, 271-75, 276-77, 278-80, 381-82
— reduction of his needs to mere bodily needs in capitalist society—220-21, 274-77, 308-09, 440-41
— his decline to a mere machine—238-39, 240, 308, 443
— as a commodity—235-36, 240, 270-72, 283-84, 312, 439
— and crude egalitarian communism—294-95
— Proudhon on—280
— Saint-Simon on—294
See also *Capitalist, Labour time, Man, Workhouses*
Workers' movement—190, 192, 313
— in England—190, 199-201, 355, 379-80, 384-85, 387, 446-47, 450, 467
— in France—200-01, 204, 313, 355, 395-97, 401-02, 411
— in Germany—191-92, 199-202, 355, 401-02, 404-05, 406-07
See also *Chartism, Class struggle, Communist movement, Lyons weavers' uprisings of 1831 and 1834, Party, proletarian, Socialism, Uprising of Silesian weavers in 1844*
Workhouses (in England)—195, 448
Working class
— conditions for its rise—187, 267, 269, 487
— in the Middle Ages—79-80, 189-90
— division of society into capitalists and workers—265-66, 431
— tendency towards numerical growth, in increasing proportion, of the working class under capitalism—434
— its impoverishment under capitalism—241, 258-59, 270-72
— its living conditions in capitalist society—307, 311
— unemployment of—239, 284
— competition among workers—238, 432
— condition of agricultural workers under capitalism—285-86
— antagonism between workers' and capitalists' interests—263-64
— capitalist as owner of workers'

conditions of life and their means of subsistence—235-38, 240, 252, 279, 283, 310-11
— development of its political consciousness—200, 202, 204, 387, 396-97, 449-50
— its emancipation as a condition for the emancipation of all classes of society—186-87, 205, 280-81, 354
— as the motive force of socialist revolution—184-87, 202, 204-05
— and progressive philosophy—187
— parties and associations of—313, 379-80, 406-07, 411
— and bourgeois reforms—191-92, 241-42, 280
— and religion—396
See also *Classes, Class struggle, Revolution, proletarian, Worker, Workers' movement, Working class in England, Working class in Germany*
Working class in England—192-94, 200-02, 263, 269-70, 308, 311, 435-36, 445-46, 447-49, 456-57, 468, 474, 486-87, 496
See also *Workers' movement*
Working class in Germany—185-87, 190-91, 196, 201-02, 204, 401
See also *Workers' movement*
World outlook—102, 173

Y

Young Hegelians—327-28, 344, 356-57, 404-06